T0385039

Service and Repair Manual
for BMW 5-Series

Martynn Randall

Models covered

(4901 - 304)

BMW 5-Series Saloon (E60) & Touring (E61)
4- and 6-cylinder turbo-diesel engines: 520d, 525d and 530d
2.0 litre (1995cc), 2.5 litre (2497cc) and 3.0 litre (2993cc) turbo-diesel

Does NOT cover petrol models, 535d twin turbo 3.0 litre diesel models, or models with xDrive transmission
Does NOT cover new 5-Series (F10/F11) range introduced during 2010

© J H Haynes & Co. Ltd. 2011

ABCDE
FGHIJ
KL

A book in the **Haynes Owners Workshop Manual Series**

Printed in India

ISBN **978 1 78521 020 4**

J H Haynes & Co. Ltd.
Sparkford, Yeovil, Somerset BA22 7JJ, England

British Library Cataloguing in Publication Data
A catalogue record for this book is available from the British Library.

Haynes North America, Inc
2801 Townsgate Road, Suite 340, Thousand Oaks, CA 91361, USA

Disclaimer

There are risks associated with automotive repairs. The ability to make repairs depends on the individual's skill, experience and proper tools. Individuals should act with due care and acknowledge and assume the risk of performing automotive repairs.

The purpose of this manual is to provide comprehensive, useful and accessible automotive repair information, to help you get the best value from your vehicle. However, this manual is not a substitute for a professional certified technician or mechanic.

This repair manual is produced by a third party and is not associated with an individual vehicle manufacturer. If there is any doubt or discrepancy between this manual and the owner's manual or the factory service manual, please refer to the factory service manual or seek assistance from a professional certified technician or mechanic.

Even though we have prepared this manual with extreme care and every attempt is made to ensure that the information in this manual is correct, neither the publisher nor the author can accept responsibility for loss, damage or injury caused by any errors in, or omissions from, the information given.

Contents

LIVING WITH YOUR BMW

Contents

Your BMW 5-Series manual

The aim of this manual is to help you get the best value from your vehicle. It can do so in several ways. It can help you decide what work must be done (even should you choose to get it done by a garage). It will also provide information on routine maintenance and servicing, and give a logical course of action and diagnosis when random faults occur. However, it is hoped that you will use the manual by tackling the work yourself. On simpler jobs it may even be quicker than booking the car into a garage and going there twice, to leave and collect it. Perhaps most important, a lot of money can be saved by avoiding the costs a garage must charge to cover its labour and overheads.

The manual has drawings and descriptions to show the function of the various components so that their layout can be understood. Tasks are described and photographed in a clear step-by-step sequence.

References to the 'left' and 'right' of the vehicle are in the sense of a person in the driver's seat facing forward.

Acknowledgements

Thanks are due to Draper Tools Limited, who provided some of the workshop tools, and to all those people at Sparkford who helped in the production of this manual.

We take great pride in the accuracy of information given in this manual, but vehicle manufacturers make alterations and design changes during the production run of a particular vehicle of which they do not inform us. No liability can be accepted by the authors or publishers for loss, damage or injury caused by any errors in, or omissions from, the information given.

The new BMW 5-Series was introduced in September 2003 and was originally available with a choice of 2.0 litre (1995 cc), 2.5 litre (2497 cc) and 3.0 litre (2993 cc) DOHC engines. In March 2007 the range was 'facelifted' with minor cosmetic revisions, and the engine range was enhanced with higher outputs and lower emissions. Both the four-door Saloon (E60) and Touring (E61) estate models were available from the models launch.

All engines are derived from the well-proven engines which have appeared in many BMW vehicles. The engines covered by this manual are of four and six-cylinder double-overhead camshaft design, mounted longitudinally with the transmission mounted on its rear. Both manual and automatic transmissions are available.

All models have fully-independent front and rear suspension, manufactured almost entirely from aluminium.

A wide range of standard and optional equipment is available within the BMW 5-Series range to suit most tastes, including central locking, electric windows, air conditioning, an electric sunroof, an anti-lock braking system, a traction control system, a dynamic stability control system, and numerous airbags.

Provided that regular servicing is carried out in accordance with the manufacturer's recommendations, the BMW should prove reliable and very economical. The engine compartment is well-designed, and most of the items requiring frequent attention are easily accessible.

Working on your car can be dangerous. This page shows just some of the potential risks and hazards, with the aim of creating a safety-conscious attitude.

General hazards

Scalding

• Don't remove the radiator or expansion tank cap while the engine is hot.
• Engine oil, transmission fluid or power steering fluid may also be dangerously hot if the engine has recently been running.

Burning

• Beware of burns from the exhaust system and from any part of the engine. Brake discs and drums can also be extremely hot immediately after use.

Crushing

• When working under or near a raised vehicle, always supplement the jack with axle stands, or use drive-on ramps.
Never venture under a car which is only supported by a jack.
• Take care if loosening or tightening high-torque nuts when the vehicle is on stands. Initial loosening and final tightening should be done with the wheels on the ground.

Fire

• Fuel is highly flammable; fuel vapour is explosive.
• Don't let fuel spill onto a hot engine.
• Do not smoke or allow naked lights (including pilot lights) anywhere near a vehicle being worked on. Also beware of creating sparks (electrically or by use of tools).
• Fuel vapour is heavier than air, so don't work on the fuel system with the vehicle over an inspection pit.
• Another cause of fire is an electrical overload or short-circuit. Take care when repairing or modifying the vehicle wiring.
• Keep a fire extinguisher handy, of a type suitable for use on fuel and electrical fires.

Electric shock

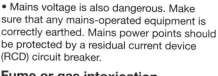

• Ignition HT and Xenon headlight voltages can be dangerous, especially to people with heart problems or a pacemaker. Don't work on or near these systems with the engine running or the ignition switched on.

• Mains voltage is also dangerous. Make sure that any mains-operated equipment is correctly earthed. Mains power points should be protected by a residual current device (RCD) circuit breaker.

Fume or gas intoxication

• Exhaust fumes are poisonous; they can contain carbon monoxide, which is rapidly fatal if inhaled. Never run the engine in a confined space such as a garage with the doors shut.
• Fuel vapour is also poisonous, as are the vapours from some cleaning solvents and paint thinners.

Poisonous or irritant substances

• Avoid skin contact with battery acid and with any fuel, fluid or lubricant, especially antifreeze, brake hydraulic fluid and Diesel fuel. Don't syphon them by mouth. If such a substance is swallowed or gets into the eyes, seek medical advice.
• Prolonged contact with used engine oil can cause skin cancer. Wear gloves or use a barrier cream if necessary. Change out of oil-soaked clothes and do not keep oily rags in your pocket.
• Air conditioning refrigerant forms a poisonous gas if exposed to a naked flame (including a cigarette). It can also cause skin burns on contact.

Asbestos

• Asbestos dust can cause cancer if inhaled or swallowed. Asbestos may be found in gaskets and in brake and clutch linings. When dealing with such components it is safest to assume that they contain asbestos.

Special hazards

Hydrofluoric acid

• This extremely corrosive acid is formed when certain types of synthetic rubber, found in some O-rings, oil seals, fuel hoses etc, are exposed to temperatures above 4000C. The rubber changes into a charred or sticky substance containing the acid. *Once formed, the acid remains dangerous for years. If it gets onto the skin, it may be necessary to amputate the limb concerned.*
• When dealing with a vehicle which has suffered a fire, or with components salvaged from such a vehicle, wear protective gloves and discard them after use.

The battery

• Batteries contain sulphuric acid, which attacks clothing, eyes and skin. Take care when topping-up or carrying the battery.
• The hydrogen gas given off by the battery is highly explosive. Never cause a spark or allow a naked light nearby. Be careful when connecting and disconnecting battery chargers or jump leads.

Air bags

• Air bags can cause injury if they go off accidentally. Take care when removing the steering wheel and trim panels. Special storage instructions may apply.

Diesel injection equipment

• Diesel injection pumps supply fuel at very high pressure. Take care when working on the fuel injectors and fuel pipes.

 Warning: Never expose the hands, face or any other part of the body to injector spray; the fuel can penetrate the skin with potentially fatal results.

Remember...

DO

• Do use eye protection when using power tools, and when working under the vehicle.

• Do wear gloves or use barrier cream to protect your hands when necessary.

• Do get someone to check periodically that all is well when working alone on the vehicle.

• Do keep loose clothing and long hair well out of the way of moving mechanical parts.

• Do remove rings, wristwatch etc, before working on the vehicle – especially the electrical system.

• Do ensure that any lifting or jacking equipment has a safe working load rating adequate for the job.

DON'T

• Don't attempt to lift a heavy component which may be beyond your capability – get assistance.

• Don't rush to finish a job, or take unverified short cuts.

• Don't use ill-fitting tools which may slip and cause injury.

• Don't leave tools or parts lying around where someone can trip over them. Mop up oil and fuel spills at once.

• Don't allow children or pets to play in or near a vehicle being worked on.

The following pages are intended to help in dealing with common roadside emergencies and breakdowns. You will find more detailed fault finding information at the back of the manual, and repair information in the main chapters.

If your car won't start and the starter motor doesn't turn

- [ ] If it's a model with automatic transmission, make sure the selector is in P or N.
- [ ] Open the right-hand storage tray in the luggage compartment and make sure that the battery terminals are clean and tight.
- [ ] Switch on the headlights and try to start the engine. If the headlights go very dim when you're trying to start, the battery is probably flat. Get out of trouble by jump starting (see next page) using a friend's car.

If your car won't start even though the starter motor turns as normal

- [ ] Is there fuel in the tank?
- [ ] Is there moisture on electrical components under the bonnet? Switch off the ignition, then wipe off any obvious dampness with a dry cloth. Spray a water-repellent aerosol product (WD-40 or equivalent) on ignition and fuel system electrical connectors like those shown in the photos.

A Check the security of the throttle body connector connector.

B Check the airflow meter wiring connector.

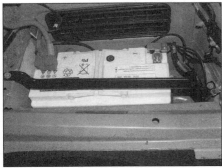

C Check the security and condition of the battery terminals (located in the luggage compartment).

D Check the glow plug control unit wiring connector (behind or under the oil filter housing)

Check that electrical connections are secure (with the ignition switched off) and spray them with a water dispersant spray like WD40 if you suspect a problem due to damp. The plastic covers on the engines either pull up from place (N47 engines), or are retained by easily visible bolts (M47 and M57 engines) – check with the relevant part of Chapter 2.

Jump starting

When jump-starting a car using a booster battery, observe the following precautions:

✔ Before connecting the booster battery, make sure that the ignition is switched off.

Caution: Remove the key in case the central locking engages when the jump leads are connected

✔ Ensure that all electrical equipment (lights, heater, wipers, etc) is switched off.

✔ Take note of any special precautions printed on the battery case.

✔ Make sure that the booster battery is the same voltage as the discharged one in the vehicle.

✔ If the battery is being jump-started from the battery in another vehicle, the two vehicles MUST NOT TOUCH each other.

✔ Make sure that the transmission is in neutral (or PARK, in the case of automatic transmission).

HAYNES HINT *Jump starting will get you out of trouble, but you must correct whatever made the battery go flat in the first place. There are three possibilities:*

1 *The battery has been drained by repeated attempts to start, or by leaving the lights on.*

2 *The charging system is not working properly (alternator drivebelt slack or broken, alternator wiring fault or alternator itself faulty).*

3 *The battery itself is at fault (electrolyte low, or battery worn out).*

1 Unclip the plastic cover from the jump-start terminal (+) adjacent to the left-hand suspension turret in the engine compartment, and connect the red jump lead to the terminal.

2 Connect the other end of the red lead to the positive (+) terminal of the booster battery.

3 Connect one end of the black jump lead to the negative (-) terminal of the booster battery.

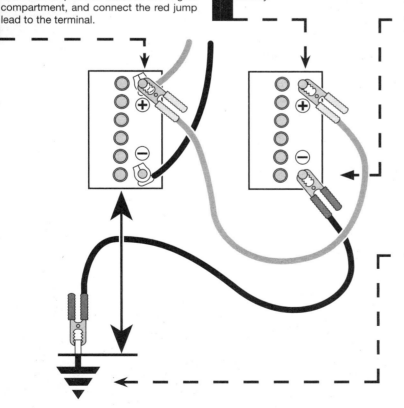

4 Connect the other end of the black jump lead to jump start negative terminal located on the left-hand suspension turret in the engine compartment.

5 Make sure that the jump leads will not come into contact with the cooling fan drivebelts or other moving parts on the engine.

6 Start the engine, then with the engine running at fast idle speed, disconnect the jump leads in the reverse order of connection, ie, negative (black) lead first. Securely refit the plastic cover to the jump start positive terminal.

Identifying leaks

Puddles on the garage floor or drive, or obvious wetness under the bonnet or underneath the car, suggest a leak that needs investigating. It can sometimes be difficult to decide where the leak is coming from, especially if an engine undershield is fitted. Leaking oil or fluid can also be blown rearwards by the passage of air under the car, giving a false impression of where the problem lies.

Warning: Most automotive oils and fluids are poisonous. Wash them off skin, and change out of contaminated clothing, without delay.

HAYNES HINT *The smell of a fluid leaking from the car may provide a clue to what's leaking. Some fluids are distinctively coloured. It may help to remove the engine undershield, clean the car carefully and to park it over some clean paper overnight as an aid to locating the source of the leak.*
Remember that some leaks may only occur while the engine is running.

Sump oil

Engine oil may leak from the drain plug...

Oil from filter

...or from the base of the oil filter.

Gearbox oil

Gearbox oil can leak from the seals at the inboard ends of the driveshafts.

Antifreeze

Leaking antifreeze often leaves a crystalline deposit like this.

Brake fluid

A leak occurring at a wheel is almost certainly brake fluid.

Power steering fluid

Power steering fluid may leak from the pipe connectors on the steering rack.

Towing

When all else fails, you may find yourself having to get a tow home – or of course you may be helping somebody else. Long-distance recovery should only be done by a garage or breakdown service. For shorter distances, DIY towing using another car is easy enough, but observe the following points:

☐ Use a proper tow-rope – they are not expensive. The vehicle being towed must display an ON TOW sign in its rear window.

☐ Always turn the ignition key to the 'on' position when the vehicle is being towed, so that the steering lock is released, and that the direction indicator and brake lights work.

☐ Only attach the tow-rope to the towing eyes provided. The towing eye is supplied as part of the tool kit which is fitted under the luggage compartment lid or floor. To fit the eye, press the arrow symbol and swing out the access cover from the front/rear bumper (as applicable). Screw the eye into position and tighten it securely **(see illustrations)**.

☐ Before being towed, release the handbrake and select neutral on the transmission. On models with automatic transmission, set the selector lever to position N. Maximum towing speed is 43 mph, and maximum distance is 90 miles.

☐ Note that greater-than-usual pedal pressure will be required to operate the brakes, since the vacuum servo unit is only operational with the engine running.

☐ On models with power steering, greater-than-usual steering effort will also be required.

☐ The driver of the car being towed must keep the tow-rope taut at all times to avoid snatching.

☐ Make sure that both driver's know the route before setting off.

☐ Only drive at moderate speeds and keep the distance towed to a minimum. Drive smoothly and allow plenty of time for slowing down at junctions.

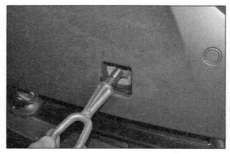

Introduction

There are some very simple checks which need only take a few minutes to carry out, but which could save you a lot of inconvenience and expense.

These *Weekly checks* require no great skill or special tools, and the small amount of time they take to perform could prove to be very well spent, for example;

☐ Keeping an eye on tyre condition and pressures, will not only help to stop them wearing out prematurely, but could also save your life.

☐ Many breakdowns are caused by electrical problems. Battery-related faults are particularly common, and a quick check on a regular basis will often prevent the majority of these.

☐ If your car develops a brake fluid leak, the first time you might know about it is when your brakes don't work properly. Checking the level regularly will give advance warning of this kind of problem.

☐ If the oil or coolant levels run low, the cost of repairing any engine damage will be far greater than fixing the leak, for example.

Underbonnet check points

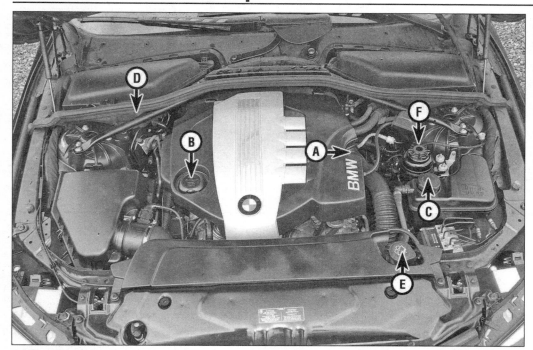

◄ 2.0 litre N47 engine

A *Engine oil level dipstick*

B *Engine oil filler cap*

C *Coolant expansion tank*

D *Brake and clutch fluid reservoir (under the pollen filter housing)*

E *Screen washer fluid reservoir*

F *Power steering fluid reservoir*

◄ 2.0 litre M47 engine

A *Engine oil level dipstick*

B *Engine oil filler cap*

C *Coolant expansion tank*

D *Brake and clutch fluid reservoir (under the pollen filter housing)*

E *Power steering fluid reservoir*

F *Screen washer fluid reservoir*

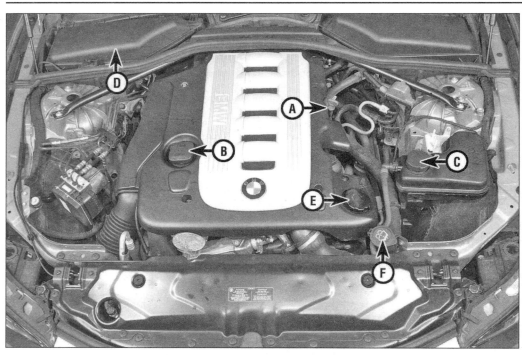

◀ 3.0 litre M57T2 engine

A Engine oil level dipstick

B Engine oil filler cap

C Coolant expansion tank

D Brake and clutch fluid reservoir (under the pollen filter housing)

E Power steering fluid reservoir

F Screen washer fluid reservoir

Coolant level

Warning: DO NOT attempt to remove the expansion tank pressure cap when the engine is hot, as there is a very great risk of scalding. Do not leave open containers of coolant about, as it is poisonous.

Car care

● With a sealed-type cooling system, adding coolant should not be necessary on a regular basis. If frequent topping-up is required, it is likely there is a leak. Check the radiator, all hoses and joint faces for signs of staining or wetness, and rectify as necessary.

● It is important that antifreeze is used in the cooling system all year round, not just during the winter months. Don't top-up with water alone, as the antifreeze will become too diluted.

1 Wait until the engine is cold. Slowly unscrew the expansion tank cap, to release any pressure present in the cooling system, and remove it.

2 The coolant expansion tank incorporates a bridge piece located under the filler cap which indicates the maximum and minimum coolant levels. See the information adjacent to the filler neck.

3 Add a mixture of water and antifreeze to the expansion tank until the level of the coolant is up to the MAX mark. Refit the cap and tighten it securely.

Engine oil level

Before you start
✔ Make sure that your car is on level ground.

The correct oil
Modern engines place great demands on their oil. It is very important that the correct oil for your car is used (see *Lubricants and fluids*).

Car care
● If you have to add oil frequently, you should check whether you have any oil leaks. Place some clean paper under the car overnight, and check for stains in the morning. If there are no leaks, the engine may be burning oil, or the oil may only be leaking when the engine is running.

● Note that models from 03/2007 do not have a traditional oil level dipstick. Instead the level is shown on the central display unit. On other engines, the oil level is checked using a traditional dipstick.

Models without a dipstick
Start the engine, and call up the 'Vehicle Status' using the iDrive controller and central display unit – select 'Engine oil level'. Follow the on-screen instructions, and add oil if directed by the instructions.

Models with a dipstick
● Check the oil level before the car is driven, or at least 5 minutes after the engine has been switched off.

 HAYNES HINT *If the oil is checked immediately after driving the vehicle, some of the oil will remain in the upper engine components, resulting in an inaccurate reading on the dipstick.*

● Always maintain the level between the upper and lower dipstick marks (see photo 3). If the level is too low severe engine damage may occur. Oil seal failure may result if the engine is overfilled by adding too much oil.

1 The dipstick top is often brightly coloured for easy identification (see *Underbonnet check points* for exact location). Withdraw the dipstick.

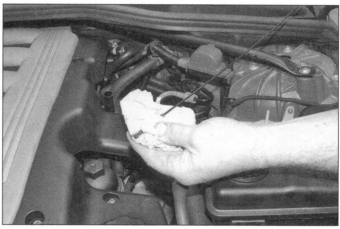

2 Using a clean rag or paper towel remove all oil from the dipstick. Insert the clean dipstick into the tube as far as it will go, then withdraw it again.

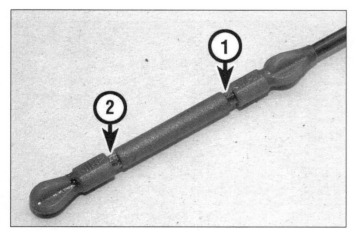

3 Note the oil level on the end of the dipstick, which should be between the upper maximum mark (1) and lower minimum mark (2). Approximately 1.0 litre of oil will raise the level from the lower mark to the upper mark.

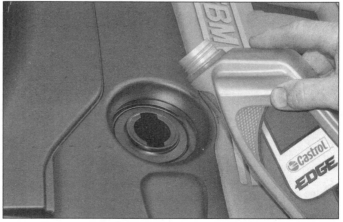

4 Oil is added through the filler cap. Unscrew the cap and top-up the level; a funnel may help to reduce spillage. Add the oil slowly, checking the level on the dipstick often. Don't overfill.

Brake and clutch fluid level

Warning:
● *Brake fluid can harm your eyes and damage painted surfaces, so use extreme caution when handling and pouring it.*
● *Do not use fluid that has been standing open for some time, as it absorbs moisture from the air, which can cause a dangerous loss of braking effectiveness.*

Before you start

✔ Make sure that your car is on level ground.

Safety first!

● If the reservoir requires repeated topping-up this is an indication of a fluid leak somewhere in the system, which should be investigated immediately.
● If a leak is suspected, the car should not be driven until the braking system has been checked. Never take any risks where brakes are concerned.

 The fluid level in the reservoir will drop slightly as the brake pads wear down, but the fluid level must never be allowed to drop below the MIN mark.

1 Fold the clip forwards, rotate the fastener 90° anti-clockwise and remove the lid from the driver's and passenger's side pollen filter housing.

2 Pull up the rubber sealing strip, then lift the clip and slide the central plastic panel to the left and remove it.

3 Lift out the plastic trim at the outer edge of the pollen filter housings.

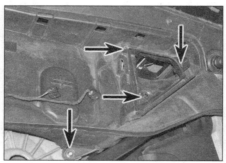

4 Undo the bolts, rotate the fasteners 90° anti-clockwise, lift the passenger's side filter housing and remove the driver's side filter housing.

5 The MAX and MIN marks are indicated on the side of the reservoir. The fluid level must be kept between the marks at all times.

6 If topping-up is necessary, first wipe clean the area around the filler cap to prevent dirt entering the hydraulic system.

7 Unscrew the reservoir cap and carefully lift it out of position, taking care not to damage the level switch float. Inspect the reservoir, if the fluid is dirty the hydraulic system should be drained and refilled (see Chapter 1).

8 Carefully add fluid taking care not to spill it onto the surrounding components. Use only the specified fluid; mixing different types can cause damage to the system. After topping-up to the correct level, securely refit the cap and wipe off any spilt fluid.

Power steering fluid level

Before you start

✔ Park the vehicle on level ground.
✔ Set the steering wheel straight-ahead.
✔ The engine should be turned off.

 HAYNES HiNT *For the check to be accurate, the steering must not be turned while the level is being checked.*

Safety first!

● The need for frequent topping-up indicates a leak, which should be investigated immediately.

1 The reservoir is located near the front of the engine compartment. Wipe clean the area around the reservoir filler neck and unscrew the filler cap/dipstick from the reservoir.

2 Insert the dipstick into the reservoir, fully screwing on the cap, then remove it. The fluid level should be at the Max mark at 20°C. Note that with the engine at normal operating temperature (fluid temperature of 50 to 60°C), it is permissible for the level to be up to 10 mm above the MAX mark. When topping-up, use the specified type of fluid and do not overfill the reservoir. When the level is correct, securely refit the cap.

Screenwasher fluid level*

On models with a headlight washer system, the screenwash is also used to clean the headlights

● Screenwash additives not only keep the windscreen clean during foul weather, they also prevent the washer system freezing in cold weather – which is when you are likely to need it most. Don't top-up using plain water as the screenwash will become too diluted, and will freeze during cold weather.

Caution: On no account use coolant antifreeze in the washer system – this could discolour or damage paintwork.

1 The screenwasher fluid reservoir is located in the front left-hand corner of the engine compartment.

2 Pull up the cap, and add a screenwash additive in the quantities recommended by the manufacturer.

Wiper blades

● Check the condition of the wiper blades; if they are cracked or show any signs of deterioration, or if the glass swept area is smeared, renew them. Wiper blades should be renewed annually.

1 To remove a wiper blade, pull the arm away from the screen until it locks. Squeeze together the clips and disengage the blade from the arm.

Tyre condition and pressure

It is very important that tyres are in good condition, and at the correct pressure - having a tyre failure at any speed is highly dangerous. Tyre wear is influenced by driving style - harsh braking and acceleration, or fast cornering, will all produce more rapid tyre wear. As a general rule, the front tyres wear out faster than the rears. Interchanging the tyres from front to rear ("rotating" the tyres) may result in more even wear. However, if this is completely effective, you may have the expense of replacing all four tyres at once!

Remove any nails or stones embedded in the tread before they penetrate the tyre to cause deflation. If removal of a nail does reveal that the tyre has been punctured, refit the nail so that its point of penetration is marked. Then immediately change the wheel, and have the tyre repaired by a tyre dealer.

Regularly check the tyres for damage in the form of cuts or bulges, especially in the sidewalls. Periodically remove the wheels, and clean any dirt or mud from the inside and outside surfaces. Examine the wheel rims for signs of rusting, corrosion or other damage. Light alloy wheels are easily damaged by "kerbing" whilst parking; steel wheels may also become dented or buckled. A new wheel is very often the only way to overcome severe damage.

New tyres should be balanced when they are fitted, but it may become necessary to re-balance them as they wear, or if the balance weights fitted to the wheel rim should fall off. Unbalanced tyres will wear more quickly, as will the steering and suspension components. Wheel imbalance is normally signified by vibration, particularly at a certain speed (typically around 50 mph). If this vibration is felt only through the steering, then it is likely that just the front wheels need balancing. If, however, the vibration is felt through the whole car, the rear wheels could be out of balance. Wheel balancing should be carried out by a tyre dealer or garage.

1 Tread Depth - visual check
The original tyres have tread wear safety bands (B), which will appear when the tread depth reaches approximately 1.6 mm. The band positions are indicated by a triangular mark on the tyre sidewall (A).

2 Tread Depth - manual check
Alternatively, tread wear can be monitored with a simple, inexpensive device known as a tread depth indicator gauge.

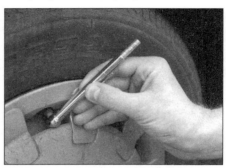

3 Tyre Pressure Check
Check the tyre pressures regularly with the tyres cold. Do not adjust the tyre pressures immediately after the vehicle has been used, or an inaccurate setting will result.

Tyre tread wear patterns

Shoulder Wear

Underinflation (wear on both sides)
Under-inflation will cause overheating of the tyre, because the tyre will flex too much, and the tread will not sit correctly on the road surface. This will cause a loss of grip and excessive wear, not to mention the danger of sudden tyre failure due to heat build-up.
Check and adjust pressures
Incorrect wheel camber (wear on one side)
Repair or renew suspension parts
Hard cornering
Reduce speed!

Centre Wear

Overinflation
Over-inflation will cause rapid wear of the centre part of the tyre tread, coupled with reduced grip, harsher ride, and the danger of shock damage occurring in the tyre casing.
Check and adjust pressures

If you sometimes have to inflate your car's tyres to the higher pressures specified for maximum load or sustained high speed, don't forget to reduce the pressures to normal afterwards.

Uneven Wear

Front tyres may wear unevenly as a result of wheel misalignment. Most tyre dealers and garages can check and adjust the wheel alignment (or "tracking") for a modest charge.
Incorrect camber or castor
Repair or renew suspension parts
Malfunctioning suspension
Repair or renew suspension parts
Unbalanced wheel
Balance tyres
Incorrect toe setting
Adjust front wheel alignment
Note: *The feathered edge of the tread which typifies toe wear is best checked by feel.*

Battery

Caution: Before carrying out any work on the vehicle battery, read the precautions given in 'Safety first!' at the start of this manual.

✔ Make sure that the battery tray is in good condition, and that the clamp is tight. Corrosion on the tray, retaining clamp and the battery itself can be removed with a solution of water and baking soda. Thoroughly rinse all cleaned areas with water. Any metal parts damaged by corrosion should be covered with a zinc-based primer, then painted.

✔ Periodically (approximately every three months), check the charge condition of the battery, as described in Chapter 5.

✔ If the battery is flat, and you need to jump start your vehicle, see *Roadside Repairs*.

HAYNES HINT

Battery corrosion can be kept to a minimum by applying a layer of petroleum jelly to the clamps and terminals after they are reconnected.

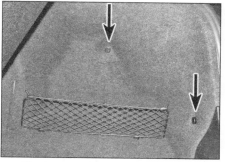

1 The battery is located in the right-hand rear corner of the luggage compartment. Lift out the luggage compartment floor panel, then rotate the fasteners 90° anti-clockwise (Saloon models) or release the clip (Touring models), and remove the right-hand side luggage compartment storage tray. On Touring models, undo the nuts/bolt and remove the cover over the battery.

3 If corrosion (white, fluffy deposits) is evident, remove the cables from the battery terminals, clean them with a small wire brush, then refit them. Automotive stores sell a tool for cleaning the battery post . . .

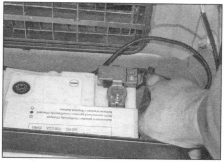

2 Check the tightness of the battery clamps to ensure good electrical connections. You should not be able to move them. Also check each cable for cracks and frayed conductors.

4 . . . as well as the battery cable clamps

Electrical systems

✔ Check all external lights and the horn. Refer to the appropriate Sections of Chapter 12 for details if any of the circuits are found to be inoperative.

✔ Visually check all accessible wiring connectors, harnesses and retaining clips for security, and for signs of chafing or damage.

✔ If a single indicator light, stop-light or headlight has failed, it is likely that a bulb has blown and will need to be renewed. Refer to Chapter 12 for details. If both stop-lights have failed, it is possible that the switch has failed (see Chapter 9).

HAYNES HINT *If you need to check your brake lights and indicators unaided, back up to a wall or garage door and operate the lights. The reflected light should show if they are working properly.*

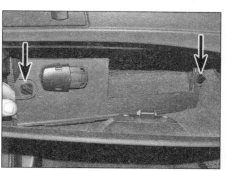

1 If more than one indicator light or tail light has failed check that a fuse has not blown or that there is a fault in the circuit (see Chapter 12). The fuses are located in the fusebox in the passenger side glovebox. Details of the circuits protected by the fuses are shown on the card in the fusebox. Open the glovebox, rotate the fasteners 90° anti-clockwise and lower the fusebox cover from the roof of the glovebox.

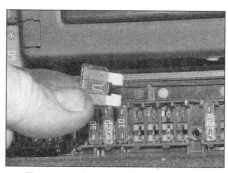

2 To renew a blown fuse, simply pull it out and fit a new fuse of the correct rating (see Chapter 12). If the fuse blows again, it is important that you find out why – a complete checking procedure is given in Chapter 12.

Lubricants and fluids

Engine

All engines . . . . BMW Long-life 04
SAE 5W-30 or 5W-40 (fully-synthetic) to ACEA A3/B4 may be used for topping-up **only**

Cooling system . . . . Long-life ethylene glycol based antifreeze*

Manual transmission

Up to March 2007 . . . . BMW Lifetime transmission oil MTF-LT-2
From March 2007 . . . . BMW Lifetime transmission oil MTF-LT-3

Automatic transmission . . . . BMW Lifetime transmission oil*

Final drive unit . . . . SAE 75W/90 EP*

Braking and clutch systems . . . . Hydraulic fluid to DOT 4

Power steering/Dynamic drive . . . . Dexron II* or Pentosin CHF11S (marked as ATF or CHF on the reservoir filler cap)

* Refer to your BMW dealer for brand name and type recommendations

Tyre pressures (cold)

The tyre pressures are given on a label affixed to the driver's door aperture.

Chapter 1
Routine maintenance and servicing

Contents

Degrees of difficulty

Easy, suitable for novice with little experience	**Fairly easy,** suitable for beginner with some experience	**Fairly difficult,** suitable for competent DIY mechanic	**Difficult,** suitable for experienced DIY mechanic	**Very difficult,** suitable for expert DIY or professional 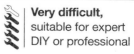

Lubricants and fluids

Refer to *Weekly checks*

General information

Engine type:

N47 D20 (1995 cc)	Four-cylinder in-line, double overhead camshaft, 16-valve, four-stroke, liquid-cooled
M47 D20 T2 (1995 cc)	Four-cylinder in-line, double overhead camshaft, 16-valve, four-stroke, liquid-cooled
M57 D25 TU (2497 cc)	Six-cylinder in-line, double overhead camshaft, 24-valve, four-stroke, liquid cooled
M57 D30 TU/T2 (2993 cc)	Six-cylinder in-line, double overhead camshaft, 24-valve, four-stroke, liquid cooled

Capacities

Note that all capacities are approximate

Engine oil (including filter)

4-cylinder engines:

M47	5.75 litres
N47	5.20 litres

6-cylinder engines:

M57TU	8.25 litres
M57T2:	
Black dipstick	7.50 litres
Red dipstick	7.70 litres

Cooling system

4-cylinder engines:

Manual transmission.	8.0 litres
Automatic transmission	8.6 litres

6-cylinder models:

Manual transmission.	8.2 litres
Automatic transmission	8.8 litres

Transmission

Manual transmission	1.4 litres
Automatic transmission	3.0 litres

Final drive unit

All models:

4-cylinder models.	1.2 litres
6-cylinder models.	1.7 litres

Fuel tank

All models.	70 litres

Cooling system

Antifreeze mixture:

50% antifreeze	Protection down to -30°C

Note: *Refer to antifreeze manufacturer for latest recommendations.*

Brakes

Brake pad friction material minimum thickness.	2.0 mm
Handbrake shoe friction material minimum thickness	1.5 mm

Note: *The wear warning symbol will illuminate when the pad wears down to 3.7 mm thick.*

Torque wrench settings

	Nm	lbf ft
Cylinder block coolant drain plug.	25	18
Engine oil filter cover	25	18
Engine sump oil drain plug:		
M12 plug.	25	18
M18 plug.	35	26
M22 plug.	60	44
Roadwheel bolts.	120	89

The service intervals are tailored according to the operating conditions, driving style, time elapsed and mileage covered, instead of set distance/time limits. These factors are taken into account, and the maintenance requirements are calculated by the vehicles on-board systems, then a symbol representing the item requiring attention is displayed in the instrument cluster. Consequently, the intervals listed below are guidelines, starting values/interval forecasts, or our recommendations. For more details, refer to the Owners Handbook supplied with the vehicle.

When the vehicle is new, it should be serviced by a dealer service department (or other workshop recognised by the vehicle manufacturer as providing the same standard of service) in order to preserve the warranty. The vehicle manufacturer may reject warranty claims if you are unable to prove that servicing has been carried out as and when specified, using only original equipment parts or parts certified to be of equivalent quality.

Remote control battery renewal

The remote control battery is recharged every time the key is inserted into the ignition switch. Battery renewal is therefore not necessary. Should the battery fail, the complete key will require renewing. Refer to a BMW dealer or specialist.

Every 250 miles or weekly
☐ Refer to *Weekly checks*

Every 15 000 miles or 2 years (whichever comes first)
☐ Oil service (Section 3)
Note: *This includes handbrake check, and air filter, main fuel filter, pollen filter and crankcase ventilation filter/depression limiting valve renewal.*
☐ Reset the service interval display (Section 4)

Every 25 000 miles
☐ Front brake service (Section 5)
☐ Reset the service interval display (Section 4)

Every 30 000 miles
☐ Rear brake service (Section 6)
☐ Reset the service interval display (Section 4)

Every 30 000 miles or 4 years (whichever comes first)
☐ Vehicle check (Section 7)
☐ Reset the service interval display (Section 4)

Every 2 years
☐ Renew the brake fluid (Section 8)
☐ Reset the service interval display (Section 4)

Every 125 000 miles
☐ Renew the diesel particulate filter (Section 9)
☐ Reset the service interval display (Section 4)

Every 4 years
Note: *The following items have no specific recommendation concerning their inspection or renewal. However, we consider it prudent to carry out these tasks at least every 4 years.*
☐ Check the condition of the auxiliary drivebelt(s), and adjust/renew if necessary (Section 10)
☐ Coolant renewal (Section 11)

Underbonnet view of the N47 engine

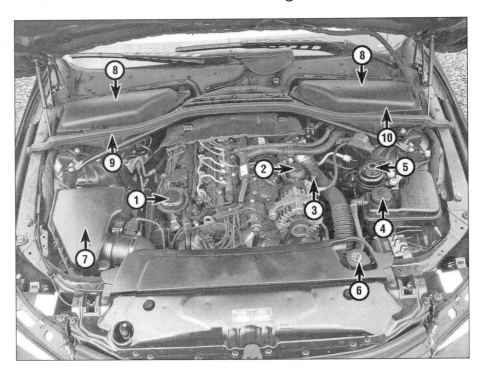

1 Engine oil filler cap
2 Engine oil filter cover
3 Engine oil level dipstick
4 Coolant expansion tank
5 Power steering fluid reservoir
6 Washer fluid reservoir
7 Air filter housing
8 Pollen filter housings
9 Brake and clutch fluid reservoir
  (under pollen filter housing)
10 Engine electrical box (under pollen
   filter housing)

Underbonnet view of the M57T2 engine – M47 engine similar

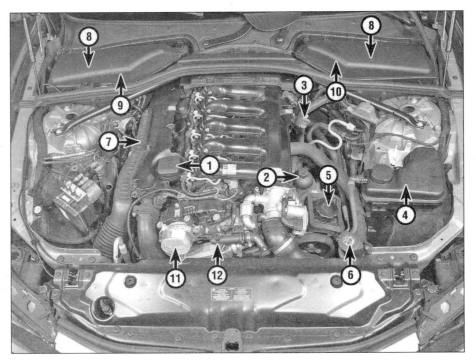

1 Engine oil filler cap
2 Engine oil filter cover
3 Engine oil level dipstick
4 Coolant expansion tank
5 Power steering fluid reservoir
6 Washer fluid reservoir
7 Air filter housing
8 Pollen filter housings
9 Brake and clutch fluid reservoir
  (under pollen filter housing)
10 Engine electrical box (under pollen
   filter housing)
11 Vacuum pump
12 Coolant bleed screw

Front underbody view

1 Engine oil (sump) drain plug
2 Front underbody reinforcement plate
3 Control arm
4 Tension strut
5 Steering track rod
6 Anti-roll bar
7 Intercooler
8 Steering rack
9 Air conditioning compressor
10 Front subframe
11 Brake caliper

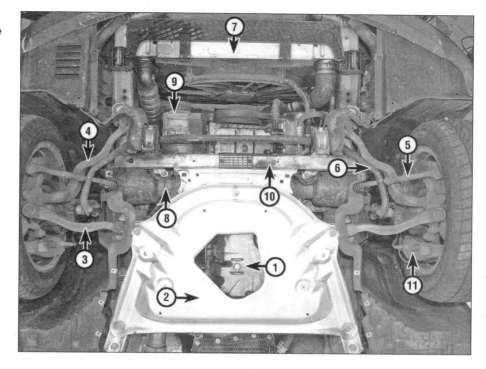

Rear underbody view – Saloon models

1 Fuel tank
2 Exhaust tail box
3 Final drive unit
4 Driveshaft
5 Handbrake cable
6 Integral link
7 Swinging arm
8 Anti-roll bar

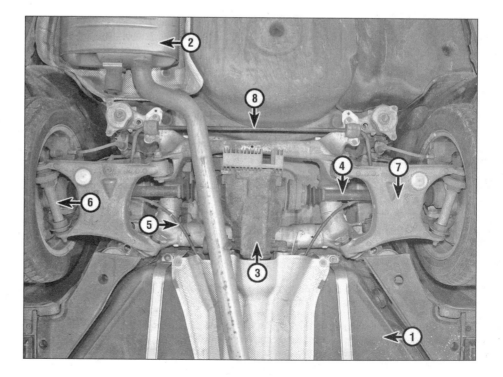

Rear underbody view – Touring models

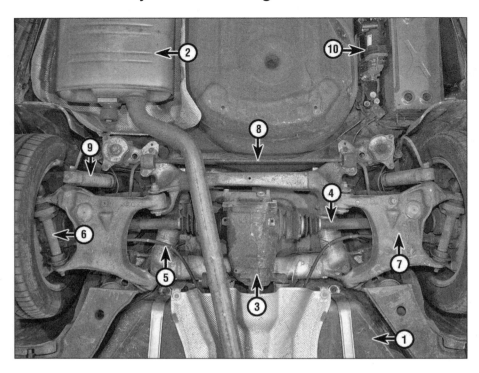

1 Fuel tank
2 Exhaust tail box
3 Final drive unit
4 Driveshaft
5 Handbrake cable
6 Integral link
7 Swinging arm
8 Anti-roll bar
9 Shock absorber
10 Air supply control unit

1 Introduction

1 This Chapter is designed to help the home mechanic maintain his/her vehicle for safety, economy, long life and peak performance.
2 The Chapter contains a master maintenance schedule, followed by Sections dealing specifically with each task in the schedule. Visual checks, adjustments, component renewal and other helpful items are included. Refer to the accompanying illustrations of the engine compartment and the underside of the vehicle for the locations of the various components.
3 Servicing your vehicle in accordance with the service indicator display and the following Sections will provide a planned maintenance programme, which should result in a long and reliable service life. This is a comprehensive plan, so maintaining some items but not others at the specified service intervals, will not produce the same results.
4 As you service your vehicle, you will discover that many of the procedures can – and should – be grouped together, because of the particular procedure being performed, or because of the proximity of two otherwise-unrelated components to one another. For example, if the vehicle is raised for any reason, the exhaust can be inspected at the same time as the suspension and steering components.
5 The first step in this maintenance programme is to prepare yourself before the actual work begins. Read through all the Sections relevant to the work to be carried out, then make a list and gather all the parts and tools required. If a problem is encountered, seek advice from a parts specialist, or a dealer service department.

2 Regular maintenance

1 If, from the time the vehicle is new, the routine maintenance schedule is followed closely, and frequent checks are made of fluid levels and high-wear items, as suggested throughout this manual, the engine will be kept in relatively good running condition, and the need for additional work will be minimised.
2 It is possible that there will be times when the engine is running poorly due to the lack of regular maintenance. This is even more likely if a used vehicle, which has not received regular and frequent maintenance checks, is purchased. In such cases, additional work may need to be carried out, outside of the regular maintenance intervals.
3 If engine wear is suspected, a compression test (refer to the relevant Part of Chapter 2) will provide valuable information regarding the overall performance of the main internal components. Such a test can be used as a basis to decide on the extent of the work to be carried out. If, for example, a compression test indicates serious internal engine wear, conventional maintenance as described in this Chapter will not greatly improve the performance of the engine, and may prove a waste of time and money, unless extensive overhaul work is carried out first.
4 The following series of operations are those most often required to improve the performance of a generally poor-running engine:

Primary operations

a) Clean, inspect and test the battery (See 'Weekly checks').
b) Check all the engine-related fluids (See 'Weekly checks').
c) Check the condition and tension of the auxiliary drivebelt(s) (Section 10).
d) Renew the main fuel filter (Section 3).
e) Check the condition of the air filter, and renew if necessary (Section 3).
f) Check the condition of all hoses, and check for fluid leaks (Section 7).

5 If the above operations do not prove fully effective, carry out the following secondary operations:

Secondary operations

All items listed under *Primary operations*, plus the following:

a) Check the charging system (see Chapter 5).
b) Check the glow plug system (see Chapter 5).
c) Check the fuel system (see Chapter 4A).

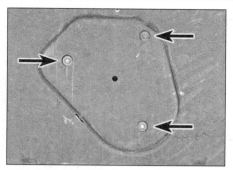

3.3a Undo the bolts (arrowed) and remove the flap in the engine undershield . . .

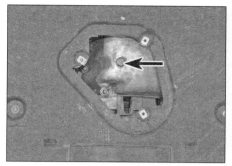

3.3b . . . to access the sump drain plug (arrowed)

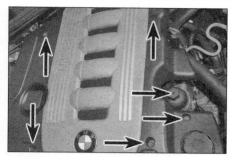

3.4 Undo the bolts (arrowed) and remove the engine cover to improve access to the oil filter housing (arrowed)

Every 15 000 miles or 2 years (whichever comes first)

3 Oil service

1 The engine oil service is made up of 5 elements: Engine oil and filter change, handbrake check, pollen filter renewal, air filter element renewal and main fuel filter change. The handbrake check and pollen filter renewal should be carried out every time the engine oil and filter are changed, whilst on models up to 03/2009, the air filter element and main fuel filter should be renewed after every 3rd engine oil and filter change, and on models after this date, every 2nd engine oil and filter change.

Engine oil and filter change

2 Frequent oil and filter changes are the most important preventative maintenance work which can be undertaken by the DIY owner. As engine oil ages, it becomes diluted and contaminated, which leads to premature engine wear.

3 Before starting this procedure, gather together all the necessary tools and materials. Also make sure you have plenty of clean rags and newspapers handy, to mop-up any spills. Ideally, the engine oil should be warm, as it will drain better, and more built-up sludge will be removed with it. Take care, however, not to touch the exhaust or any other hot parts of the engine when working under the car. To avoid any possibility of scalding, and to protect yourself

from possible skin irritants and other harmful contaminants in used engine oils, it is advisable to wear gloves. Access to the underside of the car will be improved if it can be raised on a lift, driven onto ramps, or jacked up and supported on axle stands (see *Jacking and vehicle support*). Whichever method is chosen, make sure the car remains level, or if it is at an angle, so that the drain plug is at the lowest point. Access to the sump plug is via a removable flap in the engine undershield **(see illustrations)**.

4 Working in the engine compartment, locate the oil filter housing on the left-hand side of the engine, beside the intake manifold. Undo the bolts (M47 and M57 engines only) and remove the plastic acoustic cover from the top of the engine **(see illustration)**. On N47 engines, simply pull the front edge of the cover upwards to release it.

5 Place a wad of rag around the bottom of the oil filter housing to absorb any spilt oil.

6 Using a spanner or socket, unscrew and remove the cover, complete with the filter element **(see illustration)**. The oil will drain from the housing back into the sump as the cover is removed.

7 Recover the O-ring from the cover.

8 Using a clean rag, wipe the mating faces of the housing and cover.

9 Fit new O-ring to the cover **(see illustration)**.

10 On M47 and M57 engines, fit the new filter element into the cover **(see illustration)**. On N47 engines, fit the new filter element into the filter housing, ensuing the lug on the base of the element aligns with the locating hole in the housing **(see illustrations)**.

3.6 Unscrew the cover complete with the filter element

3.9 Renew the O-ring seal

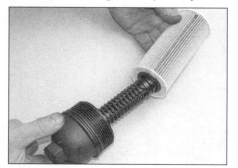

3.10a Fit the new element to the cover – M47 and M57 engines

3.10b Align the lug on the base of the filter element (arrowed) . . .

3.10c . . . with the locating hole (arrowed) in the housing – N47 engines

3.11 Tighten the oil filter cover to the specified torque

3.15 Renew the sump drain plug sealing washer

11 Smear a little clean engine oil on the O-rings, refit the cover and tighten it to 25 Nm (18 lbf ft) if using the special filter removal tool, or securely if using a strap wrench **(see illustration)**.

12 Working under the car, slacken the sump drain plug about half a turn **(see illustration 3.3b)**. Position the draining container under the drain plug, then remove the plug completely. If possible, try to keep the plug pressed into the sump while unscrewing it by hand the last couple of turns.

13 Recover the drain plug sealing ring.

14 Allow some time for the old oil to drain, noting that it may be necessary to reposition the container as the oil flow slows to a trickle.

15 After all the oil has drained, wipe off the drain plug with a clean rag. Check the sealing washer condition, and renew it if necessary. Clean the area around the drain plug opening, then refit and tighten the plug **(see illustration)**.

16 Remove the old oil and all tools from under the car, then lower the car to the ground (if applicable).

Models without a level dipstick

17 Add a little less than the correct amount of oil (see *Capacities* at the start of this Chapter) to the engine through the oil filler cap orifice,

using the correct grade and type of oil (see *Lubricants and fluids*). An oil can spout or funnel may help to reduce spillage.

18 Start the engine and run it for 3 minutes; check for leaks around the oil filter seal and the sump drain plug. Note that there may be a delay of a few seconds before the oil pressure warning light goes out when the engine is first started, as the oil circulates through the engine oil galleries and the new oil filter, before the pressure builds-up.

19 Select 'Vehicle Status' then 'Engine Oil' level through the iDrive menu system. If necessary, stop the engine and add engine oil until the level is correct. Refer to the owners handbook for details of the electronic oil level monitor.

Models with a level dipstick

20 Remove the dipstick then unscrew the oil filler cap from the cylinder head cover. Fill the engine, using the correct grade and type of oil (see *Lubricants and fluids*). An oil can spout or funnel may help to reduce spillage. Pour in half the specified quantity of oil first, then wait a few minutes for the oil to fall to the sump. Continue adding oil a small quantity at a time until the level is up to the lower mark on the dipstick. Finally, bring the level up to the upper mark on the dipstick. Insert the dipstick, and refit the filler cap.

21 Start the engine and run it for a few minutes; check for leaks around the oil filter seal and the sump drain plug. Note that there may be a delay of a few seconds before the oil pressure warning light goes out when the engine is first started, as the oil circulates through the engine oil galleries and the new oil filter, before the pressure builds-up.

22 Switch off the engine, and wait a few minutes for the oil to settle in the sump once more. With the new oil circulated and the filter completely full, recheck the level on the dipstick, and add more oil as necessary.

All models

23 Dispose of the used engine oil safely, with reference to *General repair procedures* in the *Reference* section of this manual.

Handbrake check

24 Check and, if necessary, adjust the handbrake as described in Chapter 9. Check that the handbrake cables are free to move easily and lubricate all exposed linkages/cable pivots.

Pollen filter renewal

25 Undo the fastener 90° anti-clockwise, fold the catch forwards and remove the upper section of the pollen filter housing each side **(see illustration)**. Note that a filter is fitted under the housing on each side of the engine compartment.

26 Remove the filter element **(see illustration)**.

27 Fit the new element into the housing, ensuring it's correctly seated.

28 Refit the upper housing and tighten the fastener.

29 Reset the CBS display as described in Section 4.

Air filter element renewal

M47 engines

30 Undo the bolts and remove the plastic acoustic cover from the top/front of the

3.25 Fold the catch forwards and undo the fastener 90° anti-clockwise (arrowed)

3.26 Slide the pollen filter element from the housing

3.31 Undo the bolt (arrowed) and pull the neck from the housing cover

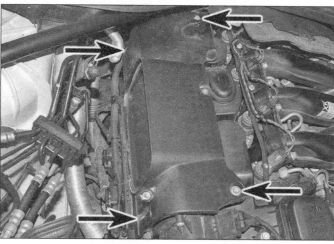

3.32a Undo the bolts (arrowed) . . .

3.32b . . . and manoeuvre the housing cover from place

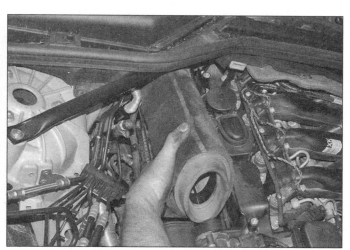

3.33 Lift the filter element from the housing

engine, then undo the bolts and move the plastic acoustic cover at the top/rear of the engine to the left-hand side a little.

31 Undo the bolt and pull the neck outwards from the housing cover **(see illustration)**.

32 Undo the 4 bolts and lift off the filter housing cover **(see illustrations)**.

33 Lift the filter element from place, noting how the support at the end of the filter element locates in the housing **(see illustration)**.

34 Clean the air filter housing, removing all debris.

35 Slide the new filter element into place, ensuring it locates correctly with the housing, with the rear locating lug at the base.

36 The remainder of refitting is a reversal of removal.

N47 engines

37 Undo the fasteners and lift the filter cover **(see illustration)**.

38 Note its fitted position, and lift the

filter element from the housing **(see illustration)**.

39 Clean the air filter housing, removing all debris.

40 Fit the new filter element into place, ensuring it locates correctly with the housing.

41 The remainder of refitting is a reversal of removal.

M57 engines

42 Undo the bolts and remove the acoustic cover from the top of the engine **(see illustration 3.4)**.

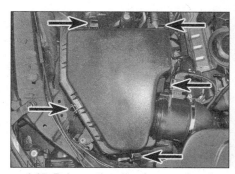

3.37 Release the clips (arrowed) and remove the air filter cover

3.38 Lift out the filter element

3.44 Undo the bolts (arrowed) and slide the intake neck forwards

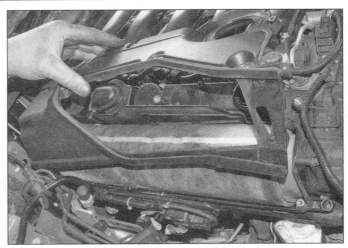

3.45 Undo the bolts and manoeuvre the air filter cover from place

3.46 Note how the front of the element locates in the housing

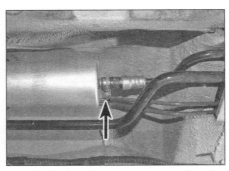

3.52 Slacken the clamp (arrowed) and disconnect the hose from the filter

Main fuel filter renewal

50 Ensure the ignition is switched off, then raise the rear of the vehicle and support it securely on axle stands (see *Jacking and vehicle support*).

51 Undo the bolts and remove the underbody protection panel to the left-hand side of the transmission.

52 Release the clamp securing the fuel hose to the front of the filter, and disconnect the hose **(see illustration)**. Be prepared for fuel spillage.

53 Undo the bolt securing the filter unit clamp to the vehicle body **(see illustration)**. The clamp must be transferred to the new filter.

54 Slide out the clip and detach the fuel preheater from the rear of the filter **(see illustration)**.

55 Refitting is a reversal of removal. Turn on the ignition and leave it for approximately 1 minute. The presupply pump in the tank is activated, and the fuel pipe to the high-pressure pump is vented. Start the engine and check for leaks.

43 Disconnect the intake hose from the air cleaner housing.

44 Undo the 3 bolts and slide the air filter intake neck forwards **(see illustration)**.

45 Unscrew the oil filler cap, then undo the 5 bolts and remove the air filter cover **(see illustration)**.

46 Lift the filter element from place, noting

how the support at the end of the filter element locates in the housing **(see illustration)**.

47 Clean the air filter housing, removing all debris.

48 Slide the new filter element into place, ensuring it locates correctly with the housing.

49 The remainder of refitting is a reversal of removal.

3.53 Undo the filter clamp retaining bolt (arrowed)

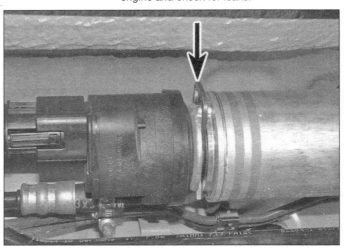

3.54 Slide out the clip (arrowed) securing the preheater

Crankcase ventilation filter/ depression limiting valve renewal

Note: *This applies to M47 engines up to 06/06 only. After this date, a different design of filter is used that requires no attention.*

56 Renew the filter in the crankcase depression limiting valve as described in Chapter 4B.

4 Resetting the service interval display

1 Ensure that all electrical items are switched off then turn on the ignition switch. **Note:** *Do not start the engine.*

2 Ensure the on-board time and date are correctly set in accordance with the instructions in the owners handbook. In order for the CBS display to function correctly, the on-board time and date must be correct. Refer to the owners handbook for details of how to set these values.

3 Each service item that appears on the instrument cluster display can be reset. Note that it is only possible to reset an item if the service life of the item is below 80%.

4 Press the trip odometer button for approximately 10 seconds until the first CBS (Condition Based Service) item appears in the instrument cluster display. Note that the most urgent item is displayed first. If this is not the item required, select the item to be reset by briefly pressing the button again.

5 When the required item is selected, press the button again until 'Reset?' appears in the display. Note that the reset process is cancelled by not pressing the button to confirm, and waiting for the display to return to its normal state.

6 Press the button again for approximately 3 seconds to confirm the reset. Note that it is only possible to reset the brake pad display if the pad sensors are working properly.

7 Turn off the ignition switch.

Every 25 000 miles

5 Front brake service

Front brake pads

1 When this CBS item is displayed, the thickness of the front brake pads friction material should be checked, and if any are approaching the minimum thickness, *all* four front pads should be renewed.

2 Firmly apply the handbrake, then jack up the front of the car and support it securely on axle stands (see *Jacking and vehicle support*). Remove the front roadwheels.

3 The brake pad warning symbol in the CBS display indicates that the pad friction material thickness is worn such that the pads require renewal. However, the warning will also be given if the wiring to and from each pads sensor is damaged or the connections are poor, dirty, etc. Check the wiring to and from the sensor for poor connections/breaks before renewing the pads.

4 The thickness of friction material remaining on each brake pad can be measured through the top of the caliper body. If any pad's friction material is worn to the specified thickness or less, all four pads must be renewed as a set. Pad renewal is described in Chapter 9.

5 Regardless of whether or not the pads have been changed, apply a light coat of anti-seize grease (eg, Copperslip) to the centre of the allow wheel prior to refitting.

Front brake disc check

6 Check the front brake disc condition, and measure the thickness of the disc as described in Chapter 9. Renew both front discs if necessary.

7 Reset the CBS display as described in Section 4.

Every 30 000 miles

6 Rear brake service

Rear brake pads

1 When this CBS item is displayed, the thickness of the rear brake pads friction material should be checked, and if any are approaching the minimum thickness, *all* four rear pads should be renewed.

2 Chock the front wheels, then jack up the rear of the car and support it on axle stands (see *Jacking and vehicle support*). Remove the rear roadwheels.

3 The thickness of friction material remaining on each brake pad can be measured through the top of the caliper body. If any pad's friction material is worn to the specified thickness or less, *all* four pads must be renewed as a set. Pad renewal is described in Chapter 9.

4 Regardless of whether or not the pads have been changed, apply a light coat of anti-seize grease (eg, Copperslip) to the centre of the allow wheel prior to refitting.

Rear brake disc check

5 Check the front brake disc condition, and measure the thickness of the disc as described in Chapter 9. Renew both front discs if necessary.

Handbrake shoe lining check

6 Inspect and the handbrake shoes lining material as described in Chapter 9. If any of the shoe's lining material has worn below the minimum thickness, renew *all* four shoes as described in Chapter 9.

7 Reset the CBS display as described in Section 4.

Every 30 000 miles or 4 years (whichever comes first)

7 Vehicle check

1 The vehicle check consists of several tasks. Before the CBS display can be reset, *all* of the following tasks must be complete.

Instruments and electrical equipment

2 Check the operation of all instruments and electrical equipment.

3 Make sure that all instruments read correctly, and switch on all electrical equipment in turn, to check that it functions properly.

Seat belt check

4 Carefully examine the seat belt webbing for cuts or any signs of serious fraying or deterioration. Pull the belt all the way out, and examine the full extent of the webbing.

5 Fasten and unfasten the belt, ensuring that the locking mechanism holds securely and releases properly when intended. Check

7.12 Use an hydrometer to check the coolant concentration

HAYNES HINT

A leak in the cooling system will usually show up as white- or antifreeze-coloured deposits on the area adjoining the leak

7.26 Check for wear in the hub bearings by grasping the wheel and trying to rock it

also that the retracting mechanism operates correctly when the belt is released.

6 Check the security of all seat belt mountings and attachments which are accessible, without removing any trim or other components, from inside the car.

Wash/wipe system check

7 Check that each of the washer jet nozzles are clear and that each nozzle provides a strong jet of washer fluid. Renew as necessary – refer to Chapter 12.

8 Check the condition of each wiper blade for damage of wear. As time passes the blades will become hardened, wipe performance will deteriorate, and noise will increase. Renew the blades as necessary – see Chapter 12.

Bodywork corrosion check

9 This work should be carried out by a BMW dealer in order to validate the vehicle warranty. The work includes a thorough inspection of the vehicle paintwork and underbody for damage and corrosion.

Tyre check

10 Check the tread depth, external condition and inflation pressure of the tyres. See *Weekly checks* for details of the procedures and tyre pressure information.

Battery check

11 Check the condition of the battery, and recharge if necessary – refer to Chapter 5.

Coolant concentration check

12 Use a hydrometer to check the strength of the antifreeze **(see illustration)**. Follow the instructions provided with your hydrometer. The antifreeze strength should be approximately 50%. If it is significantly less than this, drain a little coolant from the radiator (see this Chapter), add antifreeze to the coolant expansion tank, then recheck the strength.

Hose and fluid leak check

13 Visually inspect the engine joint faces, gaskets and seals for any signs of water or oil leaks. Pay particular attention to the areas around the camshaft cover, cylinder head, oil filter and sump joint faces. Bear in mind that, over a period of time, some very slight seepage from these areas is to be expected – what you are really looking for is any indication of a

serious leak. Should a leak be found, renew the offending gasket or oil seal by referring to the appropriate Chapters in this manual.

14 Also check the security and condition of all the engine-related pipes and hoses. Ensure that all cable-ties or securing clips are in place and in good condition. Clips which are broken or missing can lead to chafing of the hoses, pipes or wiring, which could cause more serious problems in the future.

15 Carefully check the radiator hoses and heater hoses along their entire length. Renew any hose which is cracked, swollen or deteriorated. Cracks will show up better if the hose is squeezed. Pay close attention to the hose clips that secure the hoses to the cooling system components. Hose clips can pinch and puncture hoses, resulting in cooling system leaks.

16 Inspect all the cooling system components (hoses, joint faces, etc) for leaks. A leak in the cooling system will usually show up as white- or antifreeze-coloured deposits on the area adjoining the leak **(see Haynes Hint)**. Where any problems of this nature are found on system components, renew the component or gasket with reference to Chapter 3.

17 Where applicable, inspect the automatic transmission fluid cooler hoses for leaks or deterioration.

18 With the car raised, inspect the petrol tank and filler neck for punctures, cracks and other damage. The connection between the filler neck and tank is especially critical. Sometimes a rubber filler neck or connecting hose will leak due to loose retaining clamps or deteriorated rubber.

19 Carefully check all rubber hoses and metal fuel lines leading away from the petrol tank. Check for loose connections, deteriorated hoses, crimped lines, and other damage. Pay particular attention to the vent pipes and hoses, which often loop up around the filler neck and can become blocked or crimped. Follow the lines to the front of the car, carefully inspecting them all the way. Renew damaged sections as necessary.

20 Closely inspect the metal brake pipes which run along the car underbody. If they show signs of excessive corrosion or damage they must be renewed.

21 From within the engine compartment, check the security of all fuel hose attachments and pipe unions, and inspect the fuel hoses and vacuum hoses for kinks, chafing and deterioration.

22 Check the condition of the power steering fluid hoses and pipes.

Suspension and steering check

23 Raise the front of the car, and securely support it on axle stands (see *Jacking and vehicle support*).

24 Visually inspect the balljoint dust covers and the steering rack-and-pinion gaiters for splits, chafing or deterioration. Any wear of these components will cause loss of lubricant, then dirt and water entry, resulting in rapid deterioration of the balljoints or steering gear.

25 Check the power steering fluid hoses for chafing or deterioration, and the pipe and hose unions for fluid leaks. Also check for signs of fluid leakage under pressure from the steering gear rubber gaiters, which would indicate failed fluid seals within the steering gear.

26 Grasp the roadwheel at the 12 o'clock and 6 o'clock positions, and try to rock it **(see illustration)**. Very slight free play may be felt, but if the movement is appreciable, further investigation is necessary to determine the source. Continue rocking the wheel while an assistant depresses the footbrake. If the movement is now eliminated or significantly reduced, it is likely that the hub bearings are at fault. If the free play is still evident with the footbrake depressed, then there is wear in the suspension joints or mountings.

27 Now grasp the wheel at the 9 o'clock and 3 o'clock positions, and try to rock it as before. Any movement felt now may again be caused by wear in the hub bearings or the steering track rod balljoints. If the inner or outer balljoint is worn, the visual movement will be obvious.

28 Using a large screwdriver or flat bar, check for wear in the suspension mounting bushes by levering between the relevant suspension component and its attachment point. Some movement is to be expected as the mountings are made of rubber, but excessive wear should be obvious. Also check the condition of any visible rubber bushes, looking for splits, cracks or contamination of the rubber.

29 With the car standing on its wheels, have

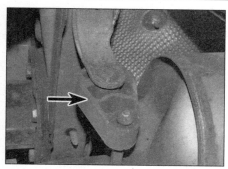

7.33 Check the condition of the exhaust mounting rubbers (arrowed)

an assistant turn the steering wheel back and forth about an eighth of a turn each way. There should be very little, if any, lost movement between the steering wheel and roadwheels. If this is not the case, closely observe the joints and mountings previously described, but in addition, check the steering column universal joints for wear, and the rack-and-pinion steering gear itself.

Strut/shock absorber check

30 Check for any signs of fluid leakage around the suspension strut/shock absorber body, or from the rubber gaiter around the piston rod. Should any fluid be noticed, the suspension strut/shock absorber is defective internally, and should be renewed. **Note:** *Suspension struts/shock absorbers should always be renewed in pairs on the same axle.*
31 The efficiency of the suspension strut/ shock absorber may be checked by bouncing the car at each corner. Generally speaking, the body will return to its normal position and stop after being depressed. If it rises and returns on a rebound, the suspension strut/shock absorber is probably suspect. Examine also the suspension strut/shock absorber upper and lower mountings for any signs of wear.

Exhaust system check

32 With the engine cold (at least an hour after

the car has been driven), check the complete exhaust system from the engine to the end of the tailpipe. The exhaust system is most easily checked with the car raised on a hoist, or suitably supported on axle stands, so that the exhaust components are readily visible and accessible.
33 Check the exhaust pipes and connections for evidence of leaks, severe corrosion and damage. Make sure that all brackets and mountings are in good condition, and that all relevant nuts and bolts are tight **(see illustration)**. Leakage at any of the joints or in other parts of the system will usually show up as a black sooty stain in the vicinity of the leak.
34 Rattles and other noises can often be traced to the exhaust system, especially the brackets and mountings. Try to move the pipes and silencers. If the components are able to come into contact with the body or suspension parts, secure the system with new mountings. Otherwise separate the joints (if possible) and twist the pipes as necessary to provide additional clearance.

Hinge and lock lubrication

35 Lubricate the hinges of the bonnet, doors and tailgate with a light general-purpose oil. Similarly, lubricate all latches, locks and lock strikers. At the same time, check the security and operation of all the locks, adjusting them if necessary (see Chapter 11). Lightly lubricate the bonnet release mechanism and cable with a suitable grease.

Road test

Steering and suspension

36 Check for any abnormalities in the steering, suspension, handling or road 'feel'.
37 Drive the car, and check that there are no unusual vibrations or noises.
38 Check that the steering feels positive, with no excessive 'sloppiness', or roughness, and check for any suspension noises when cornering and driving over bumps.

Drivetrain

39 Check the performance of the engine,

clutch (where applicable), gearbox/ transmission and driveshafts.
40 Listen for any unusual noises from the engine, clutch and gearbox/transmission.
41 Make sure that the engine runs smoothly when idling, and that there is no hesitation when accelerating.
42 Check that, where applicable, the clutch action is smooth and progressive, that the drive is taken up smoothly, and that the pedal travel is not excessive. Also listen for any noises when the clutch pedal is depressed.
43 On manual gearbox models, check that all gears can be engaged smoothly without noise, and that the gear lever action is smooth and not abnormally vague or 'notchy'.
44 On automatic transmission models, make sure that all gearchanges occur smoothly, without snatching, and without an increase in engine speed between changes. Check that all the gear positions can be selected with the car at rest. If any problems are found, they should be referred to a BMW dealer or suitably-equipped specialist.

Braking system

45 Make sure that the car does not pull to one side when braking, and that the wheels do not lock when braking hard.
46 Check that there is no vibration through the steering when braking.
47 Check that the handbrake operates correctly without excessive movement of the lever, and that it holds the car stationary on a slope.
48 Test the operation of the brake servo unit as follows. With the engine off, depress the footbrake four or five times to exhaust the vacuum. Hold the brake pedal depressed, then start the engine. As the engine starts, there should be a noticeable 'give' in the brake pedal as vacuum builds-up. Allow the engine to run for at least two minutes, and then switch it off. If the brake pedal is depressed now, it should be possible to detect a hiss from the servo as the pedal is depressed. After about four or five applications, no further hissing should be heard, and the pedal should feel much harder.

Every 2 years

8 Brake fluid renewal

⚠️ *Warning: Brake hydraulic fluid can harm your eyes and damage painted surfaces, so use extreme caution when handling and pouring it. Do not use fluid that has been standing open for some time, as it absorbs moisture from the air. Excess moisture can cause a dangerous loss of braking effectiveness.*

1 The procedure is similar to that for the bleeding of the hydraulic system as described in Chapter 9, except that the brake fluid reservoir should be emptied by siphoning,

using a clean poultry baster or similar before starting, and allowance should be made for the old fluid to be expelled when bleeding a section of the circuit.
2 Working as described in Chapter 9, open the first bleed screw in the sequence, and pump the brake pedal gently until nearly all the old fluid has been emptied from the master cylinder reservoir.
3 Top-up to the MAX level with new fluid, and continue pumping until only the new fluid remains in the reservoir, and new fluid can be seen emerging from the bleed screw. Tighten the screw, and top the reservoir level up to the MAX level line.
4 Work through all remaining bleed screws in the sequence until new fluid can be seen

at all of them. Be careful to keep the master cylinder reservoir topped-up to above the MIN level at all times, or air may enter the system and increase the length of the task.

 Old hydraulic fluid is usually much darker in colour than the new, making it easy to distinguish the two.

5 When the operation is complete, check that all bleed screws are securely tightened, and that their dust caps are refitted. Wash off all traces of spilt fluid, and recheck the master cylinder reservoir fluid level.
6 Check the operation of the brakes before taking the car on the road.

Every 125 000 miles

9 Diesel particulate filter renewal

Note: *This procedure is only necessary on engines equipped with a particulate filter.*

Renewal of the diesel particulate filter is described in Chapter 4B.

Every 4 years

10 Auxiliary drivebelt(s) check and renewal

Drivebelt(s) checking

1 Due to their function and construction, the belts are prone to failure after a period of time, and should be inspected periodically to prevent problems.

10.6 Lever the lower edge of the compressor belt forwards and rotate the crankshaft pulley

2 The number of belts used on a particular car depends on the accessories fitted. Drivebelts are used to drive the coolant pump, alternator, power steering pump and air conditioning compressor (where applicable).

3 To improve access for belt inspection, if desired, remove the cooling fan and shroud as described in Chapter 3.

4 With the engine stopped, using your fingers (and an electric torch if necessary), move along the belts, checking for cracks and separation of the belt plies. Also check for fraying and glazing, which gives the belt a shiny appearance. Both sides of the belts should be inspected, which means the belt will have to be twisted to check the underside. If necessary turn the engine using a spanner or socket on the crankshaft pulley bolt to that the whole of the belt can be inspected.

Drivebelt(s) renewal

5 Open the bonnet. Remove the cooling fan and shroud as described in Chapter 3.

M47 engine

6 If the drivebelt is to be re-used, mark the running direction of the belt before removal.

Using a large flat bar, lever the lower edge of the air conditioning compressor (where fitted) belt forwards, and rotate the crankshaft pulley clockwise and remove the belt from the pulleys **(see illustration)**.

7 If the drivebelt is to be re-used, mark the running direction of the belt before removal.

8 Using a ½ inch drive extension bar, rotate the belt tensioner assembly clockwise to compress the tensioner, and slide the drivebelt from the pulleys **(see illustration)**.

9 If desired, to aid refitting the tensioner can be compressed fully and locked in position using a metal rod through the hole in the tensioner – note that the tensioner has a powerful spring, so a strong rod will be required **(see illustration 10.8)**.

10 If the original belt is being refitted, observe the running direction mark made before removal.

11 If the tensioner has not been locked in position, compress the tensioner, and engage the belt with the pulleys, ensuring that it is routed as noted before removal **(see illustration)**. Make sure that the belt engages correctly with the grooves in the pulleys.

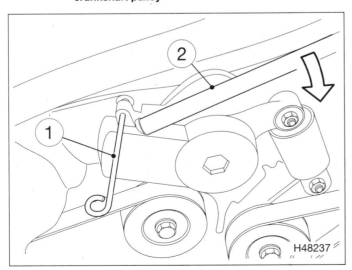

10.8 Position the ½" drive extension bar (2), press down, and lock it in place with a suitable rod/drill bit (1)

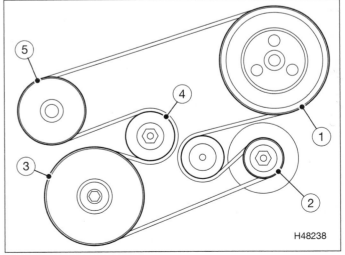

10.11 Auxiliary drivebelt routing – M47 engine

1 *Power steering pump pulley*	3 *Crankshaft pulley*
2 *Alternator pulley*	4 *Tensioner pulley*
	5 *Coolant pump pulley*

10.13a The BMW tool fits into the centre of the pulley, and feeds the belt into place as it's rotated

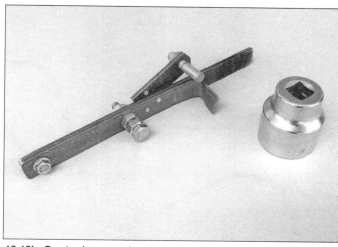

10.13b Our tool uses strip steel, a couple of bolts, some studding and a large socket

10.13c Position the socket in the pulley, the tool in the socket, fit the belt to the top edge of the tool . . .

10.13d . . . then rotate the tool clockwise and seat the belt in the pulley grooves

12 Where applicable, compress the tensioner until the locking rod can be removed, then withdraw the rod and release the tensioner.

13 Position the air conditioning compressor belt around the pump pulley and the upper half of the crankshaft pulley. Position BMW special tool No 11 0 330 on the crankshaft pulley, then rotate the pulley clockwise. As the pulley rotates, the power steering pump belt will be pulled into place. We made an alternative tool using strips of steel (see illustrations).

N47 engine

14 If the drivebelt is to be re-used, mark the running direction of the belt before removal.

15 Using a Torx bit, rotate the tensioner (clockwise), and slide the drivebelt from the pulleys (see illustration).

16 If desired, to aid refitting, the tensioner can be compressed fully and locked in position using a metal rod engaged with the

holes in the tensioner and backplate – note that the tensioner has a powerful spring, so a strong rod/drill bit will be required (see illustration).

17 If the original belt is being refitted, observe

the running direction mark made before removal.

18 If the tensioner has not been locked in position, compress the tensioner, and engage the belt with the pulleys, ensuring

10.15 Insert a Torx bit into the bolt head (arrowed) and rotate the tensioner clockwise

10.16 Lock the tensioner using a drill bit/rod (arrowed)

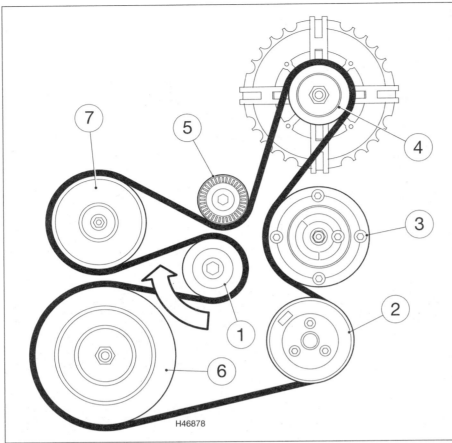

10.18 Auxiliary belt routing – N47 engines

1	Tensioner pulley	4	Alternator pulley
2	Power steering pump pulley	5	Idler pulley
3	Air conditioning compressor pulley	6	Crankshaft pulley
		7	Coolant pump pulley

that it is routed as noted before removal **(see illustration)**. Make sure that the belt engages correctly with the grooves in the pulleys.

19 Where applicable, compress the tensioner until the locking rod can be removed, then withdraw the rod and release the tensioner.

20 Refit the cooling fan and shroud as described in Chapter 3.

M57 engine

21 Raise the front of the vehicle and support it securely on axle stands (see *Jacking and vehicle support*). Undo the fasteners, remove the front section of the engine undershield **(see illustration)**.

22 Remove the cooling fan and shroud as described in Chapter 3.

23 Remove the air conditioning compressor drivebelt as described in Paragraph 6 of this Section.

24 If the main drivebelt is to be re-used, mark the running direction of the belt before removal.

25 Using a spanner or socket, rotate the tensioner pulley (clockwise) to compress the tensioner, and slide the drivebelt from the pulleys **(see illustration)**.

26 If the original belt is being refitted, observe the running direction mark made before removal.

27 Compress the tensioner, and engage the belt with the pulleys, ensuring that it is routed as noted before removal **(see illustration)**. Make sure that the belt engages correctly with the grooves in the pulleys.

10.25 Rotate the tensioner pulley clockwise

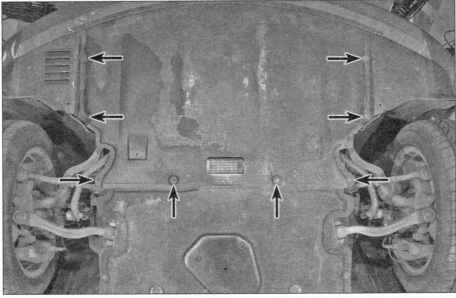

10.21 Undo the fasteners (arrowed) and remove the front section of the engine undershield

10.27 Auxiliary belt routing – M57 engines. Note the extra pulley (arrowed) is only fitted to automatic transmission models

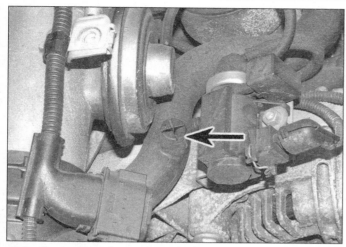

11.3a Coolant bleed screws may be located on the coolant return hose (arrowed) . . .

11.3b . . . and the EGR cooler (arrowed), according to model

28 Refit the air conditioning compressor drivebelt.
29 Refit the cooling fan and shroud as described in Chapter 3.

11 Coolant renewal

⚠️ *Warning: Wait until the engine is cold before starting this procedure. Do not allow antifreeze to come in contact with your skin, or with the painted surfaces of the car. Rinse off spills immediately with plenty of water. Never leave antifreeze lying around in an open container, or in a puddle in the driveway or on the garage floor. Children and pets are attracted by its sweet smell, but antifreeze can be fatal if ingested.*

Cooling system draining

1 With the engine completely cold, cover the expansion tank cap with a wad of rag, and slowly turn the cap anti-clockwise to relieve the pressure in the cooling system (a hissing sound may be heard). Wait until any pressure in the system is released, then continue to turn the cap until it can be removed.
2 Remove the intercooler as described in Chapter 4A. **Note:** *On 6-cylinder engines, we found it possible to access the radiator drain plug without removing the intercooler. On these models, raise the front of the vehicle, undo the fasteners and remove the engine/radiator undershield (see illustration 10.21).*
3 Bleed screws may be fitted to the EGR cooler, the coolant return hose and the coolant expansion tank **(see illustrations)**. Undo the bolts (where applicable), remove the

plastic cover from the top of the engine **(see illustration 3.4)** and open the bleed screws.
4 Position a suitable container beneath the drain plug(s) on the base of the radiator. Unscrew the drain plug(s) and allow the coolant to drain into the container **(see illustration)**. On models without a radiator drain plug, release the clamp and disconnect the radiator lower hose.
5 To fully drain the system, also unscrew the coolant drain plug from the right-hand side of the cylinder block and allow the remainder of the coolant to drain into the container **(see illustration)**. Access to the plug is extremely limited.
6 If the coolant has been drained for a reason other than renewal, then provided it is clean it can be re-used, though this is not recommended.
7 Once ali the coolant has drained, fit a new

11.4 The drain plug is located at the left-hand end of the radiator (arrowed – viewed from underneath)

11.5 The cylinder block coolant drain plug is located on the right-hand side of the cylinder block (arrowed). Shown with the air conditioning compressor removed

sealing washer to the block drain plug and tighten it to the specified torque.

Cooling system flushing

8 If the antifreeze mixture has become diluted, then in time, the cooling system may gradually lose efficiency, as the coolant passages become restricted due to rust, scale deposits, and other sediment. The cooling system efficiency can be restored by flushing the system clean.

9 The radiator should be flushed independently of the engine, to avoid unnecessary contamination.

Radiator flushing

10 To flush the radiator, disconnect the top and bottom hoses and any other relevant hoses from the radiator, with reference to Chapter 3.

11 Insert a garden hose into the radiator top inlet. Direct a flow of clean water through the radiator, and continue flushing until clean water emerges from the radiator bottom outlet.

12 If after a reasonable period, the water still does not run clear, the radiator can be flushed with a good proprietary cooling system cleaning agent. It is important that their manufacturer's instructions are followed carefully. If the contamination is particularly bad, insert the hose in the radiator bottom outlet, and reverse-flush the radiator.

Engine flushing

13 To flush the engine, remove the thermostat as described in Chapter 3, then temporarily refit the thermostat cover. On models where the thermostat is integral with the housing, remove the housing to allow the water to flow out.

14 With the top and bottom hoses disconnected from the radiator, insert a garden hose into the radiator top hose. Direct a clean flow of water through the engine, and continue flushing until clean water emerges from the radiator bottom hose.

15 On completion of flushing, refit the thermostat and reconnect the hoses with reference to Chapter 3.

Cooling system filling

16 Before attempting to fill the cooling system, make sure that all hoses and clips are in good condition, and that the clips are tight and the radiator and cylinder block drain plugs are securely tightened. Note that an antifreeze mixture must be used all year round, to prevent corrosion of the engine components (see following sub-Section).

17 Slacken the bleed screw(s) **(see illustrations 11.3a and 11.3b)**.

18 Turn on the ignition, and set the heater control to maximum temperature, with the fan speed set to 'low'. This opens the heating valves.

19 Remove the expansion tank filler cap. Fill the system by slowly pouring the coolant into the expansion tank to prevent airlocks from forming.

20 If the coolant is being renewed, begin by pouring in a couple of litres of water, followed by the correct quantity of antifreeze, then top-up with more water.

21 As soon as coolant free from air bubbles emerges from the bleed screw(s), tighten the screw(s) securely.

22 Once the level in the expansion tank starts to rise, squeeze the radiator top and bottom hoses to help expel any trapped air in the system. Once all the air is expelled, top-up the coolant level to the maximum level, then refit the expansion tank cap **(see illustration)**.

23 Start the engine and run it until it reaches normal operating temperature, then stop the engine and allow it to cool.

24 Check for leaks, particularly around disturbed components. Check the coolant level in the expansion tank, and top-up if necessary. Note that the system must be cold before an accurate level is indicated in the expansion tank. If the expansion tank cap is removed while the engine is still warm, cover

11.22 Top-up the coolant to the MAX level indicated in the expansion tank filler neck

the cap with a thick cloth, and unscrew the cap slowly to gradually relieve the system pressure (a hissing sound will normally be heard). Wait until any pressure remaining in the system is released, then continue to turn the cap until it can be removed.

Antifreeze mixture

25 Always use an ethylene-glycol based antifreeze which is suitable for use in mixed-metal cooling systems. The quantity of antifreeze and levels of protection are indicated in the Specifications.

26 Before adding antifreeze, the cooling system should be completely drained, preferably flushed, and all hoses checked for condition and security.

27 After filling with antifreeze, a label should be attached to the expansion tank, stating the type and concentration of antifreeze used, and the date installed. Any subsequent topping-up should be made with the same type and concentration of antifreeze.

Caution: Do not use engine antifreeze in the windscreen/tailgate washer system, as it will damage the vehicle paintwork. A screenwash additive should be added to the washer system in the quantities stated on the bottle.

Chapter 2 Part A:
N47 engine in-car repair procedures

Contents

Degrees of difficulty

Easy, suitable for novice with little experience 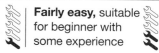	**Fairly easy,** suitable for beginner with some experience	**Fairly difficult,** suitable for competent DIY mechanic	**Difficult,** suitable for experienced DIY mechanic	**Very difficult,** suitable for expert DIY or professional

Specifications

General

Engine type:

N47 D20 .... Four-cylinder in-line, double overhead camshaft, 16-valve, four-stroke, liquid-cooled

Bore	84.0 mm
Stroke	90.0 mm
Capacity	1995 cc
Direction of crankshaft rotation	Clockwise (seen from the front of the engine)
Compression ratio	16.0 : 1
Compression pressure:	
Minimum.	16 bar

Lubrication system

Minimum system pressure:

Idle speed (hot)	1.3 bar
3500 rpm (hot)	4.0 to 6.0 bar

Torque wrench settings	Nm	lbf ft
Balance shaft idler gear to crankcase*	70	52
Balance shaft drivegear:*		
Stage 1	40	30
Stage 2	Angle-tighten a further 90°	
Camshaft bearing cap bolts	10	7
Camshaft carrier to cylinder head	13	10
Camshaft cover bolts:		
M6	10	7
M7	15	11
Camshaft sprocket to gearwheel – intake camshaft	14	10
Connecting rod big-end bearing cap bolts:*		
Stage 1	5	4
Stage 2	20	15
Stage 3	Angle-tighten a further 70°	
Crankshaft pulley/vibration damper bolts:*		
Stage 1	40	30
Stage 2	Angle-tighten a further 120°	
Cylinder block drain plug	25	18

Torque wrench settings (continued)

	Nm	lbf ft
Cylinder head bolts:*		
Stage 1	70	52
Stage 2	Slacken 180°	
Stage 3	50	37
Stage 4	Angle-tighten a further 120°	
Stage 5	Angle-tighten a further 120°	
Cylinder head-to-timing cover bolts:		
M7	15	11
M8	20	15
Engine mountings:		
Mounting to front subframe:		
M8	21	15
M10	56	41
Mounting to engine support bracket	56	41
Engine support bracket to engine	38	28
Flywheel/driveplate bolts*	120	89
Front underbody reinforcement plate:*		
Stage 1	56	41
Stage 2	Angle tighten a further 90°	
Front subframe mounting bolts:		
M10:		
Stage 1	56	41
Stage 2	Angle-tighten a further 90°	
M12	100	74
Fuel injection pump sprocket retaining bolt	65	48
Main bearing cap bolts:*		
Stage 1	25	18
Stage 2	50	37
Stage 3	Angle-tighten a further 60°	
Stage 4	Angle-tighten a further 60°	
Oil cooler-to-oil filter housing bolts	22	16
Oil filter cap	25	18
Oil filter housing bolts	25	18
Oil level sensor	8	6
Oil pressure sensor	28	21
Oil pump:		
M7	25	18
M8:*		
Stage 1	15	11
Stage 2	Angle-tighten a further 90°	
Oil pump intake pipe	20	15
Oil pump sprocket:†		
Stage 1	5	4
Stage 2	Angle-tighten a further 90°	
Piston oil spray jet bolts	10	7
Roadwheel bolts	120	89
Suspension turret/tension braces*	30	22
Sump bolts:		
M6	10	7
M8	25	18
Sump drain plug	25	18
Timing chain cover bolts:		
M6:		
Stage 1	8	6
Stage 2	Angle-tighten a further 90°	
Timing chain cover to fuel pump	11	8
M6	10	7
M7	15	11
M8	22	16
Timing chain cover plug:*		
M34	20	15
M40	30	22
Timing chain lower guide pins	20	15
Timing chain lower tensioner bolts	10	7
Timing chain upper tensioner	70	52

† Left-hand thread
* Do not re-use
Always renew aluminium bolts.

1 General information and precautions

How to use this Chapter

This Part of the Chapter describes those repair procedures that can reasonably be carried out on the engine whilst it remains in the vehicle. If the engine has been removed from the vehicle and is being dismantled as described in Part C of this Chapter, any preliminary dismantling procedures can be ignored.

Note that whilst it may be possible physically to overhaul items such as the piston/connecting rod assemblies with the engine in the vehicle, such tasks are not usually carried out as separate operations and usually require the execution of several additional procedures (not to mention the cleaning of components and of oilways). For this reason, all such tasks are classed as major overhaul procedures and are described in Part C of this Chapter.

Engine description

This Chapter covers 4-cylinder N47 diesel engines fitted to the E60/61 5-Series range.

The aluminium cylinder block is of the dry-liner type. The crankshaft is supported within the cylinder block on five shell-type main bearings. Thrustwashers are integral with the No 3 main bearing shells to control crankshaft endfloat.

The cylinder head is of the double overhead camshaft, 4-valve per cylinder design – two intake and two exhaust valves per cylinder. The valves are operated by one intake camshaft and one exhaust camshaft, via rocker fingers. One end of each finger acts upon the valve stem, whilst the other end pivots on a support pillar. Valve clearances are maintained automatically by hydraulic compensation elements incorporated within the support pillars. In order to achieve high levels of combustion efficiency, the cylinder head has two intake ports for each cylinder. One port is tangential, whilst the other is helical.

The connecting rods rotate on horizontally-split bearing shells at their big-ends. The pistons are attached to the connecting rods by gudgeon pins which are secured in position with circlips. The aluminium alloy pistons are fitted with three piston rings, comprising two compression rings and an oil control ring.

The intake and exhaust valves are each closed by coil springs and operate in guides pressed into the cylinder head. Valve guides cannot be renewed.

A timing chain at the rear of the engine, driven by the crankshaft, drives the high-pressure fuel pump sprocket, which in turn drives the intake camshaft. The camshafts are geared together. The vacuum pump is integral with the oil pump. The coolant pump is driven by the auxiliary drivebelt.

On all engines, lubrication is by means of an eccentric-rotor type pump driven by the crankshaft via a Simplex chain. The pump draws oil through a strainer located in the sump, and then forces it through an externally-mounted full-flow paper element type oil filter into galleries in the cylinder block/crankcase, from where it is distributed to the crankshaft (main bearings), timing chain (sprayed by a jet), and camshafts. The big-end bearings are supplied with oil via internal drillings in the crankshaft, while the camshaft bearings and the followers receive a pressurised supply via drillings in the cylinder head. The camshaft lobes and valves are lubricated by oil splash, as are all other engine components. An oil cooler (integral with the oil filter housing) is fitted to keep the oil temperature stable under arduous operating conditions.

The cylinder block is fitted with counter-rotating balance shafts, driven by a gear on the crankshaft.

Operations with engine in car

The following work can be carried out with the engine in the vehicle:

a) Compression pressure – testing.
b) Camshaft cover – removal and refitting.
c) Crankshaft pulley – removal and refitting.
d) Camshafts and rocker arms – removal, inspection and refitting.
e) Cylinder head – removal and refitting.
f) Cylinder head and pistons – decarbonising.
g) Sump – removal and refitting.
h) Oil pump – removal, overhaul and refitting.
i) Oil filter housing/cooler – removal and refitting.
j) Crankshaft oil seals – renewal.
k) Engine/transmission mountings – inspection and renewal.
l) Flywheel/driveplate – removal, inspection and refitting.

Note: Although in theory it is possible to remove the timing cover and timing chains with the engine fitted, in practice access is extremely limited, special BMW tools are needed, and the cylinder head and sump must be removed. Consequently, it is recommended that the engine is removed prior to timing cover and chains removal.

2 Compression test – description and interpretation

Compression test

Note: A compression tester specifically designed for diesel engines must be used for this test.

1 When engine performance is down, or if misfiring occurs which cannot be attributed to the fuel system, a compression test can provide diagnostic clues as to the engine's condition. If the test is performed regularly, it can give warning of trouble before any other symptoms become apparent.

2 The tester is connected to an adapter which screws into the glow plug hole. It is unlikely to be worthwhile buying such a tester for occasional use, but it may be possible to borrow or hire one – if not, have the test performed by a garage.

3 Unless specific instructions to the contrary are supplied with the tester, observe the following points:

a) *The battery must be in a good state of charge, the air filter must be clean, and the engine should be at normal operating temperature.*
b) *All the glow plugs should be removed before starting the test (see Chapter 5).*
c) *Disconnect the wiring plugs from the injectors (see Chapter 4A).*

4 There is no need to hold the accelerator pedal down during the test, because the engine air intake is not throttled.

5 Crank the engine on the starter motor; after one or two revolutions, the compression pressure should build up to a maximum figure, and then stabilise. Record the highest reading obtained.

6 Repeat the test on the remaining cylinders, recording the pressure in each.

7 All cylinders should produce very similar pressures; a difference of more than 2 bars between any two cylinders indicates a fault. Note that the compression should build-up quickly in a healthy engine; low compression on the first stroke, followed by gradually-increasing pressure on successive strokes, indicates worn piston rings. A low compression reading on the first stroke, which does not build-up during successive strokes, indicates leaking valves or a blown head gasket (a cracked head could also be the cause). Deposits on the undersides of the valve heads can also cause low compression.

Note: *The cause of poor compression is less easy to establish on a diesel engine than on a petrol one. The effect of introducing oil into the cylinders ('wet' testing) is not conclusive, because there is a risk that the oil will sit in the swirl chamber or in the recess on the piston crown instead of passing to the rings.*

8 Refer to a BMW dealer or other specialist if in doubt as to whether a particular pressure reading is acceptable.

9 On completion of the test, refit the glow plugs as described in Chapter 5, and reconnect the injector wiring plugs.

Leakdown test

10 A leakdown test measures the rate at which compressed air fed into the cylinder is lost. It is an alternative to a compression test, and in many ways it is better, since the escaping air provides easy identification of where pressure loss is occurring (piston rings, valves or head gasket).

11 The equipment needed for leakdown testing is unlikely to be available to the home mechanic. If poor compression is suspected, have the test performed by a suitably-equipped garage.

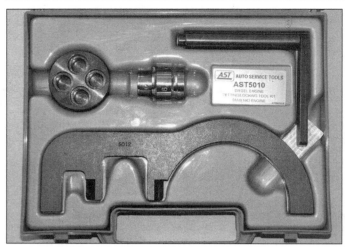

3.1 This kit includes crankshaft and camshaft setting tools, along with a tool that fits over the pulley bolts to facilitate crankshaft rotation

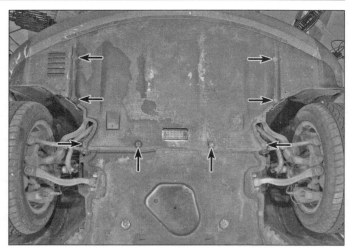

3.3a Engine/radiator undershield fasteners (arrowed)

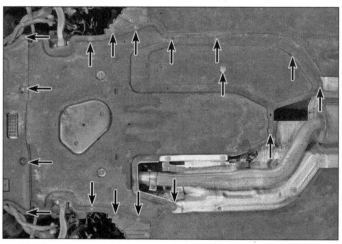

3.3b Engine/transmission undershield fasteners (arrowed)

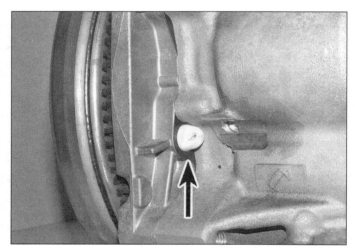

3.5 Pull the blanking plug (arrowed) from the timing pin hole

3 Engine assembly/valve timing settings – general information and usage

Note: BMW tool No 11 5 320 or suitable equivalent will be required to lock the crankshaft in position, and access to BMW tool No 11 8 760 or equivalent is required to position the camshafts.

1 The flywheel is equipped with an indent, which aligns with a hole in the engine block when No 1 piston is at TDC (top dead centre). In this position, if No 1 piston is at TDC on its compression stroke, it must be possible to fit a BMW special tool (No 11 8 760) or equivalent, over the square sections of the exhaust camshaft (with all four No 1 cylinder camshaft lobes pointing towards the right-hand side). **Note:** The inexpensive, high quality setting tools featured in this manual were supplied and manufactured by Auto Service Tools ltd **(see illustration)**.

2 Firmly apply the handbrake then jack up the front of the vehicle and support it securely on axle stands (see Jacking and vehicle support).
3 Undo the retaining bolts/clips and remove the engine undershields **(see illustrations)**.
4 Remove the camshaft cover and gasket, as described in Section 4.
5 Pull out the blanking plug from the timing pin hole in the engine block above the starter motor **(see illustration)**. Access is limited – with difficulty, we removed the plug using a length of welding rod. To Improve access, remove the catalytic converter/particulate filter as described in Chapter 4B.
6 Using a socket and extension bar on one of the crankshaft pulley centre bolts, turn the crankshaft clockwise whilst keeping an eye on the No 1 cylinder camshaft lobes. BMW tool No 11 6 480 or equivalent is available to rotate the crankshaft pulley bolts. The tool fits over all 4 bolts **(see illustration)**. **Note:** Do not turn the engine anti-clockwise.

7 Rotate the crankshaft clockwise until the No 1 cylinder camshaft lobes approach the point where all four lobes are pointing upwards. Have an assistant insert BMW tool No 11 5 320 or equivalent into the timing pin hole, and press the pin gently against the flywheel. Continue to slowly turn the crankshaft slowly until the pin is

3.6 The tool fits over the heads of the pulley bolts

3.7 Insert the crankshaft timing pin and engage it with the indent in the flywheel

3.8a The marks on the sprocket faces must align

felt to engage in the indent in the flywheel, and the crankshaft locks (see illustration).

8 With the crankshaft in this position, all four camshaft lobes of No 1 cylinder should be pointing to the right-hand side. Check that the 2 marks on the front of the exhaust camshaft sprocket align with the single mark on the front of the intake camshaft sprocket. Fit BMW tool No 11 8 760 or equivalent over the flats on the exhaust camshaft collar, adjacent to No 1 camshaft bearing cap. If the camshaft is timed correctly, the tool will contact both sides of the camshaft cover gasket face on the cylinder head (see illustrations). Note: To avoid confusion, bear in mind that the timing chain and sprockets are fitted at the rear of the engine.

4 Camshaft cover –
removal and refitting

Removal

1 Disconnect the battery negative lead (refer to Chapter 5).
2 With reference to Chapter 4A, remove the intake manifold, common rail and fuel injectors.
3 Note their fitted positions and routing,

3.8b Fit the setting tool over the flats on the exhaust camshaft collar

then undo the bolts and move the wiring harness and cable holders to one side (see illustration). Note that there are 3 bolts securing the cable holder on the right-hand side of the camshaft cover. Disconnect the wiring plugs as necessary, and place the wiring harness assembly over the left-hand side of the engine compartment.
4 Release the clips and detach the engine breather hose from the camshaft cover, and the glow plug wiring harness from the retaining clips on the cover (see illustration).
5 Open the oil filler cap, rotate it until the marks align, and remove it. Release the clips

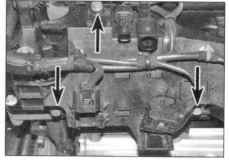

4.3 The cable holder on the right-hand side is retained by 3 bolts (arrowed)

on the underside and remove the oil filler cap flange rubber seal (see illustration).
6 Working in from the outside-in, evenly slacken and remove the bolts securing the camshaft cover to the cylinder head.
7 Remove the cover and discard its gaskets.

Refitting

8 Ensure the mating surfaces are clean and dry then fit the new gaskets to the cover (see illustration).
9 Refit the cover to the cylinder head, ensuring that the gaskets remain correctly seated.
10 Insert the cover retaining bolts and tighten

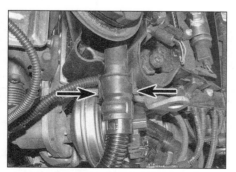

4.4 Squeeze together the clips (arrowed) and disconnect the breather hose

4.5 Align the marks (arrowed) and remove the oil filler cap

4.8 Don't forget to renew the seals around the injector apertures

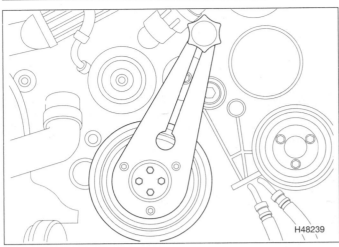

5.4 The tool to prevent crankshaft rotation locates in the centre of the pulley, and is secured into the threaded hole vacated by the auxiliary belt idler pulley

5.5 Crankshaft pulley retaining bolts

them all by hand. Once all bolts are in position, tighten them to the specified torque setting starting from the inside, working outwards.

11 The remainder of refitting is a reversal of removal.

5 Crankshaft pulley/vibration damper – removal and refitting

Removal

1 Firmly apply the handbrake then jack up the front of the vehicle and support it securely on axle stands (see *Jacking and vehicle support*).

2 Remove the auxiliary drivebelt(s) as described in Chapter 1.

3 If further dismantling is to be carried out (beyond pulley removal), align the engine assembly/valve timing settings as described in Section 3.

4 Slacken the crankshaft pulley retaining bolts. To prevent crankshaft rotation, (the pulley retaining bolts are extremely tight) a special BMW tool (No 11 7 221) is available. This tool is secured to the front of the engine using the mounting hole vacated by the auxiliary drivebelt idler pulley, and located in the lugs in the centre of the crankshaft pulley **(see illustration)**. This

tool may also be available from automotive tool specialists. In the absence of the tool, remove the starter motor as described in Chapter 5 to expose the flywheel ring gear, and have an assistant insert a wide-bladed screwdriver between the ring gear teeth and the transmission bellhousing whilst the pulley retaining bolts are slackened. If the engine is removed from the vehicle it will be necessary to lock the flywheel (see Section 13).

Caution: Do not be tempted to use the crankshaft locking pin (see Section 3) to prevent rotation as the centre bolts are slackened.

5 Unscrew the retaining bolts, and remove the pulley from the crankshaft **(see illustration)**. Discard the bolts, new ones must be fitted.

Refitting

6 Fit the pulley to the crankshaft and screw in the new retaining bolts.

7 Lock the crankshaft by the method used on removal, and tighten the pulley retaining bolts to the specified Stage 1 torque setting then angle-tighten the bolt(s) through the specified Stage 2 angle, using a socket and extension bar. It is recommended that an angle-measuring gauge is used during the final stages of the tightening, to ensure accuracy. If a gauge is not available, use paint to make

alignment marks between the bolt heads and pulley prior to tightening; the marks can then be used to check that the bolt has been rotated through the correct angle.

8 Refit the auxiliary drivebelt(s) as described in Chapter 1.

6 Camshafts, rocker arms and hydraulic tappets – removal, inspection and refitting

Removal

1 Remove the cylinder head cover as described in Section 4.

2 Firmly apply the handbrake, then jack up the front of the vehicle and support it securely on axle stands (see *Jacking and vehicle support*).

3 Undo the fasteners and remove the engine undershields **(see illustrations 3.3a and 3.3b)**.

4 Set the engine to TDC on No 1 cylinder as described in Section 3. Insert the flywheel locking tool, but do not fit the camshaft locking tool.

5 Undo and release the timing chain tensioner **(see illustration)**. Discard the seal, a new one must be fitted.

6 Undo and remove the bolts securing the sprocket to the camshaft. Pull the sprocket from the camshaft, and place the chain in the cylinder head **(see illustrations)**.

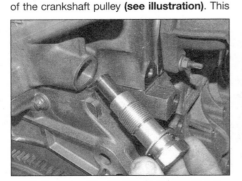

6.5 Unscrew the timing chain tensioner

6.6a Undo the sprocket retaining bolts . . .

6.6b . . . then remove the sprocket and lay the chain to one side

6.7 The camshaft bearing caps are marked A for exhaust, and E for intake. No 1 is at the front of the engine – the timing chain is at the **rear**

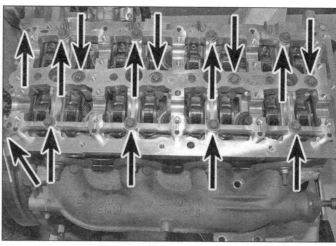

6.10 Working from the outside-in, undo the camshaft carrier bolts (arrowed)

7 Identify the camshaft bearing caps, to ensure they are refitted to their original positions. The exhaust camshaft is marked A, so mark the exhaust camshaft bearing caps as A1, A2, A3, etc, starting with the cap at the front of the engine. The intake camshaft is marked E, so repeat the procedure for the intake camshaft starting with E1 at the front of the engine (furthest from the timing chain) **(see illustration)**.

8 Evenly and progressively, slacken and remove the retaining bolts, and remove the camshaft bearing caps.

9 Remove the camshafts from the cylinder head.

10 Working from the outside towards the centre, undo the bolts and remove the camshaft carrier **(see illustration)**. Recover the seals between the carrier and the cylinder head.

11 Lift the rocker arms from the cylinder head, and lay them out in order on a clean surface, so that they can be fitted into their original positions – if they are to be reused. Note that the rocker arms are clipped to the tappets – unless required, there is no need to separate the two – lift the rockers and tappets together.

12 Obtain sixteen small, clean plastic containers, and label them for identification. Alternatively, divide a larger container into compartments. Withdraw each hydraulic tappet in turn, and place it in its respective container, which should then be filled with clean engine oil.

Caution: Do not interchange the tappets, and do not allow the tappets to lose oil, as they will take a long time to refill with oil on restarting the engine, which could result in incorrect valve clearances. Absolute cleanliness is essential at all times when handling the tappets.

Inspection

13 Examine the camshaft bearing surfaces and cam lobes for signs of wear ridges and scoring. Renew the camshaft if any of these conditions are apparent. Examine the condition of the bearing surfaces both on the camshaft journals and in the cylinder head. If the head bearing surfaces are worn excessively, the cylinder head will need to be renewed.

14 Examine the rocker bearing surfaces which contact the camshaft lobes for wear ridges and scoring. If the engine's valve clearances have sounded noisy, particularly if the noise persists after initial start-up from cold, then there is reason to suspect a faulty tappet. If any tappet is thought to be faulty or is visibly worn it should be renewed.

Refitting

15 Where removed, lubricate the tappets with clean engine oil and carefully insert each one into its original location in the cylinder head **(see illustration)**.

16 Refit the rocker arms to their original locations, ensuring that they are correctly orientated, and clipped onto the tappets (if removed).

17 Ensure the mating surfaces of the camshaft carrier and cylinder head are clean, then refit the camshaft carrier using new seals. Tighten the bolts to the specified torque working from the centre to the outside **(see illustration)**.

18 Remove the crankshaft locking tool, and rotate the crankshaft 45° anti-clockwise to prevent any accidental piston-to-valve contact. Ensure the timing chain does not fall into the timing cover, or jam on the crankshaft sprocket.

19 Engage the gear on the exhaust camshaft with the gear on the intake camshaft, so the 2 dots on the front of the intake camshaft gear are each side of the dot on the exhaust camshaft gear, then lay the camshafts in place on the cylinder head so the dots are flush with the upper surface of the cylinder head **(see illustration 3.8a)**.

20 Lubricate the bearing surfaces of the camshaft with clean engine oil, then refit the bearing caps to their original positions.

21 Insert the bearing cap bolts, then evenly and progressively tighten the retaining bolts to draw the bearing caps squarely down into contact with the cylinder head. Once the caps are in contact with the head, tighten the retaining bolts to the specified torque.

Caution: If the bearing caps bolts are carelessly tightened, the caps might break. If the caps are broken then the complete cylinder head assembly must be renewed; the caps are matched to the head and are not available separately.

6.15 Refit the hydraulic tappets and rocker arms to their original positions

6.17 Renew the seals between the camshaft carrier and the cylinder head

6.22a Rotate the exhaust camshaft using a 10 mm Allen bit/key . . .

6.22b . . . in the hexagonal section in the centre of the camshaft

6.24 The sprocket bolts holes should be almost in the centre of the slots

6.26 Compress the tensioner piston to evacuate any oil

22 With the camshafts in this position, it should be possible to fit BMW tool No 11 8 760 (or equivalent) over the square section on the exhaust camshaft, as described in Section 3. If not, rotate the camshafts using a 10 mm Allen key in the hexagonal section in the centre of the exhaust camshaft **(see illustrations)**.

23 With the camshafts held in position, rotate the crankshaft 45° clockwise (back to TDC) so the flywheel locking tool can be reinserted. Ensure the timing chain doesn't fall inside the cover, or jam on the crankshaft sprocket.

24 Engage the timing chain with the sprocket, and position the sprocket on the end of the intake camshaft so the bolt holes are in the centre of the slots **(see illustration)**.

25 Fit the sprocket retaining bolts into the holes and tighten them to 10 Nm (7 lbf ft), then slacken them 90° each.

26 The oil within the chain tensioner must be evacuated. Hold the tensioner on a hard, level surface and slowly compress to squeeze out the oil **(see illustration)**. Repeat this procedure twice. With a new seal fitted, refit the chain tensioner and tighten it to the specified torque.

27 Make a final check to ensure the camshaft and flywheel locking tools are correctly fitted, then tighten the camshaft sprocket bolts to the specified torque.

28 Remove the camshaft and flywheel locking tools, then rotate the crankshaft two complete revolutions clockwise, and check the camshaft and flywheel tools can still be installed. If they cannot, repeat the fitting procedure from paragraph 24 onwards.

29 The remainder of refitting is a reversal of removal.

7 Cylinder head – removal and refitting

Removal

1 Remove the camshafts, rocker arms and tappets as described in Section 6.

2 Drain the cooling system, as described in Chapter 1.

3 Remove the turbocharger as described in Chapter 4A.

4 Remove the EGR cooler as described in Chapter 4B.

5 Release the retaining clips, and disconnect the various coolant hoses from the cylinder head **(see illustration)**.

6 Undo the plug on the right-hand side of the cylinder block and drain the coolant **(see illustration)**. Fit a new sealing washer and tighten the drain plug to the specified torque.

7 Undo the 2 bolts at the rear of the cylinder head **(see illustration)**. Where applicable, undo the 3 bolts and remove the wiring harness support bracket from the cylinder head and right-hand engine mounting bracket.

8 Undo the 3 bolts at the rear, left-hand corner or the cylinder head **(see illustration)**.

9 Make a final check to ensure that all relevant hoses, pipes and wires, etc, have been disconnected.

10 Working in the **reverse** of the tightening sequence **(see illustration 7.27)**, progressively slacken the cylinder head bolts by a third of a turn at a time until all bolts can be unscrewed

7.5 Prise out the clips (arrowed) and disconnect the various coolant hoses from the cylinder head

7.6 The cylinder block drain plug (arrowed) is located on the right-hand side of the block

7.7 Undo the 2 bolts at the rear of the cylinder head (arrowed) . . .

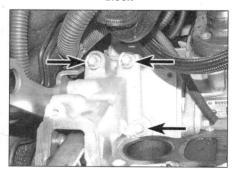

7.8 . . . and the 3 at the rear, left-hand corner (arrowed)

7.18 Cylinder head gasket identification holes (arrowed – see text)

7.20 Measure the piston protrusion using a DTI gauge

holes in the gasket next to the timing chain area **(see illustration)**.

Holes in gasket	Largest piston protrusion
One hole	Up to 0.92 mm
Two holes	0.92 to 1.03 mm
Three holes	1.03 to 1.18 mm

Select the new gasket which has the same thickness/number of holes as the original, unless new piston and connecting rod assemblies have been fitted. In that case, the correct thickness of gasket required is selected by measuring the piston protrusions as follows.

19 Remove the locking pin from the flywheel and mount a dial test indicator securely on the block so that its pointer can be easily pivoted between the piston crown and block mating surface.

20 Ensure the piston is at exactly TDC then zero the dial test indicator on the gasket surface of the cylinder block. Carefully move the indicator over No 1 piston, taking measurements in line with the gudgeon pin axis, measure the protrusion on both the left-hand and right-hand side of the piston **(see illustration)**. **Note:** *When turning the crankshaft, ensure that the timing chain does not jam in the timing cover.*

21 Rotate the crankshaft to bring the remaining pistons to TDC in turn. Ensure the crankshaft is accurately positioned then measure the protrusions of the remaining pistons, taking two measurements for each piston. Once all the pistons have been measured, rotate the crankshaft to bring No 1 piston back to TDC. Then rotate it 45° anti-clockwise.

22 Use the table in paragraph 18 to select the appropriate gasket.

Refitting

23 Wipe clean the mating faces of the head and block and ensure that the two locating dowels are in position on the cylinder block/crankcase surface **(see illustration)**.

24 Apply a little sealant (Drei Bond 1209) to the area where the timing chain cover meets the cylinder block **(see illustration)**, then fit

by hand. Withdraw and discard the bolts, new ones must be fitted.

11 Lift the cylinder head from the cylinder block. If necessary, tap the cylinder head gently with a soft-faced mallet to free it from the block, but **do not** lever at the mating faces.

12 When the joint is broken, lift the cylinder head away then remove the gasket. Note the fitted positions of the two locating dowels, and remove them for safe-keeping if they are loose. Keep the gasket for identification purposes (see paragraph 18).

Caution: Do not lay the head on its lower mating surface; support the head on wooden blocks, ensuring each block only contacts the head mating surface not the glow plugs. The glow plugs protrude out the bottom of the head and they will be damaged if the head is placed directly onto a bench.

13 If the cylinder head is to be dismantled, refer to the relevant Sections of Part C of this Chapter.

Preparation for refitting

14 The mating faces of the cylinder head and block must be perfectly clean before refitting the head. Use a scraper to remove all traces of gasket and carbon, and also clean the tops of the pistons. Take particular care with the aluminium surfaces, as the soft metal is damaged easily. Also, make sure that debris

is not allowed to enter the oil and water channels – this is particularly important for the oil circuit, as carbon could block the oil supply to the camshaft or crankshaft bearings. Using adhesive tape and paper, seal the water, oil and bolt holes in the cylinder block. To prevent carbon entering the gap between the pistons and bores, smear a little grease in the gap. After cleaning the piston, rotate the crankshaft so that the piston moves down the bore, then wipe out the grease and carbon with a cloth rag. Clean the piston crowns in the same way.

15 Check the block and head for nicks, deep scratches and other damage. If slight, they may be removed carefully with a file. More serious damage may be repaired by machining, but this is a specialist job.

16 If warpage of the cylinder head gasket surface is suspected, use a straight-edge to check it for distortion. Refer to Part C of this Chapter if necessary.

17 Ensure that the cylinder head bolt holes in the crankcase are clean and free of oil. Syringe or soak up any oil left in the bolt holes. This is most important in order that the correct bolt tightening torque can be applied and to prevent the possibility of the block being cracked by hydraulic pressure when the bolts are tightened.

18 On these engines, the cylinder head-to-piston clearance is controlled by fitting different thickness head gaskets. The piston protrusion is represented by the number of

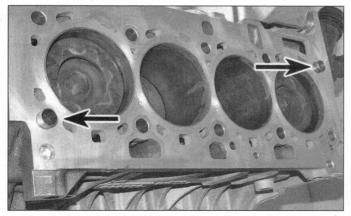

7.23 Ensure the locating dowels are in place (arrowed)

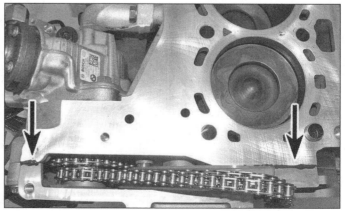

7.24 Apply sealant where the cylinder block meets the timing chain cover (arrowed)

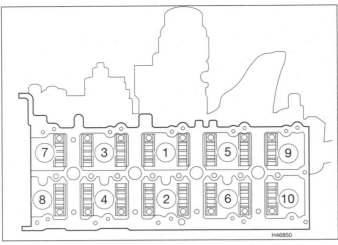

7.27 Cylinder head bolt tightening sequence

7.29 Tighten the cylinder head bolts using an angle-gauge

the new gasket to the cylinder block, ensuring that it fits correctly over the locating dowels.

25 Carefully refit the cylinder head, locating it on the dowels. Make sure the timing chain can be pulled up through the cylinder head tunnel.

26 The new cylinder head bolts are supplied pre-coated – do not wash the coating off, or apply grease/oil to them. Carefully enter the main bolts (1 to 10) into the holes and screw them in, by hand only, until finger-tight.

Caution: Do not drop the bolts into their holes.

27 Working progressively and in the sequence shown, first tighten all the cylinder head bolts to the Stage 1 torque setting **(see illustration)**.

28 Slacken all the bolts half a turn (180°), then tighten them in sequence to the Stage 3 setting.

29 Again, in sequence, angle-tighten them to Stage 4, and then Stage 5, using an angle-measuring gauge **(see illustration)**.

30 Refit and tighten the bolts at the rear/corner securing the cylinder head to the timing cover, to the specified torque **(see illustrations 7.7 and 7.8)**.

31 The remainder of refitting is a reversal of removal, noting the following points:

a) Renew all gaskets/seals disturbed during the removal procedure.

b) Tighten all fasteners to their specified torque where given.

c) Refill the cooling system as described in Chapter 1.

8 Sump – removal and refitting

Removal

1 Drain the engine oil and remove the oil filter as described in Chapter 1. Refit the sump plug with a new washer and tighten the plug to the specified torque.

2 Remove the acoustic cover from the top of the engine **(see illustration)**.

3 Remove the cooling fan and shroud as described in Chapter 3.

4 The front subframe must be lowered a little as follows:

5 Jack up the front of the vehicle and support it securely on axle stands (see *Jacking and vehicle support*). Remove the retaining bolts and fasteners and remove the engine undershield.

6 Remove the exhaust system as described in Chapter 4A.

7 Remove the bonnet as described in Chapter 11.

8 Remove the wiper arms as described in Chapter 12.

9 Undo the bolts and remove the front underbody reinforcement plate **(see illustration)**. Discard the bolts – new ones must be fitted.

10 The engine must be supported in position using an engine hoist or engine crossbeam. Attach the hoist/crossbeam to the engine lifting eyes at the front and rear of the engine. Take the weight of the engine.

11 Undo the nut each side securing the engine mounting support brackets to the mountings, then raise the engine approximately 10 mm.

12 Remove driver's side lower facia panel above the pedals as described in Chapter 11.

13 Remove the steering column lower universal joint pinch-bolt and lift the column shaft upwards from the steering rack pinion **(see illustration)**. Discard the pinch-bolt – a new one must be used.

Caution: Ensure the steering wheel/column is not rotated with the universal joint disconnected from the steering rack pinion. Damage to the column could result.

14 Disconnect the wiring plugs from the ride height sensors (where fitted), then disconnect the vacuum hoses from the engine mountings (where applicable).

15 On models with electric power steering,

8.2 Pull up the front edge and slide the engine cover forwards

8.9 Front underbody reinforcement plate bolts (arrowed)

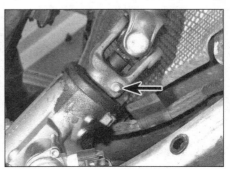

8.13 Steering column lower universal joint pinch-bolt (arrowed)

8.20 The oil level dipstick guide tube is bolted to the oil filter housing

8.25 Oil pump intake pipe bolts (arrowed)

8.28 Apply sealant to the area where the cylinder block meets the timing chain cover (arrowed)

cut the cable-tie securing the wiring harness to the subframe.

16 On models with Dynamic Drive active suspension system, place a container beneath the pipes, undo the unions and drain the fluid from the return and pressure pipes.

17 Examine the front subframe, and identify any remaining wiring looms/connectors which will be affected by the lowering of the subframe. Note their fitted positions, and disconnect/release them.

18 Support the front subframe using a workshop jack and lengths of wood, etc, then undo the 3 bolts each side and carefully lower the subframe a maximum of 10 cm. Pay attention to the power steering hoses/pipes as the subframe is being lowered – do not allow them to be bent or stretched. When refitting, tighten down the front bolts first.

19 Remove the starter motor as described in Chapter 5.

20 Undo the bolt securing the oil level dipstick guide tube and pull the tube from the sump **(see illustration)**. Renew the guide tube O-ring seal.

21 Disconnect the wiring plug from the engine oil level sensor.

22 Slacken and remove the bolts securing the transmission casing to the sump.

23 Progressively slacken and remove the bolts securing the sump to the base of the cylinder block.

24 Break the sump joint by striking the sump with the palm of the hand, then lower the sump away from the engine. Remove the

gasket and discard it, a new one should be used on refitting.

25 While the sump is removed, take the opportunity to check the oil pump intake pipe for signs of clogging or splitting. If necessary, unbolt the intake pipe, and remove it from the engine along with its gasket **(see illustration)**. The strainer can then be cleaned easily in solvent. Inspect the strainer mesh for signs of clogging or splitting and renew if necessary. If the intake pipe bolts are damaged they must be renewed.

Refitting

26 Clean all traces of gasket from the mating surfaces of the cylinder block and sump, then use a clean rag to wipe out the sump and the engine interior.

27 Where necessary, fit a new seal to the oil pump intake pipe then carefully refit the pipe. Refit the retaining bolts, and tighten them to the specified torque setting.

28 Apply a bead of suitable sealant (Drei Bond 1209 is available from your BMW dealer) to the area where the cylinder block meets the timing cover **(see illustration)**.

29 Fit the gasket to the sump then offer up the sump to the cylinder block/crankcase **(see illustration)**. Refit the sump retaining bolts, and tighten the bolts finger-tight only.

30 Fit the bolts securing the sump to the gearbox. In order to align the rear sump flange with the gearbox, lightly tighten the bolts, then slacken them. If the sump is being refitted to the engine with the gearbox removed, use a straight-edge to ensure that the sump casting

is flush with the end of the cylinder block **(see illustration)**.

31 Tighten the sump-to-engine block bolts, and then the sump-to-transmission bolts to the specified torque.

32 Refit the oil dipstick tube, with a new O-ring, and tighten the bolts securely.

33 The remainder of refitting is a reversal of removal, noting the following points:

a) Renew all gaskets/seals where disturbed.

b) Tighten all fasteners to their specified torque where given.

c) Renew the engine oil and filter as described in Chapter 1.

d) Where applicable, fill and bleed the Dynamic Drive hydraulic system as described in Chapter 10.

e) If necessary, have the front wheel alignment checked by a BMW dealer or suitably-equipped specialist.

9 Oil/vacuum pump – removal, inspection and refitting

Removal

1 Remove the sump and oil pump intake pipe as described in Section 8.

2 Undo the bolt(s) down the centre line of the pump, then remove the spacers (where fitted) by rotating them anti-clockwise **(see illustration)**. Discard the bolts – new ones must be fitted.

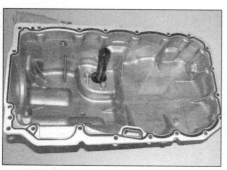

8.29 Fit the new gasket to the sump

8.30 Use a straight-edge to ensure the sump is flush with the cylinder block

9.2 Rotate the spacers (arrowed) anti-clockwise and remove them

11.3 Disconnect the air temperature sensor (arrowed) from the intake pipe

11.4 The glow plug control unit (arrowed) is located behind the oil filter housing

11.7 Oil filter housing bolts (arrowed)

3 Undo the 8 pump retaining bolts.

4 Lift up the front edge of the pump assembly, and manoeuvre the drive sprocket out from the chain. BMW insist that the drive sprocket is not removed.

Inspection

5 At the time of writing, no new parts are available for the oil/vacuum pump. If defective, the complete assembly must be renewed. Consult a BMW dealer or parts specialist.

Refitting

6 Ensure the mating surfaces of the pump and cylinder block are clean and dry. Ensure all mounting holes are clean and free from oil.

7 Engage the pump drive sprocket with the chain and with the pump in place, insert the 8 retaining bolts.

8 Refit the 3 spacers (where applicable) to the pump by rotating them clockwise, then refit the pump centre line bolt(s) **(see illustration 9.2)**.

9 Tighten the pump retaining bolts to their specified torque.

10 Refit the sump as described in Section 8.

10 Balance shaft assembly – general information

These shafts are fitted into the cylinder block each side of the crankshaft, and are gear-driven from the crankshaft. In order to remove the balance shafts, the crankshaft must first be removed. Refer to Chapter 2C.

11 Oil cooler – removal and refitting

Removal

1 Drain the coolant and engine oil, and remove the oil filter as described in Chapter 1.

2 Remove the front section of the acoustic cover from the top of the engine.

3 Disconnect the intake air temperature sensor wiring plug, then release the clamp at each end and disconnect the air intake duct from the throttle body/intake manifold **(see**

illustration). Check the condition of the seals at each end of the air duct, and renew them if damaged or defective.

4 Disconnect the wiring plug from the glow plug control unit **(see illustration)**.

5 Release the cable-tie securing the wiring harness, then undo the bolt and pull the engine oil level dipstick guide tube from position **(see illustration 8.20)**. Renew the guide tube O-ring seal.

6 Disconnect the oil pressure switch wiring plug.

7 Undo the bolts and remove the oil filter housing **(see illustration)**. Discard the sealing gasket.

8 Undo the bolts and detach the oil cooler from the oil filter housing. Renew the seals **(see illustrations)**.

Refitting

9 Ensure the mating surfaces of the oil cooler and oil filter housing are clean and dry, and with a new gasket, fit the cooler to the housing. Tighten the bolts securely or clip the cooler into the housing as applicable.

10 The remainder of refitting is a reversal of removal.

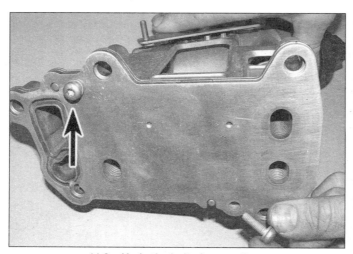

11.8a Undo the bolts (arrowed) . . .

11.8b . . . and pull the cooler from the housing

12 Crankshaft oil seals – renewal

Front end seal

1 Remove the crankshaft pulley/vibration damper as described in Section 5.

2 Lever out the seal using a flat-bladed screwdriver (or similar).
Caution: Great care must be taken to avoid damage to the crankshaft.

3 Clean the seal housing and polish off any burrs or raised edges which may have caused the seal to fail in the first place.

4 Do not lubricate the new seal with engine oil or lubricant – the seal must be installed dry. BMW specify a special tool (No 11 8 501) to guide the seal over the crankshaft shoulders. However, with care, it is possible to fit the seal without the tool. Ensure the lips of the seal are around the outer edge of the crankshaft. Press the seal squarely into position until it is flush with the housing. If necessary, a suitable tubular drift, such as a socket, which bears only on the hard outer edge of the seal can be used to tap the seal into position. Take great care not to damage the seal lips during fitting and ensure that the seal lips face inwards.

5 Refit the crankshaft pulley as described in Section 5.

Flywheel/driveplate end seal

6 Remove the flywheel or driveplate as described in Section 13, then remove the end cap **(see illustration)**. Avoid touching the outer edge of the end cap with fingers, as the crankshaft position sensor wheel is embedded in the rubber.

7 Lever out the seal using a flat-bladed screwdriver (or similar) **(see illustration)**.
Caution: Great care must be taken to avoid damage to the crankshaft.

8 Do not lubricate the new seal with engine oil or lubricant – the seal must be installed dry. BMW specify a special tool (No 11 8 815) to guide the seal over the crankshaft shoulders. However, with care, it is possible to fit the seal without the tool **(see illustration)**.

9 Press the seal squarely into position until it is flush with the housing. If possible, a suitable tubular drift, such as a socket, which bears

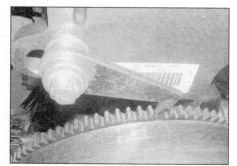

13.2 Lock the flywheel using a similar tool

12.6 Remove the end cap from the crankshaft

12.8 Guide the seal lips over the crankshaft shoulders . . .

only on the hard outer edge of the seal can be used to tap the seal into position. Take great care not to damage the seal lips during fitting and ensure that the seal lips face inwards **(see illustration)**. If available, BMW specify tools No 11 8 10, 11 8 811, 11 8 812, 11 8 813 and 11 8 814 to draw the seal into position in the timing chain cover. Although desirable, the use of these tools is not essential.

10 Refit the end cap, followed by the flywheel/driveplate as described in Section 13.

13 Flywheel/driveplate – removal, inspection and refitting

Flywheel

Note: *New flywheel retaining bolts must be used on refitting.*

13.3a Note the locating dowel (arrowed) . . .

12.7 Lever out the seal using a hooked tool or screwdriver

12.9 . . . then press it into place until it's flush with the housing

Removal

1 Remove the clutch assembly as described in Chapter 6.

2 Prevent the flywheel from turning by locking the ring gear teeth with a similar arrangement to that shown **(see illustration)**. Alternatively, bolt a strap between the flywheel and the cylinder block/crankcase.

3 Slacken and remove the retaining bolts and remove the flywheel, noting its locating dowel **(see illustrations)**. **Do not** drop it, as it is very heavy. Discard the bolts, they must be renewed whenever they are disturbed.

Inspection

4 If the flywheel-to-clutch mating surface is deeply scored, cracked or otherwise damaged, then the flywheel must be renewed, unless it is possible to have it surface ground. Seek the advice of a BMW dealer or engine reconditioning specialist.

13.3b . . . which corresponds with the hole (arrowed) in the flywheel

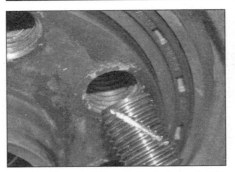

13.8a Clean out the crankshaft flywheel bolt threads using an old bolt with a saw cut across it

5 If the ring gear is badly worn or has missing teeth, then it must be renewed. This job is best left to a BMW dealer or engine reconditioning specialist.

6 These vehicles are fitted with dual mass flywheels. Whilst BMW do not publish any checking procedures, rotate the inner mass by hand anti-clockwise, mark its position in relation to the outer mass, then rotate it by hand clockwise and measure the travel. As a general rule, if the movement is more than 30 mm or less than 15 mm, consult a BMW dealer or transmission specialist as to whether a new unit is needed.

Refitting

7 Clean the mating surfaces of the flywheel and crankshaft and remove all traces of locking compound from the crankshaft threaded holes.

8 Fit the flywheel to the crankshaft, engaging it with the crankshaft locating dowel, and fit the new retaining bolts **(see illustrations)**. **Note:** *If the new bolts are not supplied pre-coated with locking compound, apply a few drops prior to fitting the bolts.*

9 Lock the flywheel using the method employed on dismantling then, working in a diagonal sequence, tighten all the retaining bolts to the specified torque setting.

10 Refit the clutch assembly as described in Chapter 6.

Driveplate

Note: *New driveplate retaining bolts must be used on refitting.*

14.7a Disconnect the earth strap (arrowed) from the mounting bracket

13.8b The new bolts should be pre-coated with thread-locking compound

Removal

11 Remove the automatic transmission as described in Chapter 7B.

12 Prevent the driveplate from turning by locking the ring gear teeth with a similar arrangement to that shown **(see illustration 13.2)**. Alternatively, bolt a strap between the driveplate and the cylinder block/crankcase.

13 Slacken and remove the retaining bolts and remove the driveplate, noting its locating dowel. Discard the bolts, they must be renewed whenever they are disturbed.

Inspection

14 If the ring gear is badly worn or has missing teeth, then it must be renewed. This job is best left to a BMW dealer or engine reconditioning specialist.

Refitting

15 Clean the mating surfaces of the driveplate and crankshaft and remove all traces of locking compound from the crankshaft threaded holes.

16 Fit the driveplate to the crankshaft, engaging it with the crankshaft locating dowel, and fit the new retaining bolts. **Note:** *If the new bolts are not supplied pre-coated with locking compound, apply a few drops prior to fitting the bolts.*

17 Lock the driveplate using the method employed on dismantling then, working in a diagonal sequence, tighten all the retaining bolts to the specified torque setting.

18 Refit the automatic transmission as described in Chapter 7B.

14.7b Undo the bracket retaining bolts (arrowed)

14 Engine mountings – inspection and renewal

Inspection

1 Two engine mountings are used, one on either side of the engine.

2 If improved access is required, raise the front of the vehicle and support it securely on axle stands (see *Jacking and vehicle support*). Undo the fasteners and remove the engine undershield.

3 Check the mounting rubber to see if it is cracked, hardened or separated from the metal at any point. Renew the mounting if any such damage or deterioration is evident.

4 Check that all the mounting fasteners are securely tightened.

5 Using a large screwdriver or a crowbar, check for wear in the mounting by carefully levering against it to check for free play. Where this is not possible, enlist the aid of an assistant to move the engine/transmission back and forth, or from side to side, while you observe the mounting. While some free play is to be expected, even from new components, excessive wear should be obvious. If excessive free play is found, check first that the fasteners are correctly secured, then renew any worn components as required.

Renewal

6 Support the engine, either using a hoist and lifting tackle connected to the engine lifting brackets (refer to *Engine – removal and refitting* in Part C of this Chapter), or by positioning a jack and interposed block of wood under the sump. Ensure that the engine is adequately supported before proceeding.

7 Unscrew the nuts securing the left- and right-hand engine mounting brackets to the mounting rubbers, then unbolt the mounting brackets from the cylinder block, and remove the mountings. Disconnect any engine earth straps from the mountings (where fitted) **(see illustrations)**.

8 Unscrew the nuts securing the mountings to the subframe, then withdraw the mountings. Disconnect the vacuum hoses from the mountings as they are withdrawn (where applicable).

14.7c Mounting retaining bolts (arrowed)

15.3 Drive the flywheel pilot bearing out from the engine side

15.4a Position the bearing . . .

15.4b . . . then fit it using a tubular spacer or socket

9 Refitting is a reversal of removal. Tighten all fasteners to their specified torque where given.

15 Flywheel pilot bearing – inspection, removal and refitting

Inspection

1 The pilot bearing is fitted into the centre of the dual mass flywheel, and provides support for the free end of the gearbox input shaft on manual transmission vehicles. It can only be examined once the clutch (Chapter 6) has been removed. Using a finger, rotate the inner race of the bearing and check for any roughness, binding or looseness in the bearing. If any of these conditions are evident, the bearing must be renewed.

Removal

2 Remove the flywheel as described in Section 13.
3 The bearing must be pressed out using a hydraulic press, with a drift that bears only on the inner bearing race. The bearing is pressed from the engine side of the flywheel and out of the clutch side **(see illustration)**. Note that the act of pressing the bearing out will render it unusable – it must be renewed.

Refitting

4 Using a suitable tubular spacer that bears

only on the hard outer edge of the bearing, press the new bearing into the flywheel until it contacts the shoulder **(see illustrations)**.
5 Refit the flywheel as described in Section.

16 Timing chains and cover – general information

On these engines, the timing chains are fitted at the rear of the engine. In order to remove the timing chains or the timing cover, it is necessary to first remove the engine. Consequently, renewal of the timing chains and covers is described in Chapter 2C.

17 Oil pressure and level sensors – removal and refitting

Oil pressure sensor

1 The oil pressure sensor is fitted into the base of the oil filter housing. Remove the oil filter element as described in Chapter 1. This allows the oil to drain from the housing, preventing excessive oil leakage as the sensor is removed.
2 Disconnect the wiring plug, and unscrew the sensor **(see illustration)**. Be prepared for oil spillage.
3 Refitting is a reversal of removal, using a

new sealing washer, and tightening the sensor to the specified torque.

Oil level sensor

4 Drain the engine oil as described in Chapter 1.
5 Undo the fasteners and remove the engine undershield **(see illustration 3.3b)**.
6 Disconnect the wiring plug, undo the three retaining nuts and remove the sensor from the base of the sump.
7 Ensure that the sump mating surface is clean.
8 Complete with a new seal, install the sensor, apply a little thread-locking compound and tighten the retaining nuts to the specified torque.
9 Refit the engine undershield, and replenish the engine oil as described in Chapter 1.

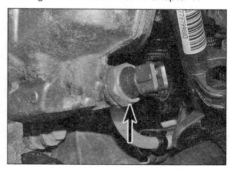

17.2 Oil pressure sensor (arrowed)

Notes

Chapter 2 Part B:
M47 and M57 engines in-car repair procedures

Contents

Degrees of difficulty

Easy, suitable for novice with little experience	**Fairly easy,** suitable for beginner with some experience	**Fairly difficult,** suitable for competent DIY mechanic	**Difficult,** suitable for experienced DIY mechanic	**Very difficult,** suitable for expert DIY or professional

Specifications

General

Engine type:

M47 D20 T2	Four-cylinder in-line, double overhead camshaft, 16-valve, four-stroke, liquid-cooled
M57 D25 TU	Six-cylinder in-line, double overhead camshaft, 24-valve, four-stroke, liquid cooled
M57 D30 TU/T2	Six-cylinder in-line, double overhead camshaft, 24-valve, four-stroke, liquid cooled

Bore	84.0 mm

Stroke:

M47 D20	90.0 mm
M57 D25	75.1 mm
M57 D30	90.0 mm

Capacity:

M47 D20	1995 cc
M57 D25	2497 cc
M57 D30	2993 cc
Direction of crankshaft rotation	Clockwise (seen from the front of the engine)

Compression ratio:

M47 D20	17.0 : 1
M57 D25	16.5 : 1
M57 D30	17.0 : 1

Compression pressure:

Minimum	10 bar

Lubrication system

Minimum system pressure:

Idle speed (hot) . . . . 1.3 bar

3500 rpm (hot) . . . . 4.0 to 6.0 bar

Torque wrench settings

	Nm	lbf ft
Acoustic cover-to-engine bolts	8	6
Camshaft bearing cap bolts:		
M6	10	7
M7	15	11
Camshaft cover bolts:		
M6	10	7
M7	15	10
Camshaft sprocket to gearwheel – intake camshaft*	14	10
Connecting rod big-end bearing cap bolts:*		
Stage 1	5	4
Stage 2	20	15
Stage 3	Angle-tighten a further 70°	
Crankshaft pulley/vibration damper bolts:*		
M47 engine:		
Stage 1	100	74
Stage 2	Angle-tighten a further 150°	
M57 engine:		
Stage 1	40	30
Stage 2	Angle-tighten a further 120°	
Crankshaft rear oil seal housing bolts:		
M6	10	7
M8	22	16
Cylinder head bolts:*		
Stage 1	80	59
Stage 2	Slacken 180°	
Stage 3	50	37
Stage 4	Angle-tighten a further 90°	
Stage 5	Angle-tighten a further 90°	
Cylinder head-to-timing cover bolts:		
M7	15	11
M8	20	15
Engine mountings:		
Mounting to front subframe:		
M8	28	21
M10	56	41
Mounting to engine support bracket	56	41
Flywheel/driveplate bolts*	120	89
Front underbody reinforcement plate:*		
Stage 1	56	41
Stage 2	Angle tighten a further 90°	
Front subframe mounting bolts:		
M10:		
Stage 1	56	41
Stage 2	Angle-tighten a further 90°	
M12	100	74
Fuel injection pump sprocket retaining nut	65	48
Main bearing cap bolts:*		
M47T2 engine:		
Stage 1	23	17
Stage 2	Angle-tighten a further 90°	
M57TU engine:		
Stage 1	23	17
Stage 2	Angle-tighten a further 90°	
M57T2 engine:		
Stage 1	50	37
Stage 2	Angle-tighten a further 90°	
Oil cooler-to-oil filter housing bolts	22	16
Oil feed guide rail bolts	10	7
Oil filter cap	25	18
Oil filter housing bolts	25	18
Oil level sensor	8	6
Oil pressure sensor	28	21

Torque wrench settings (continued)

	Nm	lbf ft
Oil pump:		
Drive sprocket to driveshaft:		
M6	10	7
M10	25	18
Retaining bolts:		
M6	14	10
M7/M8	25	18
Cover bolts	10	7
Intake pipe	10	7
Piston oil spray jet bolts	10	7
Roadwheel bolts	120	89
Suspension turret/tension brace*	30	22
Sump bolts:		
M6	10	7
M8	19	14
Sump drain plug:		
M12	25	18
M18	35	26
Timing chain cover bolts:		
M6	10	7
M7	15	11
M8	20	15
Timing chain cover plug:		
M30	70	52
M40	30	22
Timing chain tensioner bolts	10	7
Vacuum pump bolts*	22	16

* Do not re-use

Always renew aluminium bolts.

1 General information and precautions

How to use this Chapter

This Part of the Chapter describes those repair procedures that can reasonably be carried out on the engine whilst it remains in the vehicle. If the engine has been removed from the vehicle and is being dismantled as described in Part C of this Chapter, any preliminary dismantling procedures can be ignored.

Note that whilst it may be possible physically to overhaul items such as the piston/connecting rod assemblies with the engine in the vehicle, such tasks are not usually carried out as separate operations and usually require the execution of several additional procedures (not to mention the cleaning of components and of oilways). For this reason, all such tasks are classed as major overhaul procedures and are described in Part C of this Chapter.

Engine description

This Chapter covers 4- and 6-cylinder diesel engines, designated M47 and M57. These engines are in most respects identical to one another, apart from the number of cylinders. The D suffix indicates engine capacity (D25 = 2.5 litre, etc), and the T suffix indicates

development stage (TU = technical upgrade, T2 = 2nd technical upgrade).

The cast-iron cylinder block is of the dry-liner type. The crankshaft is supported within the cylinder block on five shell-type main bearings. Thrustwashers are integral with the No 4 (4-cylinder engine) or No 6 (6-cylinder engine) main bearing shells to control crankshaft endfloat.

The cylinder head is of the double overhead camshaft, 4-valve per cylinder design – two intake and two exhaust valves per cylinder. The valves are operated by one intake camshaft and one exhaust camshaft, via rocker fingers. One end of each finger acts upon the valve stem, whilst the other end pivots on a support pillar. Valve clearances are maintained automatically by hydraulic compensation elements incorporated within the support pillars. In order to achieve high levels of combustion efficiency, the cylinder head has two intake ports for each cylinder. One port is tangential, whilst the other is helical.

The connecting rods rotate on horizontally-split bearing shells at their big-ends. The pistons are attached to the connecting rods by gudgeon pins which are secured in position with circlips. The aluminium alloy pistons are fitted with three piston rings, comprising two compression rings and an oil control ring.

The intake and exhaust valves are each closed by coil springs and operate in guides

pressed into the cylinder head. Valve guides cannot be renewed.

A timing chain, driven by the crankshaft, drives the high pressure fuel pump sprocket, which in turn drives the intake camshaft. The camshafts are geared together. The vacuum pump is fitted to the front of the cylinder head, and is driven by the exhaust camshaft. The coolant pump is driven by the auxiliary drivebelt.

On 6-cylinder engines, lubrication is by means of an eccentric-rotor type pump driven by the crankshaft via a Simplex chain. The pump draws oil through a strainer located in the sump, and then forces it through an externally-mounted full-flow paper element type oil filter into galleries in the cylinder block/crankcase, from where it is distributed to the crankshaft (main bearings), timing chain (sprayed by a jet), and camshafts. The big-end bearings are supplied with oil via internal drillings in the crankshaft, while the camshaft bearings and the followers receive a pressurised supply via drillings in the cylinder head. The camshaft lobes and valves are lubricated by oil splash, as are all other engine components. An oil cooler (integral with the oil filter housing) is fitted to keep the oil temperature stable under arduous operating conditions.

On 4-cylinder engines, the oil pump is gear-driven from a gear integral with the rear of the crankshaft. The oil pump gear also drives a balance shaft assembly fitted to the base of the cylinder block.

Operations with engine in car

The following work can be carried out with the engine in the vehicle:

a) *Compression pressure – testing.*
b) *Camshaft cover – removal and refitting.*
c) *Crankshaft pulley – removal and refitting.*
d) *Balance shaft housing – removal and refitting.*
e) *Camshafts and rocker arms – removal, inspection and refitting.*
f) *Cylinder head – removal and refitting.*
g) *Cylinder head and pistons – decarbonising.*
h) *Sump – removal and refitting.*
i) *Oil pump – removal, overhaul and refitting.*
j) *Oil filter housing/cooler – removal and refitting.*
k) *Crankshaft oil seals – renewal.*
l) *Engine/transmission mountings – inspection and renewal.*
m) *Flywheel/driveplate – removal, inspection and refitting.*
n) *Timing chains – removal, inspection and refitting.*

2 Compression test – description and interpretation

Compression test

Note: *A compression tester specifically designed for diesel engines must be used for this test.*

1 When engine performance is down, or if misfiring occurs which cannot be attributed to the fuel system, a compression test can provide diagnostic clues as to the engine's condition. If the test is performed regularly, it can give warning of trouble before any other symptoms become apparent.

2 The tester is connected to an adapter which screws into the glow plug hole. It is unlikely to be worthwhile buying such a tester for occasional use, but it may be possible to borrow or hire one – if not, have the test performed by a garage.

3 Unless specific instructions to the contrary are supplied with the tester, observe the following points:

a) *The battery must be in a good state of charge, the air filter must be clean, and the engine should be at normal operating temperature.*
b) *All the glow plugs should be removed before starting the test (see Chapter 5).*
c) *Disconnect the wiring plugs from the injectors (see Chapter 4A).*

4 There is no need to hold the accelerator pedal down during the test, because the diesel engine air intake is not throttled.

5 Crank the engine on the starter motor; after one or two revolutions, the compression pressure should build-up to a maximum figure,

and then stabilise. Record the highest reading obtained.

6 Repeat the test on the remaining cylinders, recording the pressure in each.

7 All cylinders should produce very similar pressures; a difference of more than 2 bars between any two cylinders indicates a fault. Note that the compression should build-up quickly in a healthy engine; low compression on the first stroke, followed by gradually-increasing pressure on successive strokes, indicates worn piston rings. A low compression reading on the first stroke, which does not build-up during successive strokes, indicates leaking valves or a blown head gasket (a cracked head could also be the cause). Deposits on the undersides of the valve heads can also cause low compression. **Note:** *The cause of poor compression is less easy to establish on a diesel engine than on a petrol one. The effect of introducing oil into the cylinders ('wet' testing) is not conclusive, because there is a risk that the oil will sit in the swirl chamber or in the recess on the piston crown instead of passing to the rings.*

8 Refer to a BMW dealer or other specialist if in doubt as to whether a particular pressure reading is acceptable.

9 On completion of the test, refit the glow plugs as described in Chapter 5, and reconnect the injectors (Chapter 4A).

Leakdown test

10 A leakdown test measures the rate at which compressed air fed into the cylinder is lost. It is an alternative to a compression test, and in many ways it is better, since the escaping air provides easy identification of where pressure loss is occurring (piston rings, valves or head gasket).

11 The equipment needed for leakdown testing is unlikely to be available to the home mechanic. If poor compression is suspected, have the test performed by a suitably-equipped garage.

3 Engine assembly/valve timing settings – general information and usage

Note: *BMW tool No 11 5 180 or suitable*

3.5 Pull the blanking plug from the timing pin hole in the engine block

home-made equivalent will be required to lock the crankshaft in position, and access to BMW tool No 11 6 321 and 11 6 322 or home-made equivalents are required to position the camshafts.

1 The flywheel is equipped with an indent, which aligns with a hole in the engine block when No 1 piston is at TDC (top dead centre). In this position, if No 1 piston is at TDC on its compression stroke, it must be possible to fit a BMW special tool (No 11 6 321) or home-made equivalent, over the square sections of the intake camshaft (with all four No 1 cylinder camshaft lobes pointing towards the right-hand side). **Note:** *As explained in the front of this manual, all references to left and right are in the sense of a person in the driver's seat facing forward.*

2 Firmly apply the handbrake then jack up the front of the vehicle and support it securely on axle stands (see *Jacking and vehicle support*).

3 Undo the retaining bolts/clips and remove the engine undershields **(see illustrations 6.3a and 6.3b)**.

4 Remove the camshaft cover and gasket, as described in Section 4.

5 Pull out the blanking plug from the timing pin hole in the engine block **(see illustration)**. The plug is more easily accessible from underneath.

6 Using a socket and extension bar on the crankshaft pulley centre bolt, turn the crankshaft clockwise whilst keeping an eye on the No 1 cylinder camshaft lobes. **Note:** *Do not turn the engine anti-clockwise.*

7 Rotate the crankshaft clockwise until the No 1 cylinder camshaft lobes approach the point where all four lobes are pointing upwards. Have an assistant insert BMW tool No 11 5 180 or home-made equivalent into the timing pin hole, and press the pin gently against the flywheel. Continue to slowly turn the crankshaft slowly until the pin is felt to engage in the indent in the flywheel, and the crankshaft locks **(see illustration)**.

8 With the crankshaft in this position, all four camshaft lobes of No 1 cylinder should be pointing to the right-hand side. Fit BMW tool No 11 6 321 over the flats on the intake camshaft collar, adjacent to No 1 camshaft bearing cap. If the camshaft is timed correctly,

3.7 Insert the timing pin through the engine block flange into the indent in the flywheel

3.8 Fit the special tool over the flats on the intake camshaft collar. The tool must contact both sides of the camshaft cover gasket face on the cylinder head

3.9 Use the clamp to lock the camshaft tool in place

the tool will contact both sides of the camshaft cover gasket face on the cylinder head **(see illustration)**.

9 To lock the intake camshaft in this position, fit BMW tool No 11 6 322. This tool clamps tool No 11 6 321 in place, preventing the tool from moving. Note that the exhaust camshaft is geared to the intake camshaft, and adjustment is not possible **(see illustration)**.

4 Camshaft cover – removal and refitting

Removal

1 Disconnect the battery negative lead (refer to Chapter 5). On 6-cylinder engines, remove the cooling fan and shroud as described in Chapter 3.

2 With reference to Chapter 4A, remove the fuel injectors.

3 Undo the bolt and detach the air intake ducting from the air filter housing.

4 Undo the bolts and remove the air filter housing cover **(see illustration)**. Remove the air filter element.

5 Undo the 2 bolts and pull the air duct forwards from the air filter housing **(see illustration)**.

6 Disconnect the wiring plugs from the camshaft position, and mass airflow/ intake air temperature sensors **(see illustrations)**.

7 Undo the bolts securing the fuel common rail to the cylinder head.

8 Slide out the rectangular wiring connector, then use a small flat-bladed screwdriver to lift the retaining clips, pull the wiring harness guide plate upwards, and detach it from the right-hand edge of the camshaft cover. Similarly, lift the clip and slide out the harness retaining clip at the rear of the cover **(see illustration)**.

4.4 Undo the air filter housing cover bolts (arrowed)

4.5 Air duct retaining bolts (arrowed)

4.6a Disconnect the wiring plug from the mass airflow sensor . . .

4.6b . . . and the camshaft position sensor

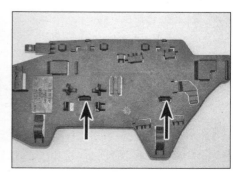

4.8 Lift the two clips (arrowed) and slide the harness guide plate upwards from the right-hand side of the camshaft cover

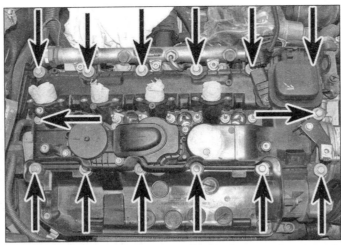

4.9 Camshaft cover bolts (arrowed) – 4-cylinder engine shown

4.12 Apply a bead of sealant to the areas shown (arrowed)

9 Working in from the outside-in, evenly slacken and remove the bolts securing the camshaft cover to the cylinder head **(see illustration)**.

10 Gently ease the common rail away, and remove the cover and discard its gasket. Note that when the gasket is removed, the bolts will fall from the cover.

Refitting

11 Ensure the mating surfaces are clean and dry then fit the new gasket to the cover. Insert the bolts into the gasket.

12 Apply a 2 mm bead of sealant (Drei Bond 1209) to the cylinder head mating surface as shown **(see illustration)**.

13 Refit the cover to the cylinder head, ensuring that the gasket remains correctly seated.

14 Insert the cover retaining bolts and tighten them all by hand. Once all bolts are in position, tighten them to the specified torque setting starting from the inside, working outwards.

15 The remainder of refitting is a reversal of removal.

5 Crankshaft pulley/vibration damper – removal and refitting

Removal

1 Firmly apply the handbrake then jack up the front of the vehicle and support it securely on axle stands (see *Jacking and vehicle support*).

2 Remove the auxiliary drivebelt(s) as described in Chapter 1.

3 If further dismantling is to be carried out (beyond pulley removal), align the engine assembly/valve timing settings as described in Section 3.

4 Slacken the crankshaft pulley retaining bolt(s). The pulley retaining bolt is extremely tight. On the 4-cylinder engine, we found it impossible to undo the bolt without applying heat to the pulley bolt, and the use of BMW tool No 11 8 182/183 and 11 8 185 (manual transmission only) to prevent crankshaft rotation. This tool fits through the hole in the base of the transmission bellhousing and engages with the starter ring gear. Slacken the bolt using a 3/4" drive socket **(see illustrations)**. On 6-cylinder engines, the crankshaft must be prevented from

5.4a We fabricated a tool . . .

5.4b . . . which is bolted to the bellhousing and locates through a hole, engaging with the flywheel starter ring gear

5.4c The part of the tool which engages with the ring gear, is an old bolt, ground at the end to match the profile of the ring gear teeth. The bolt must be a good fit in the bellhousing hole

5.5a Unscrew the retaining bolt and washer . . .

5.5b . . . and remove the crankshaft pulley

5.5c On 6-cylinder engines, the crankshaft pulley is retained by 4 bolts

5.7 Use paint to make alignment marks between the bolt head and the pulley prior to tightening

rotating using BMW tool No 11 8 182/183, fitted through the hole in the base of the transmission bellhousing, as described for the 4-cylinder engine – the vibration damper is retained by 4 bolts. If the engine is removed from the vehicle it will be necessary to lock the flywheel (see Section 13).

Caution: Do not be tempted to use the crankshaft locking pin (see Section 3) to prevent rotation as the centre bolt is slackened.

5 Unscrew the retaining bolt(s) and washer (where applicable), and remove the pulley from the crankshaft (see illustrations).

Refitting

6 Fit the pulley to the crankshaft and screw in the retaining bolt(s) with the washer fitted (where applicable).
7 Lock the crankshaft by the method used on removal, and tighten the pulley retaining bolt(s) to the specified Stage 1 torque setting then angle-tighten the bolt(s) through the

specified Stage 2 angle, using a socket and extension bar. It is recommended that an angle-measuring gauge is used during the final stages of the tightening to ensure accuracy. If a gauge is not available, use paint to make alignment marks between the bolt head(s) and pulley prior to tightening; the marks can then be used to check that the bolt has been rotated through the correct angle (see illustration).
8 Refit the auxiliary drivebelt(s) as described in Chapter 1.
9 Refit the roadwheel then lower the vehicle to the ground.

6 Camshafts, rocker arms and hydraulic tappets – removal, inspection and refitting

Removal

1 Remove the cylinder head cover as described in Section 4, and the vacuum pump as described in Chapter 9.
2 Firmly apply the handbrake, then jack up the front of the vehicle and support it securely on axle stands (see *Jacking and vehicle support*).
3 Undo the fasteners and remove the engine undershields (see illustrations).

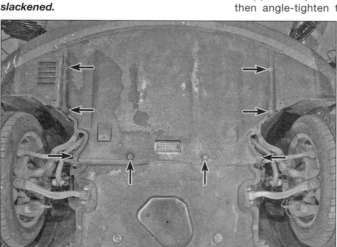

6.3a Engine/radiator undershield fasteners (arrowed)

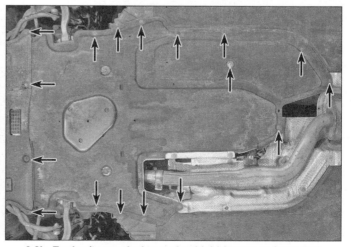

6.3b Engine/transmission undershield fasteners (arrowed)

6.4 With all the camshaft lobes of No 1 cylinder pointing downwards . . .

6.5 . . . remove the camshaft sprocket upper bolt

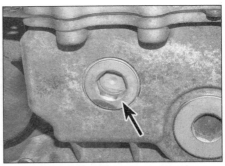

6.6 Unscrew the plug (arrowed) from the timing chain cover

4 Using a socket and ratchet, rotate the crankshaft pulley clockwise until the lobes of the No 1 cylinder intake camshaft are pointing downwards **(see illustration)**.

5 Undo and remove the upper bolt securing the sprocket to the camshaft **(see illustration)**.

6 Remove the plug in the timing chain cover **(see illustration)**.

7 Fit an open-ended spanner to the hexagonal section of the exhaust camshaft, and rotate the camshaft anti-clockwise slightly, to force the timing chain tensioner to compress. Whilst the tensioner is compressed, insert a 4.0 mm diameter rod/drill bit through the plug hole in the timing cover to lock the tensioner in place **(see illustrations)**.

8 Pull out the blanking plug from the timing

pin hole in the engine block **(see illustration 3.5)**.

9 Using a socket and extension bar on the crankshaft pulley centre bolt, turn the crankshaft clockwise whilst keeping an eye on the No 1 cylinder camshaft lobes.

10 Rotate the crankshaft clockwise until the No 1 cylinder camshaft lobes approach the point where all four lobes are pointing upwards. Have an assistant insert BMW tool No 11 5 180 or home-made equivalent into the timing pin hole, and press the pin gently against the flywheel – see Section 3. Continue to slowly turn the crankshaft slowly until the pin is felt to engage in the indent in the flywheel, and the crankshaft locks **(see illustration 3.7)**.

11 Undo the 2 bolts securing the sprocket to the intake camshaft **(see illustration)**.

12 Unscrew and remove the timing chain guide bearing pins from the timing cover **(see illustration)**. Where necessary, undo the bolts and remove the lifting eye bracket to access the left-hand pin.

13 Pull the sprocket from the intake camshaft, hold it across to the right-hand side, then pull the left-hand timing chain guide upwards from the timing cover **(see illustrations)**.

14 Disengage the sprocket from the timing chain, then lay the chain to the left-hand side of the cylinder head. Secure the chain in place with tape, etc, to prevent it falling into the timing cover.

15 Identify the camshaft bearing caps, to ensure they are refitted to their original positions. The exhaust camshaft is marked A, so mark the exhaust camshaft bearing

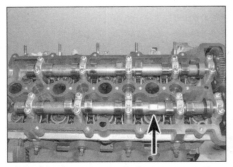

6.7a Use an open-ended spanner on the hexagonal section (arrowed) of the exhaust camshaft

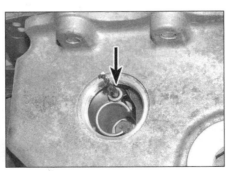

6.7b Insert a 4.0 mm drill bit/rod into the tensioner (arrowed)

6.11 Remove the remaining camshaft sprocket bolts

6.12 Unscrew the timing chain guide bearing pins (arrowed)

6.13a Pull the sprocket from the camshaft, hold it to the right-hand side . . .

6.13b . . . then pull the left-hand chain guide upwards

6.15 The camshaft bearing caps are marked E for intake, and A for exhaust, and numbered from the timing chain end (arrowed)

caps as A1, A2, A3, etc, starting with the cap nearest the timing chain. The intake camshaft is marked E, so repeat the procedure for the intake camshaft starting with E1 adjacent to the timing chain **(see illustration)**.

16 Evenly and progressively, slacken and remove the retaining bolts, and remove the camshaft bearing caps. **Note:** *Do not undo the bolts securing the vacuum pump guide to the cylinder head.*

17 Remove the camshafts from the cylinder head.

18 Lift the rocker arms from the cylinder head, and lay them out in order on a clean surface, so that they can be fitted into their original positions – if they are to be re-used.

19 Obtain 16 (4-cylinder engines) or 24 (6-cylinder engines) small, clean plastic containers, and label them for identification. Alternatively, divide a larger container into compartments. Withdraw each hydraulic tappet in turn, and place it in its respective container, which should then be filled with clean engine oil.

Caution: Do not interchange the tappets, and do not allow the tappets to lose oil, as they will take a long time to refill with oil on restarting the engine, which could result in incorrect valve clearances. Absolute cleanliness is essential at all times when handling the tappets.

Inspection

20 Examine the camshaft bearing surfaces

6.25a The 2 dots on the rear of the exhaust camshaft gear must align with the dot on the intake gear

and cam lobes for signs of wear ridges and scoring. Renew the camshaft if any of these conditions are apparent. Examine the condition of the bearing surfaces both on the camshaft journals and in the cylinder head. If the head bearing surfaces are worn excessively, the cylinder head will need to be renewed.

21 Examine the rocker bearing surfaces which contact the camshaft lobes for wear ridges and scoring. If the engine's valve clearances have sounded noisy, particularly if the noise persists after initial start-up from cold, then there is reason to suspect a faulty tappet. If any tappet is thought to be faulty or is visibly worn it should be renewed.

Refitting

22 Where removed, lubricate the tappets with clean engine oil and carefully insert each one into its original location in the cylinder head **(see illustration)**.

23 Refit the rocker arms to their original locations, ensuring that they are correctly orientated **(see illustration)**.

24 Remove the crankshaft locking tool, and rotate the crankshaft 45° anti-clockwise (if not already done so) to prevent any accidental piston-to-valve contact. Ensure the timing chain does not fall into the timing cover, or jam on the crankshaft sprocket.

25 Engage the gear on the exhaust camshaft with the gear on the intake camshaft, so the 2 dots on the rear of the exhaust camshaft gear are each side of the dot on the intake gear, then lay the camshafts in place on the

6.25b The dots on the gears must be approximately flush with the upper surface of the cylinder head

6.22 Refit each hydraulic tappet to its original location

6.23 Refit the rocker arms, ensuring they locate on the top of the tappets correctly

cylinder head so the dots are flush with the upper surface of the cylinder head **(see illustrations)**.

26 Lubricate the bearing surfaces of the camshaft with clean engine oil, then refit the bearing caps to their original positions.

27 Insert the bearing cap bolts, then evenly and progressively tighten the retaining bolts to draw the bearing caps squarely down into contact with the cylinder head. Once the caps are in contact with the head, tighten the retaining bolts to the specified torque.

Caution: If the bearing caps bolts are carelessly tightened, the caps might break. If the caps are broken then the complete cylinder head assembly must be renewed; the caps are matched to the head and are not available separately.

28 With the camshafts in this position, it should be possible to fit BMW tool No 11 6 321 (or equivalent) over the flat in the collar on the intake camshaft, as described in Section 3. If it is not, adjust the position of the camshafts slightly using an open-ended spanner on the hexagonal section of the exhaust camshaft.

29 With the camshafts held in position, rotate the crankshaft 45° clockwise (back to TDC) so the flywheel locking tool can be reinserted. Ensure the timing chain doesn't fall inside the cover, or jam on the crankshaft sprocket.

30 Lower the left-hand timing chain guide into position.

31 Engage the timing chain with the sprocket, and position the sprocket on the end of the intake camshaft so the bolt holes align **(see illustration)**. Fit the new retaining bolts, but

6.31 Align the sprocket with the bolt holes

only finger-tighten them at this stage – the sprocket must be able to rotate independently of the camshaft.

32 Apply a little thread-locking compound, then refit and tighten the timing chain guide bearing pins.

33 Remove the rod/drill bit locking the timing chain tensioner

34 Tighten the new sprocket retaining bolts to the specified torque.

35 Remove the flywheel and camshaft locking tools, then rotate the crankshaft so the remaining sprocket bolt can be inserted and tightened.

36 Refit and tighten the plug to the timing chain cover.

37 Rotate the crankshaft clockwise until the third camshaft sprocket bolt can be installed and tightened.

38 The remainder of refitting is a reversal of removal.

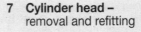

7 Cylinder head –
removal and refitting

Removal

1 Remove the camshafts, rocker arms and tappets as described in Section 6, then lift out the right-hand upper timing chain guide.

2 Drain the cooling system, as described in Chapter 1.

3 Remove the EGR cooler as described in Chapter 4B.

4 Disconnect the fuel pressure sensor wiring plug, and release the harness grommet from the cylinder head.

5 Disconnect the engine coolant temperature sensor wiring plug.

6 Undo the high-pressure fuel pipe unions, remove the pipe from the pump to the common rail, then undo the bolts and remove the common rail. Disconnect the wiring plugs and return hose as the common rail is withdrawn **(see illustration)**. Note that a new high-pressure fuel pipe must be fitted.

7 Gently pull the connectors from the glow plugs.

8 On 4-cylinder engines, undo the 3 retaining bolts, and pull the coolant hose

7.10a The coolant rail is secured by a bolt at the front (arrowed) . . .

7.6 Common fuel rail mounting bolts (arrowed)

connector away from the cylinder head **(see illustration)**.

9 Release the retaining clips, and disconnect the various coolant hoses from the cylinder head.

10 Unscrew the bolts securing the coolant rail, release the clips and manoeuvre the coolant rail to one side **(see illustrations)**.

4-cylinder engines

11 Unscrew the 3 bolts securing the turbocharger to the exhaust manifold, and discard the gasket.

6-cylinder engines

12 Slacken the bolts securing the turbocharger to the cylinder block.

13 Slacken the clamp securing the turbocharger to the exhaust manifold. Once the cylinder head has been removed, renew the clamp.

14 Undo the bolts securing the wiring guide and bracket to the rear of the cylinder head.

All engines

15 Unscrew the bolts securing the cylinder head to the timing cover **(see illustration)**.

16 Make a final check to ensure that all relevant hoses, pipes and wires, etc, have been disconnected.

17 Working in the **reverse** of the tightening sequence **(see illustration 7.34a or 7.34b)**, progressively slacken the cylinder head bolts by a third of a turn at a time until all bolts can be unscrewed by hand. Withdraw and discard the bolts, new ones must be fitted.

18 Lift the cylinder head from the cylinder block. If necessary, tap the cylinder head

7.10b . . . and one at the rear (arrowed)

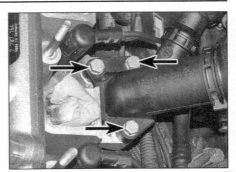

7.8 Undo the bolts (arrowed) and remove the coolant hose connector

gently with a soft-faced mallet to free it from the block, but **do not** lever at the mating faces.

19 When the joint is broken, lift the cylinder head away then remove the gasket. Note the fitted positions of the two locating dowels, and remove them for safe-keeping if they are loose. Keep the gasket for identification purposes (see paragraph 25).

Caution: Do not lay the head on its lower mating surface; support the head on wooden blocks, ensuring each block only contacts the head mating surface not the glow plugs. The glow plugs protrude out the bottom of the head and they will be damaged if the head is placed directly onto a bench.

20 If the cylinder head is to be dismantled, refer to the relevant Sections of Part C of this Chapter.

Preparation for refitting

21 The mating faces of the cylinder head and block must be perfectly clean before refitting the head. Use a scraper to remove all traces of gasket and carbon, and also clean the tops of the pistons. Take particular care with the aluminium surfaces, as the soft metal is damaged easily. Also, make sure that debris is not allowed to enter the oil and water channels – this is particularly important for the oil circuit, as carbon could block the oil supply to the camshaft or crankshaft bearings. Using adhesive tape and paper, seal the water, oil and bolt holes in the cylinder block. To prevent carbon entering the gap between the pistons

7.15 Undo the bolts (arrowed) securing the cylinder head to the timing chain cover

and bores, smear a little grease in the gap. After cleaning the piston, rotate the crankshaft so that the piston moves down the bore, then wipe out the grease and carbon with a cloth rag. Clean the piston crowns in the same way.

22 Check the block and head for nicks, deep scratches and other damage. If slight, they may be removed carefully with a file. More serious damage may be repaired by machining, but this is a specialist job.

23 If warpage of the cylinder head gasket surface is suspected, use a straight-edge to check it for distortion. Refer to Part C of this Chapter if necessary.

24 Ensure that the cylinder head bolt holes in the crankcase are clean and free of oil. Syringe or soak up any oil left in the bolt holes. This is most important in order that the correct bolt tightening torque can be applied and to prevent the possibility of the block being cracked by hydraulic pressure when the bolts are tightened.

25 On these engines, the cylinder head-to-piston clearance is controlled by fitting different thickness head gaskets. The piston protrusion is represented by the number of holes in the gasket next to the timing chain area **(see illustration)**.

M47 and M57TU engines

Holes in gasket	Largest piston protrusion
One hole	0.72 to 0.83 mm
Two holes	0.83 to 0.93 mm
Three holes	0.93 to 1.04 mm

M57T2 engines

Holes in gasket	Largest piston protrusion
One hole	0.77 to 0.92 mm
Two holes	0.92 to 1.03 mm
Three holes	1.03 to 1.18 mm
Zero holes	more than 1.18 mm

Select the new gasket which has the same thickness/number of holes as the original, unless new piston and connecting rod assemblies have been fitted. In that case, the correct thickness of gasket required is selected by measuring the piston protrusions as follows.

26 Remove the locking pin from the flywheel and mount a dial test indicator securely on the block so that its pointer can be easily pivoted between the piston crown and block mating surface.

27 Ensure No 1 piston is at exactly TDC then zero the dial test indicator on the gasket surface of the cylinder block. Carefully move the indicator over No 1 piston, taking measurements in line with the gudgeon pin axis, measure the protrusion on both the left-hand and right-hand side of the piston **(see illustration)**. **Note:** When turning the crankshaft, ensure that the timing chain does not jam in the timing cover.

28 Rotate the crankshaft to bring the

7.25 Cylinder head gasket identification holes (arrowed)

7.30 Ensure the dowels are in position (arrowed)

7.27 Measure the piston protrusion with a DTI gauge

7.33 Insert the new bolts and washers into place

remaining pistons to TDC in turn. Ensure the crankshaft is accurately positioned then measure the protrusions of the remaining pistons, taking two measurements for each piston. Once both pistons have been measured, rotate the crankshaft to bring No 1 piston back to TDC. Then rotate it 45° anti-clockwise.

29 Use the table in paragraph 25 to select the appropriate gasket.

Refitting

30 Wipe clean the mating faces of the head and block and ensure that the two locating dowels are in position on the cylinder block/crankcase surface **(see illustration)**.

31 Fit the new gasket to the cylinder block,

ensuring that it fits correctly over the locating dowels.

32 Carefully refit the cylinder head, locating it on the dowels. Make sure the timing chain can be pulled up through the cylinder head tunnel.

33 The new cylinder head bolts are supplied pre-coated – do not wash the coating off, or apply grease/oil to them. Carefully enter the main bolts (1 to 10 – 4-cylinder engines, or 1 to 14 – 6-cylinder engines) into the holes and screw them in, by hand only, until finger-tight **(see illustration)**.
Caution: Do not drop the bolts into their holes.

34 Working progressively and in the sequence shown, first tighten all the cylinder head bolts to the Stage 1 torque setting **(see illustrations)**.

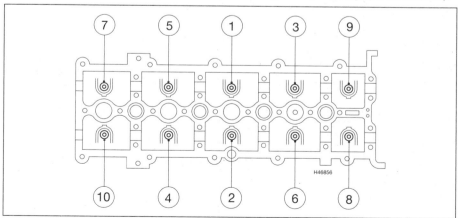
7.34a Cylinder head bolt tightening sequence – 4-cylinder engines

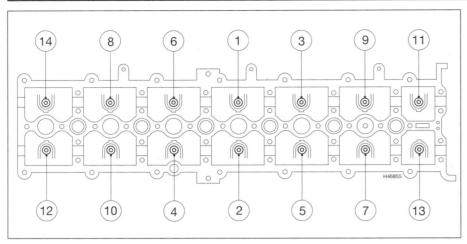

7.34b Cylinder head bolt tightening sequence – 6-cylinder engines

35 Slacken all the bolts half a turn (180°), then tighten them in sequence to the Stage 3 setting.

36 Again, in sequence, angle-tighten them 90° (Stage 4), and another 90° (Stage 5), using an angle-measuring gauge **(see illustration)**.

37 Refit and tighten the bolts securing the cylinder head to the timing cover, to the specified torque. **Note:** *Take great care not to drop the inner bolt down the timing chain tunnel **(see illustration 7.15)**.*

38 The remainder of refitting is a reversal of removal, noting the following points:
   a) *Renew all gaskets/seals disturbed during the removal procedure.*
   b) *Refit the right-hand upper timing chain guide before installing the camshafts.*
   c) *Tighten all fasteners to their specified torque where given.*
   d) *Refill the cooling system as described in Chapter 1.*

8 Sump – removal and refitting

Removal

1 Drain the engine oil and remove the oil filter as described in Chapter 1. Refit the sump plug with a new washer and tighten the plug to the specified torque.

2 Remove the acoustic cover from the top of the engine **(see illustration)**.

3 Remove the cooling fan and shroud as described in Chapter 3.

4 The front subframe must be lowered a little as follows:

5 Jack up the front of the vehicle and support it securely on axle stands (see *Jacking and vehicle support*). Remove the retaining bolts and fasteners and remove the engine undershield **(see illustrations 6.3a and 6.3b)**.

6 Remove the exhaust system as described in Chapter 4.

7 Remove the bonnet as described in Chapter 11.

8 Rotate the fastener 90° anti-clockwise, release the clip and remove the pollen filter covers from the housing each side **(see illustration)**.

9 Pull up the rubber sealing strip, then release the clip and slide the plastic cover from the centre of the panel **(see illustrations)**.

7.36 Use an angle gauge to accurately tighten the cylinder head bolts

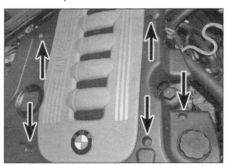

8.2 Undo the bolts (arrowed) and remove the acoustic cover from the engine – 6-cylinder engine shown

8.8 Rotate the fastener 90° anti-clockwise and fold the clip forwards (arrowed)

8.9a Pull up the rubber sealing strip

8.9b Lift the clip and slide the cover to the passenger's side

8.10a Lift out the plastic trim . . .

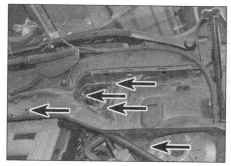

8.10b . . . undo the fasteners/bolt (arrowed) and lift out the cover each side

8.11 Undo the bolts and remove the strut brace (arrowed)

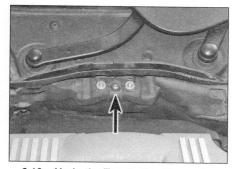

8.12a Undo the Torx bolt in the centre (arrowed) . . .

8.12b . . . the 2 bolts each side (arrowed) . . .

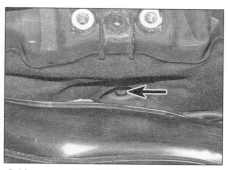

8.12c . . . rotate the fastener (arrowed) in the centre 90° anti-clockwise . . .

10 Lift out the plastic trim, undo the bolts/fasteners and remove the left- and right-hand plastic covers from behind the suspension turret each side of the engine compartment. Unclip the wiring where applicable **(see illustrations)**.

11 Undo the 4 bolts and remove the strut brace **(see illustration)**. Discard the bolts – new ones must be fitted.

12 Remove the Torx bolt, the 2 bolts each side, and the fastener in the centre, then pull the fresh air duct forwards **(see illustrations)**. Undo the bolt securing the pipe clamp (where fitted).

13 Undo the bolts and remove the front underbody reinforcement plate **(see illustration)**. Discard the bolts – new ones must be fitted.

14 The engine must be supported in position using an engine hoist or engine crossbeam.

Attach the hoist/crossbeam to the engine lifting eyes at the front and rear of the engine. Take the weight of the engine.

Caution: Note that if using the crossbeam, mount the crossbeam on the suspension turrets and the front panel adjacent to the bonnet catch each side. The inner wings are not strong enough to take the weight of the engine.

15 Undo the nut each side securing the engine mounting support brackets to the mountings, then raise the engine approximately 10 mm.

16 Remove driver's side lower facia panel as described in Chapter 11.

17 Remove the steering column lower universal joint pinch-bolt and lift the column shaft upwards from the steering rack pinion **(see illustration)**. Discard the pinch-bolt – a new one must be used.

Caution: Ensure the steering wheel/column is not rotated with the universal joint disconnected from the steering rack pinion. Damage to the column could result.

18 Disconnect the wiring plugs from the ride height sensors (where fitted), then disconnect the vacuum hoses from the engine mountings (where applicable).

19 On models with electric power steering, cut the cable-tie securing the wiring harness to the subframe.

20 On models with Dynamic Drive active suspension system, place a container beneath the pipes, undo the unions and drain the fluid from the return and pressure pipes.

21 Examine the front subframe, and identify any remaining wiring looms/connectors which will be affected by the lowering of the subframe. Note their fitted positions, and disconnect/release them.

8.12d . . . and remove the fresh air duct

8.13 Front underbody reinforcement plate bolts (arrowed)

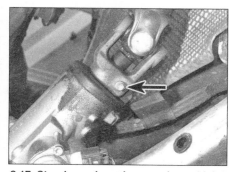

8.17 Steering column lower universal joint pinch-bolt (arrowed)

8.29 Oil pump pick-up/strainer bolts (arrowed)

8.32a Apply a bead of sealant to the areas indicated – 4-cylinder engines

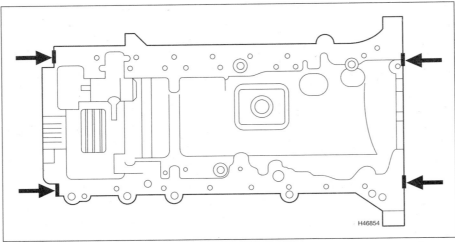

8.32b Apply a 2 mm wide bead of sealant to the areas arrowed – 6-cylinder engines

22 Support the front subframe using a workshop jack and lengths of wood, etc, then undo the 3 bolts each side and carefully lower the subframe a maximum of 100 mm. Pay attention to the power steering hoses/pipes as the subframe is being lowered – do not allow them to be bent or stretched. When refitting, tighten down the front bolts first.

23 Remove the starter motor as described in Chapter 5.

24 Undo the bolt securing the oil level dipstick guide tube and pull the tube from the sump. Renew the guide tube O-ring seal.

25 Disconnect the wiring plug from the engine oil level sensor.

26 Slacken and remove the bolts securing the transmission casing to the sump.

27 Progressively slacken and remove the bolts securing the sump to the base of the cylinder block.

28 Break the sump joint by striking the sump with the palm of the hand, then lower the sump away from the engine. Remove the gasket and discard it, a new one should be used on refitting.

29 While the sump is removed, take the

opportunity to check the oil pump intake pipe for signs of clogging or splitting. If necessary, unbolt the intake pipe, and remove it from the engine along with its gasket **(see illustration)**. The strainer can then be cleaned easily in solvent. Inspect the strainer mesh for signs of clogging or splitting and renew if necessary. If the intake pipe bolts are damaged they must be renewed.

Refitting

30 Clean all traces of gasket from the mating surfaces of the cylinder block and sump, then use a clean rag to wipe out the sump and the engine interior.

31 Where necessary, fit a new seal to the oil pump intake pipe then carefully refit the pipe. Refit the retaining bolts, and tighten them to the specified torque setting.

32 Apply a bead of suitable sealant (Drei Bond 1209 is available from your BMW dealer) to the area where the cylinder block meets the timing cover **(see illustrations)**.

33 Fit the gasket to the sump then offer up the sump to the cylinder block/crankcase **(see illustration)**. Refit the sump retaining bolts, and tighten the bolts finger-tight only.

34 Fit the bolts securing the sump to the gearbox. In order to align the rear sump flange with the gearbox, lightly tighten the bolts, then slacken them. If the sump is being refitted to the engine with the gearbox removed, use a straight-edge to ensure that the sump casting is flush with the end of the cylinder block **(see illustration)**.

35 Tighten the sump-to-engine block bolts, and then the sump-to-transmission bolts to the specified torque.

36 Refit the oil dipstick tube, with a new O-ring, and tighten the bolts securely.

37 The remainder of refitting is a reversal of removal, noting the following points:

   a) *Renew all gaskets/seals where disturbed.*

   b) *Tighten all fasteners to their specified torque where given.*

   c) *Renew the engine oil and filter as described in Chapter 1.*

   d) *Where applicable, fill and bleed the Dynamic Drive hydraulic system as described in Chapter 10.*

   e) *If necessary, have the front wheel alignment checked by a BMW dealer or suitably equipped-specialist.*

8.33 Offer the sump up into position, and insert a couple of the retaining bolts

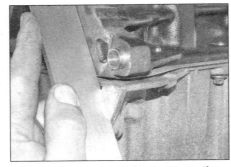

8.34 Use a straight-edge to ensure the sump casting is flush with the end of the engine block

9 Oil pump – removal, inspection and refitting

4-cylinder engines

Note: *BMW insist that a removed oil pump must not be refitted. It must be renewed. The drivegear of the new pump is coated with paint to ensure correct backlash adjustment.*

9.1 Plastic cover retaining bolts (arrowed)

9.7 Insert two 5.0 mm drill bits/rods into the holes in the balance shaft assembly

Removal

1 Remove the sump as described in Section 8, then undo the bolts and remove the plastic cover from the pump **(see illustration)**.

2 Undo the retaining bolts and remove the oil pump. Discard the bolts, new ones must be fitted.

Inspection

3 At the time of writing, no new parts are available for the oil pump. If defective, the complete assembly must be renewed. Consult a BMW dealer or parts specialist.

Refitting

4 Ensure the mating surfaces of the oil pump and cylinder block are clean and dry. Ensure all mounting holes are clean and free from oil.

5 Pull out the blanking plug from the timing pin hole in the engine block **(see illustration 3.5)**.

6 Using a socket and extension bar on the crankshaft pulley centre bolt, turn the crankshaft clockwise and insert BMW tool

No 11 5 180 or home-made equivalent into the timing pin hole, and press the pin gently against the flywheel. Continue to slowly turn the crankshaft slowly until the pin is felt to engage in the indent in the flywheel, and the crankshaft locks **(see illustrations 3.7)**.

7 Insert 5.0 mm rods or pins into the holes in the base of the balance shaft assembly to lock the shafts in position **(see illustration)**.

8 Offer the oil pump into position, ensuring the drivegear engages with the crankshaft drivegear and the balance shaft gear. The marks on the oil pump drivegear must point towards the other gears **(see illustration)**. Insert the pump retaining bolts and finger-tighten them. It must be possible to still move the pump.

9 Push the pump forwards into position whilst holding it against the balance shaft and crankshaft gears.

10 Tighten the pump retaining bolts to their specified torque in the sequence shown **(see illustration)**.

11 Refit the sump as described in Section 8.

9.8 The painted marks (arrowed) must point towards the other gears

6-cylinder engines

Removal

12 Remove the sump as described in Section 8.

13 Undo the bolt securing the sprocket to the pump shaft **(see illustration)**.

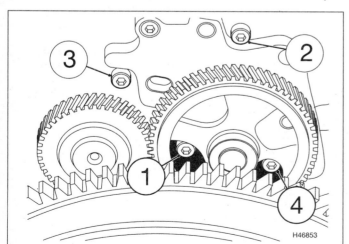

9.10 Oil pump bolts tightening sequence

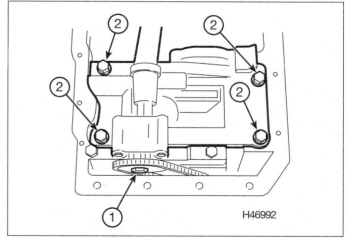

9.13 Oil pump sprocket bolt (1) and mounting bolts (2)

11.3 Fold the clip forwards, and undo the fastener 90° anti-clockwise (arrowed)

14 Undo the bolts and remove the oil pick-up assembly. Discard the O-ring seal, a new one must be fitted.

15 Undo the four bolts and remove the oil pump.

Inspection

16 At the time of writing, no new parts are available for the oil pump. If defective, the complete assembly must be renewed. Consult a BMW dealer or parts specialist.

Refitting

17 Offer the pump into position and engage the sprocket (with the chain still in place) with the pump driveshaft.

18 Insert the pump retaining bolts and tighten them to the specified torque.

19 Refit the sprocket retaining bolt and tighten it to the specified torque.

20 Fit a new O-ring seal to the pick up tube and refit it. Tighten the bolts securely.

21 Refit the sump as described in Section 8.

---

10 Balance shaft assembly – removal and refitting

Note: *Only the 4-cylinder engine is equipped with a balance shaft assembly.*

Removal

1 Remove the oil pump as described in Section 9.

11.8 Oil cooler bolts (arrowed)

11.7 Glow plug control unit retaining bolts (arrowed)

2 Undo the bolts and detach the balance shaft assembly from the base of the cylinder block. Note that no separate parts are available for the balance shaft assembly – if defective, the complete assembly must be renewed.

Refitting

3 Ensure the mating surface of the balance shaft assembly and the cylinder block is clean, then position the assembly on the cylinder block and tighten the bolts securely.

4 Refit the oil pump as described in Section 9.

---

11 Oil cooler – removal and refitting

Removal

4-cylinder engines

1 Drain the engine coolant and engine oil, and remove the oil filter as described in Chapter 1.

2 Undo the bolts and remove the front section of the acoustic cover from the top of the engine.

3 Fold forwards the clip, undo the bolt and remove the left-hand pollen filter cover **(see illustration)**.

4 Pull up the rubber sealing strip, lift the clip and slide the central plastic panel to

11.10 Disconnect the coolant hose from the oil cooler (arrowed)

the left-hand side **(see illustrations 8.9a and 8.9b)**.

5 Lift up the trim at the outer edge, then undo the fasteners/bolt and remove the left-hand side pollen filter housing **(see illustrations 8.10a and 8.10b)**.

6 Release the clip securing, and disconnect the hose from the oil cooler.

7 Undo the bolts and move the glow plug control unit and bracket to one side **(see illustration)**. The control unit is located under the oil cooler.

8 Unscrew the three bolts and remove the oil cooler from the oil filter housing. Discard the gasket. Be prepared for fluid spillage **(see illustration)**.

6-cylinder engines

9 Drain the engine coolant and engine oil, and remove the oil filter as described in Chapter 1.

10 Release the clamp and disconnect the coolant hose from the oil cooler **(see illustration)**.

11 Disconnect the wiring plug, then undo the bolts and remove the oil filter housing from the left-hand side of the cylinder block **(see illustration)**.

12 Undo the bolts and detach the oil cooler from the filter housing. Renew the gasket.

Refitting

13 Ensure the mating surfaces of the oil cooler and oil filter housing are clean and dry, and with a new gasket, fit the cooler to the housing. Tighten the bolts to the specified torque.

14 The remainder of refitting is a reversal of removal.

---

12 Crankshaft oil seals – renewal

Timing chain end seal

1 Remove the crankshaft pulley/vibration damper as described in Section 5.

2 Very carefully punch or drill two small holes opposite each other in the oil seal. Screw a

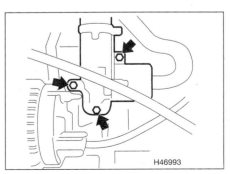

11.11 Oil filter housing retaining bolts (arrowed)

12.2 Remove the crankshaft oil seal using a self-tapping screw

12.4 Press the seal squarely into position until it's flush with the timing chain cover

12.7 Remove the cap from the end of the crankshaft

self-tapping screw into each and pull on the screws with pliers to extract the seal **(see illustration)**.
Caution: Great care must be taken to avoid damage to the crankshaft.
3 Clean the seal housing and polish off any burrs or raised edges which may have caused the seal to fail in the first place.
4 Ease the new seal into position on the end of the shaft – do not oil the seal lips. Press the seal squarely into position until it is flush with the housing. If necessary, a suitable tubular drift, such as a socket, which bears only on the hard outer edge of the seal can be used to tap the seal into position. Take great care not to damage the seal lips during fitting and ensure that the seal lips face inwards **(see illustration)**.
5 Refit the crankshaft pulley as described in Section 5.

Flywheel/driveplate end oil seal

6 Remove the flywheel or driveplate as described in Section 13.
7 Carefully remove the cap from the end of the crankshaft **(see illustration)**.
8 Undo the bolt and pull the crankshaft position sensor from the oil seal housing **(see illustration)**.
9 Undo the retaining bolts, then carefully detach the oil seal housing from the cylinder block and sump, without damaging the sump gasket **(see illustration)**. If the gasket is damaged, the sump will have to be removed

12.8 Undo the bolt (arrowed) and pull the crankshaft position sensor from place

as described in Section 8. Note that oil seal is integral with the housing.
10 The new seal and housing assembly is supplied with a seal protector installed. Lubricate the end of the crankshaft with a little clean engine oil, then position the seal protector, complete with seal, over the end of the crankshaft, and ease the seal and housing over the crankshaft shoulder **(see illustrations)**.
11 Refit the oil seal housing bolts, and tighten them to the specified torque.
12 Refit the crankshaft position sensor and tighten the bolt securely.
13 Ensure the dowel is correctly fitted in the end of the crankshaft, and refit the end cap.
14 Wash off any oil then refit the flywheel/driveplate as described in Section 13.

12.9 Undo the bolts and pull the seal housing from the engine block. Take care not to damage the sump gasket

13 Flywheel/driveplate – removal, inspection and refitting

Flywheel

Note: *New flywheel retaining bolts must be used on refitting.*

Removal

1 Remove the clutch assembly as described in Chapter 6.
2 Prevent the flywheel from turning by locking the ring gear teeth with a similar arrangement to that shown **(see illustration)**. Alternatively, bolt a strap between the flywheel and the cylinder block/crankcase.

12.10a With the seal protector (arrowed) installed . . .

12.10b . . . position the assembly over the end of the crankshaft

13.2 Lock the flywheel using a similar tool

13.3 Note the locating dowel (arrowed)

3 Slacken and remove the retaining bolts and remove the flywheel, noting its locating dowel **(see illustration)**. **Do not** drop it, as it is very heavy. Discard the bolts, they must be renewed whenever they are disturbed.

Inspection

4 If the flywheel-to-clutch mating surface is deeply scored, cracked or otherwise damaged, then the flywheel must be renewed, unless it is possible to have it surface ground. Seek the advice of a BMW dealer or engine reconditioning specialist.
5 If the ring gear is badly worn or has missing teeth, then it must be renewed. This job is best left to a BMW dealer or engine reconditioning specialist.
6 These vehicles are fitted with dual mass flywheels. Whilst BMW do not publish any checking procedures, rotate the inner mass by hand anti-clockwise, mark its position in relation to the outer mass, then rotate it by hand clockwise and measure the travel. As a general rule, if the movement is more than 30 mm or less than 15 mm, consult a BMW dealer or transmission specialist as to whether a new unit is needed.

Refitting

7 Clean the mating surfaces of the flywheel and crankshaft, and remove all traces of locking compound from the crankshaft threaded holes.
8 Fit the flywheel to the crankshaft, engaging it with the crankshaft locating dowel, and fit the new retaining bolts. **Note:** *If the new bolts are not supplied pre-coated with locking*

compound, apply a few drops prior to fitting the bolts.
9 Lock the flywheel using the method employed on dismantling then, working in a diagonal sequence, tighten all the retaining bolts to the specified torque setting.
10 Refit the clutch assembly as described in Chapter 6.

Driveplate

Note: *New driveplate retaining bolts must be used on refitting.*

Removal

11 Remove the automatic transmission and torque converter as described in Chapter 7B.
12 Prevent the driveplate from turning by locking the ring gear teeth with a similar arrangement to that shown **(see illustration 13.2)**. Alternatively, bolt a strap between the driveplate and the cylinder block/crankcase.
13 Slacken and remove the retaining bolts and remove the driveplate, noting its locating dowel. Discard the bolts, they must be renewed whenever they are disturbed.

Inspection

14 If the ring gear is badly worn or has missing teeth, then it must be renewed. This job is best left to a BMW dealer or engine reconditioning specialist.

Refitting

15 Clean the mating surfaces of the driveplate and crankshaft and remove all traces of locking compound from the crankshaft threaded holes.
16 Fit the driveplate to the crankshaft, engaging it with the crankshaft locating dowel, and fit the new retaining bolts. **Note:** *If the new bolts are not supplied pre-coated with locking compound, apply a few drops prior to fitting the bolts.*
17 Lock the driveplate using the method employed on dismantling then, working in a diagonal sequence, tighten all the retaining bolts to the specified torque setting.
18 Refit the torque converter and automatic transmission as described in Chapter 7B.

14 Engine mountings –
inspection and renewal

Inspection

1 Two engine mountings are used, one on either side of the engine.
2 If improved access is required, raise the front of the vehicle and support it securely on axle stands (see *Jacking and vehicle support*). Undo the fasteners and remove the engine undershield.
3 Check the mounting rubber to see if it is cracked, hardened or separated from the metal at any point. Renew the mounting if any such damage or deterioration is evident.
4 Check that all the mounting fasteners are securely tightened.
5 Using a large screwdriver or a crowbar, check for wear in the mounting by carefully levering against it to check for free play. Where this is not possible, enlist the aid of an assistant to move the engine/transmission back and forth, or from side to side, while you observe the mounting. While some freeplay is to be expected, even from new components, excessive wear should be obvious. If excessive freeplay is found, check first that the fasteners are correctly secured, then renew any worn components as required.

Renewal

6 Support the engine, either using a hoist and lifting tackle connected to the engine lifting brackets (refer to *Engine – removal and refitting* in Part C of this Chapter), or by positioning a jack and interposed block of wood under the sump. Ensure that the engine is adequately supported before proceeding.
7 Unscrew the nuts securing the left- and right-hand engine mounting brackets to the mounting rubbers, then unbolt the mounting brackets from the cylinder block, and remove the mounting brackets. Disconnect any engine earth straps from the mountings **(see illustrations)**.
8 Unscrew the bolts securing the mountings to the subframe, then withdraw the mountings **(see illustration)**. Disconnect the vacuum

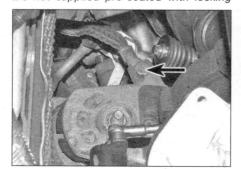

14.7a Disconnect the earth strap (arrowed) from the mounting bracket

14.7b Undo the bracket retaining bolts (arrowed)

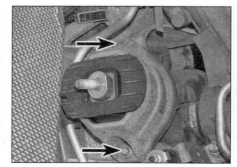

14.8 Mounting retaining bolts (arrowed)

15.3 Drive the flywheel pilot bearing out from the engine side

15.4a Position the bearing . . .

15.4b . . . then fit it using tubular spacer or socket

hoses from the mountings as they are withdrawn (where applicable)

9 Refitting is a reversal of removal. Tighten all fasteners to their specified torque where given.

15 Flywheel pilot bearing – inspection, removal and refitting

Inspection

1 The pilot bearing is fitted into the centre of the dual mass flywheel, and provides support for the free end of the gearbox input shaft on manual transmission vehicles. It can only be examined once the clutch (Chapter 6) has been removed. Using a finger, rotate the inner race of the bearing and check for any roughness, binding or looseness in the bearing. If any of these conditions are evident, the bearing must be renewed.

Removal

2 Remove the flywheel as described in Section 13.

3 Ideally the bearing should be pressed out using a hydraulic press. However, we managed

to remove the old bearing and fit the new one using a hammer, drift and socket. Position the flywheel over a 27 mm socket that bears on the flywheel centre immediately surrounding the bearing. Then drive the bearing from the flywheel with a drift. The bearing is driven from the engine side of the flywheel and out of the clutch side **(see illustration)**. Note that the act of pressing the bearing out will render it unusable – it must be renewed.

Refitting

4 Using a suitable tubular spacer that bears only on the hard outer edge of the bearing, press/drive the new bearing into the flywheel until it contacts the shoulder **(see illustrations)**.

5 Refit the flywheel as described in Section 13.

16 Timing chains and cover – removal and refitting

Removal

1 Remove the cylinder head as described in Section 7.

2 Remove the sump as described in Section 8.

3 Remove the crankshaft timing chain end oil seal as described in Section 12.

4 On models with conventional power steering, undo the 3 bolts securing the pulley to the power steering pump, then undo the 3 mounting bolts and move the pump to one side. There's no need to disconnect the hoses/pipes.

5 Remove the alternator as described in Chapter 5.

6 Undo the bolt and remove the alternator drivebelt tensioner **(see illustration)**.

7 Remove the coolant pump as described in Chapter 3.

8 Undo the 2 bolts securing the EGR solenoid valve bracket (where fitted) to the timing cover.

9 Undo the bolts and pull the timing cover from place **(see illustration)**.

10 In order to renew the timing cover gasket, the timing chain from the crankshaft to the fuel injection pump must be removed as follows:

11 Compress the timing chain tensioner by

16.6 Drivebelt tensioner bolt (arrowed)

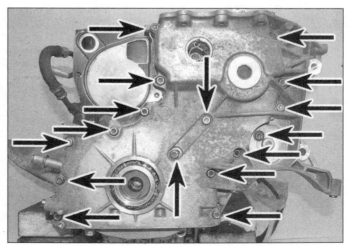

16.9 Timing chain cover bolts (arrowed)

16.11 Push back the tensioner piston, then lock it in place with a 4.0 mm drill bit

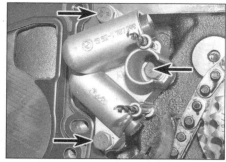

16.12a Tensioner retaining bolts (arrowed)

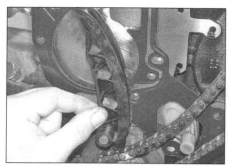

16.12b Slide the upper guide rail from place

hand, and lock it in place using a 4.0 mm drill bit **(see illustration)**.

12 Undo the bolts and remove the chain tensioner, followed by the upper guide rail **(see illustrations)**.

13 Undo the nut securing the sprocket to the fuel injection pump **(see illustration)**.

14 Carefully pull the timing chains, the sprockets from the crankshaft and fuel injection pump shaft, and the lower guide rail from place. If necessary, use a two-legged puller to release the fuel pump sprocket from the shaft taper **(see illustrations)**

15 Remove the old gasket.

Refitting

16 Ensure the timing chain cover and cylinder block mating surfaces are clean and free from oil and debris. Ensure the dowels in the

cylinder block are undamaged and in place.

17 Locate the new gasket over the dowels on the cylinder block **(see illustration)**.

18 Refit the timing chains and sprockets, and lower guide rail as an assembly to the crankshaft and fuel injection pump shaft. Ensure the crankshaft sprocket locates correctly over the shaft key **(see illustration)**.

19 Tighten the fuel injection pump sprocket retaining nut to the specified torque.

20 Refit the upper timing chain guide rail and tensioner. Tighten the fasteners to the specified torque, then pull out the tensioner locking drill bit.

21 Apply a little sealant (Drei Bond 1209) to the base of the gasket each side **(see illustration)**, then refit the timing chain cover over the dowels in the cylinder block.

22 Insert the timing chain cover bolts and

tighten them evenly to their specified torque.

23 Fit a new crankshaft/timing cover oil seal as described in Section 12.

24 The remainder of refitting is a reversal of removal.

17 Oil pressure and level sensors – removal and refitting

Oil pressure sensor

1 The oil pressure sensor is located on the left-hand side of the engine block behind the oil filter housing. Remove the oil filter element as described in Chapter 1. This allows the oil to drain from the housing, preventing

16.13 Undo the fuel injection pump sprocket nut

16.14a Remove the chain sprockets and lower guide rail

16.14b If necessary, use a puller to extract the fuel pump sprocket

16.17 Locate the new gasket over the dowels on the engine block

16.18 Ensure the sprocket locates over the crankshaft key

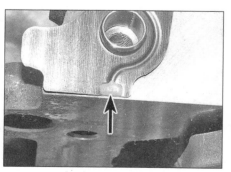

16.21 Apply a little sealant to the base of the gasket each side (arrowed)

17.2 Oil pressure sensor (arrowed)

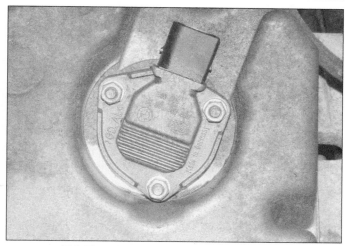

17.6 The oil level sensor is retained by 3 nuts

excessive oil leakage as the sensor is removed.

2 Disconnect the wiring plug, and unscrew the sensor **(see illustration)**. Be prepared for oil spillage.

3 Refitting is a reversal of removal, using a new sealing washer, and tightening the sensor to the specified torque.

Oil level sensor

4 Drain the engine oil as described in Chapter 1.

5 Undo the fasteners and remove the engine undershield.

6 Disconnect the wiring plug, undo the three retaining nuts and remove the sensor **(see illustration)**.

7 Ensure that the sump mating surface is clean.

8 Complete with a new seal, install the sensor, apply a little thread-locking compound and tighten the retaining nuts to the specified torque.

9 Refit the engine undershield, and replenish the engine oil as described in Chapter 1.

Notes

Chapter 2 Part C:
General engine overhaul procedures

Contents

Degrees of difficulty

Easy, suitable for novice with little experience	Fairly easy, suitable for beginner with some experience	Fairly difficult, suitable for competent DIY mechanic	Difficult, suitable for experienced DIY mechanic	Very difficult, suitable for expert DIY or professional

Specifications

Cylinder head

Maximum gasket face distortion:
All engines	0.050 mm

New cylinder head height:
N47 engine	No machining possible
M47T2 engine	Not available
M57TU engine	No machining possible
M57T2 engine	130.70 ± 0.05 mm

Minimum cylinder head height after machining:
N47 engine	No machining possible
M47T2 engine	Not available
M57TU engine	No machining possible
M57T2 engine	Not available

Valves

Valve head diameter:
N47 engine:	
Intake	24.50 mm
Exhaust	27.30 mm
M47T2 engine	Not available
M57TU engine	Not available
M57T2 engine:	
Intake	25.90 mm
Exhaust	25.90 mm

Cylinder block

Cylinder bore diameter:
N47 engine	84.00 mm (nominal)
M47T2 engine	Not available
M57TU engine	Not available
M57T2 engine:	
2.5 litre	82.00 mm (nominal)
3.0 litre	84.00 mm (nominal)
Maximum cylinder bore ovality	0.005 mm
Maximum cylinder bore taper	0.010 mm

Crankshaft

Endfloat (all engines) . . . .   0.060 to 0.250 mm

Piston rings

End gaps:
  N47 engines:
    Top compression ring . . . .   0.20 to 0.30 mm
    Second compression ring . . . .   0.30 to 0.45 mm
  M47T2 engines:
    Top compression ring . . . .   0.20 to 0.35 mm
    Second compression ring . . . .   0.30 to 0.45 mm
    Oil control ring . . . .   Not applicable
  M57TU engine . . . .   Not available
  M57T2 engine:
    Top compression ring . . . .   0.20 to 0.35 mm
    Second compression ring . . . .   0.30 to 0.45 mm
    Oil control ring . . . .   Not applicable

Torque wrench settings

Refer to Chapter 2A or 2B Specifications as applicable

1 General information

Included in this Part of Chapter 2 are details of removing the engine/transmission from the car and general overhaul procedures for the cylinder head, cylinder block/crankcase and all other engine internal components.

The information given ranges from advice concerning preparation for an overhaul and the purchase of new parts, to detailed step-by-step procedures covering removal, inspection, renovation and refitting of engine internal components.

After Section 5, all instructions are based on the assumption that the engine has been removed from the car. For information concerning in-car engine repair, as well as the removal and refitting of those external components necessary for full overhaul, refer to Part A or B of this Chapter, as applicable and to Section 5. Ignore any preliminary dismantling operations described in Parts A or B that are no longer relevant once the engine has been removed from the car.

Apart from torque wrench settings, which are given at the beginning of Parts A or B all specifications relating to engine overhaul are at the beginning of this Part of Chapter 2.

2 Engine overhaul – general information

1 It is not always easy to determine when, or if, an engine should be completely overhauled, as a number of factors must be considered.
2 High mileage is not necessarily an indication that an overhaul is needed, while low mileage does not preclude the need for an overhaul. Frequency of servicing is probably the most important consideration. An engine which has had regular and frequent oil and filter changes, as well as other required maintenance, should give many thousands of miles of reliable service. Conversely, a neglected engine may require an overhaul very early in its life.
3 Excessive oil consumption is an indication that piston rings, valve seals and/or valve guides are in need of attention. Make sure that oil leaks are not responsible before deciding that the rings and/or guides are worn. Perform a compression test, as described in Part A or B of this Chapter, to determine the likely cause of the problem.
4 Check the oil pressure with a gauge fitted in place of the oil pressure switch, and compare it with that specified. If it is extremely low, the main and big-end bearings, and/or the oil pump, are probably worn out.
5 Loss of power, rough running, knocking or metallic engine noises, excessive valve gear noise, and high fuel consumption may also point to the need for an overhaul, especially if they are all present at the same time. If a complete service does not remedy the situation, major mechanical work is the only solution.
6 A full engine overhaul involves restoring all internal parts to the specification of a new engine. During a complete overhaul, the pistons and the piston rings are renewed, and the cylinder bores are reconditioned. New main and big-end bearings are generally fitted; if necessary, the crankshaft may be reground, to compensate for wear in the journals. The valves are also serviced as well, since they are usually in less-than-perfect condition at this point. Always pay careful attention to the condition of the oil pump when overhauling the engine, and renew it if there is any doubt as to its serviceability. The end result should be an as-new engine that will give many trouble-free miles.
7 Critical cooling system components such as the hoses, thermostat and water pump should be renewed when an engine is overhauled.

The radiator should be checked carefully, to ensure that it is not clogged or leaking. Also, it is a good idea to renew the oil pump whenever the engine is overhauled.
8 Before beginning the engine overhaul, read through the entire procedure, to familiarise yourself with the scope and requirements of the job. Overhauling an engine is not difficult if you follow carefully all of the instructions, have the necessary tools and equipment, and pay close attention to all specifications. It can, however, be time-consuming. Plan on the car being off the road for a minimum of two weeks, especially if parts must be taken to an engineering works for repair or reconditioning. Check on the availability of parts and make sure that any necessary special tools and equipment are obtained in advance. Most work can be done with typical hand tools, although a number of precision measuring tools are required for inspecting parts to determine if they must be renewed. Often the engineering works will handle the inspection of parts and offer advice concerning reconditioning and renewal.
9 Always wait until the engine has been completely dismantled, and until all components (especially the cylinder block/crankcase and the crankshaft) have been inspected, before deciding what service and repair operations must be performed by an engineering works. The condition of these components will be the major factor to consider when determining whether to overhaul the original engine, or to buy a reconditioned unit. Do not, therefore, purchase parts or have overhaul work done on other components until they have been thoroughly inspected. As a general rule, time is the primary cost of an overhaul, so it does not pay to fit worn or sub-standard parts.
10 As a final note, to ensure maximum life and minimum trouble from a reconditioned engine, everything must be assembled with care, in a spotlessly-clean environment.

3 Engine removal – methods and precautions

1 If you have decided that the engine must be removed for overhaul or major repair work, several preliminary steps should be taken.

2 Locating a suitable place to work is extremely important. Adequate work space, along with storage space for the car, will be needed. If a workshop or garage is not available, at the very least, a flat, level, clean work surface is required.

3 Cleaning the engine compartment and engine/transmission before beginning the removal procedure will help keep tools clean and organised.

4 An engine hoist or A-frame will also be necessary. Make sure the equipment is rated in excess of the weight of the engine. Safety is of primary importance, considering the potential hazards involved in lifting the engine/transmission out of the car.

5 If this is the first time you have removed an engine, an assistant should ideally be available. Advice and aid from someone more experienced would be helpful. There are many instances when one person cannot simultaneously perform all of the operations required when lifting the engine out of the vehicle.

6 Plan the operation ahead of time. Before starting work, arrange for the hire of or obtain all of the tools and equipment you will need. Some of the equipment necessary to perform engine/transmission removal and installation safely and with relative ease (in addition to an engine hoist) is as follows: a heavy duty trolley jack, complete sets of spanners and sockets (see *Tools and working facilities*), wooden blocks, and plenty of rags and cleaning solvent for mopping-up spilled oil, coolant and fuel. If the hoist must be hired, make sure that you arrange for it in advance, and perform all of the operations possible without it beforehand. This will save you money and time.

7 Plan for the car to be out of use for quite a while. An engineering works will be required to perform some of the work which the do-it-yourselfer cannot accomplish without special equipment. These places often have

a busy schedule, so it would be a good idea to consult them before removing the engine, in order to accurately estimate the amount of time required to rebuild or repair components that may need work.

8 Always be extremely careful when removing and refitting the engine/transmission. Serious injury can result from careless actions. Plan ahead and take your time, and a job of this nature, although major, can be accomplished successfully.

9 On all models, then engine is removed by first removing the gearbox/transmission, then lifting the engine out from above the vehicle.

4 Engine – removal and refitting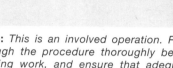

Note: *This is an involved operation. Read through the procedure thoroughly before starting work, and ensure that adequate lifting tackle and jacking/support equipment is available. Make notes during dismantling to ensure that all wiring/hoses and brackets are correctly repositioned and routed on refitting. The use of a digital camera to record there fitted positions could be invaluable.*

Removal

1 Remove the bonnet as described in Chapter 11.

2 Disconnect the battery negative lead (see Chapter 5).

3 Drain the cooling system as described in Chapter 1.

4 Drain the engine oil, referring to Chapter 1.

5 Remove the manual gearbox (Chapter 7A) or the automatic transmission (Chapter 7B), as applicable.

6 Remove the auxiliary drivebelt(s) as described in Chapter 1, then unbolt the air conditioning compressor from the engine where applicable, release the pipes from the retaining clips, and support the compressor clear of the working area, as described in Chapter 3. Secure the compressor to the chassis leg using cable-ties or similar.

> ⚠ **Warning: Do not disconnect the refrigerant lines – refer to Chapter 3 for precautions to be taken.**

7 Make a note of their fitted locations, then disconnect the engine wiring loom plugs from the electric box.

8 Remove the intake manifold and air cleaner assembly as described in the relevant part of Chapter 4.

9 Remove the radiator, cooling fan and shroud as described in Chapter 3.

10 Make a note of their fitted positions, then disconnect the various coolant hoses from the engine.

11 If not already done so, disconnect and remove the intake and outlet hoses from the intercooler – see Chapter 4A.

12 Disconnect the fuel feed and return pipes **(see illustration)**. Plug/seal the openings to prevent contamination.

13 On models with conventional power steering, remove the power steering pump as described in Chapter 10. Note there is no need to disconnect the hoses – place the pump to one side.

14 Unless a hoist is available which is capable of lifting the engine out over the front of the vehicle with the vehicle raised, it will now be necessary to remove the axle stands and lower the vehicle to the ground. Ensure that the engine is adequately supported during the lowering procedure.

15 Unbolt the earth lead(s) from the engine mounting bracket(s), and the earth lead from the cylinder head to the right-hand inner wing (where fitted) **(see illustration)**.

16 Make a final check to ensure that all relevant hoses, pipes and wiring have been disconnected from the engine and moved clear to allow the engine to be lifted out.

17 Position the lifting tackle and hoist to support the engine both from the lifting eye at the rear left-hand corner of the cylinder block, and from the lifting bracket at the front of the cylinder head. Raise the hoist to just take the weight of the engine.

18 Undo the nuts securing the engine mountings to the mounting bracket each side, then undo the bolts and remove the right-hand mounting bracket from the cylinder block. Where applicable, disconnect the vacuum hose from the solenoid valve on the engine block.

19 With the aid of an assistant, raise the hoist, and manoeuvre the engine from the engine compartment. Access is limited – take care not to damage and wiring, hoses, etc, as the engine is removed.

Refitting

20 Refitting is a reversal of removal, bearing in mind the following points.

   a) *Tighten all fixings to the specified torque where given.*

   b) *Ensure that all wiring, hoses and brackets are positioned and routed as noted before removal.*

   c) *Refit the auxiliary drivebelt with reference to Chapter 1.*

   d) *Refit the intake manifold as described in the relevant part of Chapter 4.*

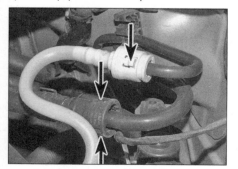

4.12 Depress the release buttons (arrowed) and disconnect the fuel pipes

4.15 Disconnect the earth lead (arrowed) from the right-hand engine mounting bracket

e) Refit the radiator, referring to Chapter 3.
f) Refit the manual gearbox or automatic transmission as described in Chapter 7A or 7B respectively.
g) On completion, refill the engine with oil, and refill the cooling system as described in Chapter 1.

5 Engine overhaul – dismantling sequence

1 It is much easier to dismantle and work on the engine if it is mounted on a portable engine stand. These stands can often be hired from a tool hire shop. Before the engine is mounted on a stand, the flywheel/driveplate should be removed, so that the stand bolts can be tightened into the end of the cylinder block/crankcase.

2 If a stand is not available, it is possible to dismantle the engine with it blocked up on a sturdy workbench, or on the floor. Be extra careful not to tip or drop the engine when working without a stand.

3 If you are going to obtain a reconditioned engine, all the external components must be removed first, to be transferred to the new engine (just as they will if you are doing a complete engine overhaul yourself). These components include the following:
a) Ancillary unit mounting brackets (oil filter, starter, alternator, power steering pump, etc).
b) Thermostat and housing (Chapter 3).
c) All electrical switches and sensors.
d) Intake and exhaust manifolds – where applicable (the relevant part of Chapter 4).
e) Flywheel/driveplate (Part A or B of this Chapter).

Note: When removing the external components from the engine, pay close attention to details that may be helpful or important during refitting. Note the fitted position of gaskets, seals, spacers, pins, washers, bolts, and other small items.

4 If you are obtaining a 'short' engine (which consists of the engine cylinder block/crankcase, crankshaft, pistons and connecting rods all assembled), then the cylinder head, sump, oil pump, and timing chain will have to be removed also.

5 If you are planning a complete overhaul, the engine can be dismantled, and the internal components removed, in the order given below, referring to Part A or B of this Chapter unless otherwise stated.
a) Intake and exhaust manifolds – where applicable (the relevant part of Chapter 4).
b) Timing chains, sprockets and tensioner(s).
c) Cylinder head.
d) Flywheel/driveplate.
e) Sump.
f) Oil pump.
g) Piston/connecting rod assemblies (Section 9).
h) Crankshaft (Section 11).

6 Before beginning the dismantling and overhaul procedures, make sure that you have all of the correct tools necessary. Refer to Tools and working facilities for further information.

6 Cylinder head – dismantling

Note: New and reconditioned cylinder heads are available from the manufacturer, and from engine overhaul specialists. Be aware that some specialist tools are required for the dismantling and inspection procedures, and new components may not be readily available. It may therefore be more practical and economical for the home mechanic to purchase a reconditioned head, rather than dismantle, inspect and recondition the original head. A valve spring compressor tool will be required for this operation.

1 Remove the cylinder head, camshafts, cam followers/rocker arms and hydraulic adjusters as described in Part A or B of this Chapter as applicable.

2 Using a valve spring compressor, compress the spring on each valve in turn until the split collets can be removed. Note that where the springs have a larger diameter at one end, this end must be placed against the cylinder head upon refitting. Release the compressor, and lift off the spring retainer, and spring. Using a pair of pliers, carefully extract the valve stem oil seal/spring seat from the top of the guide **(see illustrations)**.

3 If, when the valve spring compressor is screwed down, the spring retainer refuses to free and expose the split collets, gently tap the top of the tool, directly over the retainer, with a light hammer. This will free the retainer.

4 Withdraw the valve through the combustion chamber.

5 It is essential that each valve is stored together with its collets, retainer, springs, and spring seats. The valves should also be kept in their correct sequence, unless they are so badly worn that they are to be renewed. If they are going to be kept and used again, place each valve assembly in a labelled polythene bag or similar small container **(see illustration)**. Note that No 1 valve is at the crankshaft pulley end of the engine.

7 Cylinder head and valves – cleaning and inspection

1 Thorough cleaning of the cylinder head and valve components, followed by a detailed inspection, will enable you to decide how much valve service work must be carried out during the engine overhaul. **Note:** If the engine has been severely overheated, it is best to assume that the cylinder head is warped – check carefully for signs of this.

Cleaning

2 Scrape away all traces of old gasket material from the cylinder head.

3 Scrape away the carbon from the combustion chambers and ports, then wash the cylinder head thoroughly with paraffin or a suitable solvent.

4 Scrape off any heavy carbon deposits that may have formed on the valves, then use a power-operated wire brush to remove deposits from the valve heads and stems.

Inspection

Note: Be sure to perform all the following inspection procedures before concluding

6.2a Compress the valve springs using a spring compressor tool

6.2b Remove the valve stem oil seals

6.5 Place each valve and its associated components in a labelled polythene bag

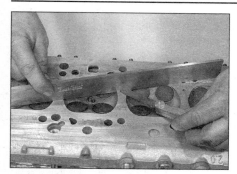

7.6 Check the cylinder head gasket face for distortion

7.12 Measure the valve stem diameter using a micrometer

7.15 Grinding-in a valve

that the services of a machine shop or engine overhaul specialist are required. Make a list of all items that require attention.

Cylinder head

5 Inspect the head very carefully for cracks, evidence of coolant leakage, and other damage. If cracks are found, a new cylinder head should be obtained.

6 Use a straight-edge and feeler blade to check that the cylinder head gasket surface is not distorted **(see illustration)**. If it is, it may be possible to have it machined, provided that the cylinder head is not reduced to less than the specified height.

7 Examine the valve seats in each of the combustion chambers. If they are severely pitted, cracked, or burned, they will need to be renewed or recut by an engine overhaul specialist. If they are only slightly pitted, this can be removed by grinding-in the valve heads and seats with fine valve-grinding compound, as described later in this Section.

8 Check the valve guides for wear by inserting the relevant valve, and checking for side-to-side motion of the valve. A very small amount of movement is acceptable. If the movement seems excessive, renew the valve. Separate valve guides are not available, although different grades (sizes) of valves (stems) may be.

9 Examine the bearing surfaces in the cylinder head or bearing castings (as applicable) and the bearing caps for signs of wear or damage.

10 Where applicable, check the camshaft bearing casting mating faces on the cylinder head for distortion.

Valves

⚠️ *Warning: The exhaust valves fitted to some engines are filled with sodium to improve their heat transfer. Sodium is a highly reactive metal, which will ignite or explode on contact with water (including water vapour in the air). These valves must NOT be disposed of as ordinary scrap. Seek advice from a BMW dealer or your local authority when disposing of the valves.*

11 Examine the head of each valve for pitting, burning, cracks, and general wear. Check the valve stem for scoring and wear ridges. Rotate the valve, and check for any obvious

indication that it is bent. Look for pits or excessive wear on the tip of each valve stem. Renew any valve that shows any such signs of wear or damage.

12 If the valve appears satisfactory at this stage, measure the valve stem diameter at several points using a micrometer **(see illustration)**. Any significant difference in the readings obtained indicates wear of the valve stem. Should any of these conditions be apparent, the valve(s) must be renewed.

13 If the valves are in satisfactory condition, they should be ground (lapped) into their respective seats, to ensure a smooth, gas-tight seal. If the seat is only lightly pitted, or if it has been recut, fine grinding compound *only* should be used to produce the required finish. Coarse valve-grinding compound should *not* be used, unless a seat is badly burned or deeply pitted. If this is the case, the cylinder head and valves should be inspected by an expert, to decide whether seat recutting, or even the renewal of the valve or seat insert (where possible) is required.

14 Valve grinding is carried out as follows. Place the cylinder head upside-down on a bench.

15 Smear a trace of (the appropriate grade of) valve-grinding compound on the seat face, and press a suction grinding tool onto the valve head **(see illustration)**. With a semi-rotary action, grind the valve head to its seat, lifting the valve occasionally to redistribute the grinding compound. A light spring placed under the valve head will greatly ease this operation.

16 If coarse grinding compound is being used, work only until a dull, matt even surface is produced on both the valve seat and the valve, then wipe off the used compound, and repeat the process with fine compound. When a smooth unbroken ring of light grey matt finish is produced on both the valve and seat, the grinding operation is complete. *Do not* grind-in the valves any further than absolutely necessary, or the seat will be prematurely sunk into the cylinder head.

17 When all the valves have been ground-in, carefully wash off *all* traces of grinding compound using paraffin or a suitable solvent, before reassembling the cylinder head.

Valve components

18 Examine the valve springs for signs of damage and discoloration. No minimum free length is specified by BMW, so the only way of judging valve spring wear is by comparison with a new component.

19 Stand each spring on a flat surface, and check it for squareness. If any of the springs are damaged, distorted or have lost their tension, obtain a complete new set of springs. It is normal to renew the valve springs as a matter of course if a major overhaul is being carried out.

20 Renew the valve stem oil seals regardless of their apparent condition.

Cam followers/valve lifters

21 Examine the contact surfaces for wear or scoring. If excessive wear is evident, the component(s) should be renewed.

8 Cylinder head – reassembly

Note: *New valve stem oil seals should be fitted, and a valve spring compressor tool will be required for this operation.*

1 Lubricate the stems of the valves, and insert the valves into their original locations **(see illustration)**. If new valves are being fitted, insert them into the locations to which they have been ground.

2 Working on the first valve, dip the new valve stem seal in fresh engine oil. New seals are normally supplied with protective

8.1 Lubricate the valve stem

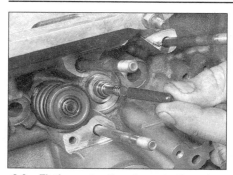

8.2a Fit the protective sleeve to the valve stem . . .

8.2b . . . then fit the oil seal using a socket

8.3a Fit the valve spring . . .

8.3b . . . followed by the spring retainer

9 Piston/connecting rod assembly – removal

⚠️ *Warning: On engines with oil spray jets fitted to the cylinder block, take care not to damage the jets as the piston/connecting rod assemblies are removed. BMW insist that if the jets are bent, they must be renewed.*

1 Remove the cylinder head, sump and balancer shaft/oil pump/vacuum housing (as applicable) as described in Part A or B.

2 If there is a pronounced wear ridge at the top of any bore, it may be necessary to remove it with a scraper or ridge reamer, to avoid piston damage during removal. Such a ridge indicates excessive wear of the cylinder bore.

3 Check the connecting rods and big-end caps for identification marks. Both rods and caps should be marked with the cylinder number. Note that No 1 cylinder is at the crankshaft pulley end of the engine. If no marks are present, using a hammer and centre-punch, paint or similar, mark each connecting rod and big-end bearing cap with its respective cylinder number on the flat machined surface provided **(see illustration)**.

4 Turn the crankshaft to bring pistons 1 and 4 (4-cylinder engines) or 1 and 6 (6-cylinder engines), as applicable, to BDC (bottom dead centre).

5 Unscrew the bolts from No 1 piston big-end bearing cap. Take off the cap, and recover the bottom half bearing shell **(see illustration)**. If the bearing shells are to be re-used, tape the cap and the shell together.

6 Using a hammer handle, push the piston up through the bore, and remove it from the top of the cylinder block. Recover the bearing shell, and tape it to the connecting rod for safe-keeping. Take great care not to damage the oil spray jets.

sleeves which should be fitted to the tops of the valve stems to prevent the collet grooves from damaging the oil seals. If no sleeves are supplied, wind a little thin tape round the top of the valve stems to protect the seals. Carefully locate the seal over the valve and onto the guide. Take care not to damage the seal as it is passed over the valve stem. Use a suitable socket or metal tube to press the seal firmly onto the guide **(see illustrations)**.

3 Locate the valve spring on top of the seat, then refit the spring retainer. Where the spring diameter is different at each end, the larger diameter end of the valve spring fits against the seat on the cylinder head **(see illustrations)**.

4 Compress the valve spring(s), and locate the split collets in the recess in the valve stem. Release the compressor, then repeat the procedure on the remaining valves.

5 With all the valves installed, support the cylinder head on blocks of wood and, using a hammer and interposed block of wood, tap the end of each valve stem to settle the components.

6 Refit the camshaft bearing castings, cam followers, camshafts and cylinder head as described in Part A or B of this Chapter.

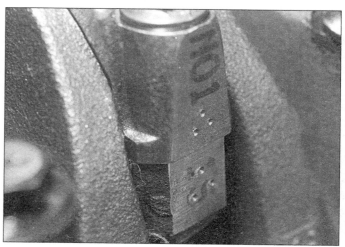

9.3 Big-end bearing cap marks

9.5 Remove the big-end bearing cap

10.2 Timing cover retaining bolts (arrowed)

10.4 The oil pump sprocket bolt has a left-hand thread

7 Loosely refit the big-end cap to the connecting rod, and secure with the bolts – this will help to keep the components in their correct order.

8 Remove No 4 piston assembly (4-cylinder engines) or No 6 piston assembly (6-cylinder engines), as applicable, in the same way.

9 Turn the crankshaft as necessary to bring the remaining pistons to BDC, and remove them in the same way.

10 Timing chains (N47 engines) – removal and refitting

Note: *The engine has to be removed for this procedure.*

Removal

1 Remove the cylinder head, flywheel and sump as described in Chapter 2A.

2 Undo the bolts and remove the timing cover from the rear of the engine **(see illustration)**.

3 Remove the metal gasket from rear of the cylinder block. Check the locating dowels are in good condition and correctly located.

4 Undo the bolt securing the sprocket to the oil pump shaft. Note that the bolt has a **left-hand thread (see illustration)**. Pull the sprocket and chain from the shaft.

5 Slide the upper timing chain guide rail from the locating pin **(see illustration)**.

6 Secure the crankshaft against rotation and slacken the fuel pump central bolt **(see illustration)**.

7 Using BMW tool No 11 8 740 or a suitable puller, release the fuel pump sprocket from the shaft **(see illustration)**.

8 Press in the chain tensioner piston, and

insert a suitable diameter rod/drill bit to lock the piston in place **(see illustration)**.

9 Slide the guide rails from each side of the fuel pump drive chain as the chain and fuel pump sprocket are removed **(see illustration)**.

Refitting

10 Position the crankshaft so piston No 1 is 45° after top dead centre (TDC). This can be verified by measuring the distance from the cylinder block upper gasket surface to the top

10.5 Slide the upper chain guide from the pin (arrowed)

10.6 Slacken the fuel pump sprocket bolt

10.7 Use a puller to remove the fuel pump sprocket

10.8 Push in the piston, then use a drill bit/rod to secure it in place

10.9 Remove the timing chain, pump sprocket and guide rails together

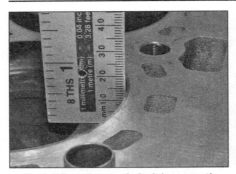

10.10 When the crankshaft is correctly positioned, the distance from the piston to the gasket surface should be 16 mm

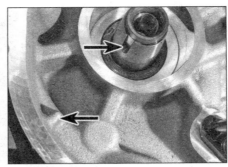

10.11 The groove on the pump shaft must align with the mark on the block (arrowed)

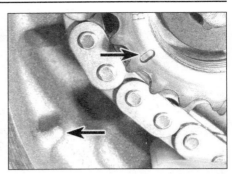

10.12 The mark on the sprocket must also align with the mark on the block (arrowed)

of the piston. When the crankshaft is correctly positioned, the distance should be 16 mm **(see illustration)**.

11 With the crankshaft correctly positioned, the groove in the fuel pump shaft must be aligned with the mark on the cylinder block **(see illustration)**.

12 Fit the fuel pump sprocket into the chain, then fit the chain around the crankshaft sprocket. Position the sprocket on the fuel pump shaft noting the mark and pin on the sprocket (which aligns with the groove on the pump shaft) must align with the mark on the cylinder block **(see illustration)**. Push the sprocket onto the pump shaft, and refit the guide rails at the same time.

13 With the crankshaft held stationary, tighten the fuel pump shaft bolt to the specified torque.

14 Pull out the locking rod/drill bit from the tensioner to release the tensioner piston.

15 Engage the upper timing chain with the fuel pump sprocket, and the lower chain with the oil pump sprocket and crankshaft sprocket. Fit the sprocket to the oil pump, noting that the flat on the pump shaft must align with the flat in the sprocket mounting hole **(see illustration)**.

16 Prevent the crankshaft from rotating, and tighten the oil pump sprocket retaining bolt to the specified torque. Note that the bolt has a **left-hand thread**.

17 Fit the new gasket over the locating dowels, then refit the timing cover to the rear of the cylinder block. Tighten the retaining bolts to the specified torque.

10.15 The flat on the oil pump shaft aligns with the flat in the mounting hole (arrowed)

18 The remainder of refitting is a reversal of removal.

11 Crankshaft – removal

Note: *On N47 4-cylinder engines, in order to remove the crankshaft, the balance shafts must first be removed. This is a complex task requiring the use of several BMW special tools. Consequently, it is recommended that this task be entrusted to a BMW dealer or suitably-equipped engine overhaul specialist.*

1 Remove the sump, timing chain, balancer shaft housing/oil pump/vacuum pump, flywheel/driveplate and crankshaft oil seals as described in Part A or B of this Chapter as applicable.

M47 engines

2 Remove the pistons and connecting rods, as described in Section 9.

3 If no work is to be done on the pistons and connecting rods, there is no need to remove the cylinder head, or to push the pistons out of the cylinder bores. The pistons should just be pushed far enough up the bores so that they are positioned clear of the crankshaft journals.

⚠ *Warning: If the pistons are pushed up the bores, and the cylinder head is still fitted, take care not to force the pistons into the open valves.*

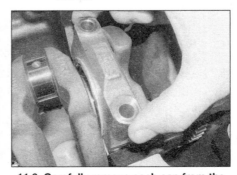

11.6 Carefully remove each cap from the cylinder block

4 Check the crankshaft endfloat as described in Section 14, then proceed as follows.

5 The main bearing caps should be numbered 1 to 5 from the timing chain end of the engine. If the bearing caps are not marked, mark them accordingly using a centre-punch.

6 Slacken and remove the main bearing cap retaining bolts, and lift off each bearing cap **(see illustration)**. Recover the lower bearing shells, and tape them to their respective caps for safe-keeping. Note that the main bearing cap bolts must be renewed.

7 Note that the lower thrust bearing shell, which controls crankshaft endfloat, may be fitted to No 4 or No 5 main bearing saddle. The correct location can be identified by the machined area for the thrust bearings to locate.

M57 engines

8 Undo the bolts and remove the reinforcement plate from the base of the cylinder block.

9 Remove the pistons and connecting rods, as described in Section 9. If no work is to be done on the pistons and connecting rods, there is no need to remove the cylinder head, or to push the pistons out of the cylinder bores. The pistons should just be pushed far enough up the bores so that they are positioned clear of the crankshaft journals.

⚠ *Warning: If the pistons are pushed up the bores, and the cylinder head is still fitted, take care not to force the pistons into the open valves.*

10 Check the crankshaft endfloat as described in Section 14, then proceed as follows.

11 The main bearing caps should be numbered 1 to 7 from the timing chain end of the engine. If the bearing caps are not marked, mark them accordingly using a centre-punch.

12 Slacken and remove the main bearing cap retaining bolts, and lift off each bearing cap **(see illustration 11.6)**. Recover the lower bearing shells, and tape them to their respective caps for safe-keeping. Note that the main bearing cap bolts must be renewed.

13 Note that the lower thrust bearing shell, which controls crankshaft endfloat, may be fitted to No 4 or No 6 main bearing saddle.

11.15 Lift the upper main bearing shells from the cylinder block

12.7 Clean the cylinder block threaded holes using a suitable tap

13.2 Remove the piston rings with the aid of a feeler gauge

The correct location can be identified by the machined area for the thrust bearings to locate.

All engines

14 Lift the crankshaft from place. Take care as the crankshaft is heavy.
15 Recover the upper bearing shells from the cylinder block **(see illustration)**. Note the location of the upper thrust bearing shell.

12 Cylinder block/crankcase – cleaning and inspection

Cleaning

 Warning: On engines with oil spray jets fitted to the cylinder block between the bearing locations, take care not to damage the jets when working on the cylinder block/crankcase. BMW insist that if the jets are bent, they must be renewed.

1 Remove all external components and electrical switches/sensors from the block. For complete cleaning, the core plugs should ideally be removed. Drill a small hole in the plugs, then insert a self-tapping screw into the hole. Pull out the plugs by pulling on the screw with a pair of grips, or by using a slide hammer.
2 Scrape all traces of gasket from the cylinder block/crankcase, taking care not to damage the gasket/sealing surfaces.
3 Remove all oil gallery plugs (where fitted). The plugs are usually very tight – they may have to be drilled out, and the holes retapped. Use new plugs when the engine is reassembled.
4 If any of the castings are extremely dirty, all should be steam-cleaned.
5 After the castings are returned, clean all oil holes and oil galleries one more time. Flush all internal passages with warm water until the water runs clear. Dry thoroughly, and apply a light film of oil to all mating surfaces, to prevent rusting. Also oil the cylinder bores. If you have access to compressed air, use it to speed up the drying process, and to blow out all the oil holes and galleries.

 Warning: Wear eye protection when using compressed air.

6 If the castings are not very dirty, you can do an adequate cleaning job with hot (as hot as you can stand), soapy water and a stiff brush. Take plenty of time, and do a thorough job. Regardless of the cleaning method used, be sure to clean all oil holes and galleries very thoroughly, and to dry all components well. Protect the cylinder bores as described above, to prevent rusting.
7 All threaded holes must be clean, to ensure accurate torque readings during reassembly. To clean the threads, run the correct-size tap into each of the holes to remove rust, corrosion, thread sealant or sludge, and to restore damaged threads **(see illustration)**. If possible, use compressed air to clear the holes of debris produced by this operation.

 HAYNES HiNT *A good alternative is to inject aerosol-applied water-dispersant lubricant into each hole, using the long spout usually supplied.*

 Warning: Wear eye protection when cleaning out these holes in this way.

8 Ensure that all threaded holes in the cylinder block are dry.
9 After coating the mating surfaces of the new core plugs with suitable sealant, fit them to the cylinder block. Make sure that they are driven in straight and seated correctly, or leakage could result.

HAYNES HiNT *A large socket with an outside diameter which will just fit into the core plug can be used to drive core plugs into position.*

10 Apply suitable sealant to the new oil gallery plugs, and insert them into the holes in the block. Tighten them securely.
11 If the engine is not going to be reassembled right away, cover it with a large plastic bag to keep it clean; protect all mating

surfaces and the cylinder bores as described above, to prevent rusting.

Inspection

12 Visually check the castings for cracks and corrosion. Look for stripped threads in the threaded holes. If there has been any history of internal water leakage, it may be worthwhile having an engine overhaul specialist check the cylinder block/crankcase with special equipment. If defects are found, have them repaired if possible, or renew the assembly.
13 Check each cylinder bore for scuffing and scoring. Check for signs of a wear ridge at the top of the cylinder, indicating that the bore is excessively worn.
14 Have the bores of the engine block measured by a BMW dealer or automotive engineering workshop. Then if the bore wear exceeds the permitted tolerances, or if the bore walls are badly scuffed or scored, then the cylinders must be rebored. Have the work carried out by a BMW dealer or automotive engineering workshop, who will also be able to supply suitable oversize pistons and rings.

13 Piston/connecting rod assembly – inspection

1 Before the inspection process can begin, the piston/connecting rod assemblies must be cleaned, and the original piston rings removed from the pistons.
2 Carefully expand the old rings over the top of the pistons. The use of two or three old feeler blades will be helpful in preventing the rings dropping into empty grooves **(see illustration)**. Be careful not to scratch the piston with the ends of the ring. The rings are brittle, and will snap if they are spread too far. They are also very sharp – protect your hands and fingers. Note that the third ring incorporates an expander. Always remove the rings from the top of the piston. Keep each set of rings with its piston if the old rings are to be re-used. Note which way up each ring is fitted.
3 Scrape away all traces of carbon from the top of the piston. A hand-held wire brush (or a piece of fine emery cloth) can be used,

13.13a Prise out the circlips . . .

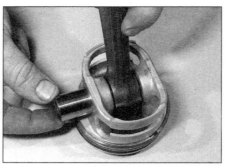

13.13b . . . and remove the gudgeon pins from the pistons

once the majority of the deposits have been scraped away.

4 Remove the carbon from the ring grooves in the piston, using an old ring. Break the ring in half to do this (be careful not to cut your fingers – piston rings are sharp). Be careful to remove only the carbon deposits – do not remove any metal, and do not nick or scratch the sides of the ring grooves.

5 Once the deposits have been removed, clean the piston/connecting rod assembly with paraffin or a suitable solvent, and dry thoroughly. Make sure that the oil return holes in the ring grooves are clear.

6 If the pistons and cylinder bores are not damaged or worn excessively, and if the cylinder block does not need to be rebored,

the original pistons can be refitted. Measure the piston diameters, and check that they are within limits for the corresponding bore diameters. If the piston-to-bore clearance is excessive, the block will have to be rebored, and new pistons and rings fitted. Normal piston wear shows up as even vertical wear on the piston thrust surfaces, and slight looseness of the top ring in its groove. New piston rings should always be used when the engine is reassembled.

7 Carefully inspect each piston for cracks around the skirt, around the gudgeon pin holes, and at the piston ring 'lands' (between the ring grooves).

8 Look for scoring and scuffing on the piston skirt, holes in the piston crown, and burned areas at the edge of the crown. If the skirt is scored or scuffed, the engine may have been suffering from overheating, and/or abnormal combustion which caused excessively high operating temperatures. The cooling and lubrication systems should be checked thoroughly. Scorch marks on the sides of the pistons show that blow-by has occurred. A hole in the piston crown, or burned areas at the edge of the piston crown, indicates that abnormal combustion (pre-ignition, knocking, or detonation) has been occurring. If any of the above problems exist, the causes must be investigated and corrected, or the damage will occur again. The causes may include intake air leaks or incorrect air/fuel mixture.

9 Corrosion of the piston, in the form of pitting, indicates that coolant has been leaking into the combustion chamber and/

or the crankcase. Again, the cause must be corrected, or the problem may persist in the rebuilt engine.

10 New pistons can be purchased from a BMW dealer.

11 Examine each connecting rod carefully for signs of damage, such as cracks around the big-end and small-end bearings. Check that the rod is not bent or distorted. Damage is highly unlikely, unless the engine has been seized or badly overheated. Detailed checking of the connecting rod assembly can only be carried out by a BMW dealer or engine repair specialist with the necessary equipment. Note that on all engines, the connecting rods can only be renewed as a complete, matched set.

12 The gudgeon pins are of the floating type, secured in position by two circlips. The pistons and connecting rods can be separated as follows. Note that the gudgeon pins are matched to the pistons, they are not available separately.

13 Using a small flat-bladed screwdriver, prise out the circlips, and push out the gudgeon pin **(see illustrations)**. Hand pressure should be sufficient to remove the pin. Identify the piston and rod to ensure correct reassembly. Discard the circlips – new ones **must** be used on refitting. Note that BMW recommend that gudgeon pins must not be renewed separately – they are matched to their respective pistons.

14 Examine the gudgeon pin and connecting rod small-end bearing for signs of wear or damage. It should be possible to push the gudgeon pin through the connecting rod by hand, without noticeable play. Wear can only be cured by renewing both the pin and piston.

15 The connecting rods themselves should not be in need of renewal, unless seizure or some other major mechanical failure has occurred. Check the alignment of the connecting rods visually, and if the rods are not straight, take them to an engine overhaul specialist for a more detailed check.

16 Examine all components, and obtain any new parts from your BMW dealer. If new pistons are purchased, they will be supplied complete with gudgeon pins and circlips. Circlips can also be purchased individually.

17 Position the piston in relation to the connecting rod, so that when the assembly is refitted to the engine, the identifying cylinder numbers on the connecting rod and big-end cap are positioned on the exhaust manifold side of the engine, and the installation direction arrow on the piston crown points towards the crankshaft pulley end of the engine **(see illustrations)**.

18 Apply a smear of clean engine oil to the gudgeon pin. Slide it into the piston and through the connecting rod small-end. Check that the piston pivots freely on the rod, then secure the gudgeon pin in position with two new circlips. Ensure that each circlip is correctly located in its groove in the piston.

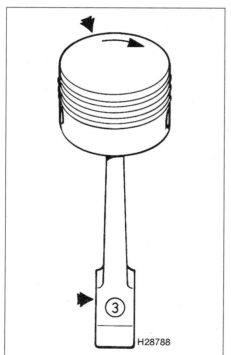

13.17a The cylinder number markings should be on the exhaust manifold side of the engine, and the arrow on the piston crown should point towards the crankshaft pulley end of the engine

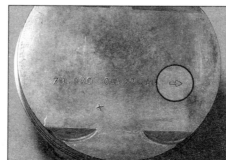

13.17b Installation direction arrow on 6-cylinder engine piston crown

14 Crankshaft – inspection

Checking crankshaft endfloat

1 If the crankshaft endfloat is to be checked, this must be done when the crankshaft is still installed in the cylinder block/crankcase, but is free to move.

2 Check the endfloat using a dial gauge in contact with the end of the crankshaft. Push the crankshaft fully one way, and then zero the gauge. Push the crankshaft fully the other way, and check the endfloat. The result can be compared with the specified amount, and will give an indication as to whether new thrust bearing shells are required **(see illustration)**.

3 If a dial gauge is not available, feeler blades can be used. First push the crankshaft fully towards the flywheel end of the engine, then use feeler blades to measure the gap between the crankshaft web and the thrust bearing shell **(see illustration)**.

Inspection

4 Clean the crankshaft using paraffin or a suitable solvent, and dry it, preferably with compressed air if available. Be sure to clean the oil holes with a pipe cleaner or similar probe, to ensure that they are not obstructed.

 Warning: Wear eye protection when using compressed air.

5 Check the main and big-end bearing journals for uneven wear, scoring, pitting and cracking.

6 Big-end bearing wear is accompanied by distinct metallic knocking when the engine is running (particularly noticeable when the engine is pulling from low speed) and some loss of oil pressure.

7 Main bearing wear is accompanied by severe engine vibration and rumble – getting progressively worse as engine speed increases – and again by loss of oil pressure.

8 Check the bearing journal for roughness by running a finger lightly over the bearing surface. Any roughness (which will be accompanied by obvious bearing wear) indicates that the crankshaft requires regrinding (where possible) or renewal.

9 If the crankshaft has been reground, check for burrs around the crankshaft oil holes (the holes are usually chamfered, so burrs should not be a problem unless regrinding has been carried out carelessly). Remove any burrs with a fine file or scraper, and thoroughly clean the oil holes as described previously.

10 Have the crankshaft journals measured by a BMW dealer or automotive engineering workshop. If the crankshaft is worn or damaged, they may be able to regrind the journals and supply suitable undersize bearing shells. If no undersize shells are available and the crankshaft has worn beyond the specified limits, it will have to be renewed. Consult your BMW dealer or engine specialist for further information on parts availability.

15 Main and big-end bearings – inspection

1 Even though the main and big-end bearings should be renewed during the engine overhaul, the old bearings should be retained for close examination, as they may reveal valuable information about the condition of the engine. The bearing shells are graded by thickness, the grade of each shell being indicated by the colour code marked on it.

2 Bearing failure can occur due to lack of lubrication, the presence of dirt or other foreign particles, overloading the engine, or corrosion **(see illustration)**. Regardless of the cause of bearing failure, the cause must be corrected (where applicable) before the engine is reassembled, to prevent it from happening again.

3 When examining the bearing shells, remove them from the cylinder block/crankcase, the connecting rods and the connecting rod big-end bearing caps. Lay them out on a clean surface in the same general position as their location in the engine. This will enable you to match any bearing problems with the corresponding crankshaft journal. *Do not* touch any shell's bearing surface with your fingers while checking it, or the delicate surface may be scratched.

4 Dirt and other foreign matter gets into the engine in a variety of ways. It may be left in the engine during assembly, or it may pass

through filters or the crankcase ventilation system. It may get into the oil, and from there into the bearings. Metal chips from machining operations and normal engine wear are often present. Abrasives are sometimes left in engine components after reconditioning, especially when parts are not thoroughly cleaned using the proper cleaning methods. Whatever the source, these foreign objects often end up embedded in the soft bearing material, and are easily recognised. Large particles will not embed in the bearing, and will score or gouge the bearing and journal. The best prevention for this cause of bearing failure is to clean all parts thoroughly, and keep everything spotlessly-clean during engine assembly. Frequent and regular engine oil and filter changes are also recommended.

5 Lack of lubrication (or lubrication breakdown) has a number of interrelated causes. Excessive heat (which thins the oil), overloading (which squeezes the oil from the bearing face) and oil leakage (from excessive bearing clearances, worn oil pump or high engine speeds) all contribute to lubrication breakdown. Blocked oil passages, which usually are the result of misaligned oil holes in a bearing shell, will also oil-starve a bearing, and destroy it. When lack of lubrication is the cause of bearing failure, the bearing material is wiped or extruded from the steel backing of the bearing. Temperatures may increase to the point where the steel backing turns blue from overheating.

6 Driving habits can have a definite effect on bearing life. Full-throttle, low-speed operation (labouring the engine) puts very high loads on bearings, tending to squeeze out the oil film. These loads cause the bearings to flex, which produces fine cracks in the bearing face (fatigue failure). Eventually, the bearing

14.2 Measure the crankshaft endfloat using a dial gauge . . .

14.3 . . . or feeler gauges

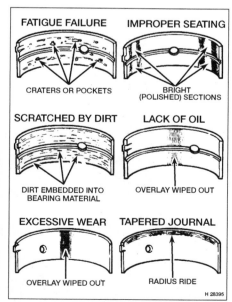

15.2 Typical bearing failures

material will loosen in pieces, and tear away from the steel backing.

7 Short-distance driving leads to corrosion of bearings, because insufficient engine heat is produced to drive off the condensed water and corrosive gases. These products collect in the engine oil, forming acid and sludge. As the oil is carried to the engine bearings, the acid attacks and corrodes the bearing material.

8 Incorrect bearing installation during engine assembly will lead to bearing failure as well. Tight-fitting bearings leave insufficient bearing running clearance, and will result in oil starvation. Dirt or foreign particles trapped behind a bearing shell result in high spots on the bearing, which lead to failure.

9 *Do not* touch any shell's bearing surface with your fingers during reassembly; there is a risk of scratching the delicate surface, or of depositing particles of dirt on it.

10 As mentioned at the beginning of this Section, the bearing shells should be renewed as a matter of course during engine overhaul; to do otherwise is false economy.

16 Engine overhaul – reassembly sequence

1 Before reassembly begins, ensure that all new parts have been obtained, and that all necessary tools are available. Read through the entire procedure to familiarise yourself with the work involved, and to ensure that all items necessary for reassembly of the engine are at hand. In addition to all normal tools and materials, thread-locking compound will be needed. A suitable sealant (available from BMW dealers) will also be required.

2 In order to save time and avoid problems, engine reassembly can be carried out in the following order, referring to the relevant Part of this Chapter unless otherwise stated:

    a) *Crankshaft (Section 18).*
    b) *Piston/connecting rod assemblies (Section 19).*
    c) *Oil pump/balancer shaft housing.*
    d) *Sump.*
    e) *Flywheel/driveplate.*
    f) *Cylinder head.*
    g) *Timing chain, tensioner and sprockets.*
    h) *Engine external components.*

17.5 Measure the piston ring end gaps

3 At this stage, all engine components should be absolutely clean and dry, with all faults repaired. The components should be laid out (or in individual containers) on a completely clean work surface.

17 Piston rings – refitting

1 Before fitting new piston rings, the ring end gaps must be checked as follows.

2 Lay out the piston/connecting rod assemblies and the new piston ring sets, so that the ring sets will be matched with the same piston and cylinder during the end gap measurement and subsequent engine reassembly.

3 Insert the top ring into the first cylinder, and push it down the bore using the top of the piston. This will ensure that the ring remains square with the cylinder walls. Position the ring near the bottom of the cylinder bore, at the lower limit of ring travel. The top and second compression rings are different. The second ring is easily identified by the step on its lower surface, and by the fact that its outer face is tapered.

4 Measure the end gap using feeler blades.

5 Repeat the procedure with the ring at the top of the cylinder bore, at the upper limit of its travel **(see illustration)**, and compare the measurements with the figures given in the Specifications.

6 If the gap is too small (unlikely if genuine BMW parts are used), it must be enlarged, or the ring ends may contact each other during engine operation, causing serious damage. Ideally, new piston rings providing the correct end gap should be fitted. As a last resort, the end gap can be increased by filing the ring ends very carefully with a fine file. Mount the

file in a vice equipped with soft jaws, slip the ring over the file with the ends contacting the file face, and slowly move the ring to remove material from the ends. Take care, as piston rings are sharp, and are easily broken.

7 With new piston rings, it is unlikely that the end gap will be too large. If the gaps are too large, check that you have the correct rings for your engine and for the particular cylinder bore size.

8 Repeat the checking procedure for each ring in the first cylinder, and then for the rings in the remaining cylinders. Remember to keep rings, pistons and cylinders matched up.

9 Once the ring end gaps have been checked and if necessary corrected, the rings can be fitted to the pistons.

10 Fit the piston rings using the same technique as for removal. Fit the bottom (oil control) ring first, and work up. When fitting a three-piece oil control ring, first insert the expander, then fit the lower rail with its gap positioned 120° from the expander gap, then fit the upper rail with its gap positioned 120° from the lower rail. When fitting a two-piece oil control ring, first insert the expander, then fit the control ring with its gap positioned 180° from the expander gap. Ensure that the second compression ring is fitted the correct way up, with its identification mark (either a dot of paint or the word TOP stamped on the ring surface) at the top, and the stepped surface at the bottom **(see illustration)**. Arrange the gaps of the top and second compression rings 120° either side of the oil control ring gap, but make sure that none of the rings gaps are positioned over the gudgeon pin hole. **Note:** *Always follow any instructions supplied with the new piston ring sets – different manufacturers may specify different procedures. Do not mix up the top and second compression rings, as they have different cross-sections.*

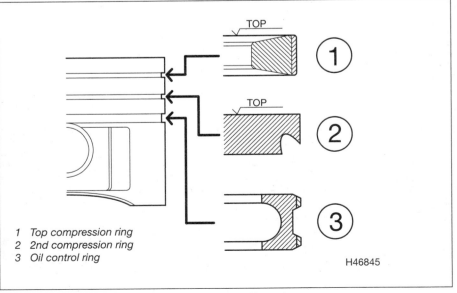

1 *Top compression ring*
2 *2nd compression ring*
3 *Oil control ring*

H46845

17.10 Piston ring orientation

18 Crankshaft – refitting

Selection of new bearing shells

1 Have the crankshaft inspected and measured by a BMW dealer or automotive engineering workshop. They will be able to carry out any regrinding/repairs, and supply suitable main and big-end bearing shells.

Crankshaft refitting

Note: *New main bearing cap/lower crankcase bolts must be used when refitting the crankshaft.*

2 Where applicable, ensure that the oil spray jets are fitted to the bearing locations in the cylinder block.

3 Clean the backs of the bearing shells, and the bearing locations in both the cylinder block/crankcase and the main bearing caps/lower crankcase/bedplate.

4 Press the bearing shells into their locations, ensuring that the tab on each shell engages in the notch in the cylinder block/crankcase or bearing cap/lower crankcase. Take care not to touch any shell's bearing surface with your fingers. Note that only the shells with a yellow paint mark on the back, or lubrication groove must be fitted to the crankcase/cylinder block. The thrust bearing shells fit in No 4 or No 5 bearing location on 4-cylinder engines, or No 4 or No 6 bearing location on 6-cylinder engines **(see illustration)**. Ensure that all traces of protective grease are cleaned off using paraffin. Wipe dry the shells with a lint-free cloth. Liberally lubricate each bearing shell in the cylinder block/crankcase and cap/lower crankcase with clean engine oil **(see illustration)**.

5 Lower the crankshaft into position so that Nos 1 and 4 cylinder crankpins (4-cylinder engines) or Nos 1 and 6 cylinder crankpins (6-cylinder engines), as applicable, will be at BDC, ready for fitting No 1 piston. Check the crankshaft endfloat as described in Section 14.

6 Lubricate the lower bearing shells in the main bearing caps with clean engine oil. Make sure that the locating lugs on the shells

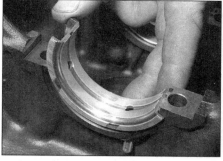

18.4a Fit the thrust bearing shell to the correct location – see text

engage with the corresponding recesses in the caps.

7 Fit the main bearing caps to their correct locations, ensuring that they are fitted the correct way round (the bearing shell tab recesses in the block and caps must be on the same side).

8 Tighten the main bearing cap bolts to the specified torque, in the stages given in the Specifications.

9 Check that the crankshaft rotates freely.

10 Refit the piston/connecting rod assemblies as described in Section 19.

19 Piston/connecting rod assembly – refitting

⚠️ **Warning: On engines with oil spray jets fitted to the cylinder block between the bearing locations, take care not to damage the jets when working on the cylinder block/crankcase. BMW insist that if the jets are bent, they must be renewed.**

Selection of bearing shells

1 There are a number of sizes of big-end bearing shell produced by BMW; a standard size for use with the standard crankshaft, and undersizes for use once the crankshaft journals have been reground.

2 Have the crankshaft inspected and measured by a BMW dealer or automotive engineering workshop. They will be able to carry out any regrinding/repairs, and

18.4b Lubricate the bearing shells

supply suitable main and big-end bearing shells.

Piston/connecting rod refitting

Note: *New big-end cap bolts must be used when finally refitting the piston/connecting rod assemblies. A piston ring compressor tool will be required for this operation.*

3 Note that the following procedure assumes that the main bearing caps are in place (see Section 18).

4 Press the bearing shells into their locations, ensuring that the tab on each shell engages in the notch in the connecting rod and cap. On M57 and N47 engines, fit the shell with the red mark on its back in to the bearing cap, and the one with the blue mark (or S mark) in to the connecting rod. Take care not to touch any shell's bearing surface with your fingers. Ensure that all traces of the protective grease are cleaned off using paraffin. Wipe dry the shells and connecting rods with a lint-free cloth.

5 Lubricate the cylinder bores, the pistons, and piston rings, then lay out each piston/connecting rod assembly in its respective position.

6 Start with assembly No 1. Make sure that the piston rings are still spaced as described in Section 17, then clamp them in position with a piston ring compressor.

7 Insert the piston/connecting rod assembly into the top of cylinder No 1. Ensure that the arrow on the piston crown points towards the crankshaft pulley end of the engine, and that the identifying marks on the connecting rods and big-end caps are positioned as noted before removal. Using a block of wood or hammer handle against the piston crown, tap the assembly into the cylinder until the piston crown is flush with the top of the cylinder **(see illustrations)**.

8 Ensure that the bearing shell is still correctly installed. Liberally lubricate the crankpin and both bearing shells. Taking care not to mark the cylinder bores, pull the piston/connecting rod assembly down the bore and onto the crankpin. Refit the big-end bearing cap. Note that the bearing shell locating tabs must abut each other.

9 Fit **new** bearing cap securing bolts, then tighten the bolts evenly and progressively to

19.7a Insert the piston/connecting rod assembly into the cylinder bore . . .

19.7b . . . then lightly tap the assembly into the cylinder

the Stage 1 torque setting. Once both bolts have been tightened to the Stage 1 setting, angle-tighten them through the specified Stage 2 angle, using a socket and extension bar. It is recommended that an angle-measuring gauge is used during this stage of the tightening, to ensure accuracy. If a gauge is not available, use a dab of white paint to make alignment marks between the bolt and bearing cap prior to tightening; the marks can then be used to check that the bolt has been rotated sufficiently during tightening.

10 Once the bearing cap bolts have been correctly tightened, rotate the crankshaft. Check that it turns freely; some stiffness is to be expected if new components have been fitted, but there should be no signs of binding or tight spots.

11 Refit the remaining piston/connecting rod assemblies in the same way.

12 Where applicable, refit the oil baffle/deflector to the bottom of the cylinder block.

13 Refit the cylinder head, balancer shaft housing/oil pump/vacuum pump, and sump as described in Part A or B of this Chapter.

20 Engine –
initial start-up after overhaul

1 With the engine refitted in the vehicle, double-check the engine oil and coolant levels. Make a final check that everything has been reconnected, and that there are no tools or rags left in the engine compartment.

2 Disable the ignition and fuel injection systems by removing the engine management relay (located in the engine electrical box), and the fuel pump fuse (located in the main fusebox – see Chapter 12), then turn the engine on the starter motor until the oil pressure warning light goes out.

3 Refit the relays (and ensure that the fuel pump fuse is fitted), and switch on the ignition to prime the fuel system.

4 Start the engine, noting that this may take a little longer than usual, due to the fuel system components having been disturbed.

Caution: When first starting the engine after overhaul, if there is a rattling noise from the valvegear, this is probably due to the hydraulic valve lifters partially draining. If the rattling persists, do not run the engine above 2000 rpm until the rattling stops.

5 While the engine is idling, check for fuel, water and oil leaks. Don't be alarmed if there are some odd smells and smoke from parts getting hot and burning off oil deposits.

6 Assuming all is well, keep the engine idling until hot water is felt circulating through the top hose, then switch off the engine.

7 After a few minutes, recheck the oil and coolant levels as described in *Weekly checks*, and top-up as necessary.

8 If new pistons, rings or crankshaft bearings have been fitted, the engine must be treated as new, and run-in for the first 500 miles. Do not operate the engine at full-throttle, or allow it to labour at low engine speeds in any gear. It is recommended that the oil and filter are changed at the end of this period.

Chapter 3
Cooling, heating and ventilation systems

Contents

Degrees of difficulty

Easy, suitable for novice with little experience	Fairly easy, suitable for beginner with some experience	Fairly difficult, suitable for competent DIY mechanic	Difficult, suitable for experienced DIY mechanic	Very difficult, suitable for expert DIY or professional

Specifications

General

Expansion tank cap opening pressure	1.4 ± 0.2 bar
Air conditioning refrigerant capacity	700 ± 10g

Refer also to the underbonnet sticker

Thermostat

Opening temperatures	Not available

Torque wrench settings

	Nm	lbf ft
Compressor mounting bolts	20	15
Coolant pump nuts/bolts:		
M6	10	7
M7	13	10
M8	22	16
Coolant temperature sensor	13	10
Facia crossmember	21	15
Refrigerant pipe unions	20	15
Thermostat cover bolts	10	7
Thermostat housing	10	7

1 General information and precautions

The cooling system is of pressurised type, comprising a pump, an aluminium crossflow radiator, cooling fan, and a thermostat. The system functions as follows. Cold coolant from the radiator passes through the hose to the coolant pump where it is pumped around the cylinder block and head passages. After cooling the cylinder bores, combustion surfaces and valve seats, the coolant reaches the underside of the thermostat, which is initially closed. The coolant passes through the heater and is returned through the cylinder block to the coolant pump.

When the engine is cold the coolant circulates only through the cylinder block, cylinder head, expansion tank and heater. When the coolant reaches a predetermined temperature, the thermostat opens and the coolant passes through to the radiator. On some models, the thermostat opening and closing is controlled by the engine management ECM by a heating element within the wax capsule of the thermostat. This allows fine control of the engine running temperature, resulting in less emissions, and better fuel consumption.

As the coolant circulates through the radiator it is cooled by the inrush of air when the car is in forward motion. Airflow is supplemented by the action of the cooling fan. Upon reaching the radiator, the coolant is now cooled and the cycle is repeated.

The cooling fan is electrically-operated, and mounted on the engine side of the radiator. The fan is controlled by the engine management ECM, which receives information from the coolant temperature sensor.

The coolant pump is driven by the auxiliary drivebelt from the crankshaft pulley.

Refer to Section 10 for information on the air conditioning system.

⚠ *Warning: Do not attempt to remove the expansion tank filler cap or disturb any part of the cooling system while the engine is hot, as there is a high risk of scalding. If the expansion tank filler cap must be removed before the engine and radiator have fully cooled (even though this is not recommended) the pressure in the cooling system must first be relieved. Cover the cap with a thick layer of cloth, to avoid scalding, and slowly unscrew the filler cap until a hissing sound can be heard. When the hissing has stopped, indicating that the pressure has reduced, slowly unscrew the filler cap until it can be removed; if more hissing sounds are heard, wait until they have stopped before unscrewing the cap completely. At all times keep well away from the filler cap opening.*

● Do not allow antifreeze to come into contact with skin or painted surfaces of the vehicle. Rinse off spills immediately with plenty of water. Never leave antifreeze lying around in an open container or in a puddle in the driveway or on the garage floor. Children and pets are attracted by its sweet smell. Antifreeze can be fatal if ingested.

● Refer to Section 10 for precautions to be observed when working on models equipped with air conditioning.

2.3a Prise up the wire locking clip ...

2.3b ... and pull the hose from the fitting

2 Cooling system hoses – disconnection and renewal

Note: Refer to the warnings given in Section 1 of this Chapter before proceeding.

1 If the checks described in Chapter 1 reveal a faulty hose, it must be renewed as follows.

2 First drain the cooling system (see Chapter 1). If the coolant is not due for renewal, it may be re-used if it is collected in a clean container.

3 To disconnect a hose, prise up the wire retaining clip and pull the hose from its fitting (**see illustrations**). Some hoses may be secured using traditional hose clamps. To disconnect these hoses, slacken the worm-drive screw, then move them along the hose, clear of the relevant inlet/outlet union. Carefully work the hose free. While the hoses can be removed with relative ease when new, or when hot, **do not** attempt to disconnect any part of the system while it is still hot.

4 Note that the radiator inlet and outlet unions are fragile; do not use excessive force when attempting to remove the hoses. If a hose proves to be difficult to remove, try to release it by rotating the hose ends before attempting to free it (**see Haynes Hint**).

> **HAYNES HiNT** *If all else fails, cut the hose with a sharp knife, then slit it so that it can be peeled off in two pieces. Although this may prove expensive if the hose is otherwise undamaged, it is preferable to buying a new radiator.*

5 To refit a hose, simply push the end over the fitting until the retaining clip engages and lock the hose in place. Pull the hose to make sure its locked in place. When fitting a hose with traditional hose clips, first slide the clips onto the hose, then work the hose into position. If the hose is stiff, use a little soapy water as a lubricant, or soften the hose by soaking it in hot water. Work the hose into position, checking that it is correctly routed, then slide each clip along the hose until it passes over the flared end of the relevant inlet/outlet union, before securing it in position with the retaining clip.

6 Refill the cooling system with reference to Chapter 1.

7 Check thoroughly for leaks as soon as possible after disturbing any part of the cooling system.

3 Radiator – removal, inspection and refitting

> **HAYNES HiNT** *If leakage is the reason for wanting to remove the radiator, bear in mind that minor leaks can be often be cured using a radiator sealant with the radiator in situ.*

Removal

1 Drain the cooling system as described in Chapter 1.

2 Undo the bolts and remove the front panel centre section (**see illustration**).

3 Undo the bolts and remove the radiator cover (**see illustration**).

3.2 Centre panel retaining bolts (right-hand bolts arrowed)

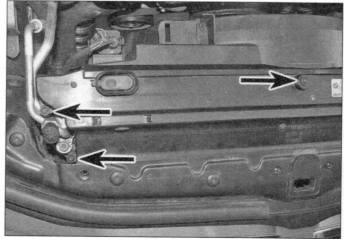

3.3 Undo the radiator cover bolts (right-hand bolts arrowed)

3.5a Disconnect the upper hose from the left-hand side of the radiator . . .

3.5b . . . and the lower hose from the right-hand side

3.6 Slide the radiator upwards from place

4 Remove the electric cooling fan and shroud as described in Section 5.

5 Prise out the wire clips and disconnect the radiator upper and lower coolant hoses **(see illustrations)**.

6 Pull the top of the radiator rearwards, and upwards from place **(see illustration)**.

Inspection

7 If the radiator has been removed due to suspected blockage, reverse flush it as described in Chapter 1. Clean dirt and debris from the radiator fins, using an airline (in which case, wear eye protection) or a soft brush. Be careful, as the fins are easily damaged, and are sharp.

8 If necessary, a radiator specialist can perform a 'flow test' on the radiator, to establish whether an internal blockage exists.

9 A leaking radiator must be referred to a specialist for permanent repair. Do not attempt to weld or solder a leaking radiator, as damage may result.

10 Inspect the radiator lower mounting rubbers for signs of damage or deterioration and renew if necessary.

Refitting

11 Refitting is the reverse of removal, noting the following points.

  a) *Lower the radiator into position, engage it with the mountings and secure it in position with the retaining bolts.*

  b) *Ensure that the fan cowl is correctly located with the lugs on the radiator and secure it in position with the clips.*

  d) *Reconnect the hoses and ensure the retaining clips engage securely.*

  e) *Check the condition of the O-ring seals in the end of the radiator fittings. Renew any that are defective.*

  f) *On completion, refill the cooling system (see Chapter 1).*

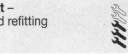

4 Thermostat – removal and refitting

Note: *A new thermostat sealing ring and (where fitted) housing gasket/seal will be required on refitting.*

Removal

1 Drain the cooling system as described in Chapter 1.

M47 and M57 engines

2 Remove the EGR cooler as described in Chapter 4B.

3 Lever out the clips and disconnect the coolant hoses from the thermostat housing.

4 Undo the bolts and remove the thermostat housing **(see illustration)**. Note that the thermostat is integral with the housing, and can only be renewed as a complete assembly. Discard the O-ring seal, a new one must be fitted.

N47 engines

5 Remove the EGR cooler as described in Chapter 4B.

6 Remove the air filter housing as described in Chapter 4A.

7 Release the clips and remove the turbocharger-to-intercooler air hose on the right-hand side of the engine.

8 Release the clamp and disconnect the coolant hose from the thermostat housing.

9 Undo the 4 bolts and remove the thermostat housing **(see illustrations)**. Pull the thermostat from the housing. Discard the O-ring seal, a new one must be fitted.

Refitting

10 Refitting is a reversal of removal, bearing in mind the following points.

  a) *Renew the thermostat cover/housing O-ring seal.*

  b) *Tighten the thermostat cover/housing bolts to the specified torque where given.*

  c) *On completion refill the cooling system as described in Chapter 1.*

4.4 Thermostat housing bolts (arrowed)

4.9a Undo the thermostat housing bolts

4.9b Pull the thermostat from the housing

4.9c Renew the thermostat housing seal

5.1 Undo the bolts (arrowed) and remove the plastic panel – M47 engine

5.3 The cooling fan wiring plug (arrowed) is located on the right-hand side of the shroud

5.4 Unclip the hose (arrowed) from the shroud

5.5 Slide the cooling fan and shroud upwards

5 Electric cooling fan and shroud – removal and refitting

Removal

1 Undo the bolts and remove the front panel centre section **(see illustration 3.2)**. On M47 engines, undo the bolts and remove the plastic panel attached to the front **(see illustration)**.
2 Undo the bolts and remove the radiator cover **(see illustration 3.3)**.
3 Disconnect the fan motor wiring plug **(see illustration)**.
4 Unclip the coolant hose from the base of the shroud (where fitted) **(see illustration)**.
5 Lift the shroud and fan from place **(see illustration)**.

Refitting

6 Refitting is a reversal of removal, ensuring the lugs on the lower edge of the shroud engage in the corresponding slots in the radiator edge.

6 Cooling system electrical switches – testing, removal and refitting

Note: *Testing of the sensors should be entrusted to a BMW dealer.*

Coolant temperature sensor

Removal – M47 and M57 engines

1 Either partially drain the cooling system to just below the level of the sensor (as described in Chapter 1), or have ready a suitable plug which can be used to plug the sensor aperture whilst it is removed. If a plug is used, take great care not to damage the sensor unit aperture, and do not use anything which will allow foreign matter to enter the cooling system.
2 The sensor is located under the intake manifold at the rear of the left-hand side of the cylinder head. Remove the intake manifold as described in Chapter 4A.
3 Release the clip, and disconnect the wiring plug from the sensor.
4 Unscrew the sensor from the cylinder head **(see illustration)**.

Removal – N47 engines

5 Either partially drain the cooling system to just below the level of the sensor (as described in Chapter 1), or have ready a suitable plug which can be used to plug the sensor aperture whilst it is removed. If a plug is used, take great care not to damage the sensor unit aperture, and do not use anything which will allow foreign matter to enter the cooling system.
6 Lift up the front edge, then slide the acoustic cover forwards from the top of the engine **(see illustration)**.
7 The sensor is located at the front of the cylinder head. Slide up the locking clip and disconnect the wiring plug from the sensor **(see illustration)**.
8 Using a deep socket, unscrew the sensor from the cylinder head.

Refitting

9 Apply a little sealant to the sensor unit threads or renew the sealing ring as applicable, and refit the sensor, tightening it to the specified torque.
10 Reconnect the wiring connector then refill the cooling system as described in Chapter 1 or top-up as described in *Weekly checks*. Check for leaks.

Coolant level switch

Removal

11 The level switch is fitted into the base of the coolant expansion tank. Disconnect the level switch wiring plug.
12 Undo the 2 retaining bolts and raise the

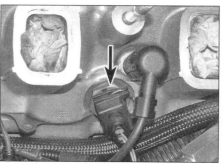

6.4 Coolant temperature sensor (arrowed) – M47 and M57 engines

6.6 Pull up the front edge, and slide the engine cover forwards

6.7 Coolant temperature sensor (arrowed) – N47 engines

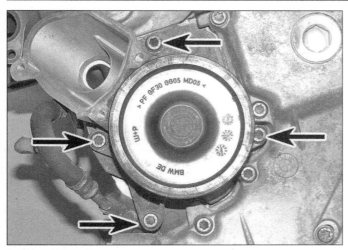

7.3 Coolant pump retaining bolts (arrowed)

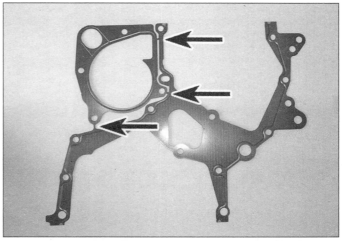

7.4 The original coolant pump gasket was part of the timing chain cover gasket. Cut where arrowed to separate the two

coolant tank. There's no need to disconnect the hoses.

13 Tilt the expansion tank so the switch is uppermost, then rotate the switch anti-clockwise and pull it from the tank.

Refitting

14 Refitting is a reversal of removal. If necessary, top-up the coolant as described in *Weekly checks*.

7 Coolant pump – removal and refitting

Note: *A new sealing ring will be required on refitting.*

Removal

1 Drain the cooling system as described in Chapter 1.

M47 and M57 engines

2 Remove the thermostat as described in Section 4.

3 Undo the 4 retaining bolts and remove the coolant pump **(see illustration)**.
4 The coolant pump gasket was originally integral with the lower timing cover gasket. In order to remove the pump gasket, cut through where the gaskets join **(see illustration)**.

N47 engines

5 Remove the thermostat as described in Section 4.
6 Undo the retaining bolts and remove the pump **(see illustration)**. Discard the pump seal.

Refitting

M47 and M57 engines

7 Cut the coolant pump gasket from the new lower timing cover gasket. Ensure it locates correctly on the cylinder block. Note that new coolant pump gaskets may be available separately from the timing cover gasket.
8 Position the pump, insert the retaining bolts and tighten them to the specified torque.
9 Refit the thermostat as described in Section 4.

N47 engines

10 Fit a new seal to the pump, then fit the pump and tighten the bolts to the specified torque **(see illustration)**.
11 Refit the thermostat as described in Section 4.

8 Heating and ventilation system – general information

1 The heating/ventilation system consists of a multi-speed blower motor, face-level vents in the centre and at each end of the facia, and air ducts to the front and rear footwells.
2 The control unit is located in the facia, and the controls operate flap valves to deflect and mix the air flowing through the various parts of the heating/ventilation system. The flap valves are contained in the air distribution housing, which acts as a central distribution unit, passing air to the various ducts and vents.

7.6 Coolant pump retaining bolts (arrowed)

7.10 Renew the pump seal

3 Cold air enters the system through the grille at the rear of the engine compartment. A pollen filter is fitted to the inlet to filter out dust, spores and soot from the incoming air.

4 The airflow, which can be boosted by the blower, then flows through the various ducts, according to the settings of the controls. Stale air is expelled through ducts at the rear of the vehicle. If warm air is required, the cold air is passed through the heater matrix, which is heated by the engine coolant.

5 If necessary, the outside air supply can be closed off, allowing the air inside the vehicle to be recirculated. This can be useful to prevent unpleasant odours entering from outside the vehicle, but should only be used briefly, as the recirculated air inside the vehicle will soon deteriorate.

6 Certain models may be fitted with heated front seats. The heat is produced by electrically-heated mats in the seat and backrest cushions (see Chapter 12). The temperature is regulated automatically by a thermostat, and can be set at one of three levels, controlled by switches on the facia.

9 Heater/ventilation components –
removal and refitting

Heater/air conditioning/ ventilation control unit

1 Disconnect the battery negative lead (see Chapter 5).

2 Using a blunt, flat-bladed tool, carefully prise the hazard switch from the centre of the facia (see Chapter 12). Disconnect the wiring plug as the switch is removed.

3 Undo the bolt (where fitted) in the switch aperture, then starting at the outside edge, carefully prise the decorative panel from the passenger's side of the facia **(see illustration)**.

9.3 Carefully prise the decorative panel from the passenger's side of the facia

9.4b Using tape to protect the lower panel, prise the facia centre panel rearwards . . .

4 Undo the bolt each side, then carefully prise the facia centre panel from place **(see illustrations)**. Disconnect the various wiring plugs as the panel is withdrawn.

5 If required, undo the bolts and separate the control unit from the panel.

6 Refitting is a reversal of removal. Note that if a new control unit has been fitted, it must be programmed using BMW test equipment. Entrust this task to a BMW dealer or suitably-equipped specialist.

Heater assembly

7 Have the air conditioning refrigerant

9.4a Undo the bolt (arrowed) each side of the control panel

9.4c . . . to release the steel clip each side

discharged by a suitably-equipped specialist.

8 Working at the rear of the engine compartment, undo the fasteners 90°, release the clips and remove the pollen filter covers each side **(see illustration)**. Slide the filters from the housings. If necessary, refer to Chapter 1.

9 Pull up the rubber sealing strip, then release the clip and slide the plastic cover from the centre of the panel **(see illustrations)**.

10 Lift out the plastic trim, undo the bolts/ fasteners and remove the left- and right-hand pollen filter housings from behind the

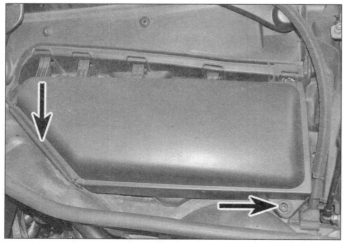

9.8 Rotate the fastener 90° anti-clockwise, press the clip forwards, and remove the pollen filter cover each side (arrowed)

9.9a Pull up the rubber sealing strip

9.9b Lift the clip and slide the cover to the passenger's side

9.10a Lift out the plastic trim . . .

9.10b . . . undo the fasteners/bolts (arrowed) and lift out the cover each side

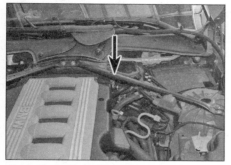

9.11 Undo the bolts and remove the strut brace (arrowed)

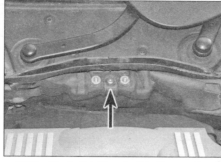

9.12a Undo the Torx bolt in the centre (arrowed) . . .

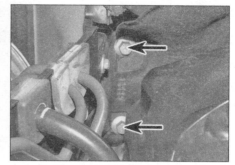

9.12b . . . the 2 bolts each side (arrowed) . . .

suspension turret each side of the engine compartment. Unclip the wiring where applicable (see illustrations).

11 Undo the 4 bolts and remove the strut brace (see illustration). Discard the bolts – new ones must be fitted.

12 Remove the Torx bolt, the 2 bolts each side, and the fastener in the centre, then pull the fresh air duct forwards (see illustrations). Undo the bolt securing the pipe clamp (where fitted).

13 Remove the complete facia as described in Chapter 11.

14 Undo the 2 nuts, and gently pull the air conditioning refrigerant pipes from the side of the engine compartment (see illustration).

15 Undo the nut and detach the refrigerant pipes from the engine compartment bulkhead (see illustration). Discard the pipe seals, new

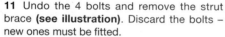
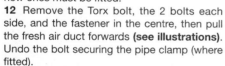

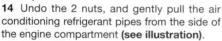

9.12c . . . rotate the fastener in the centre 90° anti-clockwise (arrowed) . . .

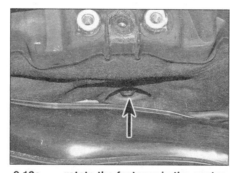

ones must be fitted. Seal/plug the openings to prevent contamination.

16 Undo the 2 nuts securing the right-hand air duct to the bulkhead (see illustration).

9.12d . . . and remove the fresh air duct

Note that the air duct is glued to the bulkhead – the nuts secure the heater assembly to the bulkhead.

17 Clamp the heater hoses as close to the

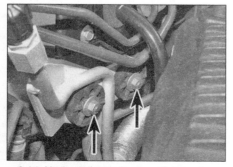

9.14 Undo the nuts (arrowed) securing the pipes to the side of the engine compartment

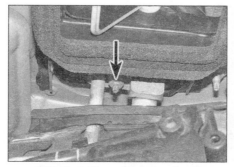

9.15 Undo the nut (arrowed) and disconnect the refrigerant pipes from the expansion valve

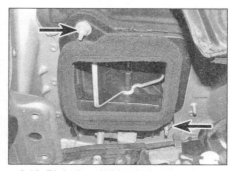

9.16 Right-hand side air duct retaining nuts (arrowed)

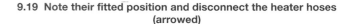

9.19 Note their fitted position and disconnect the heater hoses (arrowed)

9.20 Unclip the left- and right-hand side footwell air duct 'elbows'

bulkhead as possible to minimise coolant loss. Alternatively, drain the cooling system as described in Chapter 1.

18 Undo the 2 nuts securing the left-hand air duct to the bulkhead.

19 Pull away the rubber grommet around the hoses, then disconnect the heater hoses at the bulkhead **(see illustration)**. If possible, use compressed air applied to one of the heater matrix pipes to evacuate coolant from the heater.

20 Working inside the vehicle, unclip the left- and right-hand footwell air ducts from the heater assembly **(see illustration)**.

21 Remove the foam packing, then undo the 2 bolts and pull the driver's side air duct from place **(see illustration)**.

22 Remove the foam packing, then undo the 3 bolts and remove the passenger's side air duct.

23 Release the clips and pull the centre air distributor housing rearwards from place **(see illustration)**. Disconnect the temperature sensor wiring plug as the housing is withdrawn.

24 Make a note of their fitted positions and routing, then unclip all wiring harnesses/cable ducts from the facia crossmember.

25 Prise open the cover each side, and undo the bolts securing the CD autochanger (where fitted) to the facia crossmember. Pull the autochanger rearwards slightly, and carefully disconnect the wiring plug. Take care not to kink the optical cable **(see illustrations)**.

26 Remove the 4 retaining bolts and lower the fusebox to the floor **(see illustration)**. There is no need to disconnect the fusebox wiring plugs.

27 Undo the 2 bolts and lower the CAS (Car Access System) module and the LCM (Light Control Module) from the right-hand side of the facia crossmember **(see illustration)**.

9.21 Driver's side air duct retaining bolts (arrowed)

9.23 Unclip the centre air distributor housing

9.25a Prise open the cover in each lower corner, undo the bolt (arrowed) . . .

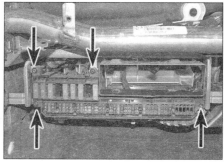

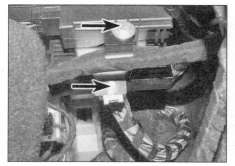

9.25b . . . and pull the CD autochanger from place

9.26 Fusebox retaining bolts (arrowed)

9.27 CAS module and LCM retaining bolts (arrowed)

9.28a The facia crossmember is secured by 2 nuts at each end (arrowed) . . .

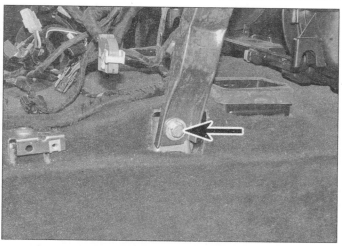

9.28b . . . a bolt each side in the centre (arrowed) . . .

9.28c . . . and 2 bolts each side of the steering column position (arrowed)

9.29 Evaporator drain grommets (arrowed)

28 Undo the various nuts and bolts, and with the help of an assistant, manoeuvre the facia crossmember from the passenger cabin **(see illustrations)**. Support the steering column with an axle stand to prevent damage to the universal joints.
Caution: The facia crossmember has a lot of sharp edges – it would be prudent to wear gloves.
29 Ensure all relevant wiring plugs have been disconnected, then with the help of an assistant, remove the heater assembly from the passenger cabin. Note the evaporator drain grommets in the floor **(see illustration)**.

30 Refitting is a reversal of removal, noting the following points:
a) *Tighten all fasteners to their specified torque, where given.*
b) *Align the drain pipes on the base of the housing with the drain hose grommets in the floor.*
c) *Renew all seals and gaskets.*
d) *Have the refrigerant circuit recharged by a suitably-equipped specialist.*
e) *Top-up the coolant system as described in Chapter 1.*

Heater matrix

31 Remove the heater assembly as described previously in this Section.
32 Carefully peel away the foam gasket, then undo the 5 bolts and remove the support bracket around the pipes **(see illustrations)**.
33 Undo the bolts, disconnect the flap linkage, release the clips, disconnect

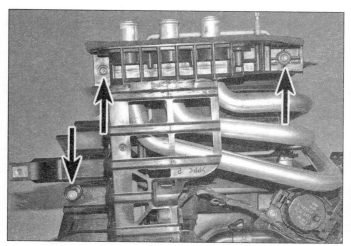

9.32a Undo the 3 bolts on the side (arrowed) . . .

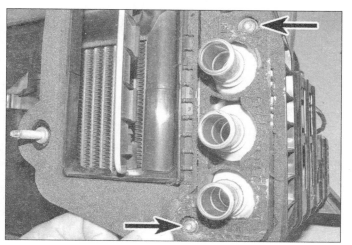

9.32b . . . and the 2 at the front (arrowed)

9.33a Undo the bolts (arrowed) and remove the small cover at the right-hand end of the matrix

9.33b The main heater housing cover is secured by various bolts and clips at the front left (arrowed) . . .

9.33c . . . front right (arrowed) . . .

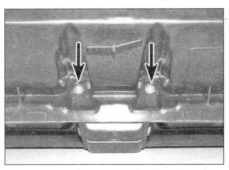

9.33d . . . centre rear (arrowed) . . .

9.33e . . . rear right (arrowed) . . .

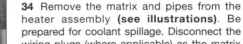

the various wiring plugs, and remove the cover from main heater housing **(see illustrations)**.

34 Remove the matrix and pipes from the heater assembly **(see illustrations)**. Be prepared for coolant spillage. Disconnect the wiring plugs (where applicable) as the matrix is withdrawn.

35 If required, prise out the clips and disconnect the coolant pipes from the matrix **(see illustration)**. Discard the seals – new ones must be fitted.

36 Refitting is a reversal of removal, noting the following points:

   a) *Use new sealing rings between the pipes and the matrix.*

   b) *When refitting the matrix, ensure it's correctly seated.*

   c) *Top-up the coolant system as described in Chapter 1.*

Heater blower motor

37 Move the driver's seat fully rearwards, and then remove the centre console and passenger's glovebox as described in Chapter 11.

38 Remove the facia audio unit and CCC (Car Communication Controller) (where fitted) as described in Chapter 12.

39 Remove the driver's side lower facia panel as described in Chapter 11.

40 Unclip the left- and right-hand rear

9.33f . . . and rear left (arrowed) of the circumference

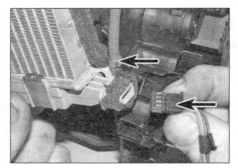

9.33g Prise apart the flap linkage

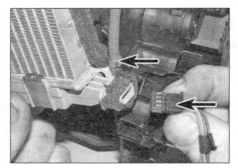

9.34a Lift the heater matrix from the housing

9.34b Disconnect the wiring plug and electric heating element current supply cable (arrowed)

9.35 Slide the clips from the pipe connections

9.40 Pull the air duct rearwards to unclip it (arrowed)

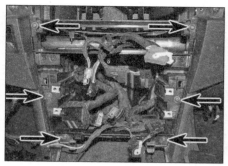

9.41 Centre bracket retaining bolts (arrowed). Note the wiring loom routing

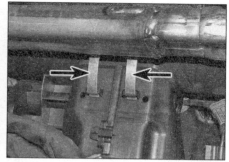

9.42a Press in the centre, and lever out the lower ends of the clips (arrowed) . . .

footwell air ducts from the heater assembly **(see illustration)**.

41 The centre bracket of the facia is secured by 6 bolts **(see illustration)**. Undo the bolts and remove the bracket assembly. Note the location of any wiring looms to aid refitment.

42 Release the clips, disconnect the wiring plugs and remove the rear section of the air distribution housing **(see illustrations)**. The clips are released by pressing in the centre and levering out the lower ends.

43 Disconnect the left- and right-hand air duct 'elbows' from the heater housing **(see illustration 9.20)**.

44 Disconnect the wiring plug, then undo the 4 bolts and remove the rear section of the cover over the blower motor **(see illustration)**.

45 Manoeuvre the blower motor from position. If required, release the clip and separate the resistor from the motor **(see illustrations)**.

46 Refitting is a reversal of the removal procedure making sure the motor is correctly clipped into the housing.

Heater blower motor resistor

47 Remove the heater blower motor as described in this Section.

48 Unclip and remove the resistor **(see illustration 9.45b)**.

49 Refitting is the reverse of removal.

9.42b . . . then remove the rear section of the air distribution housing

10 Air conditioning system – general information and precautions

General information

1 An air conditioning system enables the temperature of incoming air to be lowered, and dehumidifies the air, which makes for rapid demisting and increased comfort.

2 The cooling side of the system works in the same way as a domestic refrigerator. Refrigerant gas is drawn into a belt-driven compressor and passes into a condenser mounted in front of the radiator, where it loses heat and becomes liquid. The liquid passes through an expansion valve to an evaporator, where it changes from liquid under

9.44 Rear section retaining bolts (arrowed)

high pressure to gas under low pressure. This change is accompanied by a drop in temperature, which cools the evaporator. The refrigerant returns to the compressor and the cycle begins again.

3 Air blown through the evaporator passes to the air distribution unit, where it is mixed with hot air blown through the heater matrix to achieve the desired temperature in the passenger compartment.

4 The operation of the system is controlled by an electronic control module, with a self-diagnosis system. Any problems with the system should be referred to a BMW dealer or suitably-equipped specialist.

5 The air conditioning refrigerant circuit high- and low-pressure service ports are located in the engine compartment **(see illustration)**.

9.45a Manoeuvre the blower motor from place (facia removed for clarity)

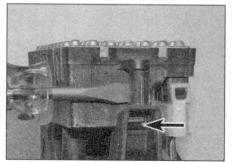

9.45b Lever out the bracket to release the clip (arrowed) and detach the resistor

10.5 Air conditioning refrigerant circuit service ports (arrowed)

Precautions

● When an air conditioning system is fitted, it is necessary to observe special precautions whenever dealing with any part of the system, its associated components and any items which require disconnection of the system. If for any reason the system must be disconnected, entrust this task to your BMW dealer or a suitably-equipped specialist.

 Warning: The refrigerant is potentially dangerous and should only be handled by qualified persons. If it is splashed onto the skin it can cause frostbite. It is not itself poisonous, but in the presence of a naked flame (including a cigarette) it forms a poisonous gas. Uncontrolled discharging of the refrigerant is dangerous and potentially damaging to the environment.

 Warning: Do not operate the air conditioning system if it is known to be short of refrigerant, as this may damage the compressor.

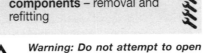

11 Air conditioning system components – removal and refitting

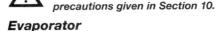

 Warning: Do not attempt to open the refrigerant circuit. Refer to the precautions given in Section 10.

Evaporator

1 Remove the heater matrix as described in Section 9.
2 Undo the retaining bolts and detach the expansion valve **(see illustration)**.
3 Release the clips, disconnect the wiring plugs and remove the rear section of the air distribution housing **(see illustrations 9.42a and 9.42b)**.
4 Disconnect the left- and right-hand air ducts from the heater housing **(see illustration 9.20)**.
5 Disconnect the wiring plug, then undo the 4 bolts and remove the rear section of the cover over the blower motor **(see illustration 9.44)**.
6 Manoeuvre the blower motor from position.
7 Release the bolts and pull out the fresh air/

recirculation servo motor and linkage from the housing **(see illustration)**.
8 Carefully remove the foam seals around the air inlet ducts on the front of the heater housing.
9 Undo the bolts, release the clips and remove the upper heater housing **(see illustration)**. Note the fitted positions of the various flaps, and wiring looms
10 Undo the 4 bolts, release the clip and remove the plastic holder **(see illustration)**.
11 Taking care not to bend the cooling fins, pull the evaporator from the housing **(see illustration)**. Check the condition of the evaporator seal and renew in necessary.
12 Refitting is a reversal of removal. Have the refrigerant recharged by a BMW dealer or specialist, and top-up the coolant level as described in *Weekly checks*.

Expansion valve

13 Have the air conditioning refrigerant discharged by a suitably-equipped specialist.
14 Working at the rear of the engine compartment, undo the bolts, release the clips and remove the pollen filter covers each side **(see illustration 9.8)**. Slide the filters from the housings. If necessary, refer to Chapter 1.
15 Pull up the rubber sealing strip, then release the clip and slide the plastic cover from the centre of the panel **(see illustrations 9.9a and 9.9b)**.
16 Lift out the plastic trim, undo the bolts/fasteners and remove the left- and right-hand plastic covers from behind the suspension turret each side of the engine compartment.

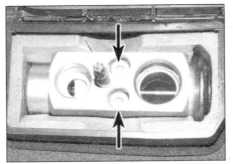

11.2 Expansion valve retaining bolts (arrowed)

Unclip the wiring where applicable **(see illustrations 9.10a and 9.10b)**.
17 Undo the 4 bolts and remove the strut brace **(see illustration 9.11)**. Discard the bolts – new ones must be fitted.
18 Remove the Torx bolt, the 2 bolts each side, and the fastener in the centre, then pull the fresh air duct forwards **(see illustrations 9.12a, 9.12b, 9.12c and 9.12d)**. Undo the bolt securing the pipe clamp (where fitted).
19 Undo the nut and detach the refrigerant pipes from the expansion valve and the engine compartment bulkhead **(see illustration 9.15)**. Discard the pipe seals, new ones must be fitted. Plug/seal the openings to prevent contamination.
20 Undo the 2 bolts and remove the expansion valve **(see illustration 11.2)**. Discard the O-ring seals, new ones must be fitted.
21 Refitting is a reversal of removal. Have the refrigerant recharged by a BMW dealer or specialist, and top-up the coolant level as described in Chapter 1.

Receiver/drier

22 The receiver/drier should be renewed when:
    a) There is dirt in the air conditioning system.
    b) The compressor has been renewed.
    c) The condenser or evaporator have been renewed.
    d) A leak has emptied the air conditioning system.
    e) The air conditioning refrigerant circuit has been opened for more than 24 hours.

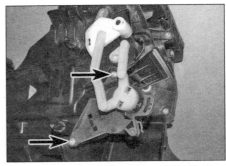

11.7 Recirculation motor retaining bolts (arrowed)

11.9 Release the clips, undo the bolts, and remove the upper heating housing

11.10 Remove the cover over the pipes

11.11 Lift the evaporator from the housing

11.25 Prise up the rubber cap and remove the circlip (arrowed)

11.26a Screw a bolt into the cap, and pull it from place . . .

23 Have the air conditioning refrigerant discharged by a BMW dealer or suitably-equipped specialist.

24 Undo the bolts and remove the bonnet slam panel without disconnecting the release cable, then undo the bolts and remove the plastic panel above the radiator **(see illustration 3.2)**.

25 Prise up the rubber cap, then remove the circlip securing the receiver/drier insert **(see illustration)**.

26 Using an old bolt, pull the cap and insert from the receiver/drier **(see illustrations)**. Note that a new cap, seals and circlip are supplied in the genuine renewal kit.

27 Fit the new insert into the condenser, followed by the new cap, seals and circlip **(see illustrations)**. The remainder of refitting is a reversal of removal.

Compressor

28 Have the air conditioning refrigerant discharged by a BMW dealer or suitably-equipped specialist.

29 Remove the auxiliary drivebelt as described in Chapter 1.

N47 engines

30 Remove the alternator as described in Chapter 5.

M47 engines

31 Raise the front of the vehicle and support

11.26b . . . followed by the insert

it on axle stands (see *Jacking and vehicle support*). Undo the fasteners and remove the engine undershield **(see illustration)**.

32 Remove the air intake hose.

M57 engines

33 Raise the front of the vehicle and support it on axle stands (see *Jacking and vehicle*

11.27a Press in the new cap complete with O-ring seals . . .

11.27b . . . then fit the new circlip

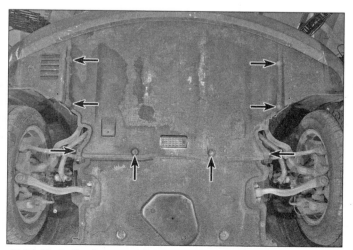

11.31 Undo the fasteners (arrowed) and remove the front section of the engine undershield

11.35 Prise out the clip (arrowed) and disconnect the charge air pipe from the intercooler

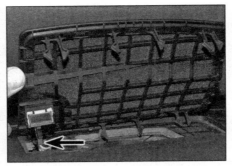

11.42 Prise up the speaker grille, and disconnect the sensor wiring plug (arrowed)

11.53 Condenser refrigerant pipe bolts (arrowed)

support). Undo the fasteners and remove the engine undershield **(see illustration 11.31)**.

34 Remove the air intake hose.

35 Remove the right-hand charge air pipe from the turbocharger to the intercooler **(see illustration)**.

36 Remove the front anti-roll bar as described in Chapter 10.

37 Where applicable, undo the fasteners and move any pipe/hose bracket to one side, in order to gain access to the compressor.

All engines

38 Disconnect the compressor wiring plug.

39 Undo the two bolts and disconnect the air conditioning pipes from the compressor. Discard the O-ring seals, new ones must be fitted. Seal/plug the openings to prevent contamination.

40 Undo the mounting bolts and remove the compressor.

41 Refitting is a reversal of removal, noting the following points:

  a) Prior to refitting the compressor, it is essential that the correct amount of refrigerant oil is added – refer to your dealer for the correct amount and specification.

  b) Always use new seals when reconnecting the refrigerant pipes.

  c) Where applicable, apply a smear of grease to the charge air pipes seals to aid refitment.

  d) Upon completion, have the refrigerant recharged by a BMW dealer or specialist.

Sunlight sensor

42 Using a blunt, flat-bladed tool, carefully prise the speaker grille from the top of the facia **(see illustration)**. Disconnect the wiring plug, and secure the harness from falling into the facia with tape.

43 Release the clips and remove the sensor from the speaker frame.

44 Refitting is a reversal of removal.

Evaporator temperature sensor

45 Remove the passenger's side lower facia panel as described in Chapter 11.

46 Undo the retaining bolt, and disconnect the footwell air vent on the left-hand side.

47 Undo the bolt and pull the rear heating duct upwards to disconnect it.

48 Disconnect the sensor wiring plug, then withdraw the sensor from the heater housing.

49 Refitting is a reversal of removal.

Condenser

50 Have the air conditioning refrigerant discharged by a BMW dealer or suitably-equipped specialist.

51 Undo the bolts and remove the bonnet slam panel without disconnecting the release cable **(see illustration 3.2)**.

52 Undo the 5 bolts and remove the radiator cover **(see illustration 3.3)**.

53 Undo the two bolts and disconnect the refrigerant pipes from the condenser **(see illustration)**. Discard the O-ring seals – new ones must be fitted.

54 Manoeuvre the condenser upwards from place.

55 Refitting is a reversal of removal, noting the following points:

  a) Prior to refitting the condenser it is essential that the correct amount of refrigerant oil is added – refer to your dealer for the correct amount and specification.

  b) Always use new seals when reconnecting the refrigerant pipes.

  c) Upon completion, have the refrigerant recharged by a BMW dealer or specialist.

Chapter 4 Part A:
Fuel and exhaust systems

Contents

Degrees of difficulty

Easy, suitable for novice with little experience	**Fairly easy,** suitable for beginner with some experience	**Fairly difficult,** suitable for competent DIY mechanic	**Difficult,** suitable for experienced DIY mechanic	**Very difficult,** suitable for expert DIY or professional

Specifications

General

System type	Direct injection common rail with Bosch high-pressure delivery pump and Electronic Diesel Control with DDE ECM
Fuel delivery pump pressure:	
N47 engine	3.5 to 4.5 bar
M47 and M57 engines	3.5 to 7.0 bar
Injection pressure	250 to 1600 bar
Level sensor resistance:	
Tank empty	15 ohms
Tank full	390 ohms

Torque wrench settings

	Nm	lbf ft
Camshaft position sensor	4	3
Common rail-to-cylinder head bolts	25	18
Crankshaft position sensor	8	6
Exhaust gas temperature sensor:		
N47 engine	45	33
M47T2	30	22
M57T2	30	22
Exhaust manifold-to-cylinder head:*		
N47 engines	13	10
M47 engines	20	15
M57TU engines	20	15
M57T2 engines	13	10
Front reinforcement plate:*		
Stage 1	56	41
Stage 2	Angle-tighten a further 90°	
Fuel injection pump mounting:		
Nuts	25	18
Bolts:		
M6	8	6
M8	19	14

Torque wrench settings (continued)

	Nm	lbf ft
Fuel injection pump sprocket retaining bolt	65	48
Fuel injector clamp bolts (N47 engines)	26	19
Fuel injector clamp nuts/studs (M47 and M57 engines)	10	7
Fuel pipe union nuts	23	17
Fuel pressure regulator	85	63
Fuel pressure sensor	70	52
Intake manifold:		
M6	10	7
M7	15	11
M8	22	16
Rear reinforcement plate	25	18
Rear tension strut	165	122
Suspension turret/tension brace:*		
M8	30	22
Throttle body to manifold:		
N47	8	6
Turbocharger-to-exhaust manifold bolts:		
N47 engine	25	18
M47 engine	50	37
Turbocharger oil feed banjo bolts	22	16
Timing cover access plug (fuel pump)	30	22

* Use new fasteners

1 General information and precautions

General information

The operation of the fuel injection system is described in more detail in Section 5.

Fuel is drawn from a tank under the rear of the vehicle by a tank-immersed electric pump, then by a filter assembly mounted under the left-hand chassis member, then to the injection pump. The chain-driven injection pump supplies very high-pressure fuel to the common fuel rail, which is connected to each individual injector. The injectors are operated by solenoids/crystals controlled by the ECM, based on information supplied by various sensors. The engine ECM also controls the preheating side of the system – refer to Chapter 5 for more details.

The EDC (electronic diesel control) system fitted incorporates a 'drive-by-wire' system, where the traditional accelerator cable is replaced by an accelerator pedal position sensor. The position and rate-of-change of the accelerator pedal is reported by the position sensor to the ECM, which then adjusts the fuel injectors to deliver the required amount of fuel, and optimum combustion efficiency

The exhaust system incorporates a turbocharger, a particulate filter (depending on model) and an EGR system. Further detail of the emission control systems can be found in Chapter 4B.

Precautions

- When working on diesel fuel system components, scrupulous cleanliness must be observed, and care must be taken not to introduce any foreign matter into fuel lines or components.
- After carrying out any work involving

disconnection of fuel lines, it is advisable to check the connections for leaks; pressurise the system by cranking the engine several times.
- Electronic control modules are very sensitive components, and certain precautions must be taken to avoid damage to these units as follows.
- When carrying out welding operations on the vehicle using electric welding equipment, the battery and alternator should be disconnected.
- Although the underbonnet-mounted modules will tolerate normal underbonnet conditions, they can be adversely affected by excess heat or moisture. If using welding equipment or pressure-washing equipment in the vicinity of an electronic module, take care not to direct heat, or jets of water or steam, at the module. If this cannot be avoided, remove the module from the vehicle, and protect its wiring plug with a plastic bag.
- Before disconnecting any wiring, or removing components, always ensure that the ignition is switched off.
- Do not attempt to improvise ECM fault diagnosis procedures using a test lamp or

2.2 Mass airflow sensor wiring plug (arrowed)

multimeter, as irreparable damage could be caused to the module.
- After working on fuel injection/engine management system components, ensure that all wiring is correctly reconnected before reconnecting the battery or switching on the ignition.

2 Air cleaner assembly – removal and refitting

M47 and M57 engines

1 The air cleaner housing is integral with the cylinder head cover – see Chapter 2B.

N47 engines

2 Disconnect the mass airflow sensor wiring plug **(see illustration)**.
3 Slacken the clamp and pull the air outlet hose from the air cleaner cover.
4 Undo the 2 air cleaner assembly mounting bolts **(see illustration)**.
5 Pull the intake 'snorkel' from the intake hood, then pull the air cleaner assembly upwards from place.
6 Refitting is a reversal of removal.

2.4 Air cleaner housing bolts (arrowed)

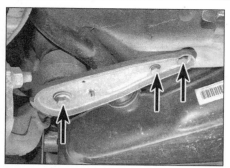

3.9 Tension strut retaining bolts (arrowed)

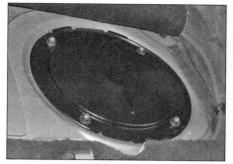

3.10 Undo the nuts and remove the access covers

3.11a Slide out the locking catch (arrowed) and disconnect the wiring plug

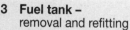

3 Fuel tank – removal and refitting

Removal

1 Disconnect the battery negative lead as described in Chapter 5.

2 Before removing the fuel tank, all fuel should be drained from the tank.

HAYNES HINT *Before removing the fuel tank, all fuel must be drained from the tank. Since a drain plug is not provided, it is therefore preferable to carry out the removal operation when the fuel tank is nearly empty. The remaining fuel can then be siphoned or hand-pumped from the tank.*

3 Remove the rear seat cushion as described in Chapter 11.

4 Jack up the rear of the vehicle, and support it securely on axle stands (see *Jacking and vehicle support*). Remove the right-hand rear roadwheel.

5 Detach the handbrake cables from the handbrake lever as described in Chapter 9.

6 Pull the handbrake cables from the guide tubes.

7 Remove the propeller shaft as described in Chapter 8.

8 The right-hand wheel arch liner is retained by a combination of bolts, plastic nuts, and plastic expansion rivets. Remove these fasteners and manoeuvre the wheel arch liner from place.

9 Working under the vehicle, undo the bolts

and remove the right-hand rear tension strut **(see illustration)**.

10 Working inside the vehicle, undo the 4 nuts, and remove the fuel tank access covers from the left- and right-hand side of the floor panel beneath the rear seat cushion location **(see illustration)**.

11 Disconnect the wiring plug from the right-hand sensor unit cover, then unlock the quick-release connectors and disconnect the fuel pipes from the left-hand sensor cover **(see illustrations)**.

12 Working in the wheel arch area, slacken the hose clip, then disconnect the fuel breather hose **(see illustration)**.

13 Undo the nut securing the filler pipe to the wing, and unclip the breather hoses from the wheel arch.

14 Support the fuel tank using a trolley jack and an interposed block of wood.

15 Undo the bolts securing the tank retaining straps. Lower the tank, and manoeuvre it from under the vehicle.

Refitting

16 Refitting is a reversal of removal. Note that once the tank is refitted, at least 5 litres of fuel must be added to allow the fuel system to function correctly.

4 Accelerator pedal – removal and refitting

1 Prise up the cap, then undo the bolt at the base of the accelerator pedal assembly **(see illustration)**.

2 Lift the throttle pedal assembly upwards, and disconnect the wiring plug. Note that the accelerator pedal is only available as a complete assembly, which includes the position sensor. If defective, the complete assembly must be renewed.

3 Refitting is a reversal of removal.

5 Fuel injection system – general information

The system is under the overall control of the Electronic Diesel Control (EDC) system, which also controls the preheating system (see Chapter 5).

Fuel is supplied from the rear-mounted fuel tank, via an electric lift pump, and fuel filter, to the fuel injection pump. The fuel injection pump supplies fuel under high pressure to the common fuel rail. The fuel rail provides a reservoir of fuel under pressure ready for the injectors to deliver direct to the combustion chamber. The individual fuel injectors incorporate solenoids, which when operated, allow the high-pressure fuel to be injected. The solenoids are controlled by the ECM. The fuel injection pump purely provides high-pressure fuel. The timing and duration of the injection is controlled by the ECM based on the information received from the various sensors. In order to increase combustion efficiency and reduce combustion noise (diesel 'knock'), a small amount of fuel is injected before the main injection takes place – this is known as Pre- or Pilot-injection.

3.11b Depress the release buttons (arrowed) and disconnect the fuel pipes

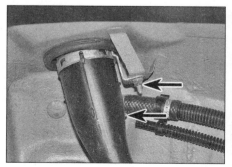

3.12 Fuel filler pipe retaining nut and breather hose clip (arrowed)

4.1 Undo the bolt (arrowed) at the base of the accelerator pedal

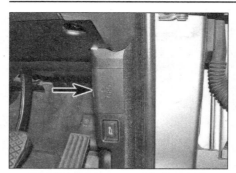

5.9a Unclip the cover labelled OBD (arrowed) . . .

Additionally, the control module activates the preheating system, and the exhaust gas recirculation (EGR) system (see Chapter 4B).

The system uses the following sensors.

a) *Crankshaft sensor – informs the ECM of the crankshaft speed and position.*
b) *Coolant temperature sensor – informs the ECM of engine temperature.*
c) *Mass airflow sensor – informs the ECM of the mass of air entering the intake tract.*
d) *Wheel speed sensor – informs the ECM of the vehicle speed.*
e) *Accelerator pedal position sensor – informs the ECM of the accelerator pedal position, and the rate of pedal opening/closing.*
f) *Fuel pressure sensor – informs the ECM of the pressure of the fuel in the common rail.*
g) *Fuel temperature sensor – informs the ECM of the temperature of the fuel returning to the tank.*
h) *Fuel pressure regulator – controls the pressure produced by the high-pressure fuel pump.*
i) *Camshaft position sensor – informs the ECM of the camshaft position so that the engine firing sequence can be established.*
j) *Stop-light switch – informs the ECM when the brakes are being applied*
k) *Turbocharger boost pressure sensor – informs the ECM of the boost pressure generated by the turbocharger.*

5.9b . . . to expose the diagnostic connector (arrowed)

l) *Intake air temperature sensor – informs the ECM of the temperature of the air entering the intake manifold.*

On all models, a 'drive-by-wire' throttle control system is used.

The signals from the various sensors are processed by the ECM, and the optimum fuel quantity and injection timing settings are selected for the prevailing engine operating conditions.

A catalytic converter and an exhaust gas recirculation (EGR) system are fitted, to reduce harmful exhaust gas emissions. Details of this and other emissions control system equipment are given in Chapter 4B.

If there is an abnormality in any of the readings obtained from any sensor, the ECM enters its back-up mode. In this event, the ECM ignores the abnormal sensor signal, and assumes a pre-programmed value which will allow the engine to continue running (albeit at reduced efficiency). If the ECM enters this back-up mode, the warning light on the instrument panel will come on, and the relevant fault code will be stored in the ECM memory.

If the warning light comes on, the vehicle should be taken to a BMW dealer or specialist at the earliest opportunity. A complete test of the Electronic Diesel Control (EDC) system can then be carried out, using a special electronic test unit which is simply plugged into the system's diagnostic connector **(see illustrations)**. The connector is located under the driver's side of the facia; to gain access to the connector, unclip the socket cover.

6 Fuel system – priming and bleeding

1 The fuel supply system is designed to be self-bleeding. After disturbing the fuel system, proceed as follows.
2 Switch on the ignition, and leave it for approximately 1 minute. Do not attempt to start the engine. During this time the electric fuel pump is activated and the system vented.
3 Depress the accelerator pedal to the floor then start the engine as normal (this may take longer than usual, especially if the fuel system has been allowed to run dry – operate the starter in ten second bursts with 5 seconds rest in between each operation). Run the engine at a fast idle speed for a minute or so to purge any remaining trapped air from the fuel lines. After this time the engine should idle smoothly at a constant speed.
4 If the engine idles roughly, then there is still some air trapped in the fuel system. Increase the engine speed again for another minute or so then recheck the idle speed. Repeat this procedure as necessary until the engine is idling smoothly.

N47 engines

5 On these engines, if the above procedure fails to allow the engine to start, proceed as follows:
6 Pull up the front edge and remove the plastic cover from the top of the engine.
7 Disconnect the camshaft position sensor wiring plug **(see illustration)**.
8 Depress the release button and disconnect the fuel return hose from the common rail **(see illustration)**.
9 Attach a hand-held vacuum pump to the return port on the common rail, and operate the pump until clear, bubble-free fuel emerges **(see illustration)**.
10 Reconnect the fuel return hose to the common rail, and refit the camshaft position sensor wiring plug.
11 Refit the engine cover, and proceed as described in paragraph 1.

6.7 Disconnect the camshaft position sensor wiring plug at the rear of the cylinder head (arrowed)

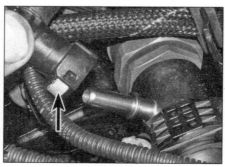

6.8 Depress the button (arrowed) and disconnect the fuel return hose from the common rail

6.9 Attach a hand-held vacuum pump and pull the fuel through

7.7 Unscrew the locking ring

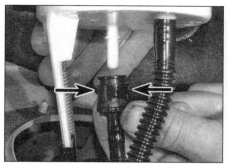

7.8 Squeeze together the release buttons (arrowed) and disconnect the fuel hose from the cover

7.9 Disconnect the wiring plug (arrowed)

7 Fuel pump/fuel level sensors – removal and refitting

Removal

1 There are two level sensors fitted to the fuel tank – one in the left-hand side of the tank, and one in the right-hand side. The pump is integral with the right-hand side sensor, and at the time of writing only the level sensor is available separately. Check with a BMW dealer or parts specialist.

Left-hand sensor

2 Before removing the fuel level sensor, all fuel should be drained from the tank. Since a fuel tank drain plug is not provided, it is preferable to carry out the removal operation when the tank is nearly empty.

3 Remove the rear seat cushion as described in Chapter 11.

4 Fold back the insulation mating to expose the access cover.

5 Undo the four nuts, and remove the access cover from the floor **(see illustration 3.10)**.

6 Disconnect the wiring plugs (where fitted) through the access hole, then depress the release buttons and disconnect the fuel pipes **(see illustration 3.11b)**. Be prepared for fuel spillage.

7 Unscrew the fuel pump/level sensor unit locking ring and remove it from the tank. Although a BMW tool (No 16 1 020) is available for this task, it can be accomplished using a large pair of grips to push on two opposite raised ribs on the locking ring. Alternatively, a home-made tool can be fabricated to engage with the raised ribs of the locking ring. Turn the ring anti-clockwise until it can be unscrewed by hand **(see illustration)**.

8 Carefully lift the fuel pump/level sensor unit cover from the tank. Note its fitted position, then disconnect the fuel hose from the underside of the cover at the quick-release connector **(see illustration)**.

9 Disconnect the wiring plug from the sensor unit **(see illustration)**.

10 Depress the clip and detach the suction jet pump assembly from the base of the unit **(see illustrations)**.

11 Carefully manoeuvre the pump/sensor unit from the tank. Take great care not to bend/damage the float arm as the unit is withdrawn.

12 If required, release the clips and slide the level sensor upwards from place. Disconnect the wiring plug as the sensor is removed **(see illustration)**. When refitting, the sensor must clip back into place.

13 If required, the level sensor can be unclipped from the pump assembly.

Right-hand sensor/pump

14 Remove the left-hand sensor as previously described.

15 Fold back the insulation mating to expose the access cover.

16 Undo the four nuts, and remove the access cover from the floor **(see illustration 3.10)**.

7.10a Depress the clip (arrowed) . . .

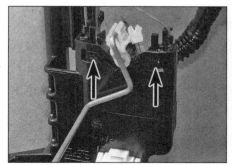

7.12 Release the clips (arrowed) and slide the sensor upwards

17 Disconnect the wiring plug from the sensor unit cover.

18 Unscrew the fuel pump/level sensor unit locking ring and remove it from the tank. Although a BMW tool (No 16 1 020) is available for this task, it can be accomplished using a large pair of grips to push on two opposite raised ribs on the locking ring. Alternatively, a home-made tool can be fabricated to engage with the raised ribs of the locking ring. Turn the ring anti-clockwise until it can be unscrewed by hand **(see illustration 7.7)**.

19 Tie a length of string/cable around the disconnected hoses accessible through the left-hand tank access hole, as these hoses will be removed with the right-hand sensor/pump unit **(see illustration)**. The idea is to pull the string/cable into the tank as the sensor/pump unit is removed, then leave it in place to facilitate refitting. Take care – the hoses must not be kinked!

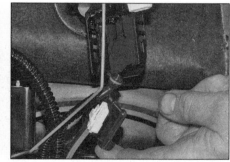

7.10b . . . and slide the suction jet pump assembly from the unit

7.19 tie a length of cable around the left-hand side disconnect hoses

7.21a Renew the sealing ring(s)

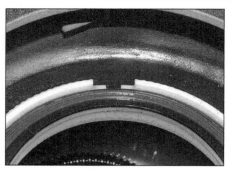

7.21b Note the notch in the tank collar

9.4 Disconnect the wiring plug (arrowed) from the regulator on the pump

20 Carefully lift the sensor/filter unit from the tank, and remove it. Untie the string/cable and leave it in place.

Refitting

21 Refitting is a reversal of removal, noting the following points:

- a) Use a new sealing ring (see illustration).
- b) To allow the unit to pass through the aperture in the fuel tank, press the float arm against the fuel pick-up strainer.
- c) When the unit is fitted, the locating lug on the unit must engage with the corresponding notch in the fuel tank collar (see illustration).
- d) The locating rods of the right-hand sensor unit cover must align with the corresponding holes in the pump/sensor unit.
- e) The locking ring must be tightened until the notch on the ring aligns with the mark on the tank.

8 Fuel injection system – testing and adjustment

Testing

1 If a fault appears in the fuel injection system, first ensure that all the system wiring connectors are securely connected and free from corrosion. Ensure that the fault is not due to poor maintenance; ie, check that the air cleaner filter element is clean, that the

cylinder compression pressures are correct (see Chapter 2A or 2B), and that the engine breather hoses are clear and undamaged (see Chapter 4B).

2 If the engine will not start, check the condition of the glow plugs (see Chapter 5).

3 If these checks fail to reveal the cause of the problem, the vehicle should be taken to a BMW dealer or specialist for testing using special electronic equipment which is plugged into the diagnostic connector (see Section 5). The tester should locate the fault quickly and simply, avoiding the need to test all the system components individually, which is time-consuming, and also carries a risk of damaging the ECM.

Adjustment

4 The engine idle speed, and maximum speed are all controlled by the ECM. Whilst in theory it is possible to check the settings, if they are found to be in need of adjustment, the car will have to be taken to a suitably-equipped BMW dealer or specialist. They will have access to the necessary diagnostic equipment required to test and (where possible) adjust the settings.

9 Fuel injection pump – removal and refitting

Caution: Be careful not to allow dirt into the injection pump or injector pipes during this procedure.

M47 and M57 engines
Removal

1 Disconnect the battery negative lead (see Chapter 5).

2 Refer to Section 16, and remove the intake manifold.

3 On 6-cylinder engines, remove the radiator cooling fan and shroud as described in Chapter 3.

4 Disconnect the wiring plug from the pressure regulator on the pump (see illustration).

5 Release the clamp, and disconnect the fuel feed pipe from the pump (see illustration). Plug or seal the openings to prevent contamination.

6 Undo the banjo bolt and disconnect the fuel return pipe from the pump.

7 Note the position of the rubber mounting, then undo the unions and disconnect the high-pressure fuel pipe from between the pump and the common rail. Discard the pipe – a new one must be fitted.

8 Undo the 3 nuts securing the injection pump to the cylinder block (see illustration).

9 Remove the auxiliary drivebelt as described in Chapter 1.

10 Undo the cap from the timing chain cover (see illustration). Discard the seal, a new one must be fitted.

11 Slacken and remove the fuel pump sprocket nut.

12 Screw BMW tool No 13 5 192 into the timing chain cover, then screw BMW tool No 13 5 191 into the fuel pump drive sprocket. Carefully tighten the centre bolt of the tool, and free the pump shaft from the sprocket

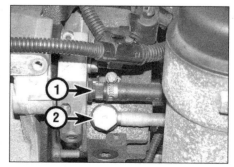

9.5 Fuel feed (1) and return (2) pipes

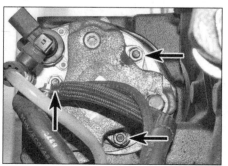

9.8 Pump retaining nuts (arrowed)

9.10 Unscrew the cap (arrowed) from the timing chain cover

9.12a Screw the tool into the timing cover . . .

9.12b . . . then screw the special tool into the pump sprocket

9.12c Tighten the centre bolt to release the pump shaft from the sprocket

(see illustrations). Do not remove tool No 13 5 192 once the shaft is free from the sprocket or the timing would be lost. If the special BMW tools are not available, the only other alternative is to remove the timing chains and pull the sprocket from the shaft as described in Chapter 2B. Although in theory it would be possible to free the sprocket from the shaft using a drift or similar, the position of the sprocket, and therefore the tension of the timing chains, would be lost.

13 Remove the fuel pump. Discard the gasket, a new one must be fitted.

Refitting

14 Ensure that the mating surfaces of the pump and engine are clean and dry, and fit the new pump gasket.

15 Unscrew tool No 13 5 191 from the centre of tool No 13 5 192.

16 Position the fuel pump on the cylinder block. Note that the position of the pump shaft in relation to the crankshaft position, is not important.

17 Fit the pump retaining nuts and tighten them to the specified torque.

18 Fit the new high-pressure fuel pipe, with the rubber mounting. Tighten the unions to the specified torque.

19 Reconnect the fuel hoses to the pump. Use a new banjo bolt seal.

20 Reconnect the wiring plug to the fuel pump.

21 If the BMW special tools were used to release the fuel pump drive sprocket, and hold the sprocket in position, unscrew the tools, fit and tighten the sprocket retaining nut to the specified torque. If the tools were not

available, refit the timing chains, sprockets and covers, as described in Chapter 2B.

22 Ensure that the timing cover access plug is clean, fit the new seal, and tighten it to the specified torque.

23 With reference to Chapter 1, refit the auxiliary drive belt.

24 Refer to Section 16, and refit the intake manifold.

25 Reconnect the battery negative lead as described in Chapter 5.

26 Bleed the fuel system as described in Section 8.

N47 engines

Removal

27 Disconnect the battery negative lead (see Chapter 5). Pull up the front edge of the acoustic cover on the top of the engine, then slide it forwards and remove it.

9.29 The glow plug control unit is located on the rear of the oil filter housing

28 Remove the air intake manifold as described in Section 16.

29 Disconnect the wiring plug, then remove the glow plug control unit **(see illustration)**.

30 Lock the crankshaft/flywheel at TDC on No 1 cylinder as described in Chapter 2A.

31 Release the locking catch, and disconnect the wiring plug from the metering unit on the injection pump **(see illustration)**.

32 Slacken the clamps and disconnect the fuel feed and return pipes from the pump **(see illustration)**. Plug or seal the openings to prevent contamination.

33 Note the fitted locations of the rubber mountings, then undo the union nuts and remove the high-pressure fuel pipe between the injection pump and the common rail **(see illustration)**.

34 Undo the sealing cap in the timing cover at the rear of the engine **(see illustration)**. Discard the sealing ring – a new one must be fitted.

9.31 Disconnect the wiring plug (arrowed) from the metering unit

9.32 Note their positions, then disconnect the fuel feed and return hoses from the pump

9.33 Note the rubber grommets (arrowed) on the high-pressure fuel pipe

9.34 Unscrew the cap (arrowed) at the rear of the engine

9.35 Screw the special tool into the timing chain cover

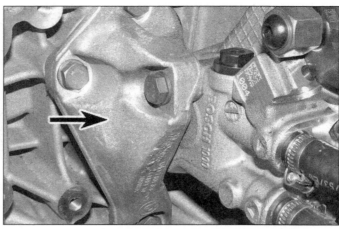

9.36 Remove the support bracket (arrowed) from the front of the pump

35 Screw BMW special tool No 11 8 741 into the cap hole in the timing chain cover **(see illustration)**. This tool traps the fuel pump sprocket and chain in place. Failure to secure the sprocket will result in the camshaft timing being lost. If the tool is not available, remove the engine and timing chain as described in Chapter 2C.

36 Undo the retaining bolts and remove the support bracket from the front of the pump **(see illustration)**.

37 Undo the bolts securing the pump to the timing chain cover. Note that it's not necessary to remove the bolts from their locations, with the exception of the outer bolt which <u>must</u> be removed and not refitted **(see illustration)**.

9.37 The outer bolt (arrowed) must not be refitted (see text)

New high-pressure pumps have no threads in this location, and can be damaged by forcing the bolt into place.

38 Undo the bolt securing the drive chain sprocket to the pump shaft. Note that the bolt remains in place in the sprocket.

39 Remove the pump from position **(see illustration)**.

Refitting

40 Ensure the pump and cylinder block mating surfaces are clean, then align the keyway on the pump shaft with the key in the tapered bore in the pump drive sprocket.

41 Fit a new O-ring seal, then offer the pump into position **(see illustration)**.

9.39 Withdraw the pump from the cylinder block

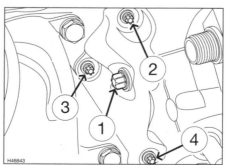

9.44 Injection pump support bracket bolts tightening sequence

42 Engage the shaft with the drive sprocket. Ensure the key and keyway engage correctly.

43 Lightly tighten the bolts securing the pump to the cylinder block/timing chain cover.

44 Refit the pump support bracket, then working in sequence, tighten the bolts hand-tight, then to their specified torque **(see illustration)**.

45 Tighten the drive sprocket retaining bolt to the specified torque.

46 Unscrew the special tool, then refit the sealing cap with a new seal. Tighten the cap to the specified torque.

47 Remove the crankshaft/flywheel locking tool, with reference to Chapter 2A.

48 Fit the new high-pressure fuel pipe between the pump and common rail, tighten the nuts to the specified torque, then refit the rubber mounting.

49 The remainder of refitting is a reversal of removal, noting the following points:
  a) Tighten all fasteners to their specified torque where given.
  b) Reconnect the battery negative lead as described in Chapter 5.
  c) Bleed the fuel system as described in Section 8.

10 Fuel injectors – removal and refitting

Caution: Be very careful not to allow dirt into the injection pump or injector pipes during this procedure. Plug/seal all openings to prevent contamination.

Removal

1 Disconnect the battery negative lead, as described in Chapter 5.

2 On M47 and M57 engines, remove the intake manifold as described in Section 16. On N47 engines, pull up the front edge and remove the plastic cover from the top of the engine.

3 Disconnect the wiring plugs from the injectors (if not already done so) **(see illustration)**.

4 Two different types of return hose

10.3 Depress the retaining clip (arrowed) and pull the wiring plug from the injector

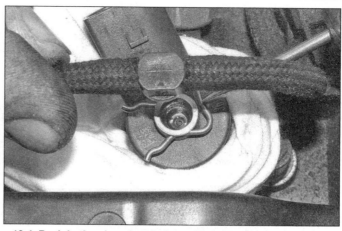

10.4 Push in the closed end of the clip and pull the return hose upwards

connections may be encountered. On the first type, push in the closed end of the clips, and remove the fuel return hoses from the injectors **(see illustration)**. If the rubber seals are damaged, the complete return hose assembly must be renewed. Plug/cover the openings to prevent contamination. Be prepared for fuel spillage – protect the alternator with clean rag.

5 On the second type of connector, carefully prise up the locking cap, then pull the return hose connection from the top of each injector **(see illustrations)**. Check the condition of the sealing rings and renew if necessary. Plug/cover the openings to prevent contamination. Be prepared for fuel spillage – protect the alternator with clean rag.

6 Slacken the pipe unions (where possible, counterhold the union on the common fuel rail and the injector), and remove the relevant injector pipe **(see illustration)**. Plug/cover the openings to prevent contamination.

M47 and M57 engines

7 Unscrew the two nuts securing each injector clamp. Use a Torx socket to unscrew the mounting studs, and force the injectors upwards from place. Discard the sealing washers – new ones must be fitted. If the injectors are to be refitted, they must be stored upright, and marked/labelled so they can be refitted into their original positions **(see illustrations)**.

10.5a Prise up the locking cap . . .

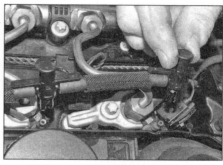

10.5b . . . and pull the return hose connection upwards

10.6 If possible, use a crows-foot adapter to slacken and tighten the high-pressure pipe unions

10.7a Undo the injector retaining nuts (arrowed) . . .

10.7b . . . undo the Torx studs (arrowed) to force the injector upwards . . .

10.7c . . . then remove the clamp jaw and injector

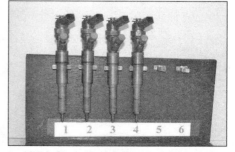

10.7d Store the injectors upright, and label them so they can be refitted to their original locations

10.8a Undo the injector retaining bolt and remove the clamping jaw

10.8b If necessary, use a spanner to rotate the injector a few degrees . . .

10.8c . . . and pull it from place

N47 engines

Note: *The high-pressure fuel pipes from the common rail to the injectors and the pump may be re-used up to 3 times providing they are not damaged or distorted.*

8 Undo the retaining bolt, remove the clamping jaw and remove the injectors. If the injectors are reluctant to move, rotate them a few degrees each way to release them **(see illustrations)**. Discard the sealing washers – new ones must be fitted. If the injectors are to be refitted, they must be stored upright, and marked/labelled so they can be refitted into their original positions **(see illustration 10.7d)**.

9 If the common fuel rail is to be removed, the intake manifold must be removed as described in Section 16. Once the manifold is withdrawn, undo the unions and remove the high-pressure fuel pipe between the pump and rail.

10 Undo the retaining bolts and remove the common rail clamps **(see illustration)**.

11 Lift the rail from place, depress the release button and disconnect the return hose from the rail **(see illustration)**.

Refitting

12 On N47 engines, where applicable, refit the common rail and clamps, then tighten the bolts to the specified torque. Fit the new high-pressure pipe (where applicable – see the Note above) between the pump and rail, and tighten the unions to the specified torque. Note the rubber sleeves fitted to the common rail locations in the camshaft cover and clamps.

13 Ensure that the injectors and seats in cylinder head are clean and dry.

14 If any of the injectors are being renewed, make a note of the 6 or 7 digit adjustment value engraved on the top of injector **(see illustrations)**. In order for the injector to function at maximum efficiency, this number must be programmed into the engine management ECM using BMW diagnostic equipment. Entrust this task to a BMW dealer or suitably-equipped specialist.

15 Fit new sealing washers to the injectors, apply a little high-temperature anti-seize grease (BMW part No 83 23 0441 070 or Copperslip) to the injector stems and refit them with the clamps **(see illustrations)**. If new injectors are not being fitted, it's absolutely essential they are refitted to their original positions. On M47 and M57 engines, tighten the clamp nuts to the specified torque. On N47 engines, refit the clamping jaw, insert the retaining bolt, and tighten it to the specified torque.

10.10 Common rail clamp bolts (arrowed)

10.11 Depress the release button (arrowed) and disconnect the return hose

10.14a Injector adjustment value (arrowed) – M47T2 and M57T2 engines

10.14b Injector adjustment value (arrowed) – N47 engine

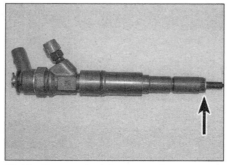

10.15a Renew the injector sealing washers (arrowed) . . .

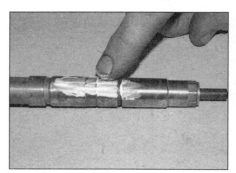

10.15b . . . and apply a little high-temperature anti-seize grease to the injector stems

10.16a Refit the injector high-pressure pipes – M47T2 engine . . .

10.16b . . . and N47 engine

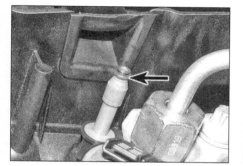

10.18 Renew the sealing ring (arrowed)

11.3 Crankshaft sensor retaining bolt (arrowed)

11 Electronic Diesel Control (EDC) system components – removal and refitting

Crankshaft sensor

M47 and M57 engines

1 The sensor is mounted on the left-hand side of the engine block. To gain access, remove the starter motor as described in Chapter 5.

2 Disconnect the wiring connector from the sensor.

3 Slacken and remove the retaining bolt and carefully remove the sensor from the engine (see illustration).

4 Refitting is the reverse of removal, tightening the retaining bolt to the specified torque.

N47 engines

5 Raise the front of the vehicle and support it securely on axle stands (see *Jacking and vehicle support*).

6 Undo the fasteners and remove the engine undershield, then undo the fasteners and remove the underbody reinforcement plate (see illustrations). Note that new

16 Refit the injection pipe(s), and tighten the unions finger-tight, then to the specified torque. Refit the pipe retaining clips (see illustrations).

17 On the first type of return hose connection, squeeze together the open ends of the clips and refit the fuel return hoses to the injectors.

18 On the second type of return hose connection, with the new sealing rings fitted

to the injectors (where necessary), press the return hose connections down on to the injectors, then press the locking caps down (see illustration).

19 On all engines, reconnect the wiring plugs to the injectors.

20 With reference to Section 16, refit the intake manifold (where applicable)

21 Reconnect the battery negative lead, as described in Chapter 5.

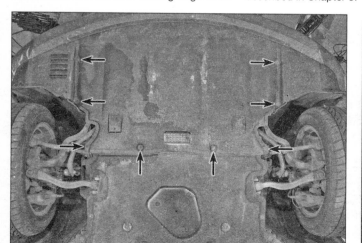

11.6a Engine/radiator undershield fasteners (arrowed)

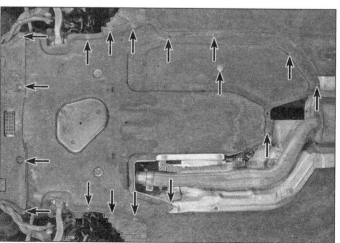

11.6b Engine/transmission undershield fasteners (arrowed)

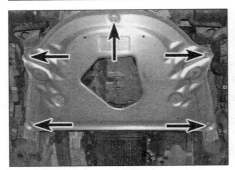

11.6c Front underbody reinforcement plate bolts (arrowed)

11.8 Crankshaft sensor retaining bolt (arrowed) – N47 engine

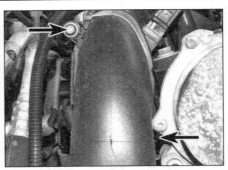

11.13a Undo the bolts (arrowed) . . .

11.13b . . . and pull the air intake pipe forwards

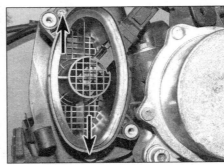

11.15 Undo the bolts (arrowed) and remove the mass airflow sensor

reinforcement plate bolts/nuts must be fitted.

7 The sensor is located beneath the fuel injection pump at the rear of the engine. Disconnect the sensor wiring plug.

8 Undo the retaining bolt and pull the sensor from position (**see illustration**).

9 Refitting is a reversal of removal.

Coolant temperature sensor

10 The sensor is screwed directly into the cylinder head. Refer to Chapter 3 for removal and refitting details.

Accelerator pedal position sensor

11 The sensor is integral with the accelerator pedal assembly – see Section 4.

Mass airflow sensor

M47 and M57T2 engines

12 Remove the acoustic cover from the top of the engine, by undoing the bolts, pulling up the front edge and sliding it forwards.

13 Undo the 2 bolts, unclip the hose, and pull the intake pipe forwards from the sensor, located at the front- right-hand corner of the engine (**see illustrations**).

14 Disconnect the wiring plug from the sensor.

15 Slacken and remove the two Torx bolts, and withdraw the sensor (**see illustration**).

16 Refitting is a reversal of removal.

N47 engines

17 The mass airflow sensor is located on the air filter cover outlet ducting. Disconnect the sensor wiring plug (**see illustration 2.2**).

18 Slacken the air outlet hose clamp and disconnect the hose.

19 Undo the 2 bolts and remove the mass airflow sensor from the filter cover (**see illustration**).

20 Refitting is a reversal of removal.

Hot film air mass meter

M57TU engines only

21 Remove the air filter element as described in Chapter 1.

22 Disconnect the wiring plug, then undo the 2 bolts and remove the sensor (**see illustration 11.19**).

23 Refitting is a reversal of removal.

11.19 Undo the bolts (arrowed) and remove the mass airflow sensor

Intake air temperature sensor

Note: On M57TU engines, the intake air temperature sensor is incorporated into the hot film air mass meter.

24 The intake air temperature sensor is located in the intake ducting on the left-hand side of the engine. Disconnect the sensor wiring plug.

25 Two different types of sensor may be fitted (**see illustration**). On the first type, a retaining clip must be pulled from place, before the sensor is removed by rotating it 45° anti-clockwise. On the second type, no clip is fitted.

26 Refitting is a reversal of removal.

Stop-light switch

27 The engine control module receives a signal from the stop-light switch which indicates when the brakes are being applied. Stop-light switch removal and refitting details can be found in Chapter 9.

Electronic control module (ECM)

Note: If a new ECM is to be fitted, it will be necessary to entrust the task to a BMW dealer or specialist. After fitting, it will be necessary to programme the ECM to enable it function correctly. This can only be done using the special BMW equipment which is plugged into the diagnostic connector (see Section 5).

28 Disconnect the battery negative lead (see Chapter 5).

29 Rotate the fastener 90° anti-clockwise, fold

11.25 To remove this type of intake air temperature sensor, rotate it 45° anti-clockwise

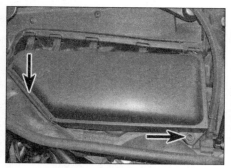

11.29 Rotate the fastener 90° anti-clockwise, press the catch forwards, and remove the pollen filter cover on the left-hand side (arrowed)

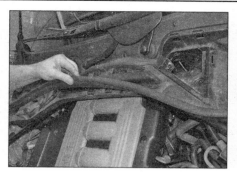

11.30a Pull up the rubber sealing strip

11.30b Lift the clip and slide the cover to the passenger's side

forwards the retaining catch and remove the left-hand pollen filter cover **(see illustration)**.

30 Pull up the rubber sealing strip, then release the clip and slide the plastic cover from the centre of the panel **(see illustration)**.

31 Lift out the plastic trim, undo the bolts/fasteners and remove the left-hand plastic cover from behind the suspension turret in the engine compartment. Unclip the wiring where applicable **(see illustrations)**.

32 Undo the bolts and remove the electrical box cover, located on the left-hand side of the engine compartment **(see illustration)**.

33 Unclip the cover, release the two retaining clips and slide up the ECM **(see illustrations)**.

34 Note their fitted locations, and disconnect

the wiring plugs from the ECM. To release these plugs, slide out the locking element, and disconnect the plugs from the ECM **(see illustration)**.

35 Refitting is the reverse of removal.

Turbocharger boost pressure sensor – M47 and M57 engines

36 Rotate the fastener 90° anti-clockwise, release the holder and remove the cover from the housing each side of the engine compartment **(see illustration 11.29)**.

37 Pull up the rubber sealing strip, then release the clip and slide the plastic cover from the centre of the panel **(see illustrations 11.30a and 11.30b)**.

38 Lift out the plastic trim, undo the bolts/

fasteners and remove the left- and right-hand plastic covers from behind the suspension turret each side of the engine compartment. Unclip the wiring where applicable **(see illustrations 11.31a and 11.31b)**.

M47 engines

39 Remove the plastic acoustic cover from the top of the engine by undoing the bolts, pulling up the front edge and sliding the cover forwards.

40 Undo the 2 bolts and remove the rear section of the plastic acoustic cover on top of the engine.

41 The sensor is located on the intake manifold. Prise out the locking clip and disconnect the sensor wiring plug.

11.31a Lift out the plastic trim . . .

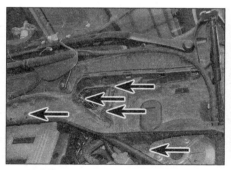

11.31b . . . undo the fasteners/bolts (arrowed) and lift out the cover on the left-hand side

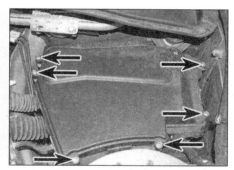

11.32 Undo the bolts (arrowed) and remove the electrical box cover

11.33a Unclip the cover, release the clip (arrowed) . . .

11.33b . . . and slide the ECM upwards

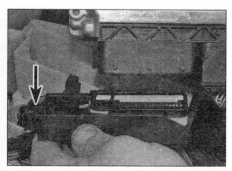

11.34 Slide out the locking element (arrowed) and disconnect the ECM wiring plugs

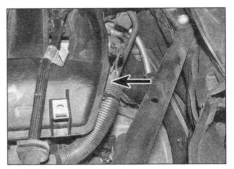

11.42 The boost pressure sensor is located under the rear end of the intake manifold (arrowed) – M47 engine

42 Undo the retaining bolt and remove the sensor **(see illustration)**.
43 Check the condition of the sensor seal, and renew if necessary.
44 Upon refitting, lubricate the sensor seal with petroleum jelly, then fit it to the manifold, and tighten the retaining bolt securely.

M57 engines

45 Undo the bolts and remove the plastic cover from the top of the engine.
46 Disconnect the sensor wiring plug, then pull if from the manifold **(see illustration)**.
47 Check the condition of the seal and renew if necessary.
48 Upon refitting, lubricate the sensor seal with petroleum jelly, then push it into the hole in the manifold.

Both engines

49 Reconnect the sensor wiring plug.
50 The remainder of refitting is a reversal of removal.

Turbocharger boost pressure sensor – N47 engines

51 Remove the plastic acoustic cover from the top of the engine by pulling up the front edge, and sliding it forwards.
52 The sensor is located at the front of the intake manifold. Disconnect the sensor wiring plug **(see illustration)**.
53 Undo the retaining bolt and pull the sensor from the manifold. Check the condition of the sealing ring, and renew if necessary.
54 Upon refitting, lubricate the sensor seal

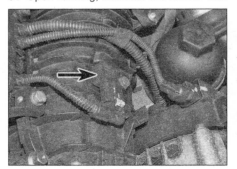

11.52 Turbocharger boost pressure sensor (arrowed) – N47 engine

11.46 Disconnect the boost pressure sensor wiring plug – M57 engine

with petroleum jelly, then fit it to the manifold, and tighten the retaining bolt securely.

Fuel pressure sensor

M47 and M57 engines

55 Remove the plastic acoustic cover from the top of the engine, by removing the retaining bolts, and sliding it forwards.
56 The fuel pressure sensor is located in the front end of the common fuel rail. Ensure that the ignition is switched off, and disconnect the wiring plug from the sensor **(see illustration)**.
57 Counterhold the sensor with a spanner to prevent rotation, then undo the locknut.
58 Ensure that the mating surfaces of the sensor and common rail are clean and dry, the screw the sensor in to position, counterhold it with a spanner to prevent rotation, and tighten the locknut to the specified torque.
59 The remainder of refitting is a reversal of removal. Note that if a new sensor has been fitted, the mean value adaptation value stored in the ECM must be reset using BMW diagnostic equipment. Entrust this task to a BMW dealer or suitably-equipped specialist.

N47 engines

60 Remove the plastic acoustic cover from the top of the engine by pulling up the front edge, and sliding it forwards.
61 Slacken the union nuts and remove the high-pressure fuel pipes from the common fuel rail to the injectors, and to the high-pressure pump. It's essential that all openings are plugged to prevent contamination. Note that

11.56 Fuel pressure sensor (arrowed) – M47 and M57 engines

the pipes must not be re-used – they must be renewed.
62 Disconnect the wiring plugs from the pressure sensor and regulator on the common fuel rail.
63 Depress the release button, and disconnect the fuel return hose from the common rail **(see illustration 6.8)**.
64 Undo the retaining bolts and remove the common fuel rail.
65 Carefully grip the common rail in a bench vice, then unscrew the sensor from place.
66 Upon refitting, apply a little grease to the sensor threads, then tighten it to the specified torque.
67 The remainder of refitting is a reversal of removal. Note that if a new sensor has been fitted, the mean adaptation value stored in the ECM must be reset using BMW diagnostic equipment. Entrust this task to a BMW dealer or suitably-equipped specialist.

Fuel pressure regulator

Note: *BMW insist that the regulator can only be used once. If removed, it must be renewed.*

M47 and M57 engines

68 With reference to Section 16, remove the intake manifold.
69 Disconnect the wiring plug from the regulator, located in the rear of the common rail **(see illustration)**.
70 Use a spanner to counterhold the regulator, then slacken the regulator locknut.
71 Ensure the common rail and regulator mating faces are clean, the screw the regulator into position. Counterhold it with a spanner and tighten the locknut to the specified torque.
72 Refit the manifold as described in Section 16.

N47 engines

73 Remove the plastic acoustic cover from the top of the engine by pulling up the front edge, and sliding it forwards.
74 Slacken the union nuts and remove the high-pressure fuel pipes from the common fuel rail to the injectors, and to the high-pressure pump. It's essential that all openings are plugged, sealed to prevent contamination. Note that the pipes must not be re-used – they must be renewed.

11.69 Fuel pressure regulator (arrowed) – M47 and M57 engines

11.84 Camshaft position sensor (arrowed) – M47 engines

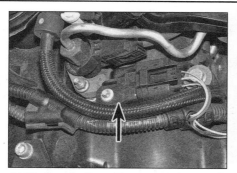

11.88 Camshaft position sensor (arrowed) – M57 engines

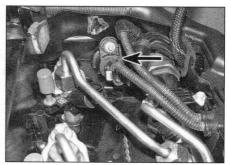

11.92 Camshaft position sensor (arrowed) – N47 engines

75 Disconnect the wiring plugs from the pressure sensor and regulator on the common fuel rail.

76 Depress the release button, and disconnect the fuel return pipe from the common rail.

77 Undo the retaining bolts and remove the common fuel rail.

78 Carefully grip the common rail in a bench vice.

79 Note the fitted position of the regulator is relation to the common rail. Counterhold the regulator with a spanner, then slacken the locknut. Unscrew the sensor from place.

80 Ensure the common rail and regulator mating faces are clean, the screw the regulator into position. Counterhold it with a spanner and tighten the locknut to the specified torque.

81 The remainder of refitting is a reversal of removal. Note that if a new regulator has been fitted, the adaptation value stored in the ECM must be reset using BMW diagnostic equipment. Entrust this task to a BMW dealer or suitably-equipped specialist.

Camshaft position sensor

M47 engines

82 Remove the acoustic cover from the top of the engine by undoing the two retaining bolts and sliding it forwards.

83 Remove the engine oil filler cap, and surrounding rubber seal.

84 Disconnect the camshaft position sensor wiring plug **(see illustration)**.

85 Undo the retaining bolt, and pull the sensor from place.

86 Upon refitting, lubricate the sealing ring with petroleum jelly, refit the sensor and tighten the retaining bolt securely.

M57 engines

87 Undo the bolts and remove the plastic acoustic cover from the top of the engine.

88 Disconnect the wiring plug, undo the retaining bolt and pull the sensor from the front of the cylinder head cover **(see illustration)**. Check the condition of the sealing ring and renew if necessary.

89 Upon refitting, lubricate the sealing ring with petroleum jelly, refit the sensor and tighten the retaining bolt securely.

N47 engines

90 Remove the plastic acoustic cover from the top of the engine by pulling up the front edge, and sliding it forwards.

91 Prise up the centre pins, lever out the plastic expansion rivets, and lift up the insulation at the rear of the cylinder head.

92 Disconnect the wiring plug from the camshaft position sensor, then undo the retaining bolt and pull the sensor from place **(see illustration)**.

93 Upon refitting, lubricate the sensor seal with a little petroleum jelly, then refit it and tighten the retaining bolt securely.

94 The remainder of refitting is a reversal of removal.

12 Turbocharger – description and precautions

Description

A turbocharger is fitted to all engines. It increases engine efficiency by raising the pressure in the intake manifold above atmospheric pressure. Instead of the air simply being sucked into the cylinders, it is forced in. Additional fuel is supplied by the injection pump in proportion to the increased air intake.

Energy for the operation of the turbocharger comes from the exhaust gas. The gas flows through a specially-shaped housing (the turbine housing) and in so doing, spins the turbine wheel. The turbine wheel is attached to a shaft, at the end of which is another vaned wheel known as the compressor wheel. The compressor wheel spins in its own housing and compresses the inducted air on the way to the intake manifold.

The compressed air passes through an intercooler. This is an air-to-air heat exchanger, mounted with the radiator at the front of the vehicle. The purpose of the intercooler is to remove from the inducted air some of the heat gained in being compressed. Because cooler air is denser, removal of this heat further increases engine efficiency.

The turbocharger has adjustable guide vanes controlling the flow of exhaust gas into the turbine. The vanes are swivelled by the boost pressure control motor (integral with

the turbocharger), controlled by the engine management ECM. At lower engine speeds, the vanes close together, giving a smaller exhaust gas entry port, and therefore higher gas speed, which increases boost pressure at low engine speed. At high engine speed, the vanes are turned to give a larger exhaust gas entry port, and therefore lower gas speed, effectively maintaining a reasonably constant boost pressure over the engine rev range.

The turbo shaft is pressure-lubricated by an oil feed pipe from the main oil gallery. The shaft 'floats' on a cushion of oil. A drain pipe/ hose returns the oil to the sump.

Precautions

The turbocharger operates at extremely high speeds and temperatures. Certain precautions must be observed to avoid premature failure of the turbo or injury to the operator.

● **Do not** operate the turbo with any parts exposed. Foreign objects falling onto the rotating vanes could cause excessive damage and (if ejected) personal injury.

● **Do not** race the engine immediately after start-up, especially if it is cold. Give the oil a few seconds to circulate.

● **Always** allow the engine to return to idle speed before switching it off – do not blip the throttle and switch off, as this will leave the turbo spinning without lubrication.

● Allow the engine to idle for several minutes before switching off after a high-speed run.

● Observe the recommended intervals for oil and filter changing, and use a reputable oil of the specified quality (see *Lubricants and fluids*). Neglect of oil changing, or use of inferior oil, can cause carbon formation on the turbo shaft and subsequent failure.

13 Turbocharger – removal and refitting

M47 and M57TU engines

Removal

1 Remove the plastic acoustic cover from the top of the engine by removing the bolts, pulling the front edge upwards, and sliding it forwards.

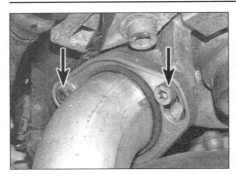

13.7 Slacken the upper bolt, remove the lower bolt, and detach the hose (arrowed)

13.8 Turbocharger oil feed banjo bolt (arrowed)

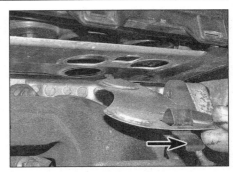

13.12a Depress the clip (arrowed) and slide the shield outwards

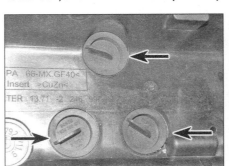

13.12b Prise out the rubber plugs (arrowed)

13.13 Undo the 3 bolts and lower the turbocharger

2 Remove the air filter element as described in Chapter 1.

3 Remove the radiator cooling fan and shroud as described in Chapter 3.

4 On 6-cylinder engines, remove the EGR cooler as described in Chapter 4B.

5 Undo the 2 bolts remove the air intake duct from the mass air flow sensor, and detach the duct from the turbocharger **(see illustrations 11.13a and 11.13b)**.

6 Remove the catalytic converter/particulate filter as described in Chapter 4B.

7 Remove the lower bolt, slacken the upper bolt, rotate the clamp anti-clockwise and detach the charge pressure hose from the base of the turbocharger **(see illustration)**. Cap/ seal the openings to prevent contamination.

8 Unscrew and remove the turbocharger oil feed banjo bolt from the turbocharger **(see illustration)**. Discard the sealing washers,

new ones must be fitted. Plug the hose and block openings to prevent contamination. Be prepared for fluid spillage.

9 Squeeze together the sides to release the clips, then disconnect the turbocharger boost control motor wiring plug.

10 Undo the bolts and remove the support bracket from the base of the turbocharger.

11 Slacken the clamps and remove the oil return hose from the base of the turbocharger and the cylinder block. Plug/seal the openings to prevent contamination.

12 Release the clip and pull out the sealing caps from the heat shield, then prise out the 3 rubber plugs from the cylinder head cover **(see illustrations)**. Where applicable, detach the refrigerant pipe bracket from the turbocharger.

13 Undo the 3 retaining bolts then manoeuvre the turbocharger from under the vehicle **(see**

illustration). Discard the gasket – a new one must be fitted.

Refitting

14 Refitting is a reversal of removal, noting the following points:
  a) *Ensure all mating surfaces are clean and dry.*
  b) *Renew all O-rings, seals and gaskets.*
  c) *Tighten all fasteners to the specified torque where available.*

M57T2 engines

Removal

15 Remove catalytic converter/particulate filter as described in Chapter 4B.

16 Undo the outer bolt, slacken the inner bolt, then rotate the clamp clockwise and detach the charge pressure hose from the top of the turbocharger **(see illustration)**. Cap/seal the openings to prevent contamination.

17 Unscrew and remove the turbocharger oil feed banjo bolt from the cylinder block **(see illustration)**. Discard the sealing washers, new ones must be fitted. Plug the hose and block openings to prevent contamination.

18 Unlock and disconnect the turbocharger boost control motor wiring plug **(see illustration)**.

19 Undo the retaining bolt and detach the oil return hose form the base of the turbocharger. Plug/seal the openings to prevent contamination.

20 Release the two retaining bolts, and disconnect the turbocharger duct from the mass air flow sensor. Remove the duct.

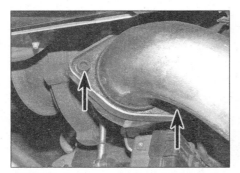

13.16 Undo the rear bolt, and slacken the front clamp bolt (arrowed)

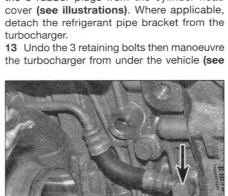

13.17 Turbocharger oil feed pipe bolt (arrowed)

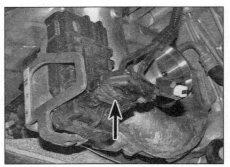

13.18 Turbocharger boost control motor wiring plug (arrowed)

13.21 Undo the turbocharger-to-manifold clamp (arrowed)

13.22a Undo the bolts (arrowed) at the rear of the turbocharger . . .

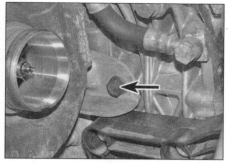

13.22b . . . and the one at the front (arrowed)

Recover the duct seal and breather pipe connector.

21 Slacken the clamp securing the turbocharger to the manifold **(see illustration)**. Note that a new clamp will be required.

22 Undo the retaining bolts and manoeuvre the turbocharger from place **(see illustrations)**.

Refitting

23 Refitting is a reversal of removal, noting the following points:

    a) *Ensure all mating surfaces are clean and dry.*

    b) *Renew all O-rings, seals and gasket.*

    c) *Tighten all fasteners to the specified torque where available.*

N47 engines

Removal

24 Remove the plastic acoustic cover from the top of the engine.

25 Remove the air cleaner assembly as described in Section 2.

26 Release the clamps and remove the charge pressure hose between the intercooler and the turbocharger.

27 Remove the catalytic converter/particulate filter as described in Chapter 4B.

28 Prise out the locking clip, undo the

bolt and detach the air intake pipe from the turbocharger.

29 Disconnect the wiring plug from the turbocharger boost control motor.

30 Undo the bolts and remove the heat shield from the exhaust manifold. Note the mounting bolt at the rear of the manifold.

31 Undo the banjo bolt and detach the oil feed pipe from the cylinder block **(see illustration)**. Discard the pipe seals, new ones must be fitted. Plug/seal the openings to prevent contamination.

32 Slacken the clamp, undo the 2 retaining bolts and remove the oil return pipe from the base of the turbocharger, then slacken the clamp and detach the pipe from the hose on the cylinder block. Discard the gasket. Plug/seal the openings to prevent contamination.

33 Undo the bolts and remove the support bracket from the base of the turbocharger and the cylinder block.

34 Undo the 3 bolts and detach the turbocharger from the exhaust manifold **(see illustration)**. Renew the gasket.

Refitting

35 Refitting is a reversal of removal, noting the following points:

    a) *Ensure all mating surfaces are clean and dry.*

    b) *Renew all O-rings, seals and gasket.*

    c) *Tighten all fasteners to the specified torque where available.*

14 Turbocharger – examination and overhaul

With the turbocharger removed, inspect the housing for cracks or other visible damage.

Spin the turbine or the compressor wheel to verify that the shaft is intact and to feel for excessive shake or roughness. Some play is normal since in use the shaft is 'floating' on a film of oil. Check that the wheel vanes are undamaged.

The variable vane assembly and actuator are integral with the turbocharger, and cannot be checked or renewed separately. Consult a BMW dealer or other specialist if it is thought that the variable vane assembly may be faulty.

If the exhaust or induction passages are oil-contaminated, the turbo shaft oil seals have probably failed. (On the induction side, this will also have contaminated the intercooler, where applicable, which if necessary should be flushed with a suitable solvent.)

No DIY repair of the turbo is possible. A new unit may be available on an exchange basis.

13.31 Turbocharger oil feed banjo bolt (arrowed)

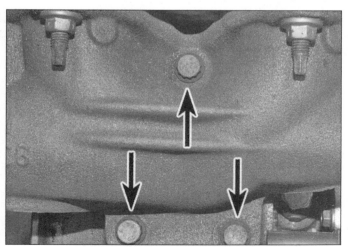

13.34 Turbocharger-to-manifold bolts (arrowed)

15.3a Prise down the wire clip (arrowed) and disconnect the hose at the left-hand end . . .

15.3b . . . and right-hand end of the intercooler (arrowed)

15.4 Squeeze together the clips and slide the fastener rearwards

15 Intercooler – removal and refitting

Removal

1 Raise the front of the vehicle and support it securely on axle stands (see *Jacking and vehicle support*). Remove the engine undershield **(see illustration 11.6a)**.
2 Remove the radiator fan and shroud as described in Chapter 3.

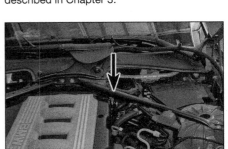

16.5 Undo the bolts and remove the strut brace (arrowed)

3 Release the clamps, and disconnect the intercooler intake and outlet hoses **(see illustrations)**. Examine the hose seals and renew if necessary.
4 Release the 2 fasteners and slide the intercooler rearwards, taking care not to damage the cooling fins **(see illustration)**.

Refitting

5 Refitting is the reverse of removal. Apply a little petroleum jelly to the intake and outlet hoses seals to aid refitting.

16 Manifolds – removal and refitting

Intake manifold

M47 and M57 engines

1 Disconnect the battery negative lead as described in Chapter 5.
2 Working at the rear of the engine compartment, undo the bolts, release the clips and remove the pollen filters covers each side **(see illustration 11.29)**. Slide the filters from the housings. If necessary, refer to Chapter 1.

3 Pull up the rubber sealing strip, then release the clip and slide the plastic cover from the centre of the panel **(see illustrations 11.30a and 11.30b)**.
4 Lift out the plastic trim, undo the bolts/fasteners and remove the left- and right-hand plastic covers from behind the suspension turret each side of the engine compartment. Unclip the wiring where applicable **(see illustrations 11.31a and 11.31b)**.
5 Undo the 4 bolts and remove the strut brace **(see illustration)**. Discard the bolts – new ones must be fitted.
6 Where fitted, remove the plastic cover at the rear of the engine.
7 Undo the bolt securing the engine oil level dipstick guide tube to the manifold **(see illustration)**.
8 Note their fitted positions and disconnect the wiring plugs/harnesses/vacuum hoses from the intake manifold/throttle body/ EGR valve/map sensor, and manifold variable geometry solenoid valve (where applicable).
9 Slacken the clamp securing the EGR pipe to the throttle body **(see illustration)**.
10 Prise out the clip and detach the charge air pipe from the throttle body.

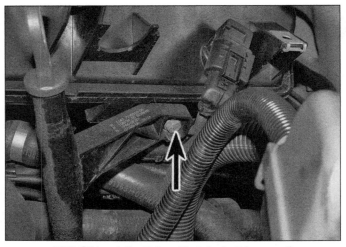

16.7 Oil level dipstick guide tube bolt (arrowed)

16.9 Slacken the clamp (arrowed) securing the EGR pipe

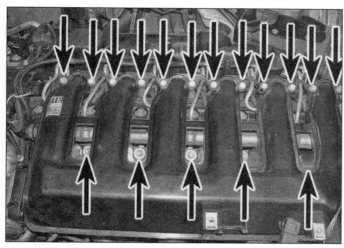

16.11a Undo the intake manifold bolts/nuts (arrowed) . . .

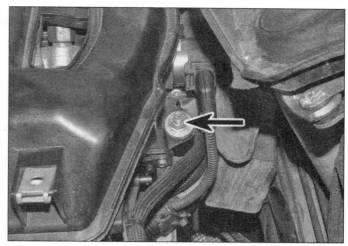

16.11b . . . not forgetting the nut at the rear (arrowed)

11 Undo the nuts/bolts and detach the intake manifold from the cylinder head **(see illustrations)**. Discard the seals.
12 Ensure the mating faces of the intake manifold and cylinder head are clean. Renew the manifold seals **(see illustration)**.
13 Position the manifold against the cylinder head, refit the nuts/bolts and tighten them to their specified torque.
14 The remainder of refitting is a reversal of removal.

N47 engine

15 Pull the plastic acoustic cover upwards and forwards from the top of the engine.
16 Disconnect the wiring plug from the intake air temperature sensor **(see illustration 11.25)**.
17 Prise out the clips and disconnect the charge air pipe from the throttle body **(see illustration)**.
18 Disconnect the wiring plugs from the throttle body and the intake air pressure sensor on the manifold.

19 Unclip the vacuum hose from the rear of the manifold, and the battery cable from the underside of the manifold.
20 Undo the 5 bolts and manoeuvre the manifold from place **(see illustration)**. Renew the manifold/EGR pipe seals.
21 Ensure the mating faces of the intake manifold and cylinder head are clean. Renew the manifold seals.
22 Position the manifold against the cylinder head, refit the bolts and tighten them to their specified torque.
23 The remainder of refitting is a reversal of removal. Note that if a new manifold has been fitted, the swirl flap stop values must be reset in the engine management ECM using BMW diagnostic equipment. Entrust this task to a BMW dealer or suitably-equipped specialist.

Exhaust manifold

M47 and M57 engines

24 Remove the cooling fan and shroud as described in Chapter 3.

16.12 Renew the manifold seals

25 Remove the air cleaner element as described in Chapter 1.
26 Remove the catalytic converter/particulate filter as described in Chapter 4B.
27 Undo the 2 retaining bolts and detach the air intake pipe from the air cleaner housing.
28 Slacken the clamp, undo the bolts and remove the EGR pipe from the front of the

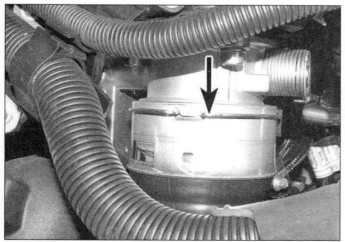

16.17 Push the pipe onto the throttle body, then prise out the clip a little (arrowed)

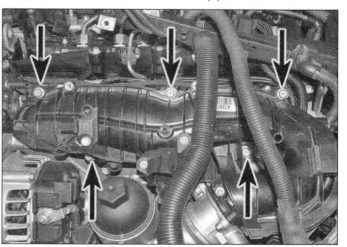

16.20 Manifold retaining bolts (arrowed)

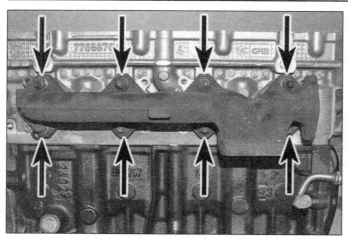

16.34 Exhaust manifold nuts (arrowed)

16.40 EGR pipe-to-manifold bolts (arrowed)

cylinder head. On engines with an EGR cooler, remove the cooler as described in Chapter 4B.

29 Slacken the front bolt, undo the rear bolt securing the charge air pipe to the turbocharger, and rotate the retaining collar clockwise **(see illustration 13.7)**.

30 Prise out the clip and disconnect the charge air pipe from the turbocharger at the quick-release coupling on the intercooler, and remove the pipe. Cap/seal the turbocharger openings to prevent contamination.

31 Prise out the sealing caps from the heat shield, then remove the 3 plugs from the cylinder head cover **(see illustrations 13.12a and 13.12b)**.

32 Undo the 3 retaining bolts securing the turbocharger to the manifold **(see illustration 13.13)**.

33 Slacken the 2 bolts securing the support bracket on the underside of the turbocharger to the cylinder block, and lower the turbocharger a little. Discard the gasket between the manifold and turbocharger – a new one must be fitted.

34 Undo the retaining nuts and withdrawn the manifold from the studs **(see illustration)**. Discard the gaskets and nuts, new ones must be fitted.

35 Examine all the manifold studs for signs of damage and corrosion; remove all traces of corrosion, and repair or renew any damaged studs.

36 Ensure the mating surfaces of the exhaust manifold and cylinder head are clean and dry. Position new gaskets, and refit the exhaust manifold to the cylinder head.

37 Apply a little high-temperature anti-seize grease (Copperslip) to the mounting studs, then tighten the new nuts to the specified torque.

38 The remainder of refitting is a reversal of removal.

N47 engines

39 Remove the turbocharger as described in Section 13.

40 Undo the bolts and remove the EGR pipe

from the exhaust manifold to the EGR valve **(see illustration)**.

41 Undo the retaining nuts and withdraw the manifold from the cylinder head studs. Recover the gaskets.

42 Examine all the manifold studs for signs of damage and corrosion; remove all traces of corrosion, and repair or renew any damaged studs.

43 Ensure the mating surfaces of the exhaust manifold and cylinder head are clean and dry. The new manifold-to-cylinder head gaskets have a graphite coating on one side. This side of the gaskets must face the manifold. Position new gaskets, and refit the exhaust manifold to the cylinder head.

44 Apply a little high-temperature anti-seize grease (Copperslip) to the mounting studs, then tighten the new nuts to the specified torque.

45 The remainder of refitting is a reversal of removal.

---

17 Exhaust system – general information and renewal

General information

1 The exhaust system consists of several sections which can be removed individually, or as a complete system.

2 The tailpipe is a sleeve fit over the end of the intermediate pipe, which is a sleeve-fit to the catalytic converter/particulate filter, and the system is suspended throughout its entire length by rubber mountings.

Removal

3 Each exhaust section can be removed individually, or alternatively, the complete system can be removed as a unit. Even if only one part of the system needs attention, it can sometimes be easier to remove the whole system and separate the sections on the bench.

4 To remove the system or part of the system, first jack up the front or rear of the car and support it securely on axle stands (see *Jacking and vehicle support*). Alternatively, position the car over an inspection pit or on car ramps.

5 Spray a little penetrating fluid around the exhaust pipe clamps, then slacken the clamp bolts/nuts **(see illustration)**.

6 Have an assistant support the exhaust system, or position a transmission jack appropriately, then undo the bolts/nuts securing the exhaust mounting brackets to the vehicle underside.

7 Manoeuvre the system from under the vehicle.

8 Heat shield(s) are fitted to the underside of the vehicle body. Each shield can be removed once its retaining bolts have been undone.

Refitting

9 Each section is refitted by reversing the removal sequence, noting the following points:

a) Inspect the rubber mountings for signs of damage or deterioration, and renew as necessary.

b) Prior to tightening the exhaust system fasteners to the specified torque, ensure that all rubber mountings are correctly located, and that there is adequate clearance between the exhaust system and vehicle underbody.

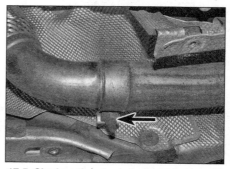

17.5 Slacken the clamp bolt/nut (arrowed)

Chapter 4 Part B:
Emission control systems

Contents

Degrees of difficulty

Easy, suitable for novice with little experience		**Fairly easy,** suitable for beginner with some experience	**Fairly difficult,** suitable for competent DIY mechanic	**Difficult,** suitable for experienced DIY mechanic	**Very difficult,** suitable for expert DIY or professional

Specifications

Torque wrench settings	Nm	lbf ft
Front reinforcement plate:*		
Stage 1	56	41
Stage 2	Angle-tighten a further 90°	
Exhaust gas recirculation (EGR) cooler to cylinder head	25	18
Exhaust gas recirculation (EGR) valve/pipe bolts:		
M6 bolts	10	7
M8 bolts	25	18
Oxygen sensors	50	37

* Do not re-use

1 General information

All diesel engine models are also designed to meet strict emission requirements. They are fitted with a crankcase emission control system, a catalytic converter and an exhaust gas recirculation (EGR) system to keep exhaust emissions down to a minimum. On some models, a combined catalytic converter and particulate filter is fitted.

The emission control systems function as follows.

Crankcase emission control

To reduce the emission of unburned hydrocarbons from the crankcase into the atmosphere, the engine is sealed and the blow-by gases and oil vapour are drawn from inside the crankcase, through a wire mesh oil separator, into the intake tract to be burned by the engine during normal combustion.

Crankcase gases are drawn via a depression limiting valve. The valve closes progressively as the engine speed increases, so limiting the maximum depression in the crankcase.

Exhaust emission control

To minimise the level of exhaust pollutants released into the atmosphere, a catalytic converter is fitted in the exhaust system of all models.

The catalytic converter consists of a canister containing a fine mesh impregnated with a catalyst material, over which the hot exhaust gases pass. The catalyst speeds up the oxidation of harmful carbon monoxide, unburned hydrocarbons and soot, effectively reducing the quantity of harmful products released into the atmosphere via the exhaust gases.

Particulate filter

This device is designed to trap carbon particulates produced by the combustion process. The particulate filter is combined with the catalytic converter. In order to prevent the filter blocking, pressure and

temperature sensors are fitted to the filter. Under high-speed driving conditions, the soot particles are burnt off in the filter by the high temperature of the exhaust gases. However, where the driving conditions are such that the exhaust gases are not sufficiently high, the engine management system injects fuel into the cylinders after the point of combustion. These are called post-injections, and raise the temperature of the exhaust gases, causing the soot particles in the filter to be burnt off.

Exhaust gas recirculation system

This system is designed to recirculate small quantities of exhaust gas into the intake tract, and therefore into the combustion process. This process reduces the level of unburnt hydrocarbons present in the exhaust gas before it reaches the catalytic converter. The system is controlled by the engine management system ECM, using the information from its various sensors, via the EGR valve which is fitted to the metal pipe connecting the intake and exhaust manifolds.

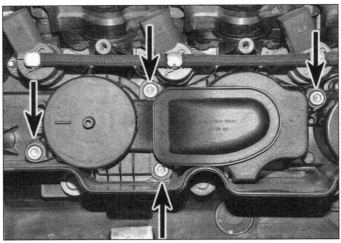

2.4 Undo the bolts (arrowed) and remove the depression limiting valve

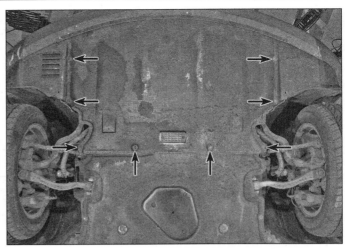

2.9a Engine/radiator undershield fasteners (arrowed)

On some models, the exhaust gases are cooled prior to entering the intake manifold by passing through a cooler mounted on the side of the EGR valve. Engine coolant circulates through the cooler.

2 Engine emission control systems – testing and component renewal

Crankcase emission control

Testing

1 The components of this system require no attention other than to check that the hose(s) are clear and undamaged at regular intervals. If the system is thought to be faulty, renew the crankcase pressure limiting valve.

Depression limiting valve renewal – M47 and M57 engines

2 Remove the plastic cover from the top of the engine.

3 Disconnect the injector wiring plugs, unscrew the three retaining bolts, and move the injector harness to one side.
4 Unscrew the four bolts, and remove the depression limiting valve complete with filter (see illustration).
5 Ensure the mating surfaces are clean and dry, renew the seals and refit the valve housing. Tighten the Allen bolts securely.
6 The remainder of refitting is a reversal of removal.

Exhaust emission control

Testing

7 The performance of the catalytic converter can be checked only by measuring the exhaust gases using a good-quality, carefully-calibrated exhaust gas analyser.
8 Before assuming that the catalytic converter is faulty, it is worth checking whether the problem is not due to a faulty injector(s). Refer to your BMW dealer or specialist for further information.

Catalytic converter/particulate filter renewal – N47, M47 and M57T2 engines

9 Remove the acoustic cover from the top of the engine, then raise the front of the vehicle, support it securely on axle stands, then undo the fasteners and remove the engine undershields (see illustrations).
10 Undo the bolts and remove the front underbody reinforcement plate (see illustration). Discard the bolts – new ones must be fitted.
11 The engine must be supported in position using an engine hoist or engine crossbeam. Attach the hoist/crossbeam to the engine lifting eyes at the front and rear of the engine. Take the weight of the engine. Note that if using the crossbeam, mount the crossbeam on the suspension turrets and the front panel adjacent to the bonnet catch each side. The inner wings are not strong enough to take the weight of the engine.
12 Undo the nut each side securing the

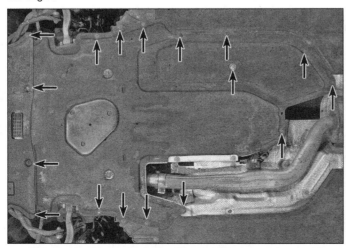

2.9b Engine/transmission undershield fasteners (arrowed)

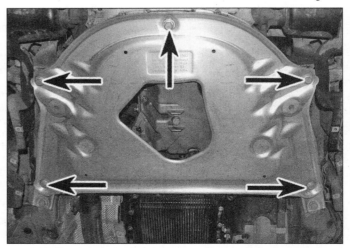

2.10 Front underbody reinforcement plate bolts (arrowed)

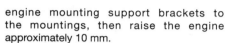

2.13 Undo the bolts (arrowed) and remove the intake neck – M57 engine shown

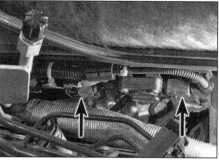

2.14 Disconnect the oxygen sensor and exhaust gas pressure sensor wiring plugs (arrowed)

2.16a Working underneath, undo the bolt (arrowed) adjacent to the steering column . . .

engine mounting support brackets to the mountings, then raise the engine approximately 10 mm.

13 On M47 and M57 engines, disconnect the air intake pipe, then undo the bolts and remove the intake neck from the side of the air filter housing **(see illustration)**.

14 Disconnect the wiring plug from the exhaust gas pressure sensor and oxygen sensor, then release the sensor/wiring plug from the mounting bracket so they can be removed along with the filter **(see illustration)**. Release the wiring looms from any retaining clips.

15 Slacken the clamp securing the front section of the exhaust to the catalytic converter/particulate filter, release the exhaust system mountings and slide the system rearwards.

16 Undo the bolts and remove the catalytic converter/particulate filter support bracket(s) **(see illustrations)**.

17 Note their fitted positions, and disconnect the pressure take-off hose(s) from the particulate filter (where applicable).

18 Slacken the clamp securing the catalytic converter/particulate filter to the turbocharger, and manoeuvre the assembly from place. Renew the sealing ring and the clamp **(see illustrations)**.

19 Refitting is a reversal of removal. Note that if a new particulate filter has been fitted, the engine management ECM adaption counter must be reset using BMW diagnostic equipment. Entrust this task to a BMW dealer or suitably-equipped specialist.

Particulate filter renewal – M57TU engines

20 Raise the front of the vehicle and support it securely on axle stands (see *Jacking and vehicle support*). Undo the fasteners and remove the engine and transmission undershields **(see illustrations 2.9a and 2.9b)**.

21 Undo the nuts securing the particulate filter to the front and rear sections of the exhaust pipe, and remove the filter. Discard the seals – new ones must be fitted.

22 Refitting is a reversal of removal. Note that if a new particulate filter has been fitted, the engine management ECM adaption

counter must be reset using BMW diagnostic equipment. Entrust this task to a BMW dealer or suitably-equipped specialist.

Catalytic converter renewal – M57TU engines

23 Raise the front of the vehicle and support it securely on axle stands (see *Jacking and vehicle support*). Undo the fasteners and remove the engine and transmission undershields **(see illustrations 2.9a and 2.9b)**.

24 Undo the bolts and remove the reinforcement plate from under the engine **(see illustration 2.10)**.

25 Remove the complete exhaust system as described in Chapter 4A.

26 Undo the nuts and remove the support brackets from the base of the catalytic converter **(see illustration)**.

2.16b . . . and the bolts (arrowed) securing the bracket at the rear of the filter

2.18b Renew the sealing ring (arrowed) between the filter and turbocharger

27 Undo the 2 nuts securing the catalytic converter to the turbocharger and manoeuvre it from place.

28 Refitting is a reversal of removal.

Exhaust gas recirculation system

Testing

29 Comprehensive testing of the system can only be carried out using specialist electronic equipment which is connected to the injection system diagnostic wiring connector (see Chapter 4A). If the EGR valve or solenoid valve are thought to be faulty, they must be renewed.

Exhaust gas recirculation (EGR) valve renewal – M47 and M57 engines

30 Release the retaining clips and disconnect the air intake ducting assembly from the EGR valve **(see illustration overleaf)**.

2.18a Slacken the clamp (arrowed) securing the filter to the turbocharger

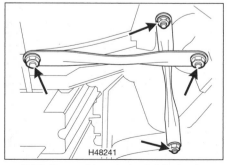

2.26 Support bracket retaining nuts (arrowed)

2.30 Prise out the clip (arrowed) a little and disconnect the intake ducting

2.31 Disconnect the vacuum hose from the EGR valve

2.32 Slacken the EGR pipe clamp bolt (arrowed)

31 Disconnect the vacuum hose (where fitted) from the EGR valve **(see illustration)**.

32 Completely slacken the clamp bolt and disconnect the EGR pipe from the valve **(see illustration)**.

33 Unscrew the four retaining bolts, and remove the EGR valve.

34 Refitting is a reversal of removal, using a new seal and tightening the valve retaining bolts to the specified torque.

Exhaust gas recirculation (EGR) valve renewal – N47 engines

35 Disconnect the wiring plug and vacuum hose from the valve **(see illustration)**.

36 Undo the 2 bolts and detach the valve from the pipe. Renew the gasket (where fitted).

37 Refitting is a reversal of removal.

Exhaust gas recirculation (EGR) solenoid valve renewal

38 Remove the intake manifold as described in Chapter 4A.

39 Disconnect the wiring plug from the solenoid.

40 Unscrew the two bolts securing the solenoid bracket to the cylinder block. Note their fitted locations then disconnect the vacuum hoses. If necessary, the solenoid can be separated from the mounting bracket by unscrewing the two retaining nuts.

41 Refitting is a reversal of removal.

Exhaust gas recirculation (EGR) cooler renewal – M47 and M57T2 engines

42 Remove the plastic cover from the top of the engine.

43 Completely slacken and remove the clamp securing the EGR pipe to the cooler.

44 Undo the bolts securing the EGR cooler to the exhaust manifold **(see illustration)**.

45 Undo the three bolts securing the EGR cooler to the cylinder head.

46 Be prepared for coolant spillage, and disconnect the coolant hoses from the cooler. Be prepared for coolant spillage – plug the openings.

47 Refitting is a reversal of removal. Top-up the coolant level as described in *Weekly checks*.

Exhaust gas recirculation (EGR) cooler renewal – M57TU engines

48 Remove the plastic cover from the top of the engine.

49 Drain the coolant as described in Chapter 1.

50 Remove the radiator cooling fan and shroud as described in Chapter 3.

51 Disconnect the coolant hoses from the EGR cooler.

52 Slacken the clamp securing the EGR pipe to the cooler.

53 Release any remaining fasteners and remove the cooler. Renew all seals/gaskets disturbed.

54 Refitting is a reversal of removal.

Exhaust gas recirculation (EGR) cooler renewal – N47 engines

55 Pull up the front edge and remove the plastic cover from the top of the engine.

56 Drain the coolant as described in Chapter 1.

57 Remove the radiator cooling fan and shroud as described in Chapter 3.

58 Undo the bolts securing the EGR pipe to the exhaust manifold and EGR cooler.

59 Undo the 2 bolts securing the EGR pipe to the cylinder head.

60 Disconnect the black vacuum hose from the valve above the cooler **(see illustration)**.

61 Remove the remaining mounting bolt and

manoeuvre the cooler from place. Be prepared for coolant spillage – plug the openings.

62 Refitting is a reversal of removal.

3 Catalytic converter – general information and precautions

1 The catalytic converter is a reliable and simple device which needs no maintenance in itself, but there are some facts of which an owner should be aware if the converter is to function properly for its full service life.

   a) *If the engine develops a misfire, do not drive the car at all (or at least as little as possible) until the fault is cured.*

   b) *DO NOT push- or tow-start the car – this will soak the catalytic converter in unburned fuel, causing it to overheat when the engine does start.*

   c) *DO NOT switch off the ignition at high engine speeds.*

   d) *DO NOT use fuel or engine oil additives – these may contain substances harmful to the catalytic converter.*

   e) *DO NOT continue to use the car if the engine burns oil to the extent of leaving a visible trail of blue smoke.*

   f) *Remember that the catalytic converter operates at very high temperatures. DO NOT, therefore, park the car in dry undergrowth, over long grass or piles of dead leaves after a long run.*

   g) *Remember that the catalytic converter is FRAGILE – do not strike it with tools during servicing work.*

2.35 EGR valve wiring plug and vacuum pipe (arrowed)

2.44 Undo the bolts (arrowed) securing the EGR cooler to the front of the exhaust manifold

2.60 Disconnect the black vacuum hose (arrowed) from the valve

Chapter 5
Starting and charging systems

Contents

Degrees of difficulty

| Easy, suitable for novice with little experience | 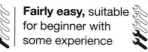 | Fairly easy, suitable for beginner with some experience | | Fairly difficult, suitable for competent DIY mechanic | | Difficult, suitable for experienced DIY mechanic | | Very difficult, suitable for expert DIY or professional | |

Specifications

System type .... 12 volt negative earth

Alternator

Regulated voltage (at 1500 rpm engine speed with no electrical
equipment switched on) .... 13.5 to 14.2 volts

Torque wrench settings

	Nm	lbf ft
Alternator to engine block	38	28
Alternator pulley retaining bolt:		
Valeo alternator	75	55
Bosch alternator	65	48
Drivebelt idler pulley	28	21
Glow plugs	18	13
Reinforcement plate:*		
Stage 1	56	41
Stage 2	Angle-tighten a further 90°	
Starter motor-to-gearbox/transmission nuts and bolts:		
M47 and M57 engines	45	33
N47 engines	19	14

* Do not re-use

1 General information and precautions

The engine electrical system consists mainly of the charging and starting systems. Because of their engine-related functions, these components are covered separately from the body electrical devices such as the lights, instruments, etc (which are covered in Chapter 12).

The electrical system is of the 12 volt negative earth type.

The battery is of the low maintenance or 'maintenance-free' (sealed for life) type and is charged by the alternator, which is belt-driven from the crankshaft pulley.

The starter motor is of the pre-engaged type incorporating an integral solenoid. On starting, the solenoid moves the drive pinion into engagement with the flywheel ring gear before the starter motor is energised. Once the engine has started, a one-way clutch prevents the motor armature being driven by the engine until the pinion disengages from the flywheel.

Precautions

Further details of the various systems are given in the relevant Sections of this Chapter. While some repair procedures are given, the usual course of action is to renew the component concerned.

It is necessary to take extra care when working on the electrical system to avoid damage to semi-conductor devices (diodes and transistors), and to avoid the risk of personal injury. In addition to the precautions given in *Safety first!* at the beginning of this manual, observe the following when working on the system:

- *Always remove rings, watches, etc, before working on the electrical system.* Even with the battery disconnected, capacitive discharge could occur if a component's live terminal is earthed through a metal object. This could cause a shock or nasty burn.

- *Do not reverse the battery connections.* Components such as the alternator, electronic control units, or any other components having semiconductor circuitry could be irreparably damaged.

- *If the engine is being started using jump leads and a slave battery, make use of the built-in jump lead connections points (see 'Jump starting' at the beginning of this manual).* This also applies when connecting a battery charger.

- *Never disconnect the battery terminals, the alternator, any electrical wiring or any test instruments when the engine is running.*

- *Do not allow the engine to turn the* alternator when the alternator is not connected.

- *Never 'test' for alternator output by 'flashing' the output lead to earth.*

- *Never use an ohmmeter of the type incorporating a hand-cranked generator for circuit or continuity testing.*

- *Always ensure that the battery negative lead is disconnected when working on the electrical system.*

- *Before using electric-arc welding equipment on the car, disconnect the battery, alternator and components such as the fuel injection electronic control module to protect them from the risk of damage.*

- If an audio unit with a built-in security code is fitted, note the following precautions. If the power source to the unit is cut, the anti-theft system will activate. Even if the power source is immediately reconnected, the audio unit will not function until the correct security code has been entered. Therefore, if you do not know the correct security code for the audio unit do not disconnect the battery negative terminal of the battery or remove the audio unit from the vehicle.

2 Electrical fault finding – general information

Refer to Chapter 12.

3 Battery – testing and charging

Note: *The following is intended as a guide only. Always refer to the manufacturer's recommendations (often printed on a label attached to the battery) before charging a battery.*

1 All models are fitted with a maintenance-free battery in production, which should require no maintenance under normal operating conditions.

2 If the condition of the battery is suspect, remove the battery as described in Section 4, and check that the electrolyte level in each cell is up to the MAX mark on the outside of the battery case (about 5.0 mm above the tops of the plates in the cells). If necessary, the electrolyte level can be topped-up by removing the cell plugs from the top of the battery and adding distilled water (**not** acid).

3 An approximate check on battery condition can be made by checking the specific gravity of the electrolyte, using the following as a guide.

4 Use a hydrometer to make the check and compare the results with the following table.

The temperatures quoted are ambient (air) temperatures. Note that the specific gravity readings assume an electrolyte temperature of 15°C; for every 10°C below 15°C subtract 0.007. For every 10°C above 15°C add 0.007.

	Ambient temperature	
	Above 25°C	**Below 25°C**
Fully-charged	*1.210 to 1.230*	*1.270 to 1.290*
70% charged	*1.170 to 1.190*	*1.230 to 1.250*
Discharged	*1.050 to 1.070*	*1.110 to 1.130*

5 If the battery condition is suspect, first check the specific gravity of electrolyte in each cell. A variation of 0.040 or more between any cells indicates loss of electrolyte or deterioration of the internal plates.

6 If the specific gravity variation is 0.040 or more, the battery should be renewed. If the cell variation is satisfactory but the battery is discharged, it should be charged in accordance with the manufacturer's instructions.

7 In cases where a 'sealed for life' maintenance-free battery is fitted, topping-up and testing of the electrolyte in each cell is not possible. The condition of the battery can therefore only be tested using a battery condition indicator or a voltmeter.

8 Models may be fitted with a battery, with a built-in charge condition indicator. The indicator is located in the top of the battery casing, and indicates the condition of the battery from its colour. If the indicator shows green, then the battery is in a good state of charge. If the indicator turns darker, eventually to black, then the battery requires charging, as described later in this Section. If the indicator shows clear/yellow, then the electrolyte level in the battery is too low to allow further use, and the battery should be renewed. **Do not** attempt to charge, load or jump start a battery when the indicator shows clear/yellow.

9 If testing the battery using a voltmeter, connect the voltmeter across the battery. A fully-charged battery should give a reading of 12.5 volts or higher. The test is only accurate if the battery has not been subjected to any kind of charge for the previous six hours. If this is not the case, switch on the headlights for 30 seconds, then wait four to five minutes before testing the battery after switching off the headlights. All other electrical circuits must be switched off, so check that the doors and tailgate are fully shut when making the test.

10 Generally speaking, if the voltage reading is less than 12.2 volts, then the battery is discharged, whilst a reading of 12.2 to 12.4 volts indicates a partially-discharged condition.

Charging

11 The battery can only be charged using the recharge points in the right-hand rear

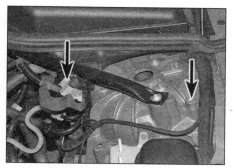

3.11 Only charge the battery using the points under the bonnet (arrowed)

corner of the engine compartment **(see illustration)**. Do not connect a battery charger directly to the battery terminals/IBS terminals of a fitted battery. These vehicles are fitted with an Intelligent Battery Sensor (IBS) incorporated into the battery negative clamp, which monitors the flow of current to and from the battery. If it calculates the state of the battery is getting low, it will ask the CAS (Car Access System) control unit to shut down certain electrical consumers. Eventually, the IBS may deem the battery state is so poor it decides the starting system must be disabled. Consequently, if a battery charger is connected directly to the terminals of the battery, even though the battery may be completely recharged, the IBS may still believe the battery state to be poor, as it has registered no current passing into the battery. Therefore, even though the battery is charged,

the starter circuit may still be disabled. Resetting of the CAS battery register must be carrier out using BMW diagnostic equipment. Entrust this task to a BMW dealer or suitably-equipped specialist.

---

4 Battery – disconnection, removal and refitting

Note: *When the battery is disconnected, any fault codes stored in the engine management ECM memory will be erased. If any faults are suspected, do not disconnect the battery until the fault codes have been read by a BMW dealer or specialist. If the vehicle is fitted with a code-protected audio unit, refer to the Owners handbook.*

Disconnection

1 The battery is located beneath a panel on the right-hand side of the luggage compartment.

Saloon models

2 Lift up the luggage compartment floor panel, then rotate the two fasteners 90° anti-clockwise and lift out the panel above the battery **(see illustration)**.

Touring models

3 Lift the catch and remove the right-hand side panel.

4 Lift the luggage compartment floor panel, then undo the 2 nuts and 1 bolt and lift out the battery cover **(see illustration)**.

All models

5 Slacken the clamp nut, and disconnect the clamp from the battery negative (earth) terminal **(see illustration)**. Position the negative lead away from the battery, so there is no risk of accidental contact between it and the battery terminal. For extra protection, cover the disconnected lead clamp with a rag or rubber glove, etc. **Note:** *The battery terminal negative clamp incorporates an IBS (Intelligent Battery Sensor), which monitors the condition of the battery. This unit is very delicate, and the following guidelines should be adhered to:*

  a) Do not attach any additional connections to the negative terminal.
  b) Do not modify the earth lead.
  c) Do not use force when disconnecting the earth terminal.
  d) Do not pull the earth cable.
  e) Do not subject the IBS to any levering, pulling, etc.
  f) Do not slacken or tighten the IBS sensor Torx bolt.

Removal

6 Disconnect the battery negative lead as described previously.

7 Prise up the plastic cover, slacken the nut and pull the positive clamp assembly from the terminal on the battery **(see illustration)**.

8 Undo the 2 bolts and remove the support bracket above the battery **(see illustration)**.

9 Unscrew the bolt, and remove the battery retaining clamp **(see illustration)**.

10 Lift the battery from its housing,

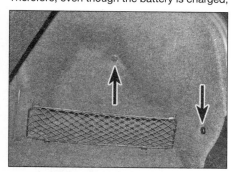

4.2 Rotate the fasteners (arrowed) 90° anti-clockwise and lift out the panel

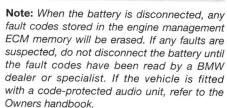

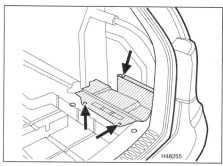

4.4 Undo the nuts/bolt (arrowed) and remove the cover over the battery

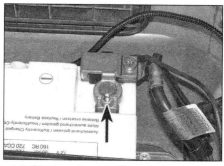

4.5 Slacken the negative terminal clamp nut (arrowed)

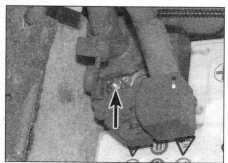

4.7 Lift the plastic cover and slacken the positive terminal clamp nut (arrowed)

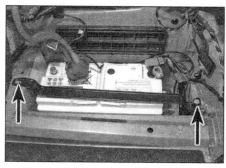

4.8 Support bracket bolts (arrowed)

4.9 Undo the battery retaining clamp bolt (arrowed)

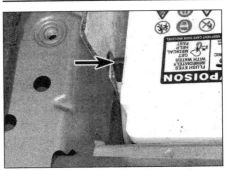

4.10 Disconnect the vent hose (arrowed) from the front of the battery

disconnect the vent hose from the front face as the battery is removed **(see illustration)**. Take care as the battery is heavy.

Refitting

11 Refitting is a reversal of removal. Always reconnect the positive lead first, and the negative lead last.

12 If a new battery has been fitted, the new unit must be registered with the CAS (Car Access System) control unit, using BMW diagnostic equipment. Entrust this task to a BMW dealer or suitably-equipped specialist. Failure to register the battery may cause the IBS to malfunction.

13 After reconnecting the battery, several of the vehicle's ECMs will require time to relearn certain values. The will normally be complete within a normal driving pattern of 15 miles (approximately). In addition, several systems may require re-initialisation as follows:

Sunroof

1) With the battery reconnected, and the ignition on, press the sunroof operating switch into the 'tilt' position and hold it there.
2) Once the sunroof has reached the 'fully-tilted' position, hold the switch in that position for approximately 30 seconds.

Active steering

1) Start the engine, and turn the steering wheel to full left lock.
2) Turn the steering wheel to full right lock.
3) Turn the steering wheel to the centre position.

4) Turn off the ignition, then turn it on again and check the steering warning light extinguishes.

Electric windows

1) Operate the button to fully open the window, then press the switch into the 'open, one-touch operation' (second switch position) and hold it there for 20 seconds.
2) Release the switch, then press the switch into the 'close, one-touch operation' (second switch position) and hold it there until the window closes completely.

5 Charging system – testing

Note: Refer to the warnings given in 'Safety first!' and in Section 1 of this Chapter before starting work.

1 If the ignition warning light fails to illuminate when the ignition is switched on, first check the alternator wiring connections for security. If satisfactory, check that the warning light bulb has not blown, and that the bulbholder is secure in its location in the instrument panel. If the light still fails to illuminate, check the continuity of the warning light feed wire from the alternator to the bulbholder. If all is satisfactory, the alternator is at fault and should be renewed or taken to an auto-electrician for testing and repair. Note that on some models, the function of the alternator is controlled by the engine management ECM, and is therefore included in the vehicle's self-diagnosis system. Should a fault occur, have the system interrogated using a code reader or scanner.

2 If the ignition warning light illuminates when the engine is running, stop the engine and check that the drivebelt is correctly tensioned (see Chapter 1) and that the alternator connections are secure. If all is so far satisfactory, have the alternator checked by an auto-electrician for testing and repair. See the note in the previous paragraph.

3 If the alternator output is suspect even though the warning light functions correctly,

the regulated voltage may be checked as follows.

4 Connect a voltmeter across the battery terminals and start the engine.

5 Increase the engine speed until the voltmeter reading remains steady; the reading should be approximately 12 to 13 volts, and no more than 14.2 volts.

6 Switch on as many electrical accessories (eg, the headlights, heated rear window and heater blower) as possible, and check that the alternator maintains the regulated voltage at around 13 to 14 volts.

7 If the regulated voltage is not as stated, the fault may be due to worn alternator brushes, weak brush springs, a faulty voltage regulator, a faulty diode, a severed phase winding or worn or damaged slip-rings. The alternator should be renewed or taken to an auto-electrician for testing and repair.

6 Alternator drivebelt – removal, refitting and tensioning

Refer to the procedure given for the auxiliary drivebelt(s) in Chapter 1.

7 Alternator – removal and refitting

Removal

1 Disconnect the battery negative lead (see Section 4).

2 Remove the alternator drivebelt as described in Chapter 1.

M47 and M57 engines

3 Disconnect the charge air pipe from the throttle body, and move it to one side.

4 Unlock and disconnect the wiring plug, then unscrew the nut and disconnect the battery lead from the rear of the alternator **(see illustration)**.

5 Undo the bolt and remove the auxiliary drivebelt idler pulley **(see illustration)**.

6 Undo the upper and lower mounting bolt, then remove the alternator **(see illustration)**.

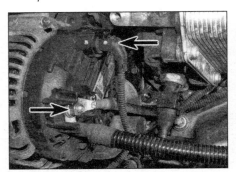

7.4 Release the clip, disconnect the wiring plug, then undo the nut (arrowed) and disconnect the lead(s)

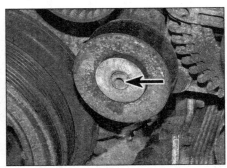

7.5 Idler pulley bolt (arrowed)

7.6 Alternator mounting bolts (arrowed)

7 To remove the alternator pulley on models with an over-running clutch, grip the alternator in a bench vice, and the pulley can be removed by inserting tool No 12 7 110 into the pulley centre and slackening the retaining bolt with a suitable Allen or Torx bit, as applicable. Suitable alternative tools are available from tool aftermarket tool manufacturers. Pull the pulley from the alternator shaft.

N47 engines

8 Unlock and disconnect the wiring plug, then unscrew the nut and disconnect the battery lead from the rear of the alternator **(see illustration)**.

9 Undo the upper and lower mounting bolt, then remove the alternator **(see illustration)**.

10 To remove the alternator pulley on models with an over-running clutch, grip the alternator in a bench vice and prise off the plastic cap, the pulley can be removed by inserting tool No 12 7 121 into the pulley centre and holding the alternator shaft with tool No 12 7 122 **(see illustrations)**. Slacken the pulley centre whilst holding the alternator shaft stationary. Suitable alternative tools are available from tool aftermarket tool manufacturers.

Refitting

11 Refitting is a reversal of removal, tightening all fasteners to their specified torque where given.

8   Alternator – testing and overhaul

If the alternator is thought to be suspect, it should be removed from the vehicle and taken to an auto-electrician for testing. Most auto-electricians will be able to supply and fit brushes at a reasonable cost. However, check on the cost of repairs before proceeding as it may prove more economical to obtain a new or exchange alternator.

9   Starting system – testing

Note: *Refer to the precautions given in 'Safety*

7.8 Disconnect the wiring from the rear of the alternator (arrowed)

first!' and in Section 1 of this Chapter before starting work.

1 If the starter motor fails to operate when the ignition key is turned to the appropriate position, the following possible causes may be to blame.

  a) *The battery is faulty.*
  b) *The electrical connections between the switch, solenoid, battery and starter motor are somewhere failing to pass the necessary current from the battery through the starter to earth.*
  c) *The solenoid is faulty.*
  d) *The starter motor is mechanically or electrically defective.*

2 To check the battery, switch on the headlights. If they dim after a few seconds, this indicates that the battery is discharged – recharge (see Section 3) or renew the battery. If the headlights glow brightly, operate the ignition switch and observe the lights. If they dim, then this indicates that current is reaching the starter motor, therefore the fault must lie in the starter motor. If the lights continue to glow brightly (and no clicking sound can be heard from the starter motor solenoid), this indicates that there is a fault in the circuit or solenoid – see following paragraphs. If the starter motor turns slowly when operated, but the battery is in good condition, then this indicates that either the starter motor is faulty, or there is considerable resistance somewhere in the circuit.

3 If a fault in the circuit is suspected, disconnect the battery leads (including the earth connection to the body), the starter/

7.9 Alternator mounting bolts (arrowed) – N47 engines

solenoid wiring and the engine/transmission earth strap. Thoroughly clean the connections, and reconnect the leads and wiring, then use a voltmeter or test lamp to check that full battery voltage is available at the battery positive lead connection to the solenoid, and that the earth is sound. Smear petroleum jelly around the battery terminals to prevent corrosion – corroded connections are amongst the most frequent causes of electrical system faults.

4 If the battery and all connections are in good condition, check the circuit by disconnecting the wire from the solenoid blade terminal. Connect a voltmeter or test lamp between the wire end and a good earth (such as the battery negative terminal), and check that the wire is live when the ignition switch is turned to the 'start' position. If it is, then the circuit is sound – if not the circuit wiring can be checked as described in Chapter 12.

5 The solenoid contacts can be checked by connecting a voltmeter or test lamp between the battery positive feed connection on the starter side of the solenoid, and earth. When the ignition switch is turned to the 'start' position, there should be a reading or lighted bulb, as applicable. If there is no reading or lighted bulb, the solenoid is faulty and should be renewed.

6 If the circuit and solenoid are proved sound, the fault must lie in the starter motor. In this event, it may be possible to have the starter motor overhauled by a specialist, but check on the cost of spares before proceeding, as it may prove more economical to obtain a new or exchange motor.

7.10a Insert the special tools into the alternator shaft and pulley centre

7.10b Hold the alternator shaft and slacken the pulley centre . . .

7.10c . . . then slide the pulley from the shaft

10 Starter motor – removal and refitting

Removal

1 Disconnect the battery negative lead (see Section 4).

M47 and M57 engines

2 Remove the air intake manifold as described in Chapter 4A.

3 Unscrew the nuts and disconnect the wiring from the starter motor **(see illustration)**. Note that the smaller connection nut is accessible once the larger, outer connection has been detached.

4 Using a socket, ratchet and long extension, undo the starter motor mounting bolts from the transmission bellhousing.

5 Pull the motor forward and manoeuvre it upwards, taking care not to damage the fuel hoses.

10.3 Starter motor wiring nuts (arrowed)

N47 engines

6 Raise the front of the vehicle and support it securely on axle stands (see *Jacking and vehicle support*).

7 Undo the fasteners and remove the engine/transmission undershields **(see illustrations)**.

8 Undo the nuts securing the wiring to the rear of the starter motor **(see illustration)**.

9 Undo the 3 bolts and remove the starter motor **(see illustration)**. **Note:** *When refitting the starter, tighten the outer mounting bolts before tightening the inner one.*

Refitting

10 Refitting is a reversal of removal. Tighten the starter motor mounting bolts to the specified torque.

11 Starter motor – testing and overhaul

If the starter motor is thought to be suspect, it should be removed from the vehicle and taken to an auto-electrician for testing. Most auto-electricians will be able to supply and fit brushes at a reasonable cost. However, check on the cost of repairs before proceeding, as it may prove more economical to obtain a new or exchange motor.

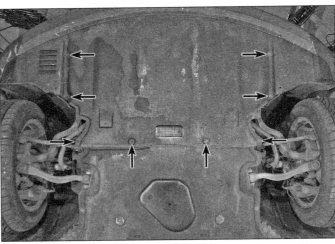

10.7a Engine/radiator undershield fasteners (arrowed)

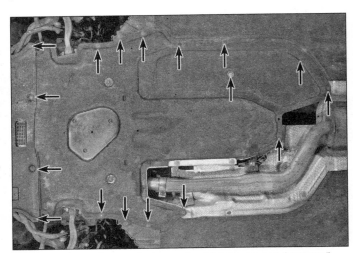

10.7b Engine/transmission undershield fasteners (arrowed)

10.8 Undo the nuts (arrowed) and disconnect the starter motor wiring

10.9 Starter motor mounting bolts (arrowed) – N47 engines

12 Diesel preheating system – description and testing

Description

1 To assist cold starting, diesel engines are fitted with a preheating system, which consists of four of glow plugs (one per cylinder), a glow plug relay unit, a facia-mounted warning lamp, the engine management ECM, and the associated electrical wiring.

2 The glow plugs are miniature electric heating elements, encapsulated in a metal case with a probe at one end and electrical connection at the other. Each combustion chamber has one glow plug threaded into it, with the tip of the glow plug probe positioned directly in line with incoming spray of fuel from the injectors. When the glow plug is energised, it heats up rapidly, causing the fuel passing over the glow plug probe to be heated to its optimum combustion temperature, ready for combustion. In addition, some of the fuel passing over the glow plugs is ignited and this helps to trigger the combustion process.

3 The preheating system begins to operate as soon as the ignition key is switched to the second position, but only if the engine coolant temperature is below 20°C and the engine is turned at more than 70 rpm for 0.2 seconds. A facia-mounted warning lamp informs the driver that preheating is taking place. The lamp extinguishes when sufficient preheating has taken place to allow the engine to be started, but power will still be supplied to the glow plugs for a further period until the engine is started. If no attempt is made to start the engine, the power supply to the glow plugs is switched off after 10 seconds, to prevent battery drain and glow plug burn-out.

4 With the electronically-controlled diesel injection systems fitted to models in this manual, the glow plug relay unit is controlled by the engine management system ECM, which determines the necessary preheating time based on inputs from the various system sensors. The system monitors the temperature of the intake air, then alters the preheating time (the length for which the glow plugs are supplied with current) to suit the conditions.

5 Post-heating takes place after the ignition key has been released from the 'Start' position, but only if the engine coolant temperature is below 20°C, the injected fuel flow is less than a certain rate, and the engine speed is less than 2000 rpm. The glow plugs continue to operate for a maximum of 60 seconds, helping to improve fuel combustion whilst the engine is warming-up, resulting in quieter, smoother running and reduced exhaust emissions.

Testing

6 If the system malfunctions, testing is ultimately by substitution of known good units, but some preliminary checks may be made as follows. Note that the preheating system is included in the vehicle's self-diagnosis system. Consequently, have the system interrogated using a fault code reader or scanner, via the vehicles diagnostic socket – see Chapter 4A.

7 Connect a voltmeter or 12 volt test lamp between the glow plug supply cable and earth (engine or vehicle metal). Make sure that the live connection is kept clear of the engine and bodywork.

8 Have an assistant switch on the ignition, and check that voltage is applied to the glow plugs. Note the time for which the warning light is lit, and the total time for which voltage is applied before the system cuts out. Switch off the ignition.

9 Warning light time will increase with lower temperatures and decrease with higher temperatures.

10 If there is no supply at all, the control unit or associated wiring is at fault.

11 To gain access to the glow plugs for further testing, refer to Chapter 4A, where necessary, and remove the intake manifold.

12 Squeeze together the side to release the clips, then pull the electrical connector from each glow plug (see illustration).

13 Use a continuity tester, or a 12 volt test lamp connected to the battery positive terminal, to check for continuity between each glow plug terminal and earth. The resistance of a glow plug in good condition is very low (less than 1 ohm), so if the test lamp does not light or the continuity tester shows a high resistance, the glow plug is certainly defective.

14 If an ammeter is available, the current draw of each glow plug can be checked. After an initial surge of 15 to 20 amps, each plug should draw 12 amps. Any plug which draws much more or less than this is probably defective.

15 As a final check, the glow plugs can be removed and inspected as described in the following Section. On completion, refit any components removed for access.

13 Glow plugs – removal, inspection and refitting

Caution: If the preheating system has just been energised, or if the engine has been running, the glow plugs will be very hot.

Removal

1 Ensure the ignition is turned off. To gain access to the glow plugs, remove the intake manifold as described in Chapter 4A.

2 Squeeze together the side to release the clips, then pull the electrical connector from each glow plug (see illustration 12.12).

3 Unscrew the glow plug(s) and remove from the cylinder head (see illustration).

Inspection

4 Inspect each glow plug for physical

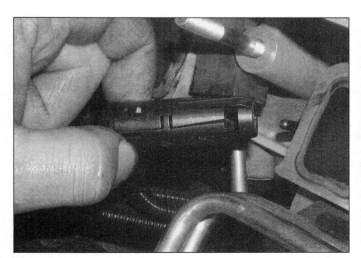

12.12 Squeeze together the ends of the connector and pull it from the glow plug

13.3 Unscrew and remove the glow plug

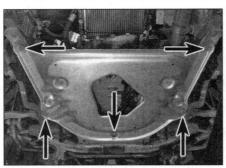

14.2 Reinforcement plate bolts (arrowed)

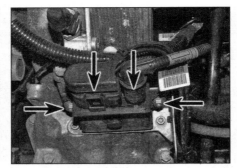

14.3 Disconnect the wiring plugs, undo the nuts and remove the glow plug control unit (arrowed) – M47 engine

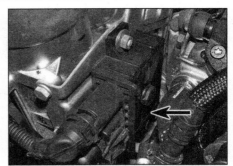

14.6 The glow plug control unit (arrowed) is located behind the oil filter housing – N47 engine

damage. Burnt or eroded glow plug tips can be caused by a bad injector spray pattern. Have the injectors checked if this sort of damage is found.

5 If the glow plugs are in good physical condition, check them electrically using a 12 volt test lamp or continuity tester as described in the previous Section.

6 The glow plugs can be energised by applying 12 volts to them to verify that they heat up evenly and in the required time. Observe the following precautions.

a) *Support the glow plug by clamping it carefully in a vice or self-locking pliers. Remember it will become red-hot.*

b) *Make sure that the power supply or test lead incorporates a fuse or overload trip to protect against damage from a short-circuit.*

c) *After testing, allow the glow plug to cool for several minutes before attempting to handle it.*

7 A glow plug in good condition will start to glow red at the tip after drawing current for 5 seconds or so. Any plug which takes much longer to start glowing, or which starts glowing in the middle instead of at the tip, is defective.

Refitting

8 Refit by reversing the removal operations. Apply a smear of copper-based anti-seize compound to the plug threads and tighten the glow plugs to the specified torque. Do not overtighten, as this can damage the glow plug element.

9 Refit any components removed for access.

14 Pre/post-heating system control/relay unit – removal and refitting

Removal

M47 engine

1 Raise the front of the vehicle and support it securely on axle stands (see *Jacking and vehicle support*). Undo the fasteners and remove the engine undershields **(see illustrations 10.7a and 10.7b)**.

2 Undo the bolts/nuts and remove the reinforcement plate from under the engine compartment **(see illustration)**. Note that new bolts/nuts will be required.

3 The relay/control unit is located on a bracket secured to the left-hand engine mounting. Disconnect the wiring plug, undo the nuts and remove the unit **(see illustration)**.

N47 engine

4 The relay is located just behind the oil filter housing. Raise the front edge, and pull the plastic cover from the top of the engine.

5 Release the clamp and disconnect the air delivery pipe from the throttle body.

6 Disconnect the wiring plug and remove the glow plug control/relay unit **(see illustration)**.

M57 engine

7 The relay is located just in front of the starter motor. Disconnect the relay wiring plugs **(see illustration)**.

8 Undo the 2 nuts and remove the relay.

Refitting

9 Refitting is a reversal of removal, ensuring that the wiring connectors are correctly connected.

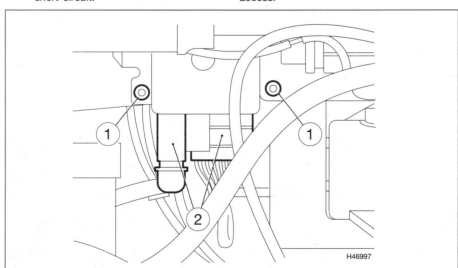

14.7 Glow plug control unit mounting nuts (1) and wiring plugs (2) – M57 engine

Chapter 6
Clutch

Contents

Degrees of difficulty

Easy, suitable for novice with little experience ≈	**Fairly easy,** suitable for beginner with some experience ≈	**Fairly difficult,** suitable for competent DIY mechanic ≈	**Difficult,** suitable for experienced DIY mechanic ≈	**Very difficult,** suitable for expert DIY or professional ≈

Specifications

Type	Single dry plate with diaphragm spring, hydraulically-operated

Driveplate

Minimum lining thickness above rivet head	1.0 mm
Diameter	240 mm

Torque wrench settings

	Nm	lbf ft
Clutch cover-to-flywheel bolts:*		
M8 grade 8.8	24	18
M8 grade 10.9	34	25
ZNS bolts:		
Stage 1	15	11
Stage 2	Angle-tighten a further 90°	
Clutch master cylinder bolts	22	16
Clutch slave cylinder nuts	22	16
Hydraulic pipe union bolts	20	15

Do not re-use

---

1 General information

All models are fitted with a single dry plate clutch, which consists of five main components; friction disc, pressure plate, diaphragm spring, cover and release bearing.

The friction disc is free to slide along the splines of the gearbox input shaft, and is held in position between the flywheel and the pressure plate by the pressure exerted on the pressure plate by the diaphragm spring. Friction lining material is riveted to both sides of the friction disc. All models are fitted with a Self-Adjusting Clutch (SAC), which compensates for friction disc wear by altering the attitude of the diaphragm spring fingers by means of a sprung mechanism within the pressure plate cover. This ensures a consistent clutch pedal 'feel' over the life of the clutch.

The diaphragm spring is mounted on pins, and is held in place in the cover by annular fulcrum rings.

The release bearing is located on a guide sleeve at the front of the gearbox, and the bearing is free to slide on the sleeve, under the action of the release arm which pivots inside the clutch bellhousing.

The release mechanism is operated by the clutch pedal, using hydraulic pressure. The pedal acts on the hydraulic master cylinder pushrod, and a slave cylinder, mounted on the gearbox bellhousing, operates the clutch release lever via a pushrod.

When the clutch pedal is depressed, the release arm pushes the release bearing forwards, to bear against the centre of the diaphragm spring, thus pushing the centre of the diaphragm spring inwards. The diaphragm spring acts against the fulcrum rings in the cover, and so as the centre of the spring is pushed in, the outside of the spring is pushed out, so allowing the pressure plate to move backwards away from the friction disc.

When the clutch pedal is released, the diaphragm spring forces the pressure plate into contact with the friction linings on the friction disc, and simultaneously pushes the friction disc forwards on its splines, forcing it against the flywheel. The friction disc is now firmly sandwiched between the pressure plate and the flywheel, and drive is taken up.

2 Clutch assembly – removal, inspection and refitting

⚠️ **Warning: Dust created by clutch wear and deposited on the clutch components may contain asbestos, which is a health hazard. DO NOT blow it out with compressed air, or inhale any of it. DO NOT use petrol (or petroleum-based solvents) to clean off the dust. Brake system cleaner or methylated spirit should be used to flush the dust into a suitable receptacle. After the clutch components are wiped clean with rags, dispose of the contaminated rags and cleaner in a sealed, marked container.**

Removal

1 Remove the gearbox, as described in Chapter 7A.
2 If the original clutch is to be refitted, make alignment marks between the clutch cover and the flywheel, so that the clutch can be refitted in its original position.
3 Progressively unscrew the bolts securing the clutch cover/pressure plate assembly to the flywheel, and where applicable recover the washers.

4 Withdraw the clutch cover from the flywheel. Be prepared to catch the clutch friction disc, which may drop out of the cover as it is withdrawn, and note which way round the friction disc is fitted – the two sides of the disc are normally marked 'Engine side' and 'Transmission side'. The greater projecting side of the hub faces away from the flywheel.

Inspection

5 With the clutch assembly removed, clean off all traces of dust using a dry cloth. Although most friction discs now have asbestos-free linings, some do not, and it is wise to take suitable precautions; *asbestos dust is harmful, and must not be inhaled.*
6 Examine the linings of the friction disc for wear and loose rivets, and the disc for distortion, cracks, and worn splines. The surface of the friction linings may be highly glazed, but, as long as the friction material pattern can be clearly seen, this is satisfactory. If there is any sign of oil contamination, indicated by a continuous, or patchy, shiny black discolouration, the disc must be renewed. The source of the contamination must be traced and rectified before fitting new clutch components; typically, a leaking crankshaft rear oil seal or gearbox input shaft oil seal – or both – will be to blame (renewal procedures are given in the relevant Part of Chapter 2, and Chapter 7A respectively). The disc must also be renewed if the lining thickness has worn down to, or just above, the level of the rivet heads. Note that BMW specify a minimum friction material thickness above the heads of the rivets (see Specifications).
7 Check the machined faces of the flywheel and pressure plate. If either is grooved, or heavily scored, renewal is necessary. The pressure plate must also be renewed if any cracks are apparent, or if the diaphragm spring is damaged or its pressure suspect.
8 With the clutch removed, it is advisable to check the condition of the release bearing, as described in Section 3.

9 Check the spigot bearing in the end of the crankshaft. Make sure that it turns smoothly and quietly. If the gearbox input shaft contact face on the bearing is worn or damaged, fit a new bearing, as described in the relevant Part of Chapter 2.

Refitting

10 If new clutch components are to be fitted, where applicable, ensure that all anti-corrosion preservative is cleaned from the friction material on the disc, and the contact surfaces of the pressure plate.
11 It is important to ensure that no oil or grease gets onto the friction disc linings, or the pressure plate and flywheel faces. It is advisable to refit the clutch assembly with clean hands, and to wipe down the pressure plate and flywheel faces with a clean rag before assembly begins.
12 Offer the disc to the flywheel, with the greater projecting side of the hub facing away from the flywheel (most friction discs will have an 'Engine side' or Transmission side' marking which should face the flywheel or gearbox as applicable) **(see illustration)**. Using a suitable BMW tool or a suitable alternative manufactured by an automotive tool specialist, centre the friction disc in the flywheel **(see illustration)**.
13 If the original pressure plate and cover is to be refitted, engage the legs of BMW tool 21 2 170 with the cover in the area of the adjusting springs. Screw down the knurled collar to lock the legs in place, then tighten down the spindle to compress the diaphragm spring. Using a screwdriver, reset the self-adjusting mechanism by pushing the adjustment ring thrust pieces fully anti-clockwise, whilst undoing the special tool spindle only enough to allow the adjustment ring to move. With the adjustment ring reset, tighten down the special tool spindle to compress the spring fingers, whilst preventing the adjustment ring thrust pieces from moving by inserting metal spacers in the gap between

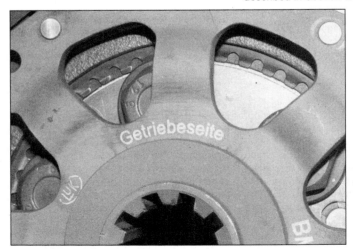

2.12a The friction disc may be marked 'Getriebeseite' meaning 'Gearbox side'

2.12b Use a suitable tool to centre the friction disc

2.13a Use BMW tool 21 2 170 to compress the diaphragm spring

2.13b Push the adjustment ring thrust pieces (arrowed) fully anti-clockwise . . .

2.13c . . . and insert metal spacers between the thrust pieces and the cover

2.13d A special BMW tool is available to reset the adjustment ring thrust pieces

2.14 Ensure the cover locates over the flywheel dowels

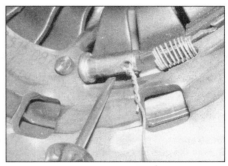

2.16 Keep all fingers away when removing the metal spacers

the thrust pieces and the cover. Note that a special tool is available from BMW to reset the adjustment ring **(see illustrations)**

14 Fit the clutch cover assembly, where applicable aligning the marks on the flywheel and clutch cover. Ensure that the clutch cover locates over the dowels on the flywheel **(see illustration)**. Insert the securing bolts and washers, and tighten them to the specified torque.

15 If a new pressure plate cover was fitted, insert a 14 mm Allen key into the centre of the diaphragm spring locking piece, and turn it clockwise and remove it to release the spring.

16 Where the original pressure plate cover was refitted, undo the spindle and knurled collar, then remove the compression tool from the cover. Prise out the metal spacers holding the adjustment ring thrust pieces in place **(see illustration)**.

Caution: As the last spacer is withdrawn, the adjustment ring may spring into place. Ensure all fingers are clear of the area.

17 If the BMW centring tool was used, remove the tool by screwing a 10 mm bolt into its end and pulling using a pair of pliers or similar **(see illustration)**.

18 Refit the gearbox as described in Chapter 7A.

3 Clutch release bearing and lever – removal, inspection and refitting

> ⚠ *Warning: Dust created by clutch wear and deposited on the clutch components may contain asbestos, which is a health hazard.*

DO NOT blow it out with compressed air, or inhale any of it. DO NOT use petrol (or petroleum-based solvents) to clean off the dust. Brake system cleaner or methylated spirit should be used to flush the dust into a suitable receptacle. After the clutch components are wiped clean with rags, dispose of the contaminated rags and cleaner in a sealed, marked container.

Removal

1 Remove the gearbox as described in Chapter 7A.

2 Slide the release lever sideways to release it from the retaining spring clip and pivot, then pull the lever and bearing forwards from the guide sleeve **(see illustration)**.

3 Do not detach the release bearing from the lever. The bearing is only available as a complete assembly with the lever.

Inspection

4 Spin the release bearing, and check it for excessive roughness. Hold the outer race, and attempt to move it laterally against the inner race. If any excessive movement or roughness is evident, renew the bearing. If a new clutch has been fitted, it is wise to renew the release bearing as a matter of course.

5 Inspect the release bearing, pivot and slave cylinder pushrod contact faces on the release lever for wear. Renew the lever if excessive wear is evident.

6 Check the release lever retaining spring clip, and renew if necessary. It is advisable to renew the clip as a matter of course.

2.17 Thread the bolt into the end of the centring tool, and pull it out

3.2 Slide the release lever sideways to disengage it from the retaining clip (arrowed)

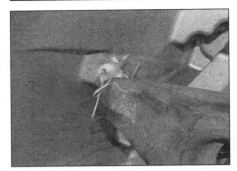

3.8 Ensure the lever engages correctly with the retaining clip

4.4 Fluid pipe union nut (arrowed)

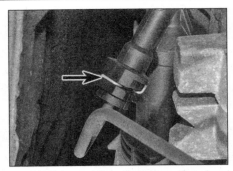

4.7 Prise out the clip (arrowed) and disconnect the fluid pipe

Refitting

7 Clean the release bearing contact surfaces on the release lever and guide sleeve. Do not apply any grease or lubricant to the sliding surfaces of the bearing or guide sleeve.

8 Slide the release lever/bearing assembly into position over the guide sleeve, then push the end of the lever over the pivot, ensuring that the retaining spring clip engages correctly over the end of the release lever **(see illustration)**.

9 Refit the gearbox, referring to Chapter 7A.

4 Hydraulic slave cylinder – removal, inspection and refitting

⚠️ **Warning: Hydraulic fluid is poisonous; wash off immediately and thoroughly in the case of skin contact, and seek immediate medical advice if any fluid is swallowed or gets into the eyes. Certain types of hydraulic fluid are inflammable, and may ignite when allowed into contact with hot components; when servicing any hydraulic system, it is safest to assume that the fluid is inflammable, and to take precautions against the risk of fire as though it is petrol that is being handled. Hydraulic fluid is also an effective paint stripper, and will attack plastics; if any is spilt, it should be washed off immediately, using copious quantities of fresh water. Finally, it is hygroscopic (it absorbs moisture from the air) – old fluid may be contaminated and unfit for further use. When topping-up or renewing the fluid, always use the recommended type, and ensure that it comes from a freshly-opened sealed container.**

Removal

1 Remove the brake fluid reservoir cap, and siphon out sufficient hydraulic fluid so that the fluid level is below the level of the reservoir fluid hose connection to the clutch master cylinder (the brake fluid reservoir feeds both the brake and clutch hydraulic systems). **Do not** empty the reservoir, as this will draw air into the brake hydraulic circuits.

2 To improve access, jack up the vehicle, and

support it securely on axle stands (see *Jacking and vehicle support*).

3 Release the bolts and remove the underbody shield (where fitted) for access to the gearbox bellhousing.

Metal slave cylinder

4 Place a container beneath the hydraulic pipe connection on the clutch slave cylinder to catch escaping hydraulic fluid. Unscrew the union nut and disconnect the fluid pipe **(see illustration)**

5 Unscrew the securing nuts, and withdraw the slave cylinder from the mounting studs on the bellhousing.

Plastic slave cylinder

6 Undo the two securing nuts and withdrawn the slave cylinder from the mounting studs on the transmission.

7 Prise out the retaining clip, and disconnect the fluid pipe from the cylinder **(see illustration)**.

Inspection

8 Inspect the slave cylinder for fluid leaks and damage, and renew if necessary. At the time of writing, no spare parts are available for the slave cylinder, and if faulty, the complete unit must be renewed. Check with your dealer or specialist.

Refitting

9 On models with a plastic slave cylinder, press the piston into the cylinder, then reconnect the fluid pipe. Refill the fluid reservoir, then extend and compress the

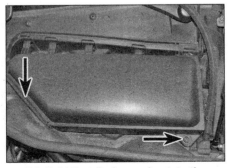

5.3 Fold the clip forward, rotate the fastener 90° anti-clockwise (arrowed) and remove the pollen filter cover each side

piston in the cylinder five times whilst holding the cylinder vertical.

10 The remainder of refitting is a reversal of removal, bearing in mind the following points.

 a) *Before refitting, clean and then lightly grease the end of the slave cylinder pushrod.*

 b) *Tighten the mounting nuts to the specified torque.*

 c) *On completion, top-up the hydraulic fluid level and bleed the clutch hydraulic circuit as described in Section 6.*

5 Hydraulic master cylinder – removal, inspection and refitting

⚠️ **Warning: Hydraulic fluid is poisonous; wash off immediately and thoroughly in the case of skin contact, and seek immediate medical advice if any fluid is swallowed or gets into the eyes. Certain types of hydraulic fluid are inflammable, and may ignite when allowed into contact with hot components; when servicing any hydraulic system, it is safest to assume that the fluid is inflammable, and to take precautions against the risk of fire as though it is petrol that is being handled. Hydraulic fluid is also an effective paint stripper, and will attack plastics; if any is spilt, it should be washed off immediately, using copious quantities of fresh water. Finally, it is hygroscopic (it absorbs moisture from the air) – old fluid may be contaminated and unfit for further use. When topping-up or renewing the fluid, always use the recommended type, and ensure that it comes from a freshly-opened sealed container.**

Removal

1 Remove the driver's side lower facia panel as described in Chapter 11.

2 Release the clip and slide the light module rearwards from the bracket. Allow the module to lay on the floor, but protect it from fluid spillage.

3 Working at the rear of the engine compartment, undo the bolt, fold forwards the clip, and remove the right- and left-hand pollen filter covers **(see illustration)**.

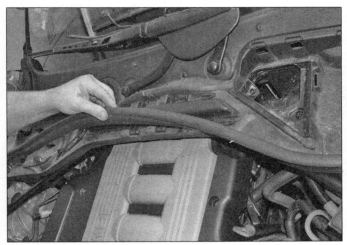

5.4a Pull up the rubber strip . . .

5.4b . . . then lift the clip and slide the panel to the left

5.5a Lift out the trim each end . . .

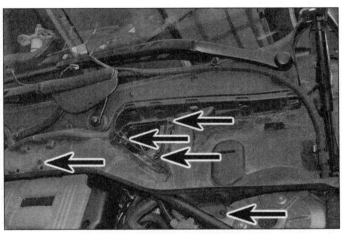

5.5b . . . then rotate the fasteners 90° anti-clockwise, undo the bolt and lift out the pollen filter housing each side (left-hand housing fasteners/bolt arrowed)

4 Pull up the rubber sealing strip, then release the clip and slide the plastic cover from the centre of the panel (see illustrations).

5 Lift out the plastic trim, undo the bolts/fasteners and remove the right-hand plastic cover from behind the suspension turret. Unclip the wiring where applicable (see illustrations).

6 Remove the brake fluid reservoir cap, and siphon out sufficient hydraulic fluid so that the fluid level is below the level of the reservoir fluid hose connection to the clutch master cylinder (the brake fluid reservoir feeds both the brake and clutch hydraulic systems). Do not empty the reservoir, as this will draw air into the brake hydraulic circuits.

7 Disconnect the clutch master cylinder hose from the brake fluid reservoir. Be prepared for fluid spillage, and plug the open end of the hose to prevent dirt entry.

8 Disconnect the lower end of the return spring from the clutch pedal.

9 Remove the retaining clip, then push out the cylinder pushrod pin from the pedal (see illustration).

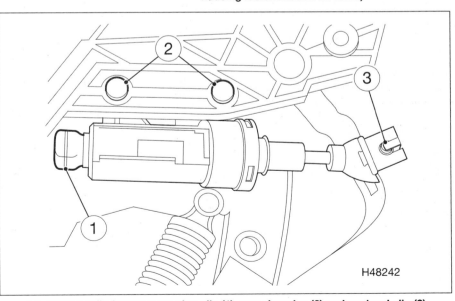

H48242

5.9 Master cylinder pressure pipe clip (1), securing pins (2) and pushrod clip (3)

10 Using a small screwdriver, prise out the retaining clip and then pull the master cylinder from the hydraulic pressure pipe **(see illustration 5.9)**. Be prepared for fluid spillage.

11 Prise out the pins securing the master cylinder to the pedal bracket, and manoeuvre the cylinder from place **(see illustration 5.9)**. Discard the pins, new ones must be fitted.

12 Depress the locking tab, and disconnect the master cylinder switch wiring plug (where fitted). If required, carefully release the clips and detach the switch from the cylinder.

Inspection

13 Inspect the master cylinder for fluid leaks and damage, and renew if necessary. At the time of writing, no spare parts were available for the master cylinder, and if faulty the complete unit must be renewed. Check with your local dealer or parts supplier.

Refitting

14 Refitting is a reversal of removal, bearing in mind the following points.
   a) Take care not to strain the master cylinder fluid pipe during refitting.
   b) On completion, top-up the level in the brake fluid reservoir, then bleed the clutch hydraulic system (see Section 6).

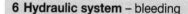

6 Hydraulic system – bleeding

⚠ *Warning: Hydraulic fluid is poisonous; wash off immediately and thoroughly in the case of skin contact, and seek immediate medical advice if any fluid is swallowed or gets into the eyes. Certain types of hydraulic fluid are inflammable, and may ignite when allowed into contact with hot components; when servicing any hydraulic system, it is safest to assume that the fluid is inflammable, and to take precautions against the risk of fire as though it is petrol that is being handled. Hydraulic fluid is also an effective paint stripper, and will attack plastics; if any is spilt, it should be washed off immediately, using copious quantities of fresh water. Finally, it is hygroscopic (it absorbs moisture from the air) – old fluid may be contaminated and unfit for further use. When topping-up or renewing the fluid, always use the recommended type, and ensure that it comes from a freshly-opened sealed container.*
Note: *BMW recommend that pressure-bleeding equipment is used to bleed the clutch hydraulic system.*

General

1 The correct operation of any hydraulic system is only possible after removing all air from the components and circuit; this is achieved by bleeding the system.

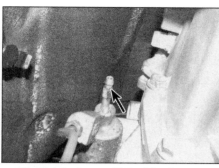

6.7 Clutch slave cylinder bleed screw (arrowed)

2 During the bleeding procedure, add only clean, unused hydraulic fluid of the recommended type; never re-use fluid that has already been bled from the system. Ensure that sufficient fluid is available before starting work.

3 If there is any possibility of incorrect fluid being already in the system, the brake and clutch components and circuit must be flushed completely with uncontaminated, correct fluid, and new seals should be fitted to the various components.

4 If hydraulic fluid has been lost from the system, or air has entered because of a leak, ensure that the fault is cured before proceeding further.

5 To improve access, apply the handbrake, then jack up the front of the vehicle, and support it securely on axle stands (see *Jacking and vehicle support*).

6 Undo the bolts and remove the underbody shield (where fitted) for access to the gearbox bellhousing.

7 Check that the clutch hydraulic pipe(s) and hose(s) are secure, that the unions are tight, and that the bleed screw on the rear of the clutch slave cylinder (mounted under the vehicle on the lower left-hand side of the gearbox bellhousing) is closed. Clean any dirt from around the bleed screw **(see illustration)**.

8 Access the fluid reservoir as described in Paragraghs 3 to 5 of Section 5, then unscrew the brake fluid reservoir cap, and top the fluid up to the MAX level line; refit the cap loosely, and remember to maintain the fluid level at least above the MIN level line throughout the procedure, or there is a risk of further air entering the system. Note that the brake fluid reservoir feeds both the brake and clutch hydraulic systems.

9 It is recommended that pressure-bleeding equipment is used to bleed the system. Alternatively, there are a number of one-man, do-it-yourself brake bleeding kits currently available from motor accessory shops. These kits greatly simplify the bleeding operation, and also reduce the risk of expelled air and fluid being drawn back into the system. If such a kit is not available, the basic (two-man) method must be used, which is described in detail below.

10 If pressure-bleeding equipment or a one-man kit is to be used, prepare the vehicle as described previously, and follow the equipment/kit manufacturer's instructions, as the procedure may vary slightly according to the type being used; generally, they are as outlined below in the relevant sub-section.

11 Whichever method is used, the same basic process must be followed to ensure that the removal of all air from the system.

Bleeding

Basic (two-man) method

12 Collect a clean glass jar, a suitable length of plastic or rubber tubing which is a tight fit over the bleed screw, and a ring spanner to fit the screw. The help of an assistant will also be required.

13 Where applicable, remove the dust cap from the bleed screw. Fit the spanner and tube to the screw, place the other end of the tube in the jar, and pour in sufficient fluid to cover the end of the tube.

14 Ensure that the reservoir fluid level is maintained at least above the MIN level line throughout the procedure.

15 Have the assistant fully depress the clutch pedal several times to build-up pressure, then maintain it on the final downstroke.

16 While pedal pressure is maintained, unscrew the bleed screw (approximately one turn) and allow the compressed fluid and air to flow into the jar. The assistant should maintain pedal pressure, following it down to the floor if necessary, and should not release it until instructed to do so. When the flow stops, tighten the bleed screw again, have the assistant release the pedal slowly, and recheck the reservoir fluid level.

17 Repeat the steps given in paragraphs 15 and 16 until the fluid emerging from the bleed screw is free from air bubbles.

18 When no more air bubbles appear, tighten the bleed screw securely. Do not overtighten the bleed screw.

19 Temporarily disconnect the bleed tube from the bleed screw, and move the container of fluid to one side.

20 Unscrew the two securing nuts, and withdraw the slave cylinder from the bellhousing, taking care not to strain the fluid hose.

21 Reconnect the bleed tube to the bleed screw, and submerge the end of the tube in the container of fluid.

22 With the bleed screw pointing vertically upwards, unscrew the bleed screw (approximately one turn), and slowly push the slave cylinder pushrod into the cylinder until no more air bubbles appear in the fluid.

23 Hold the pushrod in position, then tighten the bleed screw.

24 Slowly allow the pushrod to return to its rest position. Do not allow the pushrod to return quickly, as this will cause air to enter the slave cylinder.

25 Remove the tube and spanner, and refit the dust cap to the bleed screw.

26 Refit the slave cylinder to the bellhousing, and tighten the securing nuts to the specified torque.

Using a one-way valve kit

27 As their name implies, these kits consist of a length of tubing with a one-way valve fitted, to prevent expelled air and fluid being drawn back into the system; some kits include a translucent container, which can be positioned so that the air bubbles can be more easily seen flowing from the end of the tube.

28 The kit is connected to the bleed screw, which is then opened. The user returns to the driver's seat, depresses the clutch pedal with a smooth, steady stroke, and slowly releases it; this is repeated until the expelled fluid is clear of air bubbles.

29 Note that these kits simplify work so much that it is easy to forget the reservoir fluid level; ensure that this is maintained at least above the MIN level line at all times.

Using a pressure-bleeding kit

30 These kits are usually operated by the reservoir of pressurised air contained in the spare tyre. However, note that it will probably be necessary to reduce the pressure to a lower level than normal; refer to the instructions supplied with the kit.

31 By connecting a pressurised, fluid-filled container to the fluid reservoir, bleeding can be carried out simply by opening the bleed screw, and allowing the fluid to flow out until no more air bubbles can be seen in the expelled fluid.

32 This method has the advantage that the large reservoir of fluid provides an additional safeguard against air being drawn into the system during bleeding.

All methods

33 If after following the instructions given, it is suspected that air is still present in hydraulic system, remove the slave cylinder (Section 4) without disconnecting the hydraulic pipes, push the cylinder piston all the way in, and holding the cylinder with the bleed screw uppermost, bleed the system again. **Note:** *Steps must be taken to ensure that the slave cylinder piston is prevented from extending during the bleeding procedure. If necessary, use a metal strip and two threaded bars to fabricate a tool to hold the piston in.*

34 When bleeding is complete, and firm pedal feel is restored, wash off any spilt fluid, check that the bleed screw is tightened securely, and refit the dust cap.

35 Check the hydraulic fluid level in the reservoir, and top-up if necessary (*Weekly checks*). Refit the plastic cover over the reservoir.

36 Discard any hydraulic fluid that has been bled from the system; it will not be fit for re-use.

37 Check the feel of the clutch pedal. If it feels at all spongy, air must still be present in the system, and further bleeding is required. Failure to bleed satisfactorily after a reasonable repetition of the bleeding procedure may be due to worn master or slave cylinder seals.

38 On completion, where applicable refit the underbody shield (where fitted) and lower the vehicle to the ground.

7 Clutch pedal – removal and refitting

Removal

1 Remove the driver's side lower facia panel as described in Chapter 11.

2 Disconnect the wiring plug, undo the retaining bolt, and remove the CAS (Car Access System) control module.

3 Remove the retaining clip, then press out the master cylinder pushrod pivot pin from the clutch pedal.

4 Disconnect the lower end of the return spring from the pedal.

5 Squeeze together the clips at the end, then prise out the pivot pin, and remove the pedal. Recover the pivot bushes if they are loose. Discard the pivot pin – a new one must be fitted.

Refitting

6 Refitting is a reversal of removal. Ensure that the clutch switch plunger is fully extended prior to refitment (where fitted).

Notes

Chapter 7 Part A:
Manual gearbox

Contents

Degrees of difficulty

Easy, suitable for novice with little experience	**Fairly easy,** suitable for beginner with some experience	**Fairly difficult,** suitable for competent DIY mechanic	**Difficult,** suitable for experienced DIY mechanic	**Very difficult,** suitable for expert DIY or professional

Specifications

Type

4-cylinder engine:	
N47	GS6-17BG/DG or 37BZ/DZ
M47T2	GS6-37BZ/DZ
6-cylinder engine	GS6-53BZ/DZ

Lubrication

Capacity (approx):

GS6-17BG/DG (I type) transmission	1.3 litres
GS6-37BZ/DZ (H type) transmission	1.5 litres
GS6-53DZ/BZ (G type) transmission	1.5 litres

Torque wrench settings

	Nm	lbf ft
Gearbox crossmember-to-body bolts:		
M8 bolts	21	15
M10 bolts	42	31
Gearbox mounting-to-gearbox nuts:		
M8 nuts	21	15
M10 nuts	42	31
Gearbox-to-engine bolts:		
Hexagon head bolts:		
M8 bolts	25	18
M10 bolts	49	36
M12 bolts	74	55
Torx head bolts:		
M8 bolts	22	16
M10 bolts	43	32
M12 bolts	72	53
Oil filler/level and drain plugs:		
GS6-17 transmission	45	33
GS6-37 transmission:		
M12	25	18
M18	35	26
GS6-53 transmission	35	26

Torque wrench settings (continued)

	Nm	lbf ft
Output flange-to-output shaft nut:*		
GS6-17 and GS6-37 transmissions:		
Stage 1	170	125
Stage 2	Fully loosen nut	
Stage 3	120	89
GS6-53 transmission:		
Stage 1	200	148
Stage 2	Fully loosen nut	
Stage 3	140	103
Reinforcement plate fasteners:†		
Stage 1	56	41
Stage 2	Angle-tighten a further 90°	
Reversing light switch	16	12

Coat the threads of the nut with thread-locking compound.

†*Do not re-use*

1 General information

The gearbox is a 6-speed unit, and is contained in a cast-alloy casing bolted to the rear of the engine.

Drive is transmitted from the crankshaft via the clutch to the input shaft, which has a splined extension to accept the clutch friction plate. The output shaft transmits the drive via the propeller shaft to the rear differential.

The input shaft runs in line with the output shaft. The input shaft and output shaft gears are in constant mesh with the layshaft gear cluster. Selection of gears is by sliding synchromesh hubs, which lock the appropriate output shaft gears to the output shaft.

Gear selection is via a floor-mounted lever and selector mechanism or, depending on model, switches mounted on the steering wheel. A Sequential Manual Gearbox (SMG) option is available for some models, where the gearchanges can be performed sequentially using the floor mounted lever, or the 'paddle' shift switches on the steering wheel. On models so equipped, the gearchanges can be performed automatically, with the electronic control module (ECM) controlling gearchange and clutch operation (via hydraulic controls), dictated by driving style and road conditions. A 'launch control' is available on some models, where at the press of a button, the ECM will control engine speed, clutch operation and gearchange functions, to achieve maximum acceleration – consult your owners handbook for further details.

The selector mechanism causes the appropriate selector fork to move its respective synchro-sleeve along the shaft, to lock the gear pinion to the synchro-hub. Since the synchro-hubs are splined to the output shaft, this locks the pinion to the shaft, so that drive can be transmitted. To ensure that gearchanging can be made quickly and quietly, a synchromesh system is fitted to all forward gears, consisting of baulk rings and spring-loaded fingers, as well as the gear pinions and synchro-hubs. The synchromesh cones are formed on the mating faces of the baulk rings and gear pinions.

The transmission is filled during production, and is then considered 'filled for life', with BMW making no recommendations concerning the changing of the fluid.

2 Manual gearbox oil level check

1 To improve access, jack up the vehicle and support on axle stands (see *Jacking and vehicle support*). Ensure that the car is level. Undo the fasteners and remove the undershield beneath the transmission (where fitted) (see illustration).

2 Unscrew the gearbox oil level/filler plug from the right-hand side of the gearbox casing (see illustration).

3 The oil level should be up to the bottom of the level/filler plug hole.

4 If necessary, top-up the level, using the correct type of fluid (see *Lubricants and fluids*) until the oil overflows from the filler/level plug hole.

5 Wipe away any spilt oil, then refit the filler/level plug, and tighten to the specified torque.

6 Refit the transmission undershield (where fitted) and lower the vehicle to the ground.

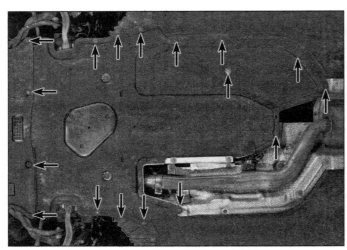

2.1 Undo the fasteners (arrowed) and remove the shield beneath the transmission

2.2 Oil filler/level plug (arrowed)

3.3 Oil drain plug (arrowed)

4.5 Squeeze in the sides, and prise up the gear lever gaiter

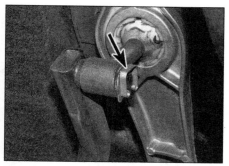

4.6 Slide the retaining clip (arrowed) from the selector rod pin

3 Manual gearbox oil renewal

Note: *New gearbox oil drain plug and oil filler/level plug sealing rings may be required on refitting.*

1 The gearbox oil should be drained with the gearbox at normal operating temperature. If the car has just been driven at least 20 miles, the gearbox can be considered warm.

2 Immediately after driving the car, park it on a level surface, apply the handbrake. If desired, jack up the car and support on axle stands (see *Jacking and vehicle support*) to improve access, but make sure that the car is level. Remove the transmission undershield **(see illustration 2.1)**.

3 Working under the car, slacken the gearbox oil drain plug about half a turn **(see illustration)**. Position a draining container under the drain plug, then remove the plug completely. If possible, try to keep the plug pressed into the gearbox while unscrewing it by hand the last couple of turns.

HAYNES HINT *As the plug releases from the threads, move it away sharply so the stream of fluid from the gearbox runs into the container, not up your sleeve.*

4 Where applicable, recover the sealing ring from the drain plug.

5 Refit the drain plug, using a new sealing ring where applicable, and tighten to the specified torque.

6 Unscrew the oil filler/level plug from the side of the gearbox, and recover the sealing ring, where applicable **(see illustration 2.2)**.

7 Fill the gearbox through the filler/level plug hole with the specified quantity and type of oil (see Specifications and *Lubricants and fluids*), until the oil overflows from the filler/level plug hole.

8 Refit the filler/level plug, using a new sealing ring where applicable, and tighten to the specified torque.

9 Where applicable, lower the car to the ground.

4 Gearchange components – removal and refitting

Manual gear lever assembly

Note: *A new gear lever bearing will be required on refitting.*

Removal

1 Jack up the car and support securely on axle stands (see *Jacking and vehicle support*). Undo the fasteners and remove the undershield beneath the transmission (where fitted) **(see illustration 2.1)**.

2 Remove the exhaust system as described in Chapter 4A.

3 Undo the fasteners and remove the heat shield from beneath the propeller shaft.

4 Pull the gear knob straight up from the lever with a sharp tug.

5 Push in the sides and free the gear lever gaiter from the centre console **(see illustration)**.

6 Prise the securing clip from the end of the gear selector rod pin. Withdraw the selector rod pin from the eye on the end of the gear lever **(see illustration)**.

7 It is now necessary to release the gear lever lower bearing retaining ring from the gear selector arm. A special tool is available for this purpose, but two screwdrivers, with the tips engaged in opposite slots in the bearing ring can be used instead. To unlock the bearing ring, turn it a quarter-turn anti-clockwise **(see illustration)**.

8 The bearing can now be pushed up through the housing, and the gear lever can be withdrawn from inside the vehicle.

9 If desired, the bearing can be removed from the gear lever ball by pressing it downwards. To withdraw the bearing over the lever eye, rotate the bearing until the eye passes through the slots provided in the bearing.

10 Fit a new bearing using a reversal of the removal process. Ensure that the bearing is pressed securely into position on the gear lever ball.

Refitting

11 Refit the lever using a reversal of the removal process, bearing in mind the following points.

  a) Grease the contact faces of the bearing before refitting.

  b) Lower the gear lever into position, ensuring that the arrow on the gear lever grommet points towards the front of the vehicle.

  c) Make sure that the gear lever grommet is correctly engaged with the gear selector arm and with the opening in the vehicle floor **(see illustration)**.

  d) When engaging the bearing with the selector arm, make sure that the arrows or tabs (as applicable) on the top of the bearing point towards the rear of the vehicle.

  e) To lock the bearing in position in the

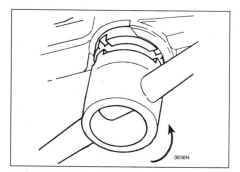

4.7 Turn the bearing ring anti-clockwise – special tool shown

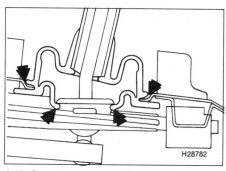

4.11 Gear lever grommet correctly engaged with the selector arm and vehicle floor

selector arm, press down on the top of the bearing retaining tab locations until the tabs are heard to click into position.

f) *Grease the selector rod pin before engaging it with the gear lever eye.*

Automatic gearchange (SMG)

12 No information was available at the time of writing.

5 Oil seals – renewal

Input shaft oil seal

1 With the gearbox removed as described in Section 7, proceed as follows.

2 Remove the clutch release bearing and lever as described in Chapter 6.

3 Unscrew the securing bolts and withdraw the clutch release bearing guide sleeve from the gearbox bellhousing **(see illustration)**.

4 Note the fitted depth of the now-exposed input shaft oil seal.

5 Drill one small hole in the oil seal (two small pilot holes should be provided at opposite points on the seal). Coat the end of the drill bit with grease to prevent any swarf from the holes entering the gearbox **(see illustration)**.

6 Using a small drift, tap one side of the seal (opposite to the hole) into the bellhousing as far as the stop.

7 Screw a small self-tapping screw into the opposite side of the seal, and use pliers to pull out the seal **(see illustration)**.

8 Clean the oil seal seating surface.

9 Lubricate the lips of the new oil seal with a little clean gearbox oil, then carefully slide the seal over the input shaft into position in the bellhousing.

10 Tap the oil seal into the bellhousing to the previously-noted depth.

11 Refit the guide sleeve to the gearbox housing, tighten the retaining bolts securely, using a drop of locking compound on the threads of the bolts.

12 Refit the clutch release lever and bearing as described in Chapter 6.

13 Refit the gearbox as described in Section 7, then check the gearbox oil level as described in Section 2.

Output flange oil seal

Note: *Thread-locking compound will be required for the gearbox flange nut on refitting.*

14 Jack up the vehicle and support securely on axle stands (see *Jacking and vehicle support*).

15 Disconnect the propeller shaft from the gearbox flange, and support it clear of the gearbox using wire or string. See Chapter 8 for details.

16 Where applicable, prise the gearbox flange nut cover plate from the flange using a screwdriver. Discard the cover plate – it is not required on refitting. If necessary, support the transmission, and remove the transmission crossmember to improve access.

17 Counterhold the gearbox flange by bolting

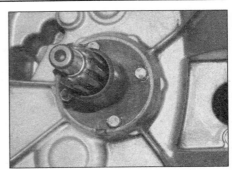

5.3 Undo the bolts securing the release bearing guide sleeve

a forked or two-legged tool to two of the flange bolt holes, then unscrew the flange securing nut using a deep socket and extension bar **(see illustration)**.

18 Using a puller, draw the flange from the end of the gearbox output shaft **(see illustration)**. Be prepared for oil spillage.

19 Note the fitted depth of the oil seal then, using an oil seal puller or remover (take care to avoid damage to the gearbox output shaft), pull/prise the oil seal from the gearbox casing **(see illustration)**.

20 Clean the oil seal seating surface.

21 Lubricate the lips of the new oil seal with a little clean gearbox oil, then carefully tap the seal into the gearbox casing to the to the previously-noted depth using a suitable tubular spacer or socket that bears only on the hard, outer edge of the seal **(see illustration)**.

5.5 Drill a small hole in the oil seal

5.7 Insert a self-tapping screw into the hole and pull the seal from place using pliers

5.17 Counterhold the output flange and undo the nut using a deep socket

5.18 Use a three-legged puller to remove the output flange

5.19 Carefully pull the seal from place

5.21 Tap the seal into place using a socket or tube

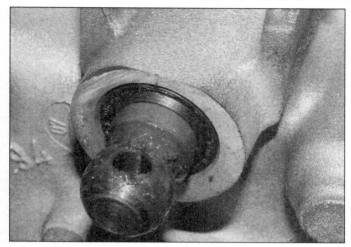

5.31 Tap the new selector shaft oil seal into position

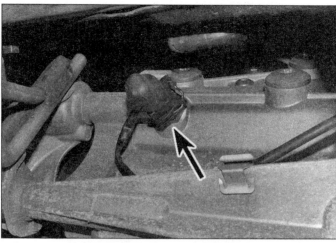

6.4 The reversing light switch (arrowed) is on the right-hand side of the transmission

22 Refit the flange to the output shaft. **Note:** *To ease refitment of the flange, immerse it in hot water for a few minutes, then install it on the shaft.*

23 Tighten the flange nut to the Stage one torque setting, then slacken and remove the nut (Stage two). Coat the threads of the flange nut with thread-locking compound, then tighten the nut to the Stage three torque as specified. Counterhold the flange as during removal.

24 If a flange nut cover plate was originally fitted, discard it. There is no need to fit a cover plate on refitting.

25 Reconnect the propeller shaft to the gearbox flange as described in Chapter 8, then check the gearbox oil level as described in Section 2, and lower the vehicle to the ground.

Gear selector shaft oil seal

Note: *A new selector shaft eye securing roll-pin will be required on refitting.*

26 Jack up the vehicle and support securely on axle stands (see *Jacking and vehicle support*).

27 Disconnect the propeller shaft from the gearbox flange, and support it clear of the gearbox using wire or string. Refer to Chapter 8 for details. For improved access, support the transmission, and remove the transmission crossmember.

28 Slide back the locking collar, then slide out the pin securing the gear selector shaft eye to the end of the gear selector shaft.

29 Pull the gear selector shaft eye (complete with gear linkage) off the end of the selector shaft, and move the linkage clear of the selector shaft.

30 Using a small flat-bladed screwdriver, prise the selector shaft oil seal from the gearbox casing.

31 Clean the oil seal seating surface, then tap the new seal into position using a small

socket or tube of the correct diameter **(see illustration)**.

32 Check the condition of the rubber washer in the end of the selector shaft eye and renew if necessary.

33 Push the selector shaft eye back onto the end of the selector shaft, then align the holes in the eye and shaft and secure the eye to the shaft using the pin.

34 Slide the locking collar into position over the roll-pin.

35 Reconnect the propeller shaft to the gearbox flange as described in Chapter 8.

36 Check the gearbox oil level as described in Section 2, then lower the vehicle to the ground.

6 Reversing light switch – testing, removal and refitting

Testing

1 The reversing light circuit is controlled by a plunger-type switch screwed into the right-hand side of the gearbox casing. If a fault develops in the circuit, first ensure that the circuit fuse has not blown.

2 To test the switch, disconnect the wiring connector, and use a multimeter (set to the resistance function) or a battery-and-bulb test circuit to check that there is continuity between the switch terminals only when reverse gear is selected. If this is not the case, and there are no obvious breaks or other damage to the wires, the switch is faulty, and must be renewed.

Removal

3 Jack up the vehicle and support securely on axle stands (see *Jacking and vehicle support*). Undo the fasteners and remove

the transmission undershield **(see illustration 2.1)**.

4 Disconnect the wiring connector, then unscrew the switch from the gearbox casing **(see illustration)**.

Refitting

5 Screw the switch back into position in the gearbox housing and tighten it securely. Reconnect the wiring connector, and test the operation of the circuit.

6 Lower the vehicle to the ground.

7 Manual gearbox – removal and refitting

Note: *This is an involved operation. Read through the procedure thoroughly before starting work, and ensure that adequate lifting tackle or jacking/support equipment is available.*

Removal

1 Disconnect the battery negative lead (see Chapter 5).

2 Jack up the car and support securely on axle stands (see *Jacking and vehicle support*). Note that the car must be raised sufficiently to allow clearance for the gearbox to be removed from under the car. Undo the bolts and remove the engine/transmission undershields, then remove the reinforcement plate from under the engine. Note that the reinforcement plate bolts/nuts must not be re-used – new ones must be fitted.

3 Remove the starter motor as described in Chapter 5.

4 Remove the propeller shaft as described in Chapter 8.

5 Working under the car, prise up the retaining clips and extract the pin each side securing the gear lever support bracket to the transmission

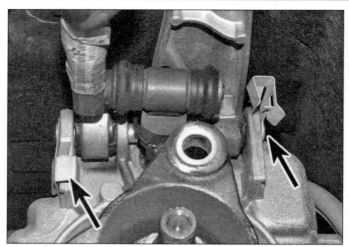

7.5 Prise up the clips (arrowed), and slide the pin each side from the casing

7.9 Adapter plate retaining bolt (arrowed)

casing **(see illustration)**. Similarly, disconnect the selector rod pin from the end of the gear lever **(see illustration 4.6)**.

6 Working at the gearbox bellhousing, unscrew the nuts, and withdraw the clutch slave cylinder from the studs on the bellhousing. Support the slave cylinder clear of the working area, but do not strain the hose.

7 Note their fitted locations, then disconnect all wiring plugs, and release any wiring harnesses from the gearbox casing.

8 Remove the particulate filter/catalytic converter as described in Chapter 4B.

9 Where applicable, unscrew the bolt securing the engine/gearbox adapter plate to the right-hand side of the gearbox bellhousing and/or remove the flywheel lower cover plate **(see illustration)**.

10 Place a suitable block of wood between the front of the engine sump and the steering rack. Once the transmission is removed, the engine will tend to tip forwards.

11 Place a trolley jack under the gearbox casing, just behind the bellhousing. Use a block of wood to spread the load, then raise the jack to just take the weight of the gearbox.

12 Remove the crossmember and mountings from the rear of the transmission, and allow the transmission/engine assembly to lower slightly.

13 Unscrew the engine-to-gearbox bolts.

14 Slide the gearbox rearwards to disengage the input shaft from the clutch. Take care during this operation to ensure that the weight of the gearbox is not allowed to hang on the input shaft.

Refitting

15 Commence refitting by checking that the clutch friction disc is centralised as described in Chapter 6 (*Clutch assembly – removal, inspection and refitting*).

16 Before refitting the gearbox, it is advisable to inspect the clutch release bearing and lever as described in Chapter 6.

17 The remainder of the refitting procedure is a reversal of removal, bearing in mind the following points.

   a) *Check that the gearbox positioning dowels are securely in place at the rear of the engine.*

   b) *Tighten all fixings to the specified torque.*

   c) *Lightly grease the gear selector arm pivot pin and the gear selector rod pin before refitting.*

   d) *Reconnect the propeller shaft to the gearbox flange as described in Chapter 8.*

   e) *Refit the starter motor as described in Chapter 5.*

8 Manual gearbox overhaul – general information

Overhauling a manual gearbox is a difficult and involved job for the DIY home mechanic. In addition to dismantling and reassembling many small parts, clearances must be precisely measured and, if necessary, changed by selecting shims and spacers. Internal gearbox components are also often difficult to obtain, and in many instances, extremely expensive. Because of this, if the gearbox develops a fault or becomes noisy, the best course of action is to have the unit overhauled by a specialist repairer, or to obtain an exchange reconditioned unit. Be aware that some gearbox repairs can be carried out with the gearbox in the car.

Nevertheless, it is not impossible for the more experienced mechanic to overhaul the gearbox, provided the special tools are available, and the job is done in a deliberate step-by-step manner, so that nothing is overlooked.

The tools necessary for an overhaul include internal and external circlip pliers, bearing pullers, a slide hammer, a set of pin punches, a dial test indicator, and possibly a hydraulic press. In addition, a large, sturdy workbench and a vice will be required.

During dismantling of the gearbox, make careful notes of how each component is fitted, to make reassembly easier and more accurate.

Before dismantling the gearbox, it will help if you have some idea what area is malfunctioning. Certain problems can be closely related to specific areas in the gearbox, which can make component examination and renewal easier. Refer to the *Fault finding* Section at the end of this manual for more information.

Chapter 7 Part B:
Automatic transmission

Contents

Degrees of difficulty

Easy, suitable for novice with little experience

Fairly easy, suitable for beginner with some experience

Fairly difficult, suitable for competent DIY mechanic

Difficult, suitable for experienced DIY mechanic

Very difficult, suitable for expert DIY or professional

Specifications

Transmission type
4-cylinder diesel engines	GA6HP19Z
6-cylinder diesel engines	GA6HP26Z

Capacities
All models	3.0 litres (approx)

Torque wrench settings

	Nm	lbf ft
Engine-to-transmission bolts:		
Hexagon bolts:		
M8 bolts	24	18
M10 bolts	45	33
M12 bolts	82	61
Torx bolts:		
M8 bolts	21	15
M10 bolts	42	31
M12 bolts	72	53
Output flange nut:*		
Stage 1	190	140
Stage 2	Slacken 360°	
Stage 3	120	89
Reinforcement plate fasteners:*		
Stage 1	56	41
Stage 2	Angle-tighten a further 90°	
Torque-converter-to-driveplate bolts:		
M8 bolts	26	19
M10 8.8 grade bolts	49	36
M10 10.9 grade bolts	56	41

Torque wrench settings (continued)

	Nm	lbf ft
Transmission crossmember-to-body bolts:		
M8 bolts	21	15
M10 bolts	42	31
Transmission mounting-to-gearbox nuts:		
M8 nuts.	21	15
M10 nuts.	42	31
Transmission oil drain plug.	8	6
Transmission oil filler/level plug:		
M18	35	26
M30	80	59

* Do not re-use. All aluminium bolts must be renewed.

1 General information

All automatic models are equipped with a six-speed automatic transmission, consisting of a torque converter, an epicyclic geartrain and hydraulically-operated clutches and brakes.

The torque converter provides a fluid coupling between engine and transmission, which acts as a clutch, and also provides a degree of torque multiplication when accelerating.

The epicyclic geartrain provides the six forward or one reverse gear ratio, according to which of its component parts are held stationary or allowed to turn. The components of the geartrain are held or released by brakes and clutches which are activated by a hydraulic control unit. A fluid pump within the transmission provides the necessary hydraulic pressure to operate the brakes and clutches.

Driver control of the transmission is by a four-position selector lever, incorporating a Steptronic function. The transmission has Park, Reverse, Neutral and Drive positions. The Drive position (D) provides automatic changing throughout the range of all forward gear ratios, and is the position selected for normal driving. An automatic kickdown facility shifts the transmission down a gear if the accelerator pedal is fully depressed.

Certain models are available with Steptronic gearchange where the driver is able to induce gearchanges with a simple movement of the lever – forward to change up, and back to change down.

Due to the complexity of the automatic transmission, any repair or overhaul work must be left to a BMW dealer or specialist with the necessary special equipment for fault diagnosis and repair. The contents of the following Sections are therefore confined to supplying general information, and any service information and instructions that can be used by the owner.

2 Gear selector lever – removal and refitting

Removal

1 Jack up the car and support securely on axle stands (see *Jacking and vehicle support*). Ensure the gear lever is in position P.
2 Working underneath the vehicle, undo the fasteners and remove the transmission undershield **(see illustration)**.

Type 1 selector cables

3 Undo the nut securing the cable support bracket to the transmission, and disengage the end of the cable from the lever.

Type 2 selector cables

4 Slacken the selector cable clamping nut on the transmission lever **(see illustration 3.8)**.
5 Undo the release the clip securing the selector outer cable and remove the cable from the support bracket on the transmission.

All types

6 Remove the centre console as described in Chapter 11.
7 Note their fitted positions, then disconnect any wiring plugs attached to the gear lever assembly.
8 Undo the three bolts securing the lever assembly to the floor, manoeuvre the assembly up from its location **(see illustration)**. Note that the lever assembly is only available complete with the selector cable. No further dismantling is recommended.

Refitting

9 Refitting is a reversal of removal, noting the following points:
  a) *Prior to refitting the gear knob, push the gaiter down the lever until the locking groove in the lever is exposed.*
  b) *On completion, adjust the selector cable as described in Section 3.*

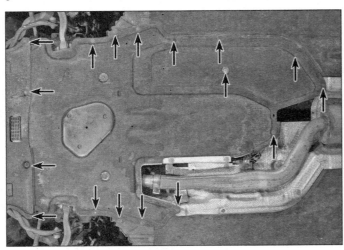

2.2 Undo the fasteners (arrowed) and remove the transmission undershield

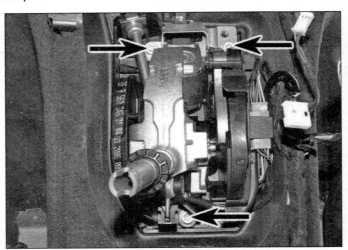

2.8 Selector lever assembly bolts (arrowed)

3 Gear selector cable –
removal, refitting and adjustment

Removal and refitting

1 The selector cable can only be renewed complete with the selector lever assembly. Removal is described in Section 2.

Adjustment

2 Move the selector lever to position P. To move the lever when the battery is disconnected, prise up the lever gaiter (where fitted), then pull up and remove the selector lever surround trim. Insert a screwdriver and press the red clip forwards to lift the locking lever, then move the selector lever to the required position. Remove the screwdriver to re-engage the selector lever locking function **(see illustrations)**.

3 Two different selector cable arrangements may be fitted. Proceed as applicable:

Type 1

4 Slacken the nut securing the cable bracket to the transmission **(see illustration)** (the car should be raised for access).

5 Adjust the position of the cable bracket so that a gap of 15 mm exists between the underside of the head of the cable end fitting, and the transmission selector lever **(see illustration 3.4)**.

6 Tighten the bracket nut securely.

7 Check that the cable is correctly adjusted by starting the engine, applying the brakes firmly, and moving the selector lever through all the selector positions.

Type 2

8 Slacken the cable end fitting bolt, then push the selector lever on the transmission fully forwards into the Park position **(see illustration)**.

3.2a Squeeze together the sides, and unclip the lever gaiter

9 Pull the inner cable towards the rear of the vehicle slightly, then tighten the cable end fitting bolt securely.

10 Check that the cable is correctly adjusted by starting the engine, applying the brakes firmly, and moving the selector lever through all the selector positions.

4 Fluid seals – renewal

Torque converter seal

1 Remove the transmission and the torque converter as described in Section 5.

2 Using a hooked tool, prise the old oil seal from the transmission bellhousing. Alternatively, drill a small hole, then screw a self-tapping screw into the seal and use pliers to pull out the seal.

3 Lubricate the lip of the new seal with clean fluid, then carefully drive it into place using a large socket or tube.

4 Remove the old O-ring seal from the input shaft, and slide a new one into place. Apply a smear of petroleum jelly to the new O-ring.

3.2b Use a screwdriver to press the red clip forwards

5 Refit the torque converter and transmission as described in Section 5.

Output flange oil seal

6 Renewal of the oil seal involves partial dismantling of the transmission, which is a complex operation – see Section 6. Oil seal renewal should be entrusted to a BMW dealer or specialist.

5 Automatic transmission –
removal and refitting

Note: *This is an involved operation. Read through the procedure thoroughly before starting work, and ensure that adequate lifting tackle and/or jacking/support equipment is available. A suitable tool will be required to align the torque converter when refitting the transmission, and new fluid pipe O-rings may be required.*

Removal

1 Disconnect the battery negative lead – see Chapter 5.

2 Jack up the car and support securely on axle stands (see *Jacking and vehicle support*). Note that the car must be raised sufficiently to allow clearance for the gearbox to be removed from under the car. Undo the bolts and remove the engine/transmission undershields from the vehicle.

3 Undo the bolts and remove the front reinforcement plate from under engine/

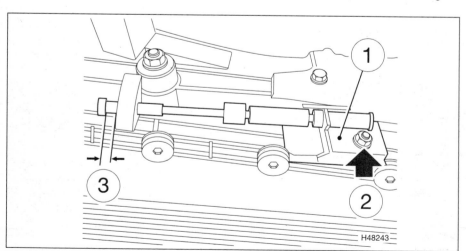

3.4 Selector cable support bracket (1), adjustment nut (2) and adjustment dimension (3)

3.8 Slacken the cable end fitting bolt (arrowed)

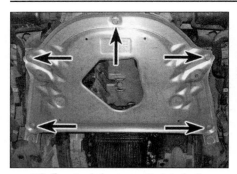

5.3 Front reinforcement plate bolts (arrowed)

5.9 Undo the bolt (arrowed) and remove the small cover

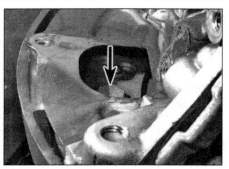

5.10 Rotate the crankshaft until the torque converter bolt (arrowed) is accessible

transmission **(see illustration)**. Note that the reinforcement plate fasteners must not be re-used.

4 Remove the starter motor as described in Chapter 5.

5 Remove the exhaust system and heat shields (see Chapter 4A), then unbolt the exhaust mounting crossmember (where fitted) from under the car.

6 Remove the catalytic converter/particulate filter as described in Chapter 4B.

7 Remove the propeller shaft as described in Chapter 8.

8 Disconnect the selector cable from the transmission with reference to Section 3.

9 Undo the retaining bolt and remove the small cover from the right-hand side of the transmission bellhousing **(see illustration)**.

10 Unscrew the three torque converter bolts, turning the crankshaft using a spanner or socket on the pulley hub bolt, for access to each bolt in turn **(see illustration)**.

11 Undo the nuts and remove the brackets from the right-hand side of the transmission sump pan, then undo the 3 bolts and remove the heat shield (where applicable).

12 Place a suitable block of wood between the engine sump casing and the steering rack, as once the transmission is removed, the engine will be front-heavy.

13 Lower the transmission a little, then rotate the collar anti-clockwise and pull the wiring plug from the transmission casing **(see illustration)**. Release the wiring harness clips on the transmission casing.

14 Unbolt the fluid cooler pipe brackets and clamps. Undo the clamp bolt and disconnect the fluid pipes – be prepared for fluid spillage **(see illustration)**. Plug/seal the openings to prevent contamination.

15 Unscrew the engine-to-transmission bolts, and recover the washers, then slide the transmission rearwards. Ensure the torque converter comes away from the driveplate, and stays in place in the transmission.

16 Insert a suitable metal or wooden lever through the slot in the bottom of the bellhousing to retain the torque converter. As the transmission is released from the engine, check to make sure that the engine is adequately supported, and no hoses are trapped.

17 Lower the transmission and carefully withdraw it from under the car, making sure that the torque converter is held in position. If the transmission is to be removed for some time, ensure that the engine is adequately supported in the engine compartment. Take measures to ensure the torque converter is prevented from sliding forwards **(see illustration)**.

⚠️ *Warning: The transmission is extremely heavy. The aid of an assistant to manoeuvre the assembly is essential.*

Refitting

18 Ensure that the transmission locating dowels are in position on the engine.

19 Before mating the transmission with the engine, it is essential that the torque converter is perfectly aligned with the driveplate.

20 Turn the driveplate to align one of the torque converter-to-driveplate bolt holes.

21 Ensure that the transmission is adequately supported, and manoeuvre it into position under the car.

22 Refit and tighten the engine-to-transmission bolts.

23 Refit the torque converter-to-driveplate bolt. Tighten the bolt to the specified torque.

24 Turn the crankshaft as during removal for access to the remaining two torque converter-to-driveplate bolt locations. Refit and tighten the bolts.

25 Further refitting is a reversal of removal, bearing in mind the following points.

  a) *Tighten all fixings to the specified torques, where applicable.*
  b) *Check the condition of the transmission fluid pipe O-rings and renew if necessary.*
  c) *Refit the propeller shaft (see Chapter 8).*
  d) *Refit the starter motor (see Chapter 5).*
  e) *Reconnect and adjust the selector cable as described in Section 3.*
  f) *On completion, check the transmission fluid as described in Section 8.*

6 Automatic transmission overhaul – general information

In the event of a fault occurring with the transmission, it is first necessary to determine whether it is of an electrical, mechanical or hydraulic nature, and to do this special test

5.13 Rotate the collar (arrowed) anti-clockwise and disconnect the wiring plug

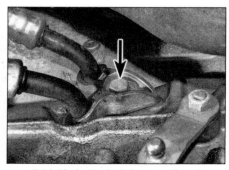

5.14 Undo the bolt (arrowed) and disconnect the fluid cooler pipes

5.17 We used some square-section steel, 2 bolts and a nut to prevent the torque converter sliding forwards

equipment is required. It is therefore essential to have the work carried out by a BMW dealer or suitably-equipped specialist if a transmission fault is suspected.

Do not remove the transmission from the car for possible repair before professional fault diagnosis has been carried out, since most tests require the transmission to be in the car.

7 Electronic components/ sensors – removal and refitting

The turbine speed sensor, output speed sensor, transmission range switch and electronic control module (ECM) are all contained within the transmission casing. Renewal of the components involves removal and the sump and partial dismantling of the transmission. Therefore renewal of these components should be entrusted to a BMW dealer or suitably-equipped specialist.

8 Automatic transmission fluid level check

Note 1: *The fluid level can only be accurately checked using BMW diagnostic equipment. The following procedure will ensure the transmission has sufficient fluid for the vehicle to be gently driven to a BMW dealer or suitably-equipped specialist, where the level can be accurately checked*

Note 2: *There is no recommendation in the BMW service schedule for the transmission fluid to be checked, or renewed. However, it may be prudent to check the fluid level every few years – especially if the vehicle is used on mostly short journeys or for towing.*

1 The fluid level is checked by removing the filler/level plug from the side of the transmission casing. If desired, jack up the car and support on axle stands (see *Jacking and vehicle support*) to improve access, but make sure that the car is level.

2 Undo the bolts and remove the undershield beneath the transmission **(see illustration 2.2)**.

3 Place a container under the transmission fluid pan, then unscrew the filler/level plug located on the right-hand side of the casing. Recover the sealing ring (where fitted).

4 The fluid level should be up to the lower edge of the filler/level plug hole.

5 If necessary, top-up the fluid until it overflows from the plug hole. Note that on some transmissions, a spring-loaded plate is fitted in the filler/level hole. It's not possible to push the plate open with a plastic filler spout – a metal spout is required.

6 Start the engine and allow it to idle. With the brake pedal depressed, shift through the gears, and return it to Park. The oil level must be checked with the engine running and the transmission oil up to the temperature indicated on a sticker affixed to the transmission casing, adjacent to the filler hole. On the vehicles we examined, the temperature range was between 30°C and 50°C. This temperature is determined by plugging in suitable diagnostic equipment into the vehicle's EOBD connector, located in the driver's footwell side panel (see Chapter 4A). In the absence of suitable equipment, err on the side of caution – check the level *before* the engine/transmission gets to normal operating temperature, then get the level checked again by a BMW dealer or suitably-equipped specialist.

7 Add oil until it begins to run out of the filler hole. Depress the brake pedal, move the selector lever through all positions and check the level again.

8 Refit the filler/level plug, using a new sealing ring (where fitted); tighten to the specified torque.

9 Automatic transmission fluid renewal

Note: *There is no recommendation in the BMW service schedule for the transmission fluid to be checked, or renewed. However, it may be prudent to renew the fluid level every few years – especially if the vehicle is used on mostly short journeys or for towing.*

1 The transmission fluid should be drained with the transmission at operating temperature. If the car has just been driven at least 20 miles, the transmission can be considered warm.

2 Immediately after driving the car, park it on a level surface, apply the handbrake. If desired, jack up the car and support on axle stands (see *Jacking and vehicle support*) to improve access, but make sure that the car is level.

9.4 Transmission fluid drain plug (arrowed)

3 Undo the bolts and remove the undershield beneath the engine/transmission **(see illustration 2.2)**.

4 Slacken the transmission fluid pan drain plug about half a turn **(see illustration)**. Position a draining container under the drain plug, then remove the plug completely. If possible, try to keep the plug pressed into the fluid pan while unscrewing it by hand the last couple of turns.

5 Discard the drain plug – BMW insist that a new one is fitted.

> **HAYNES HiNT** *As the plug releases from the threads, move it away sharply so the stream of fluid issuing from the fluid pan runs into the container, not up your sleeve.*

6 Fit the new drain plug and tighten to the specified torque.

7 With reference to Section 8, fill the transmission with the specified quantity of the correct type of fluid (see Specifications and *Lubricants and fluids*) – fill the transmission through filler/level plug hole.

8 Check the fluid level as described in Section 8, bearing in mind that the new fluid will not yet be at operating temperature.

9 With the handbrake applied, and the transmission selector lever in position P, start the engine and run it at idle for a few minutes to warm up the new fluid, then recheck the fluid level as described in Section 8. Note that it may be necessary to drain off a little fluid once the new fluid has reached operating temperature.

Notes

Chapter 8
Final drive, driveshafts and propeller shaft

Contents

Degrees of difficulty

Easy, suitable for novice with little experience 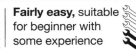	**Fairly easy,** suitable for beginner with some experience	**Fairly difficult,** suitable for competent DIY mechanic	**Difficult,** suitable for experienced DIY mechanic	**Very difficult,** suitable for expert DIY or professional

Specifications

Final drive
Type . . . .   Unsprung, attached to rear suspension crossmember

Driveshaft
Type . . . .   Steel shafts with ball-and-cage type constant velocity joints at each end
Constant velocity joint grease capacity . . . .   80g in each joint

Propeller shaft
Type . . . .   Two-piece tubular shaft with centre bearing, centre and rear universal joint. Front joint is either rubber coupling or universal joint (depending on model)

Torque wrench settings
Note: *On some fixings different grades of bolt can be used; the grade of each bolt is stamped on the bolt head. Ensure that each bolt is tightened to the correct torque for its specific grade.*

Final drive unit	Nm	lbf ft
Mounting bolts:		
Front bolts	100	74
Rear bolt.	165	122
Oil filler plug	60	44
Vibration damper on bracket (where fitted)	68	50
Driveshaft		
Driveshaft retaining nut:*		
Touring	420	310
Saloon	300	221
Shaft-to-final drive flange bolts:*		
M8 bolts	52	38
M10 bolts	80	59
M12 bolts	135	100

Torque wrench settings (continued)

Propeller shaft

Centre joint bolt	97	72
Flexible disc to transmission:		
M10 (Grade 8.8) bolts	48	35
M10 (Grade 10.9) bolts	64	47
ZNS (external Torx) bolts/nuts:*		
M10 (Grade 10.9) bolts:		
Stage 1	20	15
Stage 2	Angle-tighten a further 90°	
M12 (Grade 10.9) bolts:		
Stage 1	55	41
Stage 2	Angle-tighten a further 90°	
Shaft/coupling to final drive:*		
M10 (Grade 10.9) bolts:		
With ribbed teeth under head:		
Stage 1	40	30
Stage 2	Angle-tighten a further 45°	
Without ribbed teeth under head:		
Stage 1	20	15
Stage 2	Angle-tighten a further 90°	
M12 (Grade 10.9) bolts:		
Stage 1	55	41
Stage 2	Angle-tighten a further 90°	
Support bearing bracket nuts/bolts	21	15
Transmission crossmember:		
Crossmember to body	21	15
Crossmember mounting to transmission	19	14

Roadwheels

Wheel bolts	120	89

* *Do not reuse*

1 General information

Power is transmitted from the transmission to the rear axle by a two-piece propeller shaft, joined behind the centre bearing by a 'slip-joint', a sliding, splined coupling. The slip-joint allows slight fore-and-aft movement of the propeller shaft. The forward end of the propeller shaft is attached to the output flange of the transmission either by a flexible rubber coupling or constant velocity joint. On some models, a vibration damper is mounted between the front of the propeller shaft and coupling. The middle of the propeller shaft is supported by the centre bearing which is bolted to the vehicle body. Universal joints are located at the centre bearing and at the rear end of the propeller shaft, to compensate for movement of the transmission and differential on their mountings, and for any flexing of the chassis.

The final drive assembly includes the drive pinion, the ring gear, the differential and the output flanges. The drive pinion, which drives the ring gear, is also known as the differential input shaft and is connected to the propeller shaft via an input flange. The differential is bolted to the ring gear and drives the rear wheels through a pair of output flanges bolted to driveshafts with constant velocity (CV) joints at either end. The differential allows the wheels to turn at different speeds when cornering.

The driveshafts deliver power from the final drive unit output flanges to the rear wheels. The inner CV joints are bolted to the differential flanges, and the outer CV joints engage the splines of the wheel hubs, and are secured by a large nut.

Major repair work on the differential assembly components (drive pinion, ring-and-pinion, and differential) requires many special tools and a high degree of expertise, and therefore should not be attempted by the home mechanic. If major repairs become necessary, we recommend that they be performed by a BMW service department or other suitably-equipped automotive engineer.

2 Final drive unit – removal and refitting

Note: *New propeller shaft rear coupling nuts and driveshaft retaining bolts will be required on refitting.*

Removal

1 Chock the front wheels. Jack up the rear of the vehicle and support it on axle stands (see *Jacking and vehicle support*). Remove both rear wheels.

2 Using paint or a suitable marker pen, make alignment marks between the propeller shaft and final drive unit flange. Unscrew the bolts/nuts securing the propeller shaft to the final drive unit and discard them; new ones must be used on refitting.

3 Slacken and remove the retaining bolts and plates securing the right-hand driveshaft to the final drive unit flange and support the driveshaft by tying it to the vehicle underbody using a piece of wire. **Note:** *Do not allow the driveshaft to hang under its own weight as the CV joint may be damaged.* Discard the bolts, new ones should be used on refitting.

4 Disconnect the left-hand driveshaft from the final drive as described in Paragraph 3.

5 Undo the nuts/bolts and remove the heat shield panel from the left-hand end of the tension strut beneath the final drive input shaft flange.

6 Move a jack and interposed block of wood into position, and raise it so that it is supporting the weight of the final drive unit.

7 Making sure the final drive unit is safely supported, slacken and remove the two bolts securing the front of the unit in position and

2.7 Final drive unit front retaining bolts (arrowed)

the single bolt securing the rear of the unit in position **(see illustration)**.

8 Carefully lower the final drive unit out of position and remove it from underneath the vehicle. Examine the final drive unit mounting rubbers for signs of wear or damage and renew if necessary.

Refitting

9 Refitting is a reversal of removal noting the following.

 a) *Raise the final drive unit into position and engage it with the propeller shaft rear joint, making sure the marks made prior to removal are correctly aligned.*

 b) *Insert the final drive unit front mounting bolts, then the rear bolt.*

 c) *Tighten the final drive unit front mounting bolts to the specified torque setting, followed by the rear one.*

 d) *Fit the new propeller shaft joint bolts/ nuts and tighten them to the specified torque.*

 e) *Fit the new driveshaft joint retaining bolts and plates and tighten them to the specified torque.*

 f) *On completion, refill/top-up the final drive unit with oil as described in Section 10.*

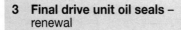

3 Final drive unit oil seals – renewal

Propeller shaft flange oil seal

Note: *A new flange nut retaining plate will be required.*

1 Remove the final drive unit as described in Section 2 and secure the unit in a vice.

2 Remove the retaining plate and make alignment marks between the propeller flange nut, the drive flange and pinion **(see illustration)**. Discard the retaining plate, a new one must be used on refitting.

3 Hold the drive flange stationary by bolting a length of metal bar to it, then unscrew the nut noting the exact number of turns necessary to remove it.

4 Using a suitable puller, draw the drive flange from the pinion and remove the dust cover. If the dust cover shows signs of wear, renew it.

5 Lever the oil seal from the final drive casing with a screwdriver. Wipe clean the oil seal seating.

6 Smear a little oil on the sealing lip of the new oil seal, then press it squarely into the casing until flush with the outer face. If necessary the seal can be tapped into position using a metal tube which bears only on its hard outer edge.

7 Fit the dust cover and locate the drive flange on the pinion aligning the marks made on removal. Refit the flange nut, screwing it on by the exact number of turns counted on removal, so that the alignment marks align.

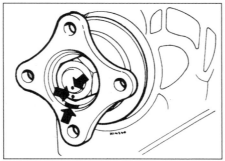

3.2 Make alignment marks (arrowed) on the flange, the pinion shaft and nut to ensure proper reassembly

> ⚠ **Warning: Do not overtighten the flange nut. If the nut is overtightened, the collapsible spacer behind the flange will be deformed necessitating its renewal. This is a complex operation requiring the final drive unit to be dismantled (see Section 1).**

8 Secure the nut in position with the new retaining plate, tapping it squarely into position.

9 Refit the final drive unit as described in Section 2 and refill it with oil as described in Section 10.

Driveshaft flange oil seal

Note: *New driveshaft joint retaining bolts and a driveshaft flange circlip will be required.*

10 Slacken and remove the bolts securing the driveshaft constant velocity joint to the final drive unit and recover the retaining plates. Position the driveshaft clear of the flange and tie it to the vehicle underbody using a piece of wire. **Note:** *Do not allow the driveshaft to hang under its own weight as the CV joint may be damaged.*

11 Using a suitable lever, carefully prise the driveshaft flange out from the final drive unit taking care not to damage the dust seal or casing **(see illustration)**. Remove the flange and recover dust seal. If the dust seal shows signs of damage, renew it.

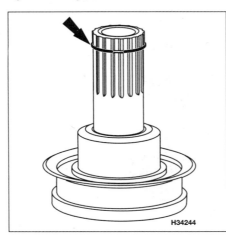

3.13 Renew the output flange circlip (arrowed)

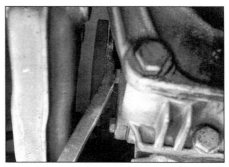

3.11 Use a lever to remove the driveshaft flange from the final drive unit

12 Carefully lever the oil seal out from the final drive unit. Wipe clean the oil seal seating.

13 With the flange removed, prise out the circlip from the end of the splined shaft **(see illustration)**.

14 Fit a new circlip, making sure it is correctly located in the splined shaft groove.

15 Smear a little final drive oil on the sealing lip of the new oil seal, then press it squarely into the casing until it reaches its stop. If necessary the seal can be tapped into position using a metal tube which bears only on its hard outer edge **(see illustration)**.

16 Fit the dust cover and insert the drive flange. Push the drive flange fully into position and check that it is securely retained by the circlip.

17 Align the driveshaft with the flange and refit the new retaining bolts and plates, tightening them to the specified torque.

18 Refill the final drive unit with oil as described in Section 10.

4 Driveshaft – removal and refitting

Note: *A new driveshaft retaining nut and bolts will be required on refitting.*

Removal

1 Remove the wheel trim/hub cap (as applicable) and slacken the driveshaft retaining

3.15 Install the new seal using a socket which bears only on the hard outer edge of the seal

4.9 Make alignment marks (arrowed) then remove the Torx bolts

4.12 Stake the driveshaft nut using a punch

nut with the vehicle resting on its wheels. Also slacken the wheel bolts.

2 Chock the front wheels, then jack up the rear of the vehicle and support it on axle stands (see *Jacking and vehicle support*).

3 Remove the relevant rear roadwheel.

4 If the left-hand driveshaft is to be removed, remove the exhaust system tailpipe to improve access (see relevant Part of Chapter 4).

5 Slacken and remove the nuts, then detach the left- and right-hand anti-roll links arms from the lower arms (see Chapter 10).

6 Place a suitable workshop trolley jack under the outer end of the lower arm/hub carrier, then undo the shock absorber lower mounting bolt/nut. Take the weight with the jack and detach the lower end of the shock absorber from the arm/carrier.

7 Raise the outer end of the lower arm/hub carrier approximately 20 mm.

8 Unscrew and remove the driveshaft nut.

9 Make alignment marks, then slacken and remove the bolts securing the driveshaft constant velocity joint to the final drive unit and recover the retaining plates (where fitted) **(see illustration)**. Position the driveshaft clear of the flange and tie it to the vehicle underbody using a piece of wire. **Note:** *Do not allow the driveshaft to hang under its own weight as the CV joint may be damaged.*

10 Withdraw the driveshaft outer constant velocity joint from the hub assembly. The outer joint will be very tight, tap the joint out of the hub using a soft-faced mallet. If this fails to free it from the hub, the joint will have to be pressed out using a suitable tool which is bolted to the hub.

11 Remove the driveshaft from underneath the vehicle.

Refitting

12 Refitting is the reverse of removal noting the following points.

   a) *Lubricate the nut-to-wheel bearing contact area and tighten the nut to the specified torque. Do not oil the threads. If necessary, wait until the vehicle is lowered to the ground and then tighten the nut to the specified torque. Once tightened, use a hammer and punch to stake the nut **(see illustration)**.*

   b) *Fit new inner joint retaining bolts and plates (where fitted) and tighten to the specified torque.*

5 Driveshaft gaiters – renewal

1 Remove the driveshaft (see Section 4).

2 Clean the driveshaft and mount it in a vice.

3 Release the two inner joint gaiter retaining clips and free the gaiter and dust cover from the joint **(see illustration)**.

4 Lever off the sealing cover from the end of the inner constant velocity (CV) joint **(see illustration)**.

5 Scoop out excess grease and remove the inner joint circlip from the end of the driveshaft **(see illustration)**.

6 Securely support the joint inner member and tap the driveshaft out of position using a hammer and suitable drift **(see illustration)**. If the joint is a tight fit, a suitable puller will be required to draw off the joint. Do not dismantle the inner joint.

7 With the joint removed, slide the inner gaiter and dust cover off from the end of the driveshaft **(see illustration)**.

8 Release the outer joint gaiter retaining clips then slide the gaiter along the shaft and remove it.

9 Thoroughly clean the constant velocity joints using paraffin, or a suitable solvent, and dry thoroughly. Carry out a visual inspection as follows.

10 Move the inner splined driving member from side to side to expose each ball in turn at the top of its track. Examine the balls for cracks, flat spots or signs of surface pitting.

11 Inspect the ball tracks on the inner and

5.3 Release the gaiter retaining clips and slide the gaiter down the shaft

5.4 Carefully remove the sealing cover from the inner end of the joint

5.5 Remove the inner joint circlip from the driveshaft

5.6 Support the inner joint inner member then tap the driveshaft out of position . . .

5.7 . . . and slide off the gaiter

5.20a Fill the inner joint with the grease supplied . . .

5.20b . . . and work it into the bearing tracks

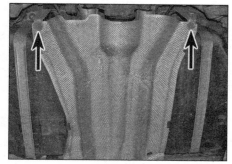

6.2 Rear heat shield fasteners (arrowed)

outer members. If the tracks have widened, the balls will no longer be a tight fit. At the same time check the ball cage windows for wear or cracking between the windows.

12 If on inspection any of the constant velocity joint components are found to be worn or damaged, it must be renewed. The inner joint is available separately but if the outer joint is worn it will be necessary to renew the complete joint and driveshaft assembly. If the joints are in satisfactory condition, obtain new gaiter repair kits which contain gaiters, retaining clips, an inner constant velocity joint circlip and the correct type and quantity of grease required.

13 Tape over the splines on the end of the driveshaft.

14 Slide the new outer gaiter onto the end of the driveshaft.

15 Pack the outer joint with the grease supplied in the gaiter kit. Work the grease well into the bearing tracks whilst twisting the joint, and fill the rubber gaiter with any excess.

16 Ease the gaiter over the joint and ensure that the gaiter lips are correctly located on both the driveshaft and constant velocity joint. Lift the outer sealing lip of the gaiter to equalise air pressure within the gaiter.

17 Fit the large metal retaining clip to the gaiter. Pull the retaining clip tight then bend it back to secure it in position and cut off any excess clip. Secure the small retaining clip using the same procedure.

18 Engage the new inner gaiter with its

dust cover and slide the assembly onto the driveshaft.

19 Remove the tape from the driveshaft splines and fit the inner constant velocity joint. Press the joint fully onto the shaft and secure it in position with a new circlip.

20 Work the grease supplied fully into the inner joint and fill the gaiter with any excess **(see illustrations)**.

21 Slide the inner gaiter into position and press the dust cover onto the joint, making sure the retaining bolt holes are correctly aligned. Lift the outer sealing lip of the gaiter, to equalise air pressure within the gaiter, and secure it in position with the retaining clips.

22 Apply a smear of suitable sealant (BMW recommend BMW sealing gel) and press the new sealing cover fully onto the end of the inner joint.

23 Check that both constant velocity joints are free to move easily then refit the driveshaft as described in Section 4.

6 Propeller shaft – removal and refitting

Removal

1 Chock the front wheels. Jack up the rear of the vehicle and support it on axle stands (see *Jacking and vehicle support*).

2 Remove the exhaust system as described

in the relevant Part of Chapter 4, then undo the fasteners and remove the various heat shields to access the propeller shaft **(see illustration)**. Where necessary, unbolt the exhaust system mounting bracket(s) in order to gain the necessary clearance required to remove the propeller shaft.

3 Support the rear end of the transmission with a workshop jack, then undo the bolts/ nuts and remove the crossmember from the rear of the transmission and vehicle body **(see illustration)**. Note that the centre bolt is accessed from above.

Caution: The transmission is heavy, so ensure that it is adequately supported. The transmission sump is plastic – ensure the transmission is supported around the edge of the sump pan.

4 If improved access in required, undo the 4 bolts and detach the mounting bracket (where fitted) from the rear of the transmission casing **(see illustration)**.

5 Make alignment marks between the shaft, transmission flange and rubber coupling at the front of the shaft. Slacken and remove the nuts and bolts securing the coupling to the transmission **(see illustration)**. Discard the nuts, new ones should be used on refitting.

6 Using paint or a suitable marker pen, make alignment marks between the propeller shaft CV joint flange and final drive unit flange. Unscrew the bolts securing the propeller shaft to the final drive unit and discard them;

6.3 Remove the crossmember from the rear of the transmission

6.4 Rear bracket bolts (arrowed)

6.5 Undo the 3 bolts/nuts (arrowed – upper bolt/nut hidden)

6.6 Note the plates (arrowed) fitted under the bolt heads

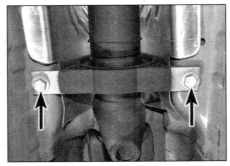

6.8 Centre support bearing bracket bolts (arrowed)

new ones must be used on refitting (**see illustration**).

7 Use a flat-bladed screwdriver to prise the CV joint flange from the final drive flange. **Note:** *If the CV joint flange is forced to an extreme angle in relation to the shaft, the joint rubber gaiter can be damaged.*

8 With the aid of an assistant, support the propeller shaft then unscrew the centre support bearing bracket retaining bolts (**see illustration**). Lower the centre of the shaft and disengage it from the transmission and final drive unit. Remove the shaft from underneath the vehicle.

9 Inspect the rubber coupling (where fitted), the support bearing and shaft joints as described in Sections 7, 8 and 9. Inspect the transmission flange locating pin and propeller shaft bush for signs of wear or damage and renew as necessary.

Refitting

10 Apply a smear of molybdenum disulphide grease (BMW recommend Molykote Long-term 2) to the transmission pin and shaft bush, and manoeuvre the shaft into position.

11 Align the marks made prior to removal and engage the shaft with the transmission and final drive unit flanges. Try not to compress the

CV joint outer flange, as this would cause the packed grease to be expelled. With the marks correctly aligned, refit the support bracket retaining bolts, tightening them lightly only at this stage.

12 Fit new retaining bolts to the rear CV joint of the propeller shaft, and tighten them evenly, working in a diagonal pattern, to the specified torque. Don't' forget to fit the plates to the bolts prior to fitting them.

13 Insert the bolts through the rubber coupling, and into the transmission output flange, then fit the new retaining nuts. Tighten them to the specified torque, noting that only the nuts should be rotated to avoid stressing the rubber coupling.

14 Tighten the centre support bearing bracket bolts to the specified torque,

15 The remainder of refitting is a reversal of removal.

7 Propeller shaft rubber coupling – check and renewal

Check

1 Firmly apply the handbrake, then jack up

the front of the vehicle and support it on axle stands (see *Jacking and vehicle support*).

2 Closely examine the rubber coupling, links the propeller shaft to the transmission, looking for signs of damage such as cracking or splitting or for signs of general deterioration. If necessary, renew the coupling as follows.

Renewal

3 Remove the propeller shaft as described in Section 6.

4 Slacken and remove the nuts securing the coupling to the shaft and remove it (**see illustration**).

5 Fit the new rubber coupling noting that the arrows on the side of the coupling must point towards the propeller shaft/transmission flanges (**see illustration**). Fit the new retaining nuts and tighten them to the specified torque.

6 Refit the propeller shaft as described in Section 6.

8 Propeller shaft support bearing – check and renewal

Check

1 Wear in the support bearing will lead to noise and vibration when the vehicle is driven. The bearing is best checked with the propeller shaft removed (see Section 6). To gain access to the bearing with the shaft in position, remove the exhaust system and heat shields as described in the relevant Part of Chapter 4.

2 Rotate the bearing and check that it turns smoothly with no sign of free play; if it's difficult to turn, or if it has a gritty feeling, renew it. Also inspect the rubber portion. If it's cracked or deteriorated, renew it.

Renewal

3 Remove the propeller shaft as described in Section 6.

7.4 Coupling-to-propeller shaft retaining nuts (arrowed)

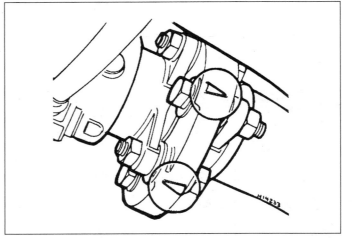

7.5 If the coupling has directional arrowed, make sure the arrows are pointing towards the propeller shaft/transmission flanges and not the bolt heads

4 Paint alignment marks between the central universal joint yoke and the propeller shaft, then undo the bolt securing the yoke to the shaft.

5 Slide off the shim and support bearing rear dust cover.

6 Draw the bearing and support bracket off from the propeller shaft using a suitable puller or hydraulic press.

7 Press/drive the new bearing and bracket assembly fully onto the shaft until it reaches the stop, using a suitable tubular spacer which bears only on the inner race of the bearing.

8 Check that the bearing is free to rotate smoothly, then fit the new dust seal.

9 Refit the shim to the end of the shaft.

10 Refit the universal joint to the shaft, aligning the previously-made marks, then apply a little thread-locking compound to the threads, and tighten the retaining bolt to the specified torque.

11 Refit the propeller shaft as described in Section 6.

9 Propeller shaft universal joints – check and renewal

Check

1 Wear in the universal joints is characterised by vibration in the transmission, noise during acceleration, and metallic squeaking and grating sounds as the bearings disintegrate. The joints can be checked with the propeller shaft still fitted, noting that it will be necessary to remove the exhaust system and heat shields (see the relevant part of Chapter 4) to gain access.

2 If the propeller shaft is in position on the vehicle, try to turn the propeller shaft while holding the transmission/final drive flange. Free play between the propeller shaft and the front or rear flanges indicates excessive wear.

3 If the propeller shaft is already removed, you can check the universal joints by holding the shaft in one hand and turning the yoke or flange with the other. If the axial movement is excessive, renew the propeller shaft.

Renewal

4 At the time of writing, no spare parts were available to enable renewal of the universal joints to be carried out. Therefore, if any joint shows signs of damage or wear the complete propeller shaft assembly must be renewed. Consult your BMW dealer for latest information on parts availability.

5 If renewal of the propeller shaft is necessary, it may be worthwhile seeking the advice of an automotive engineering specialist. They may be able to repair the original shaft assembly or supply a reconditioned shaft on an exchange basis.

10.2 Final drive filler plug (arrowed)

10 Final drive oil level check

1 BMW described the final drive as 'filled for life'. There is no requirement in the service schedule to check or change the final drive oil. However, it may be prudent to check the fluid level every few years as follows:

2 With the vehicle level, unscrew the filler plug from the rear of the final drive casing **(see illustration)**.

3 The oil level should be up to the lower edge of the filler hole. If it's not, add the specified fluid until the level is up to the bottom of the filler hole.

4 Refit the oil filler plug and tighten it to the specified torque.

Notes

Chapter 9
Braking system

Contents

Degrees of difficulty

Easy, suitable for novice with little experience	Fairly easy, suitable for beginner with some experience	Fairly difficult, suitable for competent DIY mechanic	Difficult, suitable for experienced DIY mechanic	Very difficult, suitable for expert DIY or professional

Specifications

Front brakes
Disc minimum thickness	Stamped on disc
Maximum disc runout	0.2 mm
Brake pad friction material minimum thickness	2.0 mm

Rear disc brakes
Disc minimum thickness:	
320 mm diameter	18.4 mm
345 mm diameter	22.4 mm
Maximum disc runout	0.2 mm
Brake pad friction material minimum thickness	2.0 mm
Handbrake drum diameter (depending on model)	160 to 185 mm
Handbrake shoe friction material minimum thickness	1.5 mm

Torque wrench settings
	Nm	lbf ft
ABS wheel sensor retaining bolts	8	6
Brake disc retaining bolt	16	12
Brake hose unions:		
M10 thread	17	13
M12 thread	19	14
Front brake caliper:		
Guide pins	30	22
Mounting bracket bolts*	110	81
Master cylinder mounting nuts*	26	19
Rear brake caliper:		
Guide pins	35	26
Mounting bracket bolts*	110	81
Roadwheel bolts	120	89
Servo unit mounting nuts	22	16

* Do not re-use

1 General information

The braking system is of the servo-assisted, dual-circuit hydraulic type. Under normal circumstances, both circuits operate in unison. However, if there is hydraulic failure in one circuit, full braking force will still be available at two wheels.

All models are fitted with front and rear disc brakes. ABS is fitted as standard to all models (refer to Section 19 for further information on ABS operation). **Note:** *On models also equipped with Dynamic Stability Control (DSC), the ABS system also operates the traction control side of the system.*

The front disc brakes are actuated by single-piston sliding type calipers, which ensure that equal pressure is applied to each disc pad.

All models are fitted with rear disc brakes, actuated by single-piston sliding calipers, and a separate drum brake arrangement is fitted in the centre of the brake disc to provide a separate means of handbrake application. **Note:** *When servicing any part of the system, work carefully and methodically; also observe scrupulous cleanliness when overhauling any part of the hydraulic system. Always renew components (in axle sets, where applicable) if in doubt about their condition, and use only genuine BMW parts, or at least those of known good quality. Note the warnings given in 'Safety first' and at relevant points in this Chapter concerning the dangers of asbestos dust and hydraulic fluid.*

2 Hydraulic system – bleeding

Warning: *Hydraulic fluid is poisonous; wash off immediately and thoroughly in the case of skin contact, and seek immediate medical advice if any fluid is swallowed or gets into the eyes. Certain types of hydraulic fluid are flammable, and may ignite when allowed into contact with hot components; when servicing any hydraulic system, it is safest to assume that the fluid IS flammable, and to take precautions against the risk of fire as though it is petrol that is being handled. Hydraulic fluid is also an effective paint stripper, and will attack plastics; if any is spilt, it should be washed off immediately, using copious quantities of fresh water. Finally, it is hygroscopic (it absorbs moisture from the air) – old fluid may be contaminated and unfit for further use. When topping-up or renewing the fluid, always use the recommended type, and ensure that it comes from a freshly-opened sealed container.*

Warning: *If the high-pressure hydraulic system linking the master cylinder, hydraulic unit and (where fitted) accumulator has been disturbed, then bleeding of the brakes should be entrusted to a BMW dealer or specialist. They will have access to the special service tester which is needed to operate the ABS modulator pump and bleed the high-pressure hydraulic system safely.*

General

1 The correct operation of any hydraulic system is only possible after removing all air from the components and circuit; this is achieved by bleeding the system.

2 During the bleeding procedure, add only clean, unused hydraulic fluid of the recommended type; never re-use fluid that has already been bled from the system. Ensure that sufficient fluid is available before starting work.

3 If there is any possibility of incorrect fluid being already in the system, the brake components and circuit must be flushed completely with uncontaminated, correct fluid, and new seals should be fitted to the various components.

4 If hydraulic fluid has been lost from the system, or air has entered because of a leak, ensure that the fault is cured before continuing further.

5 Park the vehicle on level ground, switch off the engine and select first or reverse gear, then chock the wheels and release the handbrake.

6 Check that all pipes and hoses are secure, unions tight and bleed screws closed. Clean any dirt from around the bleed screws.

7 Unscrew the master cylinder reservoir cap, and top the master cylinder reservoir up to the MAX level line; refit the cap loosely, and remember to maintain the fluid level at least above the MIN level line throughout the procedure, or there is a risk of further air entering the system.

8 There are a number of one-man, do-it-yourself brake bleeding kits currently available from motor accessory shops. It is recommended that one of these kits is used whenever possible, as they greatly simplify the bleeding operation, and reduce the risk of expelled air and fluid being drawn back into the system. If such a kit is not available, the basic (two-man) method must be used, which is described in detail below.

9 If a kit is to be used, prepare the vehicle as described previously, and follow the kit manufacturer's instructions, as the procedure may vary slightly according to the type being used; generally, they are as outlined below in the relevant sub-section.

10 Whichever method is used, the same sequence must be followed (paragraphs 11 and 12) to ensure the removal of all air from the system.

Bleeding sequence

11 If the system has been only partially disconnected, and suitable precautions were taken to minimise fluid loss, it should be necessary only to bleed that part of the system.

12 If the complete system is to be bled, then it should be done working in the following sequence:

   a) *Right-hand rear brake.*
   b) *Left-hand rear brake.*
   c) *Right-hand front brake.*
   d) *Left-hand front brake.*

Warning: *On models with Dynamic Stability Control (DSC), after bleeding, the operation of the braking system should be checked at the earliest possible opportunity by a BMW dealer or suitably-equipped specialist.*

Bleeding

Basic (two-man) method

13 Collect a clean glass jar, a suitable length of plastic or rubber tubing which is a tight fit over the bleed screw, and a ring spanner to fit the screw. The help of an assistant will also be required.

14 Remove the dust cap from the first screw in the sequence. Fit the spanner and tube to the screw, place the other end of the tube in the jar, and pour in sufficient fluid to cover the end of the tube.

15 Ensure that the master cylinder reservoir fluid level is maintained at least above the MIN level line throughout the procedure.

16 Have the assistant fully depress the brake pedal several times to build-up pressure, then maintain it on the final downstroke.

17 While pedal pressure is maintained, unscrew the bleed screw (approximately one turn) and allow the compressed fluid and air to flow into the jar. The assistant should maintain pedal pressure, following it down to the floor if necessary, and should not release it until instructed to do so. When the flow stops, tighten the bleed screw again, have the assistant release the pedal slowly, and recheck the reservoir fluid level.

18 Repeat the steps in paragraphs 16 and 17 until the fluid emerging from the bleed screw is free from air bubbles. If the master cylinder has been drained and refilled, and air is being bled from the first screw in the sequence, allow about 5 seconds between cycles for the master cylinder passages to refill.

19 When no more air bubbles appear, tighten the bleed screw securely, remove the tube and spanner, and refit the dust cap. Do not overtighten the bleed screw.

20 Repeat the procedure on the remaining screws in the sequence, until all air is removed from the system and the brake pedal feels firm again.

Using a one-way valve kit

21 As their name implies, these kits consist of a length of tubing with a one-way valve fitted, to prevent expelled air and fluid being drawn back into the system; some kits include a translucent container, which can

2.21 Bleeding a front brake caliper using a one-way valve kit

be positioned so that the air bubbles can be more easily seen flowing from the end of the tube **(see illustration).**

22 The kit is connected to the bleed screw, which is then opened. The user returns to the driver's seat, depresses the brake pedal with a smooth, steady stroke, and slowly releases it; this is repeated until the expelled fluid is clear of air bubbles.

23 Note that these kits simplify work so much that it is easy to forget the master cylinder reservoir fluid level; ensure that this is maintained at least above the MIN level line at all times.

Using a pressure-bleeding kit

24 These kits are usually operated by the reservoir of pressurised air contained in the spare tyre. However, note that it will probably be necessary to reduce the pressure to a lower level than normal; refer to the instructions supplied with the kit. **Note:** *BMW specify that a pressure of 2 bar (29 psi) should not be exceeded.*

25 By connecting a pressurised, fluid-filled container to the master cylinder reservoir, bleeding can be carried out simply by opening each screw in turn (in the specified sequence), and allowing the fluid to flow out until no more air bubbles can be seen in the expelled fluid.

26 This method has the advantage that the large reservoir of fluid provides an additional safeguard against air being drawn into the system during bleeding.

27 Pressure-bleeding is particularly effective when bleeding 'difficult' systems, or when bleeding the complete system at the time of routine fluid renewal.

All methods

28 When bleeding is complete, and firm pedal feel is restored, wash off any spilt fluid, tighten the bleed screws securely, and refit their dust caps.

29 Check the hydraulic fluid level in the master cylinder reservoir, and top-up if necessary (Chapter 1).

30 Discard any hydraulic fluid that has been bled from the system; it will not be fit for re-use.

31 Check the feel of the brake pedal. If it feels at all spongy, air must still be present in the system, and further bleeding is required.

Failure to bleed satisfactorily after a reasonable repetition of the bleeding procedure may be due to worn master cylinder seals.

3 Hydraulic pipes and hoses – renewal

⚠️ **Warning: Under no circumstances should the hydraulic pipes/ hoses linking the master cylinder, hydraulic unit and (where fitted) the accumulator be disturbed. If these unions are disturbed and air enters the high-pressure hydraulic system, bleeding of the system can only be safely carried out by a BMW dealer or suitably-equipped specialist using the special service tester.**

Note: *Before starting work, refer to the warnings at the beginning of Section 2.*

1 If any pipe or hose is to be renewed, minimise fluid loss by first removing the master cylinder reservoir cap, then tightening it down onto a piece of polythene to obtain an airtight seal. Alternatively, flexible hoses can be sealed, if required, using a proprietary brake hose clamp; metal brake pipe unions can be plugged (if care is taken not to allow dirt into the system) or capped immediately they are disconnected. Place a wad of rag under any union that is to be disconnected, to catch any spilt fluid.

2 If a flexible hose is to be disconnected, unscrew the brake pipe union nut before removing the spring clip which secures the hose to its mounting bracket.

3 To unscrew the union nuts, it is preferable to obtain a brake pipe spanner of the correct size; these are available from most large motor accessory shops. Failing this, a close-fitting open-ended spanner will be required, though if the nuts are tight or corroded, their flats may be rounded-off if the spanner slips. In such a case, using self-locking pliers is often the only way to unscrew a stubborn union, but it follows that the pipe and the damaged nuts must be renewed on reassembly. Always clean a union and surrounding area before disconnecting it. If disconnecting a component with more than one union, make a careful note of the connections before disturbing any of them.

4 If a brake pipe is to be renewed, it can be obtained, cut to length and with the union nuts and end flares in place, from BMW dealers. All that is then necessary is to bend it to shape, following the line of the original, before fitting it to the car. Alternatively, most motor accessory shops can make up brake pipes from kits, but this requires very careful measurement of the original, to ensure that the new one is of the correct length. The safest answer is usually to take the original to the shop as a pattern.

5 On refitting, do not overtighten the union nuts. It is **not** necessary to exercise brute force to obtain a sound joint.

6 Ensure that the pipes and hoses are correctly routed, with no kinks, and that they

are secured in the clips or brackets provided. After fitting, remove the polythene from the reservoir, and bleed the hydraulic system as described in Section 2. Wash off any spilt fluid, and check carefully for fluid leaks.

4 Front brake pads – renewal

⚠️ **Warning: Renew both sets of front brake pads at the same time – never renew the pads on only one wheel, as uneven braking may result. Note that the dust created by wear of the pads may contain asbestos, which is a health hazard. Never blow it out with compressed air, and don't inhale any of it. An approved filtering mask should be worn when working on the brakes. DO NOT use petrol or petroleum-based solvents to clean brake parts; use brake cleaner or methylated spirit only.**

1 Apply the handbrake, then slacken the front roadwheel bolts. Jack up the front of the vehicle and support it on axle stands (see *Jacking and vehicle support*). Remove both front roadwheels.

Type 1 caliper

2 Follow the relevant accompanying photos **(illustrations 4.2a to 4.2u)** for the pad renewal procedure. Be sure to stay in order and read the caption under each illustration, and note the following points:

   a) *New pads may have an adhesive foil on the backplates. Remove this foil prior to installation.*
   b) *Thoroughly clean the caliper guide surfaces, and apply a little brake assembly grease (BMW pad paste 83 23 9 407 830 or Copperslip).*
   c) *When pushing the caliper piston back to accommodate new pads, keep a close eye on the fluid level in the reservoir.*
   d) *BMW insist that the brake pad wear sensor must be renewed if it has been removed.*
   e) *On vehicles over 2 years old, BMW recommend that a new retaining clip is fitted.*

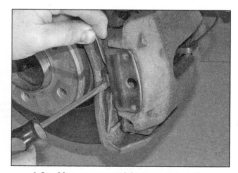

4.2a Use a screwdriver to prise the retaining clip rewards from place

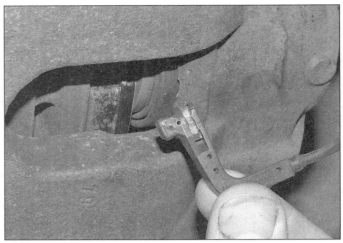

4.2b Pull the wear sensor from the inner pad, and unclip the sensor wiring from the bleed screw. Note that BMW insist the sensor is not re-used, as the retaining clip distorts during removal

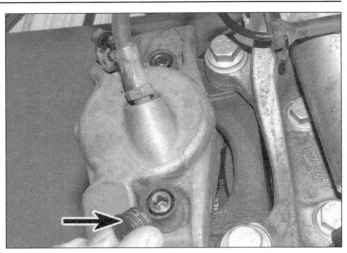

4.2c Prise out the rubber caps (arrowed) . . .

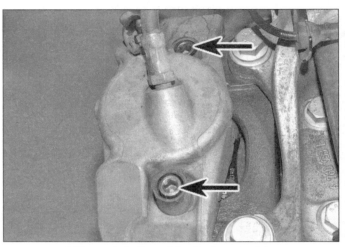

4.2d . . . undo the guide pins (arrowed) . . .

4.2e . . . and pull them from place

4.2f Slide the caliper and pads from the disc

4.2g Pull the inner pad from the piston . . .

4.2h . . . and the outer pad from the caliper

4.2i Suspend the caliper from the coil spring. Don't strain the brake hose

4.2j If a pad's friction material is 2.0 mm or less, renew all four pads

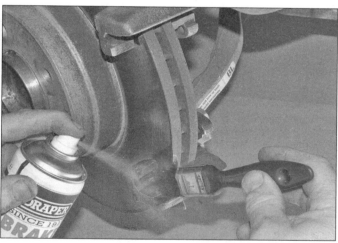

4.2k Use brake cleaner and a soft brush to clean the caliper/bracket mounting surfaces

4.2l If new pads are to be fitted, push the piston back into the caliper body using a retraction tool. Keep an eye on the brake fluid level whilst pushing the piston back

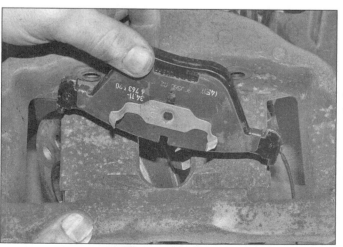

4.2m Clip the outer pad into place . . .

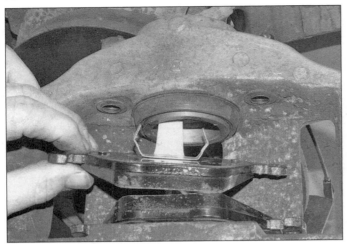

4.2n . . . then fit the inner pad to the piston . . .

4.2o . . . and slide the caliper/pads over the disc

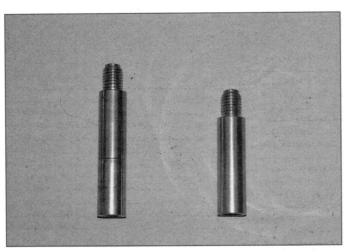

4.2p Refit the guide pins, noting that the longer pin locates in the lower hole

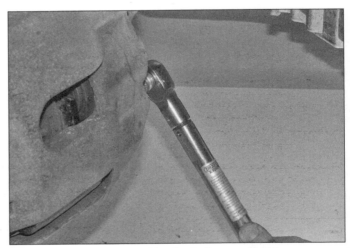

4.2q Tighten the guide pins to the specified torque

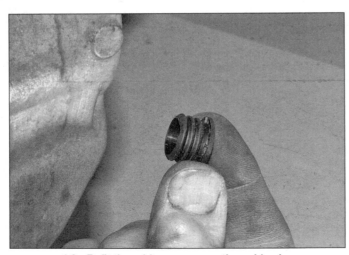

4.2r Refit the rubber caps over the guide pins

4.2s Locate the new wear sensor wiring loom over the bleed screw . . .

4.2t . . . and push the sensor into place in the inner pad

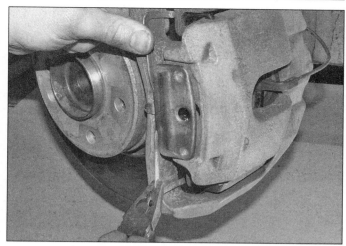

4.2u Use pliers to help refit the retaining clip

Type 2 caliper

3 Follow the relevant accompanying photos **(illustrations 4.3a to 4.3u)** for the pad renewal procedure. Be sure to stay in order and read the caption under each illustration, and note the following points:

a) *New pads may have an adhesive foil on the backplates. Remove this foil prior to installation.*

b) *Thoroughly clean the caliper guide surfaces, and apply a little brake assembly grease (BMW pad paste 83 23 9 407 830 or Copperslip).*

c) *When pushing the caliper piston back to accommodate new pads, keep a close eye on the fluid level in the reservoir.*

d) *BMW insist that the brake pad wear sensor must be renewed if it has been removed.*

e) *On vehicles over 2 years old, BMW*

recommend that a new retaining clip is fitted.

All calipers

4 Depress the brake pedal repeatedly, until the pads are pressed into firm contact with the brake disc, and normal (non-assisted) pedal pressure is restored.

5 Repeat the relevant procedure on the remaining front brake caliper.

6 Apply the little anti-seize grease to the hub surface, then refit the roadwheels, lower the vehicle to the ground and tighten the roadwheel bolts to the specified torque.

7 Check the hydraulic fluid level as described in *Weekly checks*.

Caution: New pads will not give full braking efficiency until they have bedded-in. Be prepared for this, and avoid hard braking as far as possible for the first hundred miles or so after pad renewal.

4.3a Use a screwdriver to prise the retaining clip rewards from place

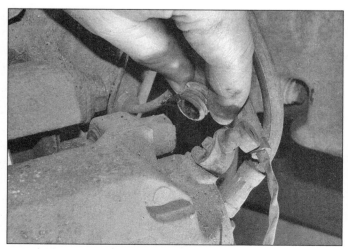

4.3b Prise out the rubber caps from the upper and lower guide pins . . .

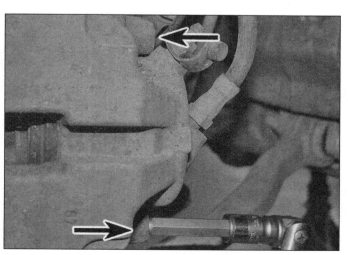

4.3c . . . then undo the guide pins

4.3d Pull the wear sensor from the inner pad, and unclip the wiring from the bleed screw

4.3e If necessary, lever the caliper outwards, to force the piston inwards . . .

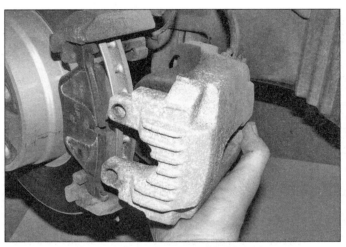

4.3f . . . so the caliper can slide from place

4.3g Pull the inner brake pad from the piston to unclip it . . .

4.3h . . . then suspend the caliper from the spring to avoid straining the rubber fluid hose

4.3i Remove the outer brake pad from the caliper mounting bracket

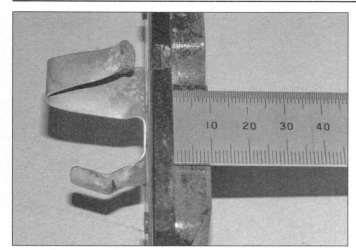

4.3j Measure the thickness of the pad's friction material

4.3k If new pads are being fitted, push the piston back into the caliper body using a retraction tool. Keep an eye on the brake fluid level whilst pushing the piston back

4.3l Use brake cleaner and a soft brush to clean the caliper/ bracket mounting surfaces

4.3m Fit the outer pad to the bracket. Ensure the friction material is against the disc surface

4.3n Press the inner pad into the piston

4.3o Slide the caliper back into place . . .

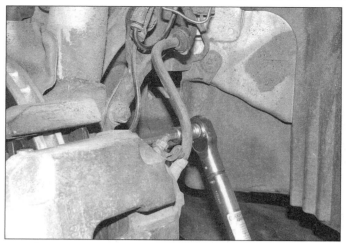

4.3p ... and tighten the guide pins to the specified torque

4.3q Refit the rubber cap to the guide pin locations

4.3r Slide the wear sensor into the slot (arrowed) in the inner pad

4.3s Clip the wear sensor wiring over the bleed screw

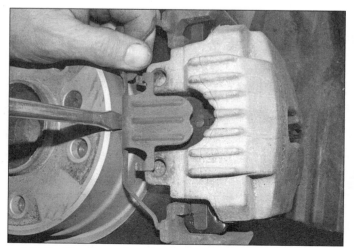

4.3t Position the ends of the retaining clip against the caliper mounting bracket, and lever the spring rearwards ...

4.3u ... so it clips into place

5 Rear brake pads – renewal

⚠️ **Warning:** *Renew both sets of rear brake pads at the same time – NEVER renew the pads on only one wheel, as uneven braking may result. Note that the dust created by wear of the pads may contain asbestos, which is a health hazard. Never blow it out with compressed air, and do not inhale any of it. An approved filtering mask should be worn when working on the brakes. DO NOT use petrol or petroleum-based solvents to clean brake parts; use brake cleaner or methylated spirit only.*

1 Chock the front wheels, then slacken the rear roadwheel bolts. Jack up the rear of the vehicle and support it on axle stands (see *Jacking and vehicle support*). Remove both rear roadwheels.

2 Follow the accompanying photos **(illustrations 5.2a to 5.2s)** for the pad renewal procedure. Be sure to stay in order and read the caption under each illustration, and note the following points:

a) *New pads may have an adhesive foil on the backplates. Remove this foil prior to installation.*

b) *Thoroughly clean the caliper guide surfaces using brake cleaner, and apply a little brake assembly (BMW pad paste 83 23 9 407 830 or Copperslip) grease.*

c) *When pushing the caliper piston back to accommodate new pads, keep a close eye on the fluid level in the reservoir.*

d) *BMW insist that the brake pad wear sensor must be renewed if it has been removed.*

3 Depress the brake pedal repeatedly, until the pads are pressed into firm contact with the brake disc, and normal (non-assisted) pedal pressure is restored.

4 Repeat the above procedure on the remaining rear brake caliper.

5 Refit the roadwheels, then lower the vehicle to the ground and tighten the roadwheel bolts to the specified torque.

6 Check the hydraulic fluid level as described in *Weekly checks*.

Caution: *New pads will not give full braking efficiency until they have bedded-in. Be prepared for this, and avoid hard braking as far as possible for the first hundred miles or so after pad renewal.*

5.2a Compress the retaining spring . . .

5.2b . . . and remove it

5.2c Pull the wear sensor from the inner brake pad

5.2d Prise out the rubber caps (arrowed) . . .

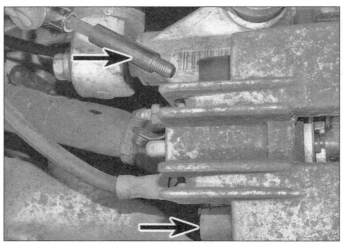

5.2e ... then unscrew the upper and lower guide pins (arrowed)

5.2f Slide the caliper, complete with inner brake pad, from the mounting bracket

5.2g Pull the inner brake pad from the caliper piston

5.2h Using wire or string, suspend the caliper from the vehicle to avoid straining the flexible brake fluid hose

5.2i Pull the outer pad from the mounting bracket

5.2j Use brake cleaner and a soft brush to clean the pad/caliper mounting surfaces

5.2k Fit the outer pad to the mounting bracket, ensuring the friction material is against the disc surface

5.2l If new pads are to be fitted, push the piston back into the caliper body using a piston retraction tool. Keep an eye on the brake fluid level in the reservoir

5.2m Push the inner pad retaining clip into the caliper piston . . .

5.2n . . . and slide the caliper back into place

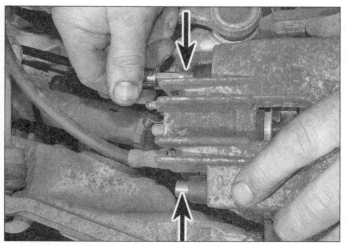

5.2o Refit the caliper guide pins (arrowed) . . .

5.2p . . . and tighten them to the specified torque

5.2q Refit the rubber caps over the guide pins

5.2r Press the retaining spring into place

5.2s Press the new wear sensor into place on the inner brake pad, then clip the wiring under the bleed screw rubber cap strap

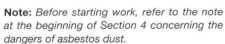

6 Front brake disc – inspection, removal and refitting

Note: *Before starting work, refer to the note at the beginning of Section 4 concerning the dangers of asbestos dust.*

Inspection

Note: *If either disc requires renewal, BOTH should be renewed at the same time, to ensure even and consistent braking. New brake pads should also be fitted.*

1 Apply the handbrake, then jack up the front of the car and support it on axle stands. Remove the appropriate front roadwheel.

2 Slowly rotate the brake disc so that the full area of both sides can be checked; remove the brake pads if better access is required to the inboard surface (see Section 4). Light scoring is normal in the area swept by the brake pads, but if heavy scoring or cracks are found, the disc must be renewed.

3 It is normal to find a lip of rust and brake dust around the disc's perimeter; this can be scraped off if required. If, however, a lip has formed due to excessive wear of the brake pad swept area, then the disc's thickness must be measured using a micrometer **(see illustration)**. Take measurements at several places around the disc, at the inside and outside of the pad swept area; if the disc has worn at any point to the specified

minimum thickness or less, the disc must be renewed.

4 If the disc is thought to be warped, it can be checked for run-out. Either use a dial gauge mounted on any convenient fixed point, while the disc is slowly rotated, or use feeler blades to measure (at several points all around the disc) the clearance between the disc and a fixed point, such as the caliper mounting bracket. If the measurements obtained are at the specified maximum or beyond, the disc is excessively warped, and must be renewed; however, it is worth checking first that the hub bearing is in good condition (Chapters 1 and/ or 10). If the run-out is excessive, the disc must be renewed.

5 Check the disc for cracks, especially around the wheel bolt holes, and any other wear or damage, and renew if necessary.

Removal

6 Unscrew the two bolts securing the brake caliper mounting bracket to the hub carrier, then slide the caliper assembly off the disc **(see illustration)**. Using a piece of wire or

6.3 Measure the thickness of the disc using a micrometer

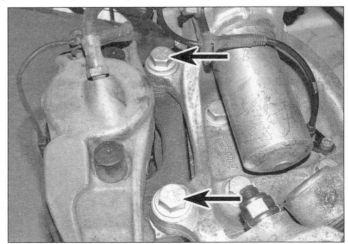

6.6 Undo the caliper mounting bracket bolts (arrowed)

6.7a Undo the retaining bolt . . .

6.7b . . . and remove the brake disc

string, tie the caliper to the front suspension coil spring, to avoid placing any strain on the hydraulic brake hose.

7 Use chalk or paint to mark the relationship of the disc to the hub, then remove the bolt securing the brake disc to the hub, and remove the disc **(see illustrations)**. If it is tight, lightly tap its rear face with a hide or plastic mallet.

Refitting

8 Refitting is the reverse of the removal procedure, noting the following points:

a) *Ensure that the mating surfaces of the disc and hub are clean and flat.*

b) *Align (if applicable) the marks made on removal, and tighten the disc retaining bolt to the specified torque.*

c) *If a new disc has been fitted, use a suitable solvent to wipe any preservative coating from the disc before refitting the caliper.*

d) *Slide the caliper into position over the disc, making sure the pads pass either side of the disc. Tighten the caliper bracket mounting bolts to the specified torque setting.*

e) *Refit the roadwheel, then lower the vehicle to the ground and tighten the roadwheel bolts to the specified torque. On completion, repeatedly depress the brake pedal until normal (non-assisted) pedal pressure returns.*

7 Rear brake disc – inspection, removal and refitting

Note: *Before starting work, refer to the note at the beginning of Section 5 concerning the dangers of asbestos dust.*

Inspection

Note: *If either disc requires renewal, BOTH should be renewed at the same time, to ensure even and consistent braking. New brake pads should also be fitted.*

1 Firmly chock the front wheels, then jack up the rear of the car and support it on axle stands. Remove the appropriate rear roadwheel. Release the handbrake.

2 Inspect the disc as described in Section 6.

Removal

3 Remove the brake pads as described in Section 5.

4 Undo the 2 bolts and remove the caliper mounting bracket. Discard the bolts – new ones must be fitted.

5 Slacken and remove the brake disc retaining bolt **(see illustration 6.7a)**.

6 It should now be possible to withdraw the brake disc from the stub axle by hand. If it is tight, lightly tap its rear face with a hide or plastic mallet. If the handbrake shoes are binding, first check that the handbrake is fully released, then continue as follows.

7 Referring to Section 14 for further details, fully slacken the handbrake adjustment, to obtain maximum free play in the cable.

8 Insert a screwdriver through one of the wheel bolt holes in the brake disc, and rotate the adjuster knurled wheel on the upper pivot to retract the shoes **(see illustration 14.6)**. The brake disc can then be withdrawn.

Refitting

9 If a new disc is been fitted, use a suitable solvent to wipe any preservative coating from the disc. Ensure the disc mounting surface on the hub is free from dirt and corrosion.

10 Align (if applicable) the marks made on removal, then fit the disc and tighten the retaining bolt to the specified torque.

11 Refit the caliper mounting bracket, and tighten the new bolts to the specified torque.

12 Adjust the handbrake shoes and cable as described in Section 14.

13 Refit the roadwheel, then lower the car to the ground, and tighten the roadwheel bolts to the specified torque. On completion, repeatedly depress the brake pedal until normal (non-assisted) pedal pressure returns. Recheck the handbrake adjustment.

8 Front brake caliper – removal, overhaul and refitting

Note: *Before starting work, refer to the note at the beginning of Section 2 concerning the dangers of hydraulic fluid, and to the warning at the beginning of Section 4 concerning the dangers of asbestos dust.*

Removal

1 Apply the handbrake, then jack up the front of the vehicle and support it on axle stands. Remove the appropriate roadwheel.

2 Minimise fluid loss by using a brake hose clamp, a G-clamp or a similar tool to clamp the flexible hose.

3 Clean the area around the union, then slacken the brake hose union nut.

4 Remove the brake pads (see Section 4).

5 Unscrew the caliper from the end of the brake hose and remove it from the vehicle.

Overhaul

6 With the caliper on the bench, wipe away all traces of dust and dirt, but *avoid inhaling the dust, as it is a health hazard.*

7 Withdraw the partially-ejected piston from the caliper body, and remove the dust seal.

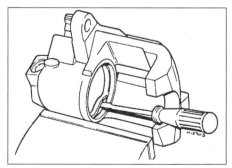

8.8 Take care not to scratch the piston bore whilst extracting the seal

HAYNES HINT *If the piston cannot be withdrawn by hand, it can be pushed out by applying compressed air to the brake hose union hole. Only low pressure should be required, such as is generated by a foot pump. As the piston is expelled, take great care not to trap your fingers between the piston and caliper.*

8 Using a small screwdriver, extract the piston hydraulic seal, taking great care not to damage the caliper bore **(see illustration)**.

9 Thoroughly clean all components, using only methylated spirit, isopropyl alcohol or clean hydraulic fluid as a cleaning medium. Never use mineral-based solvents such as petrol or paraffin, as they will attack the hydraulic system's rubber components. Dry the components immediately, using compressed air or a clean, lint-free cloth. Use compressed air to blow clear the fluid passages.

10 Check all components, and renew any that are worn or damaged. Check particularly the cylinder bore and piston; these should be renewed (note that this means the renewal of the complete body assembly) if they are scratched, worn or corroded in any way. Similarly check the condition of the guide pins and their bushes; both pins should be undamaged and (when cleaned) a reasonably tight sliding fit in the bushes. If there is any doubt about the condition of any component, renew it.

11 If the assembly is fit for further use, obtain the appropriate repair kit; the components are available from BMW dealers in various combinations. All rubber seals should be renewed as a matter of course; these should never be re-used.

12 On reassembly, ensure that all components are clean and dry.

13 Soak the piston and the new piston (fluid) seal in clean hydraulic fluid. Smear clean fluid on the cylinder bore surface.

14 Fit the new piston (fluid) seal, using only your fingers (no tools) to manipulate it into the cylinder bore groove.

15 Fit the new dust seal to the piston. Locate the rear of the seal in the recess in the caliper

body, and refit the piston to the cylinder bore using a twisting motion. Ensure that the piston enters squarely into the bore, and press it fully into the bore.

Refitting

16 Screw the caliper fully onto the flexible hose union.

17 Refit the brake pads (see Section 4).

18 Securely tighten the brake pipe union nut.

19 Remove the brake hose clamp, and bleed the hydraulic system as described in Section 2. Note that, providing the precautions described were taken to minimise brake fluid loss, it should only be necessary to bleed the relevant front brake.

20 Refit the roadwheel, then lower the vehicle to the ground and tighten the roadwheel bolts to the specified torque. On completion, check the hydraulic fluid level as described in *Weekly checks*.

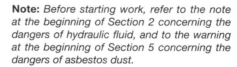

9 Rear brake caliper – removal, overhaul and refitting

Note: Before starting work, refer to the note at the beginning of Section 2 concerning the dangers of hydraulic fluid, and to the warning at the beginning of Section 5 concerning the dangers of asbestos dust.

Removal

1 Chock the front wheels, then jack up the rear of the vehicle and support on axle stands. Remove the relevant rear wheel.

2 Minimise fluid loss by using a brake hose clamp, a G-clamp or a similar tool to clamp the flexible hose.

3 Clean the area around the union, then loosen the brake hose union nut.

4 Remove the brake pads as described in Section 5.

5 Unscrew the caliper from the end of the flexible hose, and remove it from the vehicle.

Overhaul

6 Refer to Section 8.

Refitting

7 Screw the caliper fully onto the flexible hose union.

8 Refit the brake pads (refer to Section 5).

9 Securely tighten the brake pipe union nut.

10 Remove the brake hose clamp, and bleed the hydraulic system as described in Section 2. Note that, providing the precautions described were taken to minimise brake fluid loss, it should only be necessary to bleed the relevant rear brake.

11 Refit the roadwheel, then lower the vehicle to the ground and tighten the roadwheel bolts to the specified torque. On completion, check the hydraulic fluid level as described in *Weekly checks*.

10 Master cylinder – removal, overhaul and refitting

Note: Although it is possible for the home mechanic to remove the master cylinder, if the hydraulic unions are disconnected from the master cylinder, air will enter the high-pressure hydraulic system linking the master cylinder and hydraulic unit. Bleeding of the high-pressure system can only be safely carried out by a BMW dealer or specialist who has access to the service tester. Consequently, once the master cylinder has been refitted, the vehicle must be taken on a trailer or transporter to a suitably-equipped BMW dealer or specialist.

Note: Before starting work, refer to the warning at the beginning of Section 2 concerning the dangers of hydraulic fluid.

Note: New master cylinder retaining nuts will be required on refitting.

Removal

1 Working at the rear of the engine compartment, undo the fastener, release the clip and remove both the left- and the right-hand pollen filter covers **(see illustration)**.

2 Pull up the rubber sealing strip, then release the clip and slide the plastic cover from the centre of the panel **(see illustrations)**.

3 Lift out the plastic trim at the outer edge,

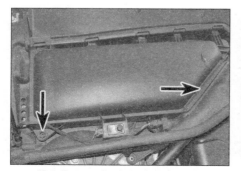

10.1 Rotate the fastener 90° anti-clockwise, and push the clip forwards

10.2a Pull up the sealing strip

10.2b Lift the clip and slide the plastic cover to the left

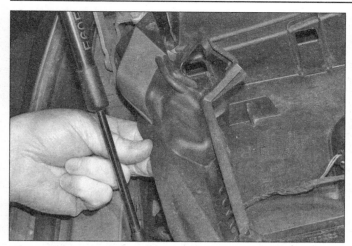

10.3a Lift out the plastic trim at the outer edges

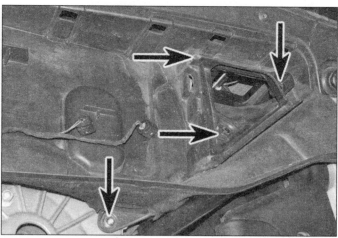

10.3b Rotate the fasteners 90° anti-clockwise and undo the bolt (arrowed)

undo the bolt/fasteners and remove the left- and right-hand pollen filter housings from behind the suspension turrets. Unclip the wiring where applicable (see illustrations).

4 Remove the master cylinder reservoir cap, and siphon the hydraulic fluid from the reservoir. **Note:** *Do not siphon the fluid by mouth, as it is poisonous; use a syringe or a hand-held vacuum pump.* Alternatively, open any convenient bleed screw in the system, and gently pump the brake pedal to expel the fluid through a plastic tube connected to the screw until the level of fluid drops below that of the reservoir (see Section 2). Disconnect the wiring connector(s) from the brake fluid reservoir **(see illustration)**.

5 Disconnect the fluid hose(s) from the side of the reservoir, and plug the hose end(s) to minimise fluid loss.

6 Unscrew and pull out the master cylinder reservoir locking pin **(see illustration)**.

7 Carefully ease the fluid reservoir out from the top of the master cylinder. Recover the reservoir seals, and plug the cylinder ports to prevent dirt entry.

8 Working under the facia, pull the lower front section trim of the centre console rearwards, undo the 4 bolts, and pull the trim panel above the driver's pedals downwards. Disconnect any wiring plugs as the panel is withdrawn.

9 Prise off the clip and remove the pin

securing the servo pushrod to the brake pedal **(see illustration)**. The servo must be slackened so the master cylinder can be removed and installed.

10 Undo the servo retaining nuts. Note that new nuts must be fitted.

11 Wipe clean the area around the brake pipe unions on the on the pipes from the master cylinder to the ABS modulator/hydraulic unit, and place absorbent rags beneath the pipe unions to catch any surplus fluid. Make a note of the correct fitted positions of the unions, then unscrew the union nuts and carefully withdraw the pipes. The pipes must not be bent. Plug or tape over the pipe ends and master cylinder orifices, to minimise the loss of brake fluid, and to prevent the entry of dirt into the system. Wash off any spilt fluid immediately with cold water.

12 Slacken and remove the two nuts and washers securing the master cylinder to the vacuum servo unit, then withdraw the unit from the engine compartment. Remove the O-ring from the rear of the master cylinder. Discard the retaining nuts, new ones should be used on refitting.

Overhaul

13 If the master cylinder is faulty, it must be renewed. Repair kits are not available from BMW dealers so the cylinder must be treated

as a sealed unit. Renew the master cylinder O-ring seal and reservoir seals regardless of their apparent condition.

Refitting

14 Remove all traces of dirt from the master cylinder and servo unit mating surfaces, and fit a new O-ring to the groove on the master cylinder body.

15 Fit the master cylinder to the servo unit, ensuring that the servo unit pushrod enters the master cylinder bore centrally. Fit the new master cylinder retaining nuts and washers, and tighten them to the specified torque.

16 Wipe clean the brake pipe unions, then refit them to the master cylinder/hydraulic unit ports and tighten them securely.

17 Press the new reservoir seals firmly into the master cylinder ports, then ease the reservoir into position. Refit the reservoir locking pin securely. Reconnect the fluid hose(s) to the reservoir, and reconnect the wiring connector(s).

18 The remainder of refitting is a reversal of removal, noting the following points:

   a) *Tighten all fasteners to their specified torque where given.*

   b) *Refill the master cylinder reservoir with new fluid, and bleed the complete hydraulic system as described in Section 2.*

10.4 Disconnect the fluid sensor wiring plug

10.6 Unscrew and remove the reservoir locking pin (arrowed)

10.9 Servo pushrod pin retaining clip (arrowed)

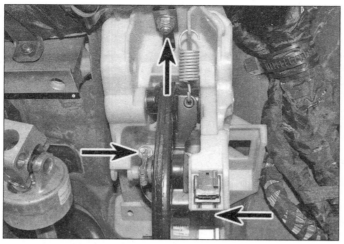

11.10 Pedal bracket retaining nuts (arrowed)

13.2 Servo unit check valve

11 Brake pedal – removal and refitting

Removal

Manual transmission

1 Remove the clutch pedal as described in Chapter 6.

2 Undo the 2 bolts and move the clutch master cylinder to one side.

3 Disconnect the stop-light switch wiring plug.

4 Slide off the retaining clip and remove the clevis pin securing the brake pedal to the servo unit pushrod.

5 Undo the 3 nuts and manoeuvre the brake pedal bracket assembly from under the facia. Discard the self-locking nuts – new ones must be fitted.

6 If required, unhook the return spring and slide the pedal from the pivot.

Automatic transmission

7 Remove the driver's side lower facia panel as described in Chapter 11.

8 Prise off the clip and remove the pin securing the servo pushrod to the brake pedal (see illustration 10.9).

9 Disconnect the stop-light switch wiring plug.

10 Undo the 3 nuts and manoeuvre the pedal and bracket assembly from under the facia (see illustration). Discard the self-locking nuts – new ones must be fitted. Note that at the time of writing, the pedal was only available as part of the complete bracket assembly. Consult your BMW dealer.

Refitting

11 Refitting is the reverse of removal. Apply a smear of multi-purpose grease to the pedal pivot and clevis pin.

12 Vacuum servo unit – testing, removal and refitting

Testing

1 To test the operation of the servo unit, depress the footbrake several times to exhaust the vacuum, then start the engine whilst keeping the pedal firmly depressed. As the engine starts, there should be a noticeable 'give' in the brake pedal as the vacuum builds-up. Allow the engine to run for at least two minutes, then switch it off. If the brake pedal is now depressed it should feel normal, but further applications should result in the pedal feeling firmer, with the pedal stroke decreasing with each application.

2 If the servo does not operate as described, first inspect the servo unit check valve as described in Section 13.

3 If the servo unit still fails to operate satisfactorily, the fault lies within the unit itself. Repairs to the unit are not possible – if faulty, the servo unit must be renewed.

Removal

4 Remove the master cylinder as described in Section 10.

5 Undo the 2 lower nuts securing the brake pedal bracket to the bulkhead (see illustration 11.10).

6 Prise the servo unit check valve from place (see illustration 13.2).

7 Manoeuvre the servo unit from place. Renew the seal between the servo and the bulkhead.

Refitting

8 Refitting is a reversal of removal.

13 Vacuum servo unit check valve – removal, testing and refitting

Removal

1 Carry out the tasks described in Paragraphs 1 to 4 of Section 10.

2 Prise the check valve from the servo, and disconnect the hose (see illustration).

Testing

3 Examine the valve for signs of damage and renew if necessary.

4 Test the valve by blowing through it in both directions; air should only flow through the valve in one direction only – when blown through from the servo end of the valve. Renew the valve if this is not the case.

Refitting

5 Refitting is a reversal of removal.

14 Handbrake – adjustment

1 Applying normal moderate pressure, pull the handbrake lever to the fully applied position, counting the number of clicks emitted from the handbrake ratchet mechanism. If adjustment is correct, there should be approximately 7 or 8 clicks before the handbrake is fully applied. If there are more than 10 clicks, adjust as follows.

2 Slacken and remove one wheel bolt from each rear wheel then chock the front wheels, jack up the rear of the vehicle and support it on axle stands.

3 Access to the handbrake cable adjuster can be gained by removing the handbrake lever gaiter from the centre console (see

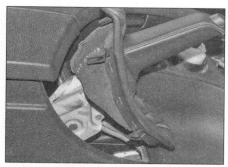

14.3 Squeeze together the sides, and unclip the handbrake lever gaiter

14.4a Push the spring stop back . . .

14.4b . . . until the retaining hook (arrowed) engages with the stop (centre console removed for clarity)

14.6 Rotate the adjuster knurled ring with a screwdriver through the wheel bolt hole at the 6 o'clock position (brake drum removed for clarity)

14.8 Press back the stop and disengage it from the hook

the roadwheels, then lower the vehicle to the ground and tighten the wheel bolts to the specified torque.

11 If after renewal of the brake shoes the performance of the handbrake is still inadequate, drive along a deserted road at 25 mph and apply the handbrake until a braking effect can be felt. Pull the lever to the next notch and drive for approximately 400 mm to bed the shoes in. Release the handbrake and allow the brakes to cool.

15 Handbrake lever – removal and refitting

Removal

1 Remove the centre console as described in Chapter 11.

2 Release the handbrake, then use a screwdriver to push the spring stop back until the retaining hook engages with the stop (**see illustrations 14.4a and 14.4b**).

3 Disconnect the handbrake warning switch, then release the clips and move the cable guide/bracket to one side.

4 Remove the retaining clip from the balance arm, then disengage ends of the handbrake cables from the balance arm (**see illustrations**).

5 Undo the 3 retaining bolts and remove the lever from the vehicle (**see illustration**).

illustration). If greater access is required, the rear section of the centre console will have to be removed (Chapter 11).

4 Release the handbrake, then use a screwdriver to push the spring stop back until the retaining hook engages with the stop (**see illustrations**).

5 Starting on the right-hand rear wheel, rotate the wheel so the adjuster knurled ring is visible through the hole.

6 Insert a screwdriver in through the bolt hole and fully expand the handbrake shoes by rotating the adjuster knurled ring. When the wheel/disc can no longer be turned, back the knurled ring off by 8 notches (185 mm diameter drum) or 9 notches 160 mm diameter drum so that the wheel is free to rotate easily (**see illustration**).

7 Repeat paragraph 5 and 6 on the left-hand wheel.

8 Unlock the cable adjuster unit by levering out the retaining hook from the spring stop with a screwdriver (**see illustration**).

9 Fully release the handbrake lever, and check that the wheels rotate freely. Slowly apply the handbrake, and check that the brake shoes start to contact the drums when the handbrake is set to the third notch of the ratchet mechanism. Check the adjustment by applying the handbrake fully, counting the clicks emitted from the handbrake ratchet and, if necessary, re-adjust.

10 Once adjustment is correct, check the operation of the handbrake warning light switch, then refit the centre console section/ handbrake lever gaiter (as applicable). Refit

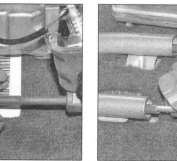

15.4a Pull up the retaining clip . . .

15.4b . . . and disengage the cable end fitting from the balance arm

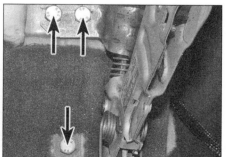

15.5 Handbrake lever retaining bolts (arrowed)

16.4 Remove the cable retaining bracket bolt (arrowed)

16.5 Disengage the cable end fitting from the expander

Refitting

6 Refitting is a reversal of the removal. Prior to refitting the centre console, adjust the handbrake as described in Section 14.

16 Handbrake cables – removal and refitting

Removal

1 Detach the front ends of the cables from the lever balance arm as described in Section 15.
2 Remove the handbrake shoes as described in Section 17.
3 Remove the exhaust system as described in Chapter 4, then release the fasteners and remove the heat shield above the exhaust system.
4 Undo the bolt and remove the cable retaining bracket from the inboard face of the hub carrier (see illustration).
5 Disengage the cable end fitting from the expander (see illustration).
6 Working back along the length of the cable, noting its correct routing, and free it from all the relevant retaining clips.

Refitting

7 Insert the cable into the brake carrier/guard plate, and push it in up to the stop on the cable outer sleeve.
8 Grip the sleeve of the cable end, and push it into the expander until it snaps into place.
9 Refitting is a reversal of the removal procedure. Prior to refitting the centre console, adjust the handbrake as described in Section 14.

17 Handbrake shoes – removal and refitting

Removal

1 Carefully prise up the handbrake lever gaiter from the centre console (see illustration 14.3). If greater access is required, the rear section of the centre console will have to be removed (Chapter 11).
2 Use a screwdriver to push the spring stop back until the retaining hook engages with the stop (see illustrations 14.4a and 14.4b).

3 Remove the rear brake disc as described in Section 7, and make a note of the correct fitted position of all components.
4 Using a pair of pliers, carefully unhook and remove the handbrake shoe return springs.
5 Release the shoe retaining pins using an Allen bit/driver, by depressing them and rotating them through 90°, then remove the pins and springs (see illustration).
6 Remove both handbrake shoes, and recover the shoe adjuster mechanism, noting which way around it is fitted.
7 Inspect the handbrake shoes for wear or contamination, and renew if necessary. It is recommended that the return springs are renewed as a matter of course. BMW state the wear limit for shoe friction material thickness is 1.5 mm.
8 While the shoes are removed, clean and inspect the condition of the shoe adjuster and expander mechanisms, renew them if they show signs of wear or damage. If all is well, apply a fresh coat of brake grease (BMW recommend Molykote Paste G) to the threads of the adjuster and sliding surfaces of the expander mechanism. Do not allow the grease to contact the shoe friction material.

Refitting

9 Prior to installation, clean the backplate, and apply a thin smear of high-temperature brake grease or anti-seize compound to all those surfaces of the backplate which bear on the shoes. Do not allow the lubricant to foul the friction material.
10 Engage the expander mechanism with the end of the handbrake cable, then offer up the handbrake shoes engaging the upper ends with the expander mechansim, and secure them in position with the retaining pins and springs (see illustration).
11 Slide the adjuster mechanism into position

17.5 Depress the pins, rotate them 90° and remove them

17.10 Position the shoes against the expander mechanism, then refit the retaining pins (driver's side shown)

17.11 Fit the adjuster between the lower ends of the shoes

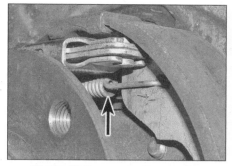

17.12a Fit the upper return spring (arrowed) . . .

17.12b . . . and the lower return spring

between the lower ends of the shoes **(see illustration)**.

12 Check all components are correctly fitted, and fit the upper and lower return springs using a pair of pliers **(see illustrations)**.

13 Centralise the handbrake shoes, and refit the brake disc as described in Section 7.

14 Prior to refitting the roadwheel, adjust the handbrake as described in Section 14.

18 Stop-light switch – removal and refitting

Removal

1 The stop-light switch is located on the pedal bracket behind the facia.

2 Working under the facia, pull the lower front section trim of the centre console rearwards, undo the 4 bolts, and pull the trim panel above the driver's pedals downwards. Disconnect any wiring plugs as the panel is withdrawn.

3 Reach up behind the facia and disconnect the wiring connector from the switch.

4 Pull the switch from the mounting. If required, depress the clips and withdraw the switch mounting from the pedal bracket **(see illustrations)**.

Refitting

5 Fully depress the brake pedal and hold it down, refit the mounting, then manoeuvre the switch into position. Push the switch fully into position, then **slowly** release the brake pedal and allow it to return to its stop. This will automatically adjust the stop-light switch. **Note:** *If the pedal is released too quickly, the switch will be incorrectly adjusted.*

6 Reconnect the wiring connector, and check the operation of the stop-lights. The stop-lights should illuminate after the brake pedal has travelled approximately 5 mm. If the switch is not functioning correctly, it is faulty and may need to be renewed; no other adjustment is possible.

7 On completion, refit the driver's side lower facia panel.

19 Anti-lock braking system (ABS) – general information

Note: *On all models the ABS unit is a dual function unit, and works both the anti-lock braking system (ABS) and traction control function of the Dynamic Stability Control (DSC) system.*

1 ABS is fitted to all models as standard. The system comprises a hydraulic block which contains the hydraulic solenoid valves and the electrically-driven return pump, the four roadwheel sensors (one fitted to each wheel), and the electronic control unit (ECU). The purpose of the system is to prevent the wheel(s) locking during heavy braking. This is achieved by automatic release of the brake on the relevant wheel, followed by re-application of the brake.

2 The solenoids are controlled by the ECU, which itself receives signals from the four wheel sensors (one fitted on each hub), which monitor the speed of rotation of each wheel. By comparing these signals, the ECU can determine the speed at which the vehicle is travelling. It can then use this speed to determine when a wheel is decelerating at an abnormal rate, compared to the speed of the vehicle, and therefore predicts when a wheel is about to lock. During normal operation, the system functions in the same way as a non-ABS braking system. In addition to this, the brake pedal position sensor (which is fitted to the vacuum servo unit) also informs the ECU of how hard the brake pedal is being depressed.

3 If the ECU senses that a wheel is about to lock, it operates the relevant solenoid valve

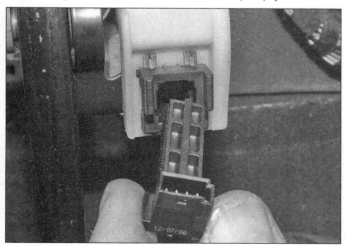

18.4a Pull the stop-light switch from the mounting

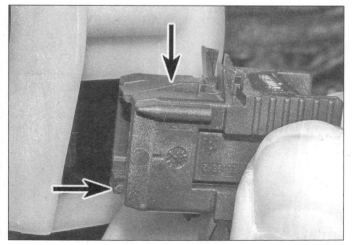

18.4b Depress the clip (arrowed) and pull the switch mounting from the bracket

in the hydraulic unit, which then isolates the brake caliper on the wheel which is about to lock from the master cylinder, effectively sealing-in the hydraulic pressure.

4 If the speed of rotation of the wheel continues to decrease at an abnormal rate, the ECU switches on the electrically-driven return pump operates, and pumps the hydraulic fluid back into the master cylinder, releasing pressure on the brake caliper so that the brake is released. Once the speed of rotation of the wheel returns to an acceptable rate, the pump stops; the solenoid valve opens, allowing the hydraulic master cylinder pressure to return to the caliper, which then re-applies the brake. This cycle can be carried out at 10 times a second.

5 The action of the solenoid valves and return pump creates pulses in the hydraulic circuit. When the ABS system is functioning, these pulses can be felt through the brake pedal.

6 The operation of the ABS system is entirely dependent on electrical signals. To prevent the system responding to any inaccurate signals, a built-in safety circuit monitors all signals received by the ECU. If an inaccurate signal or low battery voltage is detected, the ABS system is automatically shut down, and the warning light on the instrument panel is illuminated, to inform the driver that the ABS system is not operational. Normal braking should still be available, however.

7 If a fault does develop in the ABS system, the vehicle must be taken to a BMW dealer or suitably-equipped specialist for fault diagnosis and repair.

8 An accumulator is also incorporated into the hydraulic system. As well as performing the ABS function as described above, the unit also works the traction/stability control side of the DSC system. If the ECU senses that the wheels are about to lose traction under acceleration, the unit momentarily applies the rear brakes to prevent the wheel(s) spinning. If the system senses that the lateral acceleration/yaw rate of the vehicle is about to

exceed a predetermined threshold – resulting in oversteer or understeer, the system can apply the brake of each individual wheel to maintain stability and prevent/control a skid.

9 The DSC system can also control the steering of the vehicle to maintain stability in an oversteer, or understeer situation – known as Active Steering. With conventional systems, the driver has to actively steer the vehicle in a straight line if the brakes are applied on a road surface with varying traction levels. Active Steering keeps the vehicle in its track and helps to achieve acceptable braking distances. In these situations, the DSC control unit calculates the yaw rate with the brake pressure sensors on the front axle, and transmits to the Active Steering control unit the yaw-moment compensation correction angle needed for stabilisation.

10 Should a fault develop with the ABS/DSC system, the vehicle must be taken to a BMW dealer or suitably-equipped specialist who will be able to interrogate the system's self-diagnosis capacity, and pin-point the fault.

20 Anti-lock braking system (ABS) components – removal and refitting

Hydraulic/modulator/accumulator unit

1 Although it is possible for the home mechanic to remove the hydraulic unit, the unit's self-diagnosis system must be interrogated by dedicated test equipment before and after removal, and the unit must be bled by BMW service test equipment. Consequently, we recommend that removal and refitting the hydraulic unit should be entrusted to a BMW dealer or suitably-equipped specialist.

Electronic control unit (ECU)

2 In order to remove the ECU, the hydraulic unit must first be removed, as the ECU is

screwed to the side of the hydraulic unit. Consequently, we recommend that removal and refitting of the ECU is entrusted to a BMW dealer or suitably-equipped specialist.

Front wheel sensor

Removal

3 Chock the rear wheels, then firmly apply the handbrake, jack up the front of the vehicle and support on axle stands. Remove the appropriate front roadwheel. Trace the wiring back from the sensor to the connector which is situated in a protective plastic box. Unclip the lid, then free the wiring connector and disconnect it from the main harness **(see illustration)**.

4 Slacken and remove the bolt securing the sensor to the hub carrier, and remove the sensor and lead assembly from the vehicle **(see illustration)**.

Refitting

5 Prior to refitting, apply a thin coat of multipurpose grease to the sensor tip (BMW recommend the use of Staburags NBU 12/k).

6 Ensure that the sensor and hub carrier sealing faces are clean, then fit the sensor to the hub. Refit the retaining bolt and tighten it to the specified torque.

7 Ensure that the sensor wiring is correctly routed and retained by all the necessary clips, and reconnect it to its wiring connector. Refit the sensor connector into the box and securely clip the lid in position.

8 Refit the roadwheel, then lower the vehicle to the ground and tighten the roadwheel bolts to the specified torque.

Rear wheel sensor

Removal

9 Chock the front wheels, then jack up the rear of the vehicle and support it on axle stands. Remove the appropriate roadwheel.

10 Remove the sensor as described in paragraphs 3 and 4. Note that the sensor

20.3 Release the clip and open the connector box and disconnect the front ABS sensor plug (arrowed)

20.4 Front ABS sensor (arrowed)

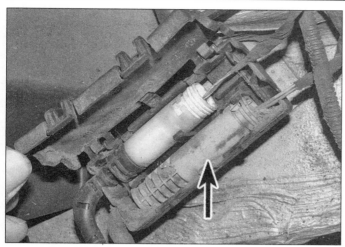

20.10 Release the clip and open the connector box, and disconnect the rear ABS sensor plug (arrowed)

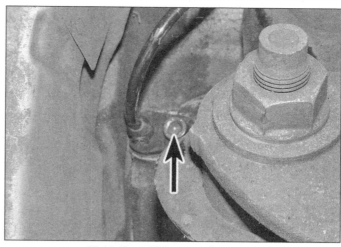

20.11 Rear ABS sensor (arrowed)

wiring connector is located behind the wheel arch liner. Undo the bolts and pull the rear section of the liner forwards to access the connector **(see illustration)**.

Refitting

11 Refit the sensor as described above in paragraphs 5 to 8 **(see illustration)**.

Front reluctor rings

12 The front reluctor rings are fixed onto the rear of the wheel hubs. Examine the rings for damage such as chipped or missing teeth. If renewal is necessary, the complete hub assembly must be dismantled and the bearings renewed, with reference to Chapter 10.

Rear reluctor rings

13 The rear reluctor rings are pressed onto the driveshaft outer joints. Examine the rings for signs of damage such as chipped or missing teeth, and renew as necessary. If renewal is necessary, the driveshaft assembly must be renewed (see Chapter 8).

21 Vacuum pump – removal and refitting

M47 and M57 engines

Removal

1 Remove the plastic cover from the top of the engine. The vacuum pump is located at the front of the engine, and is driven by the camshaft.
2 Remove the EGR pipe/cooler as described in Chapter 4B. There is no need to drain the coolant or disconnect the coolant pipes – pull the pipe/cooler forwards slightly to facilitate vacuum pump removal. **Note:** *If the vacuum pump is being removed as part of the camshaft*

removal procedure, the EGR pipe/cooler must be completely removed.
3 Undo the bolt and disconnect the hose connection from the vacuum pump **(see illustration)**. Renew the connection O-ring seal.
4 Undo the bolts and remove the vacuum pump. Renew the O-ring seal **(see illustrations)**.

Refitting

5 Refitting is a reversal of removal, ensuring

the drive lug of the pump engages correctly with the slot in the camshaft **(see illustration)**. Apply a little silicone sealant to the threads, then tighten the pump retaining bolts securely.

N47 engines

6 On these engines, the vacuum pump is integral with the oil pump. Refer to Chapter 2A for the oil pump removal procedure.

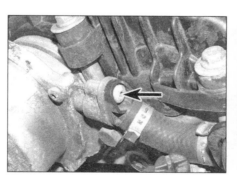

21.3 Undo the bolt (arrowed) and disconnect the vacuum hose

21.4a Undo the vacuum pump retaining bolts (arrowed)

21.4b Renew the pump O-ring seal

21.5 The pump drive engages with the slot in the end of the camshaft

Notes

Chapter 10
Suspension and steering

Contents

Degrees of difficulty

Easy, suitable for novice with little experience	**Fairly easy,** suitable for beginner with some experience	**Fairly difficult,** suitable for competent DIY mechanic	**Difficult,** suitable for experienced DIY mechanic	**Very difficult,** suitable for expert DIY or professional

Specifications

Front suspension

Type . . . . Independent, with MacPherson struts incorporating coil springs and telescopic shock absorbers. Steel anti-roll bar, with Dynamic Drive (hydraulically variable roll bar stiffness) available as an option

Rear suspension

Type . . . . Independent, lower arms located by front and rear upper control arms with McPherson struts incorporating coil springs and telescopic shock absorbers (Saloon models) or air springs and separate telescopic shock absorbers (Touring models). Steel anti-roll bar, with Dynamic Drive (hydraulically variable roll bar stiffness) available as an option

Steering

Type . . . . Rack and pinion. Power assistance standard on all models. Active electronically-controlled steering available as an option

Wheel alignment and steering angles

Vehicle must be laden to simulate front and rear passengers, and a full fuel tank

Front wheel:
   Camber angle:
      Standard suspension . . . .   -12' ± 30'
      Sports suspension . . . .   -30' ± 30'
      Maximum difference between sides . . . .   30'
   Castor angle:
      Standard suspension . . . .   Not available
      Sports suspension . . . .   Not available
      Maximum difference between sides . . . .   30'
   Toe setting (total):
      Saloon . . . .   0° 08' ± 12'
      Touring . . . .   0° 12' ± 10'
Rear wheel:
   Camber angle:
      Standard suspension . . . .   -2° 00' ± 25'
      Sports suspension . . . .   -2° 00' ± 25'
      Maximum difference between sides . . . .   30'
   Toe setting (total) . . . .   0° 18' ± 12'

Torque wrench settings

	Nm	lbf ft
Front suspension		
Anti-roll bar connecting link nuts*	65	48
Anti-roll bar link bracket to hub carrier	58	43
Anti-roll bar mounting clamp nuts	30	22
Hub/bearing assembly*	110	81
Control arm balljoint nut*	165	122
Control arm-to-subframe nut:*		
Stage 1	100	74
Stage 2	Angle-tighten a further 90°	
DSC sensor bolts	8	6
Strut piston rod nut*	64	47
Strut-to-hub carrier nut and bolt:*		
M10	45	33
M12	81	59
Strut mounting-to-body nuts*	34	25
Tension strut balljoint nut*	165	122
Tension strut-to-subframe nut:*		
Stage 1	100	74
Stage 2	Angle-tighten a further 90°	
Rear suspension		
Anti-roll bar clamps	28	21
Anti-roll bar link nut*	65	48
Hub bearing housing-to-hub carrier:		
Saloon:*		
Stage 1	30	22
Stage 2	Angle-tighten a further 90°	
Touring	100	74
Integral link to hub carrier	100	74
Integral link-to-swinging arm nut*	240	177
Shock absorber upper mounting nuts*	28	21
Shock absorber lower mounting bolt*	165	122
Swinging arm-to-subframe nut:*		
Front bolt	100	74
Rear bolt	175	129
Control arm-to-subframe nut*	100	74
Control arm-to-hub carrier nut*	165	122
Traction strut-to-hub carrier nut*	65	48
Traction strut-to-subframe nut*	65	48
Steering		
DSC/active steering acceleration sensor	8	6
Power steering pipe union bolts:		
M10 union bolt	12	9
M14 union bolt	35	26
M16 union bolt	40	30
M18 union bolt	45	33

Torque wrench settings (continued)

	Nm	lbf ft
Steering (continued)		
Power steering pump bolts	22	16
Steering column bolts	22	16
Steering column universal joint clamp/pinch-bolt*.	22	16
Steering rack mounting bolts/nuts:*		
Stage 1	56	41
Stage 2	Angle-tighten a further 90°	
Steering wheel	63	46
Suspension turret/tension braces*	30	22
Track rod end balljoint retaining nut*	165	122
Track rod end locknut.	51	38
Track rod to steering rack.	110	81
Roadwheels		
Roadwheel bolts.	120	89

* Do not re-use

1   General information

The independent front suspension is of the MacPherson strut type, incorporating coil springs and integral telescopic shock absorbers. The MacPherson struts are located by transverse lower suspension arms, which use rubber inner mounting bushes, and incorporate a balljoint at the outer ends. The front hub carriers, which carry the brake calipers and the hub/disc assemblies, are bolted to the MacPherson struts, and connect to the lower arms through balljoints. A front anti-roll bar is fitted to all models. The anti-roll bar is rubber-mounted and is connected to both suspension struts/lower arms (as applicable) by connecting links **(see illustration)**. On models with 'Dynamic Drive' the stiffness of the front and rear anti-roll bar is altered by an hydraulic actuator mounted on the bar itself. As the vehicle corners, the bar is stiffened to reduce body roll.

The rear suspension is of the fully independent type consisting of lower swinging arms, which are linked to the rear axle carrier by various control arms/struts. MacPherson struts incorporating coil springs and telescopic shock absorbers are fitted to Saloon models, whereas Touring models are equipped with 'air springs' and separate shock absorbers. These springs, in conjunction with height sensors and an air supply unit, allow

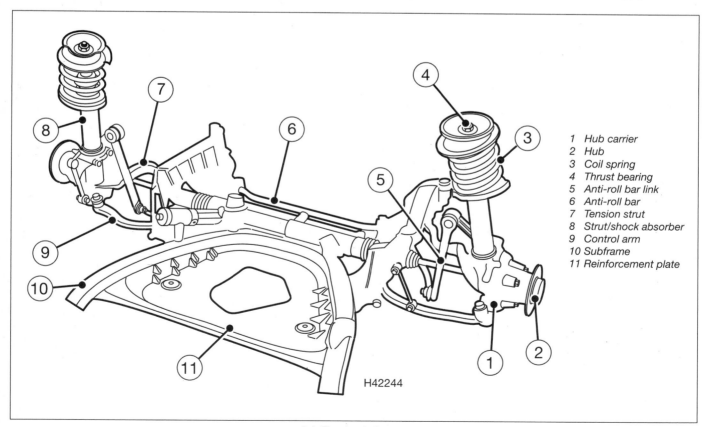

1 Hub carrier
2 Hub
3 Coil spring
4 Thrust bearing
5 Anti-roll bar link
6 Anti-roll bar
7 Tension strut
8 Strut/shock absorber
9 Control arm
10 Subframe
11 Reinforcement plate

H42244

1.1 Front axle layout

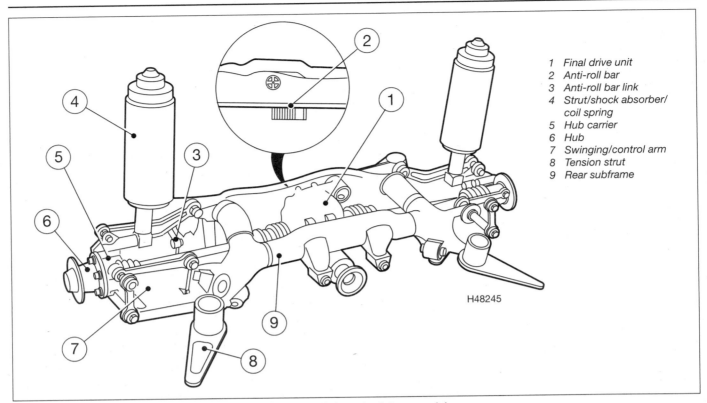

1 Final drive unit
2 Anti-roll bar
3 Anti-roll bar link
4 Strut/shock absorber/
   coil spring
5 Hub carrier
6 Hub
7 Swinging/control arm
8 Tension strut
9 Rear subframe

H48245

1.2a Rear axle layout – Saloon models

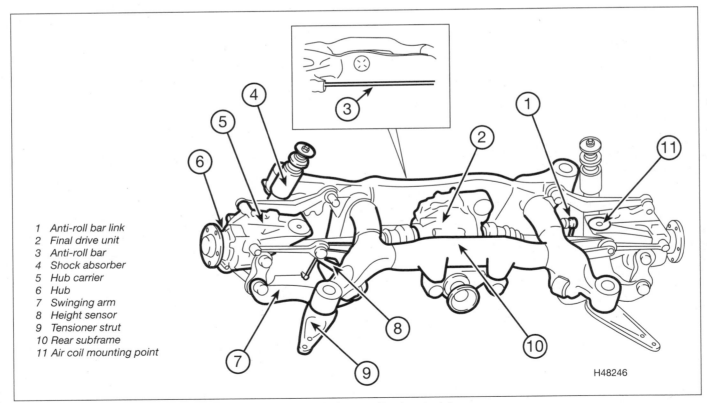

1 Anti-roll bar link
2 Final drive unit
3 Anti-roll bar
4 Shock absorber
5 Hub carrier
6 Hub
7 Swinging arm
8 Height sensor
9 Tensioner strut
10 Rear subframe
11 Air coil mounting point

H48246

1.2b Rear axle layout – Touring models

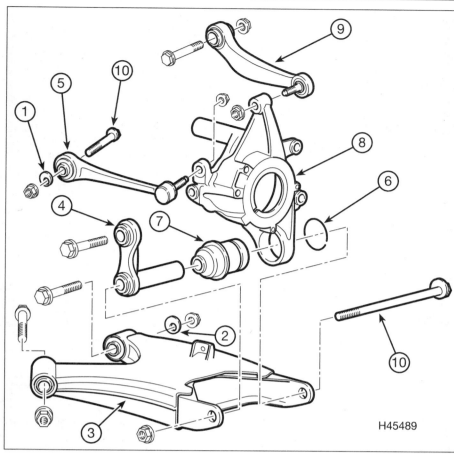

1.2c Rear suspension arms

1 Eccentric washer	5 Traction arm	9 Control arm
2 Eccentric washer	6 Circlip	10 Bolt with integral
3 Swinging arm	7 Balljoint	eccentric washer
4 Integral link	8 Hub carrier	

the rear suspension to be 'self-levelling', to compensate for various vehicle loads **(see illustrations)**. A rear anti-roll bar is fitted to all models, and may be of the 'Dynamic Drive' type as described in the previous paragraph.

The steering column is connected to the steering rack by an intermediate shaft, which incorporates a universal joint.

The steering rack is mounted onto the front

subframe, and is connected by two track rods, with balljoints at their outer ends, to the steering arms projecting forwards from the hub carriers. The track rod ends are threaded, to facilitate adjustment.

Power-assisted steering is fitted as standard to all models. The hydraulic steering system is powered by a belt-driven pump, which is driven off the crankshaft pulley, whilst on some models a fully electronic system is

available, which has a rack-mounted electric motor to provide the power assistance.
Note: *The information contained in this Chapter is applicable to the standard suspension set-up. On models with M-Technic sports suspension, slight differences will be found. Refer to your BMW dealer for detail.*

2 Front hub assembly – removal and refitting

Removal

1 Remove the hub carrier as described in Section 3.
2 Undo the 4 retaining bolts and remove the hub and bearing assembly **(see illustration)**. Discard the bolts, new ones must be fitted. Note that the hub and bearing is only available as a complete assembly.

Refitting

3 Ensure the mating surfaces of the hub and hub carrier as clean, then position the hub on the carrier.
4 Fit the new retaining bolts and tighten them to the specified torque.
5 Refit the brake disc as described in Chapter 9.

3 Front hub carrier – removal and refitting

Removal

1 Firmly apply the handbrake, then jack up the front of the car and support it on axle stands. Remove the relevant front roadwheel, then undo the fasteners and remove the engine undershield **(see illustrations 5.1a and 5.1b)**.
2 Remove the brake disc and ABS wheel speed sensor as described in Chapter 9.
3 On models with Xenon gas discharge headlights, release the clamp and detach the ride height sensor rod from the control arm **(see illustration)**.
4 Slacken the bolt securing the control arm to the front subframe **(see illustration)**. This is to

2.2 Front hub and bearing retaining bolts

3.3 Undo the height sensor rod nut (arrowed)

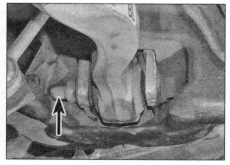

3.4 Slacken the control arm-to-subframe bolt (arrowed)

3.7 Counterhold the anti-roll bar link balljoint shank with a Torx key

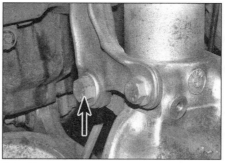

3.8a Undo the suspension strut clamp bolt (arrowed)

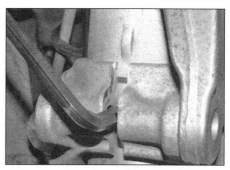

3.8b Use a large Allen key (or similar) to slightly spread the hub carrier clamp

prevent damage to the mounting bush as the hub carrier is removed.

5 Detach the control arm and tension strut from the hub carrier as described in Section 5 **(see illustrations 5.3a, 5.3b and 5.8)**.

6 Undo the nut and detach the track rod end from the hub carrier as described in Section 25.

7 Undo the bolt securing the anti-roll bar link to the bracket on the hub carrier **(see illustration)**.

8 Slacken and remove the bolt securing the suspension strut to the hub carrier. Note that the bolt is inserted from the front. Slide the hub carrier down and off from the end of the strut. Discard the nut and bolt – new ones must be fitted. To ease removal, insert a large screwdriver or Allen key into the slot on the back of the hub carrier and slightly spread the hub carrier clamp **(see illustrations)**. Take care to spread the carrier clamp only as much as absolutely necessary, as excessive force will cause damage.

9 Examine the hub carrier for signs of wear or damage, and renew if necessary.

Refitting

10 Prior to refitting, clean the threads of the strut-to-hub carrier bolt hole by running a tap of the correct thread size and pitch down it.

HAYNES HINT *If a suitable tap is not available, clean out the holes using the old bolt with slots cut in its threads.*

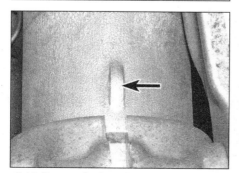

3.11 Ensure the locating notch (arrowed) aligns with the hub carrier slot

11 Locate the hub carrier correctly with the suspension strut, ensuring that the locating notch on the strut slides into the slot in the hub carrier clamp **(see illustration)**. Slide the hub carrier up until it contacts the 'stop' on the strut. Fit the new bolt from the front and tighten the new nut to the specified torque.

12 Engage the hub carrier with the control arm balljoint stud, and fit the new retaining nut. Tighten the nut to the specified torque.

13 Engage the tension strut balljoint with the hub carrier, fit the new nut and tighten it to the specified torque.

14 Engage the track rod balljoint in the hub carrier, then fit a new retaining nut and tighten it to the specified torque.

15 The remainder of refitting is a reversal of removal.

4 Front strut – removal, overhaul and refitting

Removal

1 Chock the rear wheels, apply the handbrake, then jack up the front of the car and support on axle stands. Remove the appropriate roadwheel. Undo the fasteners and remove the engine undershield.

2 Remove the hub carrier as described in Section 3.

3 Remove the plastic expansion rivets, and

4.5a Upper strut mounting nuts. Note the centring pin (arrowed)

unclip the plastic cover (where fitted) over the relevant strut upper mounting in the engine compartment.

4 Place a trolley jack under the hub carrier to prevent it falling as the upper mounting nuts are removed.

5 From within the engine compartment, unscrew the strut upper mounting nuts, then carefully lower the strut assembly out from underneath the wing. **Note:** *On some models, a centring pin fixed to the strut upper mounting plate aligns with a corresponding hole in the vehicle body work* **(see illustrations)**. *On models where no centring pin is fitted, make alignment marks between the mounting plate and vehicle body. It is essential that the mounting plate is fitted to its original location to preserve the strut camber angle.*

Overhaul

⚠ *Warning: Before attempting to dismantle the front suspension strut, a suitable tool to hold the coil spring in compression must be obtained. Adjustable coil spring compressors are readily available, and are recommended for this operation. Any attempt to dismantle the strut without such a tool is likely to result in damage or personal injury.*

6 With the strut removed from the car, clean away all external dirt, then mount it upright in a vice.

7 Fit the spring compressor, and compress the coil spring until all tension is relieved

4.5b Lower the strut from the wheel arch

4.7 Compress the spring until all tension on the upper seat is relieved

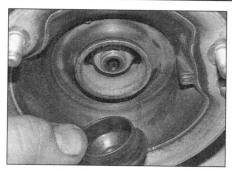

4.8a Remove the cap . . .

4.8b . . . and slacken the retaining nut whilst counterholding the piston with an Allen key/bit

from the upper spring seat **(see illustration)**.

8 Remove the cap from the top of the strut to gain access to the strut upper mounting retaining nut. Slacken the nut whilst retaining the strut piston with a suitable Allen bit **(see illustrations)**.

9 Remove the mounting nut, and lift off the mounting plate complete with thrust bearing, followed by the mounting dished washer, shim, and upper seat.

10 Lift off the coil spring, followed by the bump stop, gaiter and lower spring seat.

11 With the strut assembly now completely dismantled, examine all the components for wear, damage or deformation, and check the upper mounting bearing for smoothness of operation. Renew any of the components as necessary.

12 Examine the strut for signs of fluid leakage. Check the strut piston for signs of pitting along its entire length, and check the strut body for signs of damage.

13 If any doubt exists about the condition of the coil spring, carefully remove the spring compressors, and check the spring for

distortion and signs of cracking. Renew the spring if it is damaged or distorted, or if there is any doubt as to its condition.

14 Inspect all other components for damage or deterioration, and renew any that are suspect.

15 Refit the lower spring seat, and slide the bump stop and gaiter onto the strut piston **(see illustrations)**.

16 Fit the coil spring onto the strut, making sure the rubber seat and spring are correctly located **(see illustrations)**.

17 Fit the upper seat/rubber, shim, and dished

4.15a Refit the lower spring seat . . .

4.15b . . . followed by the bump stop and gaiter

4.16a Refit the coil spring . . .

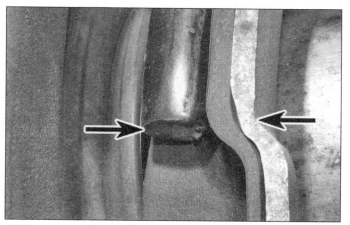

4.16b . . . and position the end of the spring level with the step in the lower seat (arrowed)

4.17a Refit the upper seat/rubber . . .

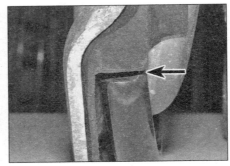

4.17b . . . with the end of the spring against the step (arrowed) . . .

4.17c . . . followed by the shim . . .

4.17d . . . and dished washer (concave side upwards)

4.18a Refit the mounting plate . . .

4.18b . . . and tighten the new nut to the correct torque

washer, so that the spring end is against the seat stop **(see illustrations)**.

18 Fit the mounting plate and new nut, and tighten it to the specified torque **(see illustrations)**. Refit the cap.

19 Ensure the spring ends and seats are correctly located, then carefully release the compressor and remove it from the strut.

Refitting

20 Refitting is a reversal of removal, noting the following points:

   a) *Tighten all fasteners to their specified torque where given.*

   b) *Renew all self-locking nuts.*
   c) *We recommend the front wheel alignment is checked at the earliest opportunity.*

5   Front arms/strut – removal, overhaul and refitting

Note: *New control arm front balljoint nuts will be required on refitting.*

Removal

1 Chock the rear wheels, firmly apply the handbrake, then jack up the front of the car and support on axle stands. Remove the appropriate front roadwheel. Undo the fasteners and remove the engine/transmission undershields **(see illustrations)**.

Control arm

2 On models fitted with suspension ride height sensors, release the nut and disconnect the sensor link from the arm.

3 Unscrew the control arm balljoint nut to the point where the edge of the nut is flush with the end of the balljoint shank, then release the arm from the hub carrier by gently tapping the end of the balljoint shank with a soft-faced

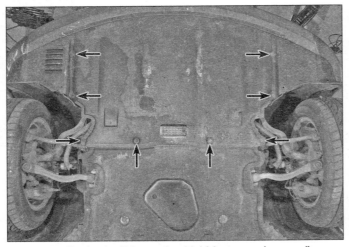

5.1a Engine/radiator undershield fasteners (arrowed)

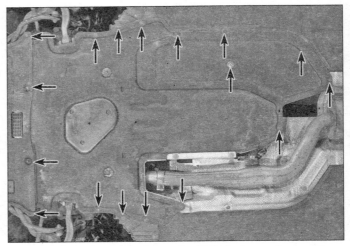

5.1b Engine/transmission undershield fasteners (arrowed)

5.3a Undo the balljoint nut using a Torx bit to counterhold the shank . . .

5.3b . . . then gently tap the balljoint from the hub carrier

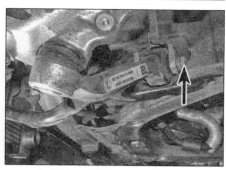

5.4 Remove the control arm inner mounting bolt (arrowed)

hammer (see illustrations). There is no need to use a balljoint separator. Discard the nut – a new one must be fitted.

4 Undo the nut and pull the inner mounting bolt from the control arm (see illustration). Note that the bolt is inserted from the rear. Discard the nut – a new one must be fitted.

5 Remove the control arm assembly from underneath the car.

Tension strut

6 Undo the nut and detach the link rod from the anti-roll bar.

7 Detach the control arm balljoint from the hub carrier as described previously in this Section.

8 Undo the tension strut balljoint nut. If necessary, use a Torx bit in the end of the balljoint shank to counterhold the nut, then release the arm from the hub carrier by gently tapping the end of the balljoint shank with a soft-faced hammer (see illustration). There is no need to use a balljoint separator. Discard the nut – a new one must be fitted.

9 Slacken the nut on the end of the bolt clamping the suspension strut to the hub carrier, then insert a large screwdriver or Allen key into the slot on the back of the hub carrier and slightly spread the hub carrier clamp (see illustrations 3.8a and 3.8b). Take care to spread the carrier clamp only as much as absolutely necessary, as excessive force will cause damage. Note that a new bolt and nut will be required.

10 Lower the hub carrier approximately 25 mm down the suspension strut, and

remove the tension strut balljoint from the hub carrier (see illustration).

11 Undo the inner mounting bolt and remove the strut from the subframe (see illustration). Discard the nut – a new one must be fitted.

Overhaul

12 Thoroughly clean the arm or strut and the area around the mountings, removing all traces of dirt and underseal if necessary, then check carefully for cracks, distortion or any other signs of wear or damage, paying particular attention to the mounting bushes and balljoint. Note that the balljoints are integral with both the arm and the strut. If the tension strut bush requires renewal, the strut should be taken to a BMW dealer or suitably-equipped garage. A hydraulic press and suitable spacers are required to press the bush out of position and install the new one.

Refitting

Control arm

13 Locate the inner end of the control arm with the subframe, insert the bolt from the rear, then fit the new nut – do not tighten the nut at this stage. On models with height sensors, refit the bracket before fitting the retaining nut.

14 Ensure the balljoint studs and mounting holes are clean and dry, then offer up the control arm, and engage the balljoint with the hub carrier. If necessary, press the inner balljoint stud into position using a jack position beneath the arm

15 Fit a new nut to the outer balljoint stud, and tighten it to the specified torque setting.

16 On models equipped with suspension ride height sensors, refit the sensor link to the control arm and secure the nut.

17 Refit the roadwheel, then lower the car to the ground and tighten the wheel bolts to the specified torque.

18 With the weight of the vehicle on the wheels, tighten the control arm inner bolt/nut to the specified torque.

19 Refit the engine undershield.

20 On models with active steering, it may be necessary to have the steering angle sensor calibration carried out using BMW diagnostic equipment. Entrust this task to a BMW dealer or suitably-equipped specialist.

21 We recommend that the front wheel alignment is checked at the earliest opportunity.

Tension strut

22 Locate the inner end of the strut in the subframe bracket, then insert the bolt and fit the new nut. Do not tighten the nut at this stage.

23 Engage the strut balljoint with the hub carrier, fit the new nut and tighten it to the specified torque.

24 Slide the hub carrier back up into position on the strut, insert the new bolt and tighten the new nut to the specified torque.

25 Reconnect the control arm balljoint to the hub carrier and tighten the new nut to the specified torque.

26 Refit the roadwheel, then lower the car to

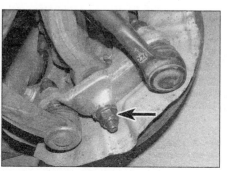

5.8 Undo the tension strut balljoint nut (arrowed)

5.10 Tension strut inner mounting bolts and nut (arrowed)

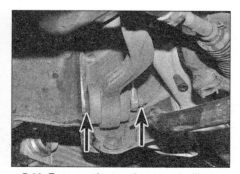

5.11 Remove the tension strut balljoint shank from the hub carrier

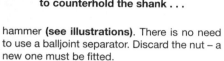

the ground and tighten the wheel bolts to the specified torque.

27 With the weight of the vehicle on the wheels, tighten the strut inner bolt/nut to the specified torque.

28 Refit the engine undershield.

6 Front arm balljoint – renewal

The balljoints on both the tension strut and control arm are integral, and cannot be renewed separately. If defective, the complete arm/strut must be renewed, as described in Section 5.

7 Front anti-roll bar – removal and refitting

Removal

1 Chock the rear wheels, firmly apply the handbrake, then jack up the front of the car and support on axle stands. Undo the fasteners and remove the engine undershield, then remove both front roadwheels.

2 On models with Dynamic Drive, undo the unions from the active anti-roll bar motors, and allow the fluid to drain into a container.

3 Unscrew the retaining nuts, and free the connecting link from each end of the anti-roll bar using a Torx bit to counterhold the balljoint stud **(see illustration)**. Discard the nuts – new ones must be fitted.

4 Make alignment marks between the mounting bushes and anti-roll bar, then slacken the anti-roll bar mounting clamp retaining nuts/bolts **(see illustration)**.

5 Undo the nuts and remove both clamps from the subframe, and manoeuvre the anti-roll bar out from underneath the car. Remove the mounting bushes from the bar. Discard the self-locking nuts – new ones must be fitted.

6 Carefully examine the anti-roll bar components for signs of wear, damage or deterioration, paying particular attention to the mounting bushes. Renew worn components as necessary.

7.3 Use a Torx bit to counterhold the anti-roll bar link balljoint stud

Refitting

7 Fit the rubber mounting bushes to the anti-roll bar, aligning them with the marks made prior to removal. Rotate each bush so that its flat surface is uppermost, and the split side on the rear. Keep the bush and bar mating faces clean and free from oil/grease.

8 Offer up the anti-roll bar, and manoeuvre it into position. Refit the mounting clamps, and fit the new retaining nuts. Ensure that the bush markings are still aligned with the marks on the bars, then tighten the mounting clamp retaining nuts to the specified torque.

9 Engage the anti-roll bar connecting links with the bar. Make sure the flats on the balljoint shank are correctly located against the lugs on the bar then fit the new retaining nuts and tighten to the specified torque.

10 Reconnect the Dynamic Drive pipe unions and tighten them securely.

11 Refit the undershield, then refit the roadwheels, lower the car to the ground and tighten the wheel bolts to the specified torque. Where applicable, fill and bleed the Dynamic Drive hydraulic system as described in Section 29.

8 Front anti-roll bar connecting link – removal and refitting

Note: *New connecting link nuts will be required on refitting.*

Removal

1 Firmly apply the handbrake, then jack up the front of the car and support it on axle stands.

2 Unscrew the retaining nut, and free the connecting link from the anti-roll bar using a Torx socket to counterhold the link balljoint stud.

3 Slacken and remove the nut securing the link to the suspension strut, using a Torx socket to counterhold the link balljoint stud **(see illustration 7.3)**.

4 Check the connecting link balljoints for signs of wear. Check that each balljoint is free to move easily, and that the rubber gaiters are undamaged. If necessary renew the connecting link.

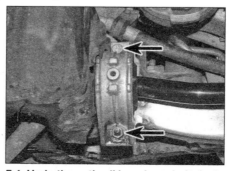

7.4 Undo the anti-roll bar clamp bolts/nuts (arrowed)

Refitting

5 Refitting is a reverse of the removal sequence, using new nuts and tightening them to the specified torque setting.

9 Rear hub assembly – removal and refitting

Note: *The hub assembly should not be removed unless it, or the hub bearing, is to be renewed. The hub is a press-fit in the bearing inner race, and removal of the hub will damage the bearings. If the hub is to be removed, be prepared to renew the hub bearing at the same time.*

Note: *A long bolt/length of threaded bar and suitable washers will be required on refitting.*

Removal

1 Remove the relevant driveshaft as described in Chapter 8.

2 Remove the brake disc as described in Chapter 9.

3 Bolt a slide hammer to the hub surface, and use the hammer to draw the hub out from the bearing. If the bearing inner race stays attached to the hub, a puller will be required to draw it off.

4 With the hub removed, renew the bearing as described in Section 10.

Refitting

5 Apply a smear of oil to the hub surface, and locate it in the bearing inner race.

6 Draw the hub into position using a long bolt or threaded length of bar and two nuts. Fit a large washer to either end of the bolt/ bar, so the inner one bears against the bearing inner race, and the outer one against the hub. Slowly tighten the nut(s) until the hub is pulled fully into position. **Note:** *Do not be tempted to knock the hub into position with a hammer and drift, as this will almost certainly damage the bearing.*

7 Remove the bolt/threaded bar and washers (as applicable), and check that the hub bearing rotates smoothly and easily.

8 Refit the brake disc as described in Chapter 9.

9 Refit the driveshaft, referring to Chapter 8.

10 Rear hub bearings – renewal

1 Remove the rear hub as described in Section 9.

2 Undo the bolts and detach the bearing housing from the hub carrier.

3 The new bearing is supplied complete with bearing housing. Ensure the mating surface of the hub carrier is clean, and free from oil and grease.

4 Position the new housing on the hub carrier, and tighten the bolts to the specified torque.

5 Fit the rear hub as described in Section 9.

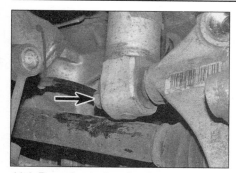

11.4 Rear shock absorber lower mounting bolt (arrowed)

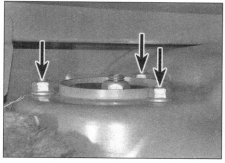

11.5a Undo the shock absorber upper mounting nuts (arrowed) . . .

11.5b . . . and lower the shock absorber from place

11 Rear shock absorber – removal, overhaul and refitting

Removal

1 Chock the front wheels, then jack up the rear of the car and support it on axle stands. To improve access, remove the rear roadwheel.

Saloon models

2 Detach the control arm from the hub carrier as described in Section 14.
3 Remove the luggage compartment side trim panel as described in Chapter 11.
4 Slacken and remove the bolt securing the shock absorber to the lower mounting **(see illustration)**. Discard the bolt – a new one must be fitted.
5 Remove the foam insulation, unscrew the upper mounting nuts, and with the help of an assistant, lower the shock absorber from the vehicle **(see illustrations)**.

Touring models

6 Remove the luggage compartment side trim panel, and floor covering as described in Chapter 11.
7 Undo the nuts and remove the floor side mouldings **(see illustration)**.
8 Place a trolley jack under the outer end of the suspension lower arm, and 'take the weight' of the arm/hub carrier – just enough to relieve the tension on the shock absorber.
9 Undo the bolt securing the shock absorber to the lower arm **(see illustration)**. Ensure all

tension is relieved from the shock absorber – if necessary adjust the trolley jack position. Discard the lower shock absorber mounting bolt – a new one must be fitted.
10 Working inside the vehicle, undo the upper securing nut and manoeuvre the shock absorber from place **(see illustration)**.

Overhaul – Saloon models only

⚠ *Warning: Before attempting to dismantle the suspension strut, a suitable tool to hold the coil spring in compression must be obtained. Adjustable coil spring compressors are readily available, and are recommended for this operation. Any attempt to dismantle the strut without such a tool is likely to result in damage or personal injury.*

11 With the strut removed from the car, clean away all external dirt, then mount it upright in a vice.

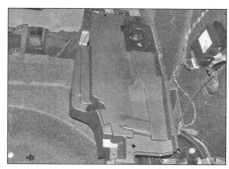

11.7 Remove the floor side mouldings

12 Fit the spring compressor, and compress the coil spring until all tension is relieved from the upper spring seat **(see illustration)**.
13 Remove the cap (where fitted) from the top of the strut to gain access to the strut upper mounting retaining nut. Slacken the nut whilst retaining the strut piston with a suitable Allen bit **(see illustration)**.
14 Remove the mounting nut, and lift off the washer and mounting plate complete with support bearing and spring seat.
15 Lift out the dished washer and bump stop, followed by the coil spring and spring seat.
16 With the strut assembly now completely dismantled, examine all the components for wear, damage or deformation, and check the upper mounting bearing for smoothness of operation. Renew any of the components as necessary.
17 Examine the strut for signs of fluid leakage. Check the strut piston for signs of

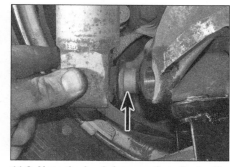

11.9 Note the bush (arrowed) on the inside of the shock absorber

11.10 Shock absorber upper mounting nut – Touring models

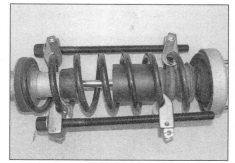

11.12 Compress the coil spring until all tension is relieved from the upper seat

11.13 Hold the piston with an Allen bit whilst slackening the nut

11.20a Fit the lower spring seat . . .

11.20b . . . followed by the bump stop . . .

11.20c . . . and dished washer

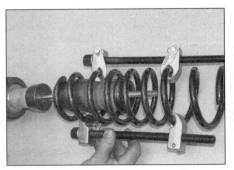

11.21 Fit the coil spring, smaller diameter at the lower end

11.22a Fit the spring seat/bearing/ mounting plate . . .

11.22b . . . and washer

pitting along its entire length, and check the strut body for signs of damage.

18 If any doubt exists about the condition of the coil spring, carefully remove the spring compressors, and check the spring for distortion and signs of cracking. Renew the spring if it is damaged or distorted, or if there is any doubt as to its condition.

19 Inspect all other components for damage or deterioration, and renew any that are suspect.

20 Refit the lower spring seat, then slide the bump stop and dished washer onto the strut piston **(see illustrations)**.

21 Fit the coil spring onto the strut, making sure the rubber seat and spring are correctly located **(see illustration)**. Note that the smaller diameter end of the spring locates on the lower spring seat.

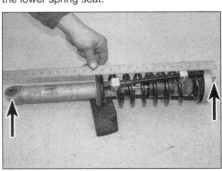

11.24 One of the mounting studs should be approximately in-line with the hole in the mounting rubber on the opposite side to the bush (arrowed)

22 Fit the spring seat/support bearing/ mounting plate and washer, so that the spring end is against the seat stop **(see illustrations)**.

23 Fit the new mounting plate nut and tighten it securely.

24 Ensure the spring ends and seats are correctly located. One of the upper mounting studs must be in-line with the hole in the lower mounting rubber on the opposite side to the bush **(see illustration)**. Carefully release the compressor and remove it from the strut. Refit the cap (where fitted) to the top of the strut.

Refitting

25 Refitting is a reversal of removal, noting the following points:

  a) *Ensure the upper mounting and body contact surfaces are clean and dry.*

  b) *Manoeuvre the shock absorber into position and fit the new upper mounting nuts.*

  c) *Tighten all fasteners to their specified torque where given.*

12 Rear air suspension – general information

The Touring models are fitted with air springs, in place of the traditional metal coil springs. In conjunction with height sensors, air supply unit and a control unit, the rear

suspension is 'self-levelling', compensating for different loads, and maintaining a constant ride height.

Prior to working on any component of the air pressure system, the circuit must be drained of compressed air, and once the work is completed, the circuit must be re-activated and pressurised. This necessitates the use of dedicated BMW diagnostic equipment. Consequently, we recommend that any task involving the air suspension system should be entrusted to a BMW dealer or suitably-equipped specialist.

Caution: It is essential that the vehicle is not driven with depressurised air springs. The springs' rubber bellows will be irretrievably damaged.

13 Rear hub carrier – removal, overhaul and refitting

Removal

Saloon models

1 Chock the front wheels, then jack up the rear of the car and support it on axle stands. Remove the relevant roadwheel.

2 Remove the relevant driveshaft (see Chapter 8).

3 Remove the brake disc and ABS wheel speed sensor as described in Chapter 9.

4 Referring to Chapter 9, disconnect the handbrake cable from the rear wheel.

14.3 Control arm-to-hub carrier balljoint nut (arrowed). Use a spanner to counterhold the shank

14.4 Control arm-to-subframe bolt (arrowed)

5 Remove the shock absorber/strut as described in Section 11.

6 Undo the bolt and detach the anti-roll bar link from the swinging arm **(see illustration 14.10)**.

7 Disconnect the integral link, traction strut, and control arm from the hub carrier as described in Section 14, then remove the hub carrier.

Touring models

8 Removal of the hub carrier on these models requires the draining, refilling, initialisation and calibration of the air suspension system. This can only be done using dedicated BMW diagnostic equipment. Consequently, we recommend this task is entrusted to a BMW dealer or suitably-equipped specialist.

Overhaul

9 Thoroughly clean the hub carrier and the area around the carrier mountings, removing all traces of dirt and underseal if necessary. Check carefully for cracks, distortion or any other signs of wear or damage, paying particular attention to the mounting bushes and balljoint. If either bushes or balljoint requires renewal, the hub carrier should be taken to a BMW dealer or suitably-equipped

garage. A hydraulic press and suitable spacers are required to press the bushes/balljoint out of position and install the new ones. Inspect the pivot bolts for signs of wear or damage, and renew as necessary.

Refitting

10 Refitting is a reversal of removal, noting the following points:
- a) Renew all self locking nuts.
- b) Only tighten the integral link, traction strut and control arm bolts/nuts when the weight of the vehicle is back on the wheels.
- c) Tighten all fasteners to their specified torque where given.
- d) Have the rear wheel alignment checked at the earliest opportunity.

14 Rear arms/struts/links – removal, overhaul and refitting

Removal

1 Chock the front wheels, then jack up the rear of the car and support it on axle stands

(see *Jacking and vehicle support)*. Remove the relevant roadwheel.

Control arm

Note: *On Touring models, the air suspension system must be depressurised prior to commencing work – refer to Section 12.*

2 Unclip the ABS sensor wiring from the retaining clip on the control arm, and, on the right-hand side (if applicable) unclip the brake pad wear sensor wiring.

3 Undo the nut securing the control arm balljoint to the hub carrier **(see illustration)**. Discard the nut – a new one must be fitted.

4 Undo the nut, and pull out the bolt securing the arm to the rear subframe **(see illustration)**. Note that the bolt is inserted from the front. Discard the nut – a new one must be fitted.

Integral link

Note: *On Touring models, the air suspension system must be depressurised prior to commencing work – refer to Section 12.*

5 Remove the relevant side driveshaft as described in Chapter 8.

6 Support the hub carrier with a trolley jack.

7 Undo the nut and pull out the bolt securing the integral link to the swinging arm **(see illustration)**. Discard the nut – a new one must be fitted.

8 Undo the upper bolt, press the swinging arm downwards a little, and remove the integral link **(see illustration 14.7)**.

Swinging arm

Note: *On Touring models, the air suspension system must be depressurised prior to commencing work – refer to Section 12.*

9 On Touring models, detach the shock absorber from the swinging arm as described in Section 11.

10 Undo the nut and detach the anti-roll bar link from the swinging arm **(see illustration)**.

11 Where applicable, disconnect the height sensor rod from the swinging arm.

12 Make alignment marks between the swinging arm front and rear inner bolts

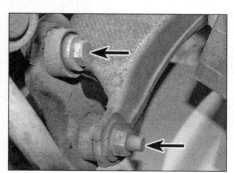

14.7 Integral link upper and lower bolts (arrowed)

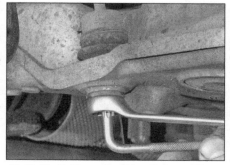

14.10 Undo the anti-roll bar link nut. Use a Torx bit to counterhold the shank

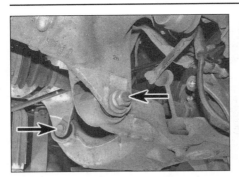

14.12 Swinging arm front and rear inner mounting bolts (arrowed)

14.17 Traction strut inner mounting bolt (arrowed)

eccentric head/washers and the subframe **(see illustration)**.

13 Undo the nut, remove the eccentric washer, then pull the swinging arm-to-integral link bolt out. Discard the nut – a new one must be fitted.

14 Undo the nuts and remove the swinging arm inner mounting bolts. Discard the nuts – new ones must be fitted.

15 Remove the swinging arm.

Traction strut

16 Undo the nut and detach the traction strut from the hub carrier **(see illustration)**. Discard the nut – a new one must be fitted.

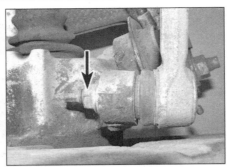

14.16 Traction strut-to-hub carrier bolt (arrowed). Counterhold the shank with a spanner

17 Make alignment marks between the traction strut inner eccentric bolt head/washer and the subframe **(see illustration)**.

18 Undo the nut, then pull the inner eccentric bolt from the subframe. On some models, it's necessary to unclip the plastic cover from the bolt head. Note that the bolt is inserted from the front. Discard the self-locking nut – a new one must be fitted.

Overhaul

19 Thoroughly clean the arms/strut and the area around the mountings, removing all traces of dirt and underseal if necessary. Check for cracks, distortion or any other wear or damage, paying particular attention to the mounting bushes. If the bushes require renewal, the arm/strut should be taken to a BMW dealer or suitably-equipped garage. A hydraulic press and suitable spacers are required to press the bushes out of position and fit the new ones.

20 Inspect the pivot bolts for signs of wear or damage, and renew as necessary.

Refitting

21 Refitting is a reversal of removal, noting the following points:

a) Renew all self-locking nuts.
b) Align any previously made-marks.

c) Only tighten the swinging arm, traction strut, integral link and control arm bolts/nuts when the weight of the vehicle is back on the wheels.
d) Tighten all fasteners to their specified torque where given.
e) Have the rear wheel alignment checked at the earliest opportunity.

15 Rear anti-roll bar – removal and refitting

Removal

1 Raise the rear of the vehicle and support it securely on axle stands (see *Jacking and vehicle support*).

2 On models with Dynamic Drive, undo the unions from the active anti-roll bar motors, and allow the fluid to drain into a container.

3 Undo the nuts and detach both anti-roll bar links from the anti-roll bar **(see illustration)**.

4 Make alignment marks between the mounting bushes and anti-roll bar, then undo the anti-roll bar mounting clamp retaining nuts **(see illustration)**.

5 Remove both clamps from the subframe, and manoeuvre the anti-roll bar out from underneath the car. Remove the mounting bushes from the bar.

6 Carefully examine the anti-roll bar components for signs of wear, damage or deterioration, paying particular attention to the mounting bushes. Renew any worn components as necessary.

Refitting

7 Fit the rubber mounting bushes to the anti-roll bar, aligning them with the marks made prior to removal.

8 Offer up the anti-roll bar, and manoeuvre it into position.

9 Refit the mounting clamps, and fit the nuts. Ensure that the bush markings are still aligned

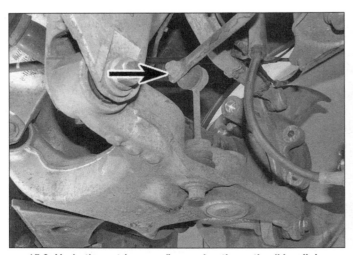

15.3 Undo the nut (arrowed) securing the anti-roll bar links

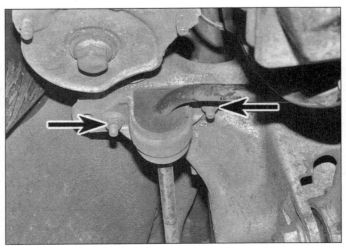

15.4 Anti-roll bar clamp nuts (arrowed)

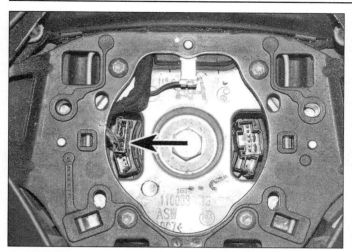

16.3 Disconnect the steering wheel wiring plug (arrowed)

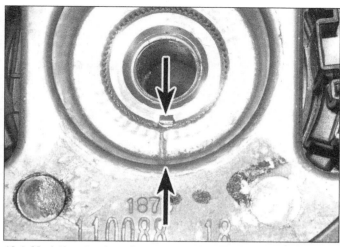

16.4 Mark the steering wheel and column shaft in relation to each other (arrowed)

with the marks on the bars, then securely tighten the mounting clamp retaining nuts.
10 Reconnect the Dynamic Drive pipe unions and tighten them securely (where applicable).
11 Refitting is a reversal of removal. On models with Dynamic Drive, fill and bleed the hydraulic system as described in Section 29.

16 Steering wheel – removal and refitting

Removal

1 Remove the airbag unit from the centre of the steering wheel, referring to Chapter 12.
2 Set the steering wheel and roadwheels in the 'straight-ahead' position.
3 Slacken and remove the steering wheel retaining bolt. Disconnect the steering wheel wiring plug(s) **(see illustration)**.
4 Mark the steering wheel and steering column shaft in relation to each other, then lift the steering wheel off the column splines. If it is tight, tap it up near the centre, using the palm of your hand, or twist it from side to side, whilst pulling upwards to release it from the shaft splines **(see illustration)**. With the steering wheel removed, apply self-adhesive tape to the airbag contact unit to prevent it from being rotated.

Refitting

5 Refitting is the reverse of removal, noting the following points.
   a) If the contact unit has been rotated with the wheel removed, centralise it by pressing down on the white button and rotating its centre fully anti-clockwise. From this position, rotate the centre back through three complete rotations in a clockwise direction.
   b) Ensure the lug on the rear of the steering wheel aligns with the corresponding slot in the contact unit.
   c) Engage the wheel with the column splines, aligning the marks made on removal, and tighten the steering wheel retaining bolt to the specified torque.
   d) Refit the airbag unit (see Chapter 12).

17 Steering column – removal, inspection and refitting

Removal

1 Disconnect the battery negative terminal (see Chapter 5).
2 Remove the driver's side lower facia panel as described in Chapter 11.
3 Make alignment marks between the steering column shaft and the intermediate

shaft universal joint to aid refitting, then undo the clamp bolt and slide the intermediate shaft downwards from the steering column **(see illustration)**. Discard the bolt – a new one must be fitted.
4 Fully extend, and set the wheel in the highest position. Remove the steering wheel as described in Section 16.
5 Unclip and remove the rear section of the steering column shroud **(see illustration)**.
6 Undo the retaining bolt and unclip the lower section of the steering column shroud **(see illustrations)**. Disconnect any wiring plugs as the shroud is removed.
7 Move the steering column to its lowest

17.3 Intermediate shaft universal joint clamp bolt (arrowed)

17.5 Unclip the steering column shroud rear section

17.6a Undo the lower shroud retaining bolt (arrowed) . . .

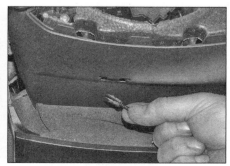

17.6b . . . and pull out the plastic expansion rivet

17.7a Unclip the front section of the upper shroud . . .

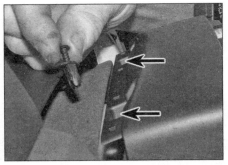

17.7b . . . then undo the bolts (arrowed) and pull out the plastic expansion rivets

17.10a Steering column upper mounting bolts (arrowed) . . .

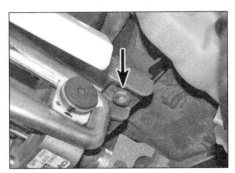

17.10b . . . and lower mounting bolts (arrowed)

position, unclip the front section of the upper steering column shroud, then undo the retaining bolts, gently bend the sides of the shroud rear section outwards and remove it from the column (see illustrations).

8 On models up to 09/2005 with automatic transmission, disconnect the interlock cable from the steering lock unit. Unclip the cable from the steering column.

9 Disconnect the wiring connectors from the column switches, and the column motors (where applicable) and free the harness from its retaining clips on the column.

10 Make alignment marks between the steering column mounting brackets and the vehicle body/facia crossmember, then undo the 4 mounting bolts and pull the column to the rear (see illustrations).

Inspection

11 The steering column incorporates a telescopic safety feature. In the event of a front-end crash, the shaft collapses and prevents the steering wheel injuring the driver. Before refitting the steering column, examine the column and mountings for damage and deformation, and renew as necessary.

12 Check the steering shaft for signs of free play in the column bushes. If any damage or wear is found on the steering column bushes, the column should be overhauled. Overhaul of the column is a complex task requiring several special tools, and should be entrusted to a BMW dealer.

Refitting

13 Manoeuvre the column into position and

engage it with the shaft splines, aligning the marks made prior to removal.

14 Locate the column in position and screw in the mounting bolts. Tighten them to the specified torque.

15 Reconnect the wiring connectors to the ignition switch and column switches, and secure the wiring to the column, ensuring it is correctly routed.

16 Ensure the shaft and column marks are correctly aligned. Fit the new clamp bolt and tighten it to the specified torque.

17 Refit the lower and upper steering column shrouds.

18 Refit the steering wheel as described in Section 16.

19 Reconnect the battery negative lead as described in Chapter 5.

20 If a new column has been fitted, it will be necessary to recalibrate the steering angle sensor using BMW diagnostic equipment. Entrust this task to a BMW dealer or suitably-equipped specialist.

18 Steering column lock – removal and refitting

Removal

1 Removal of the steering column lock is only possible on models from 09/2005 with electric column adjustment.

2 Remove the driver's side lower facia panel as described in Chapter 11.

3 Disconnect the wiring plug from the steering lock, then drill out the 2 shear bolts securing the lock to the column (see illustration).

Refitting

4 Position the lock again the column. Note that the spherical side of the shim must point to the steering column lock.

5 Insert the new shear bolts, and tighten them until the heads of the bolts shear off.

6 The remainder of refitting is a reversal of removal.

19 Steering column intermediate shaft – removal and refitting

Removal

1 Chock the rear wheels, firmly apply the handbrake, then jack up the front of the car and support on axle stands. Set the front wheels in the straight-ahead position. Undo the bolts and remove the engine undershield (see illustrations 5.1a and 5.1b).

2 Remove the driver's side lower facia panel as described in Chapter 11.

3 Prise the rubber gaiter upwards from the base of the bulkhead.

4 Where fitted, undo the bolts and remove the heat shield over the lower intermediate shaft universal joint (see illustration).

18.3 Drill out the steering column lock shear bolts (arrowed)

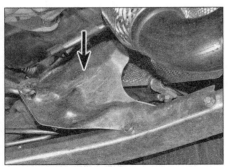

19.4 Remove the heat shield over the lower intermediate shaft universal joint (arrowed)

20.4 Undo the fastener and fold the clip forwards (arrowed)

20.5 Lift the clip and slide the central panel to the left

5 Using paint or a suitable marker pen, make alignment marks between the intermediate shaft universal joint and the steering column, and the lower universal joint and the steering rack pinion **(see illustration 20.16)**.

6 Slacken and remove the clamp bolts, then slide the two halves of the shaft together and remove the shaft assembly from the car. Discard the bolts – new ones are required. **Note:** *Do not rotate the steering wheel with the shaft removed.*

7 Inspect the intermediate shaft universal joints for signs of roughness and ease of movement. If the universal joints are suspect, the complete intermediate shaft should be renewed.

Refitting

8 Check that the front wheels are still in the straight-ahead position, and that the steering wheel is correctly positioned.

9 Align the marks made on removal, and engage the intermediate shaft joints with the steering column and pinion.

10 Insert the new clamp bolts, and tighten them to the specified torque setting.

11 The remainder of refitting is a reversal of removal. If a new shaft has been fitted, it will be necessary to recalibrate the steering angle sensor using BMW diagnostic equipment. Entrust this task to a BMW dealer or suitably-equipped specialist.

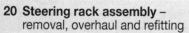

20 Steering rack assembly –
removal, overhaul and refitting

Removal

1 Chock the rear wheels, firmly apply the handbrake, then jack up the front of the car and support on axle stands. Remove both front roadwheels, undo the fasteners and remove

the engine undershield **(see illustrations 5.1a and 5.1b)**.

2 Remove the exhaust system as described in the relevant part of Chapter 4.

3 Remove the bonnet as described in Chapter 11.

4 Rotate the fastener 90° anti-clockwise, release the clip and remove the pollen filter cover each side from the housing **(see illustration)**.

5 Release the clip and slide the central plastic panel towards the left-hand side and remove it **(see illustration)**.

6 Remove the plastic cover (where fitted) from

20.6 Remove the plastic cover behind the suspension turrets

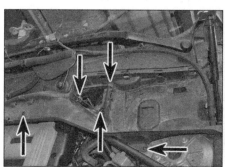

20.7b Lower pollen filter housing retaining bolt and fasteners (arrowed)

behind the left- and right-hand suspension turrets. Take care not to damage the retaining lug at the front edge of the cover **(see illustration)**.

7 Pull up the rubber seal from the bulkhead, then undo the bolt, rotate the fasteners 90° anti-clockwise, and remove the pollen filter lower housing each side **(see illustrations)**. Unclip any hoses or wiring as the housing is removed.

8 Undo the 4 bolts and remove the brace **(see illustration)**. Discard the bolts – new ones must be fitted.

9 Rotate the central fastener anti-clockwise

20.7a Pull up the rubber seal

20.8 Undo the bolts (right-hand side arrowed) and remove the brace

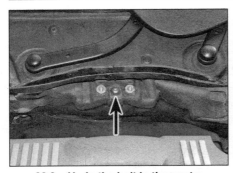

20.9a Undo the bolt in the centre (arrowed) . . .

20.9b . . . rotate the fastener (arrowed) anti-clockwise . . .

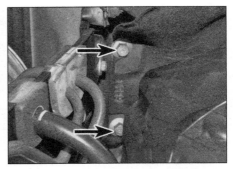

20.9c . . . undo the 2 bolts each side (arrowed) . . .

20.9d . . . and release the pipe clamp (arrowed)

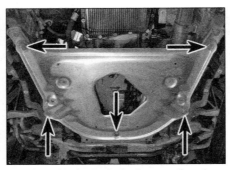

20.11 Undo the bolts (arrowed) and remove the front reinforcement plate

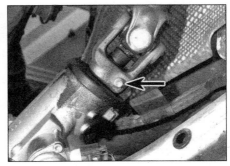

20.16 Steering column intermediate shaft lower universal joint pinch-bolt (arrowed)

90°, undo the bolts, and pull the turret braces centre panel (where fitted) forwards **(see illustrations)**. Release the pipe clamp where applicable.

10 Remove the acoustic cover from the top of the engine.

11 Undo the bolts and remove the front underbody reinforcement plate **(see illustration)**. Discard the bolts – new ones must be fitted.

12 The engine must be supported in position using an engine hoist or engine crossbeam. Attach the hoist/crossbeam to the engine lifting eyes at the front and rear of the engine. Take the weight of the engine.

Caution: Note that if using the crossbeam, mount the crossbeam on the suspension turrets and the front panel adjacent to the bonnet catch each side. The inner wings are not strong enough to take the weight of the engine.

13 Undo the nut each side securing the engine mounting support brackets to the mountings, then raise the engine approximately 10 mm.

14 Disconnect the track rod ends from the hub carriers as described in Section 25.

15 Undo the bolts and remove the heat shield from the steering rack pinion.

16 Remove the steering column lower universal joint pinch-bolt and lift the column shaft upwards from the steering rack pinion **(see illustration)**. Discard the pinch-bolt – a new one must be used.

Caution: Ensure the steering wheel/ column is not rotated with the universal

joint disconnected from the steering rack pinion. Damage to the column could result.

17 Disconnect the wiring plugs from the ride height sensors (where fitted), then disconnect the vacuum hoses from the engine mountings (where applicable).

18 On models with electric power steering, cut the cable-tie securing the wiring harness to the subframe.

19 On models with Dynamic Drive active suspension system, place a container beneath the pipes, undo the unions and drain the fluid from the return and pressure pipes.

20 Examine the front subframe, and identify any remaining wiring looms/connectors which will be affected by the lowering of the subframe. Note their fitted positions, and disconnect/release them.

21 Support the front subframe using a workshop jack and lengths of wood, etc, then undo the 3 bolts each side and carefully lower the subframe a maximum of 100 mm. Pay attention to the power steering hoses/pipes as the subframe is being lowered – do not allow them to be bent or stretched. When refitting, tighten down the front bolts first.

Conventional power steering

22 Using brake hose clamps, clamp both the supply and return hoses near the power steering fluid reservoir. This will minimise fluid loss. Mark the unions to ensure they are correctly positioned on reassembly, then slacken and remove the feed and return pipe union bolts from the steering rack pinion housing, and recover the sealing washers

– remove the heat shield if necessary. Be prepared for fluid spillage, and position a suitable container beneath the pipes whilst unscrewing the bolts. Plug the pipe ends and steering rack orifices, to prevent fluid leakage and to keep dirt out of the hydraulic system.

23 Release the power steering pipes from the retaining clips on the steering rack.

Electric power steering

24 Release the steering rack wiring harness from the cable-ties, then disconnect the wiring plug from the rack motor.

All models

25 Slacken and remove the steering rack mounting bolt/nuts, and remove the steering rack from underneath the car. Discard the nuts and bolt – new ones must be fitted.

Overhaul

26 Examine the steering rack assembly for signs of wear or damage, and check that the rack moves freely throughout the full length of its travel, with no signs of roughness or excessive free play between the steering rack pinion and rack. It is not possible to overhaul the steering rack assembly housing components; if it is faulty, the assembly must be renewed. The only components which can be renewed individually are the steering rack gaiters, the track rod balljoints and the track rods. These procedures are covered later in this Chapter.

Refitting

27 Offer up the steering rack, and insert the mounting bolts. Fit new nuts and bolt, and tighten them to the specified torque setting.
28 The remainder of refitting is a reversal of removal, noting the following points:
 a) *Reconnect the fluid pipes to the steering rack using new sealing washers, then tighten the banjo bolts to the specified torque.*
 b) *Align the marks made on removal, and connect the intermediate shaft to the steering rack, using a new pinch-bolt.*
 c) *Bleed the hydraulic system as described in Section 22.*
 d) *If a new steering rack has been fitted, it must be programmed/initialised/calibrated using BMW diagnostic equipment. Entrust this task to a BMW dealer or suitably-equipped specialist.*
 e) *Have the front wheel alignment checked at the earliest opportunity.*

21 Power steering pump – removal and refitting

Removal

1 Chock the rear wheels, then jack up the front of the car and support it on axle stands (see *Jacking and vehicle support*). Undo the fasteners and remove the engine undershield.
2 On 6-cylinder models with Dynamic Drive, remove the alternator as described in Chapter 5.
3 Working as described in Chapter 1, release the drivebelt tension and unhook the drivebelt from the pump pulley, noting that the steering pump pulley retaining bolts should be slackened prior to releasing the tension.
4 Unscrew the retaining bolts and remove the pulley from the power steering pump, noting which way around it is fitted.
5 On all models, using brake hose clamps, clamp both the supply and return hoses near the power steering fluid reservoir. This will minimise fluid loss during subsequent operations.
6 Mark the unions to ensure they are correctly positioned on reassembly, then slacken and remove the feed and return pipe union bolts and recover the sealing washers. Be prepared for fluid spillage, and position a suitable container beneath the pipes whilst unscrewing the bolts. Plug the pipe ends and steering pump orifices, to prevent fluid leakage and to keep dirt out of the hydraulic system.
7 Undo the bolts securing the fluid pressure/Dynamic Drive pressure pipes support bracket to the pump.
8 Slacken and remove the mounting bolts and remove the pump **(see illustration)**. Disconnect any wiring plugs as the pump is withdrawn.

9 If the power steering pump is faulty, seek the advice of your BMW dealer as to the availability of spare parts. If spares are available, it may be possible to have the pump overhauled by a suitable specialist, or alternatively obtain an exchange unit. If not, the pump must be renewed.

Refitting

10 Where necessary, transfer the rear mounting bracket to the new pump, and securely tighten its mounting bolts.
11 Prior to refitting, ensure that the pump is primed by injecting the specified type of fluid in through the supply hose union and rotating the pump shaft.
12 Manoeuvre the pump into position and refit the pivot bolts, tightening them to the specified torque.
13 Position a new sealing washer on each side of the pipe hose unions and refit the union bolts. Tighten the union bolts to the specified torque.
14 Remove the hose clamps and refit the pump pulley (where applicable). Ensure the pulley is the right way around, and securely tighten its retaining bolts.
15 Refit the auxiliary drivebelt and tension it as described in Chapter 1.
16 On completion, lower the car to the ground and bleed the hydraulic system as described in Section 22. **Note:** *On models with Dynamic Drive, it may be necessary to initialise the operation of the system. This can only be carried out using BMW diagnostic equipment. Entrust this task to a BMW dealer or suitably-equipped speciliast.*

22 Power steering system – bleeding

1 With the engine stopped, fill the fluid reservoir right up to the top with the specified type of fluid.
2 With the engine running, slowly move the steering from lock-to-lock twice to purge out the trapped air, then stop the engine and top-up the level in the fluid reservoir. Repeat this procedure until the

21.8 Steering pump retaining bolts (arrowed)

fluid level in the reservoir does not drop any further.
3 If, when turning the steering, an abnormal noise is heard from the fluid lines, it indicates that there is still air in the system. Check this by turning the wheels to the straight-ahead position and switching off the engine. If the fluid level in the reservoir rises, then air is present in the system and further bleeding is necessary.

23 Active steering control unit – removal and refitting

1 Disconnect the battery negative lead as described in Chapter 5.
2 Remove the driver's seat as described in Chapter 11.
3 Carefully, pull the up front part of the driver's door sill trim, then slide it rearwards to release the rear clips **(see illustration)**.
4 Remove the bonnet release handle as described in Chapter 11, then remove the lower A-pillar trim.
5 Carefully fold back the driver's side carpet to access the control unit.
6 The control unit is secured by 4 bolts. Note the earth cable secured by one of the bolts. Undo the bolts.
7 Turn the control unit over and disconnect the wiring plugs.
8 Refitting is a reversal of removal, noting that if a new unit is fitted, it must be programmed/coded using BMW diagnostic equipment. Entrust this task to a BMW dealer or suitably-equipped specialist.

24 Steering rack rubber gaiters – renewal

1 Raise the front of the vehicle and support it securely on axle stands (see *Jacking and vehicle support*). Undo the fasteners and remove the engine undershield.
2 Remove the track rod end as described in Section 25.
3 Release the clip securing the rubber gaiter

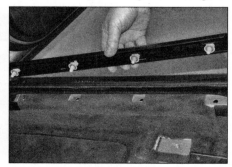

23.3 Pull up the front edge, then slide the door sill trim rearwards

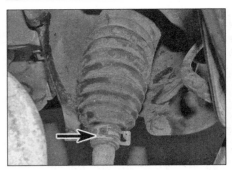

24.3 Steering rack gaiter clip (arrowed)

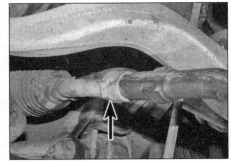

25.3 Track rod end locknut (arrowed)

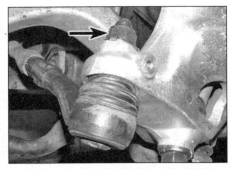

25.4 Track rod end-to-hub carrier balljoint locknut (arrowed)

to the track rod **(see illustration)**. Note the fitted position of the gaiter on the track rod.

4 Release the clamp securing the gaiter to the steering rack, and pull the gaiter over the track rod.

5 Thoroughly clean the track rod and the steering rack housing, using fine abrasive paper to polish off any corrosion, burrs or sharp edges which might damage the new gaiter's sealing lips on installation. Scrape off all the grease from the old gaiter, and apply it to the track rod inner balljoint. (This assumes that grease has not been lost or contaminated as a result of damage to the old gaiter. Use fresh grease if in doubt – consult a BMW dealer or parts specialist.) Renew the O-ring seal between the housing and gaiter.

6 Apply a little grease to the track rod so the gaiter will slide, then carefully slide the new gaiter (with the retaining clips in place) over the track rod, and locate it on the steering rack housing. Position the outer edge of the gaiter on the track rod.

7 Secure the gaiter to the rack with the retaining clamp.

8 Refit the track rod end as described in Section 25.

9 Ensure the outer end of the gaiter is still in the correct position, then secure it with the retaining clip.

10 Refit the engine undershield and lower the vehicle to the ground.

11 Upon completion, it is recommended that the front wheel alignment is checked at the earliest opportunity. On models with active steering, have the steering angle sensor calibration checked using BMW diagnostic equipment. Entrust this task to a BMW dealer or suitably-equipped specialist.

25 Track rod end/balljoint – removal and refitting

Removal

1 Apply the handbrake, then jack up the front of the car and support it on axle stands (see *Jacking and vehicle support*). Remove the appropriate front roadwheel.

2 Make a mark on the track rod and measure

the distance from the mark to the centre of the balljoint. Note this measurement down, as it will be needed to ensure the wheel alignment remains correctly set when the balljoint is installed.

3 Unscrew the track rod end locknut **(see illustration)**.

4 Undo the nut securing the track rod balljoint to the hub carrier, and unscrew it until the edge of the nut is flush with the end of the balljoint shank. Release the balljoint by gently tapping the end of the shank with a soft-faced hammer **(see illustration)**. There is no need to use a balljoint seperator tool – a new one must be fitted.

5 Counting the **exact** number of turns necessary to do so, unscrew the balljoint from the track rod end.

6 Carefully clean the balljoint and the threads. Renew the balljoint if its movement is sloppy or too stiff, if excessively worn, or if damaged in any way; carefully check the stud taper and threads. If the balljoint gaiter is damaged, the complete balljoint assembly must be renewed; it is not possible to obtain the gaiter separately.

Refitting

7 Screw the balljoint onto the track rod by the number of turns noted on removal. This should position the balljoint at the relevant distance from the track rod mark that was noted prior to removal.

8 Refit the balljoint shank to the hub carrier, then fit a new retaining nut and tighten it to the specified torque.

9 Insert the new track rod end clamp bolt, and tighten it to the specified torque.

10 Refit the roadwheel, then lower the car to

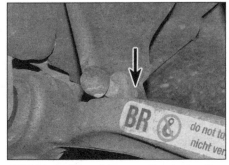

27.3 Undo the nut (arrowed) securing the height sensor rod to the control arm

the ground and tighten the roadwheel bolts to the specified torque.

11 Upon completion, it is recommended that the front wheel alignment is checked at the earliest opportunity. On models with active steering, have the steering angle sensor calibration checked using BMW diagnostic equipment. Entrust this task to a BMW dealer or suitably-equipped specialist.

26 Track rod – renewal

1 Remove the steering rack gaiter as described in Section 24.

2 Move the rack in as far as possible, then unscrew the track rod nut from the end of the steering rack.

3 Position the track rod on the end of the rack and tighten the retaining nut to the specified torque.

4 Refit the steering gaiter as described in Section 24.

27 Dynamic Stability Control – general information and component renewal

General information

1 Dynamic Stability Control (DSC) is standard on most models, and available as an option on all other models. Strictly speaking, DSC includes ABS and Traction control, but this Section is concerned with Cornering Brake Control (CBC). By monitoring steering wheel movements, suspension ride heights, roadspeed and lateral acceleration, the system controls the pressure in the brake lines to each of the four brake calipers during braking, reducing the possibility of understeer or oversteer.

Component renewal
Steering angle sensor

2 The steering angle sensor is integral with the steering column switch module – refer to Chapter 12.

Front ride height sensor

3 Undo the nut securing the sensor rod to the control arm **(see illustration)**.

27.4 Front ride height sensor wiring plug (arrowed)

27.6 Undo the rear ride height sensor rod nut (arrowed)

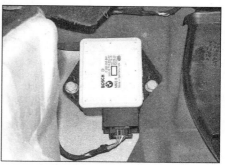

27.12 The DSC/active steering sensor located under the driver's side carpet

4 Remove the two retaining bolts, and withdraw the ride sensor. Disconnect the wiring plug as the sensor is removed **(see illustration)**.

5 Refitting is a reversal of removal. Have the headlight alignment check on completion.

Rear ride height sensor

6 Undo the nut securing the jointed rod to the sensor **(see illustration)**.

7 Undo the bolt securing the sensor mounting bracket to the subframe, and disconnect the sensor wiring plug.

8 If required, undo the 2 bolts and separate the sensor from the mounting bracket.

9 Refitting is a reversal of removal.

DSC control unit

10 The DSC control unit is integral with the ABS control unit, renewal of which should be entrusted to a BMW dealer or suitably-equipped specialist – see Chapter 9.

DSC/active steering sensor

11 Remove the driver's side front seat as described in Chapter 11, then fold back the carpet adjacent to the centre console.

12 Undo the 2 bolts and remove the sensor **(see illustration)**. Disconnect the wiring plug as the sensor is withdrawn.

13 Refitting is a reversal of removal, but tighten the sensor retaining bolts to the specified torque.

---

28 Wheel alignment and steering angles – general information

Definitions

1 A car's steering and suspension geometry is defined in four basic settings **(see illustration)** – all angles are usually expressed in degrees (toe settings are also expressed as a measurement); the steering axis is defined as an imaginary line drawn through the axis of the suspension strut, extended where necessary to contact the ground.

2 Camber is the angle between each roadwheel and a vertical line drawn through its centre and tyre contact patch, when viewed from the front or rear of the car. Positive

camber is when the roadwheels are tilted outwards from the vertical at the top; negative camber is when they are tilted inwards.

3 The front camber angle is not adjustable, and is given for reference only (see paragraph 5). The rear camber angle is adjustable and can be adjusted using a camber angle gauge.

4 Castor is the angle between the steering axis and a vertical line drawn through each roadwheel's centre and tyre contact patch, when viewed from the side of the car. Positive castor is when the steering axis is tilted so that it contacts the ground ahead of the vertical; negative castor is when it contacts the ground behind the vertical.

5 Castor is not adjustable, and is given for reference only; while it can be checked using a castor checking gauge, if the figure obtained is significantly different from that specified, the car must be taken for careful checking by a professional, as the fault can only be caused by wear or damage to the body or suspension components.

6 Toe is the difference, viewed from above, between lines drawn through the roadwheel centres and the car's centre-line. 'Toe-in' is when the roadwheels point inwards, towards each other at the front, while 'toe-out' is when they splay outwards from each other at the front.

7 The front wheel toe setting is adjusted by screwing the track rods in or out of their balljoints, to alter the effective length of the track rod assembly.

8 Rear wheel toe setting is also adjustable. The toe setting is adjusted by slackening the trailing arm mounting bracket bolts and repositioning the bracket.

Checking and adjustment

Front wheel toe setting

9 Due to the special measuring equipment necessary to check the wheel alignment, and the skill required to use it properly, the checking and adjustment of these settings is best left to a BMW dealer or similar expert. Note that most tyre-fitting shops now possess sophisticated checking equipment.

10 To check the toe setting, a tracking gauge must first be obtained. Two types of gauge are available, and can be obtained from motor

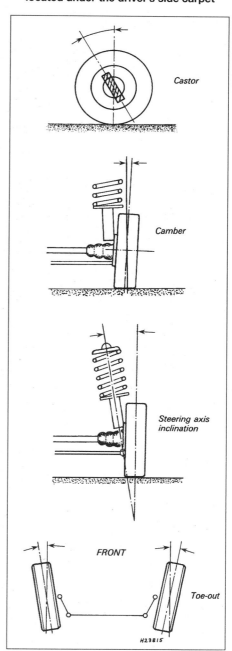

28.1 Steering geometry details

accessory shops. The first type measures the distance between the front and rear inside edges of the roadwheels, as previously described, with the car stationary. The second type, known as a 'scuff plate', measures the actual position of the contact surface of the tyre, in relation to the road surface, with the car in motion. This is achieved by pushing or driving the front tyre over a plate, which then moves slightly according to the scuff of the tyre, and shows this movement on a scale. Both types have their advantages and disadvantages, but either can give satisfactory results if used correctly and carefully.

11 Make sure that the steering is in the straight-ahead position when making measurements.

12 If adjustment is necessary, apply the handbrake then jack up the front of the car and support it securely on axle stands.

13 First clean the track rod threads; if they are corroded, apply penetrating fluid before starting adjustment. Release the rubber gaiter outer clips, peel back the gaiters and apply a smear of grease so that both are free and will not be twisted or strained as their respective track rods are rotated.

14 Retain the track rod with a suitable spanner and slacken the balljoint locknut. Alter the length of the track rod, by screwing them into or out of the balljoints by rotating the track rod using an open-ended spanner fitted to the track rod flats provided; shortening the track rods (screwing them onto their balljoints) will reduce toe-in/increase toe-out.

15 When the setting is correct, hold the track rod and tighten the balljoint locknut to the specified torque setting. If after adjustment, the steering wheel spokes are no longer horizontal when the wheels are in the straight-ahead position, remove the steering wheel and reposition it (see Section 18).

16 Check that the toe setting has been correctly adjusted by lowering the car to the ground and rechecking the toe setting; re-adjust if necessary. Ensure that the rubber gaiters are seated correctly and are not twisted or strained, and secure them in position with the retaining clips; where necessary fit a new retaining clip (see Section 24).

Rear wheel toe setting

Note: *Prior adjusting the toe setting, the camber angle should first be checked.*

17 The procedure for checking the rear toe setting is same as described for the front in paragraph 10.

18 To adjust the setting, slacken the traction strut-to-subframe nut, and rotate the bolt with the integral eccentric washer. Once the toe setting is correct, tighten the nut to specified torque.

Rear wheel camber angle

19 Checking and adjusting of the camber angle should be entrusted to a BMW dealer or other suitably-equipped specialist. Note that most tyre-fitting shops now possess sophisticated checking equipment. For reference, adjustments are made by slackening the integral link-to-hub carrier pivot bolts, and rotating the eccentric washer. Once adjustment is correct, tighten the bolt to the specified torque.

29 Dynamic Drive – general information, system filling and bleeding

General information

1 On models with 'Dynamic Drive' the stiffness of the front and rear anti-roll bar is altered by an hydraulic actuator mounted on the bar itself. As the vehicle corners, the bar is stiffened to reduce body roll. The system consists of the front and rear active anti-roll bars, height sensors (shared by the DSC systems), a control unit, valve block and the associated pressure/vent pipes. Due to the complex nature of the system, and the need for specialist diagnostic equipment, the only tasks described below is the topping-up of the hydraulic system. All other tasks should be entrusted to a BMW dealer or suitably-equipped specialist.

System filling and bleeding

2 The fluid reservoir is located in the engine compartment, and its cap is identified by the CHF 11S marking. Unscrew the cap and add fluid until its level is 15 mm above the MAX mark at 20°C (engine switched off, but at normal operating temperature).

3 Start the engine, and turn the steering wheel from lock to lock twice. If the reservoir completely drains, add fluid.

4 Turn the steering wheel to the straight-ahead position, and switch off the engine.

5 Check the fluid level and top it up to the MAX mark.

6 After bleeding, it may be necessary to have the system initialised using dedicated BMW diagnostic equipment. Entrust this task to a BMW dealer or suitably-equipped specialist.

Chapter 11
Bodywork and fittings

Contents

Degrees of difficulty

Easy, suitable for novice with little experience	**Fairly easy,** suitable for beginner with some experience	**Fairly difficult,** suitable for competent DIY mechanic	**Difficult,** suitable for experienced DIY mechanic	**Very difficult,** suitable for expert DIY or professional

Specifications

Torque wrench settings

	Nm	lbf ft
Seat belt mountings*	36	26
Seat mounting bolts*	44	32

* Do not re-use

---

1 General information

The bodyshell is made of pressed-steel and aluminium sections. Most components are welded together, but some use is made of structural adhesives.

The door and some other vulnerable panels are made of zinc-coated metal, whilst the bonnet and front wings are aluminium. All are further protected by being coated with an anti-chip primer before being sprayed.

Extensive use is made of plastic materials, mainly in the interior, but also in exterior components. The front and rear bumpers, and front grille are injection-moulded from a synthetic material that is very strong and yet light. Plastic components such as wheel arch liners are fitted to the underside of the vehicle, to improve the body's resistance to corrosion.

2 Maintenance – bodywork and underframe

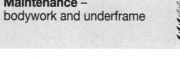

1 The condition of a vehicle's bodywork is the one thing that significantly affects its value. Maintenance is easy, but needs to be regular. Neglect, particularly after minor damage, can lead quickly to further deterioration and costly repair bills. It is important also to keep watch on those parts of the vehicle not immediately visible, for instance the underside, inside all the wheel arches, and the lower part of the engine compartment.

2 The basic maintenance routine for the bodywork is washing – preferably with a lot of water, from a hose. This will remove all the loose solids which may have stuck to the vehicle. It is important to flush these off in such a way as to prevent grit from scratching the finish. The wheel arches and underframe need washing in the same way, to remove any accumulated mud which will retain moisture and tend to encourage rust. Oddly enough, the best time to clean the underframe and wheel arches is in wet weather, when the mud is thoroughly wet and soft. In very wet weather, the underframe is usually cleaned of large accumulations automatically, and this is a good time for inspection.

3 Periodically, except on vehicles with a wax-based underbody protective coating, it is a good idea to have the whole of the underframe of the vehicle steam-cleaned, engine compartment included, so that a thorough inspection can be carried out to see what minor repairs and renovations are necessary. Steam cleaning is available at many garages, and is necessary for the removal of the accumulation of oily grime, which sometimes is allowed to become thick in certain areas. If steam-cleaning facilities are not available, there are some excellent grease solvents available which can be brush-applied; the dirt can then be simply hosed off. Note that these methods should not be used on vehicles with wax-based underbody protective coating, or the coating will be removed. Such vehicles should be inspected annually, preferably just before Winter, when the underbody should be washed down, and repair any damage to the wax coating. Ideally, a completely fresh coat should be applied. It would also be worth considering the use of such wax-based protection for injection into door panels, sills, box sections, etc, as an additional safeguard against rust damage, where such protection is not provided by the vehicle manufacturer.

4 After washing paintwork, wipe off with a chamois leather to give an unspotted clear finish. A coat of clear protective wax polish will give added protection against chemical pollutants in the air. If the paintwork sheen has dulled or oxidised, use a cleaner/polisher combination to restore the brilliance of the shine. This requires a little effort, but such dulling is usually caused because regular washing has been neglected. Care needs to be taken with metallic paintwork, as special non-abrasive cleaner/polisher is required to avoid damage to the finish. Always check that the door and ventilator opening drain holes and pipes are completely clear, so that water can be drained out. Brightwork should be treated in the same way as paintwork. Windscreens and windows can be kept clear of the smeary film which often appears, by proprietary glass cleaner. Never use any form of wax or other body or chromium polish on glass.

3 Maintenance – upholstery and carpets

Mats and carpets should be brushed or vacuum-cleaned regularly, to keep them free of grit. If they are badly stained, remove them from the vehicle for scrubbing or sponging, and make quite sure they are dry before refitting. Seats and interior trim panels can be kept clean by wiping with a damp cloth and a proprietary brand of cleaner. If they do become stained (which can be more apparent on light-coloured upholstery), use a little liquid detergent and a soft nail brush to scour the grime out of the grain of the material. Do not forget to keep the headlining clean in the same way as the upholstery. When using liquid cleaners inside the vehicle, do not over-wet the surfaces being cleaned. Excessive damp

could get into the seams and padded interior, causing stains, offensive odours or even rot. If the inside of the vehicle gets wet accidentally, it is worthwhile taking some trouble to dry it out properly, particularly where carpets are involved. Do not leave oil or electric heaters inside the vehicle for this purpose.

4 Minor body damage – repair

Repairs of minor scratches

1 If the scratch is very superficial, and does not penetrate to the metal of the bodywork, repair is very simple. Lightly rub the area of the scratch with a paintwork renovator or a very fine cutting paste to remove loose paint from the scratch, and to clear the surrounding bodywork of wax polish. Rinse the area with clean water.

2 Apply touch-up paint to the scratch using a fine paint brush; continue to apply fine layers of paint until the surface of the paint in the scratch is level with the surrounding paintwork. Allow the new paint at least two weeks to harden, then blend it into the surrounding paintwork by rubbing the scratch area with a paintwork renovator or a very fine cutting paste. Finally, apply wax polish.

3 Where the scratch has penetrated right through to the metal of the bodywork, causing the metal to rust, a different repair technique is required. Remove any loose rust from the bottom of the scratch with a penknife, then apply rust-inhibiting paint to prevent the formation of rust in the future. Using a rubber or nylon applicator, fill the scratch with bodystopper paste. If required, this paste can be mixed with cellulose thinners to provide a very thin paste which is ideal for filling narrow scratches. Before the stopper-paste in the scratch hardens, wrap a piece of smooth cotton rag around the top of a finger. Dip the finger in cellulose thinners, and quickly sweep it across the surface of the stopper-paste in the scratch; this will ensure that the surface of the stopper-paste is slightly hollowed. The scratch can now be painted over as described earlier in this Section.

Repairs of dents

4 When deep denting of the vehicle's bodywork has taken place, the first task is to pull the dent out, until the affected bodywork almost attains its original shape. There is little point in trying to restore the original shape completely, as the metal in the damaged area will have stretched on impact, and cannot be reshaped fully to its original contour. It is better to bring the level of the dent up to a point which is about 3 mm below the level of the surrounding bodywork. In cases where the dent is very shallow anyway, it is not worth trying to pull it out at all. If the underside of the dent is accessible, it can be hammered

out gently from behind, using a mallet with a wooden or plastic head. Whilst doing this, hold a suitable block of wood firmly against the outside of the panel, to absorb the impact from the hammer blows and thus prevent a large area of the bodywork from being 'belled-out'.

5 Should the dent be in a section of the bodywork which has a double skin, or some other factor making it inaccessible from behind, a different technique is called for. Drill several small holes through the metal inside the area – particularly in the deeper section. Then screw long self-tapping screws into the holes, just sufficiently for them to gain a good purchase in the metal. Now the dent can be pulled out by pulling on the protruding heads of the screws with a pair of pliers.

6 The next stage of the repair is the removal of the paint from the damaged area, and from an inch or so of the surrounding 'sound' bodywork. This is accomplished most easily by using a wire brush or abrasive pad on a power drill, although it can be done just as effectively by hand, using sheets of abrasive paper. To complete the preparation for filling, score the surface of the bare metal with a screwdriver or the tang of a file, or alternatively, drill small holes in the affected area. This will provide a good 'key' for the filler paste.

7 To complete the repair, see the Section on filling and respraying.

Repairs of rust holes or gashes

8 Remove all paint from the affected area, and from an inch or so of the surrounding 'sound' bodywork, using an abrasive pad or a wire brush on a power drill. If these are not available, a few sheets of abrasive paper will do the job most effectively. With the paint removed, you will be able to judge the severity of the corrosion, and therefore decide whether to renew the whole panel (if this is possible) or to repair the affected area. New body panels are not as expensive as most people think, and it is often quicker and more satisfactory to fit a new panel than to attempt to repair large areas of corrosion.

9 Remove all fittings from the affected area, except those which will act as a guide to the original shape of the damaged bodywork (eg, headlamp shells, etc). Then, using tin snips or a hacksaw blade, remove all loose metal and any other metal badly affected by corrosion. Hammer the edges of the hole inwards, to create a slight depression for the filler paste.

10 Wire-brush the affected area to remove the powdery rust from the surface of the remaining metal. Paint the affected area with rust-inhibiting paint; if the back of the rusted area is accessible, treat this also.

11 Before filling can take place, it will be necessary to block the hole in some way. This can be achieved with aluminium or plastic mesh, or aluminium tape.

12 Aluminium or plastic mesh, or glass-fibre matting, is probably the best material to use for a large hole. Cut a piece to the approximate size and shape of the hole to be filled, then position it in the hole so that its edges are below the level of the surrounding bodywork. It can be retained in position by several blobs of filler paste around its periphery.

13 Aluminium tape should be used for small or very narrow holes. Pull a piece off the roll, trim it to the approximate size and shape required, then pull off the backing paper (if used) and stick the tape over the hole; it can be overlapped if the thickness of one piece is insufficient. Burnish down the edges of the tape with the handle of a screwdriver or similar, to ensure that the tape is securely attached to the metal underneath.

Filling and respraying

14 Before using this Section, see the Sections on dent, deep scratch, rust holes and gash repairs.

15 Many types of bodyfiller are available, but generally speaking, those proprietary kits which contain a tin of filler paste and a tube of resin hardener are best for this type of repair which can be used directly from the tube. A wide, flexible plastic or nylon applicator will be found invaluable for imparting a smooth and well-contoured finish to the surface of the filler.

16 Mix up a little filler on a clean piece of card or board – measure the hardener carefully (follow the maker's instructions on the pack), otherwise the filler will set too rapidly or too slowly. Using the applicator, apply the filler paste to the prepared area; draw the applicator across the surface of the filler to achieve the correct contour and to level the surface. When a contour that approximates to the correct one is achieved, stop working the paste – if you carry on too long, the paste will become sticky and begin to 'pick-up' on the applicator. Continue to add thin layers of filler paste at 20-minute intervals, until the level of the filler is just proud of the surrounding bodywork.

17 Once the filler has hardened, the excess can be removed using a metal plane or file. From then on, progressively-finer grades of abrasive paper should be used, starting with a 40-grade production paper, and finishing with a 400-grade wet-and-dry paper. Always wrap the abrasive paper around a flat rubber, cork, or wooden block – otherwise the surface of the filler will not be completely flat. During the smoothing of the filler surface, the wet-and-dry paper should be periodically rinsed in water. This will ensure that a very smooth finish is imparted to the filler at the final stage.

18 At this stage, the 'dent' should be surrounded by a ring of bare metal, which in turn should be encircled by the finely 'feathered' edge of the good paintwork. Rinse the repair area with clean water, until all the dust produced by the rubbing-down operation has gone.

19 Spray the whole area with a light coat of primer – this will show up any imperfections in the surface of the filler. Repair these imperfections with fresh filler paste or bodystopper, and again smooth the surface with abrasive paper. If bodystopper is used, it can be mixed with cellulose thinners, to form a thin paste which is ideal for filling small holes. Repeat this spray-and-repair procedure until you are satisfied that the surface of the filler, and the feathered edge of the paintwork, are perfect. Clean the repair area with clean water, and allow to dry fully.

20 The repair area is now ready for final spraying. Paint spraying must be carried out in a warm, dry, windless and dust-free atmosphere. This condition can be created artificially if you have access to a large indoor working area, but if you are forced to work in the open, you will have to pick your day very carefully. If you are working indoors, dousing the floor in the work area with water will help to settle the dust which would otherwise be in the atmosphere. If the repair area is confined to one body panel, mask off the surrounding panels; this will help to minimise the effects of a slight mis-match in paint colours. Bodywork fittings (eg chrome strips, door handles etc) will also need to be masked off. Use genuine masking tape, and several thickness of newspaper, for the masking operations.

21 Before starting to spray, agitate the aerosol can thoroughly, then spray a test area (an old tin, or similar) until the technique is mastered. Cover the repair area with a thick coat of primer; the thickness should be built up using several thin layers of paint, rather than one thick one. Using 400 grade wet-and-dry paper, rub down the surface of the primer until it is smooth. While doing this, the work area should be thoroughly doused with water, and the wet-and-dry paper periodically rinsed in water. Allow to dry before spraying on more paint.

22 Spray on the top coat, again building up the thickness by using several thin layers of paint. Start spraying at the top of the repair area, and then, using a side-to-side motion, work downwards until the whole repair area and about 2 inches of the surrounding original paintwork is covered. Remove all masking material 10 to 15 minutes after spraying on the final coat of paint.

23 Allow the new paint at least two weeks to harden, then, using a paintwork renovator or a very fine cutting paste, blend the edges of the paint into the existing paintwork. Finally, apply wax polish.

Plastic components

24 With the use of more and more plastic body components by the vehicle manufacturers (eg bumpers. spoilers, and in some cases major body panels), rectification of more serious damage to such items has become a matter of either entrusting repair work to a specialist in this field, or renewing complete components. Repair of such damage by the DIY owner is not feasible, owing to the cost of the equipment and materials required for effecting such repairs. The basic technique involves making a groove along the line of the crack in the plastic, using a rotary burr in a power drill. The damaged part is then welded back together, using a hot air gun to heat up and fuse a plastic filler rod into the groove. Any excess plastic is then removed, and the area rubbed down to a smooth finish. It is important that a filler rod of the correct plastic is used, as body components can be made of different types (eg polycarbonate, ABS, polypropylene).

25 Damage of a less serious nature (abrasions, minor cracks etc) can be repaired by the DIY owner using a two-part epoxy filler repair material which can be used directly from the tube. Once mixed in equal proportions, this is used in similar fashion to the bodywork filler used on metal panels. The filler is usually cured in twenty to thirty minutes, ready for sanding and painting.

26 If the owner is renewing a complete component himself, or if he has repaired it with epoxy filler, he will be left with the problem of finding a suitable paint for finishing which is compatible with the type of plastic used. At one time, the use of a universal paint was not possible, owing to the complex range of plastics met with in body component applications. Standard paints, generally speaking, will not bond to plastic or rubber satisfactorily, but professional matched paints, to match any plastic or rubber finish, can be obtained from some dealers. However, it is now possible to obtain a plastic body parts finishing kit which consists of a pre-primer treatment, a primer and coloured top coat. Full instructions are normally supplied with a kit, but basically the method of use is to first apply the pre-primer to the component concerned, and allow it to dry for up to 30 minutes. Then the primer is applied, and left to dry for about an hour before finally applying the special-coloured top coat. The result is a correctly coloured component, where the paint will flex with the plastic or rubber, a property that standard paint does not normally posses.

5 Major body damage – repair

Where serious damage has occurred, or large areas need renewal due to neglect, it means that complete new panels will need welding-in, and this is best left to professionals. If the damage is due to impact, it will also be necessary to check completely the alignment of the bodyshell, and this can only be carried out accurately by a BMW dealer using special jigs. If the body is left misaligned, it is primarily dangerous, as the car will not handle properly, and secondly, uneven stresses will be imposed on the steering, suspension and possibly transmission, causing abnormal wear, or complete failure, particularly to such items as the tyres.

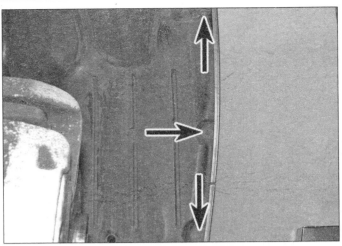

6.1 Undo the bolts (arrowed) securing the wheel arch liner each side

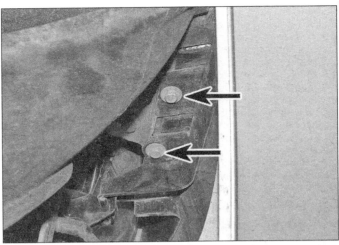

6.2 Pull back the wheel arch liner, and undo the bumper-to-wing bolts (arrowed)

6 Front bumper – removal and refitting

Removal

1 Undo the bolts each side securing the rear edge of the bumper to the wheel arch liner **(see illustration)**.

2 Pull back the wheel arch liner, and remove the 2 bolts each side securing the bumper to the front wing **(see illustration)**.

3 Undo the four bolts at the upper edge of the centre, lower grille aperture **(see illustration)**.

4 Unclip the strip at the top edge of the bumper and undo the four bolts exposed **(see illustration)**.

5 Press the front sides of the bumper rearwards a little, to release the retaining catches each side, press in the top edges each side to disengage the guides, then pull out the rear edges a little **(see illustrations)**.

6 Pull the bumper forward a little, note their fitted locations, and disconnect the various wiring plugs.

7 With the help of an assistant, remove the bumper forwards and away from the vehicle.

Refitting

8 Refitting is a reverse of the removal procedure, ensuring that the bumper mounting bolts are securely tightened.

7 Rear bumper – removal and refitting

Removal
Saloon models

1 Remove the luggage compartment side trim panels as described in Section 26.

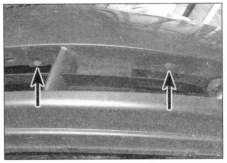

6.3 In the centre, lower grille aperture, undo the bolts (left-hand bolts arrowed)

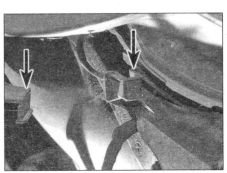

6.4a Pull up the rubber sealing strip . . .

6.4b . . . and undo the bolts (left-hand bolts arrowed)

6.5a Press the bumper rearwards a little . . .

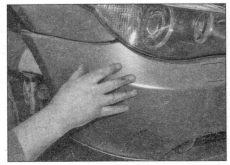

6.5c . . . then pull the edges outwards a little and slide the bumper forwards

6.5b . . . to release the hook from the catch (arrowed) . . .

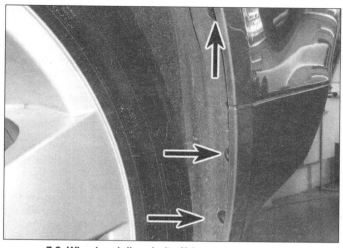

7.2 Wheel arch liner bolts (3 lower ones arrowed)

7.4 Prise down the centre pin (arrowed) and lever out the expansion rivet

2 Undo the 4 bolts securing the rear section of the wheel arch liners each side **(see illustration)**.

3 Prise down the centre pin, and lever out the plastic expansion rivet each side securing the front, lower edge of the rear bumper.

4 Prise up the centre pin, and lever out the plastic expansion rivets on the underside of the centre section of the rear bumper **(see illustration)**.

5 Undo the 2 bolts each side in the luggage compartment beneath the rear lights **(see illustration)**.

6 Pull out the front edges of the bumper each side, and with the help of an assistant, withdrawn the bumper from the vehicle. Disconnect any wiring plugs as the bumper is withdrawn.

Touring models

7 Prise down the centre pin, then lever out the plastic expansion rivet each side in the centre, underside of the bumper, and one each side at the front, lower edge **(see illustrations)**.

8 Prise open the cover and undo the bolt each side adjacent to the tail lights **(see illustrations)**.

9 Undo the 4 bolts each side securing the wheel arch liner to the bumper **(see illustration 7.2)**.

10 With the help of an assistant, pull out the front edges slightly, and slide the bumper to the rear, releasing the lower centre catches as the bumper is withdrawn. On models with PDC, disconnect the sensor wiring plug as the bumper is withdrawn **(see illustration)**.

11 Undo the nuts each side securing the bumper bar to the impact absorbers.

Refitting

12 Refitting is a reverse of the removal procedure, ensuring that the front of the bumper engages correctly with the plastic guides, and the mounting bolts/nuts are tightened securely.

7.5 Undo the bolts (arrowed) under each rear light

7.7a Prise down the centre pins and remove the plastic expansion rivets at the ends . . .

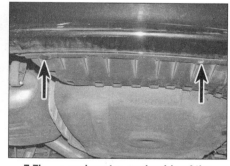

7.7b . . . and centre, underside of the bumper (arrowed)

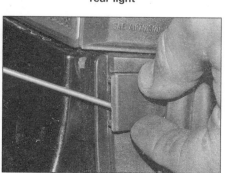

7.8a Prise open the cover . . .

7.8b . . . and undo the bolt each side

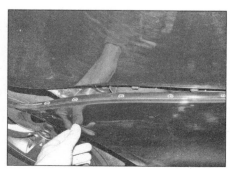

7.10 Pull out the front edges slightly

8.2 Disconnect the windscreen washer jet hoses

8.3 Note the earth lead (arrowed) under the right-hand bonnet hinge bolt/nut

8 Bonnet and support struts – removal, refitting and adjustment

Bonnet

Removal

1 Open the bonnet and have an assistant support it. Using a pencil or felt tip pen, mark the outline of each bonnet hinge relative to the bonnet, to use as a guide on refitting.
2 Disconnect the hose from the washer jets. On models with heated jets also disconnect the wiring connectors **(see illustration)**. Free the harness/hose from any retaining clips.
3 With the aid of an assistant, support the bonnet in the open position then slacken and remove the left and right-hand hinge-to-bonnet bolts **(see illustration)**. Remove the bonnet.

Refitting and adjustment

4 With the aid of an assistant, position the bonnet against the hinges. Refit the bolts and tighten them by hand only. Align the hinges with the marks made on removal, then tighten the retaining bolts securely.
5 Close the bonnet, and check for alignment with the adjacent panels. If necessary, slacken the hinge bolts and re-align the bonnet to suit. Once the bonnet is correctly aligned, securely tighten the hinge bolts, and check that the bonnet fastens and releases satisfactorily. Reconnect the hose and wiring.

Support struts

6 Open the bonnet and have an assistant support it. Prise out the retaining clips at the top and bottom of the struts **(see illustration 15.16)**.
7 Refitting is a reversal of removal.

9 Bonnet release cable – removal and refitting

Removal

1 The bonnet release cable is in three sections, the main first cable from the release lever to the connection at the right-hand side inner wing (adjacent to the windscreen washer reservoir), the second from the connection to the right-hand bonnet lock, and also one linking the two bonnet locks.

Release lever-to-connection cable

2 Unclip the connection housing from the inner wing. Prise open the connection housing and disconnect the inner and outer cables **(see illustration)**.
3 Rotate the fastener 90° anti-clockwise, release the clip and remove the pollen filter cover on the driver's side.
4 Pull up the rubber seal from the bulkhead, then undo the bolt, rotate the fasteners 90° anti-clockwise, and remove the lower housing on the driver's side. Unclip any hoses or wiring as the housing is removed.

5 Remove the driver's side lower facia panel as described in Section 26.
6 Open the driver's door, and carefully pull up the door sill trim panel.
7 Pull up the rubber weatherstrip from the door aperture adjacent to the footwell kick panel.
8 Undo the bolt and remove the bonnet release lever.
9 Undo the bolt and remove the footwell kick panel **(see illustration)**. Disconnect any wiring plugs as the panel is withdrawn.
10 Undo the 3 bolts, remove the bracket and separate the cable inner end fitting from the release lever **(see illustration)**.
11 Push/pull the outer release cable end fitting from the engine compartment bulkhead, and pull the cable into the engine compartment.

Connection-to-bonnet lock cable

12 Unclip the connection housing from the inner wing. Prise open the housing and disconnect the inner and outer cables **(see illustration 9.2)**
13 Remove the driver's side bonnet lock as described in Section 10.

Lock linking cable

14 The linking cable is removed as part of the bonnet lock removal procedure, as described in Section 10.

Refitting

15 Refitting is the reverse of removal ensuring that the cable is correctly routed, and secured to all the relevant retaining clips. Check that the bonnet locks operate correctly before closing the bonnet.

10 Bonnet lock(s) – removal and refitting

Removal

1 Unclip the connection housing from the inner wing. Prise open the housing and disconnect the inner and outer cables **(see illustration 9.2)**
2 Release the cable from the retaining clips under the front panel.

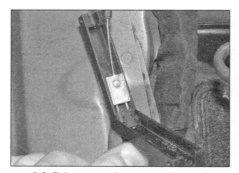

9.2 Prise open the connection and disconnect the release cable

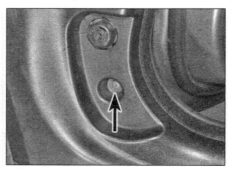

9.9 Undo the bolt (arrowed) and remove the panel

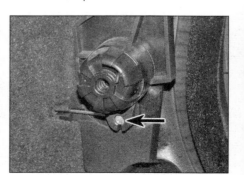

9.10 Detach the inner cable (arrowed) from the lever

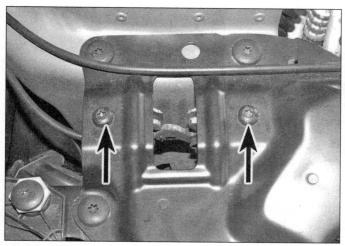

10.3 Undo the Torx bolts (arrowed) securing the bonnet lock . . .

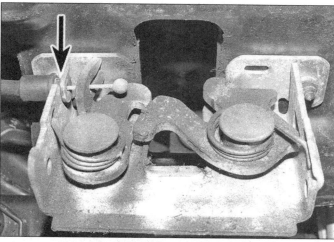

10.4 . . . and disengage the cable (arrowed)

3 Undo the 2 bolts and move the lock assembly outwards from place **(see illustration)**.

4 Disconnect the release cable from the lock **(see illustration)**.

Refitting

5 Refitting is a reversal of removal.

11 Door – removal, refitting and adjustment

Removal

1 Disconnect the battery negative terminal (see Chapter 5). This is essential, as all 5 Series models covered by this manual have front door airbags as standard, with rear door side airbags available as an option. Wait at lease 1 minute after disconnecting the battery before disconnecting the loom wiring plug (paragraph 5).
2 Undo the bolt securing the door wiring loom connector to the pillar **(see illustration)**.
3 Undo the bolt securing the check strap to the pillar **(see illustration)**.
4 Unscrew the upper and lower hinge pins **(see illustration)**.
5 With the help of an assistant, lift the door, withdraw the door wiring connector from the pillar, pull out the locking element and unplug the connector.
6 Remove the door from the vehicle.

Refitting

7 Refitting is a reversal of removal.

Adjustment

8 Always adjust the rear doors first. Close the door and check the door alignment with surrounding body panels. If necessary, slight adjustment of the door position can be made by slackening the hinge retaining nuts and repositioning the hinge/door as necessary. Once the door is correctly positioned,

securely tighten the hinge nuts. If the paint work around the hinges has been damaged, paint the affected area with a suitable touch-in brush to prevent corrosion.

12 Door inner trim panel – removal and refitting

Removal – front door

1 Disconnect the battery negative terminal then open the door (see Chapter 5). This is

essential, as all 5 Series models covered by this manual have front door airbags as standard. Wait at least 1 minute before commencing work after disconnecting the battery.
2 Carefully prise out the footwell light (where fitted) from the base of the door trim. Disconnect the wiring plug as the light is withdrawn.
3 Using a flat, blunt tool, prise out the airbag emblem from the rear of the door trim, and undo the bolt exposed **(see illustration)**.
4 Prise out the cap at the front of the door

11.2 Undo the connector retaining bolt (arrowed)

11.3 Check strap bolt (arrowed)

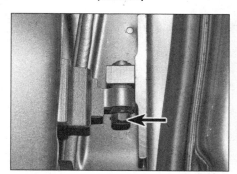

11.4 Unscrew the hinge pin (arrowed)

12.3 Prise out the airbag emblem

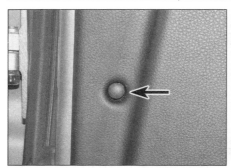

12.4 Prise out the cap (arrowed) at the front edge of the door trim

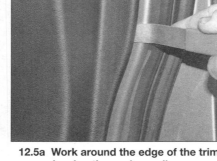

12.5a Work around the edge of the trim, releasing the push-on clips . . .

12.5b . . . and pull the top edge inwards before lifting the panel upwards

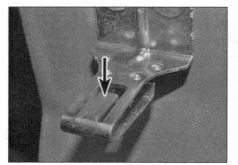

12.5c Spread the upper (arrowed) and lower tangs of the clip apart before refitting the trim panel

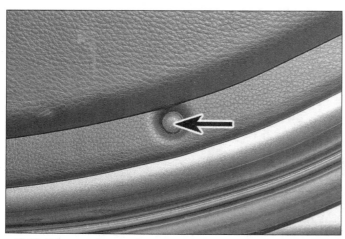

12.6 Pull out the rear edge first, then disconnect the release cable from the lever

trim and undo the bolt exposed **(see illustration)**.

5 Release the door trim panel clips, carefully levering between the panel and door with a flat-bladed screwdriver or similar blunt tool. Work around the outside of the panel, and when all the studs are released, lift the panel **(see illustration)**. Note that the clip behind the door grab handle may have to be spread apart a little prior to refitment **(see illustration)**. Transfer the plastic part of the clip to the trim panel so that it simply presses onto the metal part.

6 Disconnect any wiring plugs and the

release cable from the lock lever as the panel is withdrawn **(see illustration)**.

7 If required, carefully prise the sound insulation panel away from the door, using a flat-bladed tool to cut through the sealant.

Removal – rear door

Models with sun roller blind

8 Fully open the window, unhook the blind starting at the top, then pull it towards the inside of the cabin, and upwards to remove it.

All models

9 Disconnect the battery negative terminal

then open the door (see Chapter 5). This is essential on models with rear side door airbags. Wait at least 1 minute after disconnecting the battery before commencing work after disconnecting the battery.

10 Carefully prise out the footwell light (where fitted) from the base of the door trim. Disconnect the wiring plug as the light is withdrawn.

11 Using a flat, blunt tool, prise out the airbag emblem (where applicable) from the rear of the door trim, and undo the bolt exposed.

12 Prise out the caps at the front and lower edges of the door trim and undo the bolts exposed **(see illustration)**.

13 Release the door trim panel clips, carefully levering between the panel and door with a flat-bladed screwdriver or similar blunt tool. Work around the outside of the panel, and when all the studs are released, lift the panel **(see illustration 12.5a and 12.5b)**. Note that the clip behind the door grab handle may have to be spread apart a little prior to refitting **(see illustration 12.5c)**. Remove the plastic part of the clip and fit it to the door trim panel prior to refitting **(see illustration)**.

14 Disconnect any wiring plugs, and the release cable from the lock lever as the panel is withdrawn **(see illustration 12.6)**.

15 If required, carefully prise the sound insulation panel away from the door, using a flat-bladed tool to cut through the sealant.

12.12 Prise out the cap (arrowed) at the lower edge of the door

12.13 Remove the plastic clip and fit it to the door trim panel (arrowed)

13.2 Undo the nuts (arrowed) and remove the retaining plate

13.3 Undo the nut (arrowed) and release the clips (arrowed)

Refitting

16 Refitting of the trim panel is the reverse of removal. Before refitting, check whether any of the trim panel retaining clips were broken on removal, and renew them as necessary. Ensure that where removed, the sound insulation panel is sealed into its original location. If the sound insulation panel is damaged on removal it must be renewed.

13 Door handle and lock components – removal and refitting

Removal

Interior door handle

Note: *It would appear that the rear interior door handles are integral with the trim panels.*

1 Remove the door inner trim panel as described in Section 12.

2 On models up to 03/2007, undo the 4 nuts and remove the retaining plate, then slide the handle assembly downwards from the panel **(see illustration)**.

3 On models from 03/2007, undo the nut, release the clips and detach the handle assembly from the panel **(see illustration)**.

Door lock assembly

4 Fully close the door window, then remove

the door inner trim panel and sound insulation as described in Section 12. Note that it's only necessary to remove the rear section of the sound insulation.

5 If removing a rear door lock, undo the bolt and remove the foam crash pad from the lock (models up to 03/2004), or remove the lower bolt, slacken the upper bolt, and remove the reinforcement bar from under the lock (models from 04/2004) as applicable.

6 Detach the exterior handle operating cable from the lock assembly **(see illustration)**.

7 Release the clips and disconnect the lock wiring plug **(see illustration)**.

13.6 Pull the end of the cable (arrowed) from the lock lever

8 Unclip the lock button rod from the lock lever **(see illustration)**.

9 On models with the automatic soft close function, disconnect the units wiring plug, then undo the 2 nuts/1 bolt securing the unit to the door frame.

10 On all models, undo the three Torx bolts, and manoeuvre the door lock downwards and out from the door **(see illustration)**.

Door exterior handle

11 Prise out upper the grommet from the door end panel to access the exterior handle retaining bolt. On rear doors, unclip the rubber seal to access the upper hole **(see illustration)**.

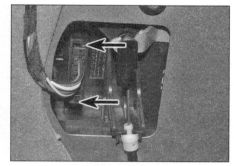

13.7 Release the clips (arrowed) and disconnect the lock wiring plug

13.8 Pull the lock button rod from the lever

13.10 Lock retaining bolts (arrowed)

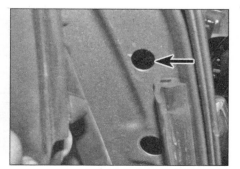

13.11 On rear doors, unclip the rubber seal to access the upper hole (arrowed)

13.12 Rotate the retaining bolt anti-clockwise until the handle is secured in the 'pulled' position

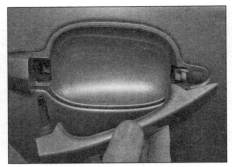

13.13 Pull the handle outwards and downwards

13.15 Prise out the lower grommet and undo the recess cover retaining bolt

12 Pull the exterior handle outwards/upwards until the handle retaining bolt it aligned with the hole in the door. Rotate the bolt anti-clockwise until the handle is secured in position **(see illustration)**.

13 Pull the rear of the handle outwards, then pull it downwards to disengage it from the lock actuator **(see illustration)**.

Door exterior handle carrier/lock cylinder

14 Remove the door lock and exterior handle assembly as described in this Section. Note that on the passenger's side or rear doors, it's not necessary to completely remove the door lock – just disconnect the exterior handle operating cable from the lock.

15 Prise out the lower rubber grommet from the door end panel, and remove the handle recess cover retaining bolt **(see illustration)**.

16 Fold forwards the rubber stop pad from the front of the handle recess cover.

17 Undo the retaining bolt at the front, then press the handle front mounting inwards, and manoeuvre the handle recess cover from place **(see illustration)**.

18 Squeeze together the upper and lower clips, then press the rear of the handle carrier/lock cylinder into the door skin slightly **(see illustration)**.

19 From inside the door, slide the carrier rearwards and manoeuvre it from place. Disconnect any wiring plugs as the unit is withdrawn.

20 No further dismantling is recommended. At the time of writing, the lock cylinder appears to only be available as an assembly with the exterior handle carrier. Check with your local BMW dealer.

Refitting

Caution: Do not close the door until you are completely satisfied that the lock is working correctly. If the door is accidentally closed, it may not be possible to open the door without cutting the door outer skin.

Interior door handle

21 Engage the inner cable with the release handle (handle closed), and press the cable lock into place.

22 The remainder of refitting is a reversal of removal.

Door lock assembly

23 Manoeuvre the lock into position, ensuring the lock cylinder shaft engages correctly (driver's door only), and refit the bolts – don't tighten them at this stage.

24 Force the lock fully into the corner of the door frame. The lock seal must fully contact the door frame to prevent water ingress. Tighten the bolts securely, and reconnect the wiring plug.

25 Refit and tighten the automatic soft close unit retaining nuts/bolt (where fitted), then reconnect the wiring plug.

26 Clip the operating cable into place on the door lock.

27 Reconnect the lock button rod.

28 The remainder of refitting is a reversal of removal, but do **not** close the door until you are completely satisfied that the lock is working correctly. If the door is accidentally closed, it may not be possible to open the door without cutting the door outer skin.

Door exterior handle

29 Insert the front end of the handle into place in the lock actuator, then engage the lug at the rear of the handle **(see illustration)**.

30 Hold the exterior handle, then tighten the retaining bolt, and refit the rubber grommet.

31 The remainder of refitting is a reversal of removal, but do **not** close the door until you are completely satisfied that the lock is working correctly. If the door is accidentally closed, it may not be possible to open the door without cutting the door outer skin.

Door exterior handle carrier/lock cylinder

32 The remainder of refitting is a reversal of removal, but do **not** close the door until you are completely satisfied that the lock is working correctly. If the door is accidentally closed, it may not be possible to open the door without cutting the door outer skin.

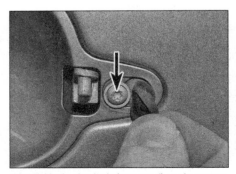

13.17 Undo the bolt (arrowed) and remove the recess cover

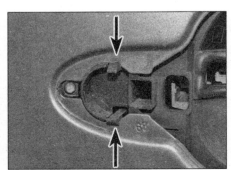

13.18 Release the clips (arrowed) and push the handle carrier into the door

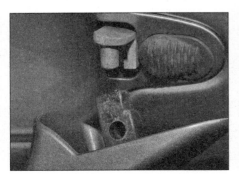

13.29 Ensure the front of the handle engages with the pin

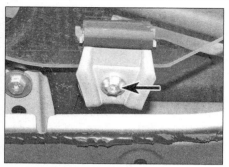

14.3a The front window has a clamping bolt at the front and rear (arrowed)

14.3b Lift the rear of the window and manoeuvre it from the door

14.5 Undo the bolt (arrowed) securing the clamp to the motor

14.6 Disconnect the motor wiring plug

14.7a Slacken the bolts (arrowed) at the lower ends of the regulator . . .

14.7b . . . and undo the upper ones (arrowed)

14 Door glass and regulator –
removal and refitting

Removal

Front door window

1 Lower the window completely.
2 Remove the door inner trim panel and sound insulation panel as described in Section 12.
3 Slacken the window clamping bolts, lift the rear of the window, and manoeuvre it from the door **(see illustrations)**.

Front door window regulator

4 Release the door window from the regulator clamps, as described earlier in this Section.

Note that there is no need to remove the window from the door, simply use adhesive tape, or rubber wedges, to secure the window in the fully-closed position.
5 Slacken the bolt and remove the clamp from the window motor **(see illustration)**.
6 Disconnect the window regulator wiring plug, and release the plastic guide **(see illustration)**.
7 Slacken the bolts at the lower ends of the window regulator frames, and remove the bolts at the upper ends **(see illustrations)**. Manoeuvre the regulator from the door. At the time of writing, it would appear that the electric motor is integral with the regulator, and must be renewed as an assembly. Check with your BMW dealer or specialist.

Rear door window

8 Lower the window approximately 345 mm then remove the door inner trim panel as described in Section 12.
9 Apply a length of insulation tape to the top edge of the door outer panel to prevent paintwork damage, then using a plastic or wooden spatula, carefully prise up the door-to-window exterior trim **(see illustration)**.
10 Carefully pull the window frame cover inwards and detach it from the door. The fixed window cover must be pulled inwards at the same time, but must not be detached from the rest of the frame cover **(see illustrations)**. On models with a rear, side roller blind, unclip the covers and remove the hook retaining bolts.
11 Pull the rubber guide from the fixed glass pillar, then undo the 3 bolts, slide the pillar

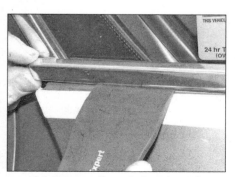

14.9 Prise up the exterior trim strip

14.10a Pull the plastic window frame cover inwards to release the clips

14.10b The fixed window cover (arrowed) must be released with the frame cover

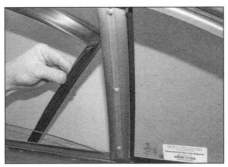

14.11a Pull the rubber guide from the pillar . . .

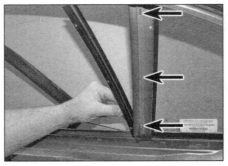

14.11b . . . then undo the 3 bolts (arrowed) and remove the pillar

14.14a Undo the window retaining bolt (arrowed) . . .

14.14b . . . and lift the window from the door

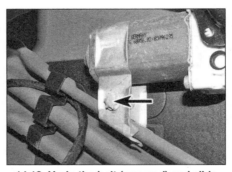

14.18 Undo the bolt (arrowed) and slide the clamp from the motor

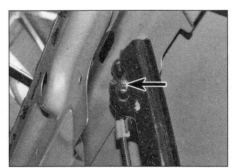

14.20 Undo the regulator upper bolt (arrowed)

downwards, and lift it from the door **(see illustrations)**.

12 Carefully prise out the rubber guide strip from the window frame channels.

13 Disconnect the electric window motor wiring plug.

14 Remove the retaining bolt and washer, the lift the rear window from the door **(see illustrations)**.

Rear door fixed window

15 As the rear door fixed window is bonded in place, renewal of the window should be entrusted to a BMW dealer or automotive window specialist.

Rear door window regulator

16 Remove the rear window as described in this Section.

17 Slacken the bolt at the lower end of the regulator frame.

18 Slacken the retaining bolt and slide the clamp from the window motor **(see illustration)**.

19 Disconnect the electric motor wiring plug.

20 Remove the bolt at the upper end of the regulator frame, and manoeuvre the regulator from the door **(see illustration)**.

21 At the time of writing, it would appear that the electric motor is integral with the regulator, and must be renewed as an assembly. Check with your BMW dealer or specialist.

Refitting

Front door window

22 Refitting is the reverse of removal, but prior to tightening the window clamp bolts, fully close the window and tighten the window clamp bolts securely. Operate the window and check that it moves easily and squarely in the door frame.

Front door window regulator

23 Refitting is the reverse of removal. Refit the window glass and adjust as described earlier in this Section. After refitting, the anti-trapping function of the window must be re-initialised as follows:

a) *Open the window completely.*
b) *Close the window, and hold the switch in this position for approximately 5 seconds.*

15.3 Undo the toolbox hinge bolts

Rear door window

24 Refitting is the reverse of removal. Prior to refitting the door sound insulation panel, check that the window operates smoothly and easily.

Rear door window regulator

25 Refitting is the reverse of removal. Prior to refitting the sound insulation panel, check that the window operates smoothly and easily. Initialise the window functions as described in Chapter 5 *Battery – disconnection, removal and refitting*.

15 Boot lid/tailgate and support struts – removal and refitting

Removal

Boot lid

1 Carefully prise the light unit (where fitted) from the boot lid trim panel, and disconnect the wiring plug.

2 On models with manual boot lid unlocking, unclip the release handle, and disconnect the operating cable from the handle.

3 Undo the toolbox lid retaining bolt, and remove the toolbox hinge bolts **(see illustration)**. Remove the toolbox from the boot trim panel.

4 Prise up the centre pins and remove the

15.4a Prise up the centre pins and remove the plastic rivets . . .

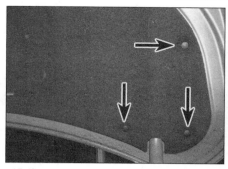

15.4b . . . around the edge of the boot lid trim (arrowed) . . .

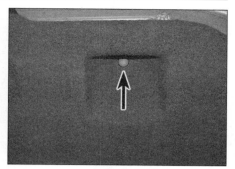

15.4c . . . and the ones in the handle recesses (arrowed)

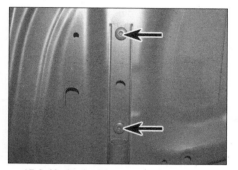

15.6 Undo the hinge-to-boot lid bolts (arrowed)

15.9 Pull the upper trim panel from place

15.11 Undo the tailgate retaining nuts (arrowed)

plastic expanding rivets, then remove the trim panel from the boot lid **(see illustrations)**.

5 Disconnect the wiring connectors from the number plate lights, luggage compartment light switch and central locking servo (as applicable) and tie a piece of string to the end of the wiring. Noting the correct routing of the wiring harness, release the harness rubber grommets from the boot lid and withdraw the wiring. When the end of the wiring appears, untie the string and leave it in position in the boot lid; it can then be used on refitting to draw the wiring into position.

6 Draw around the outline of each hinge plate with a suitable marker pen then slacken and remove the hinge retaining bolts and remove the boot lid from the vehicle **(see illustration)**.

7 Inspect the hinges for signs of wear or damage and renew if necessary; the hinges are secured to the vehicle by bolts.

Tailgate/rear window

8 Open the tailgate a little, and have an assistant standby ready to support the tailgate.

9 Open the rear window and pull the upper trim panel from the window aperture **(see illustration)**.

10 Note their fitted positions, then disconnect the various wiring plugs from the tailgate.

11 Make alignment marks between the tailgate and the hinges, then undo the nuts and remove the tailgate **(see illustration)**.

12 To remove the rear window, prise out

the grommets, undo the 4 bolts and pull the tailgate spoiler rearwards a little **(see illustration)**. Disconnect the wiring/hose connections and remove the spoiler.

13 Lift the cover over the aerial amplifier, and undo the 2 nuts, disconnect the wiring plugs and remove the amplifier **(see illustration)**.

14 Make alignment marks between the window and the hinges.

15 Slacken the window hinge nuts, and remove any spacers. Undo the bolt, completely undo the nuts and, with the help of an assistant, remove the window **(see illustration)**.

Tailgate support struts

16 Use a screwdriver to prise out the spring

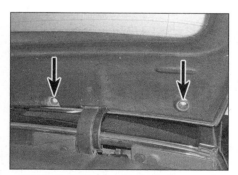

15.12 Undo the spoiler bolts (arrowed)

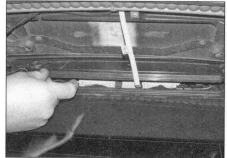

15.13 Lift the cover over the amplifier

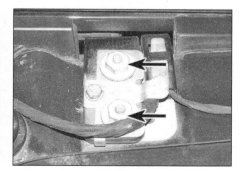

15.15 Undo the window hinge nuts (arrowed)

15.16 Prise out the spring clips at the end of the struts

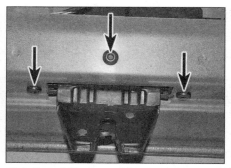

16.2 Boot lid lock retaining bolts (arrowed)

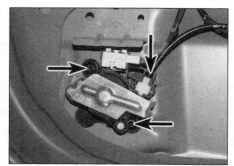

16.5 Boot lock operating cable and retaining bolts (arrowed)

clip each end of the support strut **(see illustration)**. Have an assistant support the tailgate, then pull the support strut from the mountings.

17 Refitting is a reversal of removal.

Refitting

Boot lid

18 Refitting is the reverse of removal, aligning the hinges with the marks made before removal.

19 On completion, close the boot lid and check its alignment with the surrounding panels. If necessary slight adjustment can be made by slackening the retaining bolts and repositioning the boot lid on its hinges. If the paint work around the hinges has been damaged, paint the affected area with a suitable touch-in brush to prevent corrosion.

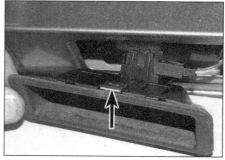

16.9 Prise out the upper edge of the button assembly to release the clip (arrowed)

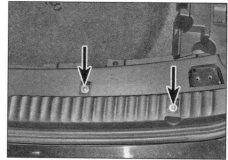

16.16 Prise out the covers each side, undo the bolts (arrowed) and remove the tailgate sill trim panel

Tailgate support struts

20 Refitting is a reverse of the removal procedure, ensuring that the strut is securely retained by its retaining clips.

Tailgate

21 Refitting is a reversal of removal, aligning the previously-made marks.

16 Boot lid/tailgate lock components – removal and refitting

Removal

Boot lid lock

1 Remove the boot lid trim panel as described in the previous Section.

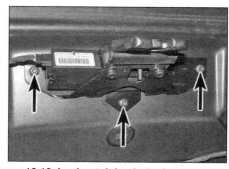

16.12 Lock retaining bolts (arrowed)

16.17 Remove the plastic expansion rivets (centre ones arrowed) and remove the wiring loom guide

2 Disconnect the lock wiring plug(s), undo the three bolts and remove the lock assembly **(see illustration)**.

3 Disconnect the lock button actuating rod.

Boot lid lock cylinder

4 Remove the boot lid trim panel as described in the previous Section.

5 Pull the operating cable outer section from place, and disconnect the inner cable end fitting from the quadrant **(see illustration)**.

6 Rotate the quadrant as necessary to access the retaining bolts. Undo the bolts, and manoeuvre the cylinder assembly from the boot lid.

Boot lid release button

7 Remove the boot lid trim panel as described in the previous Section.

8 Disconnect the button wiring plug.

9 Carefully prise out the upper edge of the button, then lift it from place **(see illustration)**. If required, slide off the clip and remove the micro switch.

Tailgate lock

10 Remove the tailgate trim panel as described in Section 26.

11 Disconnect the emergency release cable (where fitted) from the lock assembly.

12 Using a marker pen, make alignment marks between the lock and the panel. Undo the three bolts and remove the lock **(see illustration)**. Disconnect the wiring plug as the lock is withdrawn.

13 If required, undo the two retaining bolts, drive out the pivot pin, and remove the lock actuator from the lock.

Tailgate closing motor

14 Remove both D-pillar trim panels as described in Section 26.

15 Prise up the plastic covers and remove the rear storage anchors.

16 Prise open the covers, undo the bolts, then prise out the 2 clips and remove the tailgate sill trim panel **(see illustration)**.

17 Remove the plastic expansion rivets, and remove the wiring loom guide from the motor/striker assembly **(see illustration)**.

18 Make alignment marks between the motor assembly and the vehicle body, then undo the 3 bolts and remove the striker/motor assembly

16.18 Motor/striker retaining bolts (arrowed)

17.4 CAS control unit wiring plug catch and retaining bolt
(arrowed – facia removed for clarity)

(see illustration). Disconnect the wiring plug as the assembly is withdrawn.

Refitting

19 Refitting is a reversal of removal, noting the following points:
a) *Reconnect all wiring plugs, and secure the wiring harnesses using the retaining clips (where applicable).*
b) *Match-up any previously made alignment marks.*
c) *Check the operation of the locks/cylinders before refitting the trim panels.*
d) *Tighten all fasteners securely.*

17 Central locking components – removal and refitting

Note: *The central locking system is equipped with a sophisticated self-diagnosis capability. Before removing any of the central locking components, have the system interrogated by a BMW dealer or suitably-equipped specialist to pin-point the fault.*

Removal

Electronic control module (ECM)

1 Disconnect the battery as described in Chapter 5.
2 The central locking system is controlled by the Car Access System (CAS) control module. The CAS ECM also controls the electronic immobiliser, electronic steering lock, and the electric windows. To access the control unit, remove the driver's side lower facia panel as described in Section 26.
3 Release the retaining clip and disconnect the ECM wiring plug.
4 Undo the retaining bolt and remove the ECM from the vehicle **(see illustration)**. **Note:** *If the control unit is renewed, it will need to be*

programmed before use. Entrust this task to a BMW dealer or specialist.

Door lock actuator

5 The lock actuator is integral with the door lock.

Boot/tailgate lock actuator

6 The lock actuator is integral with the boot/tailgate lock.

Refitting

7 Refitting is the reverse of removal. Prior to refitting any trim panels removed for access thoroughly check the operation of the central locking system.

18 Electric window components – removal and refitting

Note: *The electric window system is equipped with a sophisticated self-diagnosis capability. Should a fault develop, before removing any of the electric window electronics, have the system interrogated by a BMW dealer or suitably-equipped specialist to pin-point the fault*

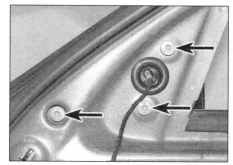

19.4 Mirror assembly retaining bolts
(arrowed)

Window switches

1 Refer to Chapter 12, Section 4.

Window motors

2 At the time of writing, it would appear that the electric motor is integral with the regulator (see Section 14), and must be renewed as an assembly. Check with your BMW dealer or specialist.

Electronic control module (ECM)

3 The electric window system is controlled by the Car Access System (CAS) ECM. Removal of the CAS ECM is described in Section 17.

19 Mirrors and associated components – removal and refitting

Exterior mirror assembly

1 Remove the door inner trim panel as described in Section 12.
2 Pull the plastic trim away from the front inner edge of the door.
3 Disconnect the mirror wiring plug(s).
4 Undo the 3 bolts, push the sealing grommet through the door frame and remove the mirror assembly **(see illustration)**.
5 Refitting is the reverse of removal.

Exterior mirror glass

Note: *If the mirror glass is removed when the mirror is cold the glass retaining clips are likely to break.*

6 Press the inner edge of the mirror glass fully forwards.
7 Insert a wide plastic or wooden wedge in between the outer edge of the mirror glass and mirror housing and carefully prise the

19.7 Prise the outer edge of the mirror glass rearwards

glass from the motor **(see illustration)**. Take great care when removing the glass; do not use excessive force as the glass is easily broken.

8 Remove the glass from the mirror and, where necessary, disconnect the wiring connectors from the mirror heating element.

9 On refitting, reconnect the wiring to the glass and clip the glass onto the motor, taking great care not to break it.

Exterior mirror switch

10 Refer to Chapter 12.

Exterior mirror cover

11 Remove the mirror glass as described above.

12 Release the four retaining clips and remove the cover **(see illustration)**.

13 Refitting is the reversal of removal.

Interior mirror

14 There are essentially two different types of mirror arms and mountings. One type has a plastic cover over the plug connection, and the other type has a mirror arm which splits in two to reveal the wiring plug.

Plastic cover type arm

15 Carefully lever out the plastic cover, and disconnect the mirror wiring plug (where applicable).

16 Strike the lower part of the mirror forwards with the ball of your hand to unclip the arm from the mounting.

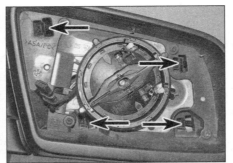

19.12 Mirror cover retaining clips (arrowed)

Caution: Do not twist the arm whilst attempting removal as the clip will be damaged, and do not pull the arm to the rear as the windscreen may be damaged.

Split cover mirror arm

17 Press the two sides of the arm covers towards the mirror and pull the two sides apart. On mirrors equipped with a rain sensor, press up at the base of the covers and pull the two sides apart **(see illustrations)**.

18 Push the right-hand side of the mirror upwards and towards the front. Swivel the left-hand arm cover to the left and unclip it from the metal part of the arm.

19 Push the left-hand side of the mirror upwards and towards the front. Swivel the right-hand arm cover to the right and unclip it from the arm.

20 Disconnect the mirror wiring plug.

21 Strike the lower part of the mirror forwards with the ball of your hand to unclip the arm from the mounting.

Caution: Do not twist the arm whilst attempting removal as the clip will be damaged, and do not pull the arm to the rear as the windscreen may be damaged.

All types

22 To refit the mirrors, position the mirror arm over the mounting at an angle of 45° to the vertical on the driver's side. Push the arm to the vertical and check that it engaged correctly **(see illustration)**. Where applicable, refit the covers and reconnect the wiring plug.

20 Windscreen and rear screen/ tailgate glass – general information

1 These areas of glass are secured by the tight fit of the weatherstrip in the body aperture, and are bonded in position with a special adhesive. Renewal of such fixed glass is a difficult, messy and time-consuming task, which is beyond the scope of the home mechanic. It is difficult, unless one has plenty of practice, to obtain a secure, waterproof fit. Furthermore, the task carries a high risk of breakage; this applies especially to the laminated glass windscreen. In view of this, owners are strongly advised to have this sort of work carried out by one of the many specialist windscreen fitters.

21 Sunroof – general information, motor renewal and initialisation

General information

1 Due to the complexity of the sunroof mechanism, considerable expertise is needed to repair, renew or adjust the sunroof components successfully. Removal of the roof first requires the headlining to be removed, which is a complex and tedious operation, and not a task to be undertaken lightly. Therefore, any problems with the sunroof (except sunroof motor renewal) should be referred to a BMW dealer or specialist.

2 On models with an electric sunroof, if the sunroof motor fails to operate, first check the relevant fuse. If the fault cannot be traced and rectified, the sunroof can be opened and closed manually using an Allen key to turn the motor spindle (a suitable key is supplied with the vehicle tool kit). To gain access to the motor, unclip the cover from the headlining. Remove the Allen key from the tool kit, remove the plastic cover and insert the Allen key into the motor spindle. Disconnect the motor wiring connector and rotate the key to move the sunroof to the required position.

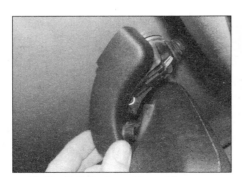

19.17a Pull the two sides of the cover apart

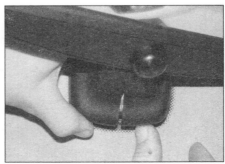

19.17b Press up at the base and pull the two sides apart

19.22 Position the mirror arm over the mounting plate at an angle of 45°

Motor renewal

3 Carefully prise the interior light unit from the headlining between the sunvisors. Disconnect the wiring plug(s) as the unit is withdrawn.
4 Carefully pull the front edge of the motor panel down and remove it complete with the switch. Disconnect the wiring plug as the panel is withdrawn.
5 Undo the three retaining bolts, and pull the motor from its location. Disconnect the wiring plug as the motor is removed.
6 Refitting is a reversal of removal, but carry out the initialisation procedure as described next.

Initialisation

7 With the battery reconnected, and the ignition on, press the sunroof operating switch into the 'tilt' position and hold it there.
8 Once the sunroof has reached the 'fully-tilted' position, hold the switch in that position for approximately 30 seconds. Initialisation is complete when the sunroof briefly lifts at the rear again.

22 Body exterior fittings – removal and refitting

Wheel arch liners and body under-panels

1 The various plastic covers fitted to the underside of the vehicle are secured in position by a mixture of bolts, nuts and retaining clips, and removal will be fairly obvious on inspection. Work methodically around, removing its retaining bolts and releasing its retaining clips until the panel is free and can be removed from the underside of the vehicle. Most clips used on the vehicle are simply prised out of position. Other clips can be released by unscrewing/prising out the centre pins and then removing the clip.
2 On refitting, renew any retaining clips that may have been broken on removal, and ensure that the panel is securely retained by all the relevant clips and bolts.

Body trim strips and badges

3 The various body trim strips and badges are held in position with a special adhesive

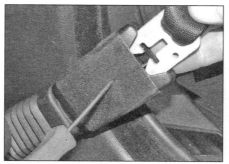
23.2 Depress the clip and disconnect the seat belt

tape. Removal requires the trim/badge to be heated, to soften the adhesive, and then cut away from the surface. Due to the high risk of damage to the vehicle's paintwork during this operation, it is recommended that this task should be entrusted to a BMW dealer or suitably-equipped specialist.

23 Seats – removal and refitting

Front seat removal

1 Slide the seat fully forwards and raise the seat cushion fully.
2 On the driver's side, use a screwdriver to depress the clip and disconnect the seat belt from the anchorage on the seat (see illustration).
3 On the passenger's side, start by lifting the rear edge, carefully pull the seat base trim from place, then undo the bolt and disconnect the seatbelt anchorage bracket from the seat (see illustration). Discard the bolt – a new one must be fitted.
4 Slacken and remove the bolts and washers securing the rear of the seat rails to the floor. Discard the bolts – new ones must be fitted.
5 Move the seat as far back as possible, then lift the centre portion of the seat inner rail trim (where fitted), and pull the trim to the front. Undo the bolt. Discard the bolt – a new one must be fitted.

23.3 Passenger's seat belt anchorage bolt (arrowed)

6 Prise up the front edge of the outer seat rail trim then unclip the inner edge and slide the trim forwards. Undo the bolt (see illustrations). Discard the bolt – a new one must be fitted.
7 Disconnect the battery negative lead as described in Chapter 5. Due to pyrotechnic pretensioners being fitted, wait at least 1 minute before proceeding.
8 Tilt the seat rearwards a little, reach under the front of the seat, pull out the front edge and unclip the plastic trim. Disconnect the wiring plug(s) and release the harness cable-ties (see illustration).
9 Lift the seat out from the vehicle.

Folding rear seat removal

Saloon

10 Pull up on the front of the seat cushion to release the left- and right-hand retaining clips, and remove it forwards and out from the vehicle. Disconnect the seat heating wiring connectors (where applicable) as the seat is withdrawn.
11 Grasp the top edge of the seat side bolster, and pull it forwards to release the clip. Lift the side bolster from place. Release the upper retaining clip from the vehicle body and fit to the bolster to aid refitting.
12 Fold the seat backs forward, undo the outer mounting bolts, and remove the seats.

Touring

13 Grasp the front edge of the seat cushion and pull it upwards with a sharp movement to release the clips. Remove the cushion.

23.6a Prise up the front edge, unclip the inner edge . . .

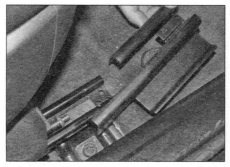
23.6b . . . and slide forwards the seat rail trim

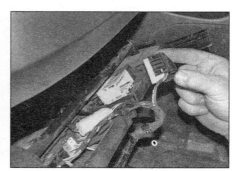
23.8 Pull forwards the plastic trim, and disconnect the wiring plugs

23.14a Note how the lug on the side bolster engages with the bracket on the vehicle body (arrowed)

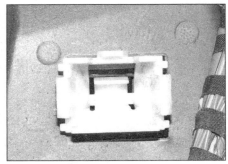

23.14b Remove the side bolster clip from the vehicle body . . .

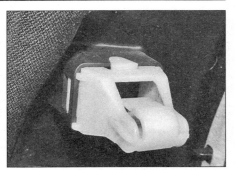

23.14c . . . and fit it to the side bolster before refitting

14 Pull the top of the side bolster forward, and then pull the whole cushion upwards to release it **(see illustrations)**. Repeat the procedure on the remaining side cushion.
15 Release the rear seat backrest, and fold it forward.
16 Undo the 2 Torx bolts at each outer edge of the backrest, and pull them from the centre mounting **(see illustrations)**.
17 Undo the centre seat belt lower anchorage, and remove the backrest.

Fixed rear seat removal

18 Pull up on the seat base cushion to release the left- and right-hand retaining clips and remove it from the vehicle. Disconnect any wiring plugs as the cushion is withdrawn.
19 Hold the centre seat belt off to one side.
20 Working in the luggage compartment, insert

a screwdriver into the holes on the underside of the parcel shelf, and lever the retaining cable outwards each side, to release the upper part of the backrest **(see illustrations)**.
21 Undo the bolt each side at the lower, centre edge of the seat back, and remove it from the vehicle **(see illustration)**.

Front seat refitting

22 Refitting is the reverse of removal, noting the following points.
   a) *On manually-adjusted seats, fit the seat retaining bolts and tighten them by hand only. Slide the seat fully forwards and then slide it back by two stops of the seat locking mechanism. Rock the seat to ensure that the seat locking mechanism is correctly engaged then tighten the mounting bolts securely.*

   b) *On electrically-adjusted seats, ensure that the wiring is connected and correctly routed then tighten the seat mounting bolts securely.*
   c) *Tighten the seat belt mounting bolt to the specified torque.*
   d) *Tighten the seat mounting bolts to the specified torque in the following sequence: Front inner, front outer, rear inner, followed by the rear outer.*

Rear seats refitting

23 Refitting is the reverse of removal. Tighten the seat belt lower mounting bolts to the specified torque setting.

24 Seat belt tensioning mechanism – general information

1 Most models are fitted with a front seat belt tensioner system. The system is designed to instantaneously take up any slack in the seat belt in the case of a sudden frontal impact, therefore reducing the possibility of injury to the front seat occupants. Each front seat is fitted with its own system, the tensioner being situated on the inboard seat rail.
2 The seat belt tensioner is triggered by a frontal impact above a predetermined force. Lesser impacts, including impacts from behind, will not trigger the system.
3 When the system is triggered, a large spring in the anchorage bracket retracts and locks

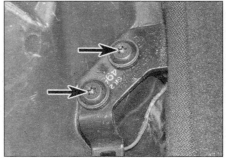

23.16a Undo the seat backrest outer mounting bolts (arrowed) . . .

23.16b . . . and pull it from the centre mounting

23.20a Working under the parcel shelf . . .

23.20b . . . lever the catch each side in the direction of the arrow to release the seat backrest

23.21 Undo the bolts (arrowed) at the lower edge of the seat backrest

the seat belt. This prevents the seat belt moving and keeps the occupant in position in the seat. Once the tensioner has been triggered, the seat belt will be permanently locked and the assembly must be renewed.

4 There is a risk of injury if the system is triggered inadvertently when working on the vehicle. If any work is to be carried out on the seat/seat belt disable the tensioner by disconnecting the battery negative lead (see Chapter 5), and waiting at least 1 minute before proceeding.

5 Also note the following warnings before contemplating any work on the front seat.

 Warning: If the tensioner mechanism is dropped, it must be renewed, even it has suffered no apparent damage.

• *Do not allow any solvents to come into contact with the tensioner mechanism.*

• *Do not subject the seat to any form of shock as this could accidentally trigger the seat belt tensioner.*

• *Check for any deformation of the seat belt stalk tensioner, and anchorage brackets. Renew any that are damaged.*

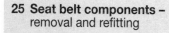
25 Seat belt components – removal and refitting

 Warning: Read Section 24 before proceeding.

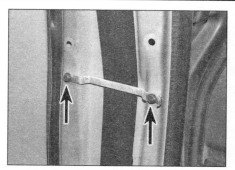

25.3 Seat belt guide bolts (arrowed)

25.4 Undo the upper seat belt mounting

Removal
Front seat belt

1 Remove the front seat as described in Section 23.

2 Remove the B-pillar trim panel as described in Section 26.

3 Undo the bolts and remove the seat belt guide from the pillar **(see illustration)**.

4 Undo the bolt securing the upper seat belt mounting **(see illustration)**. Discard the bolt – a new one must be fitted.

5 Unscrew the inertia reel retaining bolt and remove the seat belt from the door pillar **(see illustration)**. Discard the bolt – a new one must be fitted.

6 If required, carefully prise off the plastic cover, undo the retaining bolt and remove the seat belt pretensioner **(see illustration)**.

Rear seat belts – Saloon

7 Remove the rear seat as described in Section 23.

8 Remove the parcel shelf as described in Section 26.

9 Slacken and remove the bolts and washers securing the rear seat belts to the vehicle body and remove the centre belt and buckle **(see illustrations)**. Discard the bolts – new ones must be fitted.

10 Unscrew the inertia reel retaining bolt and remove the seat belt(s) **(see illustrations)**. Discard the bolt(s) – new ones must be fitted.

Rear seat belts – Touring

11 Remove the rear seat as described in Section 23.

25.5 Front seat belt inertia reel retaining bolt (arrowed)

25.6 Seat belt pretensioner bolt (arrowed)

25.9a Rear seat belt outer lower mounting (arrowed)

25.9b Rear seat belt centre stalk mounting (arrowed)

25.10a Rear centre seat belt inertia reel bolt (arrowed) – Saloon

25.10b Rear outer seat belt inertia reel bolt (arrowed) – Saloon

25.12 Rear outer seat belt inertia reel bolt (arrowed) – Touring

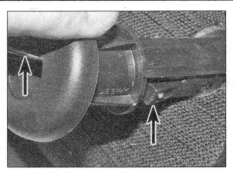

25.15 Use a length of hooked rod (arrowed) to pull the headrest tube catch (arrowed) inwards

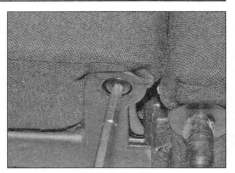

25.16a Undo the bolt . . .

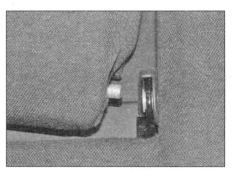

25.16b . . . and remove the armrest

25.17 Unclip the panel in the armrest aperture

12 Undo the bolt securing the inertia reel (see illustration).

Rear centre inertia reel – Touring

13 Removal of the centre inertia reel involves removal of the seat cover. This is an involved procedure, which requires some patience to accomplish successfully.

14 Remove the rear seat backrest as described in Section 23, then pull the headrests from place.

15 Using a length of stiff welding rod (or similar) with a hook on the end, release the catch and pull the headrest guide tubes from the backrest (see illustration).

16 Undo the bolt and remove the armrest (see illustrations).

17 Starting at the bottom, unclip and remove the plastic panel in the armrest aperture (see illustration).

18 Undo the 2 bolts and remove the seat belt guide trim. Feed the seat belt through the slot in the trim (see illustration).

19 Unclip the seat cover in the area of the armrest and rear, upper edge (see illustrations).

20 Undo the two bolts and remove the cover over the inertia reel (see illustration).

21 Undo the inertia reel retaining bolt and manoeuvre the assembly from position (see illustration). Discard the bolt – a new on must be fitted.

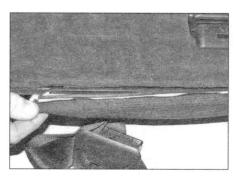

25.18 Seat belt guide bolts (arrowed)

25.19a Unclip the seat cover in the armrest area . . .

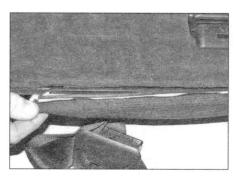

25.19b . . . and the rear, upper edge of the seat backrest

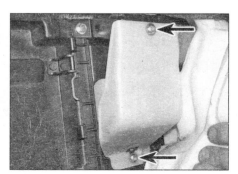

25.20 Undo the bolts (arrowed) and remove the cover

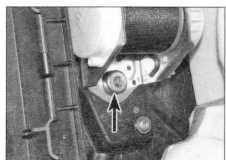

25.21 Rear, centre seat belt inertia reel bolt (arrowed)

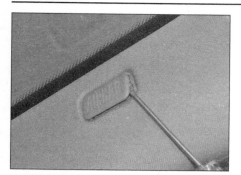

26.8 Prise out the airbag emblem and undo the bolt beneath

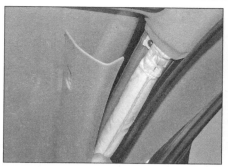

26.9a Pull the A-pillar trim inwards to release the clips

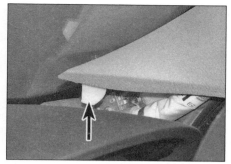

26.9b Note the lug at the base of the A-pillar trim (arrowed)

Rear seat belt stalk

22 Remove the rear seat cushion as described in Section 23.

23 Slacken and remove the bolt and washer and remove the stalk from the vehicle. Discard the bolt(s) – new ones must be fitted.

Rear centre belt and buckle – Saloon

24 Remove the rear parcel shelf as described in Section 26.

25 Slacken and remove the bolt securing the centre belt/buckle to the body and remove it from the vehicle. Discard the bolt – a new one must be fitted.

Refitting

26 Refitting is a reversal of the removal procedure, renewing the mounting bolts where specified, and tightening them to the specified torque where given.

26 Interior trim – removal and refitting

Interior trim panels

1 The interior trim panels are secured using either bolts or various types of trim fasteners, usually studs or clips.

2 Check that there are no other panels overlapping the one to be removed; usually there is a sequence that has to be followed that will become obvious on close inspection.

3 Remove all obvious fasteners, such as bolts. If the panel will not come free, it is held by hidden clips or fasteners. These are usually situated around the edge of the panel and can be prised up to release them; note, however, that they can break quite easily so new ones should be available. The best way of releasing such clips, without the correct type of tool, is to use a large flat-bladed screwdriver. Note that some panels are secured by plastic expanding rivets, where the centre pin must be prised up before the rivet can be removed. Note in many cases that the adjacent sealing strip must be prised back to release a panel.

4 When removing a panel, never use excessive force or the panel may be damaged; always check carefully that all fasteners have been removed or released before attempting to withdraw a panel.

5 Refitting is the reverse of the removal procedure; secure the fasteners by pressing them firmly into place and ensure that all disturbed components are correctly secured to prevent rattles.

A-pillar trim

6 Due to the proximity of the headlining airbag, disconnect the battery negative lead as described in Chapter 5. Wait at least 1 minute for any residual electrical energy to dissipate before proceeding.

7 Pull the rubber weatherstrip away from the door apertures, adjacent to the A-pillar.

8 Prise out the airbag emblem, and remove the bolt exposed **(see illustration)**.

9 Pull the trim inwards from the pillar to release the clips, then lift if from the facia. Note how the lug at the base of the trim engages with the facia **(see illustrations)**

10 Refitting is the reverse of the removal procedure; secure the fasteners by pressing them firmly into place and ensure that all disturbed components are correctly secured to prevent rattles.

B-pillar trim

Lower section

11 Pull up the front door sill trim panel to release the retaining clips **(see illustration)**.

12 Pull away the rubber weatherstrip from the door aperture adjacent to the pillar trim.

13 Using a wooden or plastic flat-bladed lever, carefully prise the bottom edge of the lower pillar trim inwards to release the clips, then slide it downwards from the upper A-pillar trim **(see illustrations)**.

Upper section

14 Begin by detaching the seat belt anchorage from the side of the front seat as described in Section 25.

15 Remove the lower section of the A-pillar trim as previously described in this Section.

16 Pull the lower edge of the trim inwards,

26.11 Pull up the front door sill trim

26.13a Pull the lower edge of the B-pillar trim inwards . . .

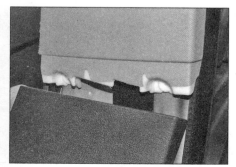

26.13b . . . and slide it down from the upper trim

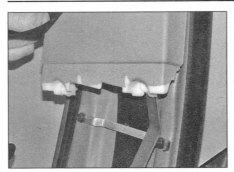

26.16a Prise the clips at the lower edge away from the pillar . . .

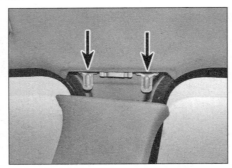

26.16b . . . and slide the A-pillar trim downwards from the clips (arrowed)

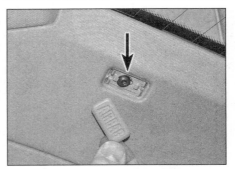

26.18 Prise out the airbag emblem and undo the bolt (arrowed)

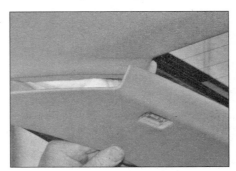

26.19 Pull the rear section of the C-pillar trim inwards to release the clips

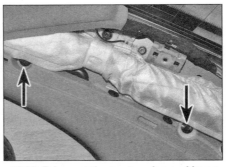

26.20 Prise out the centre pins and lever out the plastic expansion rivets (arrowed)

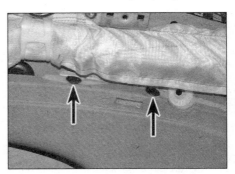

26.21 Prise out the clips (arrowed) . . .

then slide it downwards from place **(see illustrations)**. If required, feed the seat belt through the trim panel.

C-pillar trim

Saloon

17 Due to the proximity of the headlining airbag, disconnect the battery negative lead as described in Chapter 5. Wait at least 1 minute for any residual electrical energy to dissipate before proceeding.
18 Prise out airbag emblem from the

pillar trim, and undo the bolt exposed **(see illustration)**.
19 Starting at the top, pull the rear section of the pillar trim inwards to release the clips, then upwards from the parcel shelf **(see illustration)**.
20 Prise out the centre pins, then lever out the two plastic expansion rivets at the rear edge of C-pillar trim front section **(see illustration)**.
21 Prise out the two press-in clips at the rear edge of the trim panel **(see illustration)**.
22 Pull the trim panel inwards and upwards from place **(see illustration)**.

23 Refitting is the reverse of the removal procedure; secure the fasteners by pressing them firmly into place and ensure that all disturbed components are correctly secured to prevent rattles.

Touring

24 On models with a headlining airbag, disconnect the battery as described in Chapter 5.
25 Prise out the airbag emblem from the rear of the C-pillar trim, and undo the bolt exposed **(see illustration)**.

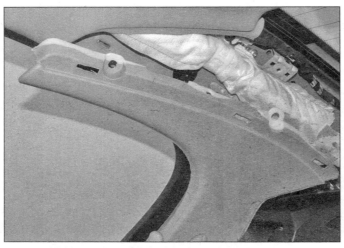

26.22 . . . then pull the trim inwards and upwards

26.25 Prise out the airbag emblem and remove the bolt beneath

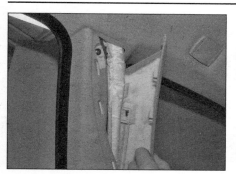

26.26 Pull the rear section of the C-pillar trim inwards

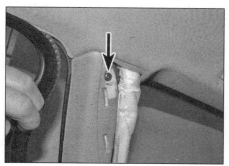

26.28 Undo the bolt (arrowed) at the top of the C-pillar trim

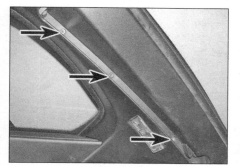

26.32 Undo the bolts (arrowed) in the D-pillar trim guide rail

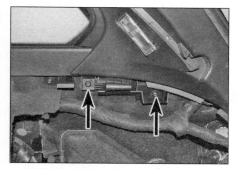

26.33 Undo the bolts (arrowed) at the lower edge of the D-pillar trim

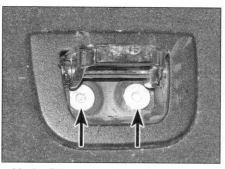

26.40a Prise up the cover and undo the bolts (arrowed)

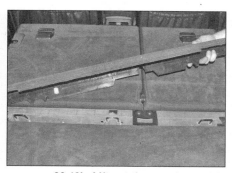

26.40b Lift out the panel

26 Pull the rear section of the C-pillar trim towards the centre of the vehicle to release the push-on clips **(see illustration)**.

27 Pull the rubber weatherstrip adjacent to the pillar from the door aperture.

28 Undo the bolt at the top of the C-pillar trim, and pull the trim in towards the centre of the vehicle to release the clip **(see illustration)**.

29 Refitting is a reversal of removal.

D-pillar trim

30 Open the luggage compartment storage compartment lids each side, and remove them.

31 On models after 03/2006 with automatic tailgate actuation, prise out the bump stop, and undo the bolt exposed.

32 Undo the 3 bolts in the guide rail **(see illustration)**.

33 Undo the 2 bolts, and pull the trim panel inwards to release the retaining clips **(see illustration)**. Disconnect any wiring plugs as the panel is withdrawn.

34 Refitting is a reversal of removal.

Luggage area side trim panel

Saloon

35 Lift the luggage compartment floor panel, and support it.

36 Rotate the fasteners anti-clockwise and manoeuvre the panel behind the rear lights from place.

37 Refitting is a reversal of removal.

Touring

38 On models with headlining airbags, disconnect the battery negative lead as described in Chapter 5.

39 Fold forwards the rear seat backrest.

40 Prise up the covers, undo the bolts and remove the luggage stowage anchors from the front of the luggage compartment floor **(see illustrations)**. Lift out the panel.

41 On models up to 04/2005 lift out the luggage compartment floor panel. On models after this date. lift the luggage compartment floor panel, prise out the clips and disconnect the upper end of the support struts from the panel, then undo the bolts at the front and remove the panel **(see illustrations)**.

42 Remove the C- and D-pillar trims as described earlier in this Section.

43 Release the clip and pull up the front section of the side trim panel top capping **(see illustration)**.

44 Pull the top of the side bolster forwards, then lift it upwards from the locating lug **(see**

26.41a Prise out the clips and disconnect the support struts

26.41b Undo the bolts (arrowed) and lift out the luggage compartment floor

26.43 Release the top capping clip

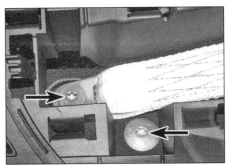

26.45 Undo the capping and airbag bolts (arrowed)

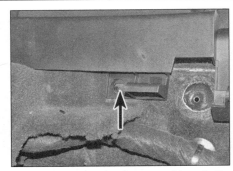

26.46a The capping is secured by a bolt underneath (arrowed) . . .

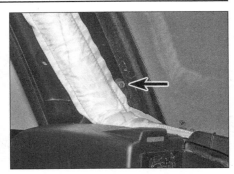

26.46b . . . a bolt on the C-pillar (arrowed) . . .

illustration 23.14a). To aid refitting, detach the upper clip from the vehicle body and fit it to the side bolster (see illustrations 23.14b and 23.14c).

45 Undo the bolt at the front of the side trim panel top capping rear section, and the bolt securing the airbag (where fitted) (see illustration).

46 Undo the 3 bolts and pull the side panel top capping front section upwards to release the retaining clips (see illustrations). If required, undo the seat belt lower anchorage bolt and feed the seat belt through the slot in the capping.

47 Prise up the centre pins, lever out the plastic expansion rivets and remove the luggage compartment side panel (see illustration). Disconnect any wiring plugs as the panel is withdrawn.

48 Refitting is a reversal of removal.

Tailgate trim panel

49 Open the tailgate, and carefully prise out the luggage compartment light from the tailgate panel. Disconnect the wiring plug as the light is withdrawn.

50 Undo the rotary fasteners, and open the flap in the tailgate panel.

51 Prise out the cover from the emergency tailgate release (where fitted), and push it back through the hole in the panel.

52 Prise out the automatic tailgate actuation switch (where fitted) and disconnect the wiring plug.

53 Unclip the hinges and remove the flap from the tailgate (see illustration).

54 Open the tailgate window, and pull up the trim panel around the wiper drive mechanism in the centre of the window aperture (see illustration).

55 Undo the two bolts in the exposed aperture.

56 Carefully unclip the trims each side, and at the top of the rear window (see illustrations).

57 The tailgate trim panel is secured by 11 bolts, and 2 plastic expansion rivets. Undo the bolts, prise up the centre pins, lever out the

26.46c . . . and one at the front edge (arrowed)

26.47 Side trim panel plastic expansion rivets (arrowed)

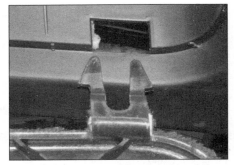

26.53 Squeeze together the side of the hinge and pull it from the panel

26.54 Pull up the panel around the wiper drive and undo the bolts (arrowed)

26.56a Pull the upper trim from the window . . .

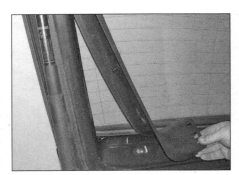

26.56b . . . then pull the side trims inwards

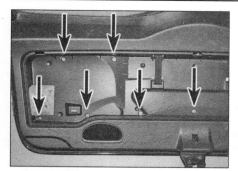

26.57 Tailgate panel bolts (arrowed)

26.59 Prise up the door sill trim

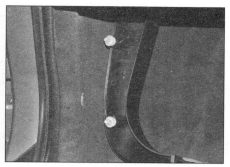

26.61 Pull the lower A-pillar trim inwards

expansion rivets, and pull the trim downwards to release it **(see illustration)**.

58 Refitting is a reversal of removal, ensuring any damaged clips are renewed.

Glovebox

59 Pull the front door sill trim panel upwards to release the retaining clips **(see illustration)**.

60 Pull away the rubber weatherstrip from the door aperture adjacent to the lower A-pillar trim.

61 Pull the lower A-pillar trim inwards to release the retaining clips **(see illustration)**.

62 Slide the front, lower section of the centre console side panel rearwards to release the clips **(see illustration 27.13)**.

63 Undo the 5 bolts and remove the lower facia panel above the footwell **(see illustration 26.90)**. Disconnect any wiring plugs as the panel is withdrawn.

64 Open the glovebox, prise off the clips securing shock absorber strut and check strap **(see illustration)**.

65 Undo the 8 bolts and pull the glovebox from the facia **(see illustrations)**. Disconnect the glovebox light wiring plug as it's withdrawn.

Glovebox lock

66 Open the glovebox, and undo the 2 bolts securing the lock to the glovebox lid.

67 Separate the upper and lower sections of the lock and remove it from the lid.

68 Insert the ignition key into the lock, release the 2 retaining clips, and pull the lock cylinder from the lock. If necessary, twist the key a little to remove the cylinder.

Carpets

69 The passenger compartment floor carpet is in one piece, secured at its edges by bolts or clips, usually the same fasteners used to secure the various adjoining trim panels.

70 Carpet removal and refitting is reasonably straightforward but very time-consuming because all adjoining trim panels must be removed first, as must components such as the seats, the centre console and seat belt lower anchorages.

Headlining

71 The headlining is clipped to the roof and can be withdrawn only once all fittings such as the grab handles, sunvisors, sunroof (if fitted), windscreen, rear quarter windows and related trim panels have been removed, and the door, tailgate and sunroof aperture sealing strips have been prised clear.

72 Note that headlining removal requires considerable skill and experience if it is to be carried out without damage and is therefore best entrusted to an expert.

Cup holders

Front cup holders

73 Open a front cup holder, peel back the

self-adhesive tape, and remove the two retaining bolts **(see illustration)**. Remove the cup holder.

74 Refitting is a reversal of removal.

Rear cup holders

75 With the armrest folded forwards, use a flat, plastic or wooden tool to release the clips and carefully prise the rear cup holder assembly from place.

76 Push cup holder assembly into place.

Parcel shelf

77 Remove both C-pillar trims as described previously in this Section.

78 Remove the rear seat as described in Section 23.

79 Undo the bolts securing the lower seat belt anchorages in the centre and each side.

26.64 Check strap pin

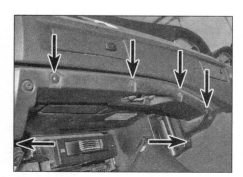

26.65a Glovebox upper bolts (arrowed) . . .

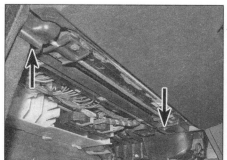

26.65b . . . and lower bolts (arrowed)

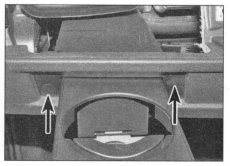

26.73 Peel away the tape (arrowed) and undo the bolts

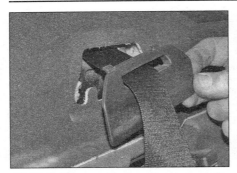

26.81 Pull the seat belt guide downwards from place

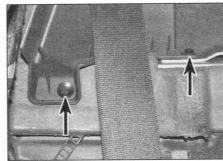

26.82 Prise up the centre pins, and remove the various plastic expansion rivets at the front edge of the parcel shelf (arrowed)

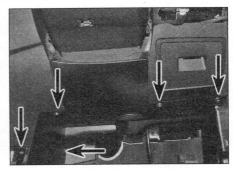

26.90 Driver's side lower facia panel bolts (arrowed)

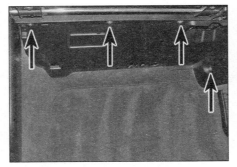

26.93a Undo the front bolts securing the passenger's side lower facia panel (arrowed) . . .

26.93b . . . and the rear one (arrowed)

80 On models with a rear roller blind, working in the luggage compartment, undo the 3 bolts on the underside of the parcel shelf, then move back to the passenger's compartment and disconnect the wiring plug for the blind (plug located at the wheel arch).
81 Pull the centre seat belt guide trim downwards and forwards from the parcel shelf, and slide it from the belt (see illustration).
82 Prise up the centre pins, lever out the plastic expansion rivets at the front edge, and slide the parcel shelf forwards. Disconnect the speaker wiring plugs, and feed the side seat belts through the parcel shelf as it's withdrawn (see illustration). Note how the shelf locates with the air grilles at the rear.
83 Refitting is a reversal of removal.

Boot lid trim panel

84 Carefully prise the light unit from the boot lid trim panel, and disconnect the wiring plug.
85 On models with manual boot lid unlocking, unclip the release handle, and disconnect the operating cable from the handle.
86 Remove the toolbox lid retaining bolt, prise off the plastic caps and remove the toolbox hinge bolts (see illustration 15.3). Remove the toolbox from the boot trim panel.
87 Prise up the centre pins and remove the plastic expanding rivets, then remove the trim panel from the boot lid (see illustrations 15.4a, 15.4b and 15.4c).
88 Refitting is a reversal of removal.

Lower facia panels

Driver's side

89 Move the driver's seat fully rearwards, then slide the front, lower panel of the centre console rearwards and remove it (see illustration 27.13).
90 Undo the 5 bolts, pull down the trim panel at the rear edge to release the clips and withdraw it from place (see illustration). Disconnect any wiring plugs as the panel is withdrawn.
91 Refitting is a reversal of removal.

Passenger's side

92 Move the passenger's seat fully rearwards, then slide the front, lower panel of the centre console rearwards and remove it (see illustration 27.13).
93 Undo the 5 bolts, then move the panel slightly forwards, pull the rear edge down a little, and manoeuvre it from place (see illustrations). Disconnect any wiring plugs as the panel is withdrawn.
94 Refitting is a reversal of removal.

27 Centre console – removal and refitting

Removal

1 On models up to 09/2008, with a central control knob equipped with just two buttons behind it (none in front), pull the knob straight upwards to remove it (see illustration). Do not attempt to remove the knob on models with the alternative buttons arrangement.

Manual transmission

2 Pull the gear knob straight upwards with a sharp tug and remove it.
3 Pull the gear lever gaiter upwards to tension the material, then squeeze the sides inwards to release the mounting frame clips (see illustration). Pull the gaiter from the lever.

Automatic transmission

4 Apply the handbrake and move the selector lever to position N.
5 On models up to 03/2007, pull the selector

27.1 Pull the central control knob straight upwards (see text)

27.3 Squeeze together the sides, and prise up the gear lever gaiter

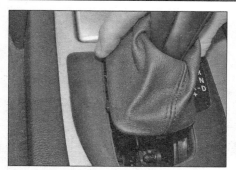

27.6a Squeeze together the sides of the gaiter and lift it from the panel

27.6b Prise the panel from the console

27.8 Undo the bolts (arrowed) in the gear/selector lever aperture

27.9 Starting at the rear, prise up the console top trim panel. Push out the switch and disconnect the wiring plug as the panel is withdrawn

27.10 Note the clip (arrowed) each side of the lower panel

27.11a Prise down the 2 clips (arrowed) . . .

lever knob straight upwards with a sharp tug and remove it.

6 On all auto models, use flat, blunt tool to carefully press in the sides of the selector lever gaiter and remove it, then prise the surround panel upwards from place **(see illustrations)**. Disconnect any wiring plugs as the cover is withdrawn.

All models

7 Remove the ashtray insert (where fitted).

8 Undo the bolts in the gear/selector lever aperture **(see illustration)**.

9 Press the release button, open the centre console cover, then carefully prise up the rear edge of the top trim panel, and manoeuvre it upwards/rearwards from place **(see illustration)**. Disconnect any wiring plugs as the panel is withdrawn. If required, press the buttons upwards from the panel.

10 Carefully prise out the lower edge of the rear panel beneath the air vents, and pull it downwards/rearwards **(see illustration)**. Disconnect any wiring plugs as the panel is withdrawn.

11 Release the 2 clips downwards, then slide the rear air vents downwards from place **(see illustrations)**. Disconnect any wiring plugs as the vents are removed.

12 Insert a long screwdriver through the aperture vacated by the control knob buttons (paragraph 1), and press the USB/audio interface socket (where fitted) from the storage compartment. Disconnect the socket wiring plug.

13 Slide rearwards the trim panels each side of the centre console rear section **(see illustration)**.

27.11b . . . the slide the rear vent downwards/rearwards

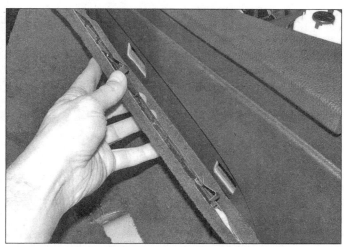

27.13 Slide the trim panel each side rearwards to release the clips

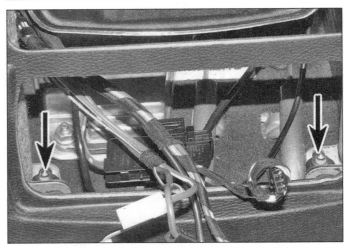

27.14 Undo the nuts at the rear (arrowed)

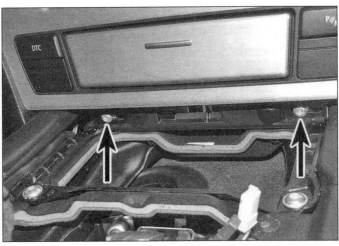

27.15a Undo the bolts (arrowed) at the front of the console

14 Undo the 2 nuts at the rear of the centre console **(see illustration)**.

15 Undo the 2 bolts at the front, centre (models from 03/2007 only), and front, sides of the centre console **(see illustrations)**.

16 Squeeze in the sides and remove the handbrake lever gaiter **(see illustrations)**.

17 Lift up the rear of the console and manoeuvre

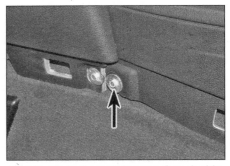

27.15b Undo the bolt (arrowed) each side at the front of the console

it from place, over the gear and handbrake levers, and remove it on the passenger side. Note their fitted locations, then disconnect any wiring plugs as the console is withdrawn. Take care not to damage the locating lugs at the front on models up to 03/2007.

Refitting

18 Refitting is the reverse of removal, making sure all fasteners are securely tightened.

---

28 Facia panel assembly – removal and refitting

HAYNES HiNT *Label each wiring connector as it is disconnected from its relevant component. The labels will prove useful on refitting, when routing the wiring and feeding the wiring through the facia apertures.*

Removal

1 Disconnect the battery negative lead as described in Chapter 5.

2 Remove the centre console as described in Section 27.

3 Remove both A-pillar trims as described in Section 26.

4 Remove the steering column switches assembly as described in Chapter 12.

5 Remove the instrument cluster and central display unit as described in Chapter 12.

6 Remove the light switch assembly as described in Chapter 12.

7 Remove the driver's and passenger's side lower facia panels as described in Section 26.

8 Remove the glovebox as described in Section 26.

9 On models with the 'Head-up' display, using a blunt, flat-bladed tool, starting at the rear edge, carefully prise up the display surround trim from the facia.

10 Remove the hazard warning light switch as described in Chapter 12.

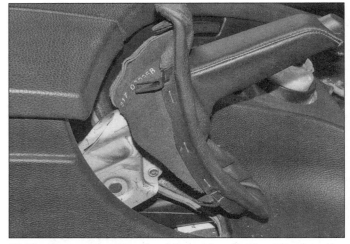

27.16a Squeeze together the sides, and unclip the gaiter from the console

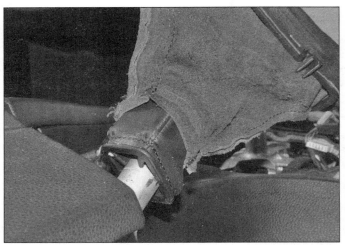

27.16b If required, cut the clip and pull the gaiter from the handbrake lever

11 Undo the bolt (where fitted) in the switch aperture, then carefully lever rearwards the decorative strip from the passenger's side of the facia **(see illustration)**. Disconnect any wiring plugs as the strip is removed.

12 Undo the 2 bolts at the upper edge, then carefully prise the centre panel trim rearwards **(see illustrations)**. Disconnect any wiring plugs as the panel is withdrawn.

13 On models with a separate lower section of the centre instrument panel trim, open the ashtray, pull the lower edge of the ashtray trim rearwards to unclip it, then carefully prise the lower section of the centre panel rearwards **(see illustrations)**. Remove the lower switches assembly as the panel is withdrawn. Disconnect any wiring plugs as the panel is withdrawn.

14 Undo the 4 bolts and pull the audio systems/Car Communication Controller rearwards from the facia. Disconnect the wiring plugs as the controller is withdrawn **(see illustrations)**.

15 Remove the front cup holders as described in Section 26.

16 Undo the bolt securing the front, outer cup holder carrier **(see illustration)**.

17 The front inner cup holder carrier must now be removed. This must be removed with the passenger's airbag assembly. Undo the bolt securing the carrier, and the 4 bolts securing the airbag assembly. Disconnect the

28.11 Carefully lever the decorative strip from the passenger's side of the facia

28.12a Undo the bolts at the top (arrowed) . . .

28.12b . . . and prise the panel rearwards. Note the tape to protect the finish

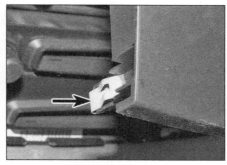

28.12c The panel is secured by clips (arrowed) each side

28.13a Pull the lower panel rearwards . . .

28.13b . . . to release the lower clips (arrowed)

28.13c Slide the lower switches assembly rearwards and disconnect the plugs

28.14a Undo the bolts (arrowed) and slide the CCC rearwards . . .

28.14b . . . then disconnect the wiring plugs

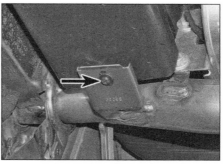

28.16 The cup holder carrier is secured by a bolt underneath (arrowed)

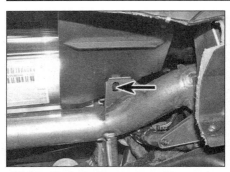

28.17a Undo the inner cup holder carrier bolt (arrowed)

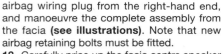

28.17b The airbag is secured by 2 bolts at the left-hand end (arrowed) . . .

airbag wiring plug from the right-hand end, and manoeuvre the complete assembly from the facia **(see illustrations)**. Note that new airbag retaining bolts must be fitted.

18 Carefully prise up the facia centre speaker panel, and remove the speaker. Disconnect the speaker and solar sensor wiring plugs (where fitted) **(see illustration)**.

19 The facia is now secured by 2 bolts in the lower, central area, 2 nuts in the upper, central area, and 1 nut at each end. Remove these fasteners, and with the help of as assistant, pull the facia slightly to the rear, lift it up and manoeuvre it through the passenger's door opening **(see illustrations)**.

Refitting

20 Refitting is a reversal of the removal procedure, noting the following points:
 a) *Manoeuvre the facia into position and, using the labels stuck on during removal, ensure that the wiring is correctly routed and securely retained by its facia clips.*
 b) *Clip the facia back into position, ensure the locating lugs at the front edge of the facia engage correctly, making sure all the wiring connectors are fed through their respective apertures, then refit all the facia fasteners, and tighten them securely.*
 c) *On completion, reconnect the battery and check that all the electrical components and switches function correctly.*

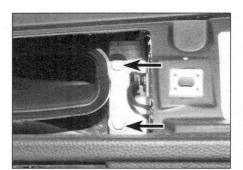

28.17c . . . and 2 at the right-hand end, accessible through the cup holder carrier aperture (arrowed)

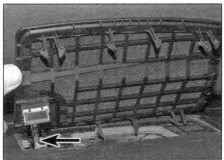

28.18 Prise up the rear edge of the grille and disconnect the solar sensor plug (arrowed)

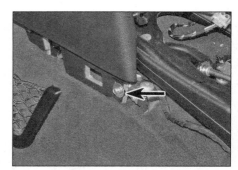

28.19a The facia is secured by bolts (arrowed) each side in the facia lower central area . . .

28.19b . . . 2 nuts (arrowed) in the upper central area . . .

28.19c . . . and a nut (arrowed) at each end

Chapter 12
Body electrical system

Contents

Degrees of difficulty

Easy, suitable for novice with little experience	Fairly easy, suitable for beginner with some experience	Fairly difficult, suitable for competent DIY mechanic	Difficult, suitable for experienced DIY mechanic	Very difficult, suitable for expert DIY or professional

Specifications

System type . . . .   12 volt negative earth

Fuses . . . .   See inside fusebox lid

Bulbs   **Wattage**

Interior lights

Front interior lights:

Base of door	5 capless
Reading lights	6
Interior lights	6
Footwell lights	5 capless
Vanity light	10 festoon
Glovebox light	5 capless
Instrument panel	LED
Luggage compartment light	10 festoon
Rear courtesy lights	6

Bulbs (continued)

	Wattage
Exterior lights	
Direction indicator side repeater	5
Direction indicator:	
Rear:	
Models up to 03/2007	21 PY
Models from 03/2007	LED
Front	21 PY
Front foglight:	
Models up to 03/2007	35 (H8 type)
Models from 03/2007	51 (HB4 type)
Headlight (halogen headlight):	
Dipped beam	55 (H7 type)
Main beam	55 (H7 type)
Sidelight:	
Models up to 03/2007	5 capless
Models from 03/2007	10 H6
Headlight (xenon HID headlight):	
Models up to 03/2007:	
Dipped beam	D2-S
Main beam	55 (H7 type)
Sidelight	10
Models from 03/2007:	
Dipped	D1-S
Main beam	55 (H7 type)
Sidelight	35 (H8 type)
Cornering light	55 (H3 type)
High-level stop-light	LED
Number plate light	5
Rear foglight	21
Reversing light:	
Models up to 03/2007	16 capless
Models from 03/2007	21
Stop-light	21
Tail light:	
Models up to 03/2007	21
Models from 03/2007	LED

Torque wrench settings

	Nm	lbf ft
Airbag system fixings*	8	6
Wiper arm-to-wiper spindle nut:		
Passenger's side:		
M8 nuts	20	15
M10 nuts	35	26
Driver's side	35	26

* Do not re-use

1 General information and precautions

⚠️ **Warning: Before carrying out any work on the electrical system, read through the precautions given in 'Safety First!' at the beginning of this manual and Chapter 5.**

The electrical system is of the 12 volt negative earth type. Power for the lights and all electrical accessories is supplied by a lead-acid type battery which is charged by the alternator.

This Chapter covers repair and service procedures for the various electrical components not associated with engine. Information on the battery, alternator and starter motor can be found in Chapter 5.

It should be noted that prior to working on any component in the electrical system, the battery negative terminal should first be disconnected to prevent the possibility of electrical short circuits and/or fires (see Chapter 5).

2 Electrical fault finding – general information

Note: Refer to the precautions given in 'Safety first!' and in Section 1 of this Chapter before starting work. The following tests relate to testing of the main electrical circuits, and should not be used to test delicate electronic circuits (such as anti-lock braking systems), particularly where an electronic control module/unit (ECM/ECU) is used.

Caution: The BMW 5-Series electrical system is extremely complex. Many of the ECMs are connected via a 'Databus' system, where they are able to share information from the various sensors, and communicate with each other. For instance, as the automatic gearbox approaches a gear ratio shift point, it signals the engine management ECM via the Databus. As the gearchange is made by the transmission ECM, the engine management ECM retards the ignition timing, momentarily reducing engine output, to ensure a smoother transition from one gear ratio to the next. Due to the design of the Databus system, it is not advisable to backprobe the ECMs with a multimeter in the traditional manner. Instead, the electrical systems are equipped with a sophisticated self-diagnosis system, which can interrogate the various ECMs to reveal stored fault codes, and help pin-point faults. In order to access the self-diagnosis system, specialist test equipment (fault code reader/scanner) is required.

General

1 A typical electrical circuit consists of an electrical component, any switches, relays, motors, fuses, fusible links or circuit breakers related to that component, and the wiring and connectors which link the component to both the battery and the chassis. To help to pin-point a problem in an electrical circuit, wiring diagrams are included at the end of this Chapter.

2 Before attempting to diagnose an electrical fault, first study the appropriate wiring diagram to obtain a complete understanding of the components included in the particular circuit concerned. The possible sources of a fault can be narrowed down by noting if other components related to the circuit are operating properly. If several components or circuits fail at one time, the problem is likely to be related to a shared fuse or earth connection.

3 Electrical problems usually stem from simple causes, such as loose or corroded connections, a faulty earth connection, a blown fuse, a melted fusible link, or a faulty relay (refer to Section 3 for details of testing relays). Visually inspect the condition of all fuses, wires and connections in a problem circuit before testing the components. Use the wiring diagrams to determine which terminal connections will need to be checked in order to pin-point the trouble spot.

4 The basic tools required for electrical fault finding include a circuit tester or voltmeter (a 12 volt bulb with a set of test leads can also be used for certain tests); a self-powered test light (sometimes known as a continuity tester); an ohmmeter (to measure resistance); a battery and set of test leads; and a jumper wire, preferably with a circuit breaker or fuse incorporated, which can be used to bypass suspect wires or electrical components. Before attempting to locate a problem with test instruments, use the wiring diagram to determine where to make the connections.

5 To find the source of an intermittent wiring fault (usually due to a poor or dirty connection,

or damaged wiring insulation), a 'wiggle' test can be performed on the wiring. This involves wiggling the wiring by hand to see if the fault occurs as the wiring is moved. It should be possible to narrow down the source of the fault to a particular section of wiring. This method of testing can be used in conjunction with any of the tests described in the following sub-Sections.

6 Apart from problems due to poor connections, two basic types of fault can occur in an electrical circuit – open circuit, or short circuit.

7 Open circuit faults are caused by a break somewhere in the circuit, which prevents current from flowing. An open circuit fault will prevent a component from working, but will not cause the relevant circuit fuse to blow.

8 Short circuit faults are caused by a 'short' somewhere in the circuit, which allows the current flowing in the circuit to 'escape' along an alternative route, usually to earth. Short circuit faults are normally caused by a breakdown in wiring insulation, which allows a feed wire to touch either another wire, or an earthed component such as the bodyshell. A short circuit fault will normally cause the relevant circuit fuse to blow.

Finding an open circuit

9 To check for an open circuit, connect one lead of a circuit tester or voltmeter to either the negative battery terminal or a known good earth.

10 Connect the other lead to a connector in the circuit being tested, preferably nearest to the battery or fuse.

11 Switch on the circuit, bearing in mind that some circuits are live only when the ignition switch is moved to a particular position.

12 If voltage is present (indicated either by the tester bulb lighting or a voltmeter reading, as applicable), this means that the section of the circuit between the relevant connector and the battery is problem-free.

13 Continue to check the remainder of the circuit in the same fashion.

14 When a point is reached at which no voltage is present, the problem must lie between that point and the previous test point with voltage. Most problems can be traced to a broken, corroded or loose connection.

Finding a short circuit

15 To check for a short circuit, first disconnect the load(s) from the circuit (loads are the components which draw current from a circuit, such as bulbs, motors, heating elements, etc).

16 Remove the relevant fuse from the circuit, and connect a circuit tester or voltmeter to the fuse connections.

17 Switch on the circuit, bearing in mind that some circuits are live only when the ignition switch is moved to a particular position.

18 If voltage is present (indicated either by the tester bulb lighting or a voltmeter reading, as applicable), this means that there is a short circuit.

19 If no voltage is present, but the fuse still blows with the load(s) connected, this indicates an internal fault in the load(s).

Finding an earth fault

20 The battery negative terminal is connected to 'earth' – the metal of the engine/transmission and the car body – and most systems are wired so that they only receive a positive feed, the current returning through the metal of the car body **(see illustrations)**. This means that the component mounting and the body form part of that circuit. Loose or corroded mountings can therefore cause a range of electrical faults, ranging from total failure of a circuit, to a puzzling partial fault. In particular, lights may shine dimly (especially when another circuit sharing the same earth point is in operation), motors (eg, wiper motors or the radiator cooling fan motor) may run slowly, and the operation of one circuit may have an apparently unrelated effect on another. Note that on many vehicles, earth straps are used between certain components, such as the engine/transmission and the body, usually where there is no metal-to-metal contact between components due to flexible rubber mountings, etc.

21 To check whether a component is properly earthed, disconnect the battery and connect one lead of an ohmmeter to a known good earth point. Connect the other lead to the wire or earth connection being tested. The resistance reading should be zero; if not, check the connection as follows.

22 If an earth connection is thought to be faulty, dismantle the connection and clean back

2.20a Earth connections below the right-hand side rear lights (arrowed) . . .

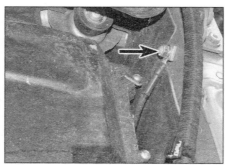

20.20b . . . left-hand corner of the engine compartment (arrowed) . . .

20.20c . . . and the right-hand engine mounting (arrowed)

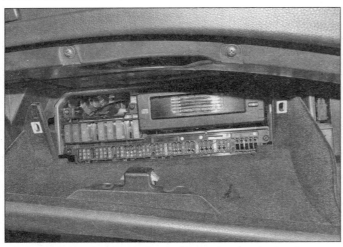

3.1a Fuses are located in front of the passenger's glovebox . . .

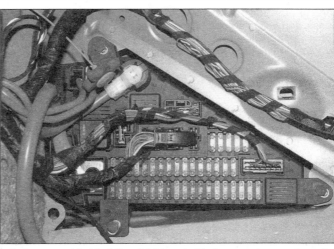

3.1b . . . and behind the right-hand side luggage compartment storage tray

to bare metal both the bodyshell and the wire terminal or the component earth connection mating surface. Be careful to remove all traces of dirt and corrosion, then use a knife to trim away any paint, so that a clean metal-to-metal joint is made. On reassembly, tighten the joint fasteners securely; if a wire terminal is being refitted, use serrated washers between the terminal and the bodyshell to ensure a clean and secure connection. When the connection is remade, prevent the onset of corrosion in the future by applying a coat of petroleum jelly or silicone-based grease or by spraying on (at regular intervals) a proprietary ignition sealer or a water dispersant lubricant.

3 Fuses and relays – general information

Main fuses

1 The majority of the fuses are located in front of passenger's side glovebox, whilst some others are located behind the right-hand storage tray in the luggage compartment (see illustrations).

2 To remove the main fusebox cover, open the glovebox, rotate 90° the two quick-release fasteners and pull down the cover (see illustration).

3 A list of the circuits each fuse protects is given on the label attached to the inside of the main fusebox cover. A pair of tweezers for removing the fuses is also clipped to the fusebox. Note that the vertical fuses are active, and the horizontal fuses are spare. High amperage fuses are located in the main fusebox.

4 To remove a fuse, first switch off the circuit concerned (or the ignition), then pull the fuse out of its terminals (see illustration). The wire within the fuse should be visible; if the fuse is blown it will be broken or melted.

5 Always renew a fuse with one of an identical rating; never use a fuse with a different rating from the original or substitute anything else. Never renew a fuse more than once without tracing the source of the trouble. The fuse rating is stamped on top of the fuse; note that the fuses are also colour-coded for easy recognition.

6 If a new fuse blows immediately, find the cause before renewing it again; a short to earth as a result of faulty insulation is most likely. Where a fuse protects more than one circuit,

try to isolate the defect by switching on each circuit in turn (if possible) until the fuse blows again. Always carry a supply of spare fuses of each relevant rating on the vehicle, a spare of each rating should be clipped into the base of the fusebox.

Relays

7 The majority of relays are located behind the passenger's side glovebox, whilst other relays are located above the battery in the luggage compartment.

8 If a circuit or system controlled by a relay develops a fault and the relay is suspect, operate the system; if the relay is functioning it should be possible to hear it click as it is energised. If this is the case the fault lies with the components or wiring of the system. If the relay is not being energised then either the relay is not receiving a main supply or a switching voltage or the relay itself is faulty. Testing is by the substitution of a known good unit but be careful; while some relays are identical in appearance and in operation, others look similar but perform different functions.

9 To renew a relay first ensure that the ignition switch is off. The relay can then simply be pulled out from the socket and the new relay pressed in.

4 Switches – removal and refitting

Note: Disconnect the battery negative lead (see Chapter 5) before removing any switch, and reconnect the lead after refitting the switch.

Ignition switch

1 Remove the steering wheel as described in Chapter 10.

2 Pull the rear section of the steering

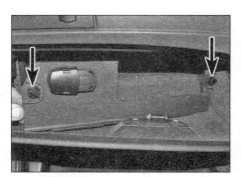

3.2 Rotate the fasteners 90° (arrowed) and remove the fusebox cover

3.4 Pull the relevant fuse from the terminals

4.2 Pull the rear section of the shroud from place

4.3a Undo the bolt (arrowed) . . .

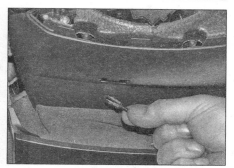

4.3b . . . pull out the plastic expansion rivet . . .

4.3c . . . and remove the steering column lower shroud

4.4a Pull up the forward section of the upper shroud

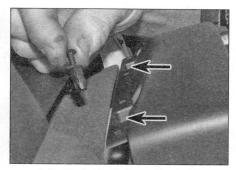

4.4b Undo the bolts, pull out the expansion rivets (arrowed)

column shroud rearwards to remove it **(see illustration)**.

3 Move the steering column to its highest position and fully extend it, then undo the bolt, pull out the expansion rivet, and unclip the column shroud lower section **(see illustrations)**. Unclip the wiring harness as the shroud is removed.

4 Fully lower the steering column, unclip the forward section of the steering column upper shroud, then undo the 2 bolts, prise out the plastic expansion rivets, pull the edges outwards a little, and remove the rear section of the upper shroud **(see illustrations)**.

5 Undo the 2 retaining bolts and remove the ignition switch **(see illustration)**. Disconnect the switch wiring plug as it's withdrawn.

6 Refitting is a reversal of removal.

Stop/start switch

7 Using a blunt, flat-bladed tool, carefully prise the light control switch/unit from the facia **(see illustration 4.22)**. Disconnect the wiring plug as the switch is withdrawn.

8 Undo the bolts and separate the switch from the panel **(see illustration)**.

9 Refitting is a reversal of removal.

Steering column switch assembly

Note: *It is possible to remove some of the steering column switches individually, as described later in this Section.*

10 Remove the steering wheel as described in Chapter 10.

11 Pull the rear section of the steering column shroud rearwards to remove it **(see illustration 4.2)**.

12 Move the steering column to its highest position and fully extend it, then undo the bolt, prise out the plastic expansion rivet and unclip the column shroud lower section **(see illustrations 4.3a, 4.3b and 4.3c)**. Unclip the wiring harness as the shroud is removed.

13 Fully lower the steering column, unclip the forward section of the steering column upper shroud, then undo the 2 bolts, prise out the plastic expansion rivets, pull the edges outwards a little, and remove the rear section of the upper shroud **(see illustrations 4.4a and 4.4b)**.

14 Disconnect the wiring plugs at the front of the assembly, then undo the 6 bolts and slide the switch assembly upwards from the column **(see illustration)**.

15 Refitting is a reversal of the removal procedure, ensuring that the wiring is correctly routed.

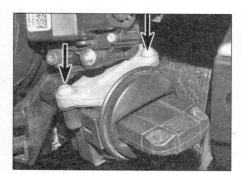

4.5 Ignition switch retaining bolts (arrowed)

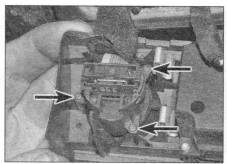

4.8 Stop/start switch retaining bolts (arrowed)

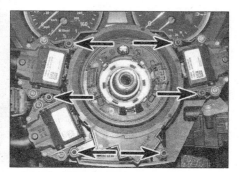

4.14 Steering column switch assembly retaining bolts (arrowed)

4.18 Wiper switch retaining bolts. Note that it's necessary to slacken the dark-coloured Torx bolt (arrowed)

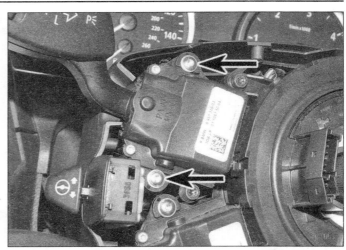

4.21 Indicator/headlight dip switch retaining bolts (arrowed)

Windscreen wiper switch

16 Remove the steering wheel as described in Chapter 10.

17 Pull the rear section of the steering column shroud rearwards to remove it **(see illustration 4.2)**.

4.22 Prise the switch and surround panel from the facia

18 Undo the 2 retaining bolts and slide the switch to the rear **(see illustration)**.

Direction indicator and headlight dipping switch

19 Remove the steering wheel as described in Chapter 10.

20 Pull the rear section of the steering column shroud rearwards to remove it **(see illustration 4.2)**.

21 Undo the 2 retaining bolts and slide the switch to the rear **(see illustration)**.

Lighting control switch/unit

22 Using a wooden or plastic tool, carefully prise the switch and surround panel from the driver's side of the facia **(see illustration)**. Take care not to damage the facia panels. Disconnect the wiring plugs as the panel is withdrawn.

23 Undo the bolts and detach the switch/unit from the panel **(see illustration)**.

24 Refitting is the reverse of removal.

Hazard warning switch and central locking switch

25 Using a wooden or plastic tool, carefully prise the switch from the facia **(see illustration)**.

26 Disconnect the wiring plugs as the switch(es) are removed.

27 Refitting is the reverse of removal.

Electric window and mirror switches

Driver's side up to 03/2007

28 Remove the door inner trim panel as described in Chapter 11.

29 Undo the nuts, remove the retaining

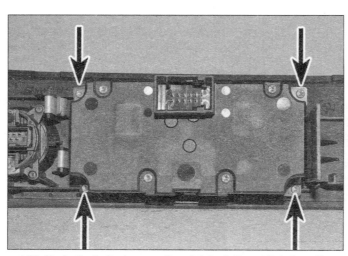

4.23 Undo the bolts (arrowed) and detach the switch from the panel

4.25 Use tape (arrowed) on the facia to prevent damage when prising out the switch

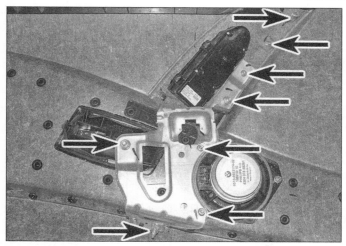

4.29a Undo the nuts (arrowed), remove the plate . . .

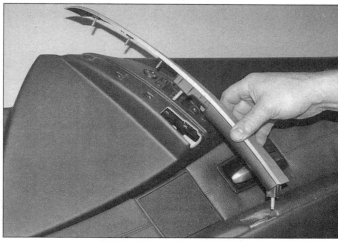

4.29b . . . and the pull handle

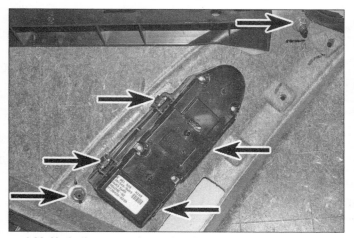

4.30 Undo the nuts, release the clips and remove the switch assembly (arrowed)

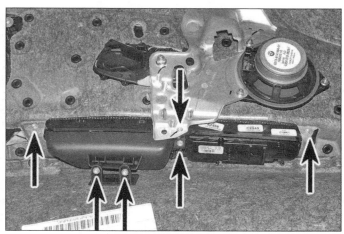

4.34a Undo the bolts (arrowed) . . .

plate and the door pull handle assembly **(see illustrations)**.

30 Undo the 2 nuts, release the clips and remove the switch assembly **(see illustration)**.

31 Refitting is the reverse of removal.

Driver's side from 03/2007

32 Remove the door inner trim panel as described in Chapter 11.

33 Unclip the speaker trim adjacent to the switch panel.

34 Undo the 6 bolts, release the catches and slide the handle recess from the door trim panel **(see illustrations)**.

35 Release the clips and detach the switch panel from the handle recess **(see illustration)**.

36 Refitting is a reversal of removal.

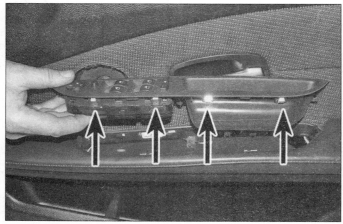

4.34b . . . and push the panel out to release the catches (arrowed)

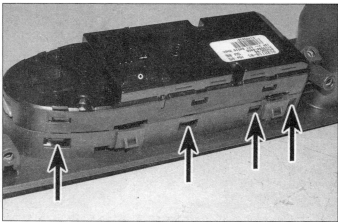

4.35 Switch retaining clips (arrowed)

4.38 Undo the nut (arrowed) release the clips and remove the rear window switch

4.40 Carefully prise up the window switch

4.50 Prise the decorative strip from the facia

4.51a Undo the 2 bolts (arrowed) at the top of the panel

4.51b Apply tape to protect the lower panel, and prise the upper panel rearwards . . .

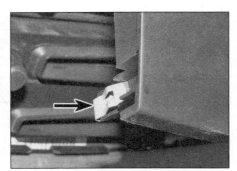

4.51c . . . to release the clip (arrowed) each side

Rear/passenger's side up to 03/2007

37 Remove the door inner trim panel as described in Chapter 11.
38 Undo the nut, release the clips and remove the switch assembly (see illustration).
39 Refitting is the reverse of removal.

Rear/passenger's side from 03/2007

40 Using a wooden or plastic tool, carefully prise the switch from the panel (see illustration). Note: *In order to eliminate the possibility of marking the interior trim, it may be prudent to remove the door trim panel as described in Chapter 11, and press the switch from the inside of the panel.*
41 Disconnect the wiring plug as the switch is withdrawn.
42 Refitting is a reversal of removal.

Clutch pedal switch

43 Remove the lower facia panel on the driver's side as described in Chapter 11.

44 Carefully release the clips and detach the switch from the master cylinder. Disconnect the wiring plug as the switch is removed.
45 Refitting is the reverse of removal.

Heated rear window switch

46 On these models the switch is an integral part of the control unit and cannot be renewed. If the switch is faulty seek the advice of a BMW dealer.

Heater blower motor switch

47 The switch is an integral part of the control unit and cannot be renewed. If the switch is faulty seek the advice of a BMW dealer.

Air conditioning system switches

48 The switch is an integral part of the control unit and cannot be renewed. If the switch is faulty seek the advice of a BMW dealer.

Centre facia panel lower switches

49 Remove the hazard warning light switch as described in this Section.
50 Undo the bolt (where fitted) in the hazard warning light switch aperture, then carefully prise the decorative strip on the passenger's side from the facia (see illustration).

Models up to 03/2007

51 Undo the 2 bolts at the top edge, and carefully prise the facia centre, middle panel from place (see illustrations). Disconnect the wiring plugs as the panel is withdrawn.
52 Open the ashtray and pull the lower edge of the ashtray trim rearwards (see illustrations).
53 Slide the switch assembly rearwards from place (see illustration). Refitting is a reversal of removal.

4.52a Pull the lower edge of the panel rearwards . . .

4.52b . . . to release the clips (arrowed)

4.53 Slide the switch assembly rearwards and disconnect the wiring plugs

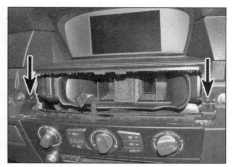

4.54a Undo the bolts (arrowed) . . .

4.54b . . . then prise the panel rearwards to release the lower clips (arrowed)

4.56 Carefully prise the lower panel rearwards

4.57 Release the 4 clips (2 on top, 2 below) and detach the switch from the panel

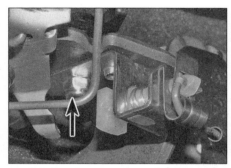

4.60 Handbrake warning light switch retaining nut (arrowed)

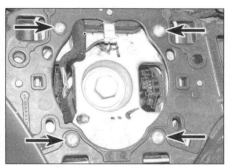

4.65 Undo the bolts (arrowed) and remove the switch retaining plate

Models from 03/2007

54 Undo the 2 bolts at the top edge, and carefully prise the facia centre, middle panel from place **(see illustrations)**. Disconnect the wiring plugs as the panel is withdrawn.

55 Ensure the ashtray is in the closed position, and the selector lever is fully rearwards (automatic transmission models only).

56 Starting at the top, carefully prise the facia centre, lower panel rearwards. Disconnect the wiring plugs as the panel is withdrawn **(see illustration)**.

57 Release the clips and detach the switch assembly from the panel **(see illustration)**.

58 Refitting is a reversal of removal.

Handbrake warning switch

59 Remove the centre console as described in Chapter 11 to gain access to the handbrake lever.

60 Disconnect the wiring connector from the warning light switch then undo the nut and remove the switch **(see illustration)**.

61 Refitting is the reverse of removal. Check the operation of the switch before refitting the centre console, the warning light should illuminate between the first and second clicks of the ratchet mechanism.

Stop-light switch

62 Refer to Chapter 9.

Courtesy light switches

63 The function of the courtesy light switches is incorporated into the door/boot lid/tailgate lock assembly. To remove the relevant lock refer to Chapter 11.

Steering wheel switches

64 Two different types of steering wheels are fitted to the 5-Series range. Either a

Multifunction steering wheel, or a Sports steering wheel. To remove the switches, remove the driver's airbag as described in Section 25, then proceed under the relevant heading.

Multifunction steering wheel

65 Undo the 4 bolts and remove the switch retaining plate **(see illustration)**. Disconnect the wiring plugs as the plate is withdrawn.

66 Undo the bolts and detach the relevant switch from the retaining plate **(see illustration)**.

Sports steering wheel

67 Undo the 2 retaining bolts and carefully unclip the switch carrier panel from the steering wheel **(see illustrations)**. Disconnect the wiring plug as the panel with withdrawn.

68 Undo the 2 bolts and detach the relevant switch from the carrier panel.

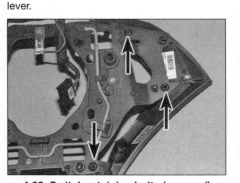

4.66 Switch retaining bolts (arrowed)

4.67a Undo the retaining bolts (arrowed) . . .

4.67b . . . and pull the switch carrier panel rearwards

4.78 Central controller retaining bolts (arrowed)

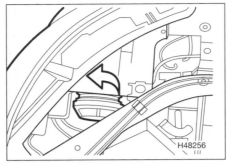

5.2 Rotate the dipped beam cap (arrowed) anti-clockwise

5.3 Press down the clip and remove the cap

Electric sunroof switch

69 Using a wooden or plastic spatula, carefully prise down the rear edge of the interior light lens and remove it.
70 Pull down the front edge of the trim just in front of the switch. Disconnect any wiring plugs as the trim is removed.
71 Depress the clips each end and detach the relevant switch from the panel.
72 Refitting is the reverse of removal.

Driving dynamics switch

73 Apply the handbrake and select neutral or position N as applicable.
74 Using a wooden or plastic spatula, press the sides inwards and prise up the lever surround trim from the console. Disconnect any wiring plugs as the trim is removed.
75 Undo the retaining bolts or release the clips (as applicable) and detach the switch from the trim.
76 Refitting is a reversal of removal.

Central controller

Controllers with 2 buttons to the rear

77 Remove the centre console top trim panel as described in Chapter 11.
78 Undo the 4 bolts and remove controller **(see illustration)**.
79 Refitting is a reversal of removal.

Controllers with 2 buttons to the rear and 5 in front

80 Remove the centre console top trim panel as described in Chapter 11.

81 Release the 6 retaining clips and detach the controller from the trim.
82 Refitting is a reversal of removal.

5 Bulbs (exterior lights) – renewal

General

1 Whenever a bulb is renewed, note the following points.
  a) *Remember that if the light has just been in use the bulb may be extremely hot.*
  b) *Always check the bulb contacts and holder, ensuring that there is clean metal-to-metal contact between the bulb and its live(s) and earth. Clean off any corrosion or dirt before fitting a new bulb.*
  c) *Wherever bayonet-type bulbs are fitted ensure that the live contact(s) bear firmly against the bulb contact.*
  d) *Always ensure that the new bulb is of the correct rating and that it is completely clean before fitting it; this applies particularly to headlight/foglight bulbs (see below).*

Headlight

Halogen dipped beam

2 On models up to 03/2007, rotate the plastic cap at the rear of the headlight anti-clockwise and remove it **(see illustration)**.
3 On models from 03/2007, release the clip at

the top of the plastic cap and pull it rearwards to remove it **(see illustration)**.
4 On all models, turn the bulbholder assembly anti-clockwise and remove it from the rear of the headlight.
5 Pull the bulb from the holder.
6 When handling the new bulb, use a tissue or clean cloth to avoid touching the glass with the fingers; moisture and grease from the skin can cause blackening and rapid failure of this type of bulb. If the glass is accidentally touched, wipe it clean using methylated spirit.
7 Insert the new bulb into the holder, the refit it to the rear of the headlight, rotating it clockwise or clipping it into place (as applicable) until the retaining clips lock.

Main beam

8 Rotate the plastic cap at the rear of the headlight anti-clockwise and remove it **(see illustration)**.
9 Turn the bulbholder assembly anti-clockwise and remove it from the rear of the headlight **(see illustration)**.
10 Pull the bulb from the holder **(see illustration)**.
11 When handling the new bulb, use a tissue or clean cloth to avoid touching the glass with the fingers; moisture and grease from the skin can cause blackening and rapid failure of this type of bulb. If the glass is accidentally touched, wipe it clean using methylated spirit.
12 Insert the new bulb into the holder, the refit it to the rear of the headlight, rotating it clockwise until the retaining clips lock. Reconnect the wiring plug.

5.8 Rotate the main beam cap (arrowed) anti-clockwise

5.9 Twist the bulbholder anti-clockwise and remove it from the reflector

5.10 Pull the main beam bulb from the bulbholder

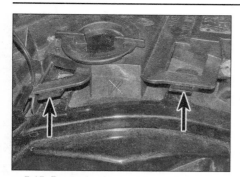

5.15 Press down and release the clips (arrowed) at the top edge of the dipped beam cap

5.16a Rotate the igniter (arrowed) anti-clockwise

5.16b Disconnect the wiring plug as the igniter is removed

13 Refit the bulb to the bulbholder, and then refit the bulbholder to the rear of the headlight, rotating it clockwise until the retaining clips lock.

Xenon dipped beam

14 On models equipped with xenon high-intensity dip beam bulbs, due to the potential high voltages involved, disconnect the battery negative lead as described in Chapter 5. In theory, it's possible to remove the bulbs with the headlight in place, but access is extremely limited. Consequently, we recommend the headlight is removed as described in Section 7.

15 Release the clips and detach the cap at the rear of the headlight **(see illustration)**.

16 Rotate the igniter unit anti-clockwise and remove it from the headlight. Note that on models up to 02/2005, the wiring plug is automatically disconnected as the igniter is released, on models after this date, disconnect the wiring plug as the igniter is removed **(see illustrations)**

17 Depending on model, the bulb may be integral with the igniter unit – check with your dealer/supplier.

18 Refitting is a reversal of removal.

Front sidelight

19 Remove the main beam bulb as previously described in this Section.

20 Rotate the bulbholder anti-clockwise and withdraw it from the headlight unit **(see illustration)**.

21 On models up to 03/2007, the bulb is of the capless type and is a push-fit in the holder.

22 On models after this date, the bulb is of the bayonet type – however, although twisting the bulb anti-clockwise will release it from the holder, there is insufficient clearance to pull it through the reflector, and the bulbholder is bonded to the rear of the sidelight reflector. BMW advise that a new sidelight reflector, complete with bulb, must be obtained. However, it is possible to cut through the bonding and pull the bulbholder from the rear of the reflector. The bulb can then be renewed **(see illustrations)**. Note that the wiring plug must be reconnected before refitting the reflector – there is insufficient clearance once the reflector is refitted.

23 Refitting is the reverse of removal.

5.20 Rotate the bulbholder/reflector (arrowed) anti-clockwise

Cornering light

24 Remove the headlight as described in Section 7.

25 Rotate the cap anti-clockwise and remove it from the headlight.

26 Disconnect the wiring plug, release the clip, and remove the bulb from the headlight.

27 Refitting is a reversal of removal.

Front direction indicator

28 Rotate the bulbholder anti-clockwise and remove it from the rear of the headlight **(see illustration)**.

29 The bulb is a bayonet fitting in the holder. Push the bulb in slightly, then rotate it anti-clockwise and pull it from the holder.

30 Refitting is a reverse of the removal procedure.

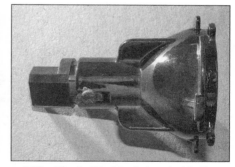

5.22a The bulbholder is bonded to the reflector

5.22b Use a sharp knife to cut-through the bonding . . .

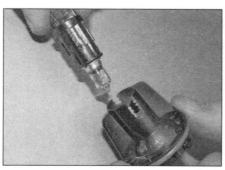

5.22c . . . and pull the bulbholder from the reflector

5.28 Rotate the front direction indicator bulbholder anti-clockwise and remove it

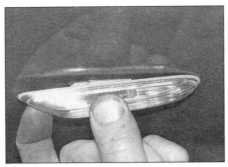

5.31 Push the side repeater lens gently rearwards

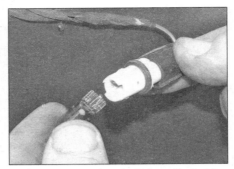

5.32 Pull the capless bulb from the holder

5.35 The front foglight bulb is integral with the holder

Side repeater

31 Using finger pressure, push the side repeater lens gently rearwards. Pull out the front edge of the lens and withdraw it from the wing **(see illustration)**.
32 Rotate the bulbholder anti-clockwise and pull it from the lens, pull the capless bulb it from the holder **(see illustration)**.
33 Refitting is a reverse of the removal procedure.

Front foglight

34 Undo the bolts and pull back the front, lower section of the front wheel arch liner. To improve access, raise the front of the vehicle, support it securely on axle stands (see *Jacking and vehicle support*). Remove the relevant front roadwheel.

35 Disconnect the wiring from the bulbholder, then rotate the bulbholder anti-clockwise and pull it from the foglight. Note that the bulb is integral with the holder **(see illustration)**.
36 When handling the new bulb, use a tissue or clean cloth to avoid touching the glass with the fingers; moisture and grease from the skin can cause blackening and rapid failure of this type of bulb. If the glass is accidentally touched, wipe it clean using methylated spirit.
37 Refitting is a reversal of removal. If necessary, adjust the aim of the light by rotating the adjusting bolt adjacent to the lens **(see illustration)**.

Rear lights – Saloon

38 Lift up the luggage compartment floor panel.
39 Rotate the fasteners anti-clockwise and

5.37 Front foglight adjustment bolt (arrowed)

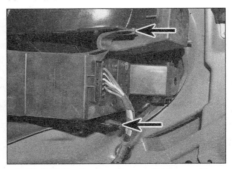

5.40 Lift the lower clip, and depress the upper clip (arrowed)

remove the trim panel behind the relevant rear light.
40 On models up to 03/2007, disconnect the wiring plug, then release the 2 clips and remove the bulbholder assembly **(see illustration)**.
41 On models from 03/2007, disconnect the wiring plug, rotate the fastener anti-clockwise and remove the bulbholder **(see illustration)**.
42 On all models, press the relevant bulb in slightly, twist it anti-clockwise, and remove it from the bulbholder **(see illustration)**. **Note:** *If renewing the indicator bulb, the bayonet fitting pins are offset and will only fit in one way.*
43 Refitting is a reversal of removal.

Body-mounted rear lights – Touring

44 Depress the clip and remove the relevant storage compartment from the corner of the luggage compartment.
45 Rotate the bulbholder anti-clockwise and remove it from the taillight **(see illustration)**.
46 Press the relevant bulb in slightly, twist it anti-clockwise, and remove it from the bulbholder.
47 Refitting is a reversal of removal.

Tailgate-mounted rear lights – Touring

Models up to 03/2007

48 Rotate the fasteners anti-clockwise and pull down the flap in the lower tailgate panel.
49 Pull out the foam insulation, then release

5.41 Rotate the fastener (arrowed) anti-clockwise

5.42 Press in the bulb, and twist it anti-clockwise

5.45 Rotate the bulbholder anti-clockwise and pull it from place

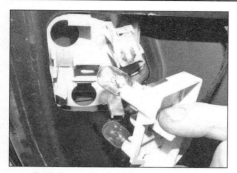

5.49 Depress the clip and pull the bulbholder from the tailgate

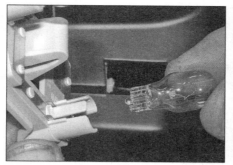

5.50 Pull the capless bulb from the holder

5.57 Push the light unit in the direction of the arrow

the clip and pull the bulbholder from the light unit **(see illustration)**.

50 Pull the relevant capless bulb from the bulbholder **(see illustration)**.

51 Refitting is a reversal of removal.

Models from 03/2007

52 Remove the rear light as described in Section 7.

53 Pull the relevant bulbholder from the light unit.

54 Press the relevant bulb in slightly, twist it anti-clockwise, and remove it from the bulbholder.

55 Refitting is a reversal of removal.

High-level stop-light

56 All models are equipped with LEDs in the high-level stop-light. If defective the complete light unit must be renewed.

Number plate light

57 Carefully push the light unit away from the end with the slot to compress the retaining spring, then lever the lens unit from place **(see illustration)**.

58 The bulb is of the 'festoon' type, and can be prised from the contacts.

59 Refitting is the reverse of removal, making sure the bulb is securely held in position by the contacts.

---

6 Bulbs (interior lights) – renewal

General

1 Refer to Section 5, paragraph 1.

Front roof lights

2 Using a wooden or plastic spatula, carefully prise down the rear edge of the interior light lens and remove it **(see illustration)**.

3 Twist the relevant bulbholder anti-clockwise and remove it **(see illustration)**.

4 Pull the relevant capless bulb from the holder.

Door-mounted footwell lights

5 Carefully prise the light lens from the base of the door **(see illustration)**.

6.2 Prise down the rear edge of the front interior light

6 Two different versions of the light may be fitted. On the first, the capless bulb pulls from the holder. On the second, rotate the bulbholder anti-clockwise, then pull the capless bulb from place.

Footwell-mounted lights

7 Carefully prise the light lens from the panel.

8 Slide the cover to one side, and pull the festoon bulb from the contacts.

Rear roof light

9 Using a wooden or plastic spatula, carefully prise down the rear edge of the interior light lens and remove it **(see illustration)**.

10 Twist the relevant bulbholder anti-clockwise and remove it **(see illustration)**.

6.3 Rotate the bulbholder (arrowed) anti-clockwise

6.5 Prise the door-mounted lights from the trim panel

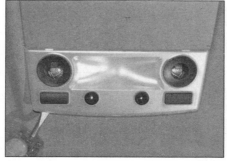

6.9 Prise down the rear edge of the light

6.10 Twist the bulbholder (arrowed) anti-clockwise

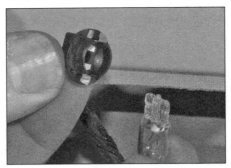

6.11 Pull the capless bulb from the holder

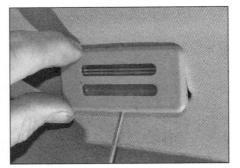

6.19 Prise the front edge of the vanity light from place

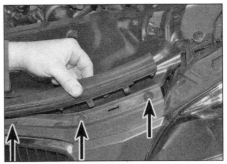

7.1 Unclip the strip, and remove the bolts (arrowed)

11 Remove the relevant bulb from the holder **(see illustration)**.

Luggage compartment light

12 Carefully prise the light unit from place. Disconnect the wiring plug as the unit is withdrawn.
13 Remove the metal cover from the light unit, and prise out the festoon bulb.

Instrument illumination and warning lights

14 Instrument illumination is provided by integral LEDs. If faulty the instrument cluster may have to be renewed. Consult your BMW dealer or specialist.

Glovebox illumination bulb

15 Carefully prise the light lens from the panel.
16 Slide the cover to one side, and pull the festoon bulb from the contacts.

Heater control panel illumination

17 The heater control panel is illuminated by LEDs which are not serviceable. If a fault develops, have the system checked by a BMW dealer or suitably-equipped specialist.

Switch illumination bulbs

18 All of the switches are fitted with LEDs. On all switches, these LEDs are an integral part of the switch assembly and cannot be obtained

separately. LED renewal will therefore require the renewal of the complete switch assembly.

Mirror illumination

19 Carefully prise the front edge of the mirror light downwards from the headlining **(see illustration)**.
20 Pull the festoon bulb from the contacts.

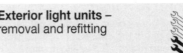

7 Exterior light units – removal and refitting

Headlight

Note: *On models with xenon HID headlights, disconnect the battery as described in Chapter 5 before commencing work.*
1 Unclip the strip at the top of the bonnet slam panel, and undo the bolts securing the top of the bumper **(see illustration)**.
2 Rotate the main beam bulb cover from the rear of the headlight anti-clockwise, and remove it **(see illustration 5.8)**.
3 Slacken the 2 bolts at the rear, lower part of the headlight, and undo the 2 bolts at the top **(see illustration)**.
4 Pull the bumper panel forwards slightly, and manoeuvre the headlight from position. Disconnect the headlight wiring plug as it's withdrawn **(see illustration)**.
5 Refitting is a direct reversal of the removal procedure. Lightly tighten the retaining bolts

and check the alignment of the headlight with the bumper and bonnet. Once the light unit is correctly positioned, securely tighten the retaining bolts and check the headlight beam alignment using the information given in Section 8.

Xenon headlight control unit

6 Remove the relevant headlight as described earlier in this Section.
7 Undo the retaining bolts, and remove the unit from the underside of the headlight **(see illustration)**.
8 Refitting is a reversal of removal.

Front direction indicator light

9 The indicator is integral with the headlight unit.

Front indicator side repeater

10 Using finger pressure, push the side repeater lens gently rearwards. Pull out the front edge of the lens and withdraw it from the wing **(see illustration 5.31)**. Disconnect the wiring plug as the unit is withdrawn.
11 Refitting is a reverse of the removal procedure.

Front foglight

12 Raise the front of the vehicle and support it securely on axle stands (see *Jacking and vehicle support*). Remove the relevant front roadwheel.
13 Undo the bolts and pull back the

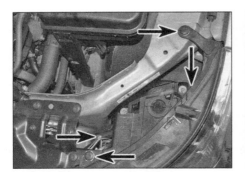

7.3 Slacken the two bolts at the rear, lower part of the headlight, and undo the ones on top (arrowed)

7.4 Pull the bumper forwards a little, and manoeuvre the headlight from place

7.7 Xenon HID control unit bolts (arrowed)

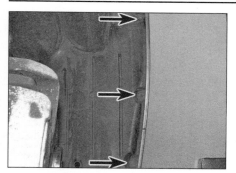

7.13 Undo the bolts (arrowed), and pull back the lower section of the front wheel arch liner

7.14 Front foglight bolts (arrowed)

7.20 Undo the rear light cluster retaining nuts (arrowed) – Saloon models

front section of the wheel arch liner **(see illustration)**.

14 Undo the two mounting bolts, and remove the foglight. Disconnect the wiring plug as the light is withdrawn **(see illustration)**.

15 Refitting is a reversal of removal. If required, the foglight aim can be adjusted by rotating the adjuster bolt adjacent to the foglight **(see illustration 5.37)**.

Rear light cluster

Saloon

16 Lift the luggage compartment floor panel.

17 Rotate the fasteners anti-clockwise and remove the trim panel behind the relevant rear light.

18 On models up to 03/2007, disconnect the wiring plug, then release the 2 clips and remove the bulbholder assembly **(see illustration 5.40)**.

19 On models from 03/2007, disconnect the wiring plug, rotate the fastener anti-clockwise and remove the bulbholder

20 On all models, undo the retaining nuts and remove the cluster from the wing **(see illustration)**.

21 Refitting is a reversal of removal.

Body-mounted lights – Touring

22 Release the clip and remove the cover each side behind the tail lights.

23 Disconnect the tail light wiring plug.

24 Undo the three retaining nuts, and remove the light cluster **(see illustration)**.

25 Refitting is a reversal of removal. Tighten the upper retaining nuts first, then the lower one.

Tailgate-mounted lights – Touring

26 Undo the rotary fasteners and open the flap in the lower section of the tailgate, then pull out the foam insulation from in front of the rear light units.

27 Disconnect the wiring plug, then undo the clamping nut and manoeuvre the light unit from the tailgate **(see illustration)**.

28 Refitting is a reversal of removal, ensuring the locating lugs are correctly positioned over the edge of the tailgate **(see illustration)**.

Number plate light

29 Carefully push the light unit away from the end with the slot to compress the retaining

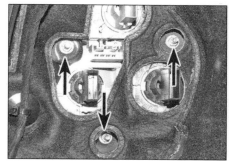

7.24 Body-mounted rear light cluster retaining nuts (arrowed) – Touring models

spring, then lever the light unit from place **(see illustration 5.57)**. Disconnect the wiring plug as the unit is withdrawn.

30 Refitting is the reverse of removal.

High-level brake light

Saloon models

31 Pull the cover downwards **(see illustration)**.

32 Press the retaining clip each side outwards, and remove the light unit. Disconnect the wiring plug as the unit is withdrawn **(see illustration)**.

33 Refitting is a reversal of removal.

Touring models

34 Prise out the grommets, undo the 4 bolts and pull the tailgate spoiler rearwards a little

7.27 Undo the clamping nut (arrowed)

7.28 Ensure the locating lugs (arrowed) are correctly located

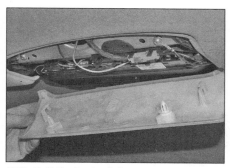

7.31 Pull the brake light cover downwards

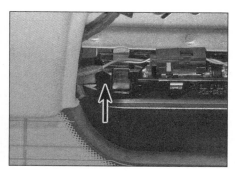

7.32 Slide the clip (arrowed) each side outwards and lower the brake light

7.34 Undo the tailgate spoiler bolts (arrowed) each side

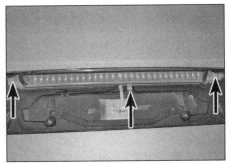

7.35 High-level brake light bolts (arrowed) – Touring models

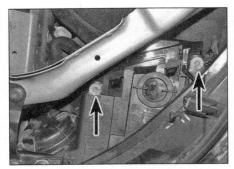

8.2 Headlight beam aim adjustment bolts (arrowed)

(see illustration). Disconnect the wiring/hose connections and remove the spoiler.

35 Undo the 3 bolts, disconnect the washer jet hose and remove the light unit **(see illustration)**.

36 Refitting is a reversal of removal.

Light Control Module (LCM)

37 The LCM controls and monitors all external light units, as well as buttons/switches, and the function of dimming the instrument cluster illumination and courtesy lights. Should a fault occur with any of these components/bulbs, the LCM will illuminate a warning light in the instrument cluster, and in some cases, storage a fault code for later retrieval. The LCM is in constant communication with the vehicle's other ECMs via BMW's databus system. By monitoring the output of various sensors, the LCM is responsible for illuminating the instrument cluster warning lights, and headlight range control. The sensors monitored are the oil temperature/level, brake fluid level, coolant level and the windscreen washer level.

38 The LCM is located behind the facia. Remove the driver's side lower facia panel as described in Chapter 11.

39 Release the clip on the side, and slide the LCM rearwards.

40 Release the locking catch and disconnect the wiring plug as the panel is withdrawn.

41 Refitting is a reversal of removal. **Note:** *If the LCM has been renewed, it must be programmed prior to use. This can only be carried out by a BMW dealer or suitably-equipped specialist.*

8 Headlight beam alignment – general information

1 Accurate adjustment of the headlight beam is only possible using optical beam setting equipment and this work should therefore be carried out by a BMW dealer or suitably-equipped workshop.

2 For reference, the headlights can be adjusted by rotating the adjuster bolts on the top of the headlight unit **(see illustration)**. The outer adjuster alters the horizontal position of the beam whilst the inner adjuster alters the vertical aim of the beam.

3 Some models have an electrically-operated headlight beam adjustment system which is controlled through the switch in the facia. On these models ensure that the switch is set to the off position before adjusting the headlight aim.

9 Instrument panel – removal and refitting

Removal

1 Disconnect the battery negative terminal (see Chapter 5).

2 Move the steering column down as far as it will go, and extend it completely.

3 Undo the 2 bolts at the top of the instrument panel trim **(see illustration)**.

4 Pull the top edge of the instrument panel rearwards, using a blunt tool **(see illustration)**. Disconnect the wiring plug as the panel is withdrawn.

5 At the time of writing, no individual components are available for the instrument panel and therefore the panel must be treated as a sealed unit. If there is a fault with one of the instruments, remove the panel and take it to your BMW dealer or specialist for testing. They have access to a special diagnostic tester which will be able to locate the fault and will then be able to advise you on the best course of action.

Refitting

6 Refitting is the reverse of removal, making sure the instrument panel wiring is correctly reconnected and securely held in position by any retaining clips. On completion reconnect the battery and check the operation of the panel warning lights to ensure that they are functioning correctly. **Note:** *If the instrument cluster has been renewed, the new unit must be coded to match the vehicle. This can only be carried out by a BMW dealer or suitably-equipped specialist.*

10 Head-up display – removal and refitting

Removal

1 Remove the complete facia as described in Chapter 11.

2 Undo the 2 bolts and remove the air duct behind the display unit.

3 Undo the locknut, remove the eccentric fastener, undo the 3 retaining bolts and remove the display unit. **Note:** *Take great care when disconnecting the fibre optic connections from the display unit. Do not place any strain, kink, or trap them. Do not subject them to bends of less than 25 mm radius.*

Refitting

4 Essentially, refitting is a reversal of removal. However, if a new unit has been fitted, it must be programmed/coded using BMW diagnostic equipment. Entrust this task to a BMW dealer or suitably-equipped specialist.

9.3 Undo the bolts (arrowed) at the top of the instrument panel trim

9.4 Pull the top edge of the panel rearwards

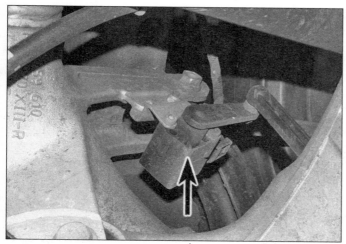

12.2 Rear suspension height sensor (arrowed)

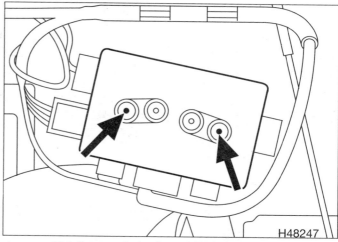

13.4 Door control unit retaining bolts (arrowed)

11 Rain/light sensor – removal and refitting

1 The rain sensor also incorporates a light sensor for automatic headlight operation.
2 Remove the interior mirror unit as described in Chapter 11.
3 Depress the locking catches, and remove the sensor.
4 Refitting is a reversal of removal. **Note:** *If the rain sensor has been renewed, the new unit must be initialised. This can only be carried out by a BMW dealer or suitably-equipped specialist.*

12 Suspension height sensor – removal and refitting

Removal

1 Vehicles equipped with xenon HID headlights or air suspension are also equipped with suspension height sensors. Ride sensors fitted to the front and rear suspension provide information on the suspension ride height, whilst the headlight range control motors alter the headlight beam angle as necessary (xenon headlights), or the suspension control unit maintains the rear ride height. The sensors are fitted between the suspension subframes and control arms. To access the sensors, jack the relevant end of the vehicle, and support securely on axle stands (see *Jacking and vehicle support*). Where applicable remove the engine undershield, or the triangular trim panel in front of the rear lower swinging arm.
2 Undo the nut securing the control rod to the sensor arm, and disconnect the rod **(see illustration)**.
3 Undo the two mounting nuts and remove the sensor. Disconnect the wiring plug as the sensor is withdrawn.

Refitting

4 Refitting is a reversal of the removal procedure, ensuring all the wiring connectors are securely reconnected.

13 Front door control unit – removing and refitting

Note: *This item is fitted to some models up to 09/2005.*
1 This unit controls the function of the door mirrors, front central locking, front electric windows, door lighting, and is also fitted with a pressure sensor as part of the side airbag system. Remove the door inner trim panel as described in Chapter 11.
2 Disconnect the battery negative lead as described in Chapter 5.
3 Note their fitted positions and disconnect the various wiring plugs.
4 Undo the 2 retaining bolts and remove the unit **(see illustration)**.
5 Refitting is a reversal of removal. If a new unit has been fitted, it must be programmed/coded using BMW diagnostic equipment. Entrust this task to a BMW dealer or suitably-equipped specialist.

14 Horn(s) – removal and refitting

Removal

1 The horn(s) is/are located behind the right-hand end of the front bumper.
2 To gain access to the horn(s) from below, apply the handbrake then jack up the front of the vehicle and support it on axle stands (see *Jacking and vehicle support*). Remove the roadwheel.
3 Undo the retaining bolts and remove the panel in front of the lower front section of the wheel arch liner.
4 Undo the retaining nuts and remove the horns, disconnecting their wiring connectors as they become accessible **(see illustration)**.

Refitting

5 Refitting is the reverse of removal.

15 Wiper arm – removal and refitting

Removal

Front wiper arm

1 Operate the wiper motor, then switch it off so that the wiper arm returns to the 'at rest' position. Open the bonnet.
2 Stick a piece of masking tape along the edge of the wiper blade to use as an alignment aid on refitting.
3 Prise off the wiper arm spindle nut cover(s) then slacken and remove the spindle nut(s). Lift the blade off the glass and pull the wiper arm off its spindle. If necessary the arm can be levered off the spindle using a suitable flat-bladed screwdriver or suitable puller.

14.4 The horns are located behind the right-hand side of the front bumper

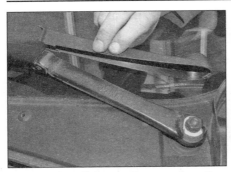

15.3a Prise off the plastic cover from the passenger's side . . .

15.3b . . . or driver's side wiper arm

15.3c Make a note of the adjusting disc fitted position in relation to the arm (arrowed)

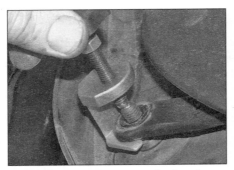

15.3d If necessary, use a puller to release the wiper arm from the spindle

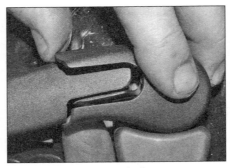

15.4 Unclip the spindle cover . . .

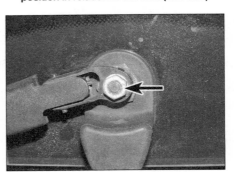

15.5 . . . and undo the wiper arm nut (arrowed)

Make a note of its fitted position prior to removal, then recover the adjusting disc from above the wiper arm on the passenger's side **(see illustrations)**.

Rear wiper arm

4 Prise apart the sides of the spindle cover slightly, then fold it out from the arm **(see illustration)**.

5 Pull the wiper arm from the window, undo the nut and remove the wiper arm **(see illustration)**. When refitting, the end of the wiper blade should be 30 mm above the window edge.

Refitting

6 Ensure that the wiper arm and spindle splines are clean and dry then refit the arm to the spindle, aligning the wiper blade with the tape fitted on removal. Where necessary, refit the adjusting disc in its original position. Refit the spindle nut, tightening it to the specified torque setting, and clip the nut cover back in position.

7 If the position of the front wiper arms has been lost, set the arms so the mounting point of the blade is approximately 69 mm above the top edge of the windscreen cowl panel (driver's side) or 87 mm (passenger's side).

8 Due the risk of the arms detaching, after allowing a 'settling' time of 50 mins, check the security of the spindle nuts.

16 Windscreen wiper motor and linkage – removal and refitting

Removal

Front windscreen wiper motor

1 Remove the wiper arms as described in the previous Section, then use a puller to remove the serrated spacer from the passenger's side spindle **(see illustration)**.

2 Working at the rear of the engine compartment, undo the bolts, release the clips and remove the pollen filter covers each

16.1 Pull the serrated spacer from the passenger's side wiper spindle

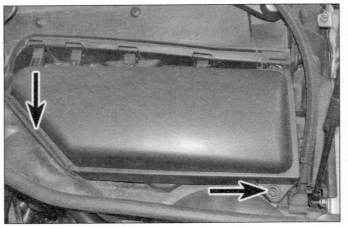

16.2 Fold the clip forwards (arrowed) and undo the fastener (arrowed)

16.3a Pull up the rubber sealing strip

16.3b Lift the clip and slide the plastic cover to the left-hand side

16.4a Lift the plastic trim at each end from place

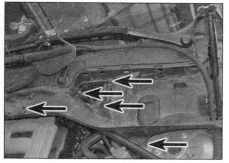

16.4b Undo the fasteners/bolt (arrowed) and remove the pollen filter lower housing each side

16.5 Remove the tension brace (arrowed)

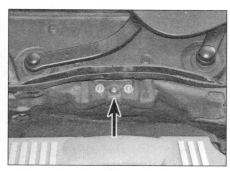

16.6a Undo the Torx bolt in the centre (arrowed) . . .

16.6b . . . the 2 bolts each side (arrowed) . . .

side (see illustration). Slide the filters from the housings. If necessary, refer to Chapter 1.

3 Pull up the rubber sealing strip, then release the clip and slide the plastic cover from the centre of the panel (see illustrations).

4 Lift out the plastic trim, undo the bolts/fasteners and remove the left- and right-hand plastic covers from behind the suspension turret each side of the engine compartment.

Unclip the wiring where applicable (see illustrations).

5 Undo the 4 bolts and remove the tension brace (see illustration). Discard the bolts – new ones must be fitted.

6 Remove the Torx bolt, the 2 bolts each side, and the fastener in the centre, then pull the fresh air duct forwards (see illustrations). Undo the bolt securing the pipe clamp (where fitted).

7 Undo the fasteners and pull the scuttle

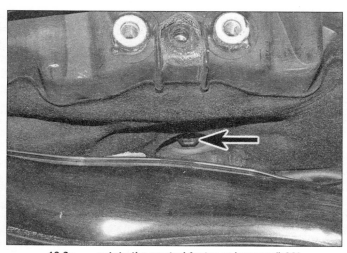

16.6c . . . rotate the central fastener (arrowed) 90° anti-clockwise . . .

16.6d . . . and remove the fresh air duct

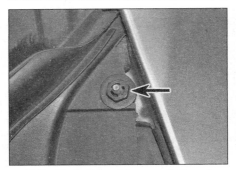

16.7a Undo the nut (arrowed) at each end . . .

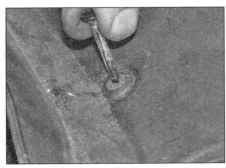

16.7b . . . prise up the centre pins and lever out the rivets in the centre . . .

16.7c . . . rotate the fasteners 90° anti clockwise along the top edge . . .

16.7d . . . and remove the scuttle cover

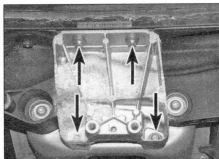

16.8 Tension brace bearing block bolts (arrowed)

cover from the base of the windscreen (see illustrations):

8 Undo the bolts and remove the tension brace bearing block (see illustration).

9 Disconnect the wiper motor wiring plug.

10 Undo the bolts securing the motor/linkage assembly and manoeuvre it from the vehicle (see illustrations). No further dismantling is recommended.

Rear windscreen wiper motor

11 Remove the tailgate lower trim panel as described in Chapter 11.

12 Disconnect the motor wiring plug.

13 Make alignment marks where the motor and bracket touch the tailgate, to aid refitting. Undo the bolts, and remove the wiper motor (see illustration).

14 If required, undo the 2 bolts and detach the rear window lock from the motor assembly.

Rear wiper arm spindle and housing

15 Remove the rear wiper arm as described in the previous Section.

16 On the outside of the windscreen, slacken and remove the wiper arm spindle nut. Recover any washers (see illustration).

17 Open the tailgate window, prise out the plastic caps and undo the two nuts and remove the cover (see illustration).

18 On the inside of the screen, disconnect the wiring plug, undo the retaining nut, and manoeuvre the housing and spindle

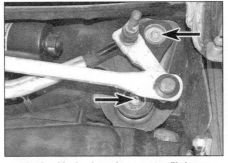

16.10a Undo the wiper motor/linkage assembly bolts (arrowed) on the passenger's side . . .

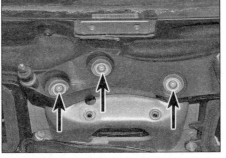

16.10b . . . and the bolts in the centre (arrowed)

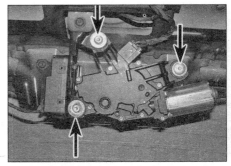

16.13 Undo the bolts (arrowed) and remove the wiper motor

16.16 Undo the wiper spindle nut (arrowed)

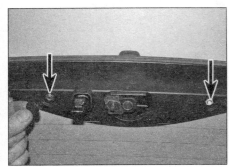

16.17 Prise out the caps and undo the nuts (arrowed)

16.18 Housing and spindle retaining nut (arrowed)

from position (see illustration). No further dismantling is recommended.

Refitting

19 Refitting is the reverse of removal. On completion refit the wiper arms as described in Section 15.

17 Washer system components – removal and refitting

Washer system reservoir

1 The windscreen washer reservoir is situated in the engine compartment. On models equipped with headlight washers the reservoir also supplies the headlight washer jets via an additional pump.
2 Empty the contents of the reservoir or be prepared for fluid spillage.
3 Jack up the front of the vehicle, and support it securely on axle stands (see *Jacking and vehicle support*). Remove the front left-hand roadwheel.
4 Undo the bolts and remove the wheel arch liner.
5 Disconnect the wiring connector(s) from the reservoir level switch and pumps, then note their fitted locations, and disconnect the various hoses from the reservoir.
6 Undo the 3 reservoir retaining bolts and manoeuvre the reservoir from position. Disconnect the filler hose as the reservoir is withdrawn. Wash off any spilt fluid with cold water.
7 Refitting is a reversal of removal. Ensure

17.15 Depress the clip (arrowed) and push the jet up through the bonnet

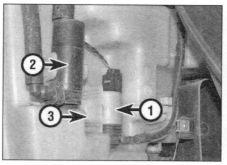

17.9 Washer pumps details

1 Windscreen washer pump
2 Headlight washer pump
3 Tailgate washer pump location

the locating lugs on the base of the reservoir engage correctly with the corresponding slots in the inner wing. Refill the reservoir and check for leakage.

Washer pumps

8 Remove the right-hand front wheel arch liner as described in Paragraphs 3 and 4.
9 Disconnect the wiring connector(s) and hose(s) from the washer pump(s). Carefully rotate the pump(s) clockwise, and pull them up from the reservoir. The left-hand pump is for the headlight washer (where fitted), then middle pump is for the rear washer (where fitted), and the right-hand pump is for the windscreen jets (see illustration). Be prepared for fluid spillage. Inspect the pump sealing grommet(s) for signs of damage or deterioration and renew if necessary. **Note:** *Take care when removing the pump(s) not to dislodge the strainer on the pump inlet. If the strainer falls into the reservoir, it will be necessary to remove reservoir to retrieve the strainer.*
10 Refitting is the reverse of removal, using a new sealing grommet if the original one shows signs of damage or deterioration. Refill the reservoir and check the pump grommet for leaks.

Washer reservoir level switch

11 Remove the left-hand front wheel arch liner as described in Paragraphs 3 and 4.
12 Rotate the level switch anti-clockwise and remove it from the reservoir.
13 Refitting is the reverse of removal, using a

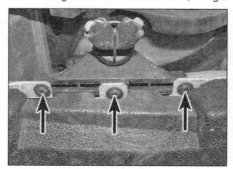

17.20 Undo the bolts (arrowed) and remove the headlight washer jet assembly

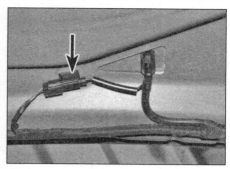

17.14 Twist the connector anti-clockwise and detach it from the bonnet

new sealing grommet if the original one shows signs of damage or deterioration. Refill the reservoir and check for leaks.

Windscreen washer jets

14 Open the bonnet and disconnect the washer hose(s) from the base of the jet. Where necessary, also disconnect the wiring connector, then twist it anti-clockwise and detach it from the bonnet (see illustration).
15 Depress the clip at the top of the jet and manoeuvre it out the top of the bonnet (see illustration).
16 On refitting, push the jet back into position in the bonnet, and securely connect the jet to the hose. Note that the aim of the jets is preset during manufacture and cannot be adjusted.

Headlight washer jets

17 Remove the front bumper as described in Chapter 11.
18 Release the retaining clip and disconnect the hose from the jet.
19 Where applicable disconnect the jet heater wiring plug.
20 Undo the 3 bolts and remove the jet (see illustration).
21 Refitting is a reversal of removal. The aim of the jets is preset during manufacture, and cannot be adjusted.

Rear screen washer jet

22 Remove the high-level brake light as described in Section 7.
23 Prise out the clip, and pull the jet and hose out through the high-level brake light assembly (see illustration).
24 Refitting is a reversal of removal.

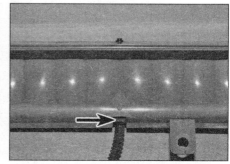

17.23 Prise out the clip (arrowed) and pull the jet/hose through the brake light assembly

18.1 Undo the bolts (arrowed) at the top of the monitor trim . . .

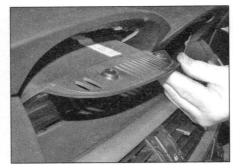

18.2 . . . then pull the top edge rearwards

18.5a Undo the bolts (arrowed) . . .

18 Infotainment units – removal and refitting

Note: *The following removal and refitting procedure is for some of the range of units which BMW fit as standard equipment. Removal and refitting procedures of non-standard will differ slightly.*

Note: *Take great care when disconnecting the fibre optic connections from the display unit. Do not place any strain, kink, or trap them. Do not subject them to bends of less than 25 mm radius.*

Removal

Central monitor/display unit

1 Undo the 2 bolts at the top of the monitor trim **(see illustration)**.

2 Pull the top edge rearwards and manoeuvre the monitor from the facia **(see illustration)**. Disconnect the various wiring plugs as the unit is withdrawn. Note that if a new unit is fitted, it must be programmed using BMW diagnostic equipment. Entrust this task to a BMW dealer or suitably-equipped specialist.

Car Infotainment Computer (CIC)

3 Disconnect the battery negative lead as described in Chapter 5.

4 Remove the centre facia panel lower switches as described in Section 4.

5 Undo the 4 retaining bolts and pull the CIC

18.5b . . . and pull the CIC rearwards from the facia

rearwards a little **(see illustrations)**. Note their fitted positions, and disconnect the various wiring plugs. Note that if a new CIC is fitted, it must be programmed using BMW diagnostic equipment. Entrust this task to a BMW dealer or suitably-equipped specialist.

DAB radio tuner

6 Disconnect the battery negative lead as described in Chapter 5.

7 Remove the left-hand side luggage compartment side panel trim as described in Chapter 11.

8 Undo the retaining bolts and slide the tuner from the mounting bracket **(see illustration)**.

9 Note their fitted positions, and disconnect the wiring plugs from the rear of the unit.

18.5c Disconnect the CIC wiring plugs

CD autochanger

10 Disconnect the battery negative lead as described in Chapter 5.

11 Open the passenger's glovebox, undo the fasteners and remove the fusebox cover from the glovebox **(see illustration 3.2)**.

12 Rotate the fasteners anti-clockwise and fold down the cover over the autochanger.

13 Prise open the covers, undo the 2 retaining bolts, and slide the unit from position **(see illustration)**. Disconnect the wiring plugs as the unit is withdrawn.

Amplifier

14 The amplifier (where fitted) is located behind the left-hand side luggage compartment trim panel. Remove the trim panel as described in Chapter 11.

15 Disconnect the amplifier wiring plugs, slide out the retaining plates and remove the unit.

Refitting

16 Refitting is a reversal of removal.

19 Loudspeakers – removal and refitting

Door main loudspeaker

1 Remove the door inner trim panel as described in Chapter 11.

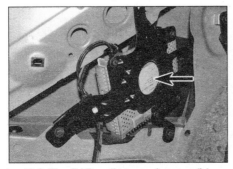

18.8 The DAB radio tuner (arrowed) is located behind the left-hand side luggage compartment side trim panel

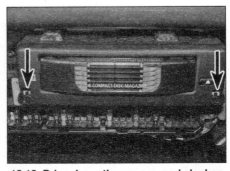

18.13 Prise down the covers, and slacken the retaining bolts (arrowed)

19.2 Undo the nuts (arrowed) securing the retaining plate and the door speaker

19.11 Prise up the front edge, and remove the parcel shelf speaker grille

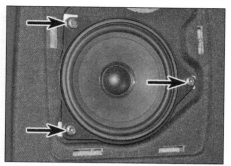

19.12 Rear speaker retaining bolts (arrowed)

2 Disconnect the wiring plugs, then unscrew the nuts and remove the retaining plate and speaker assembly from the door **(see illustration)**.

3 Refitting is the reverse of removal.

Door upper loudspeaker

4 Remove the door inner trim as described in Chapter 11.

5 Slightly lift and pull the plastic trim away from the front inner edge of the door.

6 Release the catches and remove the speaker from the door. Disconnect the wiring plug as the speaker is withdrawn.

7 Refitting is a reversal of removal.

Headlining loudspeaker

8 Starting at the front edge, carefully prise the speaker from the headlining.

9 Undo the retaining bolts and remove the speaker, disconnect its wiring connectors as they become accessible.

10 Refitting is the reverse of removal, making sure the speaker is correctly located. Fit the steel clips into the speaker surround prior to refitting the trim.

Rear loudspeaker

11 Carefully prise up the plastic grille over the speaker(s) **(see illustration)**.

12 Undo the retaining bolts, and lift the speaker from place **(see illustration)**. Disconnect the speaker wiring plug as it is withdrawn.

13 Refitting is the reverse of removal.

Facia speaker

14 Starting at the rear edge, carefully prise up and remove the plastic grille over the speaker **(see illustration)**.

15 Undo the retaining bolts, and lift the speaker from place. Disconnect the speaker wiring plug as it is withdrawn.

16 Refitting is a reversal of removal.

20 Radio aerial –
general information

The radio aerial is built into the rear screen. In order to improve reception an amplifier is fitted to boost the signal to the radio.

Saloon models

1 Remove the left-hand C-pillar trim panel as described in Chapter 11.

2 Unclip the cover from the high-level brake light as described in Section 6.

3 Release the clips around the amplifier, and remove it from position. Disconnect the wiring plugs as the unit is withdrawn.

4 Refitting is a reversal of removal.

Touring models

5 Remove the rear upper brake light as described in Section 7.

6 Unclip the cover over the amplifier, undo the retaining nuts and manoeuvre the amplifier from place **(see illustration)**. Disconnect the wiring plugs as the amplifier is withdrawn.

7 Refitting is a reversal of removal.

21 Cruise control/traction control systems – information and component renewal

1 The cruise control function is incorporated into the engine management ECM. The only renewable external component is the clutch pedal switch. Renewal of the switch is described in Section 4.

2 The traction control system incorporates elements of the ABS braking system (see Chapter 9), as well as an engine power reduction system.

22 Anti-theft alarm system – general information

The 5-Series models are equipped with a sophisticated anti-theft alarm and immobiliser system. Should a fault develop, the system's self-diagnosis facility should be interrogated using dedicated test equipment. Consult your BMW dealer or suitably-equipped specialist.

23 Heated front seat components – removal and refitting

Heater mats

On models equipped with heated front seats, a heater pad is fitted to the both the seat back and seat cushion. Renewal of either heater mat involves peeling back the upholstery, removing the old mat, sticking the new mat in position and then refitting the upholstery. Note that upholstery removal and refitting requires considerable skill and experience if it is to be carried out successfully and is therefore best entrusted to your BMW dealer or specialist. In practice, it will be very difficult for the home mechanic to carry out the job without ruining the upholstery.

Heated seat switches

Refer to Section 4 (*Centre facia panel lower switches*).

19.14 Prise up the rear edge of the facia speaker grille

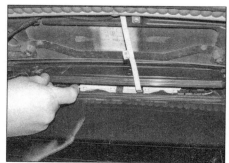

20.6 Unclip the cover over the aerial amplifier

24 Airbag system – general information and precautions

The models covered by this manual are equipped with a driver's airbag mounted in the centre of the steering wheel, a passenger's airbag located behind the facia, two head airbags located in each A-pillar/headlining, two airbags located in each front door trim panel and, on some models, behind each rear door trim. The airbag system comprises the airbag unit(s) (complete with gas generators), impact sensors, the control unit and a warning light in the instrument panel.

The airbag system is triggered in the event of a heavy frontal or side impact above a predetermined force; depending on the point of impact. The airbag(s) is inflated within milliseconds and forms a safety cushion between the cabin occupants and the cabin interior, and therefore greatly reduces the risk of injury. The airbag then deflates almost immediately.

Every time the ignition is switched on, the airbag control unit performs a self-test. The self-test takes approximately 2 to 6 seconds and during this time the airbag warning light on the facia is illuminated. After the self-test has been completed the warning light should go out. If the warning light fails to come on, remains illuminated after the initial period, or comes on at any time when the vehicle is being driven, there is a fault in the airbag system. The vehicle should be taken to a

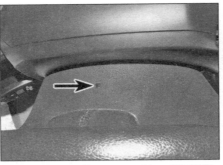

25.2a Insert a Torx screwdriver T25/T27 (or rod of 3 mm diameter) into the hole (arrowed) in the base of the steering wheel . . .

BMW dealer for examination at the earliest possible opportunity.

⚠️ *Warning: Before carrying out any operations on the airbag system, disconnect the battery negative terminal, and wait for at least 1 minute. This will allow the capacitors in the system to discharge. When operations are complete, make sure no one is inside the vehicle when the battery is reconnected.*
- *Note that the airbag(s) must not be subjected to temperatures in excess of 90°C. When the airbag is removed, ensure that it is stored the correct way up to prevent possible inflation (padded surface uppermost).*
- *Do not allow any solvents or cleaning agents to contact the airbag assemblies. They must be cleaned using only a damp cloth.*
- *The airbags and control unit are both*

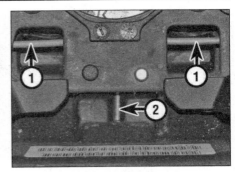

25.2b . . . and press the airbag retaining spring/clip upwards to release it (shown with the airbag removed for clarity)

1 Clip/spring   2 Screwdriver/rod

sensitive to impact. If either is dropped or damaged they should be renewed.
- *Disconnect the airbag control unit wiring plug prior to using arc-welding equipment on the vehicle.*

25 Airbag system components – removal and refitting

Note: *Refer to the warnings in Section 24 before carrying out the following operations.*

1 Disconnect the battery negative terminal (see Chapter 5), then continue as described under the relevant heading.

Driver's airbag

2 With the wheel in the straight-ahead position, insert a T25/T27 Torx screwdriver into the hole in the base of the steering wheel boss until it contact the retaining clip/spring. Continue to press until the airbag unit can be felt to release **(see illustrations)**.

3 Carefully lift the airbag assembly away from the steering wheel. Note their fitted positions and disconnect the wiring plugs from the airbag unit **(see illustration)**. Note that the airbag must not be knocked or dropped and should be stored the correct way up with its padded surface uppermost.

4 On refitting reconnect the wiring connector(s) and seat the airbag unit in the steering wheel, making sure the wire does not become trapped. Reconnect the battery as described in Chapter 5.

Passenger airbag

5 Remove the passenger's glovebox and front cup holders as described in Chapter 11.

6 Undo the bolt and remove the front, outer cup holder carrier panel **(see illustration)**.

7 The front inner cup holder carrier panel must now be removed. This must be removed with the passenger's airbag assembly. Undo the bolt securing the carrier panel, and the 4 bolts securing the airbag assembly. Disconnect the airbag wiring plug, and manoeuvre the complete assembly rearwards from the facia **(see illustrations)**.

25.3 Disconnect the driver's airbag wiring plug

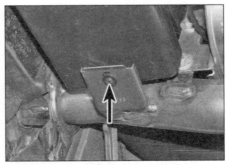

25.6 Undo the bolt (arrowed) and remove the outer cup holder carrier panel

25.7a Undo the bolt on the underside of the cup holder carrier panel (arrowed)

25.7b Undo the 2 bolts (arrowed) at each end of the passenger's airbag

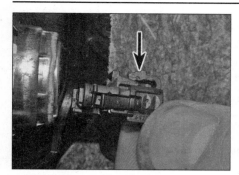

25.10 Depress the clip (arrowed) and disconnect the door airbag wiring plug

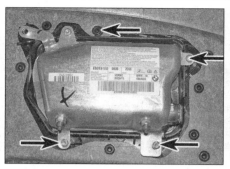

25.11 Door airbag retaining bolts (arrowed)

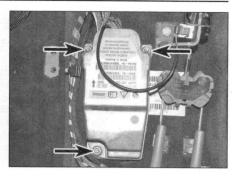

25.15 Airbag central sensor/control unit retaining nuts (arrowed)

8 Refitting is a reversal of removal. Tighten the airbag retaining bolts to the specified torque, and reconnect the battery negative terminal. Note that new airbag bolts must be fitted.

Door airbags

9 Remove the door inner trim panel as described in Chapter 11.
10 Disconnect the airbag wiring plug **(see illustration)**.
11 Undo the retaining bolts and lift the airbag from position **(see illustration)**. Note that new bolts must be fitted.
12 Refitting is a reversal of removal. Tighten the airbag retaining bolts to the specified torque, and reconnect the battery negative terminal as described in Chapter 5.

Head airbags

13 On each side of the passenger cabin, a Head Protection Airbag (HPS) is fitted. The airbag runs from the lower part of the windscreen pillar to above the rear door, and on some models, down to the rear parcel shelf. The airbag is approximately 1.5 metres in length, and 130 mm in diameter when inflated. To remove the airbag, the entire facia and headlining must be removed. This task is outside the scope of the DIYer, and therefore we recommend that the task be entrusted to a BMW dealer or specialist.

Airbag central sensor/ control unit

14 Remove the centre console as described in Chapter 11.
15 Undo the retaining nuts and lift the module. Disconnect the wiring plug as the unit is withdrawn **(see illustration)**.
16 Refitting is the reverse of removal. Note that if a new unit is fitted, it must be programmed using BMW diagnostic equipment. Entrust this task to a BMW dealer or suitably-equipped specialist.

26 Parking distance control (PDC) – information and component renewal

General information

1 In order to aid parking, a models in the 5-Series range can be equipped with a system that informs the driver of the distance between the vehicle and any vehicle/obstacle behind whilst reversing or manoeuvring forwards. The system consists of several ultrasonic sensors mounted in the bumpers which measure the distance to the nearest object. The distance is indicated by an audible signal in the passenger cabin. The closer the object, the more frequent the signals, until at less than 30 cm, the signal becomes continuous.

PDC electronic control module

2 Remove the spare wheel and the cover beneath.
3 Note their fitted positions, and disconnect the module's wiring plugs. Unclip and remove the control module **(see illustration)**.
4 Refitting is a reversal of removal. Note that if a new module has been fitted, it must be programmed using BMW diagnostic equipment. Entrust this task to a BMW dealer or suitably-equipped specialist.

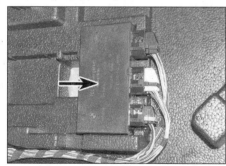

26.3 The PDC control module (arrowed) is under the spare wheel well in the luggage compartment

Ultrasonic sensors

5 Remove the bumper as described in Chapter 11.
6 Disconnect the sensor wiring plugs, release the retaining clips and remove the sensors from the bumper **(see illustration)**.
7 Refitting is the reverse of removal.

27 Wiring diagrams – general information

1 The wiring diagrams which follow only offer limited coverage of the electrical systems fitted to the BMW 5-Series.
2 Due to the sheer volume of wiring circuits applicable to the 5-Series, comprehensive coverage of all the vehicle's systems is not possible.
3 Bear in mind that, while wiring diagrams offer a useful quick-reference guide to the vehicle electrical systems, it is still possible to trace faults, and to check for supplies and earths, using a simple multimeter. Refer to the general fault finding methods described in Section 2 of this Chapter (ignoring the references to wiring diagrams if one is not provided for the system concerned).

26.6 Spread out the clips (arrowed) a little and remove the PDC sensor

BMW 5 Series wiring diagrams

Diagram 1

 WARNING: *This vehicle is fitted with a supplemental restraint system (SRS) consisting of a combination of driver (and passenger) airbag(s), side impact protection airbags and seatbelt pre-tensioners. The use of electrical test equipment on any SRS wiring systems may cause the seatbelt pre-tensioners to abruptly retract and airbags to explosively deploy, resulting in potentially severe personal injury. Extreme care should be taken to correctly identify any circuits to be tested to avoid choosing any of the SRS wiring in error.*
For further information see airbag system precautions in body electrical systems chapter.
Note: The SRS wiring harness can normally be identified by yellow and/or orange harness or harness connectors.

Key to symbols

Solenoid actuator	
Earth point and location	E7
Wire colour (blue with red tracer)	BL/RT
Dashed outline denotes part of a larger item, containing in this case an electronic or solid state device (pins 31 and 32 of a connector X14270).	X14270/31 X14270/32 (K)
Bulb	
Switch	
Fuse/Fusible link	F26
Resistor	
Variable resistor	
Variable resistor	
Wire splice, soldered joint, or unspecified connector	
Connecting wires	
Diode	
Light-emitting diode	
Item number	12
Motor/pump	M
Heating element	

Typical earth locations

E1 Engine bay, on cylinder head cover
E2 Engine bay, on cylinder head cover
E3 Engine bay, near ignition coils
E4 Engine bay, near ignition coils
E5 Engine bay, on cylinder head cover
E6 Engine bay, on cylinder head cover
E7 Passenger compartment, LH footwell
E8 Passenger compartment, LH footwell
E9 Passenger compartment, driver's seat rail
E10 Passenger compartment, driver's seat rail
E11 Passenger compartment, LH C-pillar
E12 Saloon - Luggage compartment, below LH tail light
     Estate - Luggage compartment, LH side
E13 Luggage compartment, below LH tail light
E14 Saloon - Luggage compartment, below RH tail light
     Estate - Luggage compartment, RH side
E15 Luggage compartment, under RH tail light
E16 Passenger compartment, RH C-pillar
E17 Passenger compartment, passenger's seat rail
E18 Passenger compartment, passenger's seat rail
E19 Passenger compartment, RH footwell
E20 Passenger compartment, RH footwell
E21 Engine bay, RH side near fusebox

Typical engine comp. fusebox 40

Fuse	Rating	Circuit protected
F01	30A	Ignition coils, interference suppressor
F02	30A	Camshaft sensors, coolant thermostat, electric coolant pump, VANOS solenoids
F03	20A	Crankshaft sensor, engine control unit, fuel tank vent valve, mass air flow sensor, oil condition sensor, variable intake manifold solenoid
F04	30A	Crankcase breather heater, oxygen sensor heaters, transmission control unit
F05	30A	Fuel injection relay
F06	10A	AUC sensor, brake air flap sensors, engine fusebox fan, fuel tank leakage diagnostic unit, nitrogen oxide control unit, radiator shutter solenoid, secondary air injection mass air flow sensor and pump relay, tail pipe flap
F07	40A	Valtronic relay
F010	5A	Engine breather heater

E12 E13 E12 E11 E10 E9 E8 E7 E6 E5

E4

E3

E14 E15 E14 E16 E17 E18 E19 E20 E21 E1 E2

H47180

BMW 5 Series wiring diagrams

Diagram 2

Typical passenger comp. fusebox 18

(models to 09/2005)

Fuse	Rating	Circuit protected
F1	50A	Dynamic stability control
F2	60A	Secondary air injection pump relay
F3	40A	Heater blower output stage
F4	40A	Active steering
F5	50A	Lighting control unit
F6	50A	Lighting control unit
F7	30A	Car access system
F8	60A	B+ power distribution, engine electronics fuse carrier, engine management control unit and relay
F9	60A	Engine cooling fan
F10	30A	Driver's door control unit
F11	5A	Body control unit
F12	30A	Passenger's door control unit
F13	7.5A	Instrument cluster
F14	30A	Driver's seat control
F15	5A	Car access system
F16	30A	Front wiper relay
F17	-	Spare
F18	30A	Headlight washer relay
F19	5A	Gear indicator lighting
F20	-	Spare
F21	30A	Passenger's seat control
F22	30A	Body control unit
F23	-	Spare
F24	30A	Body control unit
F25	30A	Dynamic stability control
F26	7.5A	Climate control
F27	30A	Body control unit
F28	20A	Steering column switch unit
F29	10A	Diagnostic connector, safety and gateway control unit
F30	15A	Climate control
F31	30A	Driver's seat control unit
F32	10A	Dynamic drive
F33	30A	Passenger seat control unit
F34	30A	Radio
F35	5A	Navigation
F36	-	Spare
F37	10A	Automatic transmission control unit
F38	10A	CD changer
F39	5A	Steering column switch unit
F40	10A	DVD changer
F41	7.5A	Instrument cluster
F42	-	Spare
F43	-	Spare
F44	-	Spare
F45	-	Spare
F46	-	Spare

Typical passenger comp. fusebox 18

(models from 09/2005)

Fuse	Rating	Circuit protected
F1	50A	Dynamic stability control
F2	-	Spare
F3	40A	Heater blower output stage
F4	-	Spare
F5	40A	Lighting control unit
F6	40A	Lighting control unit
F7	30A	Car access system
F8	60A	B+ power distribution, engine electronics fuse carrier, engine management control unit and relay
F9	60A	Engine cooling fan
F10	30A	Body gateway control unit
F11	5A	Body control unit
F12	30A	Body gateway control unit
F13	30A	Transfer case control unit
F14	30A	Driver's seat control
F15	5A	Car access system
F16	30A	Front wiper relay
F17	5A	Steering column switch unit
F18	30A	Body gateway control unit
F19	5A	Gear indicator lighting
F20	20A	On-board diagnostics
F21	30A	Passenger's seat control
F22	30A	Body control unit
F23	30A	Engine management control unit
F24	30A	Body control unit
F25	30A	Dynamic stability control
F26	20A	Unloading relay
F27	30A	Body control unit
F28	20A	Steering column switch unit
F29	10A	Diagnostic connector, body gateway control unit
F30	20A	Fuel pump relay
F31	10A	Engine management control unit
F32	10A	Driver's door switch unit, mirror control switch
F33	30A	Instrument cluster, seat heating
F34	20A	Radio
F35	5A	Navigation
F36	10A	Comfort access control unit, door handle control unit
F37	5A	Telematics control unit, telephone
F38	5A	CD changer
F39	5A	Steering column switch unit
F40	10A	DVD changer
F41	7.5A	Instrument cluster
F42	-	Spare
F43	-	Spare
F44	-	Spare
F45	-	Spare
F46	-	Spare

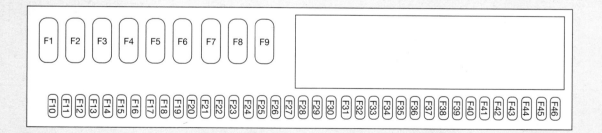

H47181

BMW 5 Series wiring diagrams

Diagram 3

Typical luggage comp. fusebox 7

(models to 09/2005)

Fuse	Rating	Circuit protected
F50	20A	Fuel pump
F51	5A	Alarm, comfort access door, electrochromic mirror
F52	10A	Micro power control unit
F53	7.5A	Models to 09/2004 - luggage compartment/tailgate lid soft-close relay
		Models from 09/2004 - comfort access, door handle control unit
F54	20A	Unloading relay
F55	5A	Rain/light sensor
F56	-	Spare
F57	20A	Micro power control unit
F58	40A	Heated rear window
F59	5A	Antenna tuner
F60	-	Spare
F61	20A	Front cigar lighter, glove box 12v socket
F62	5A	Unloading relay
F63	5A	Electrochromic mirror, park distance control
F64	10A	Central information display, iDrive controller
F65	10A	Head-up display, headset control unit
F66	5A	Dynamic stability control, transfer box
F67	10A	Video control unit
F68	5A	Seats
F69	5A	Park distance control
F70	5A	Adaptive headlights
F71	20A	Rear wiper
F72	40A	Electronic height control compressor
F73	30A	Trailer
F74	20A	Trailer
F75	30A	Transfer box
F76	40A	Luggage compartment lid lift
F77	5A	Antenna
F78	-	Spare
F79	7.5A	Electronic height control
F80	30A	Amplifier
F81	-	Spare
F82	20A	Rear cigar lighter, rear 12v socket
F83	20A	Sunroof
F84	10A	Active cruise control
F85	-	Spare
F86	15A	Transmission
F87	-	Spare
F88	30A	Centre console switches
F89	15A	Gearshift lighting, telephone

Typical luggage comp. fusebox 7

(models from 09/2005)

Fuse	Rating	Circuit protected
F50	30A	Headlight washer pump
F51	5A	Alarm, comfort access door, electrochromic mirror
F52	40A	Electronic height control compressor
F53	30A	Active seat backrest
F54	30A	Heater rear window
F55	40A	Luggage compartment lid lift
F56	5A	Rain/light sensor
F57	7.5A	Climate control, washer system
F58	20A	Rear wiper
F59	5A	Antenna tuner
F60	10A	DVD changer
F61	7.5A	Rear armrest cooler box
F62	30A	Window control
F63	20A	Climate control
F64	15A	Climate control
F65	20A	Trailer connection
F66	20A	Window control
F67	20A	Window control
F68	20A	Left doors soft close
F69	5A	Park distance control
F70	10A	Active cruise control
F71	30A	Centre console switches
F72	20A	Fuel pump
F73	30A	Models to 09/2007 - amplifier
	40A	Models from 09/2007 - amplifier
F74	5A	Models to 09/2007 - dynamic stability control, seat control
	7.5A	Models from 09/2007 - seats
F75	10A	Radio, video control unit
F76	10A	Dynamic drive
F77	10A	Engine cooling fan, head-up display
F78	5A	Dynamic stability control, transfer case
F79	10A	Central information display, iDrive
F80	10A	Gearshift light, telephone
F81	7.5A	Electronic height control
F82	7.5A	Tyre pressure control
F83	30A	Active backrest
F84	15A	Transmission
F85	7.5A	Transmission
F86	40A	Active steering
F87	20A	Front cigar lighter, glove box 12v socket
F88	20A	Rear 12v socket
F89	5A	Electrochromic mirror, unloading relay

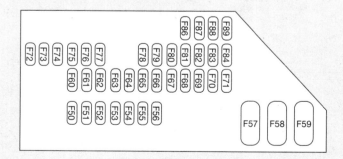

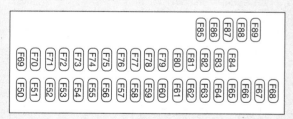

Typical rear power distribution fuses 7

Fuse	Rating	Circuit protected
F90	200A	Passenger fusebox
F91	100A	Valvetronic power supply
F92	100A	Auxiliary heater

H47182

Colour codes

WS	White	**RT**	Red
BL	Blue	**GN**	Green
GR	Grey	**VI**	Violet
GE	Yellow	**SW**	Black
BR	Brown	**OR**	Orange

Key to items

1 Battery
2 Jump start terminal point
4 Starter motor
5 Alternator
6 Intelligent battery sensor
7 Luggage compartment fusebox
    a = terminal 15 relay
8 Engine management control unit
9 Car access system
10 Ignition switch
11 Reader coil
12 Safety and gateway control unit
13 Stop light switch
14 Clutch switch control unit
15 Automatic transmission control unit
16 Sequential gearbox control unit
17 Dynamic stability control unit
18 Passenger compartment fusebox
19 Tyre pressure control unit
20 LH front wheel module
21 RH front wheel module
22 LH rear wheel module
23 RH rear wheel module
24 LH front wheel transmitter
25 RH front wheel transmitter
26 LH rear wheel transmitter
27 RH rear wheel transmitter
28 RDC antenna
29 Diagnostic connector

Diagram 4

H47183

Typical starting & charging

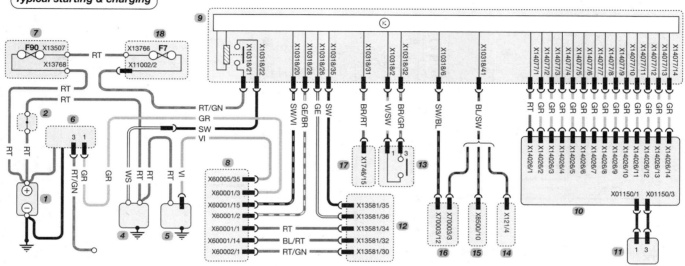

Typical tyre pressure control

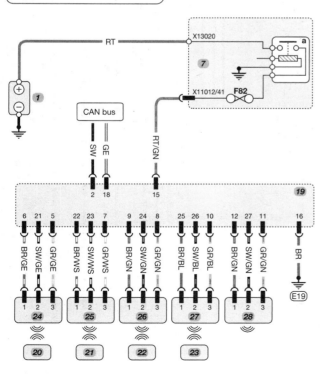

Typical diagnostic socket (OBDII)

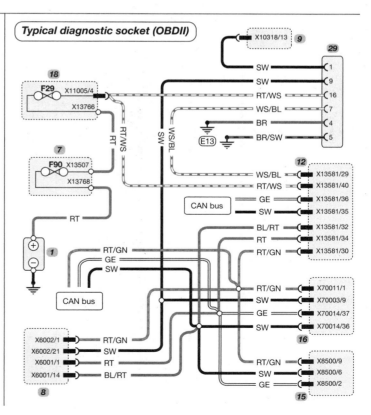

Colour codes

WS	White	**RT**	Red
BL	Blue	**GN**	Green
GR	Grey	**VI**	Violet
GE	Yellow	**SW**	Black
BR	Brown	**OR**	Orange

Key to items

1 Battery
7 Luggage compartment fusebox
   b = terminal 30g relay
8 Engine management control unit
18 Passenger compartment fusebox
29 Engine compartment fusebox
30 Engine management relay
31 Engine cooling fan
32 Engine coolant pump

33 Radiator outlet temperature sensor
34 Engine coolant temperature sensor
35 Characteristic map thermostat
36 B+ potential distributor
37 Radiator shutter motor
38 Radiator shutter solenoid
39 Engine cooling fan cut-out relay
40 Engine compartment fusebox

Diagram 5

H47184

Typical engine cooling fan (early models)

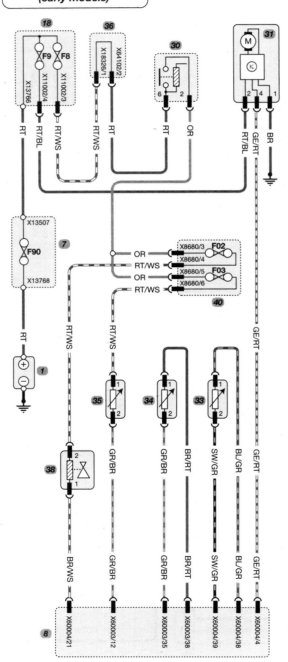

Typical engine cooling fan (later models)

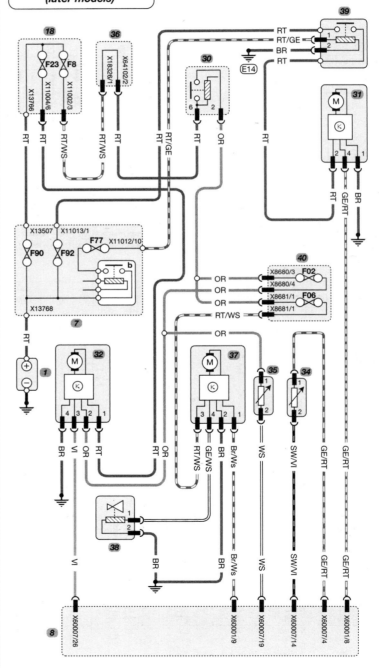

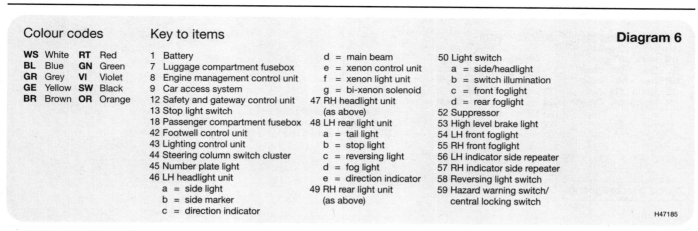

Colour codes

WS	White	RT	Red
BL	Blue	GN	Green
GR	Grey	VI	Violet
GE	Yellow	SW	Black
BR	Brown	OR	Orange

Key to items

1 Battery
7 Luggage compartment fusebox
8 Engine management control unit
9 Car access system
12 Safety and gateway control unit
13 Stop light switch
18 Passenger compartment fusebox
42 Footwell control unit
43 Lighting control unit
44 Steering column switch cluster
45 Number plate light
46 LH headlight unit
   a = side light
   b = side marker
   c = direction indicator

   d = main beam
   e = xenon control unit
   f = xenon light unit
   g = bi-xenon solenoid
47 RH headlight unit
   (as above)
48 LH rear light unit
   a = tail light
   b = stop light
   c = reversing light
   d = fog light
   e = direction indicator
49 RH rear light unit
   (as above)

50 Light switch
   a = side/headlight
   b = switch illumination
   c = front foglight
   d = rear foglight
52 Suppressor
53 High level brake light
54 LH front foglight
55 RH front foglight
56 LH indicator side repeater
57 RH indicator side repeater
58 Reversing light switch
59 Hazard warning switch/
   central locking switch

Diagram 6

H47185

Typical exterior lighting

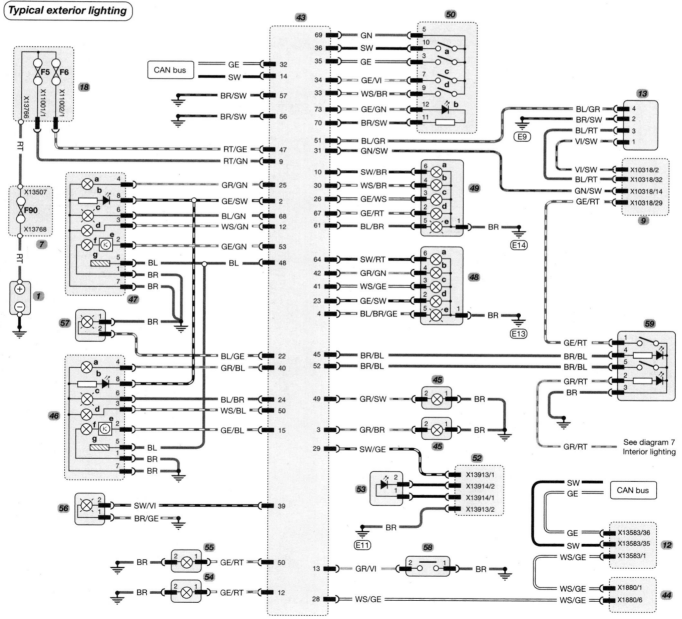

Colour codes

WS	White	**RT**	Red
BL	Blue	**GN**	Green
GR	Grey	**VI**	Violet
GE	Yellow	**SW**	Black
BR	Brown	**OR**	Orange

Key to items

1 Battery
7 Luggage compartment fusebox
18 Passenger compartment fusebox
63 Body control unit
74 Glove compartment light switch
75 LH footwell light
76 RH footwell light
77 Front interior light

78 Rear interior light
79 LH vanity mirror light
80 LH vanity mirror light switch
81 RH vanity mirror light
82 RH vanity mirror light switch
83 Glove compartment light
84 Luggage compartment light
85 Luggage compartment lock motor

Diagram 7

H47186

Typical interior lighting

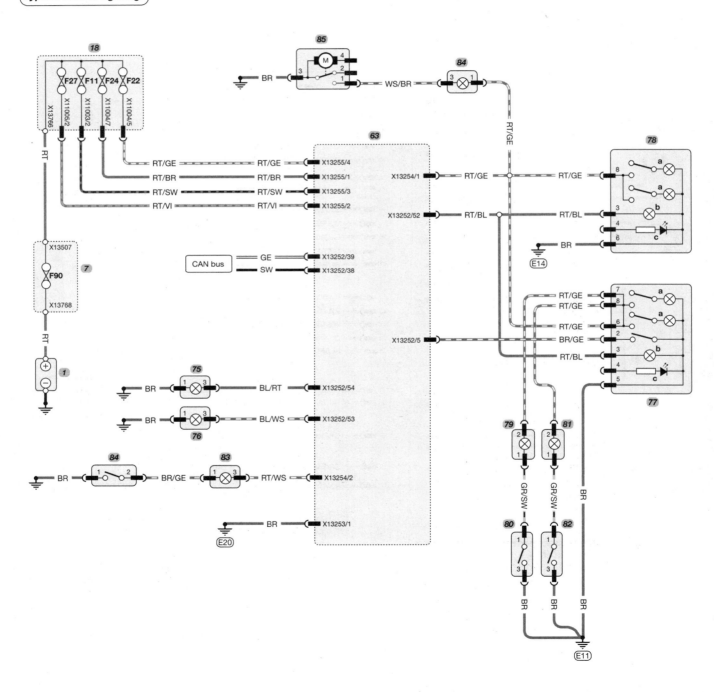

Colour codes

WS	White	RT	Red
BL	Blue	GN	Green
GR	Grey	VI	Violet
GE	Yellow	SW	Black
BR	Brown	OR	Orange

Key to items

1 Battery
7 Luggage compartment fusebox
18 Passenger compartment fusebox
63 Body control unit
86 Rear wiper relay
87 Front wiper motor
88 Rear wiper motor
89 Front washer pump
90 Rear washer pump
91 Headlight washer pump
92 Headlight washer relay

Diagram 8

H47187

Typical wash/wipe

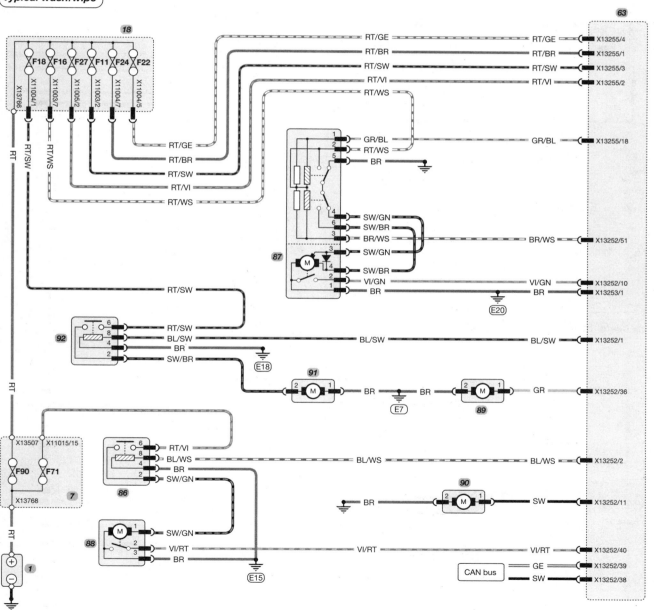

Colour codes

WS	White	**RT**	Red
BL	Blue	**GN**	Green
GR	Grey	**VI**	Violet
GE	Yellow	**SW**	Black
BR	Brown	**OR**	Orange

Key to items

1 Battery
7 Luggage compartment fusebox
  b = terminal 30g relay
  c = heated rear window relay
9 Car access system
18 Passenger compartment fusebox
93 LH heated washer jet
94 RH heated washer jet
95 Sunroof switch
96 Sunroof
97 Instrument cluster control unit

98 Wave trap 1
99 Wave trap 2
101 Washer fluid level switch
102 Handbrake switch
103 Coolant level switch
104 Heating and air conditioning control unit
105 Heater blower output stage
106 Heater blower
107 Heated rear window
108 Heated rear window lockout circuit

Diagram 9

H47188

Typical instruments & indicator lights

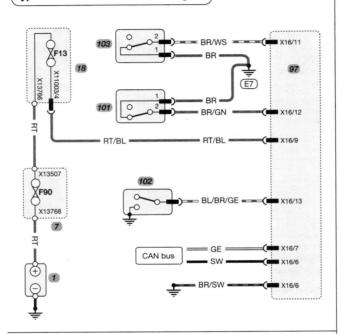

Typical heater blower

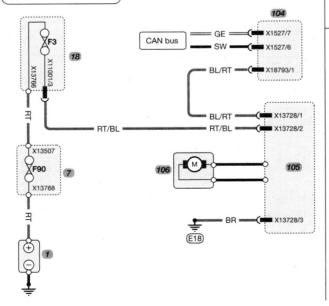

Typical heated rear window

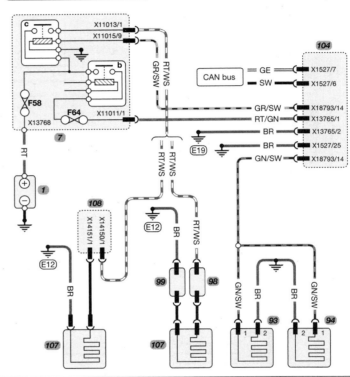

Typical electric sunroof

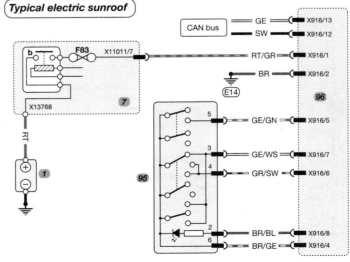

Colour codes

WS White **RT** Red
BL Blue **GN** Green
GR Grey **VI** Violet
GE Yellow **SW** Black
BR Brown **OR** Orange

Key to items

1 Battery
7 Luggage compartment fusebox
12 Safety and gateway control unit
18 Passenger compartment fusebox
63 Body control unit
111 Driver's switch cluster
112 Driver's window motor
113 Passenger's window motor
114 LH rear window motor
115 RH rear window motor

116 Passenger window switch
117 LH rear window switch
118 RH rear window switch
119 Driver's door control unit
120 Passenger's door control unit

Diagram 10

H47189

Typical electric windows

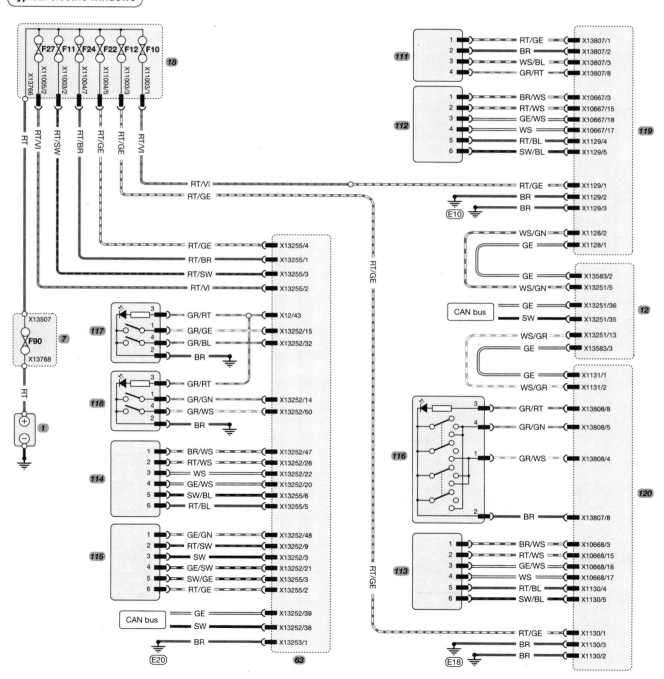

Colour codes

WS White **RT** Red
BL Blue **GN** Green
GR Grey **VI** Violet
GE Yellow **SW** Black
BR Brown **OR** Orange

Key to items

1 Battery
7 Luggage compartment fusebox
9 Car access system
12 Safety and gateway control unit
18 Passenger compartment fusebox
43 Lighting control unit
63 Body control unit
85 Luggage compartment lock motor
109 Driver's door lock assembly
110 Passenger's door lock assembly
119 Driver's door control unit
120 Passenger's door control unit
121 Luggage compartment exterior switch
122 Fuel filler flap lock
124 Luggage compartment interior release switch
125 LH rear door lock assembly
126 RH rear door lock assembly
127 Luggage compartment lock switch

Diagram 11

H47190

Typical central locking

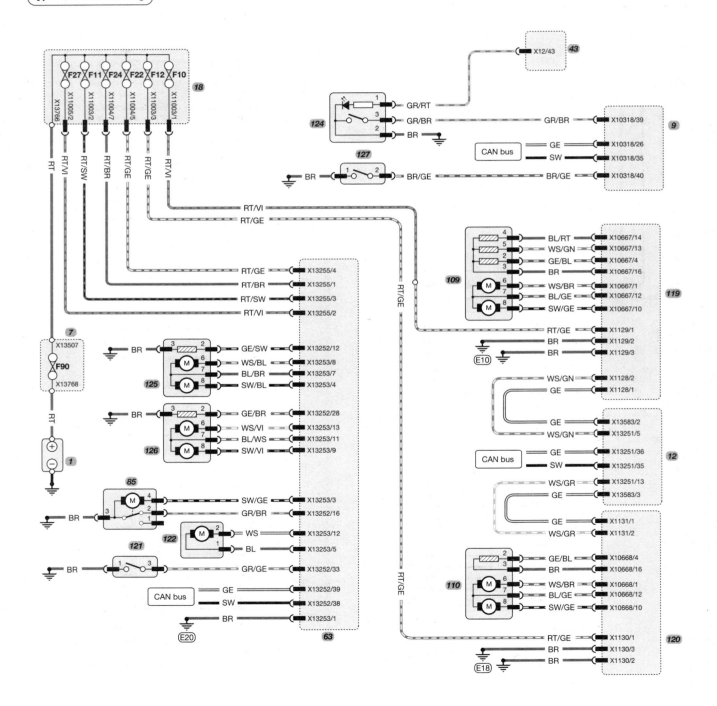

Dimensions and weights

Note: *All figures are approximate, and may vary according to model. Refer to manufacturer's data for exact figures.*

Dimensions
Overall length:
  Saloon . . . . 4841 mm
  Touring . . . . 4843 mm
Overall width* . . . . 2030 mm
Overall height (unladen):
  Saloon . . . . 1468 mm
  Touring . . . . 1492 mm
Wheelbase . . . . 2888 mm
* Including wing mirrors

Weights
Kerb weight*:
  Saloon . . . . 1585 to 1675 kg
  Touring . . . . 1675 to 1775 kg
Maximum gross vehicle weight:*
  Saloon . . . . 2050 to 2160 kg
  Touring . . . . 2200 to 2300 kg
  Maximum roof rack load. . . . . 100 kg
Maximum towing weight:**
  Unbraked trailer . . . . 750 kg
  Braked trailer . . . . 1800 to 2000 kg
* Depending on model and specification
** Refer to BMW dealer for exact recommendation

Fuel economy

Although depreciation is still the biggest part of the cost of motoring for most car owners, the cost of fuel is more immediately noticeable. These pages give some tips on how to get the best fuel economy.

Working it out

Manufacturer's figures

Car manufacturers are required by law to provide fuel consumption information on all new vehicles sold. These 'official' figures are obtained by simulating various driving conditions on a rolling road or a test track. Real life conditions are different, so the fuel consumption actually achieved may not bear much resemblance to the quoted figures.

How to calculate it

Many cars now have trip computers which will

display fuel consumption, both instantaneous and average. Refer to the owner's handbook for details of how to use these.

To calculate consumption yourself (and maybe to check that the trip computer is accurate), proceed as follows.

1. Fill up with fuel and note the mileage, or zero the trip recorder.
2. Drive as usual until you need to fill up again.
3. Note the amount of fuel required to refill the tank, and the mileage covered since the previous fill-up.
4. Divide the mileage by the amount of fuel used to obtain the consumption figure.

For example:

Mileage at first fill-up (a) = 27,903
Mileage at second fill-up (b) = 28,346
Mileage covered (b - a) = 443
Fuel required at second fill-up = 48.6 litres

The half-completed changeover to metric units in the UK means that we buy our fuel in litres, measure distances in miles and talk about fuel consumption in miles per gallon. There are two ways round this: the first is to convert the litres to gallons before doing the calculation (by dividing by 4.546, or see Table 1). So in the example:

48.6 litres ÷ 4.546 = 10.69 gallons
443 miles ÷ 10.69 gallons = 41.4 mpg

The second way is to calculate the consumption in miles per litre, then multiply that figure by 4.546 (or see Table 2).

So in the example, fuel consumption is:

443 miles ÷ 48.6 litres = 9.1 mpl
9.1 mpl x 4.546 = 41.4 mpg

The rest of Europe expresses fuel consumption in litres of fuel required to travel 100 km (l/100 km). For interest, the conversions are given in Table 3. In practice it doesn't matter what units you use, provided you know what your normal consumption is and can spot if it's getting better or worse.

Table 1: conversion of litres to Imperial gallons

litres	1	2	3	4	5	10	20	30	40	50	60	70
gallons	0.22	0.44	0.66	0.88	1.10	2.24	4.49	6.73	8.98	11.22	13.47	15.71

Table 2: conversion of miles per litre to miles per gallon

miles per litre	5	6	7	8	9	10	11	12	13	14
miles per gallon	23	27	32	36	41	46	50	55	59	64

Table 3: conversion of litres per 100 km to miles per gallon

litres per 100 km	4	4.5	5	5.5	6	6.5	7	8	9	10
miles per gallon	71	63	56	51	47	43	40	35	31	28

Maintenance

A well-maintained car uses less fuel and creates less pollution. In particular:

Filters

Change air and fuel filters at the specified intervals.

Oil

Use a good quality oil of the lowest viscosity specified by the vehicle manufacturer (see *Lubricants and fluids*). Check the level often and be careful not to overfill.

Spark plugs

When applicable, renew at the specified intervals.

Tyres

Check tyre pressures regularly. Under-inflated tyres have an increased rolling resistance. It is generally safe to use the higher pressures specified for full load conditions even when not fully laden, but keep an eye on the centre band of tread for signs of wear due to over-inflation.

When buying new tyres, consider the 'fuel saving' models which most manufacturers include in their ranges.

Driving style

Acceleration

Acceleration uses more fuel than driving at a steady speed. The best technique with modern cars is to accelerate reasonably briskly to the desired speed, changing up through the gears as soon as possible without making the engine labour.

Air conditioning

Air conditioning absorbs quite a bit of energy from the engine – typically 3 kW (4 hp) or so. The effect on fuel consumption is at its worst in slow traffic. Switch it off when not required.

Anticipation

Drive smoothly and try to read the traffic flow so as to avoid unnecessary acceleration and braking.

Automatic transmission

When accelerating in an automatic, avoid depressing the throttle so far as to make the transmission hold onto lower gears at higher speeds. Don't use the 'Sport' setting, if applicable.

When stationary with the engine running, select 'N' or 'P'. When moving, keep your left foot away from the brake.

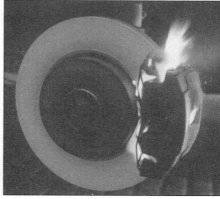

Braking

Braking converts the car's energy of motion into heat – essentially, it is wasted. Obviously some braking is always going to be necessary, but with good anticipation it is surprising how much can be avoided, especially on routes that you know well.

Carshare

Consider sharing lifts to work or to the shops. Even once a week will make a difference.

Electrical loads

Electricity is 'fuel' too; the alternator which charges the battery does so by converting some of the engine's energy of motion into electrical energy. The more electrical accessories are in use, the greater the load on the alternator. Switch off big consumers like the heated rear window when not required.

Freewheeling

Freewheeling (coasting) in neutral with the engine switched off is dangerous. The effort required to operate power-assisted brakes and steering increases when the engine is not running, with a potential lack of control in emergency situations.

In any case, modern fuel injection systems automatically cut off the engine's fuel supply on the overrun (moving and in gear, but with the accelerator pedal released).

Gadgets

Bolt-on devices claiming to save fuel have been around for nearly as long as the motor car itself. Those which worked were rapidly adopted as standard equipment by the vehicle manufacturers. Others worked only in certain situations, or saved fuel only at the expense of unacceptable effects on performance, driveability or the life of engine components.

The most effective fuel saving gadget is the driver's right foot.

Journey planning

Combine (eg) a trip to the supermarket with a visit to the recycling centre and the DIY store, rather than making separate journeys.

When possible choose a travelling time outside rush hours.

Load

The more heavily a car is laden, the greater the energy required to accelerate it to a given speed. Remove heavy items which you don't need to carry.

One load which is often overlooked is the contents of the fuel tank. A tankful of fuel (55 litres / 12 gallons) weighs 45 kg (100 lb) or so. Just half filling it may be worthwhile.

Lost?

At the risk of stating the obvious, if you're going somewhere new, have details of the route to hand. There's not much point in achieving record mpg if you also go miles out of your way.

Parking

If possible, carry out any reversing or turning manoeuvres when you arrive at a parking space so that you can drive straight out when you leave. Manoeuvering when the engine is cold uses a lot more fuel.

Driving around looking for free on-street parking may cost more in fuel than buying a car park ticket.

Premium fuel

Most major oil companies (and some supermarkets) have premium grades of fuel which are several pence a litre dearer than the standard grades. Reports vary, but the consensus seems to be that if these fuels improve economy at all, they do not do so by enough to justify their extra cost.

Roof rack

When loading a roof rack, try to produce a wedge shape with the narrow end at the front. Any cover should be securely fastened – if it flaps it's creating turbulence and absorbing energy.

Remove roof racks and boxes when not in use – they increase air resistance and can create a surprising amount of noise.

Short journeys

The engine is at its least efficient, and wear is highest, during the first few miles after a cold start. Consider walking, cycling or using public transport.

Speed

The engine is at its most efficient when running at a steady speed and load at the rpm where it develops maximum torque. (You can find this figure in the car's handbook.) For most cars this corresponds to between 55 and 65 mph in top gear.

Above the optimum cruising speed, fuel consumption starts to rise quite sharply. A car travelling at 80 mph will typically be using 30% more fuel than at 60 mph.

Supermarket fuel

It may be cheap but is it any good? In the UK all supermarket fuel must meet the relevant British Standard. The major oil companies will say that their branded fuels have better additive packages which may stop carbon and other deposits building up. A reasonable compromise might be to use one tank of branded fuel to three or four from the supermarket.

Switch off when stationary

Switch off the engine if you look like being stationary for more than 30 seconds or so. This is good for the environment as well as for your pocket. Be aware though that frequent restarts are hard on the battery and the starter motor.

Windows

Driving with the windows open increases air turbulence around the vehicle. Closing the windows promotes smooth airflow and

reduced resistance. The faster you go, the more significant this is.

And finally . . .

Driving techniques associated with good fuel economy tend to involve moderate acceleration and low top speeds. Be considerate to the needs of other road users who may need to make brisker progress; even if you do not agree with them this is not an excuse to be obstructive.

Safety must always take precedence over economy, whether it is a question of accelerating hard to complete an overtaking manoeuvre, killing your speed when confronted with a potential hazard or switching the lights on when it starts to get dark.

Conversion factors

Length (distance)

Inches (in)	x 25.4	=	Millimetres (mm)	x 0.0394 =	Inches (in)
Feet (ft)	x 0.305	=	Metres (m)	x 3.281 =	Feet (ft)
Miles	x 1.609	=	Kilometres (km)	x 0.621 =	Miles

Volume (capacity)

Cubic inches (cu in; in³)	x 16.387	=	Cubic centimetres (cc; cm³)	x 0.061 =	Cubic inches (cu in; in³)
Imperial pints (Imp pt)	x 0.568	=	Litres (l)	x 1.76 =	Imperial pints (Imp pt)
Imperial quarts (Imp qt)	x 1.137	=	Litres (l)	x 0.88 =	Imperial quarts (Imp qt)
Imperial quarts (Imp qt)	x 1.201	=	US quarts (US qt)	x 0.833 =	Imperial quarts (Imp qt)
US quarts (US qt)	x 0.946	=	Litres (l)	x 1.057 =	US quarts (US qt)
Imperial gallons (Imp gal)	x 4.546	=	Litres (l)	x 0.22 =	Imperial gallons (Imp gal)
Imperial gallons (Imp gal)	x 1.201	=	US gallons (US gal)	x 0.833 =	Imperial gallons (Imp gal)
US gallons (US gal)	x 3.785	=	Litres (l)	x 0.264 =	US gallons (US gal)

Mass (weight)

Ounces (oz)	x 28.35	=	Grams (g)	x 0.035 =	Ounces (oz)
Pounds (lb)	x 0.454	=	Kilograms (kg)	x 2.205 =	Pounds (lb)

Force

Ounces-force (ozf; oz)	x 0.278	=	Newtons (N)	x 3.6 =	Ounces-force (ozf; oz)
Pounds-force (lbf; lb)	x 4.448	=	Newtons (N)	x 0.225 =	Pounds-force (lbf; lb)
Newtons (N)	x 0.1	=	Kilograms-force (kgf; kg)	x 9.81 =	Newtons (N)

Pressure

Pounds-force per square inch (psi; lbf/in²; lb/in²)	x 0.070	=	Kilograms-force per square centimetre (kgf/cm²; kg/cm²)	x 14.223 =	Pounds-force per square inch (psi; lbf/in²; lb/in²)
Pounds-force per square inch (psi; lbf/in²; lb/in²)	x 0.068	=	Atmospheres (atm)	x 14.696 =	Pounds-force per square inch (psi; lbf/in²; lb/in²)
Pounds-force per square inch (psi; lbf/in²; lb/in²)	x 0.069	=	Bars	x 14.5 =	Pounds-force per square inch (psi; lbf/in²; lb/in²)
Pounds-force per square inch (psi; lbf/in²; lb/in²)	x 6.895	=	Kilopascals (kPa)	x 0.145 =	Pounds-force per square inch (psi; lbf/in²; lb/in²)
Kilopascals (kPa)	x 0.01	=	Kilograms-force per square centimetre (kgf/cm²; kg/cm²)	x 98.1 =	Kilopascals (kPa)
Millibar (mbar)	x 100	=	Pascals (Pa)	x 0.01 =	Millibar (mbar)
Millibar (mbar)	x 0.0145	=	Pounds-force per square inch (psi; lbf/in²; lb/in²)	x 68.947 =	Millibar (mbar)
Millibar (mbar)	x 0.75	=	Millimetres of mercury (mmHg)	x 1.333 =	Millibar (mbar)
Millibar (mbar)	x 0.401	=	Inches of water (inH₂O)	x 2.491 =	Millibar (mbar)
Millimetres of mercury (mmHg)	x 0.535	=	Inches of water (inH₂O)	x 1.868 =	Millimetres of mercury (mmHg)
Inches of water (inH₂O)	x 0.036	=	Pounds-force per square inch (psi; lbf/in²; lb/in²)	x 27.68 =	Inches of water (inH₂O)

Torque (moment of force)

Pounds-force inches (lbf in; lb in)	x 1.152	=	Kilograms-force centimetre (kgf cm; kg cm)	x 0.868 =	Pounds-force inches (lbf in; lb in)
Pounds-force inches (lbf in; lb in)	x 0.113	=	Newton metres (Nm)	x 8.85 =	Pounds-force inches (lbf in; lb in)
Pounds-force inches (lbf in; lb in)	x 0.083	=	Pounds-force feet (lbf ft; lb ft)	x 12 =	Pounds-force inches (lbf in; lb in)
Pounds-force feet (lbf ft; lb ft)	x 0.138	=	Kilograms-force metres (kgf m; kg m)	x 7.233 =	Pounds-force feet (lbf ft; lb ft)
Pounds-force feet (lbf ft; lb ft)	x 1.356	=	Newton metres (Nm)	x 0.738 =	Pounds-force feet (lbf ft; lb ft)
Newton metres (Nm)	x 0.102	=	Kilograms-force metres (kgf m; kg m)	x 9.804 =	Newton metres (Nm)

Power

Horsepower (hp)	x 745.7	=	Watts (W)	x 0.0013 =	Horsepower (hp)

Velocity (speed)

Miles per hour (miles/hr; mph)	x 1.609	=	Kilometres per hour (km/hr; kph)	x 0.621 =	Miles per hour (miles/hr; mph)

Fuel consumption*

Miles per gallon, Imperial (mpg)	x 0.354	=	Kilometres per litre (km/l)	x 2.825 =	Miles per gallon, Imperial (mpg)
Miles per gallon, US (mpg)	x 0.425	=	Kilometres per litre (km/l)	x 2.352 =	Miles per gallon, US (mpg)

Temperature

Degrees Fahrenheit = (°C x 1.8) + 32   Degrees Celsius (Degrees Centigrade; °C) = (°F - 32) x 0.56

It is common practice to convert from miles per gallon (mpg) to litres/100 kilometres (l/100km), where mpg x l/100 km = 282

Spare parts are available from many sources, including maker's appointed garages, accessory shops, and motor factors. To be sure of obtaining the correct parts, it will sometimes be necessary to quote the vehicle identification number. If possible, it can also be useful to take the old parts along for positive identification. Items such as starter motors and alternators may be available under a service exchange scheme – any parts returned should be clean.

Our advice regarding spare parts is as follows.

Officially appointed garages

This is the best source of parts which are peculiar to your car, and which are not otherwise generally available (eg, badges, interior trim, certain body panels, etc). It is also the only place at which you should buy parts if the car is still under warranty.

Accessory shops

These are very good places to buy materials and components needed for the maintenance of your car (oil, air and fuel filters, light bulbs, drivebelts, greases, brake pads, touch-up paint, etc). Components of this nature sold by a reputable shop are usually of the same standard as those used by the car manufacturer.

Besides components, these shops also sell tools and general accessories, usually have convenient opening hours, charge lower prices, and can often be found close to home. Some accessory shops have parts counters where components needed for almost any repair job can be purchased or ordered.

Motor factors

Good factors will stock all the more important components which wear out comparatively quickly, and can sometimes supply individual components needed for the overhaul of a larger assembly (eg, brake seals and hydraulic parts, bearing shells, pistons, valves). They may also handle work such as cylinder block reboring, crankshaft regrinding, etc.

Engine reconditioners

These specialise in engine overhaul and can also supply components. It is recommended that the establishment is a member of the Federation of Engine Re-Manufacturers, or a similar society.

Tyre and exhaust specialists

These outlets may be independent, or members of a local or national chain. They frequently offer competitive prices when compared with a main dealer or local garage, but it will pay to obtain several quotes before making a decision. When researching prices, also ask what extras may be added – for instance fitting a new valve, balancing the wheel and tyre disposal all both commonly charged on top of the price of a new tyre.

Other sources

Beware of parts or materials obtained from market stalls, car boot sales, on-line auctions or similar outlets. Such items are not invariably sub-standard, but there is little chance of compensation if they do prove unsatisfactory. In the case of safety-critical components such as brake pads, there is the risk not only of financial loss, but also of an accident causing injury or death.

Second-hand components or assemblies obtained from a car breaker can be a good buy in some circumstances, but this sort of purchase is best made by the experienced DIY mechanic.

Vehicle identification

Modifications are a continuing and unpublicised process in vehicle manufacture, quite apart from major model changes. Spare parts manuals and lists are compiled upon a numerical basis, the individual vehicle identification numbers being essential to correct identification of the component concerned.

When ordering spare parts, always give as much information as possible. Quote the car model, year of manufacture and registration, chassis and engine numbers as appropriate.

The *Vehicle Identification Number (VIN)* plate is stamped onto the right-hand suspension turret in the engine compartment, stamped onto a plate in the right-hand corner of the engine compartment, and visible through the passenger side of the windscreen (**see illustrations**).

The *engine number* is stamped on the left-hand face of the cylinder block near the base of the oil level dipstick.

The VIN is stamped onto the right-hand suspension turret in the engine compartment . . .

. . . onto a plate in the right-hand front corner of the engine compartment . . .

. . . and is visible through the passenger side of the windscreen

Whenever servicing, repair or overhaul work is carried out on the car or its components, observe the following procedures and instructions. This will assist in carrying out the operation efficiently and to a professional standard of workmanship.

Joint mating faces and gaskets

When separating components at their mating faces, never insert screwdrivers or similar implements into the joint between the faces in order to prise them apart. This can cause severe damage which results in oil leaks, coolant leaks, etc upon reassembly. Separation is usually achieved by tapping along the joint with a soft-faced hammer in order to break the seal. However, note that this method may not be suitable where dowels are used for component location.

Where a gasket is used between the mating faces of two components, a new one must be fitted on reassembly; fit it dry unless otherwise stated in the repair procedure. Make sure that the mating faces are clean and dry, with all traces of old gasket removed. When cleaning a joint face, use a tool which is unlikely to score or damage the face, and remove any burrs or nicks with an oilstone or fine file.

Make sure that tapped holes are cleaned with a pipe cleaner, and keep them free of jointing compound, if this is being used, unless specifically instructed otherwise.

Ensure that all orifices, channels or pipes are clear, and blow through them, preferably using compressed air.

Oil seals

Oil seals can be removed by levering them out with a wide flat-bladed screwdriver or similar implement. Alternatively, a number of self-tapping screws may be screwed into the seal, and these used as a purchase for pliers or some similar device in order to pull the seal free.

Whenever an oil seal is removed from its working location, either individually or as part of an assembly, it should be renewed.

The very fine sealing lip of the seal is easily damaged, and will not seal if the surface it contacts is not completely clean and free from scratches, nicks or grooves. If the original sealing surface of the component cannot be restored, and the manufacturer has not made provision for slight relocation of the seal relative to the sealing surface, the component should be renewed.

Protect the lips of the seal from any surface which may damage them in the course of fitting. Use tape or a conical sleeve where possible. Where indicated, lubricate the seal lips with oil before fitting and, on dual-lipped seals, fill the space between the lips with grease.

Unless otherwise stated, oil seals must be fitted with their sealing lips toward the lubricant to be sealed.

Use a tubular drift or block of wood of the appropriate size to install the seal and, if the seal housing is shouldered, drive the seal down to the shoulder. If the seal housing is unshouldered, the seal should be fitted with its face flush with the housing top face (unless otherwise instructed).

Screw threads and fastenings

Seized nuts, bolts and screws are quite a common occurrence where corrosion has set in, and the use of penetrating oil or releasing fluid will often overcome this problem if the offending item is soaked for a while before attempting to release it. The use of an impact driver may also provide a means of releasing such stubborn fastening devices, when used in conjunction with the appropriate screwdriver bit or socket. If none of these methods works, it may be necessary to resort to the careful application of heat, or the use of a hacksaw or nut splitter device. Before resorting to extreme methods, check that you are not dealing with a left-hand thread!

Studs are usually removed by locking two nuts together on the threaded part, and then using a spanner on the lower nut to unscrew the stud. Studs or bolts which have broken off below the surface of the component in which they are mounted can sometimes be removed using a stud extractor.

Always ensure that a blind tapped hole is completely free from oil, grease, water or other fluid before installing the bolt or stud. Failure to do this could cause the housing to crack due to the hydraulic action of the bolt or stud as it is screwed in.

For some screw fastenings, notably cylinder head bolts or nuts, torque wrench settings are no longer specified for the latter stages of tightening, "angle-tightening" being called up instead. Typically, a fairly low torque wrench setting will be applied to the bolts/nuts in the correct sequence, followed by one or more stages of tightening through specified angles.

When checking or retightening a nut or bolt to a specified torque setting, slacken the nut or bolt by a quarter of a turn, and then retighten to the specified setting. However, this should not be attempted where angular tightening has been used.

Locknuts, locktabs and washers

Any fastening which will rotate against a component or housing during tightening should always have a washer between it and the relevant component or housing.

Spring or split washers should always be renewed when they are used to lock a critical component such as a big-end bearing retaining bolt or nut. Locktabs which are folded over to retain a nut or bolt should always be renewed.

Self-locking nuts can be re-used in non-critical areas, providing resistance can be felt when the locking portion passes over the bolt or stud thread. However, it should be noted that self-locking stiffnuts tend to lose their effectiveness after long periods of use, and should then be renewed as a matter of course.

Split pins must always be replaced with new ones of the correct size for the hole.

When thread-locking compound is found on the threads of a fastener which is to be re-used, it should be cleaned off with a wire brush and solvent, and fresh compound applied on reassembly.

Special tools

Some repair procedures in this manual entail the use of special tools such as a press, two or three-legged pullers, spring compressors, etc. Wherever possible, suitable readily-available alternatives to the manufacturer's special tools are described, and are shown in use. In some instances, where no alternative is possible, it has been necessary to resort to the use of a manufacturer's tool, and this has been done for reasons of safety as well as the efficient completion of the repair operation. Unless you are highly-skilled and have a thorough understanding of the procedures described, never attempt to bypass the use of any special tool when the procedure described specifies its use. Not only is there a very great risk of personal injury, but expensive damage could be caused to the components involved.

Environmental considerations

When disposing of used engine oil, brake fluid, antifreeze, etc, give due consideration to any detrimental environmental effects. Do not, for instance, pour any of the above liquids down drains into the general sewage system, or onto the ground to soak away, as this is likely to pollute your local environment. Many local council refuse tips provide a facility for waste oil disposal, as do some garages. You can find your nearest disposal point by calling the Environment Agency on 03708 506 506 or by visiting www.oilbankline.org.uk.

Note: It is illegal and anti-social to dump oil down the drain. To find the location of your local oil recycling bank, call 03708 506 506 or visit www.oilbankline.org.uk.

When carrying out any kind of work, raise the vehicle using a hydraulic (or 'trolley') jack, and always supplement the jack with axle stands positioned under the vehicle jacking points.

When using a hydraulic jack or axle stands, always position the jack head or axle stand head under the relevant rubber lifting blocks. These are situated directly underneath the vehicle jack location holes in the sill – the vehicle can also be raised with a trolley jack positioned under the jacking point on the front subframe, and under the rear differential (not the end cover) **(see illustration)**.

The jack available with the vehicle locates in the holes provided in the sill. Ensure that the jack head is correctly engaged before attempting to raise the vehicle. The locations are indicated by triangular marks in the sills each side.

Never work under, around, or near a raised vehicle, unless it is adequately supported in at least two places.

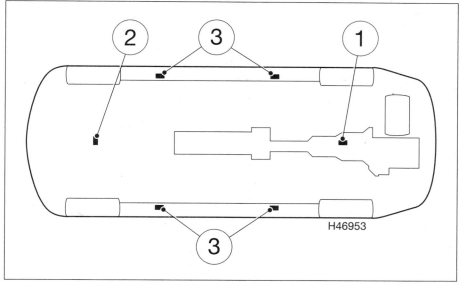

Vehicle jacking points

1 Rear differential 2 Jacking point on front subframe 3 Side jacking points

Infotainment unit anti-theft system

The Infotainment unit fitted as standard equipment by BMW is equipped with a built-in security code, to deter thieves. If the power source to the unit is cut, the anti-theft system will activate. Even if the power source is immediately reconnected, the unit may not function until the correct security code has been entered. Therefore if you do not know the correct security code for the unit, **do not** disconnect the battery negative lead, or remove the unit from the vehicle.

The procedure for reprogramming a unit that has been disconnected from its power supply varies from model to model – consult the handbook supplied with the unit for specific details or refer to your BMW dealer.

Introduction

A selection of good tools is a fundamental requirement for anyone contemplating the maintenance and repair of a motor vehicle. For the owner who does not possess any, their purchase will prove a considerable expense, offsetting some of the savings made by doing-it-yourself. However, provided that the tools purchased meet the relevant national safety standards and are of good quality, they will last for many years and prove an extremely worthwhile investment.

To help the average owner to decide which tools are needed to carry out the various tasks detailed in this manual, we have compiled three lists of tools under the following headings: *Maintenance and minor repair, Repair and overhaul,* and *Special.* Newcomers to practical mechanics should start off with the *Maintenance and minor repair* tool kit, and confine themselves to the simpler jobs around the vehicle. Then, as confidence and experience grow, more difficult tasks can be undertaken, with extra tools being purchased as, and when, they are needed. In this way, a *Maintenance and minor repair* tool kit can be built up into a *Repair and overhaul* tool kit over a considerable period of time, without any major cash outlays. The experienced do-it-yourselfer will have a tool kit good enough for most repair and overhaul procedures, and will add tools from the *Special* category when it is felt that the expense is justified by the amount of use to which these tools will be put.

Maintenance and minor repair tool kit

The tools given in this list should be considered as a minimum requirement if routine maintenance, servicing and minor repair operations are to be undertaken. We recommend the purchase of combination spanners (ring one end, open-ended the other); although more expensive than open-ended ones, they do give the advantages of both types of spanner.

☐ *Combination spanners:*
   Metric - 8 to 19 mm inclusive
☐ *Adjustable spanner - 35 mm jaw (approx.)*
☐ *Spark plug spanner (with rubber insert) - petrol models*
☐ *Spark plug gap adjustment tool - petrol models*
☐ *Set of feeler gauges*
☐ *Brake bleed nipple spanner*
☐ *Screwdrivers:*
   Flat blade - 100 mm long x 6 mm dia
   Cross blade - 100 mm long x 6 mm dia
   Torx - various sizes (not all vehicles)
☐ *Combination pliers*
☐ *Hacksaw (junior)*
☐ *Tyre pump*
☐ *Tyre pressure gauge*
☐ *Oil can*
☐ *Oil filter removal tool (if applicable)*
☐ *Fine emery cloth*
☐ *Wire brush (small)*
☐ *Funnel (medium size)*
☐ *Sump drain plug key (not all vehicles)*

Repair and overhaul tool kit

These tools are virtually essential for anyone undertaking any major repairs to a motor vehicle, and are additional to those given in the *Maintenance and minor repair* list. Included in this list is a comprehensive set of sockets. Although these are expensive, they will be found invaluable as they are so versatile - particularly if various drives are included in the set. We recommend the half-inch square-drive type, as this can be used with most proprietary torque wrenches.

The tools in this list will sometimes need to be supplemented by tools from the *Special* list:

☐ *Sockets to cover range in previous list (including Torx sockets)*
☐ *Reversible ratchet drive (for use with sockets)*
☐ *Extension piece, 250 mm (for use with sockets)*
☐ *Universal joint (for use with sockets)*
☐ *Flexible handle or sliding T "breaker bar" (for use with sockets)*
☐ *Torque wrench (for use with sockets)*
☐ *Self-locking grips*
☐ *Ball pein hammer*
☐ *Soft-faced mallet (plastic or rubber)*
☐ *Screwdrivers:*
   Flat blade - long & sturdy, short (chubby), and narrow (electrician's) types
   Cross blade – long & sturdy, and short (chubby) types
☐ *Pliers:*
   Long-nosed
   Side cutters (electrician's)
   Circlip (internal and external)
☐ *Cold chisel - 25 mm*
☐ *Scriber*
☐ *Scraper*
☐ *Centre-punch*
☐ *Pin punch*
☐ *Hacksaw*
☐ *Brake hose clamp*
☐ *Brake/clutch bleeding kit*
☐ *Selection of twist drills*
☐ *Steel rule/straight-edge*
☐ *Allen keys (inc. splined/Torx type)*
☐ *Selection of files*
☐ *Wire brush*
☐ *Axle stands*
☐ *Jack (strong trolley or hydraulic type)*
☐ *Light with extension lead*
☐ *Universal electrical multi-meter*

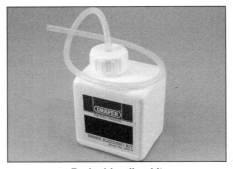

Sockets and reversible ratchet drive

Brake bleeding kit

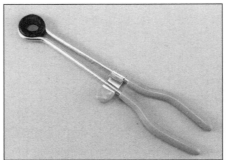

Torx key, socket and bit

Hose clamp

Angular-tightening gauge

Special tools

The tools in this list are those which are not used regularly, are expensive to buy, or which need to be used in accordance with their manufacturers' instructions. Unless relatively difficult mechanical jobs are undertaken frequently, it will not be economic to buy many of these tools. Where this is the case, you could consider clubbing together with friends (or joining a motorists' club) to make a joint purchase, or borrowing the tools against a deposit from a local garage or tool hire specialist.

The following list contains only those tools and instruments freely available to the public, and not those special tools produced by the vehicle manufacturer specifically for its dealer network. You will find occasional references to these manufacturers' special tools in the text of this manual. Generally, an alternative method of doing the job without the vehicle manufacturers' special tool is given. However, sometimes there is no alternative to using them. Where this is the case and the relevant tool cannot be bought or borrowed, you will have to entrust the work to a dealer.

- ☐ *Angular-tightening gauge*
- ☐ *Valve spring compressor*
- ☐ *Valve grinding tool*
- ☐ *Piston ring compressor*
- ☐ *Piston ring removal/installation tool*
- ☐ *Cylinder bore hone*
- ☐ *Balljoint separator*
- ☐ *Coil spring compressors (where applicable)*
- ☐ *Two/three-legged hub and bearing puller*
- ☐ *Impact screwdriver*
- ☐ *Micrometer and/or vernier calipers*
- ☐ *Dial gauge*
- ☐ *Tachometer*
- ☐ *Fault code reader*
- ☐ *Cylinder compression gauge*
- ☐ *Hand-operated vacuum pump and gauge*
- ☐ *Clutch plate alignment set*
- ☐ *Brake shoe steady spring cup removal tool*
- ☐ *Bush and bearing removal/installation set*
- ☐ *Stud extractors*
- ☐ *Tap and die set*
- ☐ *Lifting tackle*

Buying tools

Reputable motor accessory shops and superstores often offer excellent quality tools at discount prices, so it pays to shop around.

Remember, you don't have to buy the most expensive items on the shelf, but it is always advisable to steer clear of the very cheap tools. Beware of 'bargains' offered on market stalls, on-line or at car boot sales. There are plenty of good tools around at reasonable prices, but always aim to purchase items which meet the relevant national safety standards. If in doubt, ask the proprietor or manager of the shop for advice before making a purchase.

Care and maintenance of tools

Having purchased a reasonable tool kit, it is necessary to keep the tools in a clean and serviceable condition. After use, always wipe off any dirt, grease and metal particles using a clean, dry cloth, before putting the tools away. Never leave them lying around after they have been used. A simple tool rack on the garage or workshop wall for items such as screwdrivers and pliers is a good idea. Store all normal spanners and sockets in a metal box. Any measuring instruments, gauges, meters, etc, must be carefully stored where they cannot be damaged or become rusty.

Take a little care when tools are used. Hammer heads inevitably become marked, and screwdrivers lose the keen edge on their blades from time to time. A little timely attention with emery cloth or a file will soon restore items like this to a good finish.

Working facilities

Not to be forgotten when discussing tools is the workshop itself. If anything more than routine maintenance is to be carried out, a suitable working area becomes essential.

It is appreciated that many an owner-mechanic is forced by circumstances to remove an engine or similar item without the benefit of a garage or workshop. Having done this, any repairs should always be done under the cover of a roof.

Wherever possible, any dismantling should be done on a clean, flat workbench or table at a suitable working height.

Any workbench needs a vice; one with a jaw opening of 100 mm is suitable for most jobs. As mentioned previously, some clean dry storage space is also required for tools, as well as for any lubricants, cleaning fluids, touch-up paints etc, which become necessary.

Another item which may be required, and which has a much more general usage, is an electric drill with a chuck capacity of at least 8 mm. This, together with a good range of twist drills, is virtually essential for fitting accessories.

Last, but not least, always keep a supply of old newspapers and clean, lint-free rags available, and try to keep any working area as clean as possible.

Micrometers

Dial test indicator ("dial gauge")

Oil filter removal tool (strap wrench type)

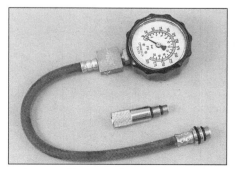

Compression tester

Fault code reader

This is a guide to getting your vehicle through the MOT test. Obviously it will not be possible to examine the vehicle to the same standard as the professional MOT tester. However, working through the following checks will enable you to identify any problem areas before submitting the vehicle for the test.

It has only been possible to summarise the test requirements here, based on the regulations in force at the time of printing. Test standards are becoming increasingly stringent, although there are some exemptions for older vehicles.

An assistant will be needed to help carry out some of these checks.

The checks have been sub-divided into four categories, as follows:

1 Checks carried out **FROM THE DRIVER'S SEAT**

2 Checks carried out **WITH THE VEHICLE ON THE GROUND**

3 Checks carried out **WITH THE VEHICLE RAISED AND THE WHEELS FREE TO TURN**

4 Checks carried out on **YOUR VEHICLE'S EXHAUST EMISSION SYSTEM**

---

1 Checks carried out **FROM THE DRIVER'S SEAT**

Handbrake

☐ Test the operation of the handbrake. Excessive travel (too many clicks) indicates incorrect brake or cable adjustment.
☐ Check that the handbrake cannot be released by tapping the lever sideways. Check the security of the lever mountings.

Footbrake

☐ Depress the brake pedal and check that it does not creep down to the floor, indicating a master cylinder fault. Release the pedal, wait a few seconds, then depress it again. If the pedal travels nearly to the floor before firm resistance is felt, brake adjustment or repair is necessary. If the pedal feels spongy, there is air in the hydraulic system which must be removed by bleeding.

☐ Check that the brake pedal is secure and in good condition. Check also for signs of fluid leaks on the pedal, floor or carpets, which would indicate failed seals in the brake master cylinder.
☐ Check the servo unit (when applicable) by operating the brake pedal several times, then keeping the pedal depressed and starting the engine. As the engine starts, the pedal will move down slightly. If not, the vacuum hose or the servo itself may be faulty.

Steering wheel and column

☐ Examine the steering wheel for fractures or looseness of the hub, spokes or rim.
☐ Move the steering wheel from side to side and then up and down. Check that the steering wheel is not loose on the column, indicating wear or a loose retaining nut. Continue moving the steering wheel as before, but also turn it slightly from left to right.
☐ Check that the steering wheel is not loose on the column, and that there is no abnormal movement of the steering wheel, indicating

wear in the column support bearings or couplings.

Windscreen, mirrors and sunvisor

☐ The windscreen must be free of cracks or other significant damage within the driver's field of view. (Small stone chips are acceptable.) Rear view mirrors must be secure, intact, and capable of being adjusted.

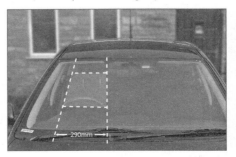

☐ The driver's sunvisor must be capable of being stored in the "up" position.

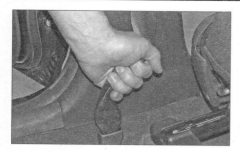

Seat belts and seats

Note: *The following checks are applicable to all seat belts, front and rear.*

☐ Examine the webbing of all the belts (including rear belts if fitted) for cuts, serious fraying or deterioration. Fasten and unfasten each belt to check the buckles. If applicable, check the retracting mechanism. Check the security of all seat belt mountings accessible from inside the vehicle.

☐ Seat belts with pre-tensioners, once activated, have a "flag" or similar showing on the seat belt stalk. This, in itself, is not a reason for test failure.

☐ The front seats themselves must be securely attached and the backrests must lock in the upright position.

Doors

☐ Both front doors must be able to be opened and closed from outside and inside, and must latch securely when closed.

2 Checks carried out WITH THE VEHICLE ON THE GROUND

Vehicle identification

☐ Number plates must be in good condition, secure and legible, with letters and numbers correctly spaced – spacing at (A) should be 33 mm and at (B) 11 mm.

☐ The VIN plate and/or homologation plate must be legible.

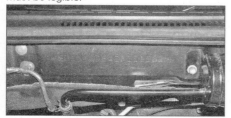

Electrical equipment

☐ Switch on the ignition and check the operation of the horn.

☐ Check the windscreen washers and wipers, examining the wiper blades; renew damaged or perished blades. Also check the operation of the stop-lights.

☐ Check the operation of the sidelights and number plate lights. The lenses and reflectors must be secure, clean and undamaged.

☐ Check the operation and alignment of the headlights. The headlight reflectors must not be tarnished and the lenses must be undamaged.

☐ Switch on the ignition and check the operation of the direction indicators (including the instrument panel tell-tale) and the hazard warning lights. Operation of the sidelights and stop-lights must not affect the indicators - if it does, the cause is usually a bad earth at the rear light cluster.

☐ Check the operation of the rear foglight(s), including the warning light on the instrument panel or in the switch.

☐ The ABS warning light must illuminate in accordance with the manufacturers' design. For most vehicles, the ABS warning light should illuminate when the ignition is switched on, and (if the system is operating properly) extinguish after a few seconds. Refer to the owner's handbook.

Footbrake

☐ Examine the master cylinder, brake pipes and servo unit for leaks, loose mountings, corrosion or other damage.

☐ The fluid reservoir must be secure and the fluid level must be between the upper (**A**) and lower (**B**) markings.

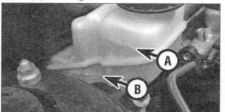

☐ Inspect both front brake flexible hoses for cracks or deterioration of the rubber. Turn the steering from lock to lock, and ensure that the hoses do not contact the wheel, tyre, or any part of the steering or suspension mechanism. With the brake pedal firmly depressed, check the hoses for bulges or leaks under pressure.

Steering and suspension

☐ Have your assistant turn the steering wheel from side to side slightly, up to the point where the steering gear just begins to transmit this movement to the roadwheels. Check for excessive free play between the steering wheel and the steering gear, indicating wear or insecurity of the steering column joints, the column-to-steering gear coupling, or the steering gear itself.

☐ Have your assistant turn the steering wheel more vigorously in each direction, so that the roadwheels just begin to turn. As this is done, examine all the steering joints, linkages, fittings and attachments. Renew any component that shows signs of wear or damage. On vehicles with power steering, check the security and condition of the steering pump, drivebelt and hoses.

☐ Check that the vehicle is standing level, and at approximately the correct ride height.

Shock absorbers

☐ Depress each corner of the vehicle in turn, then release it. The vehicle should rise and then settle in its normal position. If the vehicle continues to rise and fall, the shock absorber is defective. A shock absorber which has seized will also cause the vehicle to fail.

Exhaust system

☐ Start the engine. With your assistant holding a rag over the tailpipe, check the entire system for leaks. Repair or renew leaking sections.

3 Checks carried out **WITH THE VEHICLE RAISED AND THE WHEELS FREE TO TURN**

Jack up the front and rear of the vehicle, and securely support it on axle stands. Position the stands clear of the suspension assemblies. Ensure that the wheels are clear of the ground and that the steering can be turned from lock to lock.

Steering mechanism

☐ Have your assistant turn the steering from lock to lock. Check that the steering turns smoothly, and that no part of the steering mechanism, including a wheel or tyre, fouls any brake hose or pipe or any part of the body structure.
☐ Examine the steering rack rubber gaiters for damage or insecurity of the retaining clips. If power steering is fitted, check for signs of damage or leakage of the fluid hoses, pipes or connections. Also check for excessive stiffness or binding of the steering, a missing split pin or locking device, or severe corrosion of the body structure within 30 cm of any steering component attachment point.

Front and rear suspension and wheel bearings

☐ Starting at the front right-hand side, grasp the roadwheel at the 3 o'clock and 9 o'clock positions and rock gently but firmly. Check for free play or insecurity at the wheel bearings, suspension balljoints, or suspension mount-ings, pivots and attachments.
☐ Now grasp the wheel at the 12 o'clock and 6 o'clock positions and repeat the previous inspection. Spin the wheel, and check for roughness or tightness of the front wheel bearing.

☐ If excess free play is suspected at a component pivot point, this can be confirmed by using a large screwdriver or similar tool and levering between the mounting and the component attachment. This will confirm whether the wear is in the pivot bush, its retaining bolt, or in the mounting itself (the bolt holes can often become elongated).

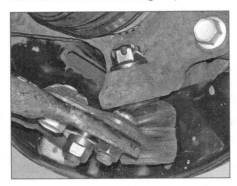

☐ Carry out all the above checks at the other front wheel, and then at both rear wheels.

Springs and shock absorbers

☐ Examine the suspension struts (when applicable) for serious fluid leakage, corrosion, or damage to the casing. Also check the security of the mounting points.
☐ If coil springs are fitted, check that the spring ends locate in their seats, and that the spring is not corroded, cracked or broken.
☐ If leaf springs are fitted, check that all leaves are intact, that the axle is securely attached to each spring, and that there is no deterioration of the spring eye mountings, bushes, and shackles.

☐ The same general checks apply to vehicles fitted with other suspension types, such as torsion bars, hydraulic displacer units, etc. Ensure that all mountings and attachments are secure, that there are no signs of excessive wear, corrosion or damage, and, on hydraulic types) that there are no fluid leaks or damaged pipes.
☐ Inspect the shock absorbers for signs of serious fluid leakage. Check for wear of the mounting bushes or attachments, or damage to the body of the unit.

Driveshafts (fwd vehicles only)

☐ Rotate each front wheel in turn and inspect the constant velocity joint gaiters for splits or damage. Also check that each driveshaft is straight and undamaged.

Braking system

☐ If possible without dismantling, check brake pad wear and disc condition. Ensure that the friction lining material has not worn excessively, (A) and that the discs are not fractured, pitted, scored or badly worn (B).

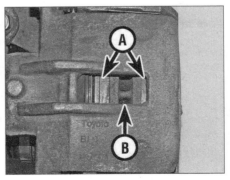

☐ Examine all the rigid brake pipes underneath the vehicle, and the flexible hose(s) at the rear. Look for corrosion, chafing or insecurity of the pipes, and for signs of bulging under pressure, chafing, splits or deterioration of the flexible hoses.
☐ Look for signs of fluid leaks at the brake calipers or on the brake backplates. Repair or renew leaking components.
☐ Slowly spin each wheel, while your assistant depresses and releases the footbrake. Ensure that each brake is operating and does not bind when the pedal is released.

□ Examine the handbrake mechanism, checking for frayed or broken cables, excessive corrosion, or wear or insecurity of the linkage. Check that the mechanism works on each relevant wheel, and releases fully, without binding.

□ It is not possible to test brake efficiency without special equipment, but a road test can be carried out later to check that the vehicle pulls up in a straight line.

Fuel and exhaust systems

□ Inspect the fuel tank (including the filler cap), fuel pipes, hoses and unions. All components must be secure and free from leaks.

□ Examine the exhaust system over its entire length, checking for any damaged, broken or missing mountings, security of the retaining clamps and rust or corrosion.

Wheels and tyres

□ Examine the sidewalls and tread area of each tyre in turn. Check for cuts, tears, lumps, bulges, separation of the tread, and exposure of the ply or cord due to wear or damage. Check that the tyre bead is correctly seated on the wheel rim, that the valve is sound and properly seated, and that the wheel is not distorted or damaged.

□ Check that the tyres are of the correct size for the vehicle, that they are of the same size

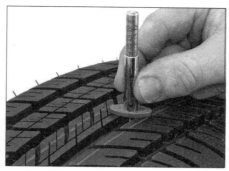

and type on each axle, and that the pressures are correct.

□ Check the tyre tread depth. The legal minimum at the time of writing is 1.6 mm over at least three-quarters of the tread width. Abnormal tread wear may indicate incorrect front wheel alignment.

Body corrosion

□ Check the condition of the entire vehicle structure for signs of corrosion in load-bearing areas. (These include chassis box sections, side sills, cross-members, pillars, and all suspension, steering, braking system and seat belt mountings and anchorages.) Any corrosion which has seriously reduced the thickness of a load-bearing area is likely to cause the vehicle to fail. In this case professional repairs are likely to be needed.

□ Damage or corrosion which causes sharp or otherwise dangerous edges to be exposed will also cause the vehicle to fail.

4 Checks carried out on YOUR VEHICLE'S EXHAUST EMISSION SYSTEM

Petrol models

□ The engine should be warmed up, and running well (ignition system in good order, air filter element clean, etc).

□ Before testing, run the engine at around 2500 rpm for 20 seconds. Let the engine drop to idle, and watch for smoke from the exhaust. If the idle speed is too high, or if dense blue or black smoke emerges for more than 5 seconds, the vehicle will fail. Typically, blue smoke signifies oil burning (engine wear); black smoke means unburnt fuel (dirty air cleaner element, or other fuel system fault).

□ An exhaust gas analyser for measuring carbon monoxide (CO) and hydrocarbons (HC) is now needed. If one cannot be hired or borrowed, have a local garage perform the check.

CO emissions (mixture)

□ The MOT tester has access to the CO limits for all vehicles. The CO level is measured at idle speed, and at 'fast idle' (2500 to 3000 rpm). The following limits are given as a general guide:

  At idle speed – Less than 0.5% CO
  At 'fast idle' – Less than 0.3% CO
  Lambda reading – 0.97 to 1.03

□ If the CO level is too high, this may point to poor maintenance, a fuel injection system problem, faulty lambda (oxygen) sensor or catalytic converter. Try an injector cleaning treatment, and check the vehicle's ECU for fault codes.

HC emissions

□ The MOT tester has access to HC limits for all vehicles. The HC level is measured at 'fast idle' (2500 to 3000 rpm). The following limits are given as a general guide:

  At 'fast idle' – Less then 200 ppm

□ Excessive HC emissions are typically caused by oil being burnt (worn engine), or by a blocked crankcase ventilation system ('breather'). If the engine oil is old and thin, an oil change may help. If the engine is running badly, check the vehicle's ECU for fault codes.

Diesel models

□ The only emission test for diesel engines is measuring exhaust smoke density, using a calibrated smoke meter. The test involves accelerating the engine at least 3 times to its maximum unloaded speed.

Note: *On engines with a timing belt, it is VITAL that the belt is in good condition before the test is carried out.*

□ With the engine warmed up, it is first purged by running at around 2500 rpm for 20 seconds. A governor check is then carried out, by slowly accelerating the engine to its maximum speed. After this, the smoke meter is connected, and the engine is accelerated quickly to maximum speed three times. If the smoke density is less than the limits given below, the vehicle will pass:

  Non-turbo vehicles: 2.5m-1
  Turbocharged vehicles: 3.0m-1

□ If excess smoke is produced, try fitting a new air cleaner element, or using an injector cleaning treatment. If the engine is running badly, where applicable, check the vehicle's ECU for fault codes. Also check the vehicle's EGR system, where applicable. At high mileages, the injectors may require professional attention.

Engine

☐ Engine fails to rotate when attempting to start
☐ Engine rotates, but will not start
☐ Engine difficult to start when cold
☐ Engine difficult to start when hot
☐ Starter motor noisy or rough in engagement
☐ Starter motor turns engine slowly
☐ Engine starts, but stops immediately
☐ Engine idles erratically
☐ Engine misfires at idle speed
☐ Engine misfires throughout the driving speed range
☐ Engine stalls
☐ Engine lacks power
☐ Engine backfires
☐ Oil pressure warning light illuminated with engine running
☐ Engine runs-on after switching off
☐ Engine noises

Cooling system

☐ Overheating
☐ Overcooling
☐ External coolant leakage
☐ Internal coolant leakage
☐ Corrosion

Fuel and exhaust systems

☐ Excessive fuel consumption
☐ Fuel leakage and/or fuel odour
☐ Excessive noise or fumes from exhaust system

Clutch

☐ Pedal travels to floor – no pressure or very little resistance
☐ Clutch fails to disengage (unable to select gears)
☐ Clutch slips (engine speed increases, with no increase in vehicle speed)
☐ Judder as clutch is engaged
☐ Noise when depressing or releasing clutch pedal

Manual transmission

☐ Noisy in neutral with engine running
☐ Noisy in one particular gear
☐ Difficulty engaging gears
☐ Jumps out of gear
☐ Vibration
☐ Lubricant leaks

Automatic transmission

☐ Fluid leakage
☐ Transmission fluid brown, or has burned smell
☐ General gear selection problems
☐ Transmission will not downshift (kickdown) with accelerator fully depressed
☐ Engine will not start in any gear, or starts in gears other than Park or Neutral
☐ Transmission slips, shifts roughly, is noisy, or has no drive in forward or reverse gears

Final drive and propeller shaft

☐ Vibration when accelerating and decelerating
☐ Low-pitched whining, increasing with road speed

Braking system

☐ Vehicle pulls to one side under braking
☐ Noise (grinding or high-pitched squeal) when brakes applied
☐ Excessive brake pedal travel
☐ Brake pedal feels spongy when depressed
☐ Excessive brake pedal effort required to stop vehicle
☐ Judder felt through brake pedal or steering wheel when braking
☐ Brakes binding

Suspension and steering systems

☐ Vehicle pulls to one side
☐ Wheel wobble and vibration
☐ Excessive pitching and/or rolling around corners, or during braking
☐ Wandering or general instability
☐ Excessively-stiff steering
☐ Excessive play in steering
☐ Lack of power assistance
☐ Tyre wear excessive

Electrical system

☐ Battery will only hold a charge for a few days
☐ Ignition/no-charge warning light remains illuminated with engine running
☐ Ignition/no-charge warning light fails to come on
☐ Lights inoperative
☐ Instrument readings inaccurate or erratic
☐ Horn inoperative, or unsatisfactory in operation
☐ Wipers inoperative, or unsatisfactory in operation
☐ Washers inoperative, or unsatisfactory in operation
☐ Electric windows inoperative, or unsatisfactory in operation
☐ Central locking system inoperative, or unsatisfactory in operation

Introduction

The vehicle owner who does his or her own maintenance according to the recommended service schedules should not have to use this section of the manual very often. Modern component reliability is such that, provided those items subject to wear or deterioration are inspected or renewed at the specified intervals, sudden failure is comparatively rare. Faults do not usually just happen as a result of sudden failure, but develop over a period of time. Major mechanical failures in particular are usually preceded by characteristic symptoms over hundreds or even thousands of miles. Those components which do occasionally fail without warning are often small and easily carried in the vehicle.

With any fault-finding, the first step is to decide where to begin investigations. Sometimes this is obvious, but on other occasions, a little detective work will be necessary. The owner who makes half a dozen haphazard adjustments or replacements may be successful in curing a fault (or its symptoms), but will be none the wiser if the fault recurs, and ultimately may have spent more time and money than was necessary. A calm and logical approach will be found to be more satisfactory in the long run. Always take into account any warning signs or abnormalities that may have been noticed in the period preceding the fault – power loss, high or low gauge readings, unusual smells,

etc – and remember that failure of components such as fuses or spark plugs may only be pointers to some underlying fault.

The pages which follow provide an easy-reference guide to the more common problems which may occur during the operation of the vehicle. These problems and their possible causes are grouped under headings denoting various components or systems, such as Engine, Cooling system, etc. The general Chapter which deals with the problem is also shown in brackets; refer to the relevant part of that Chapter for system-specific information. Whatever the fault, certain basic principles apply. These are as follows:

Verify the fault. This is simply a matter of

being sure that you know what the symptoms are before starting work. This is particularly important if you are investigating a fault for someone else, who may not have described it very accurately.

Don't overlook the obvious. For example, if the vehicle won't start, is there fuel in the tank? (Don't take anyone else's word on this particular point, and don't trust the fuel gauge either!) If an electrical fault is indicated, look for loose or broken wires before using the test gear.

Cure the disease, not the symptom. Substituting a flat battery with a fully-charged one will get you off the hard shoulder, but if the underlying cause is not attended to, the new battery will go the same way. Similarly, changing oil-fouled spark plugs for a new set will get you moving again, but remember that the reason for the fouling (if it wasn't simply an incorrect grade of plug) will have to be established and corrected.

Don't take anything for granted. Particularly, don't forget that a 'new' component may itself be defective (especially if it's been rattling around in the boot for months), and don't leave components out of a fault diagnosis sequence just because they are new or recently-fitted. When you do finally diagnose a difficult fault, you'll probably realise that all the evidence was there from the start.

Diesel fault diagnosis

The majority of starting problems on small diesel engines are electrical in origin. The mechanic who is familiar with petrol engines but less so with diesel may be inclined to view the diesel's injectors and pump in the same light as the spark plugs and distributor, but this is generally a mistake.

When investigating complaints of difficult starting for someone else, make sure that the correct starting procedure is understood and is being followed. Some drivers are unaware of the significance of the preheating warning light – many modern engines are sufficiently forgiving for this not to matter in mild weather, but with the onset of winter, problems begin. Glow plugs in particular are often neglected – just one faulty plug will make cold-weather starting very difficult.

As a rule of thumb, if the engine is difficult to start but runs well when it has finally got going, the problem is electrical (battery, starter motor or preheating system). If poor performance is combined with difficult starting, the problem is likely to be in the fuel system. The low-pressure (supply) side of the fuel system should be checked before suspecting the injectors and high-pressure pump. The most common fuel supply problem is air getting into the system, and any pipe from the fuel tank forwards must be scrutinised if air leakage is suspected.

Engine

Engine fails to rotate when attempting to start

☐ Battery terminal connections loose or corroded (*Weekly checks*)
☐ Battery discharged or faulty (Chapter 5)
☐ Broken, loose or disconnected wiring in the starting circuit (Chapter 5)
☐ Defective starter solenoid or switch (Chapter 5)
☐ Defective starter motor (Chapter 5)
☐ Starter pinion or flywheel ring gear teeth loose or broken (Chapter 2 or 5)
☐ Engine earth strap broken or disconnected (Chapter 5 or 12)

Engine rotates, but will not start

☐ Fuel tank empty
☐ Battery discharged (engine rotates slowly) (Chapter 5)
☐ Battery terminal connections loose or corroded (*Weekly checks*)
☐ Air filter element dirty or clogged (Chapter 1)
☐ Low cylinder compressions (Chapter 2)
☐ Major mechanical failure (eg, broken timing chain) (Chapter 2)
☐ Fuel injection system fault (Chapter 4)

Engine difficult to start when cold

☐ Battery discharged (Chapter 5)
☐ Battery terminal connections loose or corroded (*Weekly checks*)
☐ Air filter element dirty or clogged (Chapter 1)
☐ Low cylinder compressions (Chapter 2)
☐ Fuel injection system fault (Chapter 4)

Engine difficult to start when hot

☐ Battery discharged (Chapter 5)
☐ Battery terminal connections loose or corroded (*Weekly checks*)
☐ Air filter element dirty or clogged (Chapter 1)
☐ Fuel injection system fault (Chapter 4)

Starter motor noisy or excessively-rough in engagement

☐ Starter pinion or flywheel ring gear teeth loose or broken (Chapter 2 or 5)
☐ Starter motor mounting bolts loose or missing (Chapter 5)
☐ Starter motor internal components worn or damaged (Chapter 5)

Starter motor turns engine slowly

☐ Battery discharged (Chapter 5)
☐ Battery terminal connections loose or corroded (*Weekly checks*)
☐ Earth strap broken or disconnected (Chapter 5)
☐ Starter motor wiring loose (Chapter 5)
☐ Starter motor internal fault (Chapter 5)

Engine starts, but stops immediately

☐ Dirt in fuel system (Chapter 4)
☐ Fuel injector fault (Chapter 4)
☐ Fuel pump fault (Chapter 4)
☐ Vacuum leak at throttle body, inlet manifold or hoses (Chapters 2 and 4)

Engine idles erratically

☐ Air filter element clogged (Chapter 1)
☐ Air in fuel system (Chapter 4)
☐ Vacuum leak at throttle body, inlet manifold or hoses (Chapters 2 and 4)
☐ Uneven or low cylinder compressions (Chapter 2)
☐ Timing chain incorrectly fitted or tensioned (Chapter 2)
☐ Camshaft lobes worn (Chapter 2)
☐ Faulty fuel injector(s) (Chapter 4)

Engine misfires at idle speed

☐ Faulty fuel injector(s) (Chapter 4)
☐ Uneven or low cylinder compressions (Chapter 2)
☐ Disconnected, leaking, or perished crankcase ventilation hoses (Chapter 4)
☐ Vacuum leak at the throttle body, inlet manifold or associated hoses (Chapter 4)

Engine misfires throughout the driving speed range

☐ Fuel filter choked (Chapter 1)
☐ Fuel pump faulty, or delivery pressure low (Chapter 4)
☐ Fuel tank vent blocked, or fuel pipes restricted (Chapter 4)
☐ Uneven or low cylinder compressions (Chapter 2)

Engine (continued)

Engine stalls

- [ ] Fuel filter choked (Chapter 1)
- [ ] Blocked injector/fuel injection system fault (Chapter 4)
- [ ] Fuel pump faulty, or delivery pressure low (Chapter 4)
- [ ] Vacuum leak at the throttle body, inlet manifold or associated hoses (Chapter 4)
- [ ] Fuel tank vent blocked, or fuel pipes restricted (Chapter 4)

Engine lacks power

- [ ] Fuel filter choked (Chapter 1)
- [ ] Timing chain incorrectly fitted or tensioned (Chapter 2)
- [ ] Fuel pump faulty, or delivery pressure low (Chapter 4)
- [ ] Vacuum leak at the throttle body, inlet manifold or associated hoses (Chapter 4)
- [ ] Uneven or low cylinder compressions (Chapter 2)
- [ ] Brakes binding (Chapters 1 and 9)
- [ ] Clutch slipping (Chapter 6)
- [ ] Blocked injector/fuel injection system fault (Chapter 4)

Engine backfires

- [ ] Timing chain incorrectly fitted (Chapter 2)
- [ ] Faulty injector/fuel injection system fault (Chapter 4).

Oil pressure warning light illuminated with engine running

Note: *Low oil pressure in a high-mileage engine at tickover is not necessarily a cause for concern. Sudden pressure loss at speed is far more significant. In any event, check the gauge or pressure sensor before condemning the engine.*

- [ ] Low oil level, or incorrect oil grade (*Weekly checks*)
- [ ] Faulty oil pressure sensor (Chapter 2)
- [ ] Worn engine bearings and/or oil pump (Chapter 2)

- [ ] Excessively high engine operating temperature (Chapter 3)
- [ ] Oil pressure relief valve defective (Chapter 2)
- [ ] Oil pick-up strainer clogged (Chapter 2)

Engine runs-on after switching off

- [ ] Excessive carbon build-up in engine (Chapter 2)
- [ ] Excessively high engine operating temperature (Chapter 3)

Engine noises

Pre-ignition (pinking) or knocking during acceleration or under load

- [ ] Excessive carbon build-up in engine (Chapter 2)
- [ ] Faulty fuel injector(s) (Chapter 4)

Whistling or wheezing noises

- [ ] Leaking exhaust manifold gasket (Chapter 4)
- [ ] Leaking vacuum hose (Chapter 4 or 9)
- [ ] Blowing cylinder head gasket (Chapter 2)

Tapping or rattling noises

- [ ] Worn valve gear or camshaft (Chapter 2)
- [ ] Ancillary component fault (coolant pump, alternator, etc) (Chapters 3, 5, etc)

Knocking or thumping noises

- [ ] Worn big-end bearings (regular heavy knocking, perhaps less under load) (Chapter 2)
- [ ] Worn main bearings (rumbling and knocking, perhaps worsening under load) (Chapter 2)
- [ ] Piston slap (most noticeable when cold) (Chapter 2)
- [ ] Ancillary component fault (coolant pump, alternator, etc) (Chapters 3, 5, etc)

Cooling system

Overheating

- [ ] Insufficient coolant in system (*Weekly checks*)
- [ ] Thermostat faulty (Chapter 3)
- [ ] Radiator core blocked, or grille restricted (Chapter 3)
- [ ] Cooling fan faulty (Chapter 3)
- [ ] Inaccurate temperature gauge sender unit (Chapter 3)
- [ ] Airlock in cooling system (Chapter 3)
- [ ] Expansion tank pressure cap faulty (Chapter 3)

Overcooling

- [ ] Thermostat faulty (Chapter 3)
- [ ] Inaccurate temperature gauge sender unit (Chapter 3)

External coolant leakage

- [ ] Deteriorated or damaged hoses or hose clips (Chapter 1)
- [ ] Radiator core or heater matrix leaking (Chapter 3)
- [ ] Pressure cap faulty (Chapter 3)
- [ ] Coolant pump internal seal leaking (Chapter 3)
- [ ] Coolant pump-to-block seal leaking (Chapter 3)
- [ ] Boiling due to overheating (Chapter 3)
- [ ] Core plug leaking (Chapter 2)

Internal coolant leakage

- [ ] Leaking cylinder head gasket (Chapter 2)
- [ ] Cracked cylinder head or cylinder block (Chapter 2)

Corrosion

- [ ] Infrequent draining and flushing (Chapter 1)
- [ ] Incorrect coolant mixture or inappropriate coolant type (Chapter 1)

Fuel and exhaust systems

Excessive fuel consumption

- [ ] Air filter element dirty or clogged (Chapter 1)
- [ ] Fuel injection system fault (Chapter 4)
- [ ] Tyres under-inflated (*Weekly checks*)

Fuel leakage and/or fuel odour

- [ ] Damaged or corroded fuel tank, pipes or connections (Chapter 4)

Excessive noise or fumes from exhaust system

- [ ] Leaking exhaust system or manifold joints (Chapters 1 and 4)
- [ ] Leaking, corroded or damaged silencers or pipe (Chapters 1 and 4)
- [ ] Broken mountings causing body or suspension contact (Chapter 1)

Clutch

Pedal travels to floor – no pressure or very little resistance

- [ ] Hydraulic fluid level low/air in the hydraulic system (Chapter 6)
- [ ] Broken clutch release bearing or fork (Chapter 6)
- [ ] Broken diaphragm spring in clutch pressure plate (Chapter 6)

Clutch fails to disengage (unable to select gears)

- [ ] Clutch disc sticking on gearbox input shaft splines (Chapter 6)
- [ ] Clutch disc sticking to flywheel or pressure plate (Chapter 6)
- [ ] Faulty pressure plate assembly (Chapter 6)
- [ ] Clutch release mechanism worn or poorly assembled (Chapter 6)

Clutch slips (engine speed increases, with no increase in vehicle speed)

- [ ] Clutch disc linings excessively worn (Chapter 6)

- [ ] Clutch disc linings contaminated with oil or grease (Chapter 6)
- [ ] Faulty pressure plate or weak diaphragm spring (Chapter 6)

Judder as clutch is engaged

- [ ] Clutch disc linings contaminated with oil or grease (Chapter 6)
- [ ] Clutch disc linings excessively worn (Chapter 6)
- [ ] Faulty or distorted pressure plate or diaphragm spring (Chapter 6)
- [ ] Worn or loose engine or gearbox mountings (Chapter 2A or 2B)
- [ ] Clutch disc hub or gearbox input shaft splines worn (Chapter 6)

Noise when depressing or releasing clutch pedal

- [ ] Worn clutch release bearing (Chapter 6)
- [ ] Worn or dry clutch pedal bushes (Chapter 6)
- [ ] Faulty pressure plate assembly (Chapter 6)
- [ ] Pressure plate diaphragm spring broken (Chapter 6)
- [ ] Broken clutch disc cushioning springs (Chapter 6)

Manual transmission

Noisy in neutral with engine running

- [ ] Input shaft bearings worn (noise apparent with clutch pedal released, but not when depressed) (Chapter 7A)*
- [ ] Clutch release bearing worn (noise apparent with clutch pedal depressed, possibly less when released) (Chapter 6)

Noisy in one particular gear

- [ ] Worn, damaged or chipped gear teeth (Chapter 7A)*

Difficulty engaging gears

- [ ] Clutch fault (Chapter 6)
- [ ] Worn or damaged gearchange linkage (Chapter 7A)
- [ ] Incorrectly-adjusted gearchange linkage (Chapter 7A)
- [ ] Worn synchroniser units (Chapter 7A)*

Jumps out of gear

- [ ] Worn or damaged gearchange linkage (Chapter 7A)

- [ ] Worn synchroniser units (Chapter 7A)*
- [ ] Worn selector forks (Chapter 7A)*

Vibration

- [ ] Lack of oil (Chapter 1)
- [ ] Worn bearings (Chapter 7A)*

Lubricant leaks

- [ ] Leaking differential output oil seal (Chapter 7A)
- [ ] Leaking housing joint (Chapter 7A)*
- [ ] Leaking input shaft oil seal (Chapter 7A)*

* Although the corrective action necessary to remedy the symptoms described is beyond the scope of the home mechanic, the above information should be helpful in isolating the cause of the condition, so that the owner can communicate clearly with a professional mechanic.

Automatic transmission

Note: *Due to the complexity of the automatic transmission, it is difficult for the home mechanic to properly diagnose and service this unit. For problems other than the following, the vehicle should be taken to a dealer service department or automatic transmission specialist. Do not be too hasty in removing the transmission if a fault is suspected, as most of the testing is carried out with the unit still fitted.*

Fluid leakage

- [ ] Automatic transmission fluid is usually dark in colour. Fluid leaks should not be confused with engine oil, which can easily be blown onto the transmission by airflow
- [ ] To determine the source of a leak, first remove all built-up dirt and grime from the transmission housing and surrounding areas using a degreasing agent, or by steam-cleaning. Drive the vehicle at low speed, so airflow will not blow the leak far from its source. Raise and support the vehicle, and determine where the leak is coming from. The following are common areas of leakage:
  - a) Oil pan (Chapter 1 and 7B).
  - b) Dipstick tube (Chapter 1 and 7B)
  - c) Transmission-to-fluid cooler pipes/unions (Chapter 7B)

Transmission fluid brown, or has burned smell

- [ ] Transmission fluid level low, or fluid in need of renewal (Chapter 7B)

General gear selection problems

- [ ] Chapter 7B deals with checking and adjusting the selector cable on automatic transmissions. The following are common problems which may be caused by a poorly-adjusted cable:
  - a) Engine starting in gears other than Park or Neutral
  - b) Indicator panel indicating a gear other than the one actually being used
  - c) Vehicle moves when in Park or Neutral
  - d) Poor gear shift quality or erratic gear changes
- [ ] Refer to Chapter 7B for the selector cable adjustment procedure

Transmission will not downshift (kickdown) with accelerator pedal fully depressed

- [ ] Low transmission fluid level (Chapter 1)
- [ ] Incorrect selector cable adjustment (Chapter 7B)
- [ ] Throttle position sensor fault (Chapter 4)

Engine will not start in any gear, or starts in gears other than Park or Neutral

- [ ] Incorrect selector cable adjustment (Chapter 7B)

Transmission slips, shifts roughly, is noisy, or has no drive in forward or reverse gears

- [ ] There are many probable causes for the above problems, but the home mechanic should be concerned with only one possibility – fluid level. Before taking the vehicle to a dealer or transmission specialist, check the fluid level and condition of the fluid as described in Chapter 1. Correct the fluid level as necessary, or change the fluid and filter if needed. If the problem persists, professional help will be necessary

Final drive and propshaft

Vibration when accelerating or decelerating

- [ ] Worn universal joint (Chapter 8)
- [ ] Bent or distorted propeller shaft (Chapter 8)

Low-pitched whining; increasing with road speed

- [ ] Worn differential (Chapter 8)

Braking system

Note: *Before assuming that a brake problem exists, make sure that the tyres are in good condition and correctly inflated, that the front wheel alignment is correct, and that the vehicle is not loaded with weight in an unequal manner. Apart from checking the condition of all pipe and hose connections, any faults occurring on the anti-lock braking system should be referred to a BMW dealer or specialist for diagnosis.*

Vehicle pulls to one side under braking

- [ ] Worn, defective, damaged or contaminated brake pads/shoes on one side (Chapters 1 and 9)
- [ ] Seized or partially-seized brake caliper (Chapters 1 and 9)
- [ ] A mixture of brake pad lining materials fitted between sides (Chapters 1 and 9)
- [ ] Brake caliper mounting bolts loose (Chapter 9)
- [ ] Worn or damaged steering or suspension components (Chapters 1 and 10)

Noise (grinding or high-pitched squeal) when brakes applied

- [ ] Brake pad friction lining material worn down to metal backing (Chapters 1 and 9)
- [ ] Excessive corrosion of brake disc. (May be apparent after the vehicle has been standing for some time (Chapters 1 and 9)
- [ ] Foreign object (stone chipping, etc) trapped between brake disc and shield (Chapters 1 and 9)

Excessive brake pedal travel

- [ ] Faulty master cylinder (Chapter 9)
- [ ] Air in hydraulic system (Chapters 1 and 9)
- [ ] Faulty vacuum servo unit (Chapter 9)

Brake pedal feels spongy when depressed

- [ ] Air in hydraulic system (Chapters 1 and 9)
- [ ] Deteriorated flexible rubber brake hoses (Chapters 1 and 9)
- [ ] Master cylinder mounting nuts loose (Chapter 9)
- [ ] Faulty master cylinder (Chapter 9)

Excessive brake pedal effort required to stop vehicle

- [ ] Faulty vacuum servo unit (Chapter 9)
- [ ] Disconnected, damaged or insecure brake servo vacuum hose (Chapter 9)
- [ ] Primary or secondary hydraulic circuit failure (Chapter 9)
- [ ] Seized brake caliper (Chapter 9)
- [ ] Brake pads incorrectly fitted (Chapters 1 and 9)
- [ ] Incorrect grade of brake pads fitted (Chapters 1 and 9)
- [ ] Brake pads contaminated (Chapters 1 and 9)

Judder felt through brake pedal or steering wheel when braking

- [ ] Excessive run-out or distortion of discs (Chapters 1 and 9)
- [ ] Brake pad linings worn (Chapters 1 and 9)
- [ ] Brake caliper mounting bolts loose (Chapter 9)
- [ ] Wear in suspension or steering components or mountings (Chapters 1 and 10)

Brakes binding

- [ ] Seized brake caliper (Chapter 9)
- [ ] Incorrectly-adjusted handbrake mechanism (Chapter 9)
- [ ] Faulty master cylinder (Chapter 9)

Suspension and steering

Note: *Before diagnosing suspension or steering faults, be sure that the trouble is not due to incorrect tyre pressures, mixtures of tyre types, or binding brakes.*

Vehicle pulls to one side

- ☐ Defective tyre (*Weekly checks*)
- ☐ Excessive wear in suspension or steering components (Chapters 1 and 10)
- ☐ Incorrect front wheel alignment (Chapter 10)
- ☐ Accident damage to steering or suspension components (Chapter 1)

Wheel wobble and vibration

- ☐ Front roadwheels out of balance (vibration felt mainly through the steering wheel) (Chapters 1 and 10)
- ☐ Rear roadwheels out of balance (vibration felt throughout the vehicle) (Chapters 1 and 10)
- ☐ Roadwheels damaged or distorted (Chapters 1 and 10)
- ☐ Faulty or damaged tyre (*Weekly checks*)
- ☐ Worn steering or suspension joints, bushes or components (Chapters 1 and 10)
- ☐ Wheel bolts loose (Chapters 1 and 10)

Excessive pitching and/or rolling around corners, or during braking

- ☐ Defective shock absorbers (Chapters 1 and 10)
- ☐ Broken or weak spring and/or suspension component (Chapters 1 and 10)
- ☐ Worn or damaged anti-roll bar or mountings (Chapter 10)

Wandering or general instability

- ☐ Incorrect front wheel alignment (Chapter 10)
- ☐ Worn steering or suspension joints, bushes or components (Chapters 1 and 10)
- ☐ Roadwheels out of balance (Chapters 1 and 10)
- ☐ Faulty or damaged tyre (*Weekly checks*)
- ☐ Wheel bolts loose (Chapters 1 and 10)
- ☐ Defective shock absorbers (Chapters 1 and 10)
- ☐ Dynamic stability system fault (Chapter 10)

Excessively-stiff steering

- ☐ Lack of steering gear lubricant (Chapter 10)
- ☐ Seized track rod end balljoint or suspension balljoint (Chapters 1 and 10)

- ☐ Broken or incorrectly-adjusted drivebelt – power steering (Chapter 1)
- ☐ Incorrect front wheel alignment (Chapter 10)
- ☐ Steering rack or column bent or damaged (Chapter 10)

Excessive play in steering

- ☐ Worn steering column intermediate shaft universal joint (Chapter 10)
- ☐ Worn steering track rod end balljoints (Chapters 1 and 10)
- ☐ Worn rack-and-pinion steering gear (Chapter 10)
- ☐ Worn steering or suspension joints, bushes or components (Chapters 1 and 10)

Lack of power assistance

- ☐ Broken or incorrectly-adjusted auxiliary drivebelt (Chapter 1)
- ☐ Incorrect power steering fluid level (*Weekly checks*)
- ☐ Restriction in power steering fluid hoses (Chapter 1)
- ☐ Faulty power steering pump (Chapter 10)
- ☐ Faulty rack-and-pinion steering gear (Chapter 10)

Tyre wear excessive

Tyres worn on inside or outside edges

- ☐ Tyres under-inflated (wear on both edges) (*Weekly checks*)
- ☐ Incorrect camber or castor angles (wear on one edge only) (Chapter 10)
- ☐ Worn steering or suspension joints, bushes or components (Chapters 1 and 10)
- ☐ Excessively-hard cornering.
- ☐ Accident damage.

Tyre treads exhibit feathered edges

- ☐ Incorrect toe setting (Chapter 10)

Tyres worn in centre of tread

- ☐ Tyres over-inflated (*Weekly checks*)

Tyres worn on inside and outside edges

- ☐ Tyres under-inflated (*Weekly checks*)

Tyres worn unevenly

- ☐ Tyres/wheels out of balance (Chapter 1)
- ☐ Excessive wheel or tyre run-out (Chapter 1)
- ☐ Worn shock absorbers (Chapters 1 and 10)
- ☐ Faulty tyre (*Weekly checks*)

Electrical system

Note: *For problems associated with the starting system, refer to the faults listed under 'Engine' earlier in this Section.*

Battery will only hold a charge for a few days

- ☐ Battery defective internally (Chapter 5)
- ☐ Battery terminal connections loose or corroded (*Weekly checks*)
- ☐ Auxiliary drivebelt worn or incorrectly adjusted (Chapter 1)
- ☐ Alternator not charging at correct output (Chapter 5)
- ☐ Alternator or voltage regulator faulty (Chapter 5)
- ☐ Short-circuit causing continual battery drain (Chapters 5 and 12)

Ignition/no-charge warning light remains illuminated with engine running

- ☐ Auxiliary drivebelt broken, worn, or incorrectly adjusted (Chapter 1)
- ☐ Alternator brushes worn, sticking, or dirty (Chapter 5)
- ☐ Alternator brush springs weak or broken (Chapter 5)

- ☐ Internal fault in alternator or voltage regulator (Chapter 5)
- ☐ Broken, disconnected, or loose wiring in charging circuit (Chapter 5)

Ignition/no-charge warning light fails to come on

- ☐ Warning light bulb blown (Chapter 12)
- ☐ Broken, disconnected, or loose wiring in warning light circuit (Chapter 12)
- ☐ Alternator faulty (Chapter 5)

Lights inoperative

- ☐ Bulb blown (Chapter 12)
- ☐ Corrosion of bulb or bulbholder contacts (Chapter 12)
- ☐ Blown fuse (Chapter 12)
- ☐ Faulty relay (Chapter 12)
- ☐ Broken, loose, or disconnected wiring (Chapter 12)
- ☐ Faulty switch (Chapter 12)

Electrical system (continued)

Instrument readings inaccurate or erratic

Instrument readings increase with engine speed
- ☐ Faulty voltage regulator (Chapter 12)

Fuel or temperature gauges give no reading
- ☐ Faulty gauge sender unit (Chapters 3 and 4)
- ☐ Wiring open-circuit (Chapter 12)
- ☐ Faulty gauge (Chapter 12)

Fuel or temperature gauges give continuous maximum reading
- ☐ Faulty gauge sender unit (Chapters 3 and 4)
- ☐ Wiring short-circuit (Chapter 12)
- ☐ Faulty gauge (Chapter 12)

Horn inoperative, or unsatisfactory in operation

Horn operates all the time
- ☐ Horn push either earthed or stuck down (Chapter 12)
- ☐ Horn cable-to-horn push earthed (Chapter 12)

Horn fails to operate
- ☐ Blown fuse (Chapter 12)
- ☐ Cable or cable connections loose, broken or disconnected (Chapter 12)
- ☐ Faulty horn (Chapter 12)

Horn emits intermittent or unsatisfactory sound
- ☐ Cable connections loose (Chapter 12)
- ☐ Horn mountings loose (Chapter 12)
- ☐ Faulty horn (Chapter 12)

Windscreen wipers inoperative, or unsatisfactory in operation

Wipers fail to operate, or operate very slowly
- ☐ Wiper blades stuck to screen, or linkage seized or binding (Chapters 1 and 12)
- ☐ Blown fuse (Chapter 12)
- ☐ Cable or cable connections loose, broken or disconnected (Chapter 12)
- ☐ Faulty wiper motor (Chapter 12)

Wiper blades sweep over too large or too small an area of the glass
- ☐ Wiper arms incorrectly positioned on spindles (Chapter 1)
- ☐ Excessive wear of wiper linkage (Chapter 12)
- ☐ Wiper motor or linkage mountings loose or insecure (Chapter 12)

Wiper blades fail to clean the glass effectively
- ☐ Wiper blade rubbers worn or perished (Weekly checks)
- ☐ Wiper arm tension springs broken, or arm pivots seized (Chapter 12)
- ☐ Insufficient windscreen washer additive to adequately remove road film (Weekly checks)

Windscreen washers inoperative, or unsatisfactory in operation

One or more washer jets inoperative
- ☐ Blocked washer jet (Chapter 1)
- ☐ Disconnected, kinked or restricted fluid hose (Chapter 12)
- ☐ Insufficient fluid in washer reservoir (Weekly checks)

Washer pump fails to operate
- ☐ Broken or disconnected wiring or connections (Chapter 12)
- ☐ Blown fuse (Chapter 12)
- ☐ Faulty washer switch (Chapter 12)
- ☐ Faulty washer pump (Chapter 12)

Washer pump runs for some time before fluid is emitted from jets
- ☐ Faulty one-way valve in fluid supply hose (Chapter 12)

Electric windows inoperative, or unsatisfactory in operation

Window glass will only move in one direction
- ☐ Faulty switch (Chapter 12)

Window glass slow to move
- ☐ Regulator seized or damaged, or in need of lubrication (Chapter 11)
- ☐ Door internal components or trim fouling regulator (Chapter 11)
- ☐ Faulty motor (Chapter 11)

Window glass fails to move
- ☐ Blown fuse (Chapter 12)
- ☐ Faulty relay (Chapter 12)
- ☐ Broken or disconnected wiring or connections (Chapter 12)
- ☐ Faulty motor (Chapter 11)

Central locking system inoperative, or unsatisfactory in operation

Complete system failure
- ☐ Blown fuse (Chapter 12)
- ☐ Faulty control unit (Chapter 12)
- ☐ Broken or disconnected wiring or connections (Chapter 12)
- ☐ Faulty motor (Chapter 11)

Latch locks but will not unlock, or unlocks but will not lock
- ☐ Faulty master switch (Chapter 12)
- ☐ Broken or disconnected latch operating rods or levers (Chapter 11)
- ☐ Faulty control unit (Chapter 12)
- ☐ Faulty motor (Chapter 11)

One solenoid/motor fails to operate
- ☐ Broken or disconnected wiring or connections (Chapter 12)
- ☐ Faulty operating assembly (Chapter 11)
- ☐ Broken, binding or disconnected latch operating rods or levers (Chapter 11)
- ☐ Fault in door latch (Chapter 11)

A

ABS (Anti-lock brake system) A system, usually electronically controlled, that senses incipient wheel lockup during braking and relieves hydraulic pressure at wheels that are about to skid.

Air bag An inflatable bag hidden in the steering wheel (driver's side) or the dash or glovebox (passenger side). In a head-on collision, the bags inflate, preventing the driver and front passenger from being thrown forward into the steering wheel or windscreen.

Air cleaner A metal or plastic housing, containing a filter element, which removes dust and dirt from the air being drawn into the engine.

Air filter element The actual filter in an air cleaner system, usually manufactured from pleated paper and requiring renewal at regular intervals.

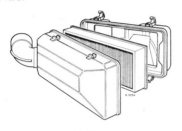

Air filter

Allen key A hexagonal wrench which fits into a recessed hexagonal hole.

Alligator clip A long-nosed spring-loaded metal clip with meshing teeth. Used to make temporary electrical connections.

Alternator A component in the electrical system which converts mechanical energy from a drivebelt into electrical energy to charge the battery and to operate the starting system, ignition system and electrical accessories.

Ampere (amp) A unit of measurement for the flow of electric current. One amp is the amount of current produced by one volt acting through a resistance of one ohm.

Anaerobic sealer A substance used to prevent bolts and screws from loosening. Anaerobic means that it does not require oxygen for activation. The Loctite brand is widely used.

Antifreeze A substance (usually ethylene glycol) mixed with water, and added to a vehicle's cooling system, to prevent freezing of the coolant in winter. Antifreeze also contains chemicals to inhibit corrosion and the formation of rust and other deposits that would tend to clog the radiator and coolant passages and reduce cooling efficiency.

Anti-seize compound A coating that reduces the risk of seizing on fasteners that are subjected to high temperatures, such as exhaust manifold bolts and nuts.

Asbestos A natural fibrous mineral with great heat resistance, commonly used in the composition of brake friction materials.

Asbestos is a health hazard and the dust created by brake systems should never be inhaled or ingested.

Axle A shaft on which a wheel revolves, or which revolves with a wheel. Also, a solid beam that connects the two wheels at one end of the vehicle. An axle which also transmits power to the wheels is known as a live axle.

Axleshaft A single rotating shaft, on either side of the differential, which delivers power from the final drive assembly to the drive wheels. Also called a driveshaft or a halfshaft.

B

Ball bearing An anti-friction bearing consisting of a hardened inner and outer race with hardened steel balls between two races.

Bearing The curved surface on a shaft or in a bore, or the part assembled into either, that permits relative motion between them with minimum wear and friction.

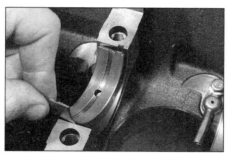

Bearing

Big-end bearing The bearing in the end of the connecting rod that's attached to the crankshaft.

Bleed nipple A valve on a brake wheel cylinder, caliper or other hydraulic component that is opened to purge the hydraulic system of air. Also called a bleed screw.

Brake bleeding Procedure for removing air from lines of a hydraulic brake system.

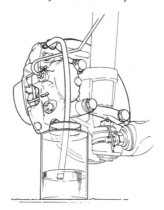

Brake bleeding

Brake disc The component of a disc brake that rotates with the wheels.

Brake drum The component of a drum brake that rotates with the wheels.

Brake linings The friction material which contacts the brake disc or drum to retard the vehicle's speed. The linings are bonded or riveted to the brake pads or shoes.

Brake pads The replaceable friction pads that pinch the brake disc when the brakes are applied. Brake pads consist of a friction material bonded or riveted to a rigid backing plate.

Brake shoe The crescent-shaped carrier to which the brake linings are mounted and which forces the lining against the rotating drum during braking.

Braking systems For more information on braking systems, consult the *Haynes Automotive Brake Manual*.

Breaker bar A long socket wrench handle providing greater leverage.

Bulkhead The insulated partition between the engine and the passenger compartment.

C

Caliper The non-rotating part of a disc-brake assembly that straddles the disc and carries the brake pads. The caliper also contains the hydraulic components that cause the pads to pinch the disc when the brakes are applied. A caliper is also a measuring tool that can be set to measure inside or outside dimensions of an object.

Camshaft A rotating shaft on which a series of cam lobes operate the valve mechanisms. The camshaft may be driven by gears, by sprockets and chain or by sprockets and a belt.

Canister A container in an evaporative emission control system; contains activated charcoal granules to trap vapours from the fuel system.

Canister

Carburettor A device which mixes fuel with air in the proper proportions to provide a desired power output from a spark ignition internal combustion engine.

Castellated Resembling the parapets along the top of a castle wall. For example, a castellated balljoint stud nut.

Castor In wheel alignment, the backward or forward tilt of the steering axis. Castor is positive when the steering axis is inclined rearward at the top.

Catalytic converter A silencer-like device in the exhaust system which converts certain pollutants in the exhaust gases into less harmful substances.

Catalytic converter

Circlip A ring-shaped clip used to prevent endwise movement of cylindrical parts and shafts. An internal circlip is installed in a groove in a housing; an external circlip fits into a groove on the outside of a cylindrical piece such as a shaft.

Clearance The amount of space between two parts. For example, between a piston and a cylinder, between a bearing and a journal, etc.

Coil spring A spiral of elastic steel found in various sizes throughout a vehicle, for example as a springing medium in the suspension and in the valve train.

Compression Reduction in volume, and increase in pressure and temperature, of a gas, caused by squeezing it into a smaller space.

Compression ratio The relationship between cylinder volume when the piston is at top dead centre and cylinder volume when the piston is at bottom dead centre.

Constant velocity (CV) joint A type of universal joint that cancels out vibrations caused by driving power being transmitted through an angle.

Core plug A disc or cup-shaped metal device inserted in a hole in a casting through which core was removed when the casting was formed. Also known as a freeze plug or expansion plug.

Crankcase The lower part of the engine block in which the crankshaft rotates.

Crankshaft The main rotating member, or shaft, running the length of the crankcase, with offset "throws" to which the connecting rods are attached.

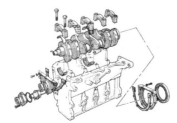

Crankshaft assembly

Crocodile clip See Alligator clip

D

Diagnostic code Code numbers obtained by accessing the diagnostic mode of an engine management computer. This code can be used to determine the area in the system where a malfunction may be located.

Disc brake A brake design incorporating a rotating disc onto which brake pads are squeezed. The resulting friction converts the energy of a moving vehicle into heat.

Double-overhead cam (DOHC) An engine that uses two overhead camshafts, usually one for the intake valves and one for the exhaust valves.

Drivebelt(s) The belt(s) used to drive accessories such as the alternator, water pump, power steering pump, air conditioning compressor, etc. off the crankshaft pulley.

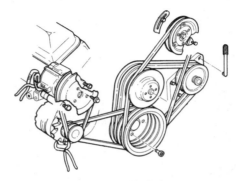

Accessory drivebelts

Driveshaft Any shaft used to transmit motion. Commonly used when referring to the axleshafts on a front wheel drive vehicle.

Drum brake A type of brake using a drum-shaped metal cylinder attached to the inner surface of the wheel. When the brake pedal is pressed, curved brake shoes with friction linings press against the inside of the drum to slow or stop the vehicle.

E

EGR valve A valve used to introduce exhaust gases into the intake air stream.

Electronic control unit (ECU) A computer which controls (for instance) ignition and fuel injection systems, or an anti-lock braking system. For more information refer to the *Haynes Automotive Electrical and Electronic Systems Manual*.

Electronic Fuel Injection (EFI) A computer controlled fuel system that distributes fuel through an injector located in each intake port of the engine.

Emergency brake A braking system, independent of the main hydraulic system, that can be used to slow or stop the vehicle if the primary brakes fail, or to hold the vehicle stationary even though the brake pedal isn't depressed. It usually consists of a hand lever that actuates either front or rear brakes mechanically through a series of cables and linkages. Also known as a handbrake or parking brake.

Endfloat The amount of lengthwise movement between two parts. As applied to a crankshaft, the distance that the crankshaft can move forward and back in the cylinder block.

Engine management system (EMS) A computer controlled system which manages the fuel injection and the ignition systems in an integrated fashion.

Exhaust manifold A part with several passages through which exhaust gases leave the engine combustion chambers and enter the exhaust pipe.

F

Fan clutch A viscous (fluid) drive coupling device which permits variable engine fan speeds in relation to engine speeds.

Feeler blade A thin strip or blade of hardened steel, ground to an exact thickness, used to check or measure clearances between parts.

Feeler blade

Firing order The order in which the engine cylinders fire, or deliver their power strokes, beginning with the number one cylinder.

Flywheel A heavy spinning wheel in which energy is absorbed and stored by means of momentum. On cars, the flywheel is attached to the crankshaft to smooth out firing impulses.

Free play The amount of travel before any action takes place. The "looseness" in a linkage, or an assembly of parts, between the initial application of force and actual movement. For example, the distance the brake pedal moves before the pistons in the master cylinder are actuated.

Fuse An electrical device which protects a circuit against accidental overload. The typical fuse contains a soft piece of metal which is calibrated to melt at a predetermined current flow (expressed as amps) and break the circuit.

Fusible link A circuit protection device consisting of a conductor surrounded by heat-resistant insulation. The conductor is smaller than the wire it protects, so it acts as the weakest link in the circuit. Unlike a blown fuse, a failed fusible link must frequently be cut from the wire for replacement.

G

Gap The distance the spark must travel in jumping from the centre electrode to the side electrode in a spark plug. Also refers to the spacing between the points in a contact breaker assembly in a conventional points-type ignition, or to the distance between the reluctor or rotor and the pickup coil in an electronic ignition.

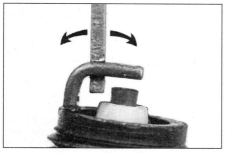

Adjusting spark plug gap

Gasket Any thin, soft material - usually cork, cardboard, asbestos or soft metal - installed between two metal surfaces to ensure a good seal. For instance, the cylinder head gasket seals the joint between the block and the cylinder head.

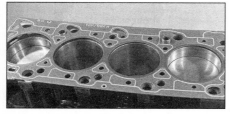

Gasket

Gauge An instrument panel display used to monitor engine conditions. A gauge with a movable pointer on a dial or a fixed scale is an analogue gauge. A gauge with a numerical readout is called a digital gauge.

H

Halfshaft A rotating shaft that transmits power from the final drive unit to a drive wheel, usually when referring to a live rear axle.

Harmonic balancer A device designed to reduce torsion or twisting vibration in the crankshaft. May be incorporated in the crankshaft pulley. Also known as a vibration damper.

Hone An abrasive tool for correcting small irregularities or differences in diameter in an engine cylinder, brake cylinder, etc.

Hydraulic tappet A tappet that utilises hydraulic pressure from the engine's lubrication system to maintain zero clearance (constant contact with both camshaft and valve stem). Automatically adjusts to variation in valve stem length. Hydraulic tappets also reduce valve noise.

I

Ignition timing The moment at which the spark plug fires, usually expressed in the number of crankshaft degrees before the piston reaches the top of its stroke.

Inlet manifold A tube or housing with passages through which flows the air-fuel mixture (carburettor vehicles and vehicles with throttle body injection) or air only (port fuel-injected vehicles) to the port openings in the cylinder head.

J

Jump start Starting the engine of a vehicle with a discharged or weak battery by attaching jump leads from the weak battery to a charged or helper battery.

L

Load Sensing Proportioning Valve (LSPV) A brake hydraulic system control valve that works like a proportioning valve, but also takes into consideration the amount of weight carried by the rear axle.

Locknut A nut used to lock an adjustment nut, or other threaded component, in place. For example, a locknut is employed to keep the adjusting nut on the rocker arm in position.

Lockwasher A form of washer designed to prevent an attaching nut from working loose.

M

MacPherson strut A type of front suspension system devised by Earle MacPherson at Ford of England. In its original form, a simple lateral link with the anti-roll bar creates the lower control arm. A long strut - an integral coil spring and shock absorber - is mounted between the body and the steering knuckle. Many modern so-called MacPherson strut systems use a conventional lower A-arm and don't rely on the anti-roll bar for location.

Multimeter An electrical test instrument with the capability to measure voltage, current and resistance.

N

NOx Oxides of Nitrogen. A common toxic pollutant emitted by petrol and diesel engines at higher temperatures.

O

Ohm The unit of electrical resistance. One volt applied to a resistance of one ohm will produce a current of one amp.

Ohmmeter An instrument for measuring electrical resistance.

O-ring A type of sealing ring made of a special rubber-like material; in use, the O-ring is compressed into a groove to provide the sealing action.

Overhead cam (ohc) engine An engine with the camshaft(s) located on top of the cylinder head(s).

Overhead valve (ohv) engine An engine with the valves located in the cylinder head, but with the camshaft located in the engine block.

Oxygen sensor A device installed in the engine exhaust manifold, which senses the oxygen content in the exhaust and converts this information into an electric current. Also called a Lambda sensor.

P

Phillips screw A type of screw head having a cross instead of a slot for a corresponding type of screwdriver.

Plastigage A thin strip of plastic thread, available in different sizes, used for measuring clearances. For example, a strip of Plastigage is laid across a bearing journal. The parts are assembled and dismantled; the width of the crushed strip indicates the clearance between journal and bearing.

Plastigage

Propeller shaft The long hollow tube with universal joints at both ends that carries power from the transmission to the differential on front-engined rear wheel drive vehicles.

Proportioning valve A hydraulic control valve which limits the amount of pressure to the rear brakes during panic stops to prevent wheel lock-up.

R

Rack-and-pinion steering A steering system with a pinion gear on the end of the steering shaft that mates with a rack (think of a geared wheel opened up and laid flat). When the steering wheel is turned, the pinion turns, moving the rack to the left or right. This movement is transmitted through the track rods to the steering arms at the wheels.

Radiator A liquid-to-air heat transfer device designed to reduce the temperature of the coolant in an internal combustion engine cooling system.

Refrigerant Any substance used as a heat transfer agent in an air-conditioning system. R-12 has been the principle refrigerant for many years; recently, however, manufacturers have begun using R-134a, a non-CFC substance that is considered less harmful to the ozone in the upper atmosphere.

Rocker arm A lever arm that rocks on a shaft or pivots on a stud. In an overhead valve engine, the rocker arm converts the upward movement of the pushrod into a downward movement to open a valve.

Rotor In a distributor, the rotating device inside the cap that connects the centre electrode and the outer terminals as it turns, distributing the high voltage from the coil secondary winding to the proper spark plug. Also, that part of an alternator which rotates inside the stator. Also, the rotating assembly of a turbocharger, including the compressor wheel, shaft and turbine wheel.

Runout The amount of wobble (in-and-out movement) of a gear or wheel as it's rotated. The amount a shaft rotates "out-of-true." The out-of-round condition of a rotating part.

S

Sealant A liquid or paste used to prevent leakage at a joint. Sometimes used in conjunction with a gasket.

Sealed beam lamp An older headlight design which integrates the reflector, lens and filaments into a hermetically-sealed one-piece unit. When a filament burns out or the lens cracks, the entire unit is simply replaced.

Serpentine drivebelt A single, long, wide accessory drivebelt that's used on some newer vehicles to drive all the accessories, instead of a series of smaller, shorter belts. Serpentine drivebelts are usually tensioned by an automatic tensioner.

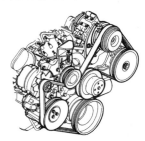

Serpentine drivebelt

Shim Thin spacer, commonly used to adjust the clearance or relative positions between two parts. For example, shims inserted into or under bucket tappets control valve clearances. Clearance is adjusted by changing the thickness of the shim.

Slide hammer A special puller that screws into or hooks onto a component such as a shaft or bearing; a heavy sliding handle on the shaft bottoms against the end of the shaft to knock the component free.

Sprocket A tooth or projection on the periphery of a wheel, shaped to engage with a chain or drivebelt. Commonly used to refer to the sprocket wheel itself.

Starter inhibitor switch On vehicles with an automatic transmission, a switch that prevents starting if the vehicle is not in Neutral or Park.

Strut See MacPherson strut.

T

Tappet A cylindrical component which transmits motion from the cam to the valve stem, either directly or via a pushrod and rocker arm. Also called a cam follower.

Thermostat A heat-controlled valve that regulates the flow of coolant between the cylinder block and the radiator, so maintaining optimum engine operating temperature. A thermostat is also used in some air cleaners in which the temperature is regulated.

Thrust bearing The bearing in the clutch assembly that is moved in to the release levers by clutch pedal action to disengage the clutch. Also referred to as a release bearing.

Timing belt A toothed belt which drives the camshaft. Serious engine damage may result if it breaks in service.

Timing chain A chain which drives the camshaft.

Toe-in The amount the front wheels are closer together at the front than at the rear. On rear wheel drive vehicles, a slight amount of toe-in is usually specified to keep the front wheels running parallel on the road by offsetting other forces that tend to spread the wheels apart.

Toe-out The amount the front wheels are closer together at the rear than at the front. On front wheel drive vehicles, a slight amount of toe-out is usually specified.

Tools For full information on choosing and using tools, refer to the *Haynes Automotive Tools Manual.*

Tracer A stripe of a second colour applied to a wire insulator to distinguish that wire from another one with the same colour insulator.

Tune-up A process of accurate and careful adjustments and parts replacement to obtain the best possible engine performance.

Turbocharger A centrifugal device, driven by exhaust gases, that pressurises the intake air. Normally used to increase the power output from a given engine displacement, but can also be used primarily to reduce exhaust emissions (as on VW's "Umwelt" Diesel engine).

U

Universal joint or U-joint A double-pivoted connection for transmitting power from a driving to a driven shaft through an angle. A U-joint consists of two Y-shaped yokes and a cross-shaped member called the spider.

V

Valve A device through which the flow of liquid, gas, vacuum, or loose material in bulk may be started, stopped, or regulated by a movable part that opens, shuts, or partially obstructs one or more ports or passageways. A valve is also the movable part of such a device.

Valve clearance The clearance between the valve tip (the end of the valve stem) and the rocker arm or tappet. The valve clearance is measured when the valve is closed.

Vernier caliper A precision measuring instrument that measures inside and outside dimensions. Not quite as accurate as a micrometer, but more convenient.

Viscosity The thickness of a liquid or its resistance to flow.

Volt A unit for expressing electrical "pressure" in a circuit. One volt that will produce a current of one ampere through a resistance of one ohm.

W

Welding Various processes used to join metal items by heating the areas to be joined to a molten state and fusing them together. For more information refer to the *Haynes Automotive Welding Manual.*

Wiring diagram A drawing portraying the components and wires in a vehicle's electrical system, using standardised symbols. For more information refer to the *Haynes Automotive Electrical and Electronic Systems Manual.*

*Note: References throughout this index are in the form "**Chapter number**" • "**Page number**". So, for example, 2C•15 refers to page 15 of Chapter 2C.*

Note: *References throughout this index are in the form* **"Chapter number"** • **"Page number"**. *So, for example, 2C•15 refers to page 15 of Chapter 2C.*

Note: *References throughout this index are in the form* "**Chapter number**" • "**Page number**". *So, for example, 2C•15 refers to page 15 of Chapter 2C.*

Preserving Our Motoring Heritage

< *The Model J Duesenberg Derham Tourster. Only eight of these magnificent cars were ever built – this is the only example to be found outside the United States of America*

Almost every car you've ever loved, loathed or desired is gathered under one roof at the Haynes Motor Museum. Over 300 immaculately presented cars and motorbikes represent every aspect of our motoring heritage, from elegant reminders of bygone days, such as the superb Model J Duesenberg to curiosities like the bug-eyed BMW Isetta. There are also many old friends and flames. Perhaps you remember the 1959 Ford Popular that you did your courting in? The magnificent 'Red Collection' is a spectacle of classic sports cars including AC, Alfa Romeo, Austin Healey, Ferrari, Lamborghini, Maserati, MG, Riley, Porsche and Triumph.

A Perfect Day Out

Each and every vehicle at the Haynes Motor Museum has played its part in the history and culture of Motoring. Today, they make a wonderful spectacle and a great day out for all the family. Bring the kids, bring Mum and Dad, but above all bring your camera to capture those golden memories for ever. You will also find an impressive array of motoring memorabilia, a comfortable 70 seat video cinema and one of the most extensive transport book shops in Britain. The Pit Stop Cafe serves everything from a cup of tea to wholesome, home-made meals or, if you prefer, you can enjoy the large picnic area nestled in the beautiful rural surroundings of Somerset.

John Haynes O.B.E., Founder and Chairman of the museum at the wheel of a Haynes Light 12. >

< *Graham Hill's Lola Cosworth Formula 1 car next to a 1934 Riley Sports.*

The Museum is situated on the A359 Yeovil to Frome road at Sparkford, just off the A303 in Somerset. It is about 40 miles south of Bristol, and 25 minutes drive from the M5 intersection at Taunton.

Open 9.30am - 5.30pm (10.00am - 4.00pm Winter) 7 days a week, *except Christmas Day, Boxing Day and New Years Day*
Special rates available for schools, coach parties and outings Charitable Trust No. 292048